GARDENERS ON THE GREENSAND

The development of a Bedfordshire family over five centuries.

REX WHITFIELD.

Cover design, maps and diagrams by James Brown, FRSA.

Published by New Generation Publishing in 2015

British Library Cataloguing Publication Data.
A catalogue record for this book is available from the British Library

ISBN 978-1-78507-378-6

www.newgeneration-publishing.com

New Generation Publishing

Contents

Index of Maps, Diagrams and Photographs

'Society is indeed a contract…it becomes a partnership not only between those who are living, but between those who are living, those who are dead, and those who are to be born'.

Edmund Burke (1729-1797)   *Reflections on the Revolution in France* (1790)

Foreword by James Brown, FRSA.

Rex Whitfield has been documenting his ancestors for forty years, and if a more thoroughly-researched or wider ranging genealogy for one ordinary yet extraordinary family exists, then it has so far escaped me.

In some ways he has been very lucky. He was fortunate to know one of his great grandfathers, born in 1874, who regaled him with tales of his Victorian childhood. One of Rex's grandfathers had been brought up by *his* grandfather, who had been born in the early 1830s, and he was able to give Rex direct oral evidence of life in rural England during the early years of Victoria's reign.

It's no wonder that Rex was entranced by these stories, nor that he has inherited the art of bringing the past to life in a similar way. But it was a chance remark by a great uncle when Rex was in his teens which turned out to be the clue which set him on his lifelong quest. The Whitfields, he claimed, were not from Potton in Bedfordshire but originated in a place called Tewin in Hertfordshire.

So far as I can recall Rex never mentioned this news at the time. We were classmates and friends at Stratton Grammar School in Biggleswade, and although we both shared a strong interest in history, I think our friendship probably sprang from the similarity of our backgrounds: we both had rural working-class roots, his in Potton and mine in Gamlingay.

After 'O' levels our paths diverged. He stayed on to complete his 'A' levels and then a University degree and I moved away from the area. We lost touch, as so many school friends do. A decade later, and now with a family of my own, I moved back to Gamlingay. My daughter was attending school in Sandy, and inevitably I had to go to a Parents' Evening. Eventually I found myself sitting opposite her Geography teacher.

"Hello, Jim", he said.

"Hello, Rex", I replied.

We picked up the broken threads of our friendship as if ten years had never passed. By then I was deeply obsessed with Gamlingay's history, while he was equally immersed in his genealogical investigations. In the thirty years since we have had countless conversations, often deep into the night, about our respective areas of interest.

Historical research is of necessity a largely solitary pursuit, and there are times when you wonder why you are spending so much time and effort doing it. The answer is that it's both rewarding and satisfying to find out what happened in the past – but it's much more so when you can share it with someone else who is equally interested. I know that being able to discuss the difficulties and share the discoveries helped me to carry on, and I like to think it helped him too.

There may be other family historians who have done as much research as Rex, though I suspect not. He has never been content with a mere list of names and dates. Beginning by resolving the Tewin connection, Rex has dug deep into the mountain of surviving historical records to unearth the evidence that brings his ancestors to life. Sometimes it was only the slightest clue that led to a new discovery or confirmed a theory, often many years later. Patience is a quality that every family historian needs. As Rex points out, genealogy isn't a race. Or if it is, it's a marathon, not a sprint.

What is so impressive about Rex's research is the breadth and depth of it. It's one thing to construct a family tree that takes a direct line back, but quite another to extend it out to the furthest branches – sometimes even to the twigs. Whitfields have lived in many places up and down the country, as well as further afield in Canada, the United States, New Zealand and India. Needless to say, Rex has tracked down most of them.

And it's something else again to take the story five centuries back in time. Most family historians consider they have done well if they make it back to the later eighteenth century, but Rex has taken the Whitfields way back to the early 1500s, to a time when England was ruled by the Tudors and parish registers were yet to be a statutory requirement.

Over the last forty years Rex has acquired a deep knowledge of social history that allows him to place his ancestors in their historical context. Many of them were market gardeners, and a high proportion of the rest grew crops in their spare time to bring in some additional cash. (If ever someone designs a Whitfield family crest – I suggest a push-hoe and spade as appropriate motifs – the family motto ought to be '*Why have one job when you can have two*'). As well as the ability to weave a story, Rex has also inherited the Whitfield market-gardening gene, and speaks from personal experience when he discusses the muscle-cracking effort involved in working a plot of land or which crops grow best on sandy soil.

Whitfields knew the abject poverty of the Victorian workhouse and the sheer slog of labouring on the land, but there were also Whitfield gamekeepers, bakers, shopkeepers, carriers, farmers, railwaymen, policemen and teachers – even a judge. A few were wealthy; most were not. They were ordinary. They were extraordinary. They were like most families, with one difference: few if any have had someone like Rex to delve as deeply into their history.

To produce such a large and impressive family tree requires the ability to collect, organise and link a huge amount of complex information into a logical sequence. No doubt there are other family historians who share these skills, but not many combine them with the ability to write about what they have found. Fewer still are able to create a readable and entertaining story that will be of interest to anyone who likes social history, as Rex has done with *Gardeners on the Greensand*. His book is a fine achievement: Whitfields past, present and future should be proud of him.

Author's Note: Setting The Scene.

This book is about people: individuals like you and me and the characters we know – or think we know. Many of them are no longer alive, but like us they once had their hopes and ambitions, their idiosyncrasies, faults and problems. These people interacted with others and played their part in society, and most of them left behind some evidence of the lives they led. Many of them lived and died in a relatively small part of rural Bedfordshire at a time when even their county town was no larger than one of today's medium sized villages.

The roughly triangular area in central Bedfordshire including the settlements of Sandy, Potton and Biggleswade was once famous for its market gardening industry, although these places - and the surrounding villages - now form part of London's commuter belt. Even on many of the modern housing estates, however, littered with the latest models of cars, the tarmac and concrete form a thin veneer over the soil based on an underlying rock laid down in the Cretaceous geological period between about 100 and 125 million years ago, give or take a year or two. This rock was formerly called the lower greensand, but more recently geologists have changed its name to the Woburn sands. Whatever its name, it was a feature of the area millions of years before humans appeared on the scene. The lower greensand outcrop within Bedfordshire extends diagonally from Leighton Buzzard and Woburn in the south-west of the county through the Ampthill, Maulden and Clophill area to Everton and Potton in the north-east; and then on to Gamlingay, just over the border in Cambridgeshire. The greensand ridge is fairly easy to spot; it would certainly be noticed by a cyclist or walker toiling up its steep scarp slope on the 1 in 7 gradient hill leading to Everton from Tempsford, for example. Once at the summit, he or she could then have a much easier journey, if desired, down the dip slope towards Potton. The soil produced as the rock weathers is not particularly fertile in its natural state, and left largely to its own devices supports a heath-like landscape, but when treated to liberal applications of manure it is suitable for the growing of vegetables on a commercial scale. The greensand contains many fossils, many of which were extracted in Victorian times and used as fertiliser. The sand is still quarried in the Potton and Sandy area for use in the building industry and so remains a valuable resource.

Members of my family have lived in this area for centuries: a comparatively long period in terms of human occupation, but a brief moment in terms of geological time. My quest to find out more about their lives and times forms the basis of this book; the backdrop for much (though not all) of it is the greensand ridge of central Bedfordshire.

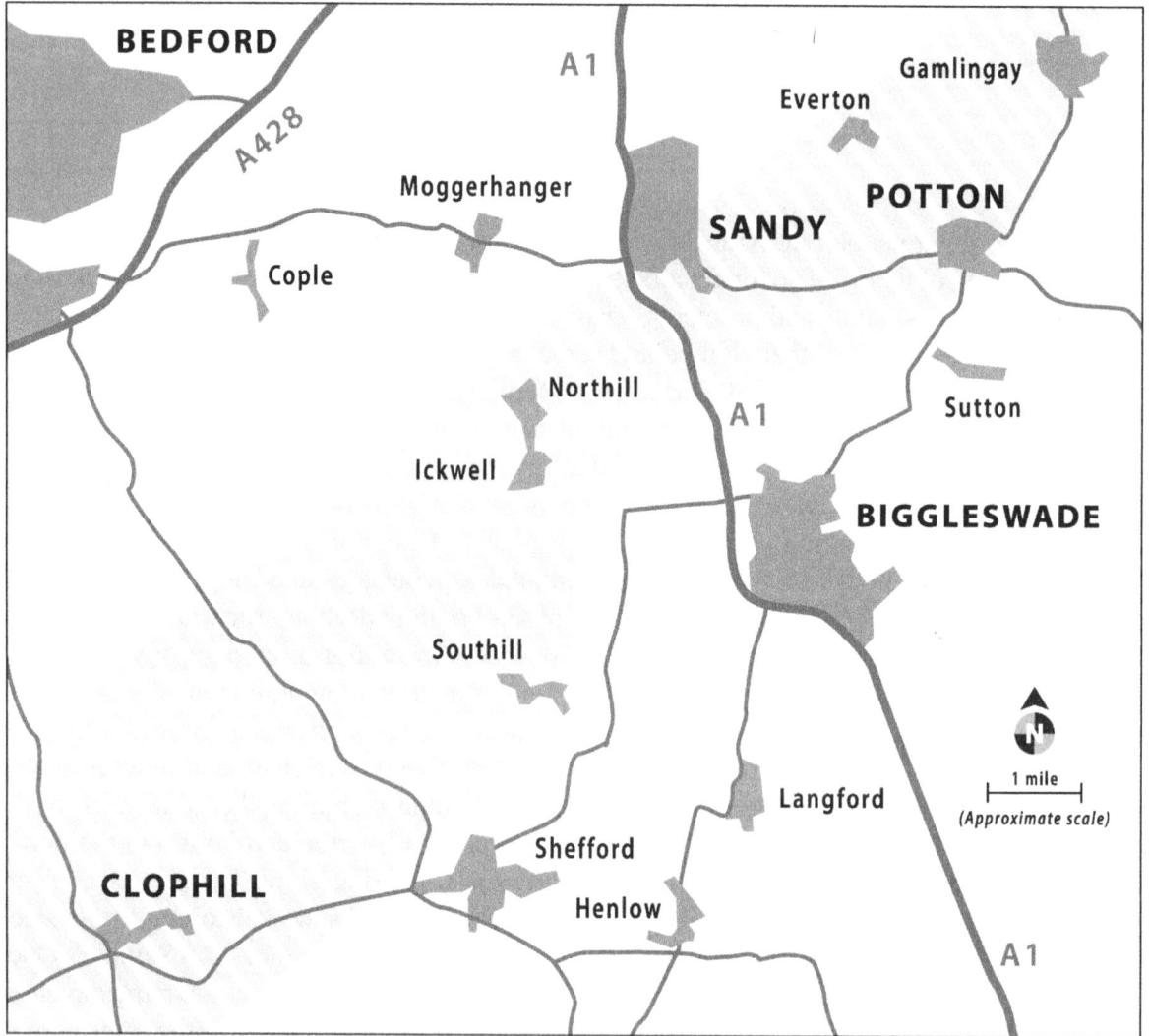

A map to show part of Central Bedfordshire

Documentary evidence shows that members of the Whitfield family have lived in this area since the sixteenth century.

Approximate extent of lower greensand

Introduction

'Compressed here in six feet by two,
In secrecy
To lie with me
Till the Call shall be
Are all these things I knew
Which cannot be handed on;
Strange happenings quite unrecorded
Lost to the world and disregarded ...'

Thomas Hardy (1840 – 1928)   *'Not only I'*

As a boy growing up in the early 1960s, I was privileged to get to know one of my great grandfathers, Philip Hiskey, who lived to the age of 91. He used to come and stay with my maternal grandparents Harry and Mildred Mingay, and I enjoyed these visits, particularly when they talked about past times.

My great grandfather was one of *fifteen* children born to Thomas and Eleanor Hiskey of Elmsett in East Suffolk. Three had died in infancy. He had left school at the age of ten, in 1885, and one of his first jobs had been to take sheep from his home village to Ipswich market, a journey of around eight miles. The job was undertaken alone, on foot. He later worked on farms as a head horseman in Suffolk and Essex, finally retiring at the age of 78, although he ploughed with horses when he was over eighty on one of his visits to my home town of Potton in Bedfordshire. Standing barely five feet tall, he had survived a lifetime of hard physical toil and he clearly enjoyed sharing his memories with his great grandson.

Granddad Harry had worked with pigs and had also spent four years somehow coping with the horrors of the trenches in the First World War before returning home to a 'Land fit for Heroes': unemployment, a brief job as a postman and a spell working for the Forestry Commission, using an axe - no chainsaws in those days. He was one of a large family, and, as his parents' cottage in Stanningfield, West Suffolk, was small, he was brought up next door by his maternal grandparents and had clearly been influenced by them. His grandfather, and thus my great great grandfather, James Limmocks, sometimes known as Lomax, was born in the early 1830s and had attended school for just one week before commencing employment at the tender age of five as a human bird-scarer on local farms in the early years of Queen Victoria's reign. James Limmocks had been renowned in his home village for his impressive physique and great physical strength. I was shown a fading photograph of him dating from about 1900. I heard about his feats of strength (he once carried four and a half hundredweight around a barn for a bet) and was given examples of some of his views and sayings, for instance "Pub talk ain't worth a farthing a bushel". Thanks to my granddad, I felt I had got to know *his* grandfather quite well and I had been mentally transported back to the days of William IV and Queen Victoria.

To hear stories related by my grandfather and great grandfather of times gone by in nineteenth century rural Suffolk was an experience to be savoured; and as their tales were often told in semi-darkness by the side of a crackling coal and wood fire and their tongues were enlivened by a glass or two of my grandmother's home-brewed beer, the stories were somehow all the more memorable. Although both men had quite different personalities, both were accomplished in the art of telling a story - an art clearly developed before the days of television. They made the past come alive for me and perhaps unwittingly encouraged a young and impressionable boy to take an interest in history in general and family history in particular. I still miss them, but their memories, in a sense, live on in me.

I grew up in the small Bedfordshire town of Potton and although we made the occasional journey to Suffolk and Essex to visit my mother's relatives, much of my regular day to day contact was with members of the Whitfield family. My grandfather Ernest Whitfield lived in King Street with his daughter Doris and his son in law Jack Sibley; I visited them every Sunday with my father, sister and brother, and their home was visited fairly regularly by my three Whitfield uncles and their families who lived in Cambridge. Unfortunately granddad Ernie died when I was nine years old, but my curiosity about the family encouraged me to obtain information from his sister Rosa, who visited occasionally, and their younger brother Arthur who lived in Potton. Both these people were interesting, larger than life characters, particularly to a rather quiet lad now in his early teens. Rosa gave me information on her father William Whitfield (my great grandfather) but always seemed reluctant to give too much information about her own earlier life. On a memorable visit to Uncle Arthur he told me that the family had come from a place called Tewin. I had never heard of it and he didn't give further details. It wasn't too difficult for me to discover that Tewin was in Hertfordshire, but I wondered why my great aunt and great uncle seemed to be withholding information about the family from me. I wanted to know more.

A few years later, a chance discovery in Reading University library of a court case in Hertford dating back to 1833 set me off on a trail of further discoveries that has so far kept me absorbed and occupied for nearly forty years. It is not and of course never will be complete. I have spent many hours poring over documents in Record Offices and elsewhere and more recently have used the internet extensively, with a fair degree of success. As a result I have been able to meet some distant Whitfield relatives and have managed to reunite, albeit temporarily, branches of the family which had been out of touch for over a century.

In the account that follows I have attempted, where possible, to give some background information to put the lives of family members into context. For example, what was it like to live in a small market town in the early Victorian period? What was a breast plough and how was it used? And what was it like to work in the Bedfordshire market gardening industry? I am conscious that on occasions I may have given a distorted view of what life was like at that particular place at that particular time. This has not been done deliberately, but historical events or geographical locations and their characteristics as they are described here are obviously subject to my interpretation of them or to the interpretation of others. This must be true of most historical writing, even in the case of 'academic' history which this case study certainly does not purport to be.

Until recently, history books have concentrated on great events which have helped to shape the way we live or have focussed on Royalty, or the rich and famous - essentially the celebrities of the day or era in any particular country or community. Village history, for instance, until recently tended to concentrate on the church, the manor house, the squire and other members of the gentry and their families. Ordinary people, as always, were given short measure and rarely featured in this type of history. Their lives seem to have been regarded as too mundane or insignificant to be worthy of any attention. Thankfully, steps are now being taken to redress the balance.

The history of an apparently ordinary family is far from dull and is documented in a surprising variety of ways, even though family members themselves may well have been illiterate or uneducated simply because they were denied the opportunity to learn even the basic skills of literacy and numeracy. However, it takes time and patience to tease out all the evidence and interpret and make sense of the story that appears to emerge from the welter of details. It would be wrong to pretend otherwise.

A leading newspaper recently gave away a booklet on tracing one's family history which gave the impression that it could be done in fourteen days. This claim was qualified by the booklet's editor who stated that these days did not need to be consecutive. I suppose that for some people a simple tree of a few generations with brief details of births, marriages and deaths *could* be produced in about a fortnight - gratifying for those who like to have almost instant results. However, my experience has been that after fourteen days I was only beginning to scratch the surface of the subject. This does not mean that I am trying to discourage anyone from embarking on a fascinating hobby - quite the reverse: I welcome the publication of *any* literature which inspires people to take an interest in their family history. My experience of family history research has been that it is necessary to take a long term view of proceedings, and 'enjoy the journey'. Genealogy is not like a race, and there are no prizes for finishing early. The early finisher in family history has probably missed some of the more interesting material which may be there to reward the more dogged and patient researcher. After spending about forty years researching my family, admittedly working on the project only when I had the opportunity between other demands on my time, I like to think I fall into this latter category, but even after this time I'm conscious of the gaps in my research, the unanswered and possibly unanswerable questions and the mistakes I may have made. I offer the account that follows rather like a cook might serve a meal, knowing that he (or she) has had to leave out a few ingredients from the recipe which were out of stock - or far too expensive - at the time the meal was being prepared. I have made use of what was available. The resulting fare may be a little nutritionally unbalanced, but it is hopefully still palatable. I have had to leave out some of the material; a diet consisting solely of carbohydrates would be substantial, but uninteresting and uninspiring. No-one, I suspect, would want to read endless lists of dates and names, for instance. It would be like reading the start of St Matthew's Gospel where he deals with the genealogy of Christ, beginning with Abraham begat Isaac and continuing in likewise manner for seventeen verses.

Obviously only a certain amount of evidence has survived, and the information I have managed to collect does not tell the *complete* story of the Whitfield family. On occasions I have had to speculate to fill in gaps and I trust that I have made it clear when I have done so. Some minor details may therefore be incorrect and may need to be revised or amended if further evidence comes to light. On the other hand, there have been occasions when the amount and nature of the material I have been able to discover about some members of the family have enabled me to get to know them very well and I have sometimes emerged from Record Offices feeling that I have been living in a previous century, with the people I have been researching.

Sometimes I have been fortunate to acquire information from family members, and I have to admit there is a possibility that their memories may have played tricks on them at times. As I have tried to be as systematic as possible I have attempted to find as many official records of family members as I can; I have also sometimes used secondary sources to put their memories into context and have thus had the opportunity to check on the information they have given me. I have been impressed with how accurate they have been.

I have come across a few controversial and colourful characters in the family during my researches. I have tried to record their lives as honestly as possible, relying on material to be found in archive collections, newspapers and in the public domain on the internet without offering further comments, although I may have speculated on possible reasons for their actions or attitudes at times. No attempt has been made to sensationalise: I am not writing for a tabloid newspaper. I am certainly not qualified or prepared to sit in judgement on fellow family members. No-one is perfect and that definitely includes me. 'He that is without sin among you, let him cast the first stone…' (This is probably a suitable place to apologise for any mistakes there may be in this book: I take sole responsibility for them and hope that they are not too numerous).

The opinions that *are* sometimes expressed in the book are mine or I am quoting from those of family members. I trust I have made it clear where I am doing this and that readers will be able to distinguish between the facts and opinions in the account which follows. Obviously, they are free to agree or disagree with my opinions. In the meantime, the search goes on, more details are discovered, events occur and the story continues to unfold. Like a map, by the time this is published it will be out of date. Today's events will be tomorrow's History.

I trust that this book will be of interest to family tree enthusiasts who may be able to learn from my mistakes, and hopefully it will encourage other people from ordinary backgrounds to write their own family histories. I began as an enthusiastic amateur genealogist and have still had no formal, professional training in the subject. My curiosity drove me on in my quest to learn more about my family. I have tried to undertake my research in a logical and systematic way using the resources available at the time, and using others which became available later, but experience has taught me that it is unwise, however theoretically desirable (and sensible) it might at first seem, to confine research to one particular member of the family at a time. In practice, it seems that researching one person tends to lead to enquiries relating to other members of the family, and following up these enquiries will often shed more light on the original person being researched in a sort of cross-fertilisation process. Being side-tracked in your quest is part of the fun - rather like making a journey in the countryside without a map. You never know where you will end up but you learn a lot about social history on the way. Of course, as in any other subject, there is always more to learn. My curiosity is insatiable.

On occasions the trail of discovery has appeared to peter out until a vital clue has emerged from another line of enquiry. This is what makes genealogy so fascinating at times and so frustrating at others, and it helps to explain why it is not ideal for those who crave instant gratification. Persistence and thinking from a different perspective are both recommended, but there is no simple recipe for success. However, beginners and more experienced researchers should not be deterred; they will find that there is a wealth of fascinating material out there waiting to be discovered and assembled into individual family stories, each one full of incident, drama and interest for the social historian as well as the general reader. People do not have to be famous, rich or influential to be interesting. They are, or can be, kind, avaricious, conceited, immoral, profligate, industrious, eccentric or saintly in any walk of life, and a few minutes spent with Quarter Sessions records or old newspapers will show that this applied to our ancestors too. Human nature doesn't seem to have changed much - if at all - over the centuries.

In the account that follows I have tried to show how my research was undertaken; readers may well be interested to see if they can follow similar lines of enquiry, hopefully without encountering some of the pitfalls which beset me. Much of my earlier work was undertaken without the use of the internet which has revolutionised genealogical research, but for detail the original documents remain invaluable. I hope that this approach is useful for readers who may be working on their own family trees.

The organisation of the book has presented me with a real challenge. I wanted to convey to the reader some sense of the excitement I had as I embarked on the project in my late teens and as I was able to take my first steps in working out my immediate family tree; the development of the internet made other discoveries possible, but of course they were not made in chronological order. Family tree research is seldom as straightforward as that. As I traced the tree further back and as I discovered more branches of the family, it became apparent that a strictly chronological approach, whether forward or backward in time, would not be entirely satisfactory. Although I wanted the 'story' to flow, the tree had become too complex. The approach I finally adopted is therefore essentially a compromise between several contesting methods of organisation. I think it works, but apologise if it is a little confusing at times. I thought it advisable to provide a few family tree diagrams and maps along the way to allow readers to navigate their way through the text. Unfortunately, limited space in the book and the size of the family tree prevented me from including the full version.

On the diagrams and sometimes within the text I have abbreviated at times by using the letter b to indicate the year when a particular member of the family was born and d to indicate when he or she died. It must be pointed out that these are only completely accurate from the year 1837, when it became a requirement to register births, marriages and deaths in England and Wales. Before this date my information was obtained mainly from parish registers, and these recorded details of *baptisms*, marriages and *burials*. Obviously there could be some potential discrepancies here: burials usually took place a few days after the death, or certainly no more than a couple of weeks later in most cases, unless an inquest was held; baptisms could occur in theory at any age, although in practice most were carried out in infancy. Later registers sometimes state the age of the person at baptism, and record the age at death. The series of censuses from 1841 from 1911 also enabled me to check on the approximate year of birth for family members, although considerable caution had to be exercised in the use of the 1841 census where ages were rounded to the nearest five years. Despite this, I have to admit that some inaccuracies may remain.

Thomas Carlyle once wrote that 'History is the essence of innumerable biographies'. This attempt to produce a history of an ordinary English family contains many small biographies, some more complete than others, and thus represents my attempt to record the contribution a family has made, simply by living day by day over five centuries, towards social history in general. How successful I have been is for the reader to decide.

Chapter 1.
The search begins.

'I keep six honest serving-men
(They taught me all I knew)
Their names are What and Why and When
And How and Where and Who'

Rudyard Kipling (1865-1936)

Do you believe in fate? My grandfather, great grandfather, great aunt and great uncle had all encouraged me to take an interest in my family background, but my family's story might never have been written if I hadn't been bored with work one evening, and decided to take a short walk from my desk. Looking back after nearly forty years, it seems strange that my search, which has required much patience, concentration and persistence started with a discovery which might not have been made if I had concentrated on what I was supposed to be doing. Perhaps I should explain.

When I went to Reading University in 1972 to study Geography I spent a great deal of time in the library in Whiteknights Park and at that time the Geography bookshelves were close to the History shelves. I soon discovered that there was a comprehensive selection of Local History books, and one evening noticed that there was a volume entitled *'Proceedings at Hertford County Assizes 1799-1833'*. It could never have been a best-seller, but idle curiosity prompted me to scan its index - a more interesting activity than grappling with the Geography essay I was supposed to be writing. To my surprise and delight I found that a Whitfield family was mentioned: the volume gave brief details of a James Whitfield, his wife Sarah and children James, George, Robert, Jonathan and David, who were to be removed from Tewin, Hertfordshire to Potton, Bedfordshire. The word 'removed' used in this context had me wondering what the family had done wrong to be treated in this way. At that time I had no idea what a removal order was, but the fact that there had been a connection between Tewin, Potton and the Whitfield family aroused my interest, bearing in mind the snippet of information I had been given by my great uncle Arthur.[1]

About this time, the Reverend Ian Stewardson became Rector of Potton, Sutton and Cockayne Hatley in Bedfordshire. His wife Margaret started to work part time at a plant nursery where I

---

1   see introduction, page xii

also worked in my University vacations; my sister Andrea became Mr Stewardson's organist at Sutton and I went out for a while with his daughter Helen. Mr Stewardson's sermons were often very relevant - even a little controversial - at times. He was prepared to state his views on contemporary issues rather than playing safe and remaining neutral and I appreciated and admired his scholarly approach and intellectual honesty. I began to attend church regularly and became a member of the church choir when I was at home in Potton. I became a fairly frequent visitor to the Rectory. Ian Stewardson was also interested in Local History and he allowed me to consult the original parish registers, many of which were still entrusted to his care.

Thanks to him I was able to take my family tree back two further generations by discovering that my great grandfather William Whitfield, so clearly described to me by various members of the family who had known him, had been baptised in 1854 in Potton, the son of James and Elizabeth Whitfield. Examination of the marriage registers showed me that James and Elizabeth had married in 1841, but also revealed that James' father had been James Whitfield, a gamekeeper. Could this latter James be the same James Whitfield mentioned in the *Proceedings at Hertford County Assizes* volume?

I could find no earlier marriages for the family in Potton. I found many later ones and the baptisms of dozens of Whitfield children. The really significant find was the record of the burial of a Sarah Whitfield, aged 48 on January 1, 1841. She would have therefore been born around 1792/3. James Whitfield's wife mentioned in the Hertford County Assizes book had been called Sarah. I searched the burial register again but could not find the burial of James recorded anywhere within its pages.

Subsequent searches revealed the marriage of a Robert Whitfield to a Catherine Jarvis in 1848. Robert's father was given as James Whitfield, gamekeeper. A Robert Whitfield, son of James, was also mentioned in the Hertford court case. I was convinced by this time that the family from Tewin was indeed my own family. I was able to draw a simple line of descent from James Whitfield to myself.

Uncle Arthur clearly knew what he was talking about. He had been born in 1895, so had obviously been given information from his father, who in turn had heard from *his* father. I had been given information in the early 1970s about an event which had occurred some 140 years previously.

As my own vicar had been so helpful, I decided to write to the vicar of Tewin to ask for further information. He kindly supplied some details from the Tewin baptism registers:

1821 Dec 16 James, son of James and Sarah Whitfield, gamekeeper.
1821 Dec 16 George, son of James and Sarah Whitfield, gamekeeper.
1825 Oct 10 David, son of James and Sarah Whitfield, gamekeeper.
1825 Oct 10 Jonathan, son of James and Sarah Whitfield, gamekeeper.
1830 April 18 David, son of James and Sarah Whitfield, gamekeeper.
1830 April 18 Henry, son of James and Sarah Whitfield, gamekeeper.

My initial reaction was one of amazement that the couple had produced three sets of twins. I later discovered that sometimes multiple baptisms were carried out at one ceremony - perhaps it was cheaper that way. The children could therefore have been born in different years. I subsequently discovered when I visited the Hertford Record Office a few years later that the Rev. Blamires Brown had missed the baptism of Robert which had taken place (on its own) in 1824.

DIAGRAM 1

My first family tree

William Whitfield
(1854 - 1930)

|

Ernest Whitfield
(1886 - 1963)

|

Hubert Whitfield
(1921 - 2006)

|

Rex Whitfield
(b 1954)

These details were obtained by talking to elderly members of the family. I soon discovered from the Potton parish registers that William Whitfield's father was James Whitfield, who married in 1841 in Potton, and died in 1895.

There also had been some burials: David Whitfield, an infant on November 6, 1825, another David Whitfield in June, 1830, aged 9 months (it was actually Henry), and finally one which I had been wondering about for a while - James Whitfield, aged 63 years, on February 21, 1833. This last burial explained why I had been unable to find James' burial in the Potton registers.

While I was there, I decided to look at the original court case and also asked for more information about removal orders. I found out that families or individuals were removed from a parish if they had settled there without having gained a legal settlement in the new parish (by certificate) and had subsequently become chargeable to the parish (in need of financial support) because they were ill or out of work. James had presumably been too ill to work as a gamekeeper in 1833 or even the previous year. There was no Social Security system as we would recognise it, administered on a national level, in those days. Instead, parish relief in the form of bread, fuel (usually coal) and sometimes money payments could be given at the discretion of parish officers like churchwardens or overseers of the poor. There was also the workhouse, where poor people were taken in to an institution, and given a very basic level of care. Here, the sexes were segregated and families were split up. This last option was a daunting prospect for most individuals and families. Presumably the Whitfield family were given some form of help by the overseers in Tewin, though as yet I have been unable to find what form this took.

Families removed from parishes were normally required to return to their parish of origin where the overseers of the poor were supposed to provide for them. It was really a method of ensuring that the new parish was not saddled with the expense and responsibility of looking after newcomers who had not gained a legal settlement and had fallen on hard times. However, I could find no firm evidence for the family having lived in Potton before 1833. What I did know was that James had been born around 1770 (as he was 63 when he died in 1833), and his wife Sarah had been born in 1792 or 1793.

In an attempt to discover more about the Whitfield family in Potton I went to the Bedford Record Office. I had never been to a record office before and I was amazed at the amount of material there was at my disposal. I was as excited as a toddler in a toyshop at the prospect of viewing original records and the staff were very helpful. Rather than looking at the parish registers for Potton (after all, I had seen the nineteenth century registers already, thanks to Ian Stewardson) they suggested that I should try the wills index. I managed to find a number of Whitfield wills, none of them made in Potton, but a couple for nearby Sandy and Biggleswade. Surprisingly, and to my delight, there was also one made by James Whitfield, yeoman, of Tewin, Hertfordshire. Why was it in the Bedfordshire Record Office, rather than at its counterpart in Hertfordshire?

James' will, made in August, 1832, stated that he was already 'very weak in body, but of perfect mind and memory'. He must have suspected that he was dying when he had his bequests formally recorded and it was touching to have the original document in my hand some 140 years or so afterwards. James left his household goods to his wife Sarah, but also mentioned that he had been left £50 by his brother Philip in *his* will. The Biggleswade will I had found was that of a Philip Whitfield. Assuming this to be the correct will I checked it for cross referencing purposes and found that James *was* mentioned in this and had indeed been left £50. Some sisters were also mentioned.

I looked at the Sandy wills, but these were much earlier (1712 and 1752). Could these have anything to do with my family? They were certainly of interest. I had copies made, but was not immediately able to connect them with James or Philip. As the men who made these wills - both called Robert Whitfield - lived in Sandy, it seemed sensible to look in the Sandy parish registers.

I was amazed to find that these registers showed that the Whitfield family had lived in Sandy since the sixteenth century. Amongst the baptism entries was one of particular interest: 1770, April 1, James, son of William and Elizabeth Whitfield. It looked as though I had found the baptism of my great-great-great grandfather, who appeared to have been born in the same year as Beethoven and Wordsworth. I suspect he never had the opportunity to hear any of Beethoven's music or read any of Wordsworth's poetry.

There was also a Sandy marriage which attracted my attention: that of James Whitfield, bachelor, a gardener aged over 21, and Elizabeth Martin, widow, by licence. It took place in 1796. Getting married by licence was regarded as more prestigious (or more discreet) than marrying by banns, where details of the parties to the forthcoming marriage were read out by the respective vicars of both parishes for their entire congregations to hear during morning service on three successive Sundays. Wealthy people got married by licence; so did couples where the bride was obviously pregnant, or where the bride or the groom - or both - had been married before.

The baptism I found in Sandy for a James Whitfield tied in well with the James who had died at Tewin aged 63 in February, 1833. However, his wife had been called Sarah, not Elizabeth and he had been a gamekeeper, not a gardener. Sarah had been born in about 1793, so a marriage between Sarah and James could, theoretically, have been from about 1809 onwards when she would have been sixteen. I could find no such marriage in Sandy.

All sorts of questions ran through my mind. Had James been a bigamist? Had he and Sarah not married at all but were *assumed* in Tewin to be a married couple? Was James the gamekeeper from Tewin a different person from the James Whitfield born in Sandy around 1770? Or had James married a second time, following the death of his first wife, Elizabeth?

I was convinced that I *was* dealing with the same person, as the baptism seemed to fit in so well with the death of a James Whitfield aged 63 in Tewin. Bigamy I felt was unlikely, though not impossible, so it seemed most likely that James' first wife had died and he had remarried. I knew, however, that my reasoning was not infallible because I was assuming that James had been baptised *as an infant* and at the back of my mind I knew that a baptism could actually occur at any age.

In order to check my remarriage theory I first needed to ascertain that his first wife had died. I was therefore looking for the death of Elizabeth Whitfield in Sandy (presumably), after 1796, but before 1821 when the first of James and Sarah's children was baptised in Tewin.

Elizabeth was clearly a popular name in the family and on checking the Sandy burial register I was surprised to find I had a choice of three:

1798 Dec 20 Elizabeth, wife of William Whitfield

1813 March 7 Elizabeth Whitfield aged 60

1820 April 24 Elizabeth Whitfield, aged 44

Unless the vicar had made a mistake with Elizabeth's husband's name, the first Elizabeth was probably not the wife of James. Subsequent research suggested that she was, in fact, James' mother. The other two were still possibilities.

Having been successful with my inspection of the index of the '*Proceedings at Hertford Assizes*' volume, it had become my habit to leaf through the index of any Bedfordshire or Hertfordshire local history book I came across for any mention of the Whitfield family. (Yes, I had become a genealogy addict). Most of these searches have proved unsuccessful over the years, but occasionally I have discovered a gem of information which has proved to be invaluable. I was now teaching at Wootton Upper School in Bedfordshire and while on duty in the library one lunchtime, I picked up a Bedfordshire Historical Society publication *Samuel Whitbread's Notebooks 1810-1811 and 1813-1814*. Samuel Whitbread, one of the brewing dynasty, held land at Southill, Beds, and was at that time a Justice of the Peace. Imagine my delight when I discovered a James Whitfield was mentioned in his notebook for 1813:

'James Whitfield, Cople. Information against Lawrence Brown and James Wilis (sic), both of Colmworth for shooting in the parish of Eaton Socon, hamlet of Wyboston, on Tuesday, September 16, 1813.'

There was a subsequent entry: Friday December 3, 1813: 'Brown and Wilis convicted of shooting. Ordered to pay the money to Mr Pearce on Saturday sennight or to me on the Sunday, done at Bedford.'

Cople is a village a few miles from Sandy on the way to Bedford. Wyboston is a hamlet four miles north of Sandy. I wasn't sure what James Whitfield was doing in either place, but if he was reporting incidents of shooting then it seemed reasonable to suppose that he might be a gamekeeper. As he was described as being of Cople, it seemed sensible to look at the Cople parish registers. It was certainly worth my while:

Marriage 30 September, 1814.

James Whitfield of this parish and Sarah Berry of this parish, married by licence.

James Whitfield x his mark

Sarah Berry x her mark

Thomas Bedford and Benjamin Twitchell, curate and churchwarden respectively, acted as witnesses; unfortunately, no other members of the Whitfield family were mentioned.

The format of the registers before 1837 is such that the fathers of brides and grooms are not recorded. However, turning to the Cople baptism registers, I found that Sarah was the daughter of a tailor, William Berry, and his wife Anna Maria, nee Lamb. Sarah's maternal grandfather, James Lamb, had been a fairly well-to-do miller and small farmer in nearby Willington. James Whitfield was 44 at the time of his marriage. Sarah's baptism was on August 19, 1792, so it seemed likely that she was about half the age of her husband. She was one of a large family (two brothers and six sisters), and James' youngest sister-in-law was only eleven. To her, James must have seemed like an old man.

Further examination of the baptism register revealed that James and Sarah had some of their family baptised in Cople:

1815 April 18, (born February 11, 1815) Naomi, daughter of James and Sarah Whitfield, Cople, gamekeeper to the Earl Ludlow.

(Sarah had clearly been about four months' pregnant when she married - a not unusual occurrence for brides in the early nineteenth century. Of course it is not unknown today. Her pregnancy would explain why James had again opted to marry by licence, rather than by banns. Having a child with an *unmarried* woman half his age might well have raised a few eyebrows in Cople and the calling of banns on three successive Sunday mornings would probably have set tongues wagging in the small rural community).

1816, September 1, Philip, son of James and Sarah Whitfield, Cople, labourer.

1818, June 12, William, son of James and Sarah Whitfield of Cople, gamekeeper to the Earl Ludlow.

It appeared, therefore, that James' first wife Elizabeth had died in 1813 aged sixty - the second one on my list of suspects mentioned earlier - and James had remarried. I was now pretty sure that James was my great-great-great- grandfather. Furthermore, it looked as though I was descended from a long line of Whitfields who had lived, loved, worked and died in Sandy

DIAGRAM 2

The Tewin connection

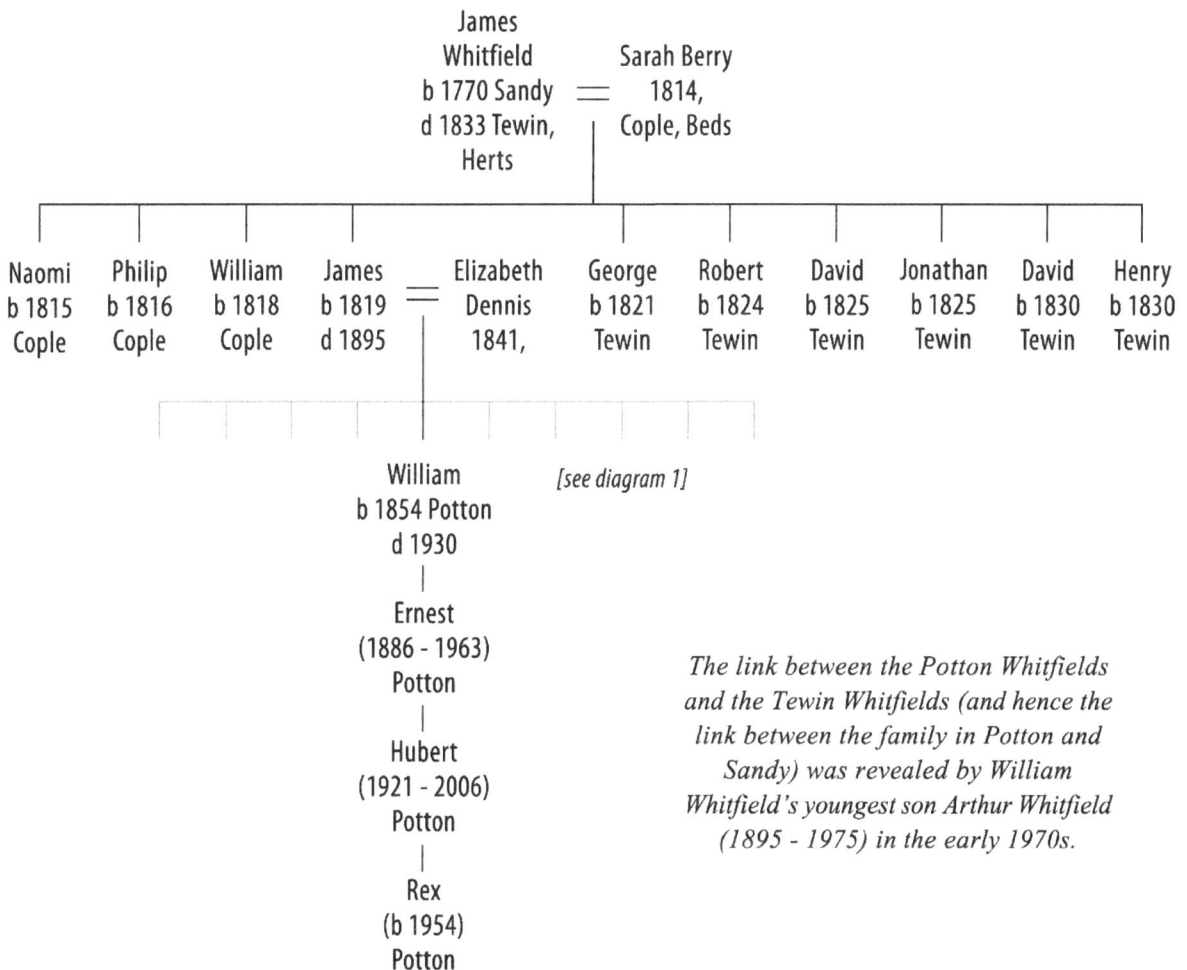

The link between the Potton Whitfields and the Tewin Whitfields (and hence the link between the family in Potton and Sandy) was revealed by William Whitfield's youngest son Arthur Whitfield (1895 - 1975) in the early 1970s.

since the sixteenth century.

James and Sarah's large number of sons and their links with Sandy, Cople, Tewin and Potton make them pivotal figures in my family history and I wanted to find out more about them, just to confirm that my conclusions were correct. Thanks to material held at the Hertfordshire and Bedfordshire Record Offices I have been able to piece together various snippets of information which, added to earlier discoveries, have enabled me to paint a reasonably complete picture of my Whitfield great-great-great grandparents. They are not necessarily in strict chronological order, but rather in the order I discovered them.

James was a 'gardener' at the time of his marriage to Elizabeth Martin in 1796, according to the marriage register. Many men in Sandy at this time were described as gardeners; the term used in this way really means a market gardener, as Sandy and Biggleswade and later Potton were centres of the market gardening industry. Domestic gardeners were usually shown as gardener to Mr.X, for example gardener to John Foster, Esquire. Land tax assessments for Sandy and Girtford, examined at the Bedford Record Office show that in 1798 James was farming land in Girtford, about half a mile from Sandy as the crow flies, as a tenant of Ann Moore. James' father's land in Swaden, Sandy, was being farmed by James' brother, Philip Whitfield. Here was more evidence that I was dealing with the same James, as Philip had been mentioned in James' will and vice versa, and both were linked with William Whitfield their father in Sandy. The names chosen by James and Sarah for their first two sons born in Cople: Philip and William, were further clues.

Gamekeepers had to obtain certificates or licences on an annual basis. From these I discovered that as early as 1796 (the year of his first marriage) James Whitfield was appointed as a gamekeeper by Sir Philip Monoux of Sandy. Certificates survive for him from 1801 to 1806 at Sandy, again registered by Sir Philip Monoux. The lists of gamekeepers for 1796 and 1806 were published in editions of the *Northampton Mercury* which I found on the internet. James continued to work on the Monoux' Sandy estate after Sir Philip's death. His new employer was Frances Monoux, one of Sir Philip's daughters. By 1815 we know, from details in the Cople baptism registers, that he was gamekeeper to Earl Ludlow. I have not discovered the reason for his move to Cople and exactly when it took place, but the entry in Samuel Whitbread's notebooks indicates that James was living there by September, 1813, some six months after his first wife, Elizabeth, died in Sandy.

The Earl Ludlow referred to in the baptism registers may have been the Right Honourable Augustus, Earl Ludlow, mentioned on some gamekeepers' certificates from 1804 to 1806. Earl Ludlow of Cople House owned Grange Farm, the Manor House and 38 acres and Water End Farm in Cople as well as Park Farm in Stevington, Bedfordshire. I later discovered (when the British Newspaper Archive appeared online) that he also owned land in Wyboston, which helped to explain James Whitfield's presence there in 1813.

The Thornton family in Moggerhanger were neighbouring landowners to Earl Ludlow at Cople. They also held the manor of Beeston, near Sandy and had an estate near Blunham called South Mills. Godfrey Thornton was a wealthy merchant, trading with Russia and was a Director of the Bank of England from 1772 to 1801, its Deputy Governor from 1791 to 1793 and Governor from 1793 to 1795. His cousin, Henry Thornton, was a prominent member of the Clapham Sect, a group of evangelical Christians, based in Clapham, London, and both Henry and Godfrey were related to the leader of the Sect, William Wilberforce. Many of the group were very wealthy; some were bankers, others were Members of Parliament; Henry Thornton was both. Members of the Sect attended Holy Trinity Church on Clapham Common. They were an influential group in the House of Commons and did much to abolish the slave trade throughout the British Empire. They have been criticised since, however, for their 'lack of political engagement with the conditions of the poor at home'. Godfrey Thornton was associated with the Clapham sect, and for a time was an employer of his cousin Henry. After Godfrey's death in 1805, Moggerhanger House and the South Mills estate passed to his eldest son Stephen Thornton (1767-1850). His (i.e. Stephen's) brother, William Thornton, assumed his grandmother's surname of Astell when he inherited Woodbury Hall between Everton and Gamlingay, close to the present day border between Bedfordshire and Cambridgeshire, from her in 1807. He married Sarah Harvey, whose father owned Ickwell Bury; more about the Harveys later. William Thornton was a director of the East India Company for nearly fifty years, its chairman four times and governor of the Russian Company. Colonel of the East Indian Volunteers and lieutenant-colonel of the Bedfordshire Militia, William Thornton was also MP for Bedfordshire until his death in 1847.

Another of Godfrey's sons, Claude George Thornton, acquired the manor of Marden Hill near Tewin in Hertfordshire in 1817 and engaged the services of a prominent architect, Sir John Soane the following year (Soane had previously worked for Godfrey Thornton at Moggerhanger) to help him get the mansion '…in a comfortable condition…with perhaps a trifling alteration to improve the dining room'. Either Sir John Soane was a very persuasive architect or Claude George Thornton suddenly felt a need to display his status (he was also a director of the Bank of England) for the mansion was in fact extensively remodelled.

I would imagine that James Whitfield's salary was not enormous when Claude George Thornton engaged *his* services by registering him as his gamekeeper in 1819, although I suspect the move to Tewin may have represented a promotion for him as James appears to have been an under-keeper in Cople. As he couldn't write and presumably had not acquired the useful skill of reading, he may well have heard about the vacancy by chatting to the Thorntons' gamekeeper at Moggerhanger, possibly over a pint at a local pub, but this is conjecture on my part.

Gamekeeping was a risky occupation in the early nineteenth century. The gamekeeper was in an awkward position in some ways; responsible for the game on his estate he was answerable to his master, usually a man of considerable wealth, status and influence. A gamekeeper clearly did not belong to the same social class as his employer and would not be part of his social circle but he did perhaps catch glimpses of a different way of life from his own. As he had to safeguard his master's game and interests on the estate it was difficult for him to be too friendly with ordinary labourers, many of whom would have regarded him with suspicion, or even hostility, and it was clearly not in the gamekeeper's interests to give away his employer's secrets or he could expect instant dismissal. For these reasons men from outside the local area were often employed as gamekeepers and this may have been why James Whitfield was selected to look after the game on the Marden Hill estate. Whatever his natural inclination, the gamekeeper often became a loner, and could expect to spend a lot of his time in secluded locations in all sorts of weather. It was most unlikely that he would ever become the most popular man in the village. Often he became a target for poachers because he stood between them and a free source of tasty meat. His job combined the duties of a rearer of livestock with those of a policeman or security guard. His status was above that of ordinary farm labourers, but essentially he was a servant of his wealthy employer, and at his beck and call.

Times were very hard for labourers in the first few decades of the nineteenth century. If they had jobs - and many did not - they worked very long hours and were paid very little. There was little job security. Families were large and had to be fed. There was every temptation, therefore - maybe even justification - for labourers to poach. Landowners were anxious to prevent poaching and trespassing on their estates and used gamekeepers to police their woods. They also placed vicious mantraps on their land. Such traps could easily break a trespasser's leg and could maim him for life. Gamekeeping was therefore a hard and dangerous way of life, not to be undertaken by those of a delicate constitution or nervous disposition.

Some Bedfordshire examples of the period illustrate this. In 1811, Thomas Delahay, gamekeeper to Samuel Whitbread (whose notebooks mentioned James Whitfield, as we have seen), wrote to his master complaining about his treatment on the Southill estate in Bedfordshire. He claimed that he had

'…laid ought many cold Nights in your Woods and Plantations wen the Rest of your Servants were a bed and doing so I have decade my Concitution for the Percivation of your Game. I have never had a pleasant word from you in the last three years'.

He apologised later for this communication, probably because his job would have been in jeopardy after such an outburst. James was not capable of writing such a letter, as he was illiterate, but it may well be that he suffered similar working conditions, and harboured similar sentiments. It was probably best not to express them. After all, he had a wife and family to support.

Poaching was not always a case of 'one for the pot'. Sometimes gangs of dangerous poachers would raid an estate. A case is quoted in *Southill and the Whitbreads*:

'On December 9, 1815 a gang of notorious and desperate poachers at Biggleswade set out after dark to shoot pheasants at Southill. Two were armed with guns and the other five with bludgeons. They agreed to stand by each other and not be taken. After shooting two pheasants they attracted the attention of the head [keeper] and underkeepers, and help was summoned from the landlord of the *White Horse*. The head keeper was shot and died of his wounds the next day, and the poachers were arrested and later committed to Bedford Prison'.

The Bedfordshire Quarter Sessions records (consulted at the Record Office) contain details of similar incidents and one I found was of particular interest because it involved James Whitfield, my great-great-great grandfather, who was watching snares set in a spinney in Willington, about a mile from Cople, for the head gamekeeper, Thomas Brampton. He had the misfortune to encounter a notorious poacher, Thomas Vintiner (or Vintner), an Old Warden labourer in his late twenties. It appears that Vintiner was not the only poacher in the spinney.

'James Whitfield watched, as described by Brampton until Monday evening between 4 and 5. He was lying among the bushes when Vintiner came up with a gun in his hand. Whitfield said "What do you do here?" and Vintiner said to Whitfield's 'holla' "I am lost". Whitfield said it was an odd place to be lost in and followed him a little way and said "Where are you going?"

Vintiner said "Damn your eyes, what is that to you?", and walked out of the spinney and said "Damn your eyes, we won't be taken now" and cried out "You who are forward come back and you who are behind come forward" and then Ashford's assistant man came out of the spinney and presented a loaded pistol to him and Vintiner presented his gun which was also loaded and they both said to Whitfield "Stand off, we won't be taken."

Whitfield had before given an alarm and the rest of his party immediately joined him. Vintiner presented his gun to Brampton and said repeatedly " Stand off, we won't be taken". Brampton and Goodship then seized the gun from Vintiner.

Clark said the same except he heard Vintiner say to Brampton on presenting his gun to him "Stand off or you shall have the contents"…'

This happened on the 13th November, 1815 and the Quarter Sessions records go on to state that James Whitfield was seriously assaulted 'so that his life was greatly despaired of '. Thomas Brampton was similarly attacked and Vintiner and Samuel Brown were also required to answer for a previous assault on another gamekeeper, William Woods of Stagsden, when they appeared in court at Bedford at its Epiphany Session in 1816. A scuffle had broken out after Woods had confiscated a hare, but Vintiner and Brown were acquitted because the plucky gamekeeper had apparently struck the first blow. However, Vintiner was sentenced to one year's imprisonment for the offence committed in Willington. He was fined one shilling and bound to keep the peace for a further two years. He had to find sureties of £100 from himself, and £50 from two others: Samuel Ashwell, a Henlow shoemaker, and Isaac Marston of Clifton. He must have found it very difficult to raise the necessary money (considerable sums in 1816/1817 when labourers were earning just a few shillings per week) because he was finally released from the Bedford Gaol on 23rd April, 1817, after having spent about sixteen months inside.

I am not sure who 'Ashford's assistant man' was, but from the context of the Willington document it would appear that he was helping the poachers. He may have been Samuel Brown, Vintiner's accomplice at Stagsden. 'Ashford' may well refer to Ezekiel Ashford, a labourer in his mid-twenties from Southill, who appears in the Bedford Gaol Register on a number of occasions from 1815 to 1819. During that period he served four separate three month sentences for poaching offences and was also fined one shilling for assault. In 1817 the Register notes that he was 'disorderly and ill-behaved'.

Samuel Brown, another labourer in his mid-twenties, lived in Cardington. He had served a three month sentence in Bedford Gaol for setting a snare in 1814, and the prison records show that he became a regular offender. He was convicted of 'snareing' again in 1816 and received a further three month sentence and in 1817, when he was caught with a pheasant in his possession and thus received a further six months inside. In 1818 he served another three months and was publicly whipped for deserting his family. Apparently unrepentant, he was back to his old poaching exploits the following year. It would appear that Vintiner, Ashford and Brown were not the sort of men anyone would want to meet in a dark alley - or spinney - anywhere. They were hardened criminals.

The Willington incident was reported in the *Cambridge Chronicle and Journal* of 19th January, 1816, and the *Bury and Norwich Post* of 31st January, 1816 - news seems to have travelled at a rather more leisurely pace in those days. Both reports state that the snares had been watched throughout the preceding night. James Whitfield had been one of *nine* assistants engaged for this purpose. I presume they operated some sort of a rota system, but unless they all had alarm clocks I suspect most of them had been awake all night, even if they weren't all in the spinney at the same time. I trust that Earl Ludlow, refreshed from a comfortable night's sleep in a warm bed, expressed his gratitude to these cold and weary men after Vintiner's capture.

James at this time was 46. Sarah, who was only about 24, must have been very worried; she had only been married about two years, and they now had young Naomi and Philip to provide for.

The year 1816 came to be known in Europe and North America as the year without a summer. James and Sarah may not have realised at the time that the weather that year had been adversely affected by the largest volcanic eruption in recorded history: the eruption of Mount Tambora on the island of Sumbawa in the Dutch East Indies (now Indonesia), which had taken place in the previous year. The phenomenal amount of ash emitted eventually encircled the earth, and entered the stratosphere, resulting in a lowering of temperatures. Unusual weather conditions were experienced in England in the summer months of 1816: in the London area, for instance, snow fell in May; temperatures were several degrees colder than usual; and rainfall totals were higher than in most summers, with rain falling on most days from May through to September. Cereal crops didn't ripen properly because of the lack of sunshine and some grains rotted on the stalk before they could be harvested. Some of the grain that was harvested went mouldy in store. Consequently, food was scarce and the price of basic foodstuffs soared. Many farm labourers found themselves without work and without money to buy food. Malnutrition was common and starvation was a definite possibility. Many labourers and their families would have been desperate for something to eat and I would imagine that James was kept busy safeguarding Earl Ludlow's land from the depredations of poachers.

It is probably safe to assume that James' and Sarah's family were well-clothed during their time at Cople because Sarah's brothers were all tailors, following their father's occupation. They were probably well-fed too; with James' former job as a market gardener he may have cultivated a garden plot for potatoes and other vegetables, and dare I suggest they may have tasted an occasional rabbit, hare and pheasant? The Duke of Bedford's wood accounts for 1817-1818 show that James bought two and three quarter yards of ash billets at four shillings and sixpence per yard at auction. He thus spent over twelve shillings on fuel, which was probably equivalent to a week's wages, to ensure that he and Sarah (now pregnant with William), Naomi and Philip were kept warm through that winter. While James was healthy and working I would imagine that he and his family were able to enjoy a few creature comforts. They would possibly have been a little better off than ordinary labourers. If James became ill or seriously injured following Vintiner's assault, the family's standard of living would have been quickly jeopardised.

Fortunately, James appears to have recovered from the injuries he received for, as we have seen, he was appointed gamekeeper to Claude George Thornton on his Marden Hill Estate near Tewin in 1819. I am not sure whether he had a period of unemployment between 1818 and 1819, but it seems possible, even likely, that he and his family settled for a brief time in Potton, before they moved to Tewin, and this is why the Removal Order required them to return there when James became too ill to work some fourteen years later. Otherwise, they would presumably have been ordered to return to Cople.

I have found very little documentary material to give a detailed picture of James and Sarah's life in Tewin, apart from that already supplied from the parish registers, which record the baptisms of their sons - and the deaths of two of them. The last two boys, Henry and David, were born when their father was about sixty years old; Sarah would have been about thirty seven. As the family's time in Tewin was before censuses were taken, I have no idea where in the village the family lived, but it is probably safe to assume that their cottage wasn't designed or improved in any way by Sir John Soane.

It seems likely that a combination of the assault at Willington, the hard physical work undertaken in all weathers and the demands of a much younger wife and growing family may have helped to undermine James' health. Alternatively he may have succumbed to disease. Cottages at this time tended to be small and overcrowded; sanitation was rudimentary and medical knowledge not very advanced. Epidemics were common and starvation was not unknown. Sixty three years was probably a fair innings for a working man in those days. Unfortunately, death certificates were not required before 1837. The cause of James' death was not recorded in the Tewin burial register, so must remain a matter for speculation. His will, drawn up in August, 1832, already refers to his weak bodily state, so it would appear that he suffered a lengthy period of illness or incapacity before he died in February, 1833. One of the witnesses to his will was Robert Ballantine, another gamekeeper, and possibly James' replacement on the Marden Hill estate.

I have searched in vain for any evidence of the Tewin overseers of the poor giving the Whitfield family some kind of help during this period; hopefully they *were* able to offer some assistance, although clearly they were unhappy about the family being chargeable to the parish. Similarly, bearing in mind the Thornton family's close connection with the Clapham Sect of evangelical Christians who advocated practical Christianity, it also seems amazing that Claude George Thornton, a man of considerable wealth and influence was unable or apparently unwilling to intervene in the Removal Order or to provide any form of assistance, financial or otherwise. James had been his gamekeeper for about fourteen years and a little compassion and practical help from his employer would not have gone amiss.

In contrast to his former gamekeeper, Claude George Thornton was able to enjoy a comfortable old age. The 1851 census shows that he had seven domestic servants to cater for his needs and whims as he continued living beyond his three score years and ten. He left around £35,000 when he died aged about ninety in 1866, a considerable sum and an advanced age for those days. There can be little doubt that his longevity was in no small part helped by the life of comparative luxury he had been able to lead in his newly enlarged mansion, while his servants and gamekeepers had taken care of the drudgery and unpleasant tasks, probably for a pittance.

Following the death of my great-great-great grandfather James Whitfield in 1833, his widow Sarah was left behind with a large family to care for. How she coped and what became of them all we shall discover in later chapters.

Footnote: Thomas Vintiner was still alive in 1851, and living in a cottage close to the *Hare and Hounds* public house in Old Warden, with his wife Mary, daughter Elizabeth, son Christopher, daughter in law Mary Ann and some young grandchildren. He was described as a pauper, formerly an agricultural labourer. I wonder whether his poaching exploits were over.

Chapter 2.
The Whitfields in Sandy – and Biggleswade.

'Fear no more the heat o' the sun
Nor the furious winter's rages
Thou thy worldly task hast done
Home art gone and ta'en thy wages…'

William Shakespeare (1564- 1616) *Cymbeline*

In the early days of tracing my family tree I was keen to see how far back in time I could get. I suppose that must be the aim of most family historians as they embark on their journey of discovery. I was excited to see that entries in the Sandy parish registers for the Whitfield family went back to the late sixteenth century and so began to try to work out how - or if - they fitted together to form separate families and different generations. It was not an easy task.

In 1538 it became a legal requirement for each parish to keep a register of births, marriages of deaths. Not all registers from this time have survived, and I was therefore fortunate in discovering that Sandy's very early registers *can* still be seen. However, I could find no mention of the family until the 1570s. Judging from the relatively small numbers of families mentioned in the registers in the sixteenth century, Sandy appears to have been a small settlement and it is likely that everybody living there knew each other during this period. Many families would have been interrelated. A former Bedfordshire archivist, Patricia Bell, has calculated that by the early eighteenth century Sandy would have contained about 150 families. From this we can estimate a population of perhaps somewhere between 600 and 750. It is likely that sixteenth century Sandy was even smaller than this – containing perhaps about four hundred people. It appears that there had been some sort of epidemic there in 1559 when seventy one burials were recorded; the average number had been just ten, according to figures given in Joyce Godber's *History of Bedfordshire*.

For a long time Sandy seems to have been overshadowed by the larger nearby market towns of Potton and Biggleswade. Its population in 1801 was still only 1115. The coming of the railway about fifty years later giving easy access to London, and the opening in 1858 of the 'Varsity' line (Oxford to Cambridge) which passed through Sandy helped the pre-existing market gardening industry to develop further by making it easier and quicker to send perishable produce to more distant markets. The railway was also used to convey horse manure from the London stables and soot from London chimneys to the hungry, light soil of the Sandy district.

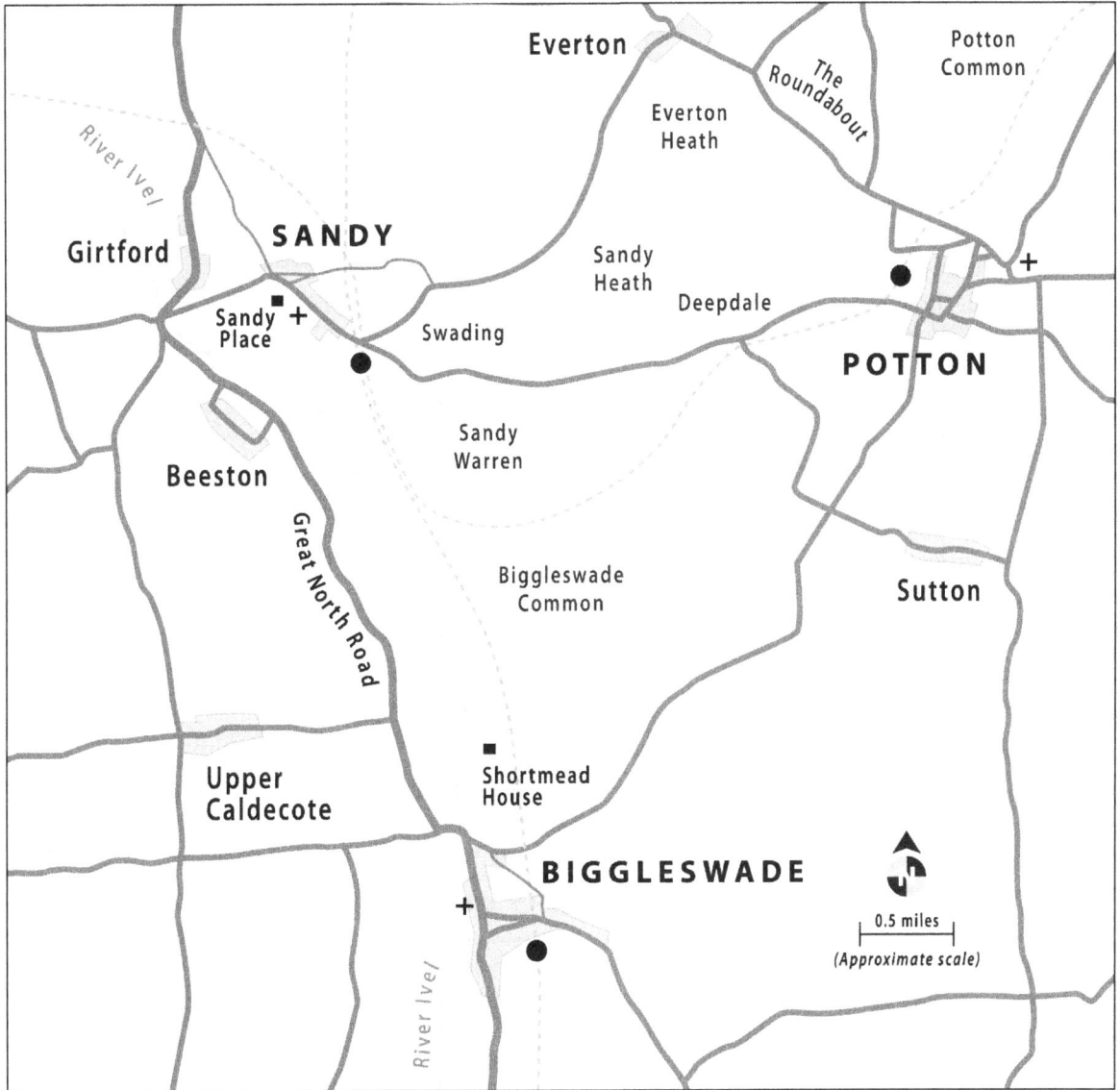

A map showing the Sandy, Potton and Biggleswade area c1870.
The Whitfield family has lived in this area of Bedfordshire from
1576 to the present day.

The manure supplied much-needed nutrients to growing plants, but would have also contained straw which helped the greensand to hold its moisture. The soot was applied, or 'sown' on still days when rain was expected. It acted as a soil conditioner, darkened the soil so that it absorbed the sun's heat more quickly and helped to deter pests in cereal and vegetable crops. Later, shoddy (waste from woollen mills in Yorkshire) was also added to the lighter soils to improve their water retention.

The population of Sandy increased during the nineteenth century so that by 1901 its population was 3110 - it was therefore still a relatively small, essentially rural community, where market gardening was important. The same surnames tend to figure repeatedly in the parish registers over the years until the start of the twentieth century. The Whitfield surname was one of these and over the years became connected by marriage to other, often long-established, families. Often these families were also connected with market gardening.

One of the problems I had in trying to make sense of the Whitfield entries in the registers was that the same Christian names tended to be used over and over again. In particular, the names Robert and William for males and Elizabeth and Susan (or Susanna) for females, were very popular over the generations. Middle Christian names were hardly ever used in my family until well into the nineteenth century and, even then, they were rare. Each family probably developed its own tradition with regard to name selection, with sons being named after their fathers and daughters after their mothers, for example, or perhaps the names of grandparents, uncles and aunts or other family members were re-cycled. The Bible and the names of members of the Royal family were often used as sources of inspiration by parents when choosing names for new family members; these were times before our present obsession with celebrities, so the names selected tended to be relatively conventional, although occasionally a son or daughter might be given their mother's maiden surname as a Christian name.

The early registers do not give addresses, and the ages of those being baptised, married or buried are often not stated. Their format is such that they give details of baptisms, marriages and burials in chronological order, year by year, but in the same register. The entries are hand written and are therefore sometimes difficult to read. *Separate* registers for each type of record were a later development. I found I had to piece together the evidence from the registers, construct some tentative trees for individual families from the entries and then look for other types of records (wills, land transaction documents and census information for example) to substantiate or disprove my theories if there was any element of doubt. A little common sense went a long way; for example I had to bear in mind that family members were unlikely to get married before their late teens, and that women were unlikely to conceive after they were in their late forties. Deaths, as now, could occur at any age, but in earlier centuries infant mortality was significantly higher, and fewer people survived into their seventies, eighties and beyond.

I used the method of listing all the children of a particular couple, together with the dates of their baptisms. I would then look at burials over the same period and a little later, and account for any infant deaths involving the children that had been baptised. Sometimes, deaths or burials would give details of a person's age, occupation and/or relationship to another member of the family. For instance I found details such as:

Elizabeth, wife of Robert Whitfield.

Elizabeth Whitfield, aged 60.

Elizabeth Whitfield, spinster.

Robert Whitfield, gardener.

Robert Whitfield, son of William Whitfield.

I was fortunate in finding some wills which were very useful in showing relationships within the family, and a land transaction document, found among the documents of the Pym family, which mentioned four generations of one branch of the Whitfield family, giving dates of death of family members as well as details relating to the reorganisation of land holdings in Sandy. Obviously of great interest, this latter document was invaluable in helping me to establish family relationships.

We saw in the previous chapter that James Whitfield (the gamekeeper) was baptised in Sandy in 1770, and was the son of William and Elizabeth Whitfield. From the baptism records I found that William and Elizabeth had produced a large family between 1759 and 1779: William, Thomas, Robert, Elizabeth, John, James, Philip, Elizabeth and Martha. There was also another daughter, Ann, mentioned in Philip's will; she was probably born between 1775 and 1779, but does not appear to have been baptised. The reason for *two* daughters being called Elizabeth was that the first Elizabeth had died in infancy. Both girls had, of course, been named after their mother.

William Whitfield, (James' father), had married Elizabeth Retchford in 1758 in Sandy. Further examination of the baptism records showed me that William had been baptised in Sandy in October,1727, but there had been two Elizabeth Retchfords. One had been baptised in Sandy in 1725, the other in 1737. Which one had married William?

Looking at the baptism of the couple's last child - Martha, in 1779 - led me to the conclusion that it was the second (younger) Elizabeth Retchford that William had married. This would explain why the marriage register stated that the consent of Elizabeth's parents was sought before the ceremony took place. She would have been 20 or 21 when she walked down the aisle (he was some ten years older) and would have had her last child when she was 42.

We have seen that James Whitfield, baptised in 1770, was originally a gardener, i.e. a market gardener. Market gardening has been practised in Sandy for centuries. The parish contains low hills of greensand, a rock which weathers to produce a soil which is light and easy to cultivate. It also warms up quickly in spring, making it suitable for growing early crops. These were highly prized in the days before refrigeration and air transport made it possible to have fruits and vegetables from all over the world displayed on supermarket shelves all the year round. The greensand is well drained, but its free-draining nature tends to make it dry out quickly in summer, making irrigation desirable. For centuries prior to the coming of the railway, liberal applications of manure from local horses, cattle and sheep helped to keep the soil fertile and ensured that it held moisture for a little longer. It is perhaps significant that some of the most important vegetable crops grown before the days of large-scale irrigation (carrots and parsnips) were root crops, able to find water below the first few dusty inches of topsoil.

Ken Quince, a retired market gardener, in his booklet *The Sandy I knew*, published in the 1980s claimed that 'Stratford [a hamlet near Sandy on the road towards Everton and Potton] in particular was noted for its early vegetables as far back as the thirteenth century. The land is protected from the north and east by woods and has a natural slope to the west'.

Market gardening seems to have started in the Stratford and Swaden (or Swading) areas of Sandy, but it later spread to the heavier land of the parish, presumably as the demand for fresh produce grew and as market gardening became more profitable. It may well be that improved ploughs and other farm implements made the cultivation of the clay land possible in later years.

Earlier writers, who, unlike Ken Quince may not have had the experience of working as market gardeners, have nevertheless commented on the distinctive nature of the agriculture of the parish, and occasionally wills left by market gardeners give clues about the types of crops grown. Throughout the seventeenth century carrots seem to have been the leading crop, but by the eighteenth century they had been superseded by onions and cucumbers. By 1810 most of the produce from Sandy was being sent up to sixty miles in all directions, by horse-drawn transport, and the inevitably slow journeys (roads were rutted and full of potholes at the best of times and sometimes virtually impassable in winter) meant that long-lasting vegetables such as onions, parsnips, carrots and cucumbers were far more suitable than crops such as lettuce and cabbages, which would soon be past their best.

In 1790, about fourteen years before land holdings were reorganised, rationalised and consolidated by enclosure in Sandy, the market garden acreage in Sandy was stated to be upwards of 60 acres, but just five years later it had grown to 150 acres. It received a further stimulus with the coming of the railway in the middle of the nineteenth century.

The Honourable J. Byng wrote in 1790 in the *Torrington Diaries* 'Passing through Sandy, any observer would be astonished at the culture and gardening of the fields; surpassing everything I saw but just about London, for every field is cropped by peas, carrots, parsnips, French beans, cucumbers etc… and you cannot prevent your horse from smashing the cucumbers. (I once told this to a friend of mine who smiled contradiction till I led him into this garden of a country, and he owned his surprise and conviction'.)

Arthur Young in his *Annals of Agriculture Volume 42 (1804)* considered that: 'This parish [Sandy] is very peculiarly circumstanced; it abounds with gardeners, many cultivate their little freeholds…there were found to be 63 proprietors; though nine tenths perhaps of the whole belonged to Sir P. Monoux and Mr Pym. These men kept cows on the boggy common and cut fern for bedding [for the cattle] on the Warren, by which means they were able to raise manure for their gardens.'

A little more information on cropping practices is given by G.A. Cooke in his *Topographical and Statistical Description of the county of Bedford (1808)*: 'They sow carrots about Lady Day [25th March] upon ground dug one spit deep, they hoe them very carefully about three times. They hoe and weed onions always five times with the expense of about £4 per acre and set them out six inches asunder. The average crop is about 200 bushels, the price varying from two to six shillings a bushel. They always manure them with great care. These gardeners give from £2 to £5 rent per acre for their land, and in some instances, considerably more.'

Thomas Batchelor, a Bedfordshire farmer, in his *General view of the agriculture of the county of Bedford* (1808) remarked on the soil found in some of the Sandy fields: it was a fine grained 'deep sand of a yellowish brown colour'; he considered that 'the depth of the soil is obviously an essential circumstance to the successful growth of carrots and other deep rooted vegetables' and recorded carrots four or five inches in diameter being grown in the district. He also mentioned crops of peas, beans, cucumbers, potatoes, parsnips, radishes, cabbages and turnips. He noted that cottagers sowed onions in drills of six inches wide and that they often grew gooseberries and currants in their gardens to 'make some profit among their more opulent neighbours'. Batchelor was aware that market gardening had been characteristic of the Sandy area for many years and commented on some of the techniques of cultivation. He considered that 'breaking the encrusted surface of the ground, and keeping it in a pulverised state' was 'essential to the growth of most kinds of vegetables'. Some larger farmers and landowners were introducing seed drills at this time; market gardeners appear to have dibbled beans (i.e. set them in individual holes made by a dibber) and it may well be that the seed of crops like turnips was still broadcast by hand. I suspect that potatoes may have been set individually, using a spade, as they still are on many allotments.

Eighteenth century market gardeners in Sandy appear to have cultivated their vegetables in relatively small strips in the open fields of the parish, or at least part of them, and it is not clear how the vegetables fitted in with the cereal crops which would also, presumably, have been grown. I have not been able to ascertain whether some market gardeners, including those in my own family, also grew cereal crops. Nor is it entirely clear how, where and when livestock dovetailed into the pattern. Arthur Young noted that cows were kept on the boggy common, but I suspect that at this time they were probably also kept, at least at times, on some of the clay ground and the land bordering the River Ivel, which could well have been too heavy and poorly drained for market gardening. Sheep appear to have been kept on some of the lighter sandy land in the early eighteenth century, but as it was recognised that they helped to compact and fertilise the soil they may have been replaced by market garden crops at times. They could have been used to graze on the remains of such crops before the vegetable remains and sheep manure were ploughed back into the soil in preparation for the next crop, although confining the wandering of the sheep might have presented a few problems in the open fields, making co-operation between neighbouring strip holders essential.

At the end of the eighteenth century there were four large open arable fields in the north of the parish: Mead, Down, Middle and Low. Mead Field was mainly on gravelly soil deposited by the River Ivel; the other three fields were on the Oxford Clay. In the centre of the parish, on the greensand, from west to east were two smaller fields, Syerholme and Chester, plus Kinwick Field, originally a larger unenclosed field which had been reduced in size to create the Hasells estate. To the south of the parish was a large sandy heath known as the Warren. Chester Field, in the Stratford area of Sandy with its north eastern extension into Swading (now called Swaden), appears to have been particularly sought after for the growing of market garden crops; it was on gently sloping land just to the west of the greensand scarp slope and was about seventy acres in size. From the documents I have seen it is clear that the large open fields had been subdivided into smaller, named sections or *furlongs*, each furlong containing numerous strips of land. A number of named tracks and baulks (uncultivated ridges of land) gave access to the strips. In addition to this already complex pattern, the heavier land bordering the river Ivel in the west of the parish was being used for grazing, and close to the settled area of Sandy were numerous large cottage gardens (sometimes also used for market gardening) and the Sandy Place estate. The system seems to have evolved to make optimum use of the variety of soils, slopes and aspects available in the area.

The individual market garden strips appear to have been cultivated at least at times by spade, (according to Cooke), as presumably many market gardeners whose land holdings often did not amount to more than a few acres would not have been able to afford a plough and a horse to draw it, but I reckon that arrangements must have been made wherever possible to borrow the necessary implements or to have the land ploughed by someone else. The individual strips on the lighter land may have made it possible for a market gardening family to carry out many tasks by hand, but it didn't necessarily encourage efficient farming practices. Much time must have been wasted in travelling from one plot to the other, for, as we shall see later, the individual strip holdings, which had been acquired in a piecemeal fashion over the centuries and had sometimes been subdivided, were, by the end of the eighteenth century, distributed in an almost random fashion over the common fields. An individual's land holding might well comprise several strips scattered all over the parish. Most gardeners would therefore have had a variety of soils to cultivate, each soil presenting its own problems and offering its own potential rewards.

All was to change in 1804 as far as Sandy was concerned, for in that year most of the land of the parish was enclosed, and the complex, and probably uneconomic pattern of land ownership and cultivation was finally swept away in an attempt to rationalise land holdings. I say *most* because some enclosure had taken place from around 1725, when Heylock Kingsley, who had purchased the Hasells in 1721, enclosed over 160 acres of his land and planted trees to improve the appearance of his estate, which later became, through marriage, the property of the Pym family. Close to his estate it was noted at the time that at least 40 acres of Kinwick Field were 'still the property of many different owners'. Enclosure in 1804 was more comprehensive, however: strips in the open fields were amalgamated and exchanged throughout the parish and the overall result appears to have been that the larger landowners and farmers received more sensibly proportioned holdings, usually on the better land. Their land was enclosed within newly-planted hedges of quick-growing hawthorn. They were now able to introduce the new farming ideas and practices being developed in arable and livestock farming, including selective breeding, new rotations, chemical fertilisers and new machinery, such as seed drills and reaper-binders. They could follow their own inclinations and there was no longer any need to co-operate with fellow farmers and market gardeners when planning and undertaking their cultivations and animal husbandry. Communal effort was being replaced by individualism.

Smaller landowners with the odd few scattered strips seem to have fared less well; they received some land, but it was more likely to be some distance from where they lived, or relatively infertile - or both. They would also have lost their rights to gather fuel and to graze animals on the common, although, of course, not all of them would have been wealthy enough to have owned livestock. Arthur Young noted at the time '…the small allotment of an acre and half, however good the land, has been no compensation for what they were deprived of. They complain heavily and know not how they will manage to raise manure'.

About thirty acres of land were allocated to the Lords of the Manors of Sandy, Hasells and Girtford, and to the rector and churchwardens 'in satisfaction of [i.e. as compensation for] the right of cutting ling and fern upon Sandy Warren for fuel, upon trust to apply the rents and profits in purchasing wood, coals and other fuel for distribution amongst the *industrious poor…*' (my italics). Presumably these good people decided whether or not a poor person was considered worthy of receiving such charity. The phrase 'hard working families who always do the right thing', uttered so frequently (and glibly) by modern politicians seems to reflect a similar kind of thinking. Clearly the distinction between the deserving and undeserving poor goes back a long way. (It's strange how we don't hear much about the deserving and undeserving rich).

As new methods were introduced the 'industrious poor' were often tempted to sell their holdings (such as they were) to the larger landowners of the parish who appear to have been keen to augment their farms and estates. They thus became landless labourers, needing to work for the larger farmers in order to be able to feed their families. The problem was, of course, that the farmers, by introducing new machinery, required fewer workers than they had before; this prompted the labourers to seek work elsewhere, and many drifted into larger towns or migrated to London. To make matters worse, it would appear that the smaller landowners and labourers were not consulted extensively in the process of land reorganisation and enclosure within their parish. As so many of them were illiterate they were unable to protest in an organised, coherent way, or to suggest an alternative. The effects of enclosure, positive and negative, agricultural and social, were to last for years, if not generations, to come; arguably to the present day. The social inequality it encouraged is now being reinforced and perpetuated, as already wealthy farmers and landowners receive extremely generous subsidies from the European fund, and conveniently manage to avoid paying inheritance tax on their agricultural assets. The early morning farming programme on the B.B.C.'s Radio 4 recently gave an example of an estate in Scotland on the market at £11million which was receiving payments of £12,000 *per week* - a fairly healthy return even in these austere times. This income was in addition to that generated by actually farming the land. Does this qualify, I wonder, as a case of the undeserving rich?

I have written about market gardening in Sandy and enclosure at some length because members of the Whitfield family, as we shall see, were involved in both, and both had an influence on the family and the way it developed over the years.

After the enclosure of Sandy, William Whitfield, (James' father), now an old man of 77, was allocated about half an acre of land in Swaden, Sandy, close to the road to Everton, on 25 January, 1804:

'...and unto William Whitfield one piece or parcel of land or ground containing 1 rood and 32 perches, situate in Swading, bounded on the NE by an allotment herein awarded to John Braybrook in right of his purchase of Thomas Croft, on the SE by Swading Road and on the SW and NW by an allotment herein awarded to the said Francis Pym. The hedges, ditches and fences of which piece or parcel of ground so awarded on the NW, NE and SE sides thereof shall be made and for ever thereafter maintained and kept in repair by and at the expense of the said William Whitfield and the owners of the allotment for the time being...'.

William was probably farming more land than this in his younger days in pre-enclosure Sandy – and, to make matters worse, he was now held officially responsible for all the hedging and ditching. I assume that this award was probably not received with too much enthusiasm, and it must have had economic implications for William and his family. It may explain why his younger sons James and Philip did not become full time market gardeners. The land their father was allocated would have been very light and sandy; in Heylock Kingsley's time it was claimed that most of this area was 'esteemed of so little value that it is wholly deserted and left

21

for a sheep common', though it should be pointed out that he was not averse to acquiring more of it for his estate if the opportunity arose.

Around the time of the enclosure award, William Whitfield appears to have been living in a cottage belonging to Sir Philip Monoux, adjoining the Mill Garden; the cottage, and William as its occupant are mentioned in Sir Philip's will, drawn up in 1797, and proved in 1805. It may be that William had worked for the Monoux family in his younger days, and worked his own land in his spare time. A document of 1784 refers to a William Whitfield formerly occupying a half acre plot called Hacksfield, abutting west on Common Lane.

Before travelling further back in time, beyond William Whitfield, I must give details of his children - James Whitfield's brothers and sisters.

His oldest brother, William, baptised in 1759 - and as the first-born boy named after his father - was a servant to Sir Philip Monoux, but died in May 1784. The next son, Thomas, baptised two years later, and named after his maternal grandfather, Thomas Retchford, also died in 1781. I have no idea why these two young men died. There was no requirement to record the cause of death in the late eighteenth century.

The next child, Robert, baptised in 1763, married Jemima Spring in Sandy in 1786 and had a large family. We will meet his children later. When his father William died in 1806, Robert, as the oldest surviving son, inherited the half acre of land in Swaden and farmed it until his death in 1841. His small land holding gave him the right to vote in elections. He appears in poll books from 1807. In this respect he was one of a privileged few: the 1831 poll book shows that he was one of just 27 Sandy men accorded this responsibility. I think he also may have worked for the Monoux family, possibly as a gardener, because he is mentioned in the will of the Honourable Frances Henley Ongley, (nee Frances Monoux). He appears to have been regarded favourably. However, the will, made in 1832, but with later codicils, wasn't proved until February, 1841; Robert died in January, 1841, so was unable to derive any benefit from Frances' bequest of the use of a cottage for the rest of his life, together with a yearly annuity of ten pounds, although his widow, Jemima, was still living in property owned by the Monoux family some ten years later. It seems that the family were benevolent employers. They were certainly wealthy: two of Frances Henley Ongley's nephews each received £15,000, and one of them was also given the freehold of the *Sun Inn*, Biggleswade. You may remember that Frances Monoux had been an early employer of my 3x great-grandfather, James Whitfield. Her will shows that she owned several horses and ponies at the time of her death and she possessed a pianoforte, so perhaps James and his older brother Robert *had* heard some of the music of their contemporary, Ludwig van Beethoven. I wouldn't think there were many pianos in Sandy in the early 1830s, when the will was first drafted.

The next two children of William and Elizabeth: Elizabeth and John, both died in infancy, and we have already met my great-great-great grandfather, James, who was their next child.

James' younger brother, Philip, baptised in 1773, appears to have started his working life as a market gardener. My guess is that he worked for at least part of the time for his father, who must have taught him the craft. I found out from land tax assessments that he farmed his father's land in Swaden between 1802 and 1804, when presumably William was too old to work the land himself, but Philip was later described as a victualler. He married a widow, Ann

DIAGRAM 3

The Sandy Whitfields - senior branch - until the late 19th century (simplified)

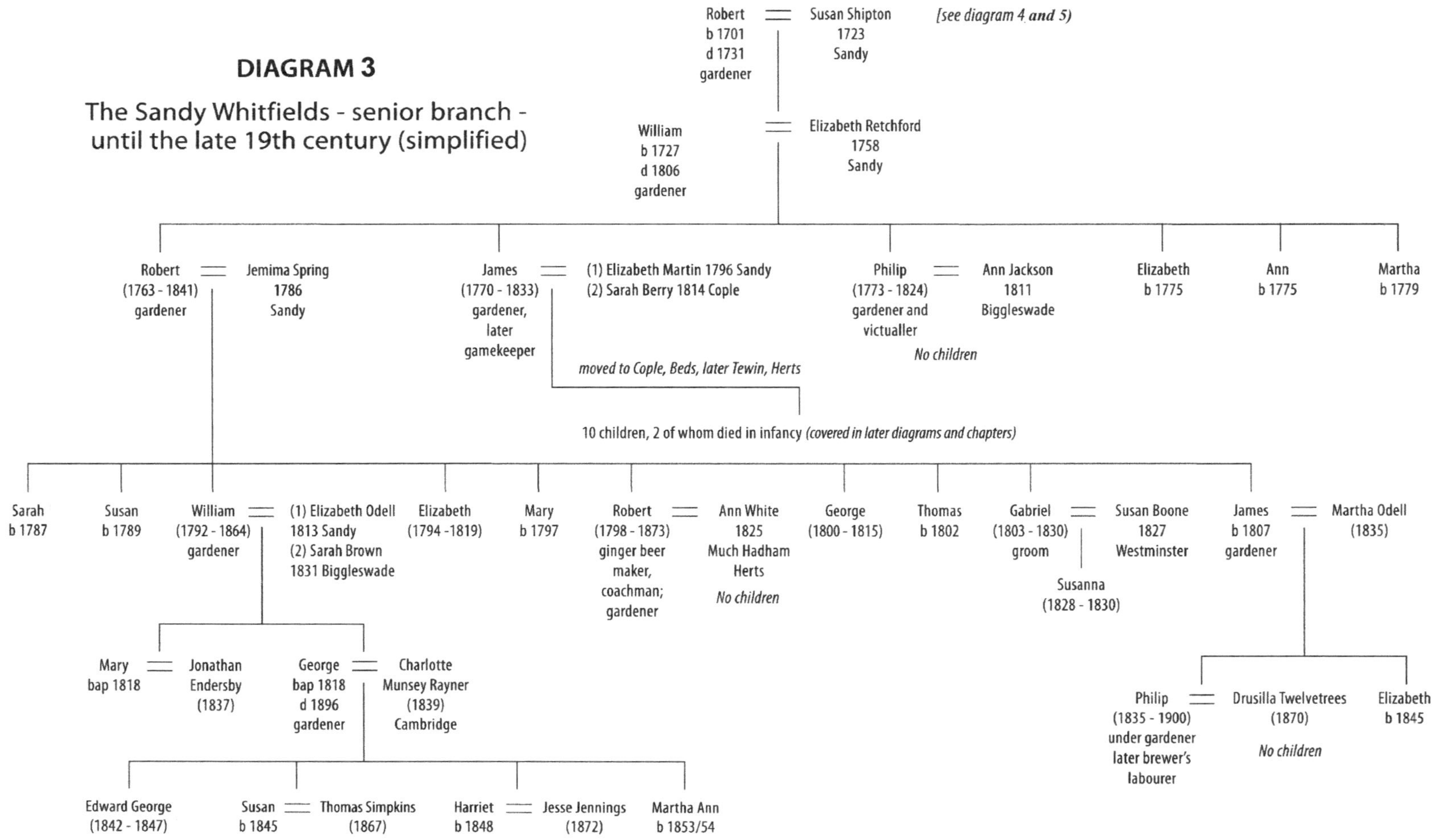

[see diagram 4 and 5]

Robert b 1701 d 1731 gardener == Susan Shipton 1723 Sandy

William b 1727 d 1806 gardener == Elizabeth Retchford 1758 Sandy

Robert (1763 - 1841) gardener == Jemima Spring 1786 Sandy

James (1770 - 1833) gardener, later gamekeeper == (1) Elizabeth Martin 1796 Sandy / (2) Sarah Berry 1814 Cople

moved to Cople, Beds, later Tewin, Herts

Philip (1773 - 1824) gardener and victualler == Ann Jackson 1811 Biggleswade

No children

Elizabeth b 1775 · Ann b 1775 · Martha b 1779

10 children, 2 of whom died in infancy (covered in later diagrams and chapters)

Sarah b 1787 · Susan b 1789

William (1792 - 1864) gardener == (1) Elizabeth Odell 1813 Sandy / (2) Sarah Brown 1831 Biggleswade

Elizabeth (1794 - 1819) · Mary b 1797

Robert (1798 - 1873) ginger beer maker, coachman; gardener == Ann White 1825 Much Hadham Herts

No children

George (1800 - 1815) · Thomas b 1802

Gabriel (1803 - 1830) groom == Susan Boone 1827 Westminster

Susanna (1828 - 1830)

James b 1807 gardener == Martha Odell (1835)

Philip (1835 - 1900) under gardener later brewer's labourer == Drusilla Twelvetrees (1870)

No children

Elizabeth b 1845

Mary bap 1818 == Jonathan Endersby (1837)

George bap 1818 d 1896 gardener == Charlotte Munsey Rayner (1839) Cambridge

Susan b 1845 == Thomas Simpkins (1867)

Harriet b 1848 == Jesse Jennings (1872)

Martha Ann b 1853/54

Edward George (1842 - 1847)

Jackson (nee Mantell or Mantle) on 24th September, 1811 in Biggleswade Church. I was rather surprised to discover that Mrs Jackson's first husband, Isaac Jackson, had only died about five weeks earlier. He had been a market gardener, and was probably well known to both Philip and his brother James, having been born in Sandy around 1770. Ann Mantell had been Isaac Jackson's *second* wife; he had formerly been married to Mary Breed. After their whirlwind courtship and subsequent marriage Philip and Ann ran the *Anchor* public house at Anchor End, Sun Street, Biggleswade, until Philip's death in 1824. Ann then continued to run the pub until 1830, when the tenancy passed to James Hide.

The *Anchor* was close to the area of Biggleswade known as Cowfairlands, a veritable warren of small, old, densely-packed cottages between Shortmead Street and Sun Street. It was not the most prosperous or salubrious area of the town. Joyce Godber in her *History of Bedfordshire* quotes from a report on housing in Biggleswade, where it was said of a house in Anchor End: 'No privy, no back door, rains in, and [inhabitants] obliged to get up or cover themselves over with sacks in bed; cesspool 6ft. from door'. This report was written in 1866; Miss Godber notes that two years later in Cowfairlands 'cowsheds and heaps of manure were close to cottages, and there were horrible sheds for privies, with faeces lying about on the floor'. I would imagine that similar conditions existed in the 1820s. The area has now been comprehensively redeveloped and most of the cottages - and the *Anchor* itself - have been demolished. Any faeces lying around on a communal grassed area, once the site of cottage gardens, are hopefully now of canine or feline origin.

It's not too difficult to suggest possible reasons for Philip's move to Biggleswade in addition to his succumbing to the attractions of Mrs Ann Jackson. It was a busy place with a greater range of employment opportunities than Sandy. There were several maltings and many pubs and inns in the town which had become an important place for London stage coaches to stop so that tired horses could be changed and weary travellers refreshed before proceeding further along the Great North Road. Several coaching inns in the centre of the town such as the *New Inn*, the *White Swan* and the *Crown* had large yards with stables and catered for this sort of trade.

The *Anchor* did not have a Market Square location, but it was, as its name suggests, closer to the River Ivel and thus to Shortmead Street which is aligned roughly parallel to the river and not much more than a stone's throw from it. This was another very busy part of the town in the early nineteenth century because of river-borne traffic. Canal barges, drawn by horses, (which were changed at regular intervals) could travel along the Ouse from King's Lynn as far as its confluence with the Ivel at Tempsford, where they then entered the Ivel Navigation system and could proceed as far as Biggleswade. In 1821, work started on extending the Ivel Navigation system as far as Shefford and took two years to complete. There were three wharves in Biggleswade: St Andrew's Wharf near the church; Middle Wharf behind Wharf House, opposite the Wesleyan chapel; and the wharf at Ivel Bury, the residence of Samuel Wells the younger, the Biggleswade brewer and banker and later the home of his son-in-law William Hogg(e).

The Ivel Navigation (completed as far as Biggleswade in 1759) made it possible to obtain bulky goods such as coal, iron, timber, tiles and other building materials; and grain, malt and flour were despatched. The *Anchor* would have been in a good position to cater for men involved in the transportation of these cargoes, although more important inns, the *Royal Oak* (owned by Samuel Wells) and the *Sun,* were even closer to the Great North Road, the bridge over the river and the Ivel Bury wharf. Both of these large inns also had more room for stabling (the *Sun* could accommodate eighty horses according to a sale notice which appeared in the *Northampton Mercury* in 1787 and the *Royal Oak* had stabling for forty in 1788) and they must have handled more of this type of trade and dealt with more prosperous customers. Philip and Ann must have struggled at times to avoid their establishment being eclipsed by the *Sun* or put into the shade by the *Royal Oak*. Clearly, in the early part of the nineteenth century, Biggleswade would have been a bustling, thriving community, with several other strings to its bow besides market gardening, and the commercial activity on the Ivel was close to its zenith. The coming of the railway to the town in the middle of the century encouraged the further growth of market gardening but heralded the steady decline of the Ivel Navigation Trust. Despite this, brewing remained important in Biggleswade.

In addition to his role as pub landlord, Philip also owned a house and some land adjoining the pub and its garden in Cowfairlands, which he purchased for £55 in 1813 (as recorded in the Biggleswade Manor Court Rolls), so it is likely that he continued with his market gardening - it was in his blood. The piece of land he purchased was one rood and fifteen poles in size - about one third of an acre. A later deed for the *Anchor* makes it clear that the pub also had a good sized garden. The house Philip bought had a well and a privy which was shared with the adjoining tenement. Hopefully these two useful facilities were not too close to each other. Joyce Godber quotes a case of cholera (an all too often fatal bacterial disease of the gut characterised by symptoms of severe abdominal pains, diarrhoea, vomiting and dehydration) in Biggleswade as late as 1868, where a well was just *four feet* from a privy which was 'in an abominable condition'. Cholera was first noted in Britain in 1831, and at first it was suspected that people caught it by breathing polluted air - a commodity not in short supply in early nineteenth century London. Dr John Snow (1813- 1858), obstetrician to Queen Victoria, published his pamphlet *The Mode of Communication of Cholera* in 1849: he considered that the disease was '…passed on through drinking water which had been polluted by sewage'. Snow plotted the addresses of his dying patients on a map and was thus able to trace the cause of an outbreak of cholera in the Broad Street district of Soho in 1854 to a water pump placed above a well which had been contaminated by a nearby cesspit; people who escaped a particularly unpleasant but mercifully rapid decline and death from the disease worked at a nearby brewery and drank only beer, where of course the water used in the brewing process had been boiled. Snow had the pump handle removed and the outbreak abated. The fear of cholera, diarrhoea or simply foul-tasting water must have encouraged people - whether in London, Biggleswade or elsewhere - to drink beer. Dr Snow advocated boiling water before drinking it. His own relatively early death was not caused by cholera, but by a stroke.

Beer was believed to be a *healthy* drink; in the previous century people had been made aware of the social problems resulting from the consumption of cheap (and sometimes adulterated) gin. William Hogarth's pictures of Beer Street and Gin Lane and the verses of the Reverend James Townley, dating from the mid-eighteenth century, sought to highlight the dangers of gin drinking and encourage people to drink beer instead. Some probably didn't need much encouragement: apart from satisfying the thirst produced by hard manual labour, the alcohol content of beer still offered a temporary, albeit illusory escape from desperate poverty. Moreover, labourers often went to pubs for company; they could chat feely in the taproom away from their masters and domestic pressures and responsibilities. Heavy drinkers neglected their families, squandered their hard-earned wages and allowed their addiction to alcohol to undermine their health, whilst lining the pockets of the brewers. Modern binge drinking merely continues a dishonourable tradition.

Pub landlords in the nineteenth century often had secondary occupations as a way of ensuring a decent income if their customers decided to transfer their allegiance to another hostelry. A landlord was often an ambitious man keen to make money from his customers who had acquired a taste for alcohol. Opening hours were long and frequently this meant that the landlord's wife looked after the pub in the daytime. There were many inns, pubs and drinking houses in Biggleswade at this time, and competition must have been intense. It may well be that Philip provided vegetables for meals served at the *Anchor* or he may have sold fresh produce from the premises. The *Anchor* was one of the many pubs owned by Samuel Wells; I would imagine that he also supplied the beer, wine and spirits. However, the success of any pub then (as now) probably depended not only on the quality of the drink and food offered, but also on the personalities of the landlord and landlady - and the service they gave to customers.

As an owner of house and land Philip was entitled to vote, according to a voters' list for 1820. His property was described as being occupied by 'himself and others' which suggested that his house was being occupied by a tenant while he and Ann lived at the *Anchor* or perhaps hinted at the ownership of other properties.

Philip's name also appears in an interesting advertisement which appeared in the *Northampton Mercury* for 7th January, 1820; the article I found showed that he was one of twenty seven Biggleswade men (and nearly sixty in the district) with commercial interests who were members of the 'Biggleswade Association for the prosecution of felons, etc.' The association offered rewards for 'the apprehension of persons convicted of … offences against any of its Members'. A long list of offences followed, together with the rewards being offered for the capture of any perpetrators. Parish constables were finding it difficult to cope with an increase in crime at a time of great social unrest. Mechanisation on the land was proceeding apace, wages were low and agricultural enclosure was resented by poor people who had lost their rights to graze animals and gather fuel from common land. Labourers, with their large families, were finding it difficult to make ends meet. Their anger and frustration was aimed at farmers and landowners; and incidents of arson, machine breaking and other damage to property, poaching and theft of fruit and vegetables became common. Not surprisingly, top of the list of offences mentioned in the advertisement with a reward of ten guineas being offered for the capture of any offenders, was murder or attempted murder; the apprehension of burglars or horse stealers or those guilty of '…wilfully or maliciously setting Fire to any House, Outhouse, Barn, Stable or Rick of Corn, Grain, Hay, Straw, Wood, Furze, Gorse or Fagots' warranted a reward of five guineas; and the capture of those guilty of stealing turnips, green peas or potatoes from the fields would be rewarded by the payment of one guinea. Also included in the list of members were Samuel Wells, banker, of Biggleswade, Stephen Thornton, Esquire, of Mogerhanger, Francis Pym, Esquire, of Sandy, and W.H.Whitbread, Esquire, M.P., of Southill, so Philip was in select company. I presume the arrangement worked rather like an insurance policy so that the rewards offered came from a communal pool of money raised by an annual subscription. Apart from protecting his commercial interests (and those of fellow members), it seems likely that Philip was well aware of the benefits offered by advertising and of associating with the local squires. The association had an annual general meeting: in 1817 it had been held at the *Crown.* I would love to know whether Philip attended. I would think that the more militant labourers were careful not to speak too freely if they drank at the *Anchor* as it would appear that Philip was not particularly sympathetic to their cause. In 1819, one of the Association's members had been the Rector of Sutton, the Reverend Doctor Edward Drax Free (1764- 1843); I wasn't too surprised to note that he was no longer a member by the following year. It *may* have had something to do with some of the Rector's exploits during his incumbency, which included selling the lead from the church roof; foddering horses and cattle in the church porch - and allowing them and un-ringed pigs to graze, root around in and churn up the churchyard; being abusive to parishioners; possessing an extensive collection of pornography and impregnating a succession of his housekeepers. (The Rector had five illegitimate children and only an assault by him on one of his pregnant housekeepers causing her to miscarry prevented the number reaching six).

Philip's will makes it clear that *he* had no children – only stepchildren: Edward Jackson, Ann Jackson and Mary, formerly Jackson, but now the wife of William Cocking. Edward Jackson was to receive £40 after his mother had died, and the three step-children were then to have equal shares of the estate. The will was a useful document to me, not only because it enabled me to find further details of some of Philip's brothers and sisters, but also, indirectly, it helped me to discover further details of his property. He had remained single until he was thirty eight and it appears that he had assiduously built up a small property empire. As we have seen, his brother James was to receive £50 after the death of Philip's widow, Ann. This £50 was not a trifling amount at a time when many labourers would have been earning about ten shillings a week - it represented about two years' wages for a labourer at that time. James did not receive this money as his sister-in-law outlived him, but the matter didn't end there, as we shall see.

Philip's will also included bequests to his sisters Ann and Martha. They were each to receive £30 on the death of his widow. There was a puzzle here because I couldn't find a baptism in Sandy for an Ann Whitfield. Philip's will mentioned that her married name was Ann Drew, so I searched for marriages between Ann Whitfield and a Mr Drew. Drew is an old Potton surname, but my search of the Potton and Sandy registers proved fruitless. I eventually discovered that the marriage of Ann Whitfield and William Drew took place at St Paul's Church, Bedford in 1801. The union produced at least one child, William junior, born in 1801, and baptised the following year, but his father appears to have died in Bedford in 1810, aged 36, after which Ann and her son moved to Potton; they were certainly there by 1817 when 'Widow Ann Drew' is mentioned in a Quarter Sessions document. Ann died in 1827, aged 52, and so was born in 1775. I wonder why she wasn't baptised. She never received her bequest from her brother Philip because her sister-in-law, Ann Whitfield (of Biggleswade) outlived her. After

This is the last Will and Testament of me
Philip Whitfield of Biggleswade in the County of Bedford
Victualler I give devise and bequeath unto my Dear wife Ann
Whitfield All and singular my Freehold and Copyhold Messuages
Cottages lands tenements hereditaments and Real Estate whatsoever
and wheresoever And also all my ready money Securities for money
debts goods chattels and personal Estate whatsoever (She paying
thereout all my just debts and funeral and testamentary expences)
To hold all and every the said Real and personal Estate and
effects unto her the said Ann Whitfield and her assigns for and
during the Term of her natural life And I direct that an —
Inventory of my said personal Estate be made by my said wife
as soon as conveniently may be after my decease and a Copy
thereof deposited with my Son in Law Edward Jackson And
I give and bequeath unto my Brother James Whitfield the sum
of Fifty pounds, unto my Sisters Martha Siles and Ann
Drew the sum of Thirty pounds each and unto my Son in
law Thomas Jackson the sum of Forty pounds Which said
several Legacies I desire may be paid within Six Calendar months
after the decease of my said wife. And I do hereby charge and
make chargeable all and every my said Messuages Cottages Lands
Tenements hereditaments and Real Estate with the payment thereof
in case my personal Estate shall not be sufficient for that purpose
And as to all and singular my said Freehold and Copyhold
lands tenements hereditaments and real Estate whatsoever and
wheresoever And the residue of my said goods Chattels monies
Securities for money and personal Estate, I do hereby give
devise and bequeath the same from and after the decease of
my said wife unto and Let the

Part of the will of Philip Whitfield of Biggleswade, Beds, 1824. The document mentions his brother, James Whitfield (my 3xgreat grandfather). Image reproduced by kind permission of the Bedfordshire and Luton Archives Service. Ref PBwP/W1824/129.

Ann Whitfield's death in 1848, the money Ann Drew (*nee* Whitfield) was to have received did eventually find its way into the Drew family, thanks to the efforts of Ann's son, William Drew and his cousin, James Whitfield, my great-great grandfather. Incidentally, one of Ann Drew's descendants, Keiron Drew, was at school with me in the 1960s. We didn't know it at the time, but we are both descended from William Whitfield (1727- 1806) and his wife Elizabeth.

Returning to Philip Whitfield's will, conspicuous by its absence was any mention of his older brother Robert, who was at that time still alive in Sandy. We have already seen that Robert had inherited the plot in Swaden from his father William in 1806, but he and his wife had produced a large family and were probably not particularly well off. It may be that he and Philip had not been on the best of terms. Philip's association with the local squires and farmers may not have been appreciated by his older brother.

A newspaper article published in the *Cambridge Independent Press* on Saturday, 14th August, 1841 (some seventeen years after Philip had died) enabled me to discover more about his property. It also made me realise that his will must have caused all sorts of problems within the family, albeit unintentionally, after his death. The article was advertising an auction to be held at the *White Horse* in Biggleswade on 25th August, as a consequence of the bankruptcy of William Cocking, a 'market gardener, dealer and chapman' of Beeston, Bedfordshire. William Cocking was the husband of one of Philip's step-daughters, the former Mary Jackson: they had married in Biggleswade in 1819. Under the terms of Philip's will, Mary was to receive a third share in the property that had been left to her mother Ann Whitfield. This property was to be lot 2 in the auction; described as 'the freehold reversion in fee simple, expectant on the decease of Ann Whitfield, widow, now aged 78, and in one equal, individual third part', it consisted of:

'...those two cottages or tenements with the barns and outbuildings thereto adjoining, now in the occupation of William Rowlett and James Langley and a close of capital garden land behind the same, containing altogether by admeasurement 3 acres, 3 roods and 13 perches (more or less) delightfully situate in the parish of Biggleswade near Road Farm, adjoining the Potton Turnpike road'.

The article went on to state that the entirety of this estate was 'subject to certain legacies payable on the death of the said Ann Whitfield, amounting altogether to £150'. These, of course, were the legacies mentioned in Philip's will in 1824. This document had specified that the bequests were to be paid within six months of Ann's death, so of course had not yet been paid. I had earlier assumed that phrases such as 'all and every my said messuages, cottages, lands, tenements, hereditaments and real estate' contained in Philip's will were *standard* phrases, to be found in many wills of the period; in fact, he had owned a house and a third of an acre in Cowfairlands, Biggleswade *and* two cottages with about three and three quarters acres in Potton Road, Biggleswade. Although he had been prudent in making a will he could not have foreseen the timing of the death of his brother James and the fact that his own wife would outlive both of them for so many years.

Both Philip's cottages are still standing. At first, I thought that one of them became the *Chequers* beerhouse in the early 1840s. The Beer Act of 1830 allowed any ratepayer to sell beer from his or her premises provided the appropriate licence fee was paid. The *Chequers'* position well outside the built up area of nineteenth century Biggleswade must have meant that it never sold much beer and it ceased trading in 1928. The house still stands close to Biggleswade Common, but when I looked at early maps of Biggleswade I concluded I was looking too far out from the town as it was in 1820.

I later realised that what appeared to be an old detached house closer to present day Biggleswade (which I had previously identified as Philip's other property or properties) had been a pair of very small cottages which would have been well outside the built up area of the town in the early part of the nineteenth century, and would have then adjoined open countryside. The house came up for sale recently, and the estate agents confirmed that it had originally been, as I had suspected, a pair of semi-detached cottages; in fact it still had two staircases. The property has been extended at the rear since the early 1820s to provide a kitchen and ground floor bathroom, so the two original cottages must have been tiny by today's standards. The house now stands somewhat incongruously, like a pensioner in a playground, amidst a mass of much more modern property; and as it is in a very poor state of repair its future must be in jeopardy. The land Philip owned at the rear of his cottages has been lost to development. Depending on its precise shape, size and alignment it is now occupied by a modern housing estate or the Edward Peake Middle School. It is perhaps worth speculating that it might have been left to my 3x great grandfather James Whitfield if he had still been living in Biggleswade or Sandy at the time of his brother's death, in which case the subsequent development and fortunes of the family could have taken a very different course.

William and Elizabeth's youngest child, and thus Philip's youngest sister, Martha, married a market gardener, Robert Surquet, or Surkitt in 1799 in Sandy. However, Robert died in 1810, and in July, 1812, Martha married a widower, William Lyles, in St Paul's Church, Bedford. I assume that Martha must have moved to Bedford in search of work after her first husband died; she may have lived with her sister Ann (Drew) for a while. William Lyles was also a gardener and the couple appear to have moved back to Potton. An entry in the Bedford Quarter Sessions records suggests that William was actually a *market* gardener because Joseph Munns stole seven bushels of potatoes from him in December, 1816. We have a slightly different picture of William ten years later from the Bedford Gaol records because *he* served a one month sentence for being a rogue and vagabond. Thanks to these records we know that he was fifty years old, 5 feet 2 inches tall, and had brown hair, hazel eyes and a fair complexion. When he rolled up his sleeves to hoe his onions or dig his potatoes, onlookers would have noticed the 'figures of ink' he had on each arm. I wonder who the local tattooist was in the early nineteenth century, where he operated and how much he charged? Unfortunately, no further details of the 'figures of ink' are given. It would have been interesting to discover the design William Lyles had selected to grace his forearms. An artistic arrangement of onions and carrots would perhaps have been appropriate.

Martha, mentioned in Philip's will, was living at Moon's Corner in Potton (where present day Chapel Street meets Blackbird Street) in a cottage adjoining the *Woolpack* public house at the time of the 1841 census. It is my theory that she was living there in 1818-1819 when her brother James left Cople, and that she offered her brother and his family a roof over their heads before they went to Tewin. Alternatively they could have lived with his other sister,

Ann Drew, for a while. It may well have been that James and Sarah Whitfield's son James was born in Potton although he was baptised in Tewin. William Lyles died in October, 1840, and Martha's brother, Robert Whitfield, died in Sandy during the following year. Martha moved back to Sandy after his death and lived with her sister in law, Jemima Whitfield, at the Old Mill House, owned by the Monoux family. Both were described in the census as paupers. The Sandy Place estate came up for auction in 1851, and the cottage they were living in was described in the catalogue: it had six rooms and a garden, was close to the banks of the River Ivel and was 'almost hid amongst the trees'. Very picturesque - but I would imagine it was also rather damp and possibly somewhat inconvenient for an old lady of eighty seven. It is likely that this was the cottage formerly occupied by William Whitfield (1727-1806) and his wife Elizabeth – Jemima's late parents-in-law. I suspect the cottage had been allocated to Robert (as William's eldest son) and his wife Jemima on William's death in 1806. Jemima was described in the catalogue as 'very aged' and 'formerly [a] Servant in the family' and it was made clear that she was to retain possession of the cottage for the rest of her life, 'under a bequest'. She was probably glad of Martha's company, but the two old ladies were clearly not in the best of health because they needed the services of an attendant, fifty eight year old Susan Lawson. I wonder if Martha ever claimed her money from her late brother Philip's estate following the death of Ann Whitfield, her sister-in-law in Biggleswade in 1848? The fact that Martha was described as a pauper in the 1851 census suggests to me that she did not. Her life came to an end a year later.

James Whitfield's descendants will be covered in later chapters, but the family of his older brother, Robert, (b.1763) for the most part, had continued to live in Sandy, possibly because, as we have seen, he had land there. It seems likely that both he and Jemima were servants to the Monoux family, and they had been living in tied accommodation. The children of Robert and Jemima were:

Sarah, b 1787. She married Samuel Lincoln in 1811. Their daughters Elizabeth and Naomi Lincoln were born in 1812 and 1816 respectively. The 1841 census of Sandy shows that Naomi was living with her newly-widowed grandmother, Jemima Whitfield. Naomi married William Denton in Goldington, just east of Bedford, a year later. I have traced some of their descendants to the present day and have found family members living in Australia and the Netherlands.

Susan, b 1789 married Sam Macklin (McClean?) in October, 1809. Unfortunately, Susan died in July, 1810. My theory is that she possibly died in childbirth.

William, b 1792, married Elizabeth Odell in Sandy in 1813. Their two children, George and Mary were baptised in 1818. They were not necessarily twins, as poorer families tended to have their children baptised in batches. There will be more about Mary and George and their respective families later. William's wife Elizabeth died in January, 1831, aged 48; it appears that the couple had moved from Sandy because Elizabeth's burial was found in the Biggleswade register. Some simple arithmetic suggested that Elizabeth had been some nine or ten years older than William. Checking in the Sandy parish registers I found the baptism of Elizabeth Odell had taken place in 1782.

William was a gardener. Documents I have seen have not enabled me to establish conclusively whether this means he was a market gardener or a gardener for a private individual. It may be that he was both: although (as oldest son) he inherited the land in Swaden from his father Robert in 1841 and farmed it until his death in 1864, the size of the plot meant that he was unlikely to have been able to make a living from it, and he probably had to use his gardening skills elsewhere. By 1831 we have seen that he was living (and probably working) in Biggleswade: he was described as being a widower 'of this parish' when he married a widow, Sarah Brown, on 1ˢᵗ November of that year. Unfortunately, the format of the entry in the marriage register has made it difficult for me to discover Sarah's maiden name and the name of her father. If the marriage had taken place six years later these details would have been recorded as a statutory requirement. However, marriages before 1837 still had to be witnessed, and I was interested to see that *James Whitfield's* cross appeared in the register. James Whitfield, the gamekeeper of Tewin, (my great-great-great grandfather), was William Whitfield's uncle, and it appears that he had made the journey from Tewin to attend the ceremony. It may well have been the last time he set foot in Bedfordshire. As is so often the case, it raised other questions in my mind: how had James travelled? Did he own a horse, for instance, had he walked, or had he made the journey by stage coach? Had he brought his family with him? And was he a fairly regular visitor to Biggleswade? After all, his brother Philip had lived there until 1824, and his brother Robert still lived in Sandy, about three miles further north. I had assumed previously that once James, Sarah and their young family had moved to Tewin they had lost all contact with their families back in Bedfordshire. I think he may have owned a horse. It would explain how he had been in Wyboston in 1813 to report a shooting incident, although of course, it didn't explain *why* he was there. I presume he had been sent there by his employer, Earl Ludlow. James' report of illegal shooting, you will remember, had been a vital clue for me, leading to many further discoveries.

In 1841, James' nephew William and his wife Sarah were living in Shortmead House, a mansion of Georgian appearance, (although parts of it are earlier), set in its own extensive grounds. Situated north of Biggleswade and east of the River Ivel, this imposing and elegant residence (now a Grade Two listed building) was only about two or three miles from Stratford and Sandy Warren, both clearly visible across the fields, and perhaps half a mile further from William's plot in Swaden. It seemed a very grand house for a gardener and his wife to own or occupy and the couple's presence there suggests two possibilities to me: either William had married a wealthy widow whose first husband had owned the property; or the owners were away on the night of the census, and William and Sarah were occupying part of the property in a 'caretaking' capacity. This latter theory seems the more likely of the two. The property and grounds have been restored in recent years and an extensive kitchen garden was discovered underneath a matted tangle of brambles, thistles and ground elder. I would imagine that this garden (hopefully then devoid of such invasive perennial weeds) had been the scene of William's labours in 1841. It would be interesting to have details of the type of work he was required to undertake. Was he, for instance, just responsible for planting, weeding and harvesting of vegetables, or did he possess skills such as budding, grafting and pruning, necessary for the establishment and maintenance of an orchard? Was he expected to provide flowers for the house? Greenhouses were becoming popular with the more affluent families at this time. Was there one at Shortmead House? If so, it may be that William was involved with the production of more exotic fruits, such as pineapples or oranges. It is interesting to speculate in the absence of any documentary evidence.

Ten years later, the childless couple were living in Conquest Buildings, Chapel Fields, Biggleswade, close to the Wesleyan chapel and just off Shortmead Street, suggesting a more modest residence. William was again described as a gardener, and it could well be that he was still in charge of vegetable and fruit production at Shortmead House. Its owner at this time was William Wells Gardner, a seventy two year old surveyor; he had his niece Temperance Gardner living with him as well as a cook, two housemaids and a groom. My guess is that Mr Gardner had possibly been employed in surveying land for Enclosure awards in his younger days. Although there were therefore two Gardners in residence, there was no *gardener* mentioned and my theory is that William (Whitfield) walked to work from his cottage in Conquest Buildings. By living away from Shortmead House William would have retained a little independence and would not have been constantly at his employer's beck and call. Incidentally, William Wells Gardner was a cousin of Frances Wells (daughter of Samuel Wells the younger, brewer and banker of Biggleswade). Frances Wells had married Robert Lindsell and the Lindsells now lived at nearby Fairfield House with a retinue of seven servants - including the aptly named cook, Caroline Giblet.

William Whitfield's ownership of the land in Swaden from 1841 meant that he was eligible to vote. He appears in a poll book for 1859, listed with Sandy men, but it is noted that he was living in *Biggleswade*. This was useful confirmation for me that I had found the correct William Whitfield. When he exercised his right to vote - a rare privilege in those days - William would have had to travel to Bedford to indicate his preference. This appears to have been for the General Election, won by the Liberals under Viscount Palmerston. A supplement to the *Bedfordshire Times* of May 14th, 1859 gives the results of the County election held at Bedford on May 6th. Bedfordshire was then a single Parliamentary constituency, returning two members to Parliament in elections until 1885, after which date the county was divided into two constituencies. Surprisingly, the supplement gives details of the preferences of each voter, and I was intrigued to read that William Whitfield had plumped for 'Russell and Higgins'. Francis Charles Hastings Russell (1819-1891) was the 9th Duke of Bedford, and was Liberal MP for Bedfordshire from 1847 to 1872. He had an interest in agriculture, particularly in new methods which he experimented with on his Woburn estate. The Higgins family were brewers in Bedford, and Charles Higgins (1789-1862) was another Liberal who had also been a much-respected mayor of Bedford in the 1840s.

William's wife, Sarah, died in the same year (1859). I was a little surprised to see that her age was said to be 81 years. William died on 14th March, 1864, aged 72. It would appear that his second wife had been fourteen years his senior at the time of their marriage: obviously William preferred older women. Somewhat surprisingly, he didn't leave a will. His half acre plot in Swaden was inherited by his son (George) from his first marriage.

Elizabeth, William's younger sister b. 1794, died unmarried in 1819.

Mary was baptised in 1797 and died in the same year.

Robert, b 1798, moved from Sandy to Hertfordshire. I have not been able to find out when he moved - or why - but as a younger son, with no land to inherit (there wasn't much anyway) he may have travelled in search of work while he was young and single. He married Ann White at Much Hadham, Hertfordshire in 1825. Subsequent census entries suggest that the couple were not blessed with children, but indicate that Robert was rather resourceful in the ways he earned his money. In 1841 the couple were living at Braughing and Robert was described as a ginger beer maker. Unfortunately, the name of his employer wasn't given. I assume it wasn't a one man enterprise. Occasionally ginger beer bottles or flagons are dug up in fields in the district, bearing the name of various Hertfordshire firms that were making ginger beer in the nineteenth century. Apparently ginger beer had originally been made in Yorkshire since the middle of the eighteenth century; its alcohol content was sometimes as high as eleven per cent. Excise regulations stipulated in 1855 that the drink should not contain any more than two per cent alcohol and it became popular with children. I have searched the Braughing census return for further information on ginger beer making. I discovered that a Rayment family were living there, including a boy called William Rayment, son of George Rayment, an agricultural labourer. By 1860 there was a brewery at nearby Furneux Pelham, established by a William Rayment, but I could find no evidence that the Rayments were involved in ginger beer manufacture in Braughing in the 1840s.

By 1851, however, Robert was working as a coachman; again, I have no idea whose brougham or coach he was driving. How long this job lasted isn't clear, but by 1861 he was following an occupation more often associated with a Whitfield: he was a *gardener*, and living at Standon, near Puckeridge. Ann died in 1862, and by 1871 Robert was an inhabitant of the rather forbidding looking workhouse at Bishop's Stortford, where he died a couple of years later aged 75.

The next son was George, baptised in 1800, who died in 1815. His younger brother, Thomas, was baptised in 1802. I presume he also died young - I have not found him in the 1841 census.

Gabriel, the youngest son of Robert and Jemima Whitfield, baptised in 1803, seems to have been a rather wayward member of the family. His name appears in a bastardy bond made in 1826:

' Be it known that on the 16th day of July in the Year of our Lord, 1826, Gabriel Whitfield of the parish of St. Martin-in-the-Strand, Middlesex, servant, acknowledged himself to owe to our Sovereign Lord the King [George IV] the sum of £20, William Dix of Sandy, victualler, to owe £10 and Samuel Sutton of Sandy aforesaid, gardener, £10 to be levied upon the several lands, tenements, goods and chattels to the use of our said Lord the King if the said Gabriel Whitfield shall make default in the condition underwritten.

Whereas Sarah Jeeves of the parish of Elstow, [Bedfordshire], single woman, hath declared she is with child, and that the said child is likely to be born a bastard and be chargeable to the said parish of Elstow, and that the above bounden Gabriel Whitfield is the father of the said child.'

The condition mentioned in the document was that Gabriel had to appear at the next session of the court held in Bedford and obey the orders made there, unless the child had died, in which case the bond or recognizance would be void. Gabriel and his two friends who had provided sureties duly appeared at the court's Michaelmas Session in 1826. I assume Gabriel had to pay maintenance towards the child's upkeep, but these details have not survived. (His

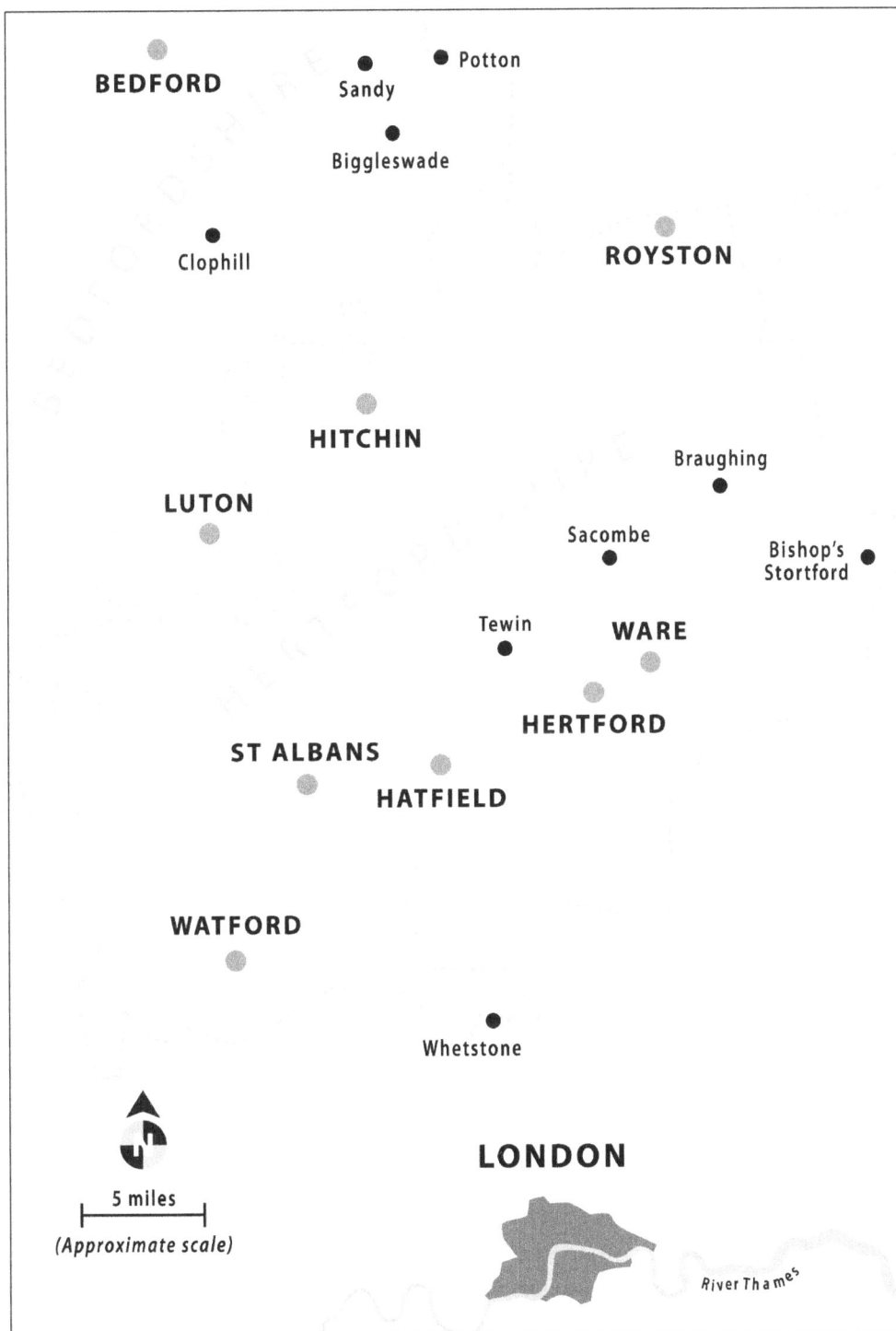

BEDFORD

Potton

Sandy

Biggleswade

Clophill

ROYSTON

HITCHIN

Braughing

LUTON

Sacombe

Bishop's
Stortford

Tewin

WARE

HERTFORD

ST ALBANS

HATFIELD

WATFORD

Whetstone

LONDON

5 miles
(Approximate scale)

River Thames

A map showing the position of Central Bedfordshire parishes
in relation to London in the nineteenth century
(Parishes associated with the Whitfield family are in lower case)

friend William Dix appears to have been an interesting character: he appeared at the Bedford court's Lent Assizes in 1829 accused of administering drugs to procure an abortion, but was acquitted).

The child fathered by Gabriel was baptised in Sandy on November 19, 1826: Joseph Gabel (sic) illegitimate son of Sarah Jeeves, spinster, Sandy.

He became known as Gabriel Jeeves and was living with his mother Sarah, now Sarah Cockings, in Sandy in 1841. Unfortunately he died in 1850.

I have not discovered the motive for Gabriel Whitfield's move to London. It may have been to avoid facing locally the scandal of fathering an illegitimate child or an attempt to escape paying for the child's upkeep. Perhaps he had intended moving to London anyway; he would not have been the first or the last Sandy resident to take this step. He was working as a groom at the time of his marriage and I suggest that he may have been looking after horses at Spitalfields, Covent Garden or Hungerford Market. All were markets for vegetables; the first two of major importance. The vegetables, of course, would have been conveyed to the markets from places like Sandy by horse and cart.

Gabriel married Susan Boone at St Martin-in-the-Fields on December 18, 1827. Their daughter, Susanna, was baptised at St Martin-in-the-Fields in 1828 and the family's address was given as Hungerford Street, a street leading from the Strand down to the Thames, and close to Hungerford Market. The family appears to have moved to Edward Street, Shoreditch, between 1828 and 1830. I have not been able to discover the reason for the move, but it is clear that they were now living in a far from salubrious area of the capital. Hector Gavin, M.D., F.R.C.S.E, produced a report on the conditions encountered in the district in 1848 - nearly twenty years after the Whitfield family were living there. He makes it clear that there had been no improvement in housing and sanitation in the previous decade (and, I suspect, in the ten years before that).

Gavin reported that Edward Street had three privies to serve all the houses, and just one water tap. The houses were very small - just two rooms - and at the time of the report were let at 3s 6d per week. Gavin noted that there was a garbage heap in the street. Edward Street was far from being the worst street in the neighbourhood: various streets nearby might have contested *that* dubious honour. Swan Street, for instance, was '....an abomination, its condition utterly disgraceful, and greatly to be reprehended...the parochial medical officer receives more orders for attendance upon the sick here than he does for any other place in his district'. Swan Court in Swan Street was

'... abominably filthy; there are three open privies belonging to it, they are full and most disgusting; dust heaps, ordure and garbage are scattered about, as are also shallow pools of liquid foetid filth. The houses convey the impression of great desolation...the whole locality that of wretchedness and misery, and disease. The medical officer at one time attended six cases of fever, being all the occupants of one room; they all lay in one bed'.

If this reads like a passage from a novel by Dickens - it would not be out of place in *Oliver Twist* for example - remember it was written by a professional medical man who was presumably not given to flights of fancy or in the habit of exaggerating what he observed.

Gabriel would have noticed conditions like these as he walked to work or to his local church - St. Leonard's at Shoreditch. Closer to Shoreditch, conditions were not much better. In Crabtree Row, Gavin noted an area of waste ground had been used to '…deposit all kinds of dirt, garbage and excrementitious matter [what a lovely euphemism] which was allowed to dry in the sun'. I can imagine the look on his face as he went on to note that 'In warm weather, a very offensive odour arises from this place'. He also complained about the '…reprobate characters in the vicinity on Sundays…who then gamble, fight and indulge in all kinds of indecencies and immoralities'. (Hopefully, Gabriel had not spent his Sundays like this a generation earlier). Austin Street, adjacent to St. Leonard's Churchyard was described as '…one of the filthiest in the metropolis'.

Gabriel and his family eluded me for many years. Searching for them in London was like looking for the proverbial needle in a haystack until the London parish registers appeared on the internet in 2009 and enabled me to discover the sorry end to this part of the family.

The burial registers for St. Leonard's Church, Shoreditch revealed that Gabriel was buried on 2 February, 1830, aged 25 years and his young daughter, Susanna some 16 days later, aged 1 year and 6 months.

Compulsory death certificates were not required before 1837, so I have not discovered why both Gabriel and Susanna died, but it is likely that they succumbed to an infectious disease. Bearing in mind the conditions described by Hector Gavin, this is hardly surprising. Sir Joseph Bazalgette would improve the health of Londoners by the middle of the nineteenth century when he developed his network of sewers, but in the 1820s and 1830s raw sewage was still being discharged into the Thames and the Lea and domestic wells and water pumps were often just a few feet from overflowing privies. A pamphlet published in 1827 noted that several thousand families in Westminster, or its suburbs were supplied with water 'in a state offensive to the sight, disgusting to the imagination, and destructive to health'. If we also add factors such as overcrowding, contaminated and adulterated food and long working hours we can understand why the average age at death for a labourer or tradesman in London at this time was disturbingly low, and why doctors like Hector Gavin were preparing reports on living conditions in the area.

Gabriel and Susanna were buried in St. Leonard's Churchyard - but did they stay there? Gabriel's widow, Susan, may well have been aware that the London Burkers, a notorious band of body snatchers or 'resurrectionists' operated in the area and lived in Nova Scotia Gardens, east of Shoreditch High Street and well within walking distance of both St. Leonard's and Edward Street.

'Resurrection', or peddling in dead bodies tended to take place between October and April each year, as this was when most hospital schools ran their course for medical students. The courses included lessons on anatomy; and for each student - there were hundreds of them each year in the early 1830s - three corpses were required: two for dissection in the anatomy course and one on which to practise operating techniques. The only problem was that suitable corpses were in short supply because they came fresh from the gallows from murderers who had been hung.

Male corpses were highly prized because they gave students a better opportunity to study well-developed muscles. Fresh corpses were obviously of much more use - and more pleasant to deal with - than ones which were beginning to putrefy. There was also a market for teeth extracted from corpses. They would be used as false teeth by people who had no teeth of their own and presumably were so desperate to be able to cut, grind and chew their food that they were happy to take advantage of this early, if rather macabre example of medical re-cycling. (I'm not sure how the teeth were fixed in their new owners' mouths; the very thought makes me want to reach for my toothbrush). Corpses fetched good money: between eight and twenty guineas, depending on freshness and the supply that had been forthcoming during that particular week. At this time male manual workers in London were earning anything between five and twenty shillings a week (25p to £1), so clearly, trading in the dead could be a lucrative, albeit illegal and risky occupation.

Sometimes the body snatchers murdered people so that they were able to deliver a fresh corpse for dissection; at other times they posed as friends or relatives of dying paupers and the corpse would be signed over for a 'private burial', which never took place. The alternative was to exhume freshly buried bodies, and as Gabriel and Susanna died in the Shoreditch area between October and April during the period in which the body snatchers were operating, I wonder whether their remains still lay in peace in St. Leonard's Churchyard.

London's Metropolitan Police were alerted in late 1831 to a series of crimes which appeared to be imitations of the notorious Burke and Hare murders for dissection in Edinburgh about three years earlier. These London crimes had taken place over a number of years before 1831, but in that year the murder of an Italian boy came to light: his clothes had been found down a well at a house in Nova Scotia Gardens in the Shoreditch area, not far from where Gabriel Whitfield and his family had lived. The occupants of the property were investigated and convicted for the murder and for many other bodysnatching incidents. One of the gang, John Bishop, was said to have sold hundreds of bodies to London surgeons (indirectly, through their porters). In an attempt to make the punishment fit the crime and to discourage others, the ringleaders were hung; the spectacle was watched by a large crowd and the bodysnatchers' own corpses were then delivered to a medical school for dissection.

I have not been able to find the death of Susan Whitfield, Gabriel's widow, who may well have maintained a graveside vigil to ensure that the corpses of her late husband and daughter did not fall prey to the body snatchers, and I have searched in vain for evidence of a remarriage, so there is still a certain degree of mystery attached to this branch of the family. Incidentally, Joyce Godber mentions that the body snatching phenomenon was also recorded in *Biggleswade* in 1826; the corpse was being conveyed in a waggon to London when the perpetrators were apprehended.

Moving to the next generation, Mary Whitfield, baptised in Sandy in 1818 with her brother George, was the daughter of William Whitfield, b. 1792 and his wife (Elizabeth, nee Odell), and the oldest of Robert and Jemima's grandchildren as she appears to have been born in 1814. She married Jonathan Endersby, a sawyer, in Wrestlingworth church in 1837. They had four daughters, Elizabeth, Mary Ann, Harriet and Emma between 1838 and 1847, before Mary died in 1848. Jonathan Endersby married Martha Freeman two years later and there were more children from this marriage. Jonathan was found in the Criminal Registers, accused of arson in 1851. He had been spotted trying to set fire to a shed belonging to Robert Lindsell and William

Hogg(e). These two men, wealthy in their own right and from well-heeled families, were now business partners, having interests in brewing and banking. They were also brothers-in-law, having both married into money by taking as their spouses the elder daughter and younger daughter respectively of Samuel Wells the younger of Biggleswade, the wealthy brewer and banker mentioned previously who had died in 1831. Wells had been an astute businessman: at his death his estate had included 46 pubs (18 outside Biggleswade), several maltings, and a large number of houses and cottages in addition to banks in Baldock and Biggleswade. Clearly, Hogge and Lindsell were unlikely to starve or end their days in the workhouse.

Lindsell, formerly a solicitor (he drew up and witnessed Philip Whitfield's will in 1824), was living at Fairfield House, Biggleswade in 1851 and was described as a banker and magistrate; his household included seven servants. He owned land and various properties in Biggleswade, including a timber yard and may have been Jonathan Endersby's employer. In his capacity as a magistrate he rather conveniently presided at Jonathan's trial at the Bedford Assizes. The understandably severe sentence (transportation for fifteen years) was subsequently commuted to seven years' imprisonment which Jonathan served at Wakefield; it would be interesting to know the reason behind his malfeasance. I suspect he may not have been too fond of Lindsell, and no doubt the feeling was mutual. Clearly, a dislike of bankers is not just a modern phenomenon: Hogg might well be an appropriate surname for some of them, although to be fair I have to admit that despite their greed, pigs do not manipulate interest rates or receive knighthoods, and exorbitant bonuses and pensions.

Jonathan Endersby returned to Biggleswade after he had completed his sentence, obtained work as a carpenter and fathered at least five more children before dying at the age of 57 in 1872. Three of the four daughters he had with Mary were looked after by his second wife who was working as a charwoman in 1851 to support them while Jonathan was in prison. Harriet Endersby, however, was brought up by her paternal grandparents in Wrestlingworth: in 1851 her grandfather was working as a sawyer, and ten years later he was running the *Three Horseshoes* public house. The girls all married later, and there were plenty of grandchildren for Jonathan (Emma, the youngest of Mary's daughters, had eleven children). Sadly, Mary did not live to see any of them.

George Whitfield, son of William Whitfield (b 1792) and his wife Elizabeth, and another one of Robert and Jemima Whitfield's grandchildren, was baptised in Sandy in 1818. He moved to Cambridge and was working as a gardener, probably for a wealthy private employer or possibly for a Cambridge college. I presume that he had learned the art of gardening from his father, and may have worked alongside him at Shortmead House. It is possible, of course, that he had moved to Cambridge to serve an apprenticeship in gardening, but I have no evidence for this. He married Charlotte Muncey Rayner, daughter of a cabinet maker, in Cambridge in May, 1839 at the church of St Andrew the Less on the Newmarket Road. At the time he was living in Jesus Terrace, and his bride (who appears to have been about ten years his senior) lived in Maid's Causeway.

George and Charlotte moved back to Biggleswade where George became gardener to John Nathaniel Foster who was living at a property known as St. Andrew's (not to be confused with the nearby St. Andrew's Church) in the town. Foster was a merchant, making good use of the navigable River Ivel; like his father before him, who had previously lived at the property, he dealt in coal, timber and wines. The 1841 census was too poorly preserved for me to draw many conclusions about when George started working for him, but the census taken ten years later was much more helpful. It shows that John Foster was living at St Andrews with his wife, two of his daughters and his son; George Whitfield lived three doors along the road with his wife Charlotte and their daughters Susan, Harriet and Martha Ann.

St Andrew's was an impressive property standing in its own grounds, close to the church, the river and to St Andrew's wharf, which would have handled John Foster's cargoes. A malting stood within the curtilage of the property. A sales catalogue produced when St Andrew's came up for auction (in 1886) refers to three dwelling houses in addition to the main property: a two bedroomed cottage adjoining the kitchen garden; a three bedroomed house also adjoined the garden; and next to this was a four bedroomed house. I wonder which one housed George and Charlotte and their family? These ancillary dwellings were all demolished in the 1960s and St Andrew's Close now occupies this part of the site. St. Andrew's itself still stands and now serves as the premises of Biggleswade's Conservative club. The catalogue also gave details of the 'pleasure grounds'. There was a vegetable border with an asparagus bed and a vinery, an orchard and a 'finely turfed lawn, studded with fine specimens of copper beech, fir and other ornamental timber… extending to the River Ivel'. There was also a 'rosery', a rustic summer house, shrubberies and a boat house. On the other side of the road were 'Two productive kitchen gardens, both walled on three sides, containing well-established espalier, pyramid, standard and wall fruit trees of the best varieties'. The soil was said to be 'principally of the greensand formation with gravelly subsoil'. George must have been kept hard at work here and was clearly a versatile and skilful gardener, presumably able to produce most types of vegetables and fruit for the delectation of the Foster family.

Proximity to a possible employer is obviously not *proof* of actual employment, but George and John Nathaniel Foster were still living at the same addresses in St. Andrew's Street in 1861. It appeared that George and his family were living in a house owned by John Foster and I already had proof that George was gardener to Foster in *Sandy* from another, later, document. Further verification came from the 1871 census which shows that *both men* and their respective families had moved to Sandy by this time. John Foster was now living at Sandy Place and George lived in a nearby cottage; Foster had actually moved there in 1867, and I presume George had also moved back to his home town at this time so that he could continue to work for him. This arrangement suggests that Foster was satisfied with George's work and that George was happy with his conditions of employment and with his employer.

John Nathaniel Foster was now a rich, powerful and influential man in the local area: county magistrate, landowner and trustee (with William Hogge and Robert Lindsell), of the Biggleswade Provident Land and Building Society. He was one of the first directors of the Great Northern Railway, a Commissioner of the Ivel Navigation and was High Sheriff of Bedfordshire in 1870. In politics, he was a Liberal. The 1871 census shows that Sandy Place was home to John Nathaniel Foster and his wife Frances, but also to their unmarried son Albert, described as a clergyman of the Church of England without cure of souls (sounds better than

Sandy Place from its grounds, 2013. The modern buildings to the right of the original house are classrooms of Sandye Place Academy. Photo by Isaac Whitfield, 2013.

an unemployed vicar) and a landowner; and two unmarried daughters, Frances and Edith. The Fosters employed a butler, a footman, a lady's maid, a cook, a housemaid and a kitchen maid in addition to those who toiled outside.

Sandy Place had been built for Humphrey Monoux in the 1740s; it had remained in the Monoux family until the early nineteenth century, when it was owned by Frances Monoux. Although she had married and become Frances Henley Ongley it had remained her property until she died in 1841. Sandy Place had 'a very capital kitchen garden of nearly an acre' according to a sale catalogue of 1851 and 'a capital Green House and Grapery, about 60 ft. long, with vines of the best sorts; Pine Pit, heated by flues and hot water [for the cultivation of pineapples], Forcing Ground, [presumably a heated area of soil used to obtain very early fruits and vegetables] and Melon Pits'. The greenhouse adjoined the kitchen garden and orchard. A later catalogue went on to state that 'The park, extending round the Mansion and Pleasure Grounds, is well Timbered, is screened from the Village and Road by a belt of Plantation, and on the South side is bounded by a branch of the River Ivel'.

I assume that the grounds and gardens were not altered substantially in the next fifteen years or so. Clearly, George would not have had to look far for something to do at Sandy Place. It would appear that he was a capable, multi-skilled gardener and I would imagine that his work there must have occupied a great deal of his time. The 1871 census suggested to me that he was helped by two under-gardeners. Thomas Barnes lived in Park Lane next door to the now widowed George and his youngest daughter, Martha Ann, (who was working as a lace milliner). Thomas Wootton lived further along Park Lane. A 'garden lad', Frank Lawson, aged thirteen, also lived in Park Lane; he may well have been George's apprentice. In 1871, George still retained a little independence from the demands of John Foster and Sandy Place because he had also inherited the half acre of land in Swaden from his father, William Whitfield (1792-1864), - and thus also from his grandfather, Robert (1763- 1841) and great grandfather William Whitfield (1727-1806). He appears to have leased this plot to a tenant, but as the freeholder he would have had the option of cultivating it himself if necessary.

According to Jennifer Davies in *The Victorian Kitchen Garden*, head gardeners at this time appear to have enjoyed a similar social standing to that of butlers, and gardening was considered a gentlemanly pursuit. A head gardener's consent would be sought, even by his employer, before any flowers were cut or any fruit was picked from the gardens he supervised. He would have liaised with the cook and recommended the fruits and vegetables to her which were at their best. His house would have been rent-free and he may have been allocated beer money in addition to his wages. At some country houses, head gardeners also charged their apprentices for the tuition they received. In her book Jennifer Davies also states that 'a head gardener wore a suit and top hat and did very little physical labour. He supervised the laying out of bedding plants in the pleasure grounds, issued orders, inspected the garden and hired and fired garden staff.' Unfortunately, I have been unable so far to find details of George's salary and conditions of employment, but as his job entailed a fair amount of responsibility I would imagine he received more money than an ordinary agricultural labourer; he was also receiving rent for his plot at Swaden. I wonder if a photograph survives of the garden staff at Sandy Place in the 1870s?

George and Charlotte's family had all been born in Biggleswade. Their first child was Edward George, who was born in 1842 and baptised at St Andrew's Church, a short stroll from where George and Charlotte were living at the time. He took his names from his grandfather Edward Rayner and his proud father, George. Unfortunately young Edward died in 1847. Susan was born in 1845, Harriet in 1848 and Martha Ann in 1850.

Susan became a dressmaker and married Thomas Simpkins in 1867 at Biggleswade Baptist Church. Thomas Simpkins' background was interesting. He was the youngest of three illegitimate children born to Kezia Simpkins, originally from Shillington, Bedfordshire. Both he and his sister Susanna Maria had been baptised in Biggleswade; his brother Charles appears to have been baptised elsewhere, possibly in Shillington or nearby Meppershall. Kezia Simpkins was not in prosperous circumstances, probably because of her illegitimate children and may have been disowned by her family back in Shillington. I discovered that in 1851 she had been living with young Thomas and his sister in Biggleswade workhouse. Presumably unemployed at the time, she was described as a general servant. Her son Charles, aged eighteen in 1851, was already fending for himself by working as a cowman. Ten years later, Thomas was working as a groom and living with his mother in Back Street, Biggleswade. Both of them were lodging with Thomas Gauge and his wife Mary.

Thomas Simpkins was described as an ironmonger at the time of his marriage to Susan Whitfield, but less than two years later he was declared bankrupt, with debts approaching £400. He ascribed his misfortune to 'want of capital, being sued and having his stock seized by the sheriff' according to an article in the *Northampton Mercury* of Saturday, 16th January, 1869. It was hardly the ideal way to start a marriage. Undaunted, he studied to become a Baptist Minister, and entered the Ministry by examination and ordination in May, 1869. The couple then emigrated to the USA in June, 1870, with their two young sons: George Whitfield Simpkins and Charles Whitfield Simpkins.

Two months later, Thomas Simpkins became pastor of the Baptist Church at Mount Bethel, New Jersey. The family were living at Johnstown in 1880 and the census shows that Thomas' mother, Kezia Simpkins, was also living with them. She had not emigrated with them, however; I found she was still lodging in Back Street, Biggleswade in 1871 and working as a straw plaiter. She had certainly arrived in America by 1875: a census of New York State taken in that year showed me that she was living with Thomas and Susan and their two children at Worcester. It would be interesting to know whether Thomas and Susan also gave Susan's father, George, the opportunity to emigrate. As far as I can tell he didn't cross the Atlantic, but surely must have been tempted to do so, particularly after 1872, for a reason which will be apparent later.

Thomas Simpkins became the pastor of the church in Adams, New Jersey, in January, 1886. He and Susan had three more children in America: Edith R., Wayne Brewster and Henry Longfellow Simpkins: presumably Thomas or Susan enjoyed reading the poetry of Henry Longfellow (1807-1882). I wonder what Henry thought of his middle name. Perhaps he was just grateful it wasn't Hiawatha.

Two tragedies - Thomas and Susan Simpkins' son Charles drowned, aged 12, in Cayadutta Creek, Johnstown in 1882 and Susan died on Christmas Day, 1891 in her mid-forties - must have severely tested Rev. Simpkins' Christian faith. His mother Kezia had also died - in 1889. Thomas remarried in October, 1893. His new wife, Miss Jennie Munson, was described as 'one of Adams' [i.e New Jersey] fairest daughters', and was some twenty six years his junior. A daughter, Jane, was born to the couple in July, 1894.

Thomas and Jennie moved to Ticonderoga, Essex, New York in January, 1896. Even today, Ticonderoga is a small settlement (its population in 2010 was just over 5,000). I was therefore very fortunate in discovering not only that Ticonderoga had an excellent local newspaper, the *Ticonderoga Sentinel,* full of interesting details for family historians, but also that its archives are available online.

Rev Thomas Simpkins died at Ticonderoga on Thursday, 23rd September, 1897. He had preached as usual on the preceding Sunday, although he clearly had been unwell, as an edition of the *Ticonderoga Sentinel* in September, 1897, had stated that he was 'dangerously ill from inflammation of the bowels'. His obituary in the *Ticonderoga Sentinel* of 8th October, 1897, describes him as 'a man of strong personality, a fine preacher [and] a devout and scholarly man'. These attributes are perhaps all the more remarkable when his humble beginnings are considered. Thomas and Susan, their son Charles and Thomas' mother Kezia are all buried in

Johnstown cemetery. I was amazed to discover that the Rev. Thomas Simpkins' second wife, Jennie, died within my lifetime – in 1957, aged 88. Jane Simpkins, the child they had together, married Clarence Parlow in 1920 and there are living descendants.

George Whitfield Simpkins, Thomas and Susan's oldest son, died at the age of 34 at Lynchburg, Virginia, where he had been a photographer. Clearly there would have been some family photographs, possibly including ones of George's parents, which may have survived as George was married with two children: Margaret S(usan?) and Charles Thomas Simpkins. It would be interesting to know whether any of these photographs were sent to his grandfather George Whitfield back in England.

By 1910, George Whitfield Simpkins' widow, May, and their two children Margaret and Charles were living in Gloversville, Fulton, New York, a settlement named after its main commercial activity, established since 1853: about ninety per cent of American gloves were made here. Such was its success that a slogan proclaiming that 'Gloversville gloves America' was later changed to 'Gloversville gloves the world'. Gloversville had large tanneries and glove shops at this time as well as related industries such as box making and sewing machine repairs, and most people's jobs were connected to glove making in some way or other. May Simpkins was working as a glove inspector and young Charles was a 'button boy', presumably responsible for stitching buttons on certain types of gloves. By 1920 the family had dispersed, and were not in Gloversville to experience its eventual decline - always a risk when a settlement becomes over-reliant on one product or industry. There are some living descendants, as both Margaret and Charles married: Margaret had the distinction of marrying Ulysses S. Grant Cure, (Junior) in 1919 - both he and his father had been named after the eighteenth President of the United States of America. Ulysses S. Grant Cure (Senior) was the editor and proprietor of the *Pine Hill Sentinel*, a paper which supported 'the principles and candidates of the Republican Party' (with a name like his it would have been a little unfortunate to be supporting the Democrat cause). His publication was 'outspoken and fearless' in advancing all measures which would 'promote the welfare of our town and country'. He also had business interests in fire insurance and real estate (property) and somehow managed to find time to be the proprietor of the Pine Hill Novelty Works which manufactured wooden souvenirs of the nearby Catskill Mountains. The internet article I found added, perhaps rather superfluously, that he was 'one of the busiest men in our community'. I haven't managed to discover whether his son followed in his father's footsteps, but he may have had a slightly less strenuous lifestyle because he lived to be nearly ninety, whereas his father had died aged fifty six.

Margaret and Ulysses' children were probably relieved to receive rather more conventional Christian names: Howard, Walter, Mary and George Thomas Cure. George Thomas Cure was presumably named after his grandfather, George Whitfield Simpkins (who in turn was named after *his* grandfather, George Whitfield, the gardener of Sandy); and his great grandfather Thomas Simpkins. You will probably be interested to learn that Howard Cure was working as a *gardener* on a private estate in Pine Hill, Ulster, New York State in 1940. I managed to find brief obituaries of Walter Cure and George Thomas Cure on the internet; they died in 2004 and 2011 respectively. George Cure was survived by children and grandchildren.

Wayne Simpkins' daughter, Elizabeth, a granddaughter of Thomas and Susan Simpkins, was born in 1906 and died in 1991. I'm sure she would have had some interesting tales to tell, and would probably have had some photographs of her grandparents. She had been an English teacher at Ticonderoga, Essex, New York for 39 years. Unfortunately, I found details of her death on the internet in 2009, so there was no opportunity to make contact. She appears to have been regarded very favourably by her former pupils. Her obituary noted that she was a member of the Ticonderoga Historical Society and of the Ticonderoga Methodist Church. She must have been very well known and respected in the small town of about five thousand inhabitants.

I searched on the internet for further details of the Simpkins family in Ticonderoga and found that both Wayne Simpkins and his younger brother Henry had continued living there after the death of their father. Wayne had been a grocer and Henry had owned a hardware shop in Ticonderoga. Once again I was able to make use of the *Ticonderoga Sentinel* which provided me with an interesting obituary for Henry Simpkins. Both he and Wayne had been very active members of the Ticonderoga Baptist Church. I have traced the line from Henry to the present day, so George Whitfield the gardener of Sandy (1818-1896) and his wife Charlotte still have several descendants living in the U.S.A. although they do not have the Whitfield surname.

Harriet, the next daughter of George and Charlotte Whitfield, baptised in Biggleswade in 1848, married Jesse Henry Jennings, a house decorator of Winslow, Buckinghamshire, in 1872. Jesse was the son of Henry Jennings who had a decorating business in the small town. It is difficult to see how Harriet and Jesse had met. I assume that Jesse had been decorating houses in the Sandy/Biggleswade area. Alternatively, Harriet could have been in domestic service in the Winslow district. Harriet's father, George, was a witness and signed his name in the register. The couple moved to Winslow, where Jesse later also became a builder and mason. They had three sons, Albert Edward, John Whitfield and William Henry. It was interesting to see that, like her sister Susan in the Simpkins family, Harriet had sought to continue the Whitfield name in the choice of a middle name for one of her sons. Harriet died in 1901, so like her sister, Susan, did not live to a great age.

Albert Jennings learned the art of painting and decorating from his father and worked alongside him in the family business in Winslow. He must have met his future wife Edith Sarah Varney in Winslow where she was working as a draper's assistant. They married in 1899; the marriage was registered at Leighton Buzzard in south west Bedfordshire. The family then moved to London. Albert and Edith were living in Clerkenwell at the time of the 1911 census, and there were no children. Albert was working as a house painter for a building firm. They appear to have had a son, John, in 1919, after about twenty years of marriage: hopefully his arrival was a pleasant surprise. Unfortunately for me his commonplace Christian name and lack of a middle name have made him difficult to trace further. It is possible that he could still be alive.

Fortunately, John Whitfield Jennings, the middle son of Jesse and Harriet was easier to trace, thanks to his distinctive middle name. After learning the painting and decorating trade with his father in Winslow he also migrated to the London area. The 1911 census showed me that he was living in Wimbledon, Surrey. I was rather surprised to discover that he was working as a footman in the household of Llewellyn Wood Longstaff, a retired lieutenant-colonel and his wife. The Longstaffs employed eleven servants in total: two lady's maids; three housemaids; a cook, assisted by a kitchen maid and a scullery maid; a coachman and a gardener in addition to their footman. The establishment appeared to be without a butler, so John must have been kept busy. Perhaps his employers were teetotal or anxious to economise. His duties could have included waiting at table, possibly accompanying the Longstaffs on social visits, cleaning boots, shoes and cutlery and a multitude of other household tasks. I would be interested to know who was asked to carry out any internal or external decorating at the property, a former convent called Ridgelands.

The Longstaff household seemed to be a little out of the ordinary and I decided to investigate further. I was intrigued by my discoveries and hope you will forgive me for a short digression. Llewellyn Wood Longstaff was the son of a consulting physician and industrial chemist, George Dixon Longstaff, one of the founders and vice-president of the Chemical Society, who had died in 1892 leaving an estate of over £107,000. Llewellyn Wood Longstaff had acquired a substantial share in a Hull-based firm: Blundell Spence and Company, which had been started by his maternal grandfather Henry Blundell and his (i.e. Henry's) brother-in-law William Spence. The firm made a range of colours (linseed oil-based paints and varnishes), and this made me wonder whether it was through the supply of these products that Longstaff was known to the Jennings family of Winslow. Otherwise, the employment of John Whitfield Jennings by the Longstaffs was an amazing coincidence.

I'm not sure when - or if - Llewellyn Wood Longstaff actually served in the army. Successive census returns gave me glimpses of his life, but obviously don't tell the complete story of a remarkable man. He appears to have made (or acquired through inheritance) his money well before middle age. At the age of just nineteen he was already described as a 'colour merchant'. In 1871, aged 29, he was described as a colour and varnish manufacturer employing 180 men and 40 boys; by 1881 he was a 'lieutenant-colonel for a voluntary force' whose income came 'from dividends, etc.'; ten years later he was 'living on his own means'. In 1901 he was 'a retired chemical merchant' and he assumed the retired lieutenant-colonel description when he completed the return for his household in 1911. What the census returns *didn't* reveal was that he was a Fellow of the Royal Geographical Society, well known to its leader Sir Clements Markham; and that he was the chief private sector promoter of the 1901 - 1904 British expedition to Antarctica, having donated £25,000 in 1899 towards the construction of the *Discovery*. Captain Scott and Ernest Shackleton had duly named a range of mountains in Antarctica in his honour in December, 1902. Longstaff died in 1918, leaving a fortune of nearly £200,000. One of his sons, Tom George Longstaff became a doctor, explorer and mountaineer and was chief medical officer on the 1922 expedition to Mount Everest. John Whitfield Jennings may well have served drinks to Markham, Scott and Shackleton planning their Antarctic expedition while they enjoyed the hospitality of their generous benefactor in an informal social setting.

I'm not sure how long John Whitfield Jennings stayed with the Longstaffs, but suspect that the First World War intervened; at the time of his marriage to Florence Gill which took place in Clerkenwell in April, 1918 he was described as a soldier. The birth of the couple's daughter, Constance M. Jennings, was registered in Holborn in the December quarter of the following year. I have not been able to discover whether John returned to domestic service or to painting and decorating after the war and know little more about him; he died in 1947 in Finsbury and the National Probate Register reveals that he left just under £450.

His younger brother, William Henry Jennings married May Marks in the spring or early summer of 1912, and their son John W. Jennings was born in the first quarter of 1913; from there the trail goes cold, and the Jennings family seems to have left Winslow. My guess is that they, too, moved to the London area. I found that a William Henry Jennings, born in 1884 or thereabouts, died in Willesden in 1954. Again, there may well be some living descendants. I would be interested to know whether Albert, John and William kept in touch with their American cousins.

It appears that George and Charlotte Whitfield's youngest child, Martha Ann, didn't marry. She was living in Bedford in 1881 and working as a milliner. By 1891 she had moved to Islington, London, and was described as a mantle (cloak) maker. She may well have been still living there ten years later, but the 1901 census shows she was visiting her brother in law, Jesse Jennings and his family in Winslow, after the death of her sister, Harriet. I was unable to find her in the 1911 census, but discovered the death of a Martha Ann Whitfield, born in 1850, which took place in 1925 in Holborn, London. It may well be that she had kept in touch with her nephew, John Whitfield Jennings who was living in the same area of London. I haven't seen the certificate, but feel fairly confident that this was the person I was looking for.

George Whitfield's wife Charlotte died in 1870. His son Edward George had died in infancy. His daughter, Susan, had married and emigrated to the U.S.A., and his daughter Harriet had moved to Winslow following her marriage. His daughter Martha had not married but had also moved away. George was fifty four when he decided to sell his half acre of land in Sandy which had been in the family for at least sixty eight years. He sold it to the Pym family, dealing initially with Alexander Pym, who was at that time looking after the family estate at Hasells Hall between Everton and Sandy, and the land was added to the Pym's landholding. A preliminary note dated 11th January, 1872, confirming details of the intended transaction, appears to be in George's own hand and suggests that he was a competent writer. Signed by George, it was witnessed by Alexander Pym and by Richard Merryweather, a woodman who still lived in Swaden; the note could have been written in his cottage, which was probably close to the plot. The indenture (sale) document of 8th April, 1872, included a small map of the Swaden area and also indicated that the purchaser was Alexander's nephew, Francis Pym, a young man in his early twenties. The £76 George received for the land must have been useful. It would probably have been roughly equivalent to a year's wages.

A document drawn up (in the presence of John Nathaniel Foster) to demonstrate George's title to the plot shows that he had been leasing it to William Darnell. At the age of fifty four, George was probably a little too old to be wanting to work an uneconomic holding by hand after tending John Foster's extensive gardens at Sandy Place all day, and he had no son or son-in-law living locally to help him. In this latter document, Samuel Barker, an old man of eighty two gave details of the plot's history, and thus, also the history of this branch of the Whitfield family. Barker was a retired market gardener, now living with his daughter and son-in-law at the *Red Lion*. He had previously lived in the Stratford area of Sandy, close to Swaden and could remember the land being allocated to George's great grandfather, William Whitfield, after Sandy had been enclosed in 1804 and could recall George's grandfather and father also working the plot. The land was a good distance from where George was living: as we have noted, the 1871 census shows that George occupied a cottage in Park Lane, next door to his wealthy employer. Unlike a lot of land in Sandy which is now occupied by housing estates, the plot which George sold can still be seen; I believe it is still part of the Pym estate, and today is being used to grow trees. John Foster's residence and grounds are now the home of a Middle School - the Sandye Place Academy. I have taught there on many occasions, and have also had the pleasure of removing several swarms of bees from old apple trees in the grounds where George Whitfield would have been working in the early 1870s.

George's ownership of his half acre plot had entitled him (like his father before him) to the privilege of voting in County and Parliamentary elections. Even as late as 1872, he was one of a small elite in this respect: in the Bedford by-election of June of that year only 101 men from Sandy voted. Possibly even in 1872 some people were disillusioned with politicians and couldn't be bothered to register their preference. George voted for Francis Bassett, the Liberal candidate. Only 28 Sandy men voted for Bassett; the other 73 voted for the Tory candidate Colonel William Stuart. Bassett came from a family of wealthy bankers whose firm was eventually amalgamated with Barclay's, but he was also a Quaker and a philanthropist, a man who put his religious principles into practice. (Perhaps Bassett's obituary - which I found in the *Bucks Herald* of 17th June, 1899, should be read by some of today's bankers as they ponder what to do with their colossal and often undeserved bonuses: it might prick their consciences). I was interested to read that Bassett was also interested in agriculture, as a noted breeder of Jersey cattle and a good judge of horses; and was at one time President of the Bedfordshire Agricultural Society. A supporter of the Bedford Infirmary, Bassett helped many other worthy causes including individuals who 'were less well off in this world's goods'.

Bassett's rival for the Bedfordshire seat, William Stuart, a Conservative, was a member of another wealthy family who resided at Tempsford Hall and Aldenham Abbey, Hertfordshire and had further property in Kempston, Bedfordshire and Sutton Cheney in Leicestershire. A grandson of John Stuart, the 3rd Earl of Bute (Tory Prime Minister of Great Britain from 1762 to 1763), and a descendant of the Royal Stuart family, William Stuart was a Colonel in the Bedfordshire Militia, and a Justice of the Peace for Hertfordshire, Bedfordshire and Huntingdonshire. He was regarded as 'one of the best type of the country squire', according to his obituary which appeared in the *Bedfordshire Times*. He had already represented Bedford as an MP on two previous occasions, and was not short of a penny or two. (He left over £226,000 when he died in 1893).The results of the election were published in the *Bedfordshire Times* of 31st August, 1872. The victorious candidate was Bassett.

I can only assume that George's land sale had not completed at the time of the election, despite the fact that the sale document was dated some two months earlier; otherwise his vote would probably have been illegal.

Despite receiving the proceeds of his land sale, George was described as a pauper in 1881 and he was living in Biggleswade workhouse. He was now clearly unemployed and I presume that he may have been incapable of doing his former job, either due to the increasing infirmity of old age or possibly because of an accident. I speculated that he may have used the money to travel to America at some time between 1872 and 1881 to visit his daughter Susan, her husband Thomas Simpkins and his Simpkins grandchildren but have so far searched in vain for any evidence of such a trip. The Sandy census of 1881 shows that the gardener at Sandy Place was now a much younger man, Joseph Holmwood, who originated from Tunbridge Wells. George was still a workhouse inmate ten years later; he had no family in Sandy to look after him. John Nathaniel Foster, his former employer, died in the same year, leaving the handsome sum of £32,000. Had he had ever spared a thought for his old gardener, now in straitened circumstances?

George endured the spartan regime of the workhouse for another five years. I have not managed to find details of the daily routine for inmates: times, meals, work undertaken, and so on, *specifically* for Biggleswade, but if the institution was typical for the period, George would have been expected to get up at six a.m. (an hour later in winter) and would be expected to start work - if he *was* still capable of undertaking any - at seven (again, an hour later in winter). He would have been allowed an hour off at mid-day for a meal, after which he would be required to work again until six in the evening. After a frugal supper he would be in bed by eight o'clock. Meals would have consisted of basic, fairly unappetising fare, such as gruel or porridge for breakfast, and bread and cheese for supper. At mid-day he might have been allowed a little poor quality meat with some potatoes and perhaps other vegetables on three days a week and soup and bread on the other days; bread was a major constituent of the workhouse diet. The portions of each type of food allocated were stipulated by rules laid down by the Poor Law commissioners: men, women and children received different sized portions. George might have undertaken gardening (just for a change) while he languished in the workhouse; alternatives for men included breaking stones (which were used for surfacing roads), chopping wood or grinding corn.

As he could sign his name, George could probably also read; if so, it is to be hoped that his family kept in touch by letter, otherwise he must have been a very lonely and possibly embittered old man. If his son, Edward George had survived to marry in Sandy, things might have turned out very differently, and perhaps a Whitfield descendant might today be cultivating a small plot on the Swaden Road just outside Sandy, unwinding after a busy day at the office. As it was, the senior branch of the Whitfield family died out in the male line when George Whitfield took his last breath in Biggleswade workhouse in 1896. His family did not live locally, so he was probably given a pauper's funeral: placed in the cheapest possible coffin and then, after a short service attended by no family mourners - possibly by no mourners at all - buried in an unmarked grave.

So far, I had traced the main trunk of my family tree back to my 4x great grandfather, William Whitfield (1727-1806), the father of James Whitfield, the gamekeeper. Using the Sandy parish registers, I was able to establish that William was the son of Robert Whitfield baptised in Sandy in 1701 and his wife Susan, nee Shipton, baptised in 1699. Robert married Susan in Sandy in 1723. He was a gardener, presumably a market gardener. He and Susan had four children:

William, baptised 1723, who died in 1724.

John, baptised and buried 1726.

William, (1727-1806), my 4x great grandfather, who was baptised in Sandy church during the same month and year as King George II's coronation in Westminster Abbey. Compared to this extravaganza, with anthems specially composed by Handel, I would imagine the ceremony in Sandy was a rather modest affair.

Susan, baptised in 1731, died as a spinster of 19 in 1750.

There were no more children from this marriage as Robert died in 1731, aged about thirty.

The cause of death was not given in the burials register. Susan, Robert's widow married again in October, 1733. Her husband was Thomas Cosyn or Cozin, and their son John was born in 1736.

Although he was only about thirty when he died, Robert survived much longer than most of his brothers and sisters. *His* parents, William Whitfield, (1673-1746) and Susan Whitfield nee Swetman, were first cousins on William's mother's side. They married in Sandy in 1700, and the union produced:

Robert, baptised 1701, died 1731.
Susan, baptised 1702, died January 15, 1706/7.
William, baptised 1703, died September 1, 1709.
Freeman, baptised 1705, died October 27, 1706.
Joseph, baptised 1706, died September 8, 1706.
Mary, baptised 1706, died September 8, 1706.
Susan, baptised 1708, died June 23, 1708.
Mary, baptised 1708, died October 31, 1708.
William, baptised 1709, who survived to marry Elizabeth Tilcock - more about these later.
Elizabeth, baptised 1711, died 1711.
Alice, baptised 1712, who died in 1720.
Freeman, baptised in 1713, died in 1714.
Susan, baptised in 1717, who died in 1719, and
Elizabeth, baptised in 1719, who died in the same year.

Susan Whitfield, William's wife then died in 1726. She must have had a hard and miserable life, coping with the births of fourteen children and the deaths of twelve of them. I have not been able to discover whether there were any epidemics in early eighteenth century Sandy, but as the couple were first cousins it is possible that there may have been some sort of genetic defect present in the children. Poor living conditions and the relatively primitive state of medicine at the time were possibly also contributory factors to this shocking example of infant mortality within the family.

William Whitfield, Susan's husband, baptised in 1673, was also a market gardener. He must have been extremely resilient, both physically and emotionally, to survive to the age of 73 after coping with the demands of a large family, the constant hard physical nature of his work and the emotional strain of losing most of his children in infancy, another son at age thirty and his wife at age fifty. He must have been a remarkable man. I found out that he owned at least 5½ acres of land in Sandy, because in 1733 when he was sixty and after his son Robert had died (in 1731), he sold the land to John Barber, a mason from nearby Moggerhanger.

These 5½ acres, which may well have represented a reasonably sized market garden holding at that time, were not situated in one convenient block, as the open fields of Sandy had not been enclosed in 1733; as we have seen, that happened about seventy years later. The document I viewed at the Bedford record office made it clear that the land was:

'…lying dispersedly in the common fields of Sandy aforesaid. That is to say in Kinwick Field one half acre abutting East on the Warren and West on the Hasells, the land of Heylock

Extract from Sandy parish register, 1709. Parish registers record in a matter of fact way the tragedies as well as the happy times of family life. Having buried their young son William in September, William and Susanna Whitfield named their next son William in the baptism ceremony which took place in St. Swithun's Church during the following month. (I have added the date at the top of the extract). Image reproduced by kind permission of the Bedfordshire and Luton Archives Service.

Married, Baptiz'd, Buried Anno Domini 1711

Susanna the daughter of Richard Ray & Margaret his wife — Baptiz'd March ye 25
Mary the daughter of John Newman & Froninny his wife — Baptiz'd April ye 8
Stephen the Son Stephen ffarrington & Mary his wife — Baptiz'd April ye 15
Thomas the Son of William Radwell & Elizabeth his wife — Baptiz'd April ye 25
John the Son of John Langley & Mary his wife — Baptiz'd May the 24
John the Son of William Richardson & Mary his wife — Baptiz'd May the 31
John the Son of William Richardson — Buried June the 1st
Elizabeth the daughter of William Whitfield & Susanna his wife — Baptiz'd June the 24
Margaret the daughter of Thomas Ireland & Elizabeth his wife — Baptiz'd July ye 15
An unbaptiz'd Child of Henry Egan of Northill — Buried July ye 2d
Stephen the Son of Stephen ffarrington — Buried July the 18
John the Son of Edward Keith & ... — ...

William Dear & Susanna Richardson — Married Augst ye 6
Elizabeth the daughter of William Dear & Susanna his wife — Baptiz'd Augst ye 9
Elizabeth the wife of William Harris of Blunham — Buried Augst ye 10
Mary the Daughter of Oliver Browning & Anne his wife — Baptiz'd Augst ye 24
John the Son of Anne Rogers widow & Thomas her late deceas'd husband — Baptiz'd Augst the 26
John the Son of John Skilliter & Margaret his wife — Baptiz'd September the 2
Daniel the Son of Daniel Thomas & Susanna his wife — Baptiz'd September ye
Elizabeth the daughter of John Cage — Buried September ye 9
Mary the daughter of Thomas Longland & Elizabeth his wife — Baptiz'd September ye
Elizabeth the daughter of Isaac Atherton & Elizabeth his wife — Baptiz'd September ye 30
Thomas Staunton & Alice Hoadey — Married October ye
Alice the daughter of Thomas Staunton & Alice his wife — Baptiz'd October
Elizabeth the daughter of William Whitfield — Buried October
John the Son of Henry Page & Mary his wife — Baptiz'd Octo
John the Son of Oliver Pygott & Anne his wife — Baptiz'd Octo
John the Son of John Grey & Jane his wife — Baptiz'd
Mary the daughter of John Brand & Mary his wife — Baptiz'd
Elizabeth the daughter of William Dear — Buried
Edward Brett — Buried
John Phileps & Mary Hodges — Married

Extract from the Sandy parish register, 1711. William and Susan(na) Whitfield baptised their daughter Elizabeth in June, 1711 and returned to St. Swithun's Church, Sandy, in October for her funeral service. They named another daughter Elizabeth in 1719, but she died in the same year. Image reproduced by kind permission of the Bedfordshire and Luton Archives Service..

1752

~~...~~ of Thomas Munns — — — — — Buried March
~~...~~ Blacksmith — — — — Buried March
William the Son of Isaac Harodine — — — — Buried March
George the Son of William Braybrook & Mary his Wife — — Baptiz'd March
Mary the Daughter of John Page & Elizabeth his Wife — — Buried April
Ann the Wife of William Brit — — — — Baptiz'd Apri
Sarah the Daughter of William Randall & Elizabeth his Wife — Baptiz'd Apri
Elizabeth the Daughter of William Christmas & Susan his Wife — Baptiz'd Apri
Ann the Daughter of Joseph Swinsco & Mary his Wife — — — Buried April
Robert Whitfield, Gardiner — — — — Baptiz'd Ma
Sarah the Daughter of Benjamin Jackson & Hanna his Wife — Baptiz'd Ma
James the Son of Mary Griffiths of ye Parish of St Luke in London — Buried Ma
John the Son of John Cullip — — — — — Married Ma
William Brit & Elizabeth Morcher — — — — Buried Ma
Thomas the Son of William Walker — — — — Buried Ma
Mary the Daughter of John Sutton — — — — Buried Ju
Thomas Walker, Farmer — — — — Married Ju
William Odell & Elizabeth Harding — — — Buried Ju
Henry Braybrook, Labourer — — — — Baptiz'd Ju
William the Son of John Tilcock & Mary his Wife — — Baptiz'd Ju
Mary the Daughter of Thomas Buxton & Sarah his Wife — — Baptiz'd Ju
Elizabeth the Daughter of William Pain & Elizabeth his Wife — Baptiz'd Ju
Thomas the Son of Thomas Perry & Elizabeth his Wife — — Baptiz'd Ju
Jeremy the Son of John Skellet & Sarah his Wife — — Buried Ju
Elizabeth Odell, Widow — — — — Baptiz'd A
Richard the Son of Richard Child & Mary his Wife — — — Buried A
Thomas the Son of Thomas Glover — — — — Buried A
Sarah the Daughter of Benjamin Jackson — — — Baptiz'd A
Thomas the Son of John Bance & Elizabeth his Wife — — Baptiz'd A
~~...~~ the Son of Francis Jewes & Rebecca his wife ~~...~~ when Baptiz'd
~~...~~ the Son of Thomas Cooper & Elizabeth his Wife — Buried A
~~...~~ the Son of John Odell — — — Buried A
~~...~~ the Son of John Tilcock — — — Married A

Sandy parish register, 1752. The burial of Robert Whitfield, 'gardiner' is recorded here. Notice that the register contains details of baptisms, marriages and burials, all in the same register. Image reproduced by kind permission of Bedfordshire and Luton Archives Service.

Kingsley, Esq., lying on both sides, one half acre more in the same field lying near to the Lord's Wood of Sandy, the land of Mr Britain lying on the East and abutting west on Paternoster Hole; in Belland Field, two selions containing one acre, the land of the Lord of Sandy in the East, a Highway leading into Belland Field on the West, abutting South on Coxwell Hill and North on a Headland of the Lord of Sandy; in Anstreet (or Austreet) Field two selions containing by estimation one acre in Coxwell Furlong, the land of John Skilleter North, abutting West on Coxwell Haydons. In the same field in Widall Furlong one rood [¼ acre], the land of the said Heylock Kingsley on the South and the land of William Randall on the North, abutting East on the Common Heath; one rood more in the same field on Church Headland furlong, the land of Robert Pulleyn, Esq., South, John Skilleter North, abutting West on Church Headland; and in the same field two selions containing an half acre more, the land of the said Robert Pulleyn lying on the South, the Lord of Sandy North and abutting West on Kinwick Broad Way; in Down Field two half acres more, one land lying between them, the land of the Lord of Sandy on the South and Thomas Single North, lying in the Upper Backside near John Richardson's hedge corner. In the same field one half acre residue thereof, lying near Sallow Close Corner, the land of the Lord of Sandy lying on the North side thereof, and John Richardson South, abutting East on the highway leading to Tempsford'.

(A selion was a cultivated strip of land in an open field, consisting of a ridge with a furrow on either side).

I have tested your patience by including the document in its entirety because it shows how complex the system of land holding had become in Sandy. Remember this document was describing just *one* man's holding.

My first reaction on finding this document was excitement; my second reaction was to conclude that a map showing these strips of land would have been very useful, not only to William Whitfield and John Barber, the parties involved in the transaction, but also to myself about 280 years later. I have looked in vain for a general map showing the layout and subdivision of the common fields of Sandy in the early eighteenth century. It is difficult to locate these picturesquely named fields in *modern* Sandy because so much of the land of the parish is now occupied by houses and factories and many of the old landmarks and features have been removed or buried under concrete. Planners and builders have done little to enhance the town in recent years. Fortunately, the River Ivel, Sandy Warren, Sandye Place, St. Swithun's Church and the scarp slope of the greensand remain to prevent a sense of total disorientation; they act as oases in a desert of undistinguished, stereotypical, high-density housing estates.

Prior to 1733, William Whitfield was clearly farming at least ten plots, ranging in size between one acre and a quarter of an acre, and these were distributed over the common fields of Sandy. Although a map has not survived, I wonder if he had drawn a plan of his own which he would keep at home to identify his plots and remember his cropping plans. Otherwise, how did he recognise his strips when he walked to them to hoe his carrots or harvest his onions? Other market gardeners' plots must have looked very similar to his. He may have had other men working for him, but he surely must have spent a fair time simply walking from one plot to another. The work involved in cultivating these strips must have been an enormous task for William as he approached the age of sixty, and in some ways perhaps it was a relief for him to sell the land to someone else. However, the sale may have caused some friction in the family at the time, and in my opinion a will made some twenty years later hints at this. After the sale, John Barber appears to have leased the land to Robert Hedge, but about three years later he sold half an acre in Kinwick Field to William Astell, esquire, of Everton. It was interesting to discover that this half acre plot had belonged originally to Robert Whitfield (1630-1714), William Whitfield's father. Later in 1737, William Astell sold the land to Heylock Kingsley, and it was added to his Hasells estate.

William Whitfield died in 1746. It would be interesting to know how he had spent his later years, without his land to cultivate. I haven't managed to find a will made by him, but his older brother Robert, another market gardener, who died unmarried in 1752, certainly *did* leave one. Robert appears to have been a shrewd businessman as well as a market gardener, taking advantage of opportunities to buy the land he tilled when they arose. William Symcotts of Clifton, Bedfordshire, was a 'gentleman' who owned some strips of land in Sandy which Robert was occupying as his tenant. When Symcotts died, his daughters sold these strips to Robert, who was described in the Indenture document of 1705-6 I found at the Bedford record office as *Robert Whitfield the younger* (to distinguish him from his father), 'gardiner'. These strips were

'…in Austreet Field in Hogsdale Furlong half an acre, the land of Mary Anger North, Thomas Skilleter South, and abutting West upon Kinwick Broadway; in Pope's Gores one rood, the Glebe Land South and abutting West upon Simsdale Furlong; in Downe Field in the Eastwell Downe Furlong one rood, the land late of Francis Bishop North, Sir Philipp Monoux South and abutting East upon Longland Furlong; in the Middle Field in Belland Furlong, one acre, the land of Thomas Vintner North, Mr Monoux South, abutting west upon the Upper Backside and East upon the Longhurst Furlong; in Mead Field in Short Lilland one rood, the land of John Smith East, Edward Spring West and abutting South upon a headland of Francis Bishop.'

In addition to these strips he also purchased, by virtue of the same agreement, some strips he was also farming that had formerly belonged to John Symcotts: '…in the said Downe Field in the Lower Backside furlong half an acre, the land of the Widdow Townsend North, the Glebe land South, abutting upon the Upper Backside Furlong and West upon London Road. In Sheep Coate Furlong two roods, the land of James Deanton the North side, the Glebe Land South and abutting East upon the Mill Way'.

Finally, there was also '…all that one rood of arable land with the appurtenances lying and being in Rye North Croft Field in Sandy aforesaid, the land of Mr Hooker West, Sir Philipp Monoux East and abutting North upon a headland of John Underwood.'

If my arithmetic is correct, it would appear that Robert had purchased nine strips in the open fields, varying between one acre and a quarter acre in size which he had been cultivating previously; it is possible that he was also involved in cultivating other land, which he may or may not have owned. For instance, a deed of exchange document drawn up in December, 1739 by the Rev. Lewis Monoux and Humphrey Monoux refers to 'a piece of garden in Chester Field, near Tower Hill (half an acre) occupied by Robert Whitfield'; it abutted east on the Sandy to Stratford Way, west on the headland of Mr Jenkin, north on the land of Sir Humphrey Monoux and south on the land of William Tilcock.

The problem for me in interpreting the other documents I found was that they mention 'Robert

Whitfield', but they do not specify whether this was Robert the younger, or Robert the elder.

A Robert Whitfield was involved in a deal whereby he, together with Baron Brittain, John Underwood, Sara Deane, Thomas Ellis, and Richard Stacey bought a messuage, cottage, 24 acres of arable land and a close of pasture in Sandy from the executors of William Symcotts for £100. How much land and property Robert received from this transaction is not clear; neither is the amount of money he contributed. The document is dated '15 days from Trinity Sunday in the fifth year of the reign of Queen Anne' (Saturday, 4th May, 1706).

Another document of 1705-1706 refers to an acre of land in the common fields of Sandy occupied by Robert Whitfield:

'…in the Middle Field, ½ acre in Whitley Furlong, abutting North and South on land of Mr Monoux, East upon woodland and West on a headland of Thomas Skilleter; and ½ acre the fifth land from the other, abutting North and South on land of Mr Pulleyn, and to East and West on the other ½ acre.'

Was this land being used by Robert Whitfield the younger, or his father Robert? *They* obviously knew, but I haven't been able to decide. In a case like this it is quite likely that if it *was* Robert the younger in 1705-6, then he was probably cultivating land which had been occupied by his father in previous years.

An article by Ronald Webber in the *Bedfordshire Magazine* (Spring, 1974) suggests that the Sandy gardeners seem to have been fairly well off on the whole. Many owned several acres of land as well as a cottage. One in 1662 bequeathed 11 acres, another in 1773 left two freehold cottages and £25 in cash; a third in 1731 owned a cottage, close and 22 acres of land.

Robert's will, dating from 1752, which I found at the Bedford Record Office, refers to his cottage, together with its barns, stables, gardens and orchards which he left to his 'kinsman' John Blane (or Blain) and his wife Anne. They were living with Robert when he wrote his will (he was over eighty years old at the time). He also left them five acres of arable land and some other leasehold land. It is likely that John Blane or Blain was Robert's nephew - probably his favourite nephew! Robert's sister, Alice Whitfield had married John Blain (senior), and John Blain (junior) was born in 1697. Another of Robert's sisters, Elizabeth Whitfield, had married Thomas Blain in 1693, so there was a double connection between the two families.

Robert left £5 to his great nephew Robert Whitfield (son of his nephew William Whitfield). Young Robert was to receive his legacy when he was fifteen years old. He was born around 1744, so would have another seven years to wait for his money. William Whitfield, another great nephew, was to receive twenty shillings. This William, my 4x great grandfather, was born in 1727 and was to become the father of James, the gamekeeper. This legacy does not appear to be over-generous, and I can only speculate about the reason for this. Thanks to Robert's will, more land was transferred away from the Whitfield family. Perhaps Robert the testator was somewhat aggrieved at his late brother's decision to sell *his* five and a half acres of land to John Barber in 1733, rather than keeping it in the family. This might explain why his late brother's grandchild William (my direct line ancestor) only received twenty shillings, although 260 years later it is difficult for us to appreciate the purchasing power this apparently modest sum might have had when the bequest was made.

Robert's will, with its bequests to nephews and great nephews was very helpful to me as I

The will of Robert Whitfield of Sandy (1674- 1752). Details are given of the land he owned in Sandy. Image reproduced by kind permission of the Bedfordshire and Luton Archives Service. Ref AD2818 tried to check the tentative family tree I had drawn. In particular, it enabled me to verify that the Robert Whitfield who had died in 1731 (my 5x great grandfather) was the Robert who had been baptised in Sandy in 1701.

The Sandy parish registers, together with land transaction documents and another will, all found at the Bedford Record Office, helped me to go back another generation: the parents of Robert Whitfield (1671-1752) whose will we have just discussed, and his younger brother William (1673-1746) were Robert Whitfield (baptised 1630 in Sandy) and his wife Alice, nee Freeman, baptised in Sandy in 1634. The couple married in Sandy Church in 1659 and were my 7x great grandparents.

Their first child, Robert, was baptised in 1660, but died the following year; Alice (junior) appears to have been born between 1660 and 1664 when her sister Elizabeth was baptised: unlike her sister, Alice does not appear to have troubled the Sandy rector to fill the font. As we have seen, Alice later married John Blain and Elizabeth took Thomas Blain as *her* husband. The next child of Robert and Alice was Mary. She was baptised in 1666 (the year of the Great Fire of London) but died in 1668. Her brother David, named after his grandfather David Freeman, was baptised in 1669, but died in the same year. As Robert, baptised in 1671 didn't marry, the continuation of the Whitfield line was thanks to his younger brother, William, baptised in 1673. He was Robert and Alice's last child.

The early life of Robert Whitfield, baptised 1630 is shrouded in mystery. Robert was the youngest child of William and Grace Whitfield nee Suttonn, who married in Potton Church in 1607. William and Grace moved back to Sandy after their wedding (marriages usually took place in the bride's parish), and the baptisms of their children are recorded in the Sandy Parish Registers:

Elizabeth, baptised 1608, died 1609.

Elizabeth, baptised 1610.

Joan, baptised 1614, died 1639.

Daniel, baptised 1617. Daniel does not appear in the Sandy marriage or burial registers, so may have left Sandy. There may therefore be generations of Whitfields descended from him of which I am unaware. Daniel appears to have been named after his paternal grandfather, whose details appear later (on page 61 and in the next chapter).

Thomas, baptised 1621, died 1625.

William, baptised 1624, but again, no further information.

Mary, baptised 1626, died 1629.

Robert, baptised 1630, whose life we are about to discuss.

Robert's early life is a mystery because his father, William, died when Robert was only four years old, and by the time he was six he was an orphan. My theory is that he was brought up by the Suttonn family, because his father William Whitfield appears to have been an only child. Whether or not he spent his formative years in Sandy is therefore a matter of conjecture, but as we have seen, he married Alice Freeman in Sandy Church in 1659, the year before Charles II came to the throne of England, following a period of Civil War.

Robert was also a market gardener in Sandy, and some documents found in the Bedfordshire Record Office give some indication of where his land was and the extent of his land holding.

The earliest document involving him that I managed to find was dated 1687; not only was it in Latin, but it also was written in a very difficult hand, consisting mainly of bold down strokes, with few obvious gaps between the words and was therefore not very helpful.

Fortunately, the slightly later documents that have survived were written in English and were much easier to read once I familiarised myself with the early eighteenth century handwriting. The problem I had, as mentioned earlier, was deciding whether the Robert Whitfield mentioned in them was actually Robert the elder (baptised 1630) or his son Robert (baptised 1671).

One document which I believe involved Robert the elder was dated 1705-1706. It is a transaction between Theophilus Cater and William Bromsall, and it refers to two and a half acres in the common fields of Sandy, occupied by Robert Whitfield. These plots were in Austreet Field in Lower Harfield Furlong and in Down Field in Delve and Upper Backside Furlongs. It would appear that Robert subsequently purchased this land, as it appears to be mentioned in his will (which is dealt with later).

As owners of land aged over 21, both Robert the elder and younger were entitled to vote. Not everyone was entitled to vote at this time; females were denied the privilege and even freeholders like the two Roberts had to possess land which had a rental value of at least forty shillings per year. There was no provision for tenants to vote. In *How Bedfordshire voted 1685-1735* by James Collett White, I found that a Robert Whitfield from Sandy had voted in the County election at the Assize House in Bedford in late October or early November, 1695. He voted for William Duncombe of Battlesden, in South West Bedfordshire, who seems to have been a supporter of King William III, but otherwise was independent, with no pronounced party views. Was the voter Robert the elder or younger? I'm not sure, but am inclined to think it was the older man. Robert senior would have been about 65 at the time, and hopefully had a little more free time to make the journey to Bedford, a distance of about eight miles, either on foot or on horseback. His son Robert might well have been too busy cultivating his strips of land, although I have to concede that late October or early November would probably not have been his busiest time of the year.

Ten years later, Robert Whitfield from Sandy voted in the poll for the Knights of the Shire for Bedfordshire, this time favouring the Tory candidates, Sir Pinsent Chernock, Bart., and John Hervey, Esquire. Was this Robert the elder or the younger making the journey to the hustings this time? There is no way of being sure. If it was Robert senior he would have been about 75 years old and he was to be commended for bothering to make the journey at what was then an advanced age. By 1710, not surprisingly, he appears to have given up his agricultural activities: a document in the Bedford Record Office refers to two closes of pasture (four acres), called Kinwick Closes in Sandy, near the Warren, '*in the late occupation of Robert Whitfield.*' Perhaps this is where Robert grazed his horse; alternatively, perhaps he kept a few cows on this light sandy land, just a few yards from where he lived in Swaden, the road leading from Sandy to Everton. Over three hundred years later, much of this land is still being used for horse grazing.

Robert had the foresight to make his will in 1712, two years before he died. He left arable land which he had *purchased from Mr Bromsall* to his son William Whitfield. I would imagine that this was the land in Austreet Field and Down Field referred to in the document of 1705-6. He also left William land which he had purchased from John Thomas (whose name was mentioned in the 1687 document). He left his house, barns and three quarters of an acre of

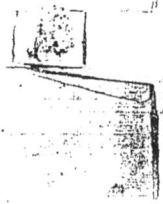

The will of Robert Whitfield, (1630 – 1714), drawn up in 1712. The spelling of some words, the formation of some of the letters and the script used testify to the age of the document, but it is still relatively easy to read. Image reproduced by kind permission of the Bedfordshire and Luton Archives Service.

land in Swaden to his son Robert Whitfield, and also bequeathed some possessions to his grandchildren, the sons and daughters of John Blain, deceased.

The preamble to Robert's will stated that he was 'of perfect mind and memory'. Whilst this was a standard opening used in those days, there can be little doubt that Robert was indeed shrewd enough to be investing in land and property when he was in his mid-seventies, and also interested enough in politics to bother to walk or ride to Bedford to exercise his right to vote. He died aged 84, a very good age for the early eighteenth century. He must have been a remarkable and resilient character. His lifetime had encompassed such national events as the Civil War, the restoration of the Monarchy, and the Great Plague and Great Fire of London to name just a few. News of these events must have reached Sandy, just fifty miles or so from the capital. Johann Sebastian Bach and George Frederick Handel, those musical geniuses of the Baroque era had been born in 1685, when Robert was well into middle age. Within Bedfordshire, John Bunyan (1628-1688), writer of *Pilgrim's*

DIAGRAM 4

The ancestry of James Whitfield (1770 - 1833)

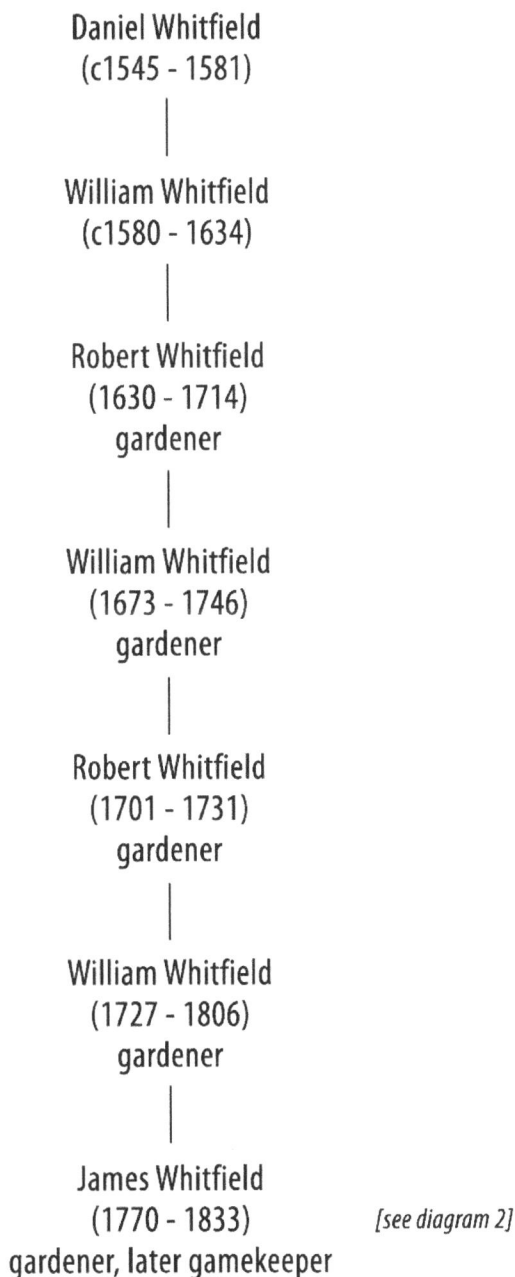

Daniel Whitfield
(c1545 - 1581)

|

William Whitfield
(c1580 - 1634)

|

Robert Whitfield
(1630 - 1714)
gardener

|

William Whitfield
(1673 - 1746)
gardener

|

Robert Whitfield
(1701 - 1731)
gardener

|

William Whitfield
(1727 - 1806)
gardener

|

James Whitfield
(1770 - 1833)   *[see diagram 2]*
gardener, later gamekeeper

I was able to discover these details from the Sandy parish registers.

Progress had been alive during Robert's lifetime - Robert may even have heard him preach.

If only, like another contemporary, Samuel Pepys (1633-1703), Robert had been able to keep a diary! There is little point in looking for one because he was only able to add his mark to his will; unlike Pepys, he had not had the opportunity to learn to write.

Unfortunately, as I went further back in time in my search of the Sandy parish registers, there seemed to be fewer documents of the same period (wills, land transactions, and so on), to substantiate the family tree I was managing to construct. I mentioned earlier that Robert Whitfield's parents were William and Grace Whitfield, who had married in Potton Church in 1607, about two years after the Gunpowder Plot. They obviously moved back to Sandy after the marriage, because the baptisms of their children are recorded in the registers there, and, later, the burials of William and Grace, in 1634 and 1636 respectively.

William's baptism is not recorded in the Sandy registers, but he appears to have been the only child of Daniel and Agnes Whitfield (nee Man or Mun), whose marriage took place in Sandy on October 30, 1576. William was presumably born no earlier than 1576 but no later than about April, 1582, because Daniel Whitfield's burial is recorded in the Sandy register in July, 1581. As usual, the cause of death is not given. My guess, for reasons I will mention later, is that Daniel was aged between his mid-thirties and mid-forties when he died. Agnes remarried in 1584. Her new husband was John Pecke. For some reason there are no baptisms recorded in the Sandy registers between July 6 1578 and April, 1579. I feel fairly sure that some did actually take place, possibly William Whitfield's amongst them; it seems unlikely that even a small settlement like Sandy would have a period of about ten months during which no infants were presented for baptism. What is more likely is that the details were written on paper, the intention being to copy them into the register later, and then the paper went missing, to the inconvenience and embarrassment of all concerned, particularly the rector, Thomas Noke. I offer this as a *possible* explanation - I have no evidence to support my theory.

William Whitfield was probably involved in agriculture as most people were in rural communities in those days, but again, this is conjecture on my part. Strangely, I have more idea of the clothes his wife, Grace, probably wore as she went about her daily tasks around 1614 or 1615. This is because she was left '… a coverlet, a gowne, a neckinger, a kercheefe and a smocke, together with a pillowe, a sheete and a stoole' in the will of Ann Scarrett of Sandy in 1614. I hope the garments were of the correct size. If the 'gowne' and 'smocke' were too large, then perhaps they were worn as maternity clothes during Grace's five pregnancies after 1614. It is, of course, a great pity that photographs were not invented in the early seventeenth century: it would be wonderful to see Grace Whitfield in her 'gowne and neckinger', and I trust that William thought so too.

I was unable to find the baptism of William's father, Daniel Whitfield, in the Sandy register, which starts in 1538, suggesting that he was born elsewhere. The marriage of Daniel to Agnes Man or Mun in 1576 is the earliest reference to the family I have found in Sandy. Daniel was presumably at least twenty years old when he married Agnes. I assumed he was born before 1556. I was still keen to trace the family further back if possible, but I had been lucky to find so many entries in the Sandy Parish Registers which I could substantiate with material from other sources. The family tree I had constructed took me back from myself some eleven generations, in fact back to the time of William Shakespeare.

DIAGRAM 5

The Sandy Whitfields descended from Daniel Whitfield (d 1581)

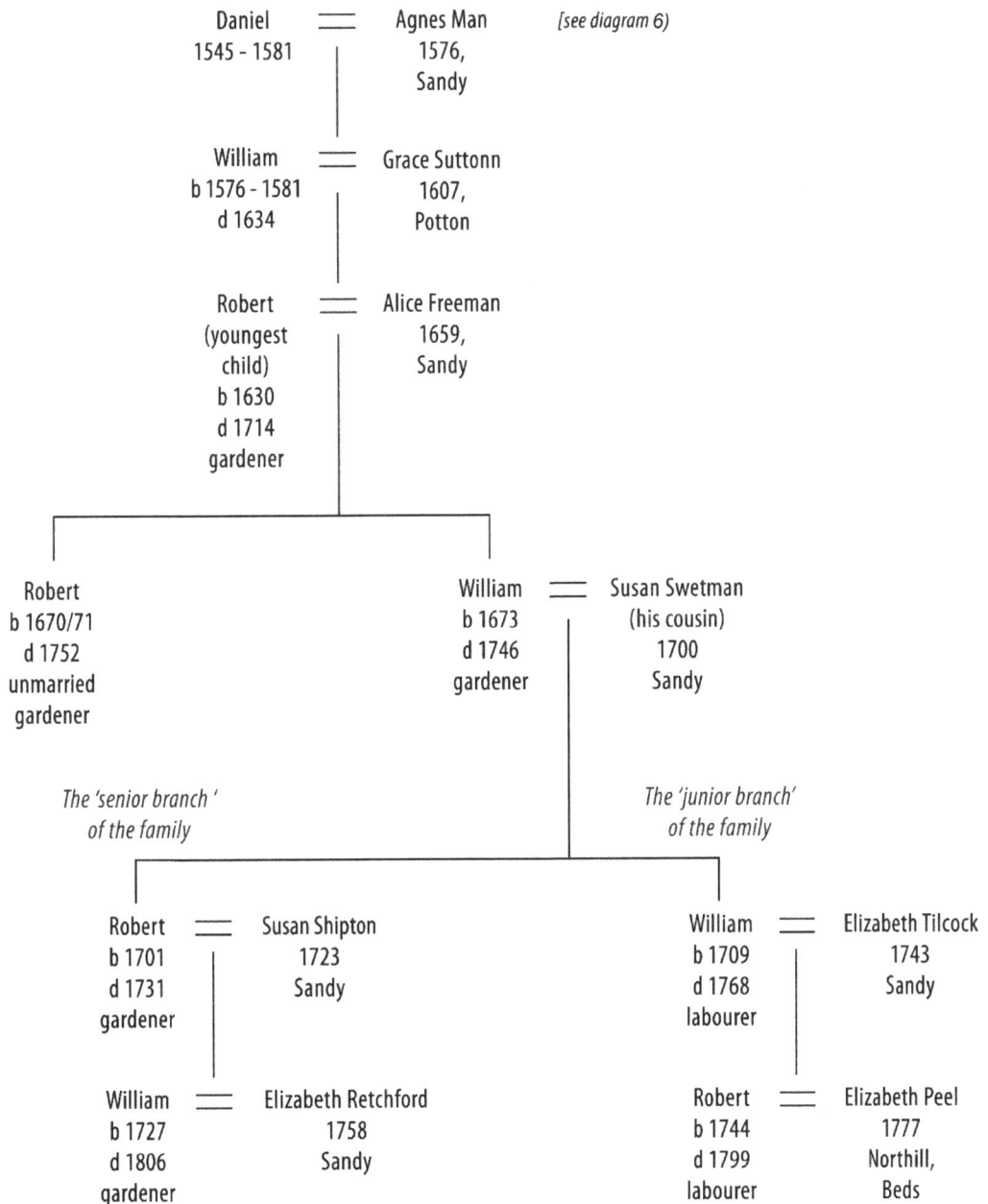

[see diagram 6]

Daniel === Agnes Man
1545 - 1581 / 1576,
Sandy

William === Grace Suttonn
b 1576 - 1581 / 1607,
d 1634 / Potton

Robert === Alice Freeman
(youngest / 1659,
child) / Sandy
b 1630
d 1714
gardener

Robert
b 1670/71
d 1752
unmarried
gardener

William === Susan Swetman
b 1673 / (his cousin)
d 1746 / 1700
gardener / Sandy

The 'senior branch'
of the family

The 'junior branch'
of the family

Robert === Susan Shipton
b 1701 / 1723
d 1731 / Sandy
gardener

William === Elizabeth Tilcock
b 1709 / 1743
d 1768 / Sandy
labourer

William === Elizabeth Retchford
b 1727 / 1758
d 1806 / Sandy
gardener

Robert === Elizabeth Peel
b 1744 / 1777
d 1799 / Northill,
labourer / Beds

[see diagram 3 and diagram 4)

This diagram, based on information gleaned from the Sandy parish registers, is a simplified version of the tree I constructed because it ignores infant mortality and family members who appear to have moved away from Sandy during this period.

Chapter 3.
Two more generations – in Clophill.

'And some there be, which have no memorial'.

Ecclesiasticus xliv 9.

Joyce Godber, in her *History of Bedfordshire*, mentioned that Clophill, a village near Shefford, and about ten miles from Sandy, had a plumber, Robert Whitfield, in the sixteenth century. As houses then would not have had flushing lavatories, kitchen sinks, washing machines, central heating, radiators and a piped water supply, I clearly needed to review my notion of what being a plumber would have entailed some 450 years ago. Plumbers at that time would have been working with lead *(plumbum* is the Latin word for lead). I assumed they would have been roofers, putting lead on the roofs of important and expensive buildings such as churches and cathedrals, (and maybe taking it off again during the time of the dissolution of the monasteries in the reign of King Henry VIII), but a document I found later has made me modify this theory. From evidence cited in this document (details of which are given later) it would appear that Robert's work, at least at times, was more akin to the work of modern plumbers than I had at first supposed.

Miss Godber's information appeared at first to have come from the will of a Robert Whitfield of Clophill which I found at the Bedford Record Office. The will was dated 1555, some 21 years before Daniel Whitfield's marriage at Sandy. Fortunately, the will was written in English rather than in Latin. The handwriting was difficult to read and the lines were very close together. The will started with a preamble which apparently was typical of this period, when so many people were Catholics:

' Fyrst I bequeath my soul unto almyghtie god , our ladye Saint Mary and to all the Saints in heaven and my bodye to be buryed in Clophill church yarde'.

Some of Robert's other bequests were of great interest:

'…I bequeathe to Alice my wyfe my house wt viij acres lande with the appurtenances… terme of her lyfe she to doo with yt what she lyste to helpe her foure children that to wete John, Nicholas, Anne and Alice and to pay my debts'

' Also I bequeath to Agnes my doughter a ffetherbed and all things thereto belonging at her daye of marriage. And also I bequeath Alyce my doughter a ffetherbedd and all things thereto belonging and she to have yt at her daye of marriage. And also I bequeath to every of them a brasse pott of the best and also three peawter dysshes a peece and also eyther of theym a

DIAGRAM 6

The Clophill Whitfields

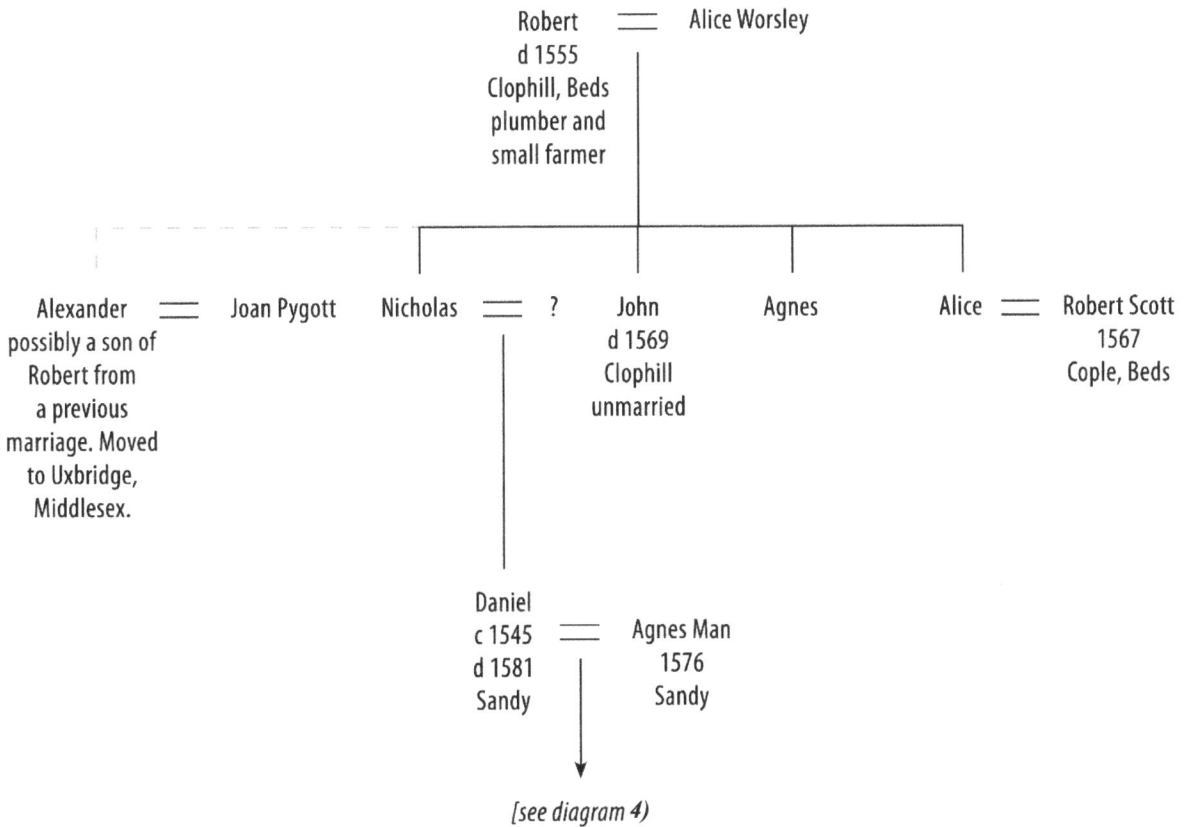

Robert === Alice Worsley
d 1555
Clophill, Beds
plumber and
small farmer

Alexander === Joan Pygott   Nicholas === ?   John   Agnes   Alice === Robert Scott
possibly a son of   d 1569   1567
Robert from   Clophill   Cople, Beds
a previous   unmarried
marriage. Moved
to Uxbridge,
Middlesex.

Daniel === Agnes Man
c 1545   1576
d 1581   Sandy
Sandy

[see diagram 4)

This tree was constructed using information gleaned from wills and land transaction documents.
Daniel Whitfield's marriage and burial dates were found in the Sandy parish registers.
Daniel was mentioned in Robert's will of 1555.

Old St Mary's Church, Clophill. The church has been a ruin for many years. Robert Whitfield, who died in 1555, and his son John Whitfield, who died in 1569 are buried in the churchyard. Photograph by Isaac Whitfield, 2013.

peawter pott and a candlestick… Also I give unto Danyell Whytfeld my sonnes childe a Calfe'.

The impression I got from the will was that Robert appeared to be a kindly and considerate family man, judging from his bequests, particularly the rather touching gift to his grandson. As he had been working with lead it is possible that he may have been suffering from the cumulative effects of lead poisoning before he died; these could have included tremors, blindness and even paralysis. I trust he had a peaceful death - which occurred in the same year as those of Hugh Latimer and Nicholas Ridley, who were burned alive at the stake on the order of Queen Mary, who was persecuting Protestants. No wonder that Robert's will included a typically Catholic preamble.

Feather beds were prized possessions in Tudor times, and not every person had the chance to experience the luxury of sleeping in one. Many people, particularly the poor, would still have slept, (rather fitfully I would think), on straw mattresses, placed on the floor, which in all likelihood was made of beaten earth. Even if widowed or single, these people would not always have slept alone: the straw inside the mattresses would have harboured fleas. Robert, presumably, possessed at least three feather beds: his wife Alice was still alive and hopefully was still entitled to sleep in the one which she had shared with him; and he was leaving his daughters Agnes and Alice one each when they married. Brass pots and pewter dishes were also treasured items, brass in particular having connotations of status as pewter became more commonplace, replacing the earlier wooden bowls and trenchers.

Unfortunately, Robert's will gives no indication of his being a plumber: it would have been interesting if he had made mention of some tools or stock-in-trade; but it does indicate that he was also a small farmer, as his house had eight acres of land, and he was keeping cattle. (Note he left '*a calf*' to his grandson, not '*the calf*', which implies to me that he had several beasts). I feel sure that 'Danyell' would have appreciated the calf which his grandfather had left him. Unfortunately, the family tree I constructed for the Clophill Whitfields was only tentative because the will didn't specify which one of Robert's two sons was Daniel's father.

I needed, if possible, to find out more about the family in Clophill, and was fortunate to discover that there were other sixteenth century documents relating to Robert Whitfield. Most of these recorded land transactions. I also found that there was another member of the family living in Clophill at this time - Alexander Whitfield. It has been impossible for me to establish whether he was a brother of Robert, or possibly another son, perhaps from a previous marriage. Life was precarious in the sixteenth century and remarriages were fairly common (perhaps about one marriage in four or five) because of the death of a previous partner. Alexander was a tailor, but also presumably a small farmer, because he figures in several land transactions in the parish, both buying and selling. The transactions were recorded in the Manor Court Rolls of the Manor of Clophill and Keynhoe (Cainhoe). From these transactions I discovered that Alexander had a wife, Joan. No children were mentioned. Alexander and Joan appear to have moved later from Clophill to Uxbridge in Middlesex, presumably at that time a relatively rural parish.

Alexander was granted land in Clophill in April, 1535 by Alexander Robynson, the rector:

'…a messuage, four acres and a parcel of meadow in Clophill….. to the use of Alexander Whitfield and if he die without heir to the use of his sister Margaret, and then to Robert Whitfield, provided that he pay ten marks for masses in Clophill Church and other good works'.

There was clearly some family connection between Alexander and Robert Whitfield and it is a pity that the document does not make this more explicit.

An internet search enabled me to find another document (in the National Archives) involving Alexander Whitfield. It is a document which was prepared for use in the (law) court of King Henry VIII, and in it, Bryan Bylby, or Byby, a Bedford 'weyver' (weaver) complains that rent and profits from property formerly owned by Alexander Robynson the 'parson of Clopphyll' have been wrongfully taken by Alexander Whitfield for three years since 'the 4th February in the 27th year of the reign of King Henry the Eighth'. This puts the date of the document at around 1539 (1509+27+3 = 1539). Bylby further claims that Alexander Whitfield had forged Alexander Robynson's will - a rather unlikely scenario I would have thought. The result of the case is not known, but it would appear that Alexander Whitfield was not the most popular man in Clophill. The controversy of the court case and the allegations made by Bylby may explain Alexander's move to Uxbridge. Bylby may have previously been connected to Alexander Whitfield by virtue of their respective occupations: he may have been supplying him with cloth, although this is speculation on my part.

The supposed transgressor did not completely sever his connections with Clophill, however, at least, not for some time after 1539: a document of 1546 shows that Alexander, now living in Uxbridge and working as a tailor, leased a tenement in Clophill 'late in the occupation of William Hede and William Smith', with 'lands in the town fields and meadows' to Thomas Pygotte of Clophill. He was thus not only a tailor, but also a businessman - *hopefully* an honest one.

Brian Bylby or Byby appears to have caused further problems to the Whitfield family in Clophill because another document makes it clear that he had trespassed on Robert's land and stolen a sheep (or possibly some sheep) and a lamb. Bylby, again described as a 'wever', had been summoned to attend court to answer for his misdemeanours, but had failed to appear. Robert was represented by his attorney, John Poley. It was ordered by the court that Byby was to be made exigent: he was on the way to being outlawed from county to county. He was given until the eighth day after Trinity to appear in court. The document was not dated and unfortunately I haven't been able to discover the final outcome of the case.

I have not been able to find when the Whitfield family arrived in Clophill, but in an attempt to do so I managed to find out a little more information about Robert. He was a witness to the will of Robert Adown or Odown of Clophill in 1536 and of Thomas Gromont in 1543; he was also the executor of the will of the Clophill rector, Alexander Robynson, who died in 1536. He must have been considered a trustworthy and competent person by the Rector to have been honoured in this way, and I wonder whether Robert held some important office at St Mary's Church, Clophill, as he appears to have been held in such high regard. Unfortunately, I have been unable to find the will, but I have discovered that Robert, in fulfilling his duties as executor, became embroiled in a dispute. A document which I was able to download from the University of Houston's website (after an internet search for Robert *Whytfeld* of Clophill) revealed that after Alexander Robynson's death, a certain Henry Albany of Bedford claimed that he had lent the Rector £20 on 14th July 1535. This money had apparently not been repaid, either by Alexander Robynson, or by Robert Whytfeld his executor and the dispute was taken to Henry VIII's Court of Common Pleas where this time Robert was represented by his attorney, Henry Joye. I was impressed that Robert had employed a man of such calibre: Henry Joye leased the manor at nearby Beadlow, which included a water mill and land in Clophill from John Gostwick as a sub-tenant: Gostwick had leased Beadlow Abbey and manor from Cardinal Wolsey. Henry Joye was also attorney in the Court of Common Pleas to Newnham Priory in Bedford. I was interested to discover that his brother, George Joye (1492 -1553) had been ordained as a sub-deacon at Newnham Priory in 1515, but had been denounced for his heretical views and had fled to mainland Europe to avoid persecution. He became the author of the first prayer book published in English and of the first English Psalter, and was also a translator and proof-reader: he was proof-reading William Tyndale's English translation of the New Testament in 1534. Apparently no-one had undertaken this task for its earlier editions. Joye had undertaken this task anonymously, without permission, and his corrections (and occasional word substitutions) were not appreciated by Tyndale. In turn, Tyndale's translation was not appreciated by Henry VIII, and copies of it were publicly burned; Tyndale was tracked down and suffered the same fate in 1536.

George Joye returned to England in the late 1540s after the death of Henry VIII. He became vicar of Blunham, Bedfordshire in 1549 and was appointed Rector of Ashwell, Hertfordshire, in the following year by Bishop Nicholas Ridley.

I have digressed to show that Clophill and mid-Bedfordshire were not as remote from significant people and national events as might be supposed, and to demonstrate that Robert and Alexander Whitfield were living in turbulent times. The outcome of the court case involving Robert is not clear; it seems to have been suggested that in the meantime Henry Albany was entitled to '… occupy and injoye all such frutys emoluments and profyts to the parsonage of Clophyll in any waye belonging as by the lawe shalbe due to the same Alexander Robynson aforesaid', but this appears to have been an intermediate judgement, and the two parties were bound to return to court fifteen days after Easter. I have not found a later document for further enlightenment.

Robert was also one of 21 Clophill men included in a muster list for Clophill in 1539.

In that year, it was thought that Emperor Charles V of the Holy Roman Empire and Francis I of France were intending to mount a joint expedition to invade England to punish Henry VIII for breaking away from the Catholic Church some five years earlier. The whole of Britain's military strength was organised in readiness for this invasion and people in the South of England were preparing to face the French. Nationally, men were sorted into groups according to their income. Those earning between £5 and £10 per year had to provide a suit of plated armour, a bill or halberd (combined spear and battle-axe), longbow and steel helmet. Central government ensured that men and equipment were ready for the threat of invasion by ordering that muster certificates were prepared and issued on a county by county basis. (It sounds a bit like an early forerunner of the Home Guard - Dad's Army - of the Second World War). In Bedfordshire, men wielding the billhook outnumbered the men using the longbow, by a ratio of three to one. It took much skill, strength and a lot of practice from an early age to master the longbow, whereas many labourers were used to wielding the billhook to great effect - when hedging - and therefore didn't need much practice. (It sounds even more like Dad's Army). Not surprisingly, Robert Whitfield - whose cattle would probably have been grazing, oblivious of the threat of a French invasion, in fields surrounded by neatly- trimmed hedges - was a billman.

Accounts for the Manor of Ampthill for August and September, 1539 mention that Robert Whitfield, plumber, and Alexander Whitfield, labourer, had been involved in the building and maintenance of the manor house in the Great Park at Ampthill for King Henry VIII. The king had acquired Ampthill Park in the 1520s and enjoyed hunting the deer there. The accounts state that the plumbers had been

'working in soldering of divers faults and cracks in two great cisterns to put in water and mending of faults and cracks on the lead over the king's great chamber and mending of leads over the great tower standing on the west side of the manor and also mending of the leads over the bowling house with other necessaries there done'. Robert had been involved in the maintenance of Henry VIII's water supply! (It was probably preferable to being his marriage guidance counsellor). The accounts record that he had provided the solder, from Bedford. It would be interesting to know how he travelled there (perhaps he owned a horse) and how he had acquired his knowledge of plumbing. I assume he would have served an apprenticeship somewhere but have been unable to find any documentary evidence.

Some other men had been given the dubious privilege of dealing with the Royal toilets. Described as 'gongfarmers', Thomas Aley (or Oaley) and John Wilkinson had been 'working as well upon cleansing and scouring of the kings jaques[2] and the queens jaques…'. Aley had been paid 6d per day and Wilkinson 8d per day for their efforts. I wonder why Wilkinson was paid at a higher rate – but perhaps it is better not to speculate. It *is* probably safe to assume that their jobs were not the most coveted positions in Ampthill. For reasons which may be readily understood, gongfermers worked at night. After dealing with the Royal faeces, their company may not have been welcomed as they trudged back to their respective families at daybreak.

Robert had been paid 7d a day for his work but may not have envied the extra penny per day earned by John Wilkinson. Assuming he worked six days a week, regular employment would have meant Robert earned just over £9 per year. I presume he had walked each day to Ampthill Park from Clophill, probably accompanied by Alexander. Their journey may well have been through Maulden, travelling on, or close to the Greensand ridge.

Alexander had only been paid 5d per day as a labourer. The accounts state that the labourers had been

'working as well in helping the carpenters and sawyers as also in digging of a foundation for a new chimney bearing down walls and … of walls in divers places in the kings lodgings there for new doors to be made with the awyd (awaying of?) the rubbish within the said place and cleansing the lodgings there'.

I was fascinated to discover that Henry VIII had been hunting in Ampthill in September, 1539, so it is possible that Robert and Alexander had viewed their monarch, who may well have inspected the work in progress. It would have made a change from pursuing deer.

We have previously seen that Alexander also worked as a tailor as well as holding land in Clophill – an early example of enterprise and versatility within the family. There can be little doubt that the Alexander Whitfield working as a labourer in Ampthill in 1539 alongside his relative Robert the plumber was the same person that had incurred the wrath of Bryan Bylby in the same year.

The earliest mention I could find of the family in Clophill was in a document dated 24 May, 1531, where John Fyndale, late citizen and 'stokfysshmonger' (vendor of dried fish) of London, granted land to Alexander Robinson, clerk, (vicar of Clophill), Robert Whitfield, John Hewett, Robert Pygott and William Wakys. John Fyndale had inherited this land from his father. The property included a tenement and eight acres of land in Clophill. A later document (1546), makes it clear that Robert Whitfield owned the tenement and eight acres of land, because the document was drawn up to enable Robert (described as a 'plumer') and his wife Alice to have the use of the property for the rest of their lives; after this the smallholding was to go to John, who was presumably the elder son, then to Nicholas. This was obviously the document which Joyce Godber had seen.

John Whitfield, Robert's son, appears not to have married. He left a will in 1569, and this document sheds further light on family relationships:

---

2   privy

' In the name of God Amen, the firste of October Anno Domini 1569 I John Whitfeld of Clophill in the counte of Bedford being sicke in bodye and holle in minde praysed be allmightye god doe ordeyne and make this my laste will and testament in manner and forme following, firste I bequeath my soell to allmyghtie god and my bodye to be buryed in the churchyard of Clophill. Item I make John Browne Clarke and Thomas Finch my trew and faythfull Executors to pay my detts and dispose my goods according to this my will. Item I wyll that my howse in Clophill wyth the appurtenances thereunto belonge to be sold for so mytch as may be by my executors and that my cosen Hary Worsley to have the firste preferment of yt unto his landlord or unto whom he will. Item I give unto Nicholas my brother xij li (£12) if he be alive. Item I give unto Agnes my sister vj li xiij s iiijd (£6 13s 4d). Item I give unto Alice my sister vj li (£6). Item I give unto Dannyell my brothers sonne vj li xiijs iiijd (£6 13s 4d). Item I give unto my cosn Hary Worsly xxs (20 shillings, i.e. £1) . Item I give unto my cosen Richard Worsly the rent of my howse he now dwellyth in for on [one] year. Item I give unto Richard Worslyes wife vs (5 shillings). Item I give unto Isabell worsly xijd (12d = I shilling).Item I give unto Richard and Roger the sonnes of Hary Worsly ich of them Xijd (12d = 1 shilling). Item I give unto Richard Worsly batchelor iijs iiijd (3s 4d)…'

Notice that unlike his father's will, John's will does *not* start with a Catholic preamble. He was dying in the reign of Queen Elizabeth I, who *supported* the Church of England. His father, Robert, had made his will in the reign of Queen Mary I who had persecuted Protestants and favoured Catholics. Another feature of John's will is that it deals almost exclusively in money rather than in property, livestock and household items, which makes it less interesting from a family historian's point of view. The money values are given in pounds (librae), shillings (solidarii) and pence (denarii). The 'j' was added instead of an 'i' to denote that this was the last written figure in each case and was meant to prevent further i's being added by scheming legatees anxious to augment, or at least contest, the sums they had been given.

It is difficult to draw too many meaningful conclusions about the value of John's estate, but the total value of his bequests where an amount of money was specified was £32 17s. Ian Mortimer in *The Time Traveller's guide to Elizabethan England* reckons that a labourer in the 1590s (admittedly over 20 years after John's death) would have been earning about 4d per day. We have already seen that Alexander Whitfield was earning 5d per day in the late 1530s. It appears, therefore, that the sum of John's bequests would have probably represented over five years' earnings for an ordinary working man, in addition to the value of his house and land. He must have been a thrifty character.

John's will, written when William Shakespeare was a little boy of five, possibly learning his alphabet in Stratford upon Avon, enabled me to draw the family tree of the 'Clophill Whitfields' with more confidence: Daniel was the son of Nicholas and the grandson of Robert.

It was interesting to note that one of the witnesses to John's will was John Browne, clerk. This would appear to be the same John Browne who became the rector of Clophill in 1570.

I returned to Robert's will. If he was leaving a calf to his grandson Daniel in 1555, then presumably Daniel would have been old enough to take an interest in it, and maybe look after it. I therefore reckoned that Daniel would have been about ten years old in 1555, and was therefore born around 1545, perhaps a little earlier or later. Robert's daughters, Agnes and

Alice had apparently not married by 1555. Of course they could have been much younger than John and Nicholas, but Robert's will stated that each daughter was to have a feather bed '*at her daye of mariage'*. If they both had not yet married, but Robert was still expecting them to do so, surely their nephew, Daniel, would not be well into his teenage years?

I think that the Daniel Whitfield mentioned in the two Clophill wills is the same Daniel Whitfield who married Agnes Man or Mun in Sandy in 1576. If he was born in 1545, then he would have been about 31 when he married and about 36 when he died. I also found the marriage of an Alice Whitfield (to Robert Scott) in the marriage registers of Cople, close to Sandy, in 1567. Was this Robert Whitfield's daughter Alice? If so, I hope the couple enjoyed the use of the feather bed bequeathed to Alice by her father in 1555. I presume it had been stored at John's house in Clophill during the intervening years.

I have tried to find more evidence to prove the link between the Clophill and Sandy Whitfields, but have been unable to do so. All I can do is state the reasons I have for asserting that they *were* connected. Obviously, the name Daniel Whitfield is common to both; I have not found that he married or died at Clophill, but have found evidence for these events at Sandy. Assuming he was born around 1545, for reasons already explained, it would appear that his age at marriage at Sandy was around 30/31, which seems plausible. An Alice Whitfield (probably his aunt) married in 1567 in a neighbouring village. Clophill and Sandy are about ten miles apart, a little less as the crow flies, well within a day's walk or a comfortable journey on horseback. There are no earlier Whitfield entries in the Sandy registers and no later entries in the Clophill registers: John Whitfield appears to have been the last member of the family to have lived (and died) in the village. Finally, there is the use of Christian names in the family: subsequent generations of Whitfields have used the name Robert for boys. The early use of this name in Sandy may well be in memory of Robert, the 'plumer' of Clophill. Is all this just coincidence? I don't think so, but have to admit that the evidence is not absolutely conclusive.

I have been unable to find any mentions of the family in Clophill before 1531. This date pre-dates parish registers, so unless other old documents come to light, it would appear that this is as far back in time that I am able to go with the family. The Clophill baptism registers start in 1567, but there is then a gap until 1579; the marriage and burials registers start in 1579. The information about my Whitfield family before these dates has all been gleaned from other sources, which may encourage readers to try more unusual documents in researching *their* families. Some Whitfield families, in Sussex, Northumberland, Northamptonshire and Yorkshire have been traced much further back, but I have been unable to establish any connection between these families and the Bedfordshire Whitfields. Geographically, it would appear that the Northamptonshire branch is the most likely one to be connected, but I have found no historical evidence in support of this assertion. There is also the problem of alternative or variant spellings of the surname, (Whytfeld, Whytefelde, Witefilde,) presumably in existence before the spelling became more or less standardised in its present form. Where should a line be drawn between these possible variant spellings and a totally different surname? In the will of John Dryver of Shillington, made in 1505 and proved the following year, a Richard Wyttefele is mentioned as one of Dryver's executors. John Dryver appears to have been a farmer judging from his bequests of barley, malt, livestock and implements, and it is likely that Richard Wyttefele was another Shillington farmer - but was he a relative of Robert Whytefeld the plumber of Clophill? The two villages are only about five or six miles apart. Similarly, I have come across members of a family called Whitefelawe in mid Bedfordshire and a Henry de Witefelde as far back as the fourteenth century. Were these people ancestors of Robert the plumber, or connected to him in some way? The matter is complicated further by the fact that there are various villages and hamlets in England with the name 'Whitfield'; for example in Northumberland, Northamptonshire and Herefordshire. In the days when surnames were just beginning to be used, someone called , simply, 'Henry', if he was born in the village of Whitfield, might have acquired the name of Henry de Whitfield, if it helped to distinguish him from another Henry living nearby who might have been called Henry Shepherd, if his job was looking after sheep. It would appear that tracing the members of ordinary English families becomes more difficult before the sixteenth century for all sorts of reasons. I may one day be able to trace the family further back in time, but I'm not holding my breath…

Chapter 4.
Labourers, plaiters and paupers.

'In the sweat of thy face shalt thou eat bread'

Genesis 3, 19.

Having established the 'trunk' or main line of my family tree, back from myself to Robert Whitfield of Clophill, I started to investigate some other branches of the family. As mentioned earlier, a number of the male members of the family remain unaccounted for because they appear to have moved away from the Sandy area. These include Alexander Whitfield who moved from Clophill to Uxbridge in the 1540s, in somewhat controversial circumstances. He and his wife Joan may have established another line of the family there. Later possible 'strays' include Daniel, b.1617 in Sandy, named after his grandfather who died in Sandy in 1581, and William, b 1624. Their names do not crop up in the Sandy marriage or burial registers for the relevant period as far as I have been able to discover, and it would appear that they moved away from Sandy. Where? At present I have no idea. If they joined the army during the Civil War, they could have been killed in their prime, or they could have settled and married elsewhere. Their Christian names are fairly widespread, and even if I found a Daniel or William Whitfield somewhere else in England in the mid-seventeenth century, there would probably be no indication that they had originated from Sandy.

I have already dealt with the brothers of James Whitfield the gamekeeper (1770-1833), because the details relating to them helped me to ascertain that James was my 3x great grandfather.

There remains the branch descended from William Whitfield, baptised in Sandy in 1709, the younger brother of my direct line ancestor Robert (1701-1731) who was the grandfather of James the gamekeeper. This younger branch of the family is not as well documented as the older branch descended from Robert. According to the Sandy burials register, William (1709-1768) was a labourer. This implies to me that he worked on the land, but didn't own any. It is interesting that he did not receive any land (or money) from his bachelor uncle Robert Whitfield (1670-1752), whose will we have already considered, although the old man did remember William's son Robert (b1744) by leaving him £5 which he must have gratefully received as a fifteen year old lad in 1759. I wonder what he did with it?

William Whitfield (1709-1768) married Elizabeth Tilcock in Sandy Church in 1743. Elizabeth came from another well-known market gardening family. It was a little confusing to ascertain the correct baptism date for her in the register because there were two Elizabeth

DIAGRAM 7

**The Sandy Whitfields - junior branch -
until the late 19th century (simplified)**

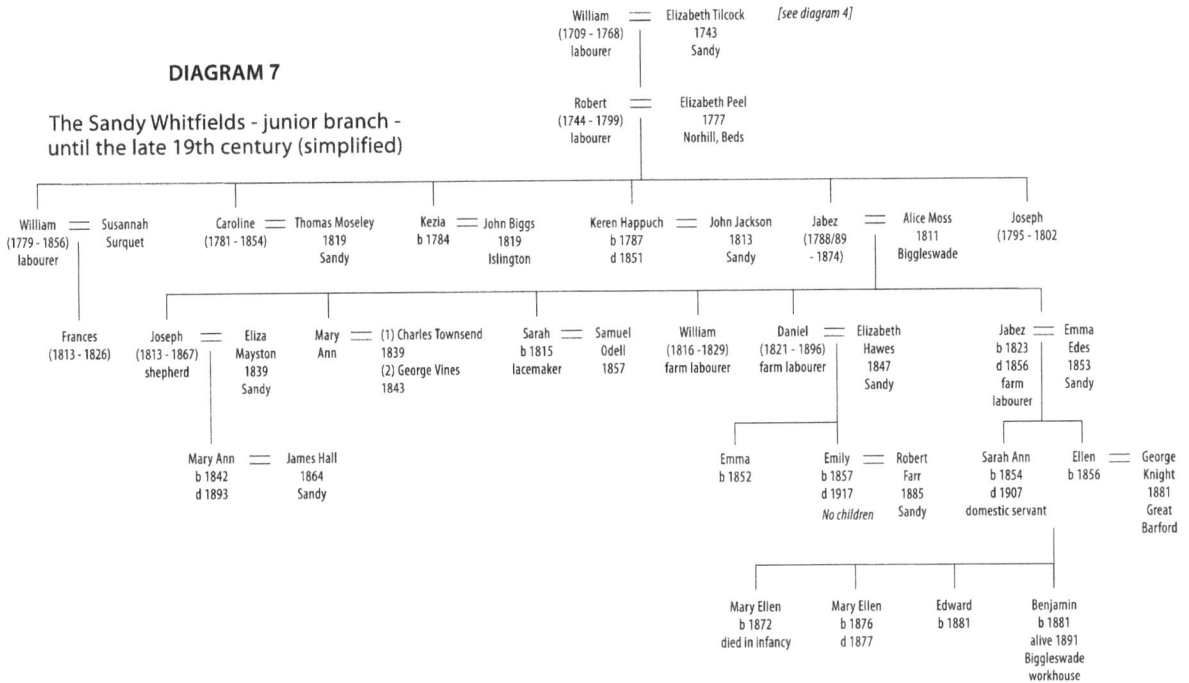

William
(1709 - 1768)
labourer
═
Elizabeth Tilcock
1743
Sandy
[see diagram 4]

Robert
(1744 - 1799)
labourer
═
Elizabeth Peel
1777
Norhill, Beds

William (1779 - 1856) labourer ═ Susannah Surquet	Caroline (1781 - 1854) ═ Thomas Moseley 1819 Sandy	Kezia b 1784 ═ John Biggs 1819 Islington	Keren Happuch b 1787 d 1851 ═ John Jackson 1813 Sandy	Jabez (1788/89 - 1874) ═ Alice Moss 1811 Biggleswade	Joseph (1795 - 1802

Frances
(1813 - 1826)

Joseph
(1813 - 1867)
shepherd
═
Eliza
Mayston
1839
Sandy

Mary
Ann
═
(1) Charles Townsend
1839
(2) George Vines
1843

Sarah
b 1815
lacemaker
═
Samuel
Odell
1857

William
(1816 -1829)
farm labourer

Daniel
(1821 - 1896)
farm labourer
═
Elizabeth
Hawes
1847
Sandy

Jabez
b 1823
d 1856
farm
labourer
═
Emma
Edes
1853
Sandy

Mary Ann
b 1842
d 1893
═
James Hall
1864
Sandy

Emma
b 1852

Emily
b 1857
d 1917
No children
═
Robert
Farr
1885
Sandy

Sarah Ann
b 1854
d 1907
domestic servant

Ellen
b 1856
═
George
Knight
1881
Great
Barford

Mary Ellen
b 1872
died in infancy

Mary Ellen
b 1876
d 1877

Edward
b 1881

Benjamin
b 1881
alive 1891
Biggleswade
workhouse

Tilcocks: one baptised in 1694, the other in 1726. William and Elizabeth had at least three children, but possibly as many as five. The last of the 'definite' family was Alice, who was baptised and died in 1755. This led me to conclude that William must have married the younger Elizabeth Tilcock (seventeen years his junior) as Elizabeth b 1694 would have been past child-bearing in 1755 at the age of 61. The other children were Robert, baptised in 1744 (the recipient of £5 in 1759), and Susan, baptised in 1751. It is possible that they had two more children: William, b 1759 and Thomas, b 1761, but these could have been children of William Whitfield (1727-1806) and *his* wife Elizabeth, nee Retchford, my 4x great grandparents. As we have seen, both William b1759 and Thomas died apparently single, both in their twenties, so in a sense their parentage is now an academic nicety.

Susan Whitfield married Thomas Endersby in nearby Northill in 1779. Her brother, Robert, appears to have moved away to Croydon in Cambridgeshire, a distance of perhaps ten miles from Sandy, presumably to work on a farm. He may well have also lived on the farm, a common practice at the time. He married Elizabeth Peel in Northill Church in 1777. I presume the couple already knew each other from when Robert was living in Sandy. The couple settled in Sandy after their marriage, and the baptisms of some of their children appear in the Sandy register:

William, b. 1779.

Caroline, b 1781.

Kezia, b 1784.

Keren Happuch, b 1787, and

Joseph, b 1795.

Robert is described as a labourer in the register, again implying that he did not own the land he cultivated. He is mentioned in a land tax assessment for Girtford (a hamlet about half a mile from Sandy) in 1783; he was a tenant of William Sirket. Robert's son William Whitfield married Susannah Surquet (or Sirket), in 1810. He was mentioned in the land tax assessments for Sandy and Girtford, where he was a tenant of Thomas Croot, and, later, Mrs Croot. He paid eighteen shillings in 1812 and 1813 for land he was cultivating, but was paying four shillings for a house and land he held as a tenant of Mrs Croot. This implies that he was cultivating less land as he grew older; perhaps he was undertaking more work for someone else, possibly for Mrs Croot herself if her husband had died. William was described as a pauper in 1851; possibly at the age of seventy three, rheumatism had got the better of him, making it difficult, or impossible to do much work. He died in 1856, and his gravestone can still be seen in Sandy churchyard. He and Susannah had produced a daughter, Caroline, named after William's sister, in 1813, but unfortunately she died in 1826. The death of their only child in her early teens must have hit them hard.

William's sister, Caroline, married a widower, Thomas Moseley, in Sandy in 1819. I know little more about her, except that she was a widow and a pauper in 1851, when she was lodging in Upper Caldecote, (between Biggleswade and Sandy), in the house of Joseph Daniels, a 73 year old pauper, his 59 year old wife Sarah, a straw plaiter, and their sons Frederick, Charles and George, all working as agricultural labourers. She died in 1854.

I have been unable to find a marriage for Kezia locally - or a burial. Obviously even if she didn't marry, she would not have avoided death. She appears to have moved away from Sandy. I have found that a Keziah Whitfield married John Biggs in the parish of St Mary, Islington in 1819. Kezia from Sandy would have been a 35 year old spinster at this time and although it it seems likely that I have found the correct person, there is no conclusive evidence. She and her sister Keren Happuch were named after two of Job's daughters in the Bible, who were born after he had recovered from all his afflictions and his fortunes were restored to him (*Job 42 vv14-15*). The Biblical passage states that '... in all the land were no women found so fair as the daughters of Job'. Unfortunately, no photographs or pictures of Kezia or Keren Happuch Whitfield have been found to testify to their beauty, which in any case would have been somewhat faded by the time photography had been invented. Incidentally, Job is said to have lived for another hundred and forty years after his fortunes were restored; Robert Whitfield, the father of Kezia and Keren Happuch wasn't so fortunate. He died in 1799, at the age of 55. I wonder if his choice of names for his daughters is an indication of some sort of religious conversion or experience he may have had? The youngest of Robert and Elizabeth Whitfield's children, Joseph, b 1795 died in 1802, aged about seven. His entry in the register states that he was the son of Elizabeth Whitfield, widow, supporting the fact that his father had died in 1799.

Keren Happuch Whitfield married an agricultural labourer, John Jackson, in Sandy church in October, 1813. Their daughter, Caroline, named after Keren Happuch's sister, was baptised a year later. Their son William was baptised in 1817, and was followed by two more daughters: Sarah in 1823 and Elizabeth in 1825. When Keren Happuch died in 1851, she was a grandmother (her daughter Caroline had married Tom Barker, an agricultural labourer, in 1841) and it may well be that there are some living descendants.

I believe that Robert and Elizabeth Whitfield had another son, Jabez, born around 1788. His baptism does not appear in the register, but the 1851 census gives his birthplace as Girtford, where I think Robert and Elizabeth were tenants of the Croot family. I managed to calculate his approximate year of birth from his date of death (1874), when his age was given as 86. The name Jabez means sorrow or trouble; it occurs in the Bible in the first Book of Chronicles, chapter 4, verse 9 where it says that 'his mother called his name Jabez, saying, Because I bare him with sorrow', and possibly superstition meant that Sandy's priest at that time (Philip Monoux) was unwilling to baptise him using this name. I have assumed his parents were Robert and Elizabeth, nee Peel. This is because the only other Whitfield married couple in Sandy at this time was Robert and Jemima, and they produced Sarah, b. 1787, Susan, b. 1789, and William, b.1792 at this time. Furthermore, if Jabez had been *their* child he would have been their eldest son, and, as such, would presumably have inherited Robert's half acre of land in Swaden when Robert died in 1841. As we have seen, this was not the case. Jabez' birth in 1788 fits into the apparent gap in Robert and Elizabeth's children: between Keren Happuch, baptised 1787 and Joseph, baptised 1795. We must remember, though, that children were not always baptised in their first year of life.

Jabez' marriage to Alice [Moss?] appeared to be equally problematic. Alice's birthplace was given in later censuses as Wrestlingworth, a village about two miles from Potton, but I was unable to find the marriage there. There was a marriage of a *Jervis* Whitfield to Alice Moss in Biggleswade in 1811, and this seemed the most likely. Among the witnesses to the marriage were a William Whitfield and a Caroline Whitfield. This made it clear to me that 'Jervis' was, in fact Jabez, as I had suspected, because Jabez had an older brother William and an older sister, Caroline. Jabez would have been about 23 at the time of the wedding ceremony, and the date of the marriage ties in with the baptisms, in Sandy, of the first two children of the couple: Joseph in 1813 and Mary Ann in 1814. The other children they had baptised were Sarah (1815), William (1816 - he died in 1829), Daniel, (1821) and Jabez, junior (1823). It seems that there was also another son, James, born around 1813, but he does not appear to have been baptised; more about him later.

Jabez senior was a farm labourer. I found a fascinating document at the Bedford Record Office which showed that Jabez was one of 27 workers employed on the farm of Thomas Croot in Girtford in 1834. (You will remember that Jabez' brother, William Whitfield, was a tenant of the Croot family). Another member of the Whitfield family was also working on this farm at times. His Christian name was not given; he was referred to as 'boy Whitfield'. I have assumed that he was a son of Jabez, probably Daniel or Jabez junior, who would have been aged around 13 and 11 respectively at the time. The document gives details of the type of work being done each week throughout the year and the rate of pay for each job. Presumably drawn up to enable Mr Croot to keep an eye on his finances, the document sheds light on early nineteenth century farming practices and represents, in effect, a sort of working diary for Jabez and his son.

As 1834 started, Jabez was felling trees and 'carving out faggots'. He was then 'allocating poles' (at 20d per day), and, as February started, he was planting trees and earning 10 shillings per week for a six day week. 'Boy Whitfield' also did three days' planting, presumably learning that farm work was a quick way to get backache but a slow way to make money: he was paid 6d per day for his efforts. Jabez was also involved in carting bushes, cutting ling and draining land. Possibly Thomas Croot, his employer, was taking in land from the waste. The land at Girtford, close to the River Ivel, is much heavier than the sandy land in Swaden in the eastern part of the parish of Sandy, where Jabez' second cousin, Robert Whitfield (1763-1841) had his half acre, and the Girtford land may well have been poorly drained and marshy. Both bush draining (presumably using the newly-cut bushes) and tile draining were mentioned, and the work, being undertaken by hand, was being paid at a piecework rate of 2s 7½ d per score of poles of land drained. A pole (sometimes called a rod or perch) was a linear unit used in land measurement and was equivalent to 5½ yards or 16½ feet. This measurement, multiplied by 1 score (20), made 330 feet, so Jabez was being paid, in modern decimal money, about 13p for every 330 feet of trench he dug. The width and depth of the trench are not recorded, but the depth would have had to be deeper than a ploughshare would normally penetrate, otherwise the bushes laid in the bottom of the trench to improve drainage would have been fetched to the surface again, and the whole exercise would have been a waste of time (and Mr Croot's money). It may be that the plough drew a furrow across the field at regular intervals, and Jabez and the other labourers had to deepen this trench by hand, using narrow, tapering drainage spades, tools specially designed for trenching. It would appear that the rate of pay was hardly generous. It must have been back-breaking work.

In May he was 'pearing' in the eight acres. At first, I thought this meant harvesting pears, but it didn't take me long to realise that pear trees would not be bearing fruit at this time; I later wondered whether I had misread Thomas Croot's handwriting and Jabez was 'peasing' i.e. picking peas. Again, this was almost certainly too early in the year. However, later entries referred to pearing and burning, and also carting and spreading ashes in the eight acres. Mr Croot's spelling was therefore possibly not as careful as his budgeting: he was referring to *paring* and burning, a technique used to clear a field of weeds and fertilise it with ashes obtained from burning the weeds. An implement called a breast plough, rather like a wide spade or shovel blade mounted at an obtuse angle on a wooden shaft with a 'T' handle at its other end, was pushed by its operator to skim off or 'pare' the top few inches of uncultivated land with its 'crop' of grass and weeds. This surface layer of vegetation, once disturbed, and with the roots of the weeds severed, would dry in the sun. The withered remains would then be collected and burnt, and the ashes returned to the soil as a fertiliser. It would have been a labour-intensive task, in dry, dusty and smoky conditions. Using the breast plough all day was a physically demanding job which taxed the stamina of the strongest men. Pushing the implement against the resistance offered by the soil and its crop of weeds involved repeated use of the chest, thigh and back muscles. It certainly wasn't a job for a man with heart trouble. Jabez must have looked forward to returning to his cottage after each working day, where, hopefully, Alice would have a hot meal ready for him: probably mainly vegetables, with bread and possibly meat if he had been able to snare a rabbit or hare on a previous occasion.

Later in May and June his jobs were more varied and a little less strenuous: he was carting wood, 'taken in oats', spreading muck and washing sheep. I hope he had several sets of clothes. He must have arrived home absolutely filthy, soaking wet, none too fragrant or a combination of all three on occasions, and Alice would have had to wash his clothes by hand. Hopefully she appreciated the steady ten shillings per week he was earning. It couldn't have gone far, with a large family to provide for, which explains why 'boy Whitfield' was also employed at times. I suspect he had to hand his few shillings to his mother.

In June, Jabez had the tedious and frustrating job of forking twitch (the brittle roots of the perennial couch grass which often invades cultivated land). Having done this job myself on many occasions I know only too well the effect it has on the back muscles and the patience required to 'tease out' and collect these rampant, spaghetti-like roots. He was also spreading muck, planting cabbages, carting hay and mowing grass. This last job would have meant Jabez was using a scythe. It was probably the start of the hay harvest, with possibly longer hours of working in a bid to make maximum use of fine weather. Jabez managed to earn 14s 6d between June 21 and 27 and was possibly on piecework. He returned to 'pearing' and burning in July, when his daily rate of pay was 22d, i.e. 11 shillings (55p) per week. It must have been warm work.

The cereal harvest, four weeks of unremitting toil in the scorching heat of high summer, began on 23 July, and Jabez earnt £5 5s in this period. He was probably using a scythe again, but this is not actually specified. The labourers may have made a harvest bargain with Thomas Croot, being paid so much per acre. Again, hours of work would probably have been extended as the men sought to ensure that 'all was safely gathered in' while the dry weather held; it was not unknown for labourers to work all day *and* all night if there was a full moon. (My great-grandfather, Philip Hiskey did when he was a young man). I hope Mr Croot provided his men with some beer in the harvest field as employers often did in those days: it would have been thirsty work.

After the harvest, Jabez was back to earning a steady ten shillings a week. He was 'burning' and spreading ashes. This probably meant that he was burning stubble after the wheat and barley had been cut. It may well be that Alice ventured on to the farm at this time to go gleaning - picking up ears of wheat or barley that the men had missed. Poor families relied on this grain to help them with bread making through the winter. Like many other labouring families at this time (and throughout the nineteenth century), Jabez and Alice probably used the extra money earnt in the harvest period to buy new boots, so that Jabez and anyone else in the household working on the land would have decent waterproof footwear through the coming winter.

In September, Jabez was spreading 'moulds' (composted material) and manure, and felling trees. In October, his job was 'water furrowing', an eighteenth and early nineteenth century method of improving surface drainage on the land, again suggesting that he was working on heavier ground, alongside the River Ivel. Later he was gathering chestnuts (presumably sweet chestnuts) and liming the autumn sown wheat.

After a week mowing brakes (bracken) which were used as animal bedding and then returned to the soil as manure, Jabez resumed his work in the plantation. It is clear that the men were being paid at a piecework rate, but I found that the accounts were rather difficult to interpret when I tried to work out how much Jabez earnt. The plantation work was clearly a large scale operation, involving all 27 men. In the week from November 29 to December 5, 4360 faggots of wood were cut. If I have pressed the correct buttons on my calculator, this represents about 23 faggots per day per man. The rate of pay for felling and tying was 4s 3d per hundred faggots, which equates to about one shilling per man per day, but in case you think Thomas Croot was being unduly careful with his money, it appears that there was a daily payment to each man in addition to this piecework incentive. To be fair to Mr Croot, he also sometimes paid his men on account, which must have helped Alice with her household budgeting.

Jabez and the other men were each paid 1s 8d for a day off on Christmas Day. They also presumably took Boxing Day as a holiday, this time unpaid. The document states that all the men were back at work on December 27 and worked through until January 2, 1835. Another year's labour had begun. I would imagine that Jabez enjoyed his two days' holiday and his Christmas dinner. Apart from anything else, the rest from toil must have been very welcome.

Jabez was clearly a hard-working man, but as we shall see, his life was far from being carefree. Unless he was very lucky, he probably suffered in his later years from arthritis or rheumatism, and bronchitis, caused by working outside in all weathers and sometimes very smoky conditions. There was no old age pension in those days and it is most unlikely that he had the opportunity to put aside any money for his declining years. His wife Alice died in 1862, and Jabez ended his days in Biggleswade workhouse, dying in 1874, at the advanced age of 86. He must have been worn out. I doubt very much whether the regime at the workhouse enabled him to enjoy any comfort in his old age.

Patchy information exists about the descendants of Jabez and Alice. Joseph, baptised in 1813 married Eliza Mayston, a dressmaker, in 1839. They appear to have had just one child - unusual in those days before reliable contraceptives became available: Mary Ann, baptised in 1842. Joseph and his family lived at Girtford. The 1851 census indicates that he was an agricultural labourer, but the 1861 census is more specific: he was a shepherd. He does not appear to have been in very prosperous circumstances, despite his smaller family, as he was in receipt of charity bread in June 1857, and again from 1865-1867.

Wynne's Charity Bread List for Sandy makes it clear that certain persons were not considered sufficiently poor to qualify for free bread: owners of either house or land; occupiers of more than two acres; single men lodgers; persons who had lived in Sandy for less than twelve months; and persons in receipt of wages of sixteen shillings (and presumably above) throughout the winter. We can assume, therefore, that Joseph was a tenant whose standard of living was, at best, modest. His wife died in 1860, and he soldiered on for another seven years before dying at the age of 55. An article in the *Bedfordshire Times* for 21st May, 1867, makes it clear that Joseph had taken his own life. Joseph had apparently been depressed for some time; he usually had breakfast with his brother-in-law who also lived in Girtford, which suggests to me that he was lonely after the death of his wife in 1860 and the marriage of his only daughter in 1864. He had not turned up for his breakfast on 16th May. Possibly suspecting the worst, neighbours had searched for him and found him hanging, lifeless, from a rope attached to a beam in his barn. Mr Piper, the deputy coroner for Bedfordshire presiding at the inquest returned a verdict of 'suicide by hanging whilst in a state of temporary insanity'. The entry in the Sandy register of deaths makes no mention of Joseph's suicide. His badly weathered gravestone still stands in Sandy churchyard.

Joseph's daughter, Mary Ann, a dressmaker in 1861, must have struggled to afford her father's headstone. She may have been helped by her husband James Hall, a Sandy market gardener, who appears to have been comfortably off. They had married on Boxing Day, 1864 at Sandy Baptist Chapel, Mary Ann signing her own name.

When Mary Ann died in 1893 'in her 52nd year', the *Bedfordshire Mercury* reported the funeral, stating that Mary Ann had endured a lingering illness. James Hall was described as 'one of the principal market gardeners of the town and a very prominent member of the Baptist denomination'. His late wife's body was 'enclosed in a splendid polished oak coffin' which was 'carried to the grave in a handsome glass hearse'. On November 17, 1894, the same newspaper reported, somewhat effusively:

'A magnificent memorial has just been erected in the [Sandy] cemetery to the memory of the late Mrs James Hall. The centre is a massive headstone of Sicilian marble with circular columns on each side with moulded bases and curved cusps to the same. Above, there are carved bosses and crotchets and two angels in prayer, supporting an elaborate shaped and carved filial. In the front there is a carved panel of lilies, roses and forget-me-nots. The headstone stands on a specially moulded base and is enclosed by a massive marble kerb supporting a neat iron palisade'.

I wonder whether the correspondent was related to the monumental mason?

I visited this 'magnificent memorial' in August, 2009. It bore the following inscription:

> *In loving memory of*
> *Mary Ann, the beloved wife of James Hall, who fell asleep*
> *Aug 14 1893 aged 52 years.*
> *Far from this world of toil and strife*
> *She's present with the Lord*
> *The labours of this mortal life*
> *End in a large reward.*

James Hall remarried in 1896. His bodily remains, together with those of his second wife are also interred beneath the memorial. James' worldly goods amounted to nearly £12,000 when he died in 1922. He must have been a thrifty, astute and hard-working market gardener. His second wife outlived him by over thirty years, dying in 1953, at the age of 104.

Mary Ann and James Hall had two children: Joseph Nathaniel Hall, baptised 1866 and named after his Whitfield grandfather, and Eliza A. Hall, baptised 1869, named after her Whitfield grandmother. Joseph Nathaniel Hall was a market gardener and vegetable merchant and I discovered he owned eight acres of land in Arlesey, Bedfordshire. However, he died in 1921, a year before his father. I was amazed to find he was a very wealthy man indeed when he died: the National Probate Register records that he left nearly £250,000. This would have been a colossal sum in those days. He had been much wealthier than his Whitfield grandfather, whose Christian name he shared, but had died at about the same age.[3]

I mentioned earlier that William Whitfield, the son of Jabez and Alice who was baptised in 1816, died in 1829. I was surprised to find his death recorded in the *Northampton Mercury* of Saturday, 7th November, 1829:

'On the 28th ultimo, an inquest was taken at Girtford, in the parish of Sandy, Bedfordshire, before F.J. Budd, gent., coroner for the county of Bedford, on view of the body of William Whitfield aged 13 years; the deceased had been at work on the preceding day chopping thistles, when he complained of a pain in his loins; he went home, and shortly afterwards went to bed, where he continued for some hours, and then expired. It appeared from evidence that the deceased was dropsical, and that the cause of his death was occasioned by water produced from the disease under which he suffered. Verdict: died by the visitation of God.'

---

3   See Appendix

Another son of Jabez and Alice - James - must have caused them many a sleepless night. He has caused me a few problems too, because I have been unable to find his baptism. The 1851 census for Sandy shows him lodging with his parents. He was 38 years old, already a widower, and working as a gardener's labourer. This suggests that he was born in 1813. James had married Martha Odell in Sandy in 1835. They had two children, Philip, b 1835, and Elizabeth, b.1845. Martha, however, died in 1847, aged only 36.

It would appear that this is the James Whitfield who appears in the Criminal Registers for Bedford Gaol, found on the internet. The gaol record gives some interesting details. It states that James was committed in 1848 for being a 'rogue and vagabond'. He had been born in Sandy and still lived there at the time of the offence, was 35 years old, 5 feet 5½ inches tall and of stout build. He had dark hair, hazel eyes, a pale complexion, and a scar on the left side of his chin. His occupation was described as a 'gamer', a somewhat ambiguous term, as it could mean that he dealt in game, or could indicate that he was a gambler. He was sentenced to three calendar months in the New House of Correction at Bedford, where he was to be kept busy on the wheel (treadmill). It may well be that he was helping to grind corn. James' committal took place a year after his wife, Martha, had died. I wondered if he was begging or dealing illegally in game to support his family. However, I discovered later that I had been unduly charitable in my supposition: the *Cambridge Independent Press* of Saturday, 27th July, 1848 revealed that James had been 'apprehended by P.C. Breakwell for leaving his family chargeable to the parish of Sandy', i.e. he had *deserted* his family and had thus been required to appear in court. It is possible that he had found a job outside Sandy as a farm labourer and that he was required to live on the premises as a farm servant. I can only assume that the stress of supporting his family in conditions of extreme poverty had become too much for him.

The presiding magistrates at Biggleswade: John Harvey, Stephen Thornton, Robert Lindsell and Francis Pym could all be described as members of the local squirearchy, with the possible exception of Lindsell who, as we have already seen, had feathered *his* nest by marrying the elder daughter of Samuel Wells II, a wealthy Biggleswade banker and brewer. However well-meaning they may have been, there can be little doubt that these men of property had considerable power and influence and their lifestyles were far removed from those of the lesser mortals over whom they were pronouncing judgement. Harvey, for instance, resided at Ickwell Bury, an imposing Queen Anne mansion set in over a hundred acres; he was able to spend his leisure hours pottering around in a lounge, staircase hall, inner hall, morning room, bird room, library, study, drawing room, dining room, justice room, music room and boudoir. The house also had sixteen main bedrooms and dressing rooms as well as a nursery. His servants (there were thirteen of them in 1851) had their own quarters. If he ventured outside, he could enjoy the use of his own tennis courts or maybe just take a pleasant stroll around his three-and-a-half acre ornamental lake. I would imagine that his servants were kept far too busy for either of these activities, but on the assumption that 'you don't keep a dog and bark yourself', concede that they may have had to retrieve the tennis balls after the Harvey family's more wayward shots and were probably required to keep the grass shorn on the tennis courts.

We met the Thornton family in an earlier chapter. You will remember that Stephen Thornton was an older brother of Claude George Thornton of Tewin and both were sons of the late

Godfrey Thornton, a former governor of the Bank of England. Stephen lived at Moggerhanger House, an impressive residence which had been extensively remodelled by the prominent architect Sir John Soane who seems to have done well out of the Thornton family.

I mention these details because they illustrate the gulf between rich and poor in early Victorian England. At the same court session (19th July, 1848) Mary Ann Haynes was accused of 'stealing one wooden rail, value two pence'. The matter was settled out of court. She may well have been looking for firewood to heat her cottage. Two labourers, William Stratton and Benjamin Ibbitt, were fined for using a gun in pursuit of game on the land of Robert Elliott, Esquire of Tempsford. They were probably after some cheap meat for their families.

As so many labourers tried to cope with dire poverty, it is easy to appreciate why some of them resorted to crime in order to survive.

In 1841, James and Martha Whitfield and their son Philip had been living in Mill Lane, Biggleswade, and James was working as a groom. Cottages in Mill Lane were not quite as luxuriously appointed as John Harvey's house at Ickwell Bury. Joyce Godber, in her *History of Bedfordshire* states that a report on housing standards in Biggleswade found that

'In Mill Lane there was only one privy to 9 cottages in which 45 persons lived. The pigsties [were] generally very close to the dwelling houses, and the accumulation of manure [was] usually kept close to the sty'

Reading between the lines, if there really *was* only one privy to 45 people the accumulation of manure referred to in the report (written in 1866) may not have owed its origin solely to the pigs. Twenty five years earlier, or thereabouts, I suspect the situation may well have been the same, if not worse. Clearly, sub-standard housing and squalid living conditions were not the preserve of large towns and cities, and it was little wonder that infectious diseases sometimes wrought havoc amongst the poor. The death of James Whitfield's wife, Martha was therefore perhaps not too much of a surprise. I haven't seen her death certificate, but doubt very much if the cause of her demise was over-exertion when playing tennis.

James served his time in prison and presumably his children were looked after by his parents for three months. He was living in Swan Lane, Sandy in 1861, and working as a gardener's labourer. He died in 1870.

James and Martha's son, Philip, was the last Whitfield I have found to live most of his life in Sandy. Born around 1835, he married Drusilla Twelvetrees, a dressmaker in June, 1870, at the Baptist Meeting, Sandy. Philip was a gardener's labourer in 1861 and was described as a 'gentleman's gardener' at the time of his marriage. Unfortunately, the register didn't specify who the 'gentleman' was and it also omitted the name of Drusilla's father, suggesting that she may have been born illegitimately.

Philip was initiated into the United Order of Free Gardeners (Sandy Lodge) in 1866. At first I thought this meant he had some sort of formal qualification in gardening, but a little research revealed that he had become a member of a Friendly Society which provided some sort of benefit for its members in instances of illness and possibly unemployment. Losing his mother at a young age may have prompted Philip to take steps to safeguard his financial security in the event of unforeseen circumstances, and it seems that he may have been a cautious, prudent character. I discovered the large framed certificate commemorating his initiation when I went to an exhibition staged by the Sandy Historical Group in 2009. The document had turned up in the loft of an old house near the parish church in Biggleswade and had been initially donated to members of the Biggleswade History Society, who had passed it on to their Sandy counterparts. I have obviously wondered how the document turned up in that particular house's loft. Is it just coincidence that a relative, George Whitfield was working next door, for John Nathaniel Foster at St. Andrew's in 1866? Perhaps Philip was also working there at that time as an under gardener. George may have recommended him to Foster.

Philip does not appear to have made much progress in his job. He was described as an *under-gardener* in 1871 (possibly working at Sandy Place with George Whitfield) and he and Drusilla received bread from Wynne's Charity in Sandy that year, and every year thereafter until 1896, apart from 1872. I wonder why they didn't qualify in that year? Little evidence appears to have survived to demonstrate the type of gardening Philip was undertaking for his employer. However, he certainly also enjoyed growing indoor plants to a high standard because he won second prize for a geranium in the 1875 Sandy Horticultural Show. In 1891 he and Drusilla were living in Bedford Road, Sandy, and he was working as a brewer's labourer. He was described as a brewer (but was presumably still a brewer's labourer) on his death certificate, which recorded that he died from nephritis (inflammation of the kidneys) and exhaustion in 1900. An advertisement extolling the virtues of pensions in the *Northampton Mercury* of 21st September 1900 recorded that Drusilla was receiving a widow's pension of 5s per week - further evidence of her late husband's prudence. In late December of the same year, Drusilla married an agricultural labourer, Arthur Reid at nearby Blunham. It was the second marriage for both bride and groom who by this time were in their sixties. Arthur Reid died in 1908, and Drusilla in December, 1916.

Mary Ann, the next child of Jabez and Alice, married Charles Townsend, a labourer and son of a wheelwright in 1839. I found Mary Ann living in Wrestlingworth, Bedfordshire in the 1841 census, and found a William Whitfield, aged two, living with her. Presumably William was born before her marriage to Charles Townsend - but was Mr Townsend the father? Charles died between April and June, 1841, and Mary Ann remarried in 1843. Her new husband was an agricultural labourer named George Vines, and the family moved to Blunham, Bedfordshire, about three miles from Sandy. I couldn't find them in the 1851 census, but they appear ten years later with their children Frederick (13), an agricultural labourer, Fanny (11), and John (9), both of whom were at school. I have found no further mention of young William.

By 1871, the children had left the household. Frederick had married and had moved to Church Gresley in Derbyshire where he was working as a coal miner, which must have been very different from working in the fresh air on the land. The 1871 census shows his parents George and Mary being visited in Blunham by Mary's widowed younger sister, Sarah Odell, nee Whitfield. Both sisters were described as lace makers, and were probably in some financial hardship: hand-produced lace was facing competition from lace made more cheaply on machines. Sarah, baptised in 1815, had married Samuel Odell, a rat catcher, in 1851. Samuel and Sarah do not appear to have had any children; the only patter of tiny feet Samuel must have heard was related to the decidedly unsavoury rodents he was paid to catch. He died in 1868. I haven't found the cause of death, but wonder if it was as a result of his occupation. Many rat catchers were bitten by rats and the bites could lead to serious infections. Death from them was not uncommon. Even Queen

Victoria's rat catcher, Jack Black, nearly died on a number of occasions from infections acquired in this way. He had numerous scars on his face and hands resulting from rat bites.

By 1881, both sisters were living together in Usher's Yard, Great Barford, a neighbouring village to Blunham. Mary was now blind. Her lacemaking had probably been responsible for this. In addition to poor posture, deteriorating eyesight was a recognised occupational hazard associated with the craft and now presumably Mary's lacemaking days were over. She died in 1887 and Sarah died five years later.

Daniel, the next child of Jabez and Alice was born in 1821 or 1822, and baptised in 1825. He married Elizabeth Hawes, a straw bonnet sewer in 1847. Their children, Emma and Emily were baptised in 1852 and 1857 respectively. Emma, like her mother was a straw bonnet sewer. At that time there was a thriving straw hat industry in Luton; it may be that the hats were made in the Sandy area from locally produced straw plaits as a cottage industry and then sold in Biggleswade, Bedford, Hitchin or Luton.

Emily, the other daughter, *was* a straw plaiter, and I imagine that the Whitfield's cottage must have been a hive of industry when the girls were younger, with Emma and her mother making straw bonnets, possibly from straw which Emily had plaited. Otherwise, the straw plaits would have been sold in Biggleswade or Shefford where there were plait markets or perhaps at a lower price to a local dealer, some of whom travelled around the district. If this sounds idyllic, remember that straw plaiting would have made plaiters' fingers, thumbs and mouths very sore and could lead to permanent scarring: the straws tended to be brittle and were often moistened with saliva to make them more pliable. They were held in the mouth until needed. The straw would probably also have been supplied by the dealer, and a certain amount of preparatory work would already have been carried out on it: it would have been bleached and fumigated by exposing it to sulphur fumes and it may have been dyed in different colours. It would have been cut to the required length. Emily Whitfield would probably not have realised that the straws she held in her mouth had been treated with potentially carcinogenic substances. She had probably been given advice from the dealer regarding the types of plait required. It was advisable for plaiters to be skilled in producing several different ones. They needed to be adaptable to cater for changing fashions.

Amounts of money earned were usually modest, at best, although hard-working and really skilful plaiters could do fairly well and maybe build up a little nest egg before marriage. Any money earned in this way was appreciated though, as it gave young women like Emily a little financial independence and it must have helped older married women to eke out family budgets. Straw plaiting could be done in any type of weather conditions and was probably preferred to agricultural work or domestic service. Plaiters could supervise younger children while they worked at home and experienced plaiters could chat while they worked, so groups of them could catch up on local news. Plaiting schools (sometimes known as sore thumb schools) were held in some villages where children were given tuition in the art of plaiting but also had basic instruction in reading. I'm not sure whether there was one at Sandy.

Straw plaiting did not meet with universal approval. As early as 1804, Arthur Young (who *did* approve of the earning potential offered) had observed that it made 'the poor saucy', and noted that in areas where straw plaiting had become established it was difficult to procure servants. Presumably this was because the plaiters could earn more money from their craft than from skivvying for middle or upper class employers. The word 'saucy' in this context possibly meant impudent, because the money earned by the plaiters gave them a certain amount of independence, but it hinted at something else: it was thought that plaiting, which sometimes brought young men and women together in close proximity, encouraged immoral behaviour which sometimes led to illegitimate births later. George Culley, giving evidence to the *Royal Commission on the Employment of Children, Young Persons and Women in Agriculture* in 1867 considered that the problem arose because young male and female plaiters were accustomed to 'go about the lanes together in summer engaged in work which *has not even the wholesome corrective of more or less physical exhaustion*' (my italics). Other criticisms levelled at the time were concerned with overcrowded, stuffy plait schools where little other than plaiting was learned, and the resulting lack of other domestic skills in the girls who had attended them.

Emily Whitfield hopefully had acquired some domestic skills by the time she married a Sandy butcher, Robert Farr, in 1885. They lived in Brickhill Road in Sandy in 1891, and by this time Emily's father, Daniel Whitfield, was living with them. Daniel, a farm labourer, despite having a small family seems to have struggled financially. He had received charity bread over a long period, from as early as 1857 (the year of Emily's birth) until he died; he also received charity coal. Hopefully in his declining years he was able to enjoy an occasional helping of meat (provided by his son-in-law) with his main meal of the day. Emily and Robert probably saved him from having to spend his last few years in the workhouse. He died of 'exhaustion and senile decay' in 1896, aged 74. He was probably worn out by his work on the land, presumably for a pittance. He is now at rest in Sandy churchyard in an unmarked grave.

Emily and Robert must have been a little concerned about Daniel's newly-dug final resting place. In September, 1896, an article in the *Bedfordshire Times* revealed that there were nearly *five hundred* dogs in Sandy (I wonder who had the job of counting them) - on average, nearly one per household - and apparently some of them were in the habit of digging in the churchyard. One hole in a grave was said to be about two feet deep. The Parish Council had responded to this unsatisfactory state of affairs by placing a notice on one of the churchyard gates. They seem to have overlooked the fact that dogs couldn't read – and neither, I suspect, could some of their owners.

By 1901, Emily and Robert had moved to Bedford where Robert was working as a jobbing gardener. They were back in Sandy ten years later, and do not appear to have been prospering: Robert stated that he was now a hawker and doing odd jobs. There were no children. I managed to discover that Robert Farr was a smoker, because John Ashwell stole tobacco and a tobacco box from him in 1895 when they were drinking in the *Black Swan* at Bedford. The incident was reported in the *Bedfordshire Times* of 1st June, and Ashwell was sentenced to four days' imprisonment for his offence.

Robert Farr died from dropsy in 1917, aged 58; at this time Emily was still alive. I haven't been able to find details of her subsequent death.

Jabez' and Alice's youngest child, also called Jabez (remember the name means sorrow or trouble), was baptised in 1823. He married another straw plaiter, Emma Edes, in July, 1853, but died in 1856. The death wasn't registered, but burial took place in Sandy churchyard. The union had produced two children: Sarah Ann, baptised 1854, and Ellen, baptised in 1857. Without a husband or father in the household, life must have been a real struggle, and in the 1861 census, Emma, described as a widow, and still working as a straw plaiter, was living with John Walkman, a brick maker, and his wife Sarah, and was described as their daughter. On her marriage certificate Emma's father was given as Philip Edes, so it may be that he had died and her mother had remarried.

By 1871, Emma, together with her two children, was living in Biggleswade workhouse, and may well have ended her days there, dying in 1877, aged 42. Her father in law, Jabez Whitfield, senior, was also a workhouse inmate in 1871; it is unlikely that they met because the sexes were segregated. Life was harsh for people who fell upon hard times in the nineteenth century, and many labouring families were so close to destitution that the untimely illness or death of a breadwinner, a period of unemployment or increasing infirmity in old age would mean a stay in the workhouse – a most unwelcome prospect. On the other hand, resorting to crime to alleviate conditions of poverty obviously carried the risk of detection and a prison sentence: the poor were between a rock and a hard place.

The elder daughter of Jabez and Emma: Sarah Ann, must have had a rather unsettled childhood and adolescence. She appears not to have married, but was clearly not without male company at times because she had four illegitimate children. These were Mary Ellen, born in 1872, who died in infancy, sometime before 1876; Mary Ellen, born in 1876 who died the following year (the same year as Sarah Ann's mother); Edward, born around 1880 and Benjamin Edgar, born in 1881. The children were all born in Biggleswade workhouse and it seems that Sarah Ann used the institution as a sort of maternity ward (there would have been free medical attention) and worked outside it when she wasn't heavily pregnant. At this time unmarried mothers were often disowned by their families and so she may have had little alternative to these arrangements. She appears to have been a domestic servant at times. She was described as such in 1881, when she was lodging at the *Rising Sun* public house in Sun Street, Biggleswade with young Edward, presumably before she was taken into the workhouse to give birth to Benjamin Edgar. I have no further details on Edward.

As a pauper and a single mother, Sarah Ann's life would not have been easy. It would be unfair to imagine her as a young lady of easy virtue: it would appear that her male friends or acquaintances had possibly taken advantage of her possibly simple and trusting nature. I discovered that she spent a significant part of her life as a patient in what was then the lunatic asylum, later the Three Counties Mental Hospital near Arlesey, Bedfordshire. I have not managed to discover the nature of her mental illness or handicap; it could have been schizophrenia, bi-polar disorder, depression or severe learning difficulties. Mental illness was not understood in those days, and to a large degree is still the 'poor relation' of the National Health Service. Her treatment could have included being handcuffed or placed in a straitjacket or padded cell. Sarah Ann was first admitted to Arlesey on 7th February, 1871. An article in the *Bedfordshire Times* of 4th February, 1871, was very useful in telling me more about the reason for her admission to the asylum: she had been charged by Harry Laney, the master of the Biggleswade Union workhouse, of absconding from that establishment on 27th January of the same year, taking a quantity of cloths with her. I wondered if this was a misprint for 'clothes'; possibly not, because the word 'cloths' was repeated in a subsequent edition of the same newspaper. Sarah had avoided a prison sentence because a 'medical certificate of insanity' had been provided for her. Her first stay at the asylum was a short one because records show that she was discharged on 1st March of the same year.

Her next admission was on 13th December, 1876, and she stayed until 23rd June, 1879, when she was discharged after having apparently made some sort of recovery. By 12th November, 1881, however, she had been admitted again, and this time her stay was a long one, lasting until 7th June, 1895. The reason for her son Benjamin Edgar being placed in Biggleswade workhouse from 1881 became clear, and it is possible that the deaths of her other children could have been from neglect. Her final stay at the asylum was from 1900 until her death on 3rd February, 1907.

I found on the BLARS (Bedfordshire and Luton Archives and Records Service) website that in April, 1881, magistrates at the Biggleswade Petty sessions had been made aware that the 'putative father' of Sarah Ann's child born on the 13th December, 1880 was James Jarvis, a labourer of Northill. Jarvis was ordered to contribute one shilling and sixpence towards the child's upkeep, 'until the child shall attain the age of 14 years', and was also fined fifteen shillings for the court costs involved. The child may well have been Benjamin Edgar Whitfield. Bearing Sarah Ann's mental illness or handicap in mind, it is possible that in the circumstances the weekly one shilling and sixpence was paid directly to the workhouse master.

Benjamin was still alive in 1891 and living in Biggleswade workhouse. I wondered if he was sent to work in Canada or the U.S.A. as some other workhouse boys were, but I was wrong. Over twenty years after I first started searching for him I found that he had left the workhouse and had been working as a labourer in Kensington, London. He then enlisted in the third battalion of the Middlesex Regiment in 1898. His attestation papers show that he had learnt to write in the workhouse and I assume that he could also read. It is likely that he fought in the Boer war but I have discovered no further information. I haven't managed to find a marriage or death for him in England, and records in South Africa are tricky to search as they are not all indexed. If he survived the Boer war he could have lived on into the 1950s or 1960s and produced a family of his own.

Ellen, the younger daughter of Jabez and Emma was in Biggleswade workhouse with her mother, sister and elderly grandfather in 1871. It was an inauspicious start for both girls, brought about by the early death of their father and hardly the ideal place to spend their childhood and early teenage years. Ellen, however, married George Knight in February, 1881 in Great Barford church. It isn't clear what she had been doing in the intervening ten years, but she would have been old enough to find a job in domestic service. By 1901, she and her family had moved to Myddleton Road, Hornsey, London, where George was working as a general labourer. No occupation was given for Ellen, but four children are listed: Mary (18) was working as a domestic servant, Walter (15) as a greengrocer's assistant; Benjamin (10) and Sidney (8) were still at school. Ellen appears to have carved out a rather more satisfying life for herself than her older sister. I couldn't find Ellen in the 1911 census; this may be explained by a death I found for an Ellen Knight, born around 1857 which took place in Edmonton, North London, in 1905.

I was surprised to see that Walter Knight had left London by 1911; he was found in Chilvers Coton near Nuneaton and had become a coal miner. Young Benjamin Knight and his brother Sidney had also left London by 1911 to work in the coal industry but had moved to Ammanford, Carmarthenshire, South Wales. Both of them were working as labourers (above ground) at a colliery and were lodging with another labourer, John Jones and his wife Martha. It seems rather strange that the three brothers should travel so far to undertake this type of work when there must have been labouring jobs available in the capital. I have not been able to trace the

Knights beyond 1911 so far. Their lack of middle Christian names has been the main problem, but this should be overcome eventually with the publication of the 1921 census.

You can see, therefore, that the Whitfields descended from William Whitfield (1709-1768) had died out in Sandy by 1900; although some of his descendants were still living they had changed their surname by marriage, moved away from Sandy, or both. Philip Whitfield (1835-1900), the son of James Whitfield and his wife Martha, nee Odell, and the grandson of Jabez Whitfield (1788-1874) was the last member of the family to live in Sandy until I lived there with my parents, sister and brother in the winter of 1971-2.

It was a similar story with the 'senior' branch of the family, descended from Robert Whitfield (1701-1731), where, as we have seen, George Whitfield, baptised in 1818, had sold his half acre of land in 1872 and died in Biggleswade workhouse twenty four years later.

The family which had owned and farmed land in Sandy since the late sixteenth century had not died out completely, however, although its economic circumstances were in decline; and we now need to return to James Whitfield, the gamekeeper, (1770-1833), my 3x great grandfather.

St. Swithun's Church, Sandy, from the grounds of Sandy Place. Many baptisms, weddings and funerals of the Whitfield family took place here between 1576 and 1900. Photo by Isaac Whitfield, 2013.

Chapter 5.
A family in crisis: the Whitfields arrive in Potton.

'O let us love our occupations
Bless the squire and his relations
Live upon our daily rations
And always know our proper stations'

Charles Dickens (1812- 1870) *The Chimes.*

You will remember from Chapter 1 that James Whitfield, the gamekeeper, who had moved to Tewin, Hertfordshire, in 1819, had not gained a legal settlement there; and when he became too ill to work and thus dependent on the parish for the support of his wife and family, the parish officers, to avoid the on-going cost of this relief, which would have been necessary even after James' death, sought to have the family removed to Potton. The Potton parish officers, anxious to minimise their expenditure, appealed against the removal order.

I returned to the court case at the Hertfordshire Record Office. The intent of the removal order was clear enough, but had any additional information survived? I found out that the case had been suspended in February, 1833 because the Justices, Thomas Daniell and the Reverend Edward Bourchier considered that James was 'unable to travel by reason of sickness and infirmity of body' and the overseers of the poor at Tewin were commanded to

'desist from conveying the said James Whitfield and his said wife and children out of the parish of Tewin until you shall make it appear unto us…that [he] hath recovered from his said illness and may without danger be conveyed…to the said parish of Potton'.

February, 1833, was one of the wettest Februarys on record and the atmosphere inside the Whitfield's cottage must have been particularly gloomy. Most cottages then had small windows and were lit by the fire in the hearth and candles for a time after dusk, although many poorer households retired to bed early to keep warm and to save the use of fuel and candles. While the rain beat down and James lay in bed seriously ill, Sarah would have had to look after her young family, prepare meals and see to other domestic tasks, with the threat of removal to Potton hanging over the family. It was probably clear to her that her husband's life was ebbing away. I doubt whether she could have afforded the expense of a doctor; it was probably a struggle to feed her children.

To their credit, the Justices had shown some compassion in suspending the court order, but the reprieve was short- lived. On 9th March a further document stated that James Whitfield was

'…dead from the sickness and infirmity of body under which he lately laboured…and his wife and five children may therefore be conveyed…to the parish of Potton.'

Potton is over twenty miles from Tewin, but only about three miles from James Whitfield's birthplace of Sandy, where, as we have seen, some of James' relatives were facing problems of their own. Potton was a fairly important small market town in the 1830s; it had a tannery, but its main economic activity was agriculture, apart from general trades. Potton's soils were mainly light and easily worked, particularly on the western side of the parish, but market gardening was not as well developed here at this time as it was in Sandy and Biggleswade; the coming of the railway, which reached the town some twenty years or so later, appears to have given the industry a boost in the latter half of the nineteenth century.

I would imagine that the journey from Tewin was made by horse and cart or waggon. In addition to Sarah and her sons James, aged 14, George (13), Robert (11) Jonathan (7) and David (4), it presumably was also carrying the few household goods that Sarah possessed, probably a few sticks of furniture, some pots and pans and some bedding. I wouldn't think it took the family long to unpack when their destination was reached. Sarah must have been tired and worried about what the future had in store for them all in Potton; the older boys probably sensed this, and must have had concerns of their own. How would they all cope with this sudden change in their circumstances?

Immediately on their arrival a bill for £1 8s was payable, presumably by the Potton parish officers to the overseers at Tewin. This sum represented the charges incurred by the suspension of the Removal Order during James' illness. The compassion shown then had come at a price.

Examination of the Potton churchwardens' accounts for this period has shown that cash payments were made to 'Widow Whitfield' in 1836. I have found just two instances: she received 4s 6d and 2 shillings. These payments do not strike me as being over-generous - Jabez Whitfield was earning about ten shillings a week for his labours in Girtford at about this time. Similarly, I was surprised not to have found some earlier payments; surely there must have been some?

It became evident that the boys - or at least some of them - had to earn their money by working. The notebooks of the overseers of the poor showed that Sarah's sons had been stone picking. These stones would probably have been removed from the newly-cultivated fields, and then broken up, in readiness for road surfacing (no tarmac in those days). I say 'probably' because in nearby Gamlingay, Cambridgeshire, stones were returned to the fields after the day's work had been completed, ready to be picked up again the following day. (It was important that the poor were kept busy, even on pointless tasks, and not receiving money for being idle).

Thus I found in one note book from 1834-1837:

William Whitfield 1 day stone picking 8d.

Whitfield boys 4 days stones 4 shillings.

Jas., Geo. and Robt Whitfield 10 loads stones 6s 8d.

Jas., Robt. and Wm. Whitfield stones 6s 6d., and in another overseer's book for 1834:

2nd month Wm. Whitfield 36 baskets stones 3s., and again

Wm. Whitfield 36 baskets stones 3s.

3rd month Wm. Whitfield 3 loads sandstones 2s.

[These would not have been just any old stones - the flat iron-rich sandstones found in the parish were used as building stones, mainly to provide decorative features and face buildings and for walls. Potton Congregational Chapel in Sun Street, and St Mary's Church Hall, both dating from 1848, made extensive use of this type of stone.]

William Whitfield 20 baskets stones 2s 6d.

(Earlier, he had been paid three shillings for 36 baskets of stones, so unless there was a difference in the size of the baskets he had, in effect, been paid just 6d for the extra 16 full baskets. Perhaps he had negotiated an increase in his rate of pay).

It looks as though Jonathan aged seven and David, aged four in 1833, were not involved, mercifully. You will probably have realised that William Whitfield was not mentioned on the final 1833 Removal document - more about this later.

Stone picking must have been a miserable, cold and back-breaking task in February and March, 1834. I have done some in my younger days when the John O'Gaunt golf club in Sutton, near Potton was preparing a new course at Deepdale. However, this was in summer, and we threw our stones onto a trailer; we didn't have to carry or drag them in baskets. It must have taken a great deal of stoicism and determination on the part of the Whitfield boys to keep going. I suppose in the circumstances they didn't have much choice. Imagine getting up in a damp and poorly-heated cottage on a bleak, dark February morning with the prospect of getting frozen fingers and toes and backache, just like on previous days and with little hope of securing any more congenial or better-paid employment. They must have hated it. Unless they were keen amateur geologists, they must have been bored stiff as well as physically very uncomfortable.

William and Robert were also required to go digging by the overseers. William received the princely sum of 2s 6d for *five days'* digging in 1835, and his younger brother Robert's handsome reward was two shillings. The boys were clearly not yet in a position to be able to avoid what appears to have been blatant exploitation. I wonder how aware they were of the economic gulf that existed between them and the 'respectable' members of Potton society - sons and daughters of parents whose well-paid occupations enabled their children to be educated and enjoy some leisure time so that they were able to read books, play games and pursue hobbies? Incidentally, one of the overseers of the poor at Potton at this time was Thomas Strickland, a brewer and farmer. He had amassed a fortune of just under £9000 by the time he died in 1872, according to the National Probate Calendar. It would be interesting to know whether stone picking had taken place on his fields, and, if so, whether he received payment from the parish for the stones picked up by others less fortunate than he was.

In case you are wondering, William Whitfield, (baptised in 1818 at Cople), was mentioned on the first 1833 Removal document, but his name had been crossed out and did not appear on the later one. At the age of about sixteen when his father died, he was presumably considered old enough to fend for himself, and may well have done so by finding a job for a while on a farm in or around Tewin. However, at the Bedford Record Office I found out that he was the subject of a separate Removal Order in 1834, so we can assume that this period of employment didn't last.

The document, dated 17th May, 1834, considered that his place of legal settlement was

Potton. William clearly had to join his mother and brothers, but judging from the overseers' notebooks appears to have done so rather earlier than the date of the document. Perhaps the document's purpose was to formalise the arrangement and make sure that William didn't try to return to Tewin.

One of the men who signed William's Removal document, thereby condemning him to months, if not years of stone picking and digging for a few pennies a day was Robert Eden, Rector of Hertingfordbury, near Tewin. A potted biography of Robert Eden should suffice to demonstrate once again the chasm that existed between rich and poor in the reigns of William IV and Victoria. Eden was born at Eden Farm, Beckenham, Kent in 1799, the third son of William Eden, first Baron Auckland; he would therefore have known one end of a spade from the other, but probably never blistered his hands by using such an implement. He probably was destined from his birth to suffer in later life from writer's cramp, dyspepsia and gout rather than rheumatism, arthritis and malnutrition, and to command rather than obey: educated at Eton College, and afterwards at Magdalene College, Cambridge, he received his M.A. in 1819, and his B.D. and D.D. in 1847. While he was at Hertingfordbury he was also chaplain to King William IV, and later, from 1837 to 1847 to the young Queen Victoria. In 1849, he became the third Baron Auckland. Five years later he became Bishop of Bath and Wells, a post he held until he resigned in 1869. In 1861, the census return shows that the Bishop and his family had no fewer than *thirteen* servants to cater for their every need and caprice when they lived at the Bishop's Palace. Next door, in a cottage, lived their gardener: I wonder how much he was paid. When the Right Honourable and Right Reverend Robert John, Baron Auckland, D.D., departed this earthly life on 25th April, 1870, he left the *enormous* sum of *£120,000*. While he had been preparing his sermons in his cosy study at Hertingfordbury in the 1830s (hopefully not with a text from St. Matthew's Gospel, chapter 19 verse 21), William Whitfield's frozen fingers were picking up sandstones from the fields of Potton for 8d per day. (A loaf of bread at this time would have cost about 4d). At this rate it would have taken William a year to earn about £10. He was earning little more than his ancestor Robert Whitfield (the plumber of Clophill) had been paid three hundred years earlier. I am assuming William had Sundays off so that he could attend divine service to hear comforting sermons preached about rich men, camels and the eyes of needles.

William's sister, Naomi, and his older brother, Philip, were also not mentioned in the Removal Documents, and at this stage in my research I wasn't sure what had happened to them.

The years between 1832 and 1841 must have been very stressful for Sarah Whitfield trying to bring up her large family while her husband was dying and the future was so uncertain and beyond her control. I don't know whether she kept in touch with any of her Berry relatives. Her mother was still alive in Cople; and although it was unlikely she could offer any financial help at least she could have given some emotional support. Sarah couldn't read or write; she was not in the best of health and she had no money. It is difficult for us today to appreciate how isolated she must have felt, as we take being able to communicate by letter, telephone, text or e-mail for granted. She had the additional worry (presumably) of not knowing how her two older children were doing. We shall find out in later chapters.

Sarah's burial is recorded in the Potton burial register on 1st January, 1841. She had died at the age of 48 from dropsy, although the water retention may have been a symptom of some other complaint or disease, for example heart disease. The boys now had to fend for themselves - no mean feat in early Victorian England.

It is a pity that the 1841 census contains so few details. Names appear, but ages are rounded in many instances to the nearest five years, and instead of a person's birthplace being stated, all the information we are given is whether they were born in the same county as the place where they were now living. Occupations, too, are not always recorded in much detail, and the document copies I have seen have always been very faded compared to later censuses, suggesting that an inferior type of ink, or perhaps even pencil, was used by the enumerators. You may have guessed by now that it has been difficult for me to establish where all the members of James' and Sarah's family were on Census Day, 1841 (6th June, 1841), and what they were doing.

David, aged ten, was living in Ostler Street (Horslow Street) Potton, in the household of John Parker (aged 60) and his wife Esther (50). There was also another lodger, Gardner Ellis, an appropriately named agricultural labourer. David's brother, Robert, aged eighteen, was also living in Horslow Street, but at a separate address. He was living with William and Mary Ann Cox and their young daughter Elizabeth (2), who had also taken in John Seamer (18), James Seamer (12), Henry Seamer (8) and Mary Ann Seamer (6). These lodging arrangements may have been made privately or they may have been organised by the overseers of the poor in Potton. I presume the Whitfield boys were paying some rent which must have come in useful to the host families concerned. As censuses were only taken every ten years I have no idea how long these arrangements lasted, but certainly by 1851 both David and Robert had moved on.

William had found his way to the Fens, another district where market gardening was becoming common. He was living and working on a farm in Manea, Cambridgeshire, over 30 miles from Potton. I have no idea what happened to him after that. He does not appear in subsequent censuses and may have died between 1841 and 1851, or emigrated. I have searched, but his commonplace Christian name and lack of a middle name have made him impossible to trace so far.

James (my great-great grandfather), George and Jonathan Whitfield were not found living in Potton in 1841. I know from later details that James was back in Potton later in the year, and George returned later in the 1840s. I suspect Jonathan may also have done, but have no evidence for this. What happened to each of them will be revealed in later chapters. It is now time to turn our attention to their sister, Naomi and their older brother, Philip.

Chapter 6.
What happened to Naomi?

'For he shall grow up before him as a tender plant'

Isaiah 42 v2.

Naomi was the eldest child of James and Sarah Whitfield and was baptised in Cople church, Bedfordshire on 18ᵗʰ April, 1815, two months before the battle of Waterloo. I assume she must have moved with her parents to Tewin as she would have only been about four years old at the time. However, I could find no mention of a Naomi Whitfield for a long time, until I was able to make use of the internet. She was not mentioned in the Removal documents.

Unfortunately, a detailed census was not taken for 1831, so I can only speculate, but it seems likely that Naomi and her two brothers Philip and William had already left home by 1833 (the date of the removal document) and were making their own way in the world. It was likely, I thought, that they were working in nearby Hertfordshire parishes if they were not in Tewin. The problem was - which ones? Searching the records of each parish within a circle whose radius was equivalent to a day's walking distance would have been a major undertaking.

The problem was solved by the coming of the internet. I managed to find that Naomi had married a labourer, William Plant, at nearby Sacombe in November, 1833, some seven or eight months after her mother Sarah and her younger sons had arrived in Potton. She was eighteen. Marriages usually took place in the bride's parish, so I have speculated that Naomi may have been in domestic service at one of the farms or larger houses in Sacombe or one of the nearby hamlets: Tonwell, Sacombe Green, Bengeo or Burrs Green. She may have been employed as a servant at Sacombe House, a mansion rebuilt between 1803-1806 for George Caswell, who became High Sheriff of Hertfordshire in 1807. As Sacombe was not far from Tewin - well within a day's comfortable walking distance across the fields - Naomi was probably aware of the death of her father in February, 1833 and the plight of her mother and brothers as they were removed to Potton. However, apart from being genuinely sympathetic, what could she do to help? Money and influence were needed to intervene, and she had neither.

By July, 1834, the couple's first child was baptised at Sacombe: Mary Ann Plant, named after William's mother. She was followed by James, named after Naomi's late father, in 1836, and Maria, named after Naomi's aunt, Maria Berry, in 1838.

The Plants appear to have left little documentary evidence, but thanks to the censuses taken every ten years we are able to have a few glimpses of the family.

The 1851 census shows that the Plant family were living in nearby Bengeo. Agricultural labourers at this time had very little job security and often moved from farm to farm as work became available. There were six children now living at home: James (15) was working as an agricultural labourer and then came Eliza (11), Sarah (9), George (7), Emma (5) and Ellen (1).

By 1861, the family had returned to Sacombe, where they were living at Burrows Green (Burrs Green). The family now included James (25), Emma (15), and working as a servant, Elizabeth (9), John (6), Charles (3) and Mary Ann (1). The name of their youngest child at this time indicates that their eldest child had died.

William and Naomi still had James living with them at Burrows Green in 1871. He was 34. The household also included George (27) a brickmaker, Charles (13) an agricultural labourer and Mary Ann (11), still at school.

The household was much smaller in 1881: James, now working as a shepherd, was living with his widowed mother at Sacombe. They were still living together in 1891.

Naomi died in 1900, aged 85. She must have had a hard life, looking after a large family of at least twelve children. Despite this, she lived longer than any of her brothers. I wonder if she kept in touch with any of them, or they with her? Naomi couldn't write and was probably unable to read. Telephones and emails were unheard of. Perhaps some of them visited her, but somehow I doubt it. They had little free time, and too many problems of their own to sort out. There were more to come, as we shall see in later chapters.

The death of his mother must have been very keenly felt by James Plant, who had lived with her all his life. He was found living in Chapmore End, a few miles south of Sacombe in 1901, with his widowed youngest sister, Mary Ann Harrison: there was the equivalent of almost a generation between them. James died six years later, aged seventy.

The 1901 census also showed that another son of William and Naomi Plant, Charles, had moved to London. He was living in Blackstock Road, Islington with his wife Sarah (born in Linton, Cambridgeshire), and working as an engineer's labourer. They had two sons: William (15), who was working as a house painter, and George J. (12). Both boys had been born in Islington. When the London parish records became available online I discovered that Charles and Sarah, nee Jobson, had married in Islington in 1885; at that time Charles was working as a warehouseman. Sarah had originally moved to London from Cambridgeshire to go into domestic service.

By 1911, Charles Plant had become a jobbing gardener, and his son William Charles was working as a compositor (type setter in the printing trade). Three years later, William Charles, now working as a motor driver, married Sophia Ablin, the daughter of a chef, in Islington. No occupation was given for Sophia on the marriage certificate, but the 1911 census showed that she had been working as a shorthand typist at a solicitor's office. William and Sophia's son, George W. Plant was born in the spring of 1916. The birth was registered in West Ham. I have not yet managed to trace the family further, but it may well be that Naomi Whitfield has some living descendants.

It is now time to follow the fortunes of Naomi's brother Philip, the eldest son of James and Sarah Whitfield.

Chapter 7
Bakers, grocers, farmers and publicans.

'….Give us this day our daily bread…'

from *The Lord's Prayer*.

'Beer, happy Produce of our Isle
Can sinewy Strength impart
And wearied with fatigue and Toil
Can cheer each manly Heart…'

Rev. James Townley, 1751.

Philip Whitfield, named after his father's younger brother, was born and baptised in Cople, Bedfordshire in 1816 and was only about three years old when the family moved to Tewin. His early life is a mystery because his name does not crop up in the Tewin records. Unlike his parents, his sister Naomi and most of his brothers, Philip could sign his name, and it is likely, though not certain, that he could also read. It may be that for a while James and Sarah were able to send their eldest son to school in Tewin, and, as their family grew, they were unable to afford to send the others, or it may be that Philip learnt the basics of literacy a little later in life. He was not mentioned in the Removal documents; by 1833 he would have been seventeen and earning a living. The problem for me was - where? Of course, finding work somewhere may have been a problem for him, too – and a far more pressing one.

Dr. Keith Snell in *Annals of the Labouring Poor: Social Change and Agrarian England 1660-1900* (1985), calculated that the average age at which boys left home to become apprentices was 14.2 years and to commence farm service 14.8 years in South East England. It seems reasonable to suppose, therefore, that Philip could have left home sometime between 1830 and 1833. It may be that he was apprenticed somewhere, and this is where he learnt to read and write. So far I have not managed to find an apprenticeship indenture for him, and as I have no idea where he was living between about 1830 and 1840, the search is likely to continue for a long time.

If Philip was working as an agricultural labourer during some of this period his chance of obtaining work would have declined once the harvest had been gathered in. He may therefore have resorted to attending a hiring fair (a sort of nineteenth century forerunner of the job centre), where unemployed labourers and farm workers such as shepherds, dairymaids and so on met

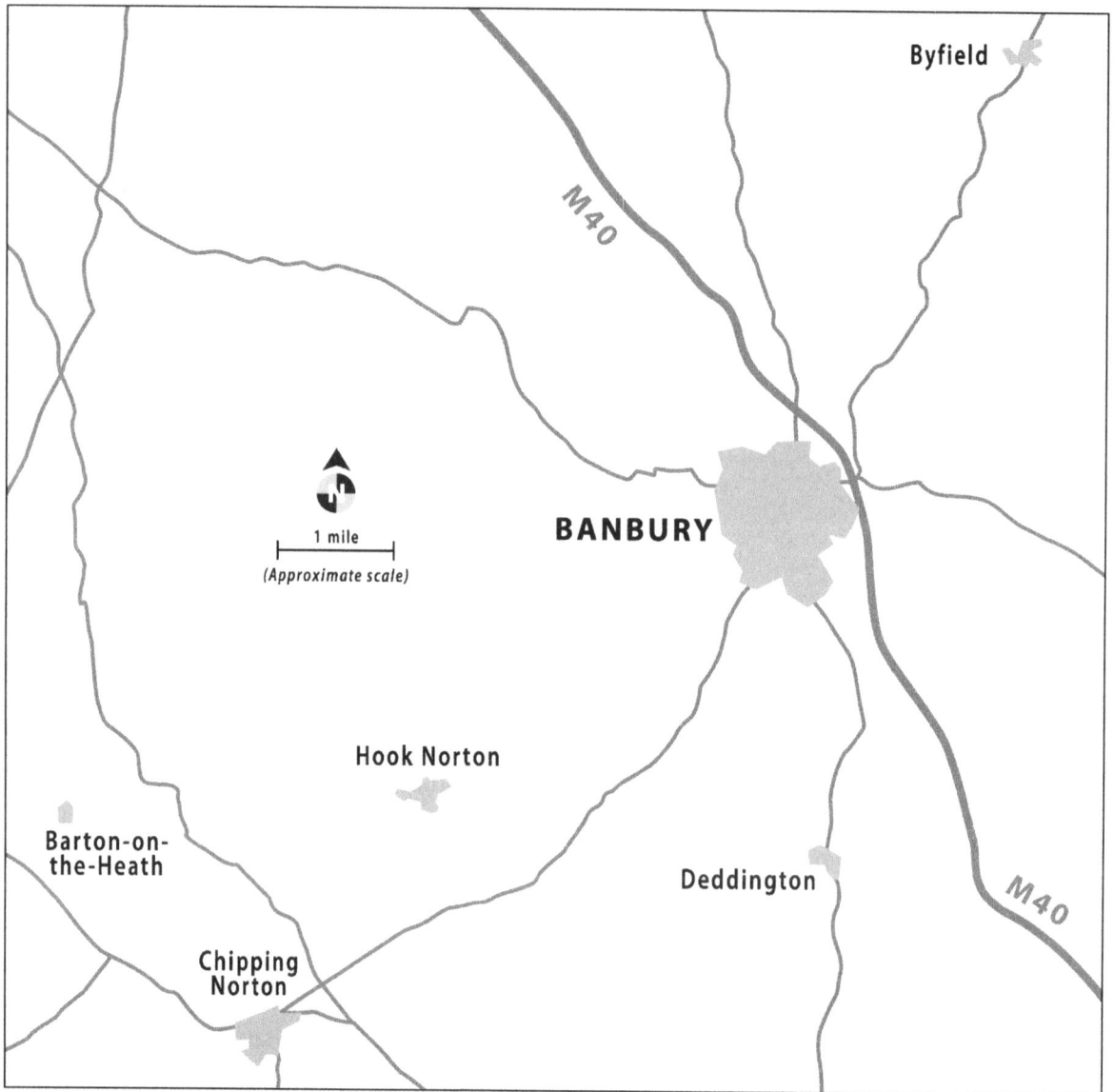

*A map showing settlements associated with the Whitfield family
in the Banbury district of Oxfordshire*

*Philip Whitfield settled in Deddington before moving to Hook Norton in 1841.
He was later joined by his brother David, who operated a carrier's service
between Hook Norton and Banbury, and Hook Norton and Chipping Norton.*

farmers and employers in the hope of securing employment for the coming season. In arable districts these were usually held in autumn around Michaelmas (September 29th) or Martinmas (November 11th). In pastoral districts the fairs were held in the spring. If written records had been kept of the transactions taking place at these events they would make fascinating reading today, enabling family historians to trace the whereabouts of their ancestors and to follow the development of their job histories over time. They would also give economic historians a good idea of the extent to which ordinary people were geographically mobile in the nineteenth century. Unfortunately, as far as I am aware, no such records exist.

For a long time I was unable to trace Philip. I wondered whether he had died in Tewin and for some reason his death hadn't been recorded, but I was grasping at straws. Then, microfiched copies of census records became available, initially, I think, on a county by county basis, and I managed to track him down. The development of the internet has now made this sort of search relatively straightforward – unless your family member was called John Smith, or some other commonplace name.

The 1841 census showed that a Philip Whitfield was living in the small town of Deddington in Oxfordshire, just beyond the Buckinghamshire border and about six miles from Banbury. When I found these details I was still not totally sure that I had found the correct person, because as we have already seen, birthplaces of people are not recorded in the 1841 census. All we get is whether or not a person had been born in the relevant county – in this case, Oxfordshire. This Philip Whitfield hadn't. Assuming that I *had* found the correct person, a number of questions almost inevitably came to my mind. How had he got to Deddington? Had he walked there over a number of days? If so, had he travelled alone? And why head for *Deddington*? It wasn't an obvious choice, at least to me, but of course I was looking at the problem from a modern perspective. I had to try to transport myself back, mentally, to the 1830s in order to try to understand Philip's motives.

Deddington was a small market town; many of its houses were built of the local amber coloured ironstone, especially along New Street, the main street through the town, running roughly North-South carrying traffic from Oxford to Banbury; and in the spacious Market Place. In addition to these substantial houses, there also existed in the nineteenth century many small cottages in courtyards and alleys off the main streets, where labourers lived. Most of these humbler dwellings have now been demolished and the modern visitor thus gets a false impression that the town always had an air of sedate and prosperous gentility. Unfortunately for the town, the weekly Saturday market, which had been held for centuries, had come to an end in 1830. Attempts were made to resurrect it but these were unsuccessful.

Deddington still held three annual fairs which attracted people from miles around. There was one on August 21st for the sale of cattle. The market on October 11th was a statute fair for the hiring of servants and the buying and selling of cattle. A feature of this fair was the ox which was roasted whole in the Market Place. The main fair, however, was held at Martinmas. It was principally for the sale of livestock, but servants and labourers were also hired at this time. The Market Place was reserved for trading in pigs, but the fair spilled over into other parts of the town: sheep were sold in the Bull Ring and horses in the Horse Fair, originally called Huff (or Hoof) Lane, where a number of iron rings, once used for tethering horses, are still fixed to some old ironstone house walls. People flocked into Deddington from far and wide, including drovers of Welsh sheep, Irish horse traders, farmers, dealers and labourers, seeking employment. Philip Whitfield may have been one of them; he had possibly read about Deddington fair in a local newspaper, or he may have heard about it from a waggoner or carrier as he travelled. Human nature being what it is, I expect the gathering also attracted its fair share of pickpockets, quack doctors, drunkards and prostitutes. A lot of money would have been exchanging hands, whether legally or illegally, for all sorts of reasons.

The small town, known by locals as 'dirty, drunken Deddington' was renowned for the quality of its ale, and the innkeepers must have rubbed their hands together gleefully as November 11th approached each year, in anticipation of the trade they would be doing. Deddington bakers also catered for the crowds by providing a local delicacy - pudding pies. These pies comprised a pre-cooked plum pudding filling contained within a pastry case, and were thus a sort of jam tart/Christmas pudding hybrid. So popular were they that the fair became known as the Pudding Pie Fair.

It may be a fanciful notion on my part, but it is possible that Philip arrived in Deddington at the time of one of its bustling fairs. He was probably seeking employment and perhaps he secured a job over a pint of Deddington beer, and one of Bennett's pudding pies. Another more prosaic possibility, of course, was that the Bennetts may have advertised, either for an apprentice, or for a baker. I have searched for such an advertisement, but without success.

The 1841 census details showed that Philip was living in the house of Elizabeth Bennett, a baker's widow. Also in the household were some of Elizabeth's children: Elizabeth, aged 29, and still single, Elias, aged 22, and Martha, aged 17. There was also a Lucy Frances Bennett, aged 3, who was probably a grandchild of Elizabeth, senior.

I have no idea when Philip arrived in Deddington or how long he had been living with the Bennetts. It may be that he learned the art of being a baker with them, or he may have joined them as a journeyman baker, having served an apprenticeship elsewhere. If so, where? There are plenty of unanswered questions. What I *do* know is that just over a fortnight after the Census enumerator knocked on the bakery door to ask Mrs Bennett about details of her household, Philip Whitfield and Elizabeth Bennett (junior) were no longer single. Their marriage took place in the church of St. Peter and St. Paul, Deddington on 23rd June, 1841. Philip's father was given as James Whitfield, gamekeeper, on the certificate, confirming that I *had* found the correct person.

I was fortunate in discovering that the vicar of Deddington at this time, the Reverend William Cotton Risley (1798- 1869) kept a diary. The volumes of this diary have been edited, and even in the edited version, mention is made of Philip and Elizabeth's wedding, at which Risley officiated. The diary also records information about the Bennett family (Philip's in-laws) and gives some details of their business interests. Many Deddington people, whether 'gentry', professionals, tradesmen or labourers feature in the diary for all sorts of reasons, and reading even the edited version enabled me to bring early Victorian Deddington to life. I was so fascinated by its contents that I decided to consult the original volumes which have been entrusted to the care of the Bodleian Library, Oxford.

The diary reveals that Thomas Bennett, Philip Whitfield's father in law, had died in 1839, aged 56. He had been well known to Risley because he had held the office of parish clerk for a while, and had been the Deddington postmaster from 1833 as well as being a baker. He appears to have been a shrewd businessman too, owning some land in Deddington and some property which was rented out to tenants. Risley mentions helping with haymaking in Thomas Bennett's field, and he also records that Bennett liked to grow auriculas. He (Bennett) presented one to Risley, and - businessman that he was - sold him another. Philip's future father-in-law was also interested in music. He certainly owned some music books, but it isn't made clear whether he played an instrument, sang, or both. He may well have been a member of a 'west gallery' band of musicians playing in the church before they were replaced by the organ; Risley's diary mentions the removal of the gallery in order to accommodate the new instrument.

After Thomas Bennett's death, his widow Elizabeth kept the bakery business going from their premises on the corner of New Street and The Stile. (The house is still there). William Cotton Risley lived on the opposite side of the street, and he was a frequent visitor to the baker's shop for a number of reasons. He bought bread, cakes, biscuits and sometimes hot cross buns, pudding pies, bacon and even (surprisingly) lollipops there; and he supplied the Bennett family with thorn faggots for their bread ovens. These were almost certainly cut from hedges on Risley's land, for, in addition to his responsibility for the cure of souls in the parish, he also had farming interests. In addition, Lucy Bennett, one of Elizabeth Bennett's daughters (who was not mentioned on the census return) was a schoolmistress, and, as Risley collected the school payments, appointed the staff and was also possibly a school governor, he often needed to speak to her. Lucy also sang at the church - Risley commented on her rich voice - and directed the girls' choir. She and Risley sometimes exchanged music and he seems to have been very fond of her.

Reading between the lines, Risley's diary suggests that he was a kindly priest, genuinely interested in, and caring for his flock of parishioners, but he was also a realist and a practical man as he attended to his farming activities. Risley was also a keen amateur gardener. From reports of prize winners at a number of Deddington Shows, I discovered that he grew apples, pears, plums, grapes, peaches, apricots, white and red currants, peas, celery, lettuce, kidney beans, onions carrots, potatoes and parsnips to a high standard. He also encouraged other gardeners in the parish by donating a prize to be awarded each year for the best-cultivated garden.

Although Risley was much richer and better educated than most of his neighbours he does not appear to have been an aloof and distant figure. The *Oxford Chronicle* reported in January, 1841, that Risley had distributed several sheep (presumably for their meat) and 'a proportionate quantity of bread' to the needy in Deddington. What a lovely man to have to conduct your wedding service! I can imagine him conducting the ceremony with muddy boots under his cassock and dirt under his fingernails and rushing off afterwards to check on his hay crop. From his accounts of his daily activities in early Victorian Deddington, fascinating in their own right, I was able to build up a picture of what life must have been like for Philip and the Bennetts.

It wasn't idyllic. A little earlier in 1841, Lucy Bennett the schoolmistress (Elizabeth's sister) had contracted a virulent fever, and despite medical attention - we have rather gruesome details of leeches and poultices being applied to her shaven head and the house being fumigated - she died in April, aged just 24. Risley conducted her funeral service and was clearly much moved by her early death. Another sister, Lydia, had also died in her twenties of a 'decline' after her father's death in 1839. This could have been due to consumption, as tuberculosis was then called, but it may have been a case of what we now call anorexia nervosa.

The Bennetts do not seem to have been a long-lived family, even by nineteenth century standards, but they were an interesting bunch of characters. As well as poor Lucy and Lydia there was their brother Elias, the baker, a rather ambitious young man who appears to have needed a little guidance at times after the death of his father. Elias later established his own butcher's shop in the town. Risley took an almost fatherly interest in him, giving him advice and sometimes practical assistance, such as the time when he presented the young man with a sheep from his farm when he was setting up the business and then ordered a leg of mutton and a leg of pork from him as one of his new customers. Risley also went on fishing trips with Elias and some other Deddington tradesmen. Elias later became a farmer in Deddington before he, like his father and grandfather before him, died in his fifties. Elias' brother Thomas (junior) joined the army and served in India. Another brother, William, was wayward and 'riotous', and probably over-fond of alcohol. He made an appearance in Deddington (and in Risley's diary) from time to time, and his visits usually caused trouble. He, too, died young. Risley asked another sister, Martha, to become a teacher at Deddington School after the death of Lucy Bennett. She declined and continued to work at the bakery, but a seed had been sown in her mind …

After he had conducted Philip and Elizabeth's marriage service, Risley noted that in the evening he went to sit with 'old Mrs Bennett' (I was somewhat disconcerted to discover that she was around sixty at the time), when the rest of the family were at the wedding reception, which was held at the house of Samuel Stilgoe and his wife Ann (Philip's new sister-in-law) at nearby Charlton. While they were making merry they were, of course, blissfully unaware that their young host and hostess would both be in their graves about two years later. Life in the early part of the nineteenth century could be harsh and unpredictable. 'Old Mrs Bennett' also died around this time, apparently from 'constipation of the bowels', although I suspect that there may have been something more sinister causing the symptoms. Risley commented with only a modicum of tact that she was '…a very large woman indeed and upwards of sixty years of age', which appears to have been considered a fairly advanced age in those days. Perhaps Mrs Bennett found it hard to resist the various tempting products of her bakery. I wonder if her daughter and namesake Elizabeth Bennett, now Elizabeth Whitfield, was also a buxom lass? Philip obviously knew, but it is unlikely that *I* shall find out because I suspect she never had her photograph taken.

Risley commented in his diary that the newly-married couple were to 'settle in Hook Norton in the bakery business'. As Philip and Elizabeth were not mentioned in the diary after a few days I suspect that the move to Hook Norton took place soon after the wedding. I have not managed to find out with certainty when Philip had bought a baker's premises and business. I wondered whether he had purchased a going concern or whether he and Elizabeth had to start from scratch. The venture appears to have been a bold move because Hook Norton already had some bakers, and I therefore figured that a pre-existing business with its (hopefully) loyal customers and goodwill had been purchased. I assumed that the premises and business would have been advertised and discovered an interesting notice of sale in the *Oxford Journal* of Saturday, 25th April, 1840:

> Hook Norton, Oxfordshire
> To Bakers and Others
> To be sold by auction, by Sotham and Wing
> At the Bell Inn, in Hook Norton, on Friday 1st day of May, 1840 at 5 o'clock in the afternoon. A freehold messuage or tenement and premises consisting of dwelling room, kitchen, good bake-house and oven, three bedrooms and attics, two meal rooms, yard, stable, hovel and other conveniences, situate at Hook Norton aforesaid, and lately occupied by Mr Richard Rowles. Immediate possession will be given…'

I feel fairly confident that Philip Whitfield was in the *Bell Inn* on that afternoon in 1840 and was successful at the auction. He probably enjoyed a celebratory drink or two before he returned to Deddington.

It would probably have taken a few months to complete the legal formalities, and it may well be that there was a certain amount of building work and general cleaning up to be done before Philip and Elizabeth were able to trade from the premises. It would appear that Richard Rowles had not been prospering there: I discovered from an earlier edition of the *Oxford Journal* that his creditors had been given notice to make their claims by 1st May, 1836. I suspect that the aptly-named baker was elderly; perhaps his bread was not liked or he had allowed standards to fall. If I am correct in my assumptions about Philip's purchase it would appear that he and Elizabeth had to work hard to build up the business and maybe tempt Mr Rowles' former customers to revisit the bakery.

Hook Norton was (and still is) a beautiful medium-sized village set in rural surroundings in North Oxfordshire, about eight miles from Banbury and five miles from Chipping Norton. As in Deddington, most of the older houses are built from the local orange/brown ironstones. Nestling amongst rolling hills which rise to around 650 feet, the village is long and straggling. Many of its streets are narrow and some are also steep, as I discovered when I trudged up from the valley of the little River Swere (after a fruitless search of the cemetery) towards St. Peter's Church. Near the church, the main street opens out into an area which could have been used as a small market place. It now serves as a car park for the *Sun* public house. According to Kate Tiller, who wrote a chapter on Hook Norton in *Rural England - an illustrated history of the Landscape*, (Oxford University Press, 2000), Hook Norton was 'a large, diverse and vigorous village society, but it never developed as a market town'. She went on to say that in the mid-nineteenth century, Hook Norton had

'….numerous farmers, high poor rates, a wide range of rural industries and crafts, many shops and pubs, a large housing stock in diverse ownership, an absence of large estates or resident gentry, a strong tradition of religious non-conformity…and a reputation for independence'.

It was ideal territory, in many ways, for an enterprising member of the Whitfield family and his wife.

Victorian trade directories testify to the number and variety of Hook Norton's tradesmen, and Philip Whitfield, as a baker, is mentioned amongst them. Other bakers are also mentioned;

perhaps Philip felt more comfortable competing with them than with his brother in law, Elias Bennett, and others, in Deddington.

Bakers were important members of any village community. Bread was one of the most important items of the Victorian diet and most people ate a lot of it; apparently it was quite common for adults to eat 1lb. of bread per person per day. It was filling and thus staved off hunger pangs, and, although they may not have realised it (vitamins had not yet been 'discovered'), it was also nutritious. It was a major component of the average labourer's weekly expenditure. Bread historian Christian Petersen states that up to eighty per cent of household expenditure in the nineteenth century was on food, and, of this, up to eighty per cent was spent on bread. This makes sense: at that time many more people would have grown their own vegetables; and meat, apart from the occasional poached rabbit, hare or pheasant, would have been an infrequent luxury for most ordinary families.

Many housewives at this time would not have done their cooking in an oven; their vegetables and the occasional piece of meat would have been cooked in a pot suspended over an open fire. Some housewives who wanted home-produced bread raised their own dough and took it to the baker to put in his oven, and in some rural or working class districts people even brought their Sunday joints of meat - if they were lucky enough to have them - to be roasted in the baker's oven, collecting them after the church service. This must have given them something else to think about during the traditionally long sermons of the period, particularly if 'burnt offerings' had been mentioned in Old Testament readings earlier.

Bread making was seen as a man's job. In the days before mechanisation it involved a lot of hard manual work: heavy sacks of flour needed to be lifted and the mixing and kneading of the dough required a lot of upper body strength. The air in the bakery would have been laden with dust from the flour and smoke from the burning thorn faggots which were placed in the brick oven to provide the necessary heat. A Parliamentary investigation undertaken in 1862 found that many bakeries also had ' … masses of cobwebs weighed down with flour dust that had accumulated upon them, hanging in strips'. Insects and vermin were other problems encountered. It may be that Richard Rowles, (Philip's predecessor) had allowed his standards of cleanliness to fall. Hopefully, Philip's premises were more hygienic. Many Victorian bakers did not live to a great age because of the unhealthy conditions they worked in which eventually took their toll and undermined the healthiest constitutions.

Baking involved a regular early morning routine which usually started while it was still dark. Firstly, ingredients would be assembled. The flour which had either been fetched from the miller or had been delivered by him, was presumably stored on the premises. Water would have to be fetched from a spring or a well: it was most unlikely that rural premises in the early Victorian period would have had piped water and the luxury of a tap to dispense it. Many Victorian bakers apparently obtained their yeast from beer brewers. It may well be that once Philip's business became established he obtained his yeast from the Hook Norton brewery which was started by John Harris, a maltster and farmer who arrived in the village in 1849. As Hook Norton's population at this time was little more than 1500 people, the two men must have known each other. (The brewery is still there today and is being run by John Harris' descendants. Naturally, I have sampled the local brew - I try to be thorough in my research.

The brewery still obtains its water from springs issuing from hills above the west of the village and produces a varied range of real ales and stouts which continue to be delivered by horse and cart to pubs in the local area).

I suspect I was not the first Whitfield to enjoy a pint of Hook Norton beer at the *Pear Tree*, an unspoilt public house literally a stone's throw from the brewery. On another occasion I was able to slake my thirst with another excellent pint of 'Old Hooky' and enjoy a steak and ale pie with a selection of vegetables at the *Sun*, opposite the parish church. It's thirsty and hungry work being a genealogist.

Philip would have mixed the wheat flour, water, yeast and salt in a wooden trough, using a wooden 'paddle'. The dough had to be worked to an even consistency and needed to be free from lumps. It was then left to rise. As this process could take several hours it could have been done the previous night.

Victorian bakers like Philip would have used a brick built oven, with a tiled floor. It would probably have had room for about 150 quartern loaves. A Deddington bakery advertised for sale in the *Oxford Journal* in October, 1835 had an oven measuring 9 feet x 7½ feet and I assume Philip's oven was of a similar size. Such ovens were heated by coal or by thorn faggots. The latter were favoured by Philip's in-laws, the Bennetts, in Deddington, and as Hook Norton was remote from coal mining areas, and there must have been a plentiful supply of faggots from hawthorn hedges nearby, presumably Philip did the same. The faggots would have been stored in an outhouse on the premises.

Having lit the oven, Philip would have had to wait until the faggots had become embers, and the cinders would have been raked over to encourage them to drop into a grate beneath the oven. By this time, the oven would have become very hot, and the smoke would have died down. While all this was going on, the dough would have been re-kneaded by Philip or his assistant, allowed to rise and then shaped into loaf-sized pieces. Philip would have tested the oven's temperature by throwing in a little flour onto the oven floor. If it browned, but didn't burn, the oven was at the correct temperature. The loaves were then fed in, using a wooden shovel-like implement called a peel. (My grandmother, Mildred Mingay, nee Hiskey (1901-2000), maker of many a tasty wholemeal loaf, recalled *her* mother making bread in a brick oven and using such an implement in Edwardian times). The larger loaves were placed at the back of the oven which tended to be hotter - they really needed to spend longer in the oven. When the oven was full, the heavy metal door was closed and the loaves were left to bake for about two hours. I would imagine that baking bread in a brick oven was an art rather than an exact science, and experience would have been essential for a successful outcome. In Philip's case, the outcome must have *been* successful, because he remained as a baker in the village for many years. Dissatisfied customers would soon have transferred their allegiance to one of his competitors; the word would have spread quickly in a small village and his reputation (and business) could have been ruined.

Cakes and biscuits were more labour-intensive but could bring in extra profit. As we have seen, a variety of these were made by the Bennetts in Deddington; Philip possibly had the skills and the experience to do the same, but from the 1840s onwards machines were invented for biscuit making on a large scale and so increasingly there was competition from firms such

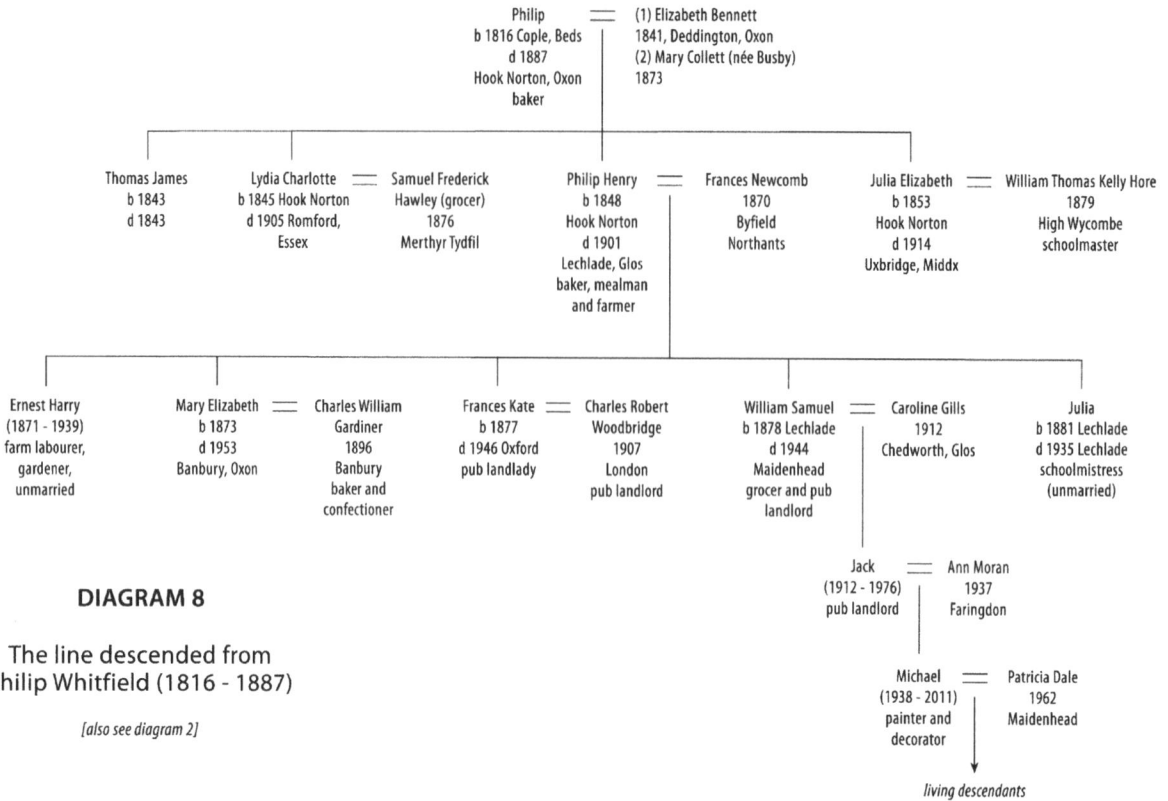

DIAGRAM 8

The line descended from
Philip Whitfield (1816 - 1887)

[also see diagram 2]

Philip
b 1816 Cople, Beds
d 1887
Hook Norton, Oxon
baker
═ (1) Elizabeth Bennett
1841, Deddington, Oxon
(2) Mary Collett (née Busby)
1873

Children of Philip:

Thomas James
b 1843
d 1843

Lydia Charlotte
b 1845 Hook Norton
d 1905 Romford,
Essex
═ Samuel Frederick
Hawley (grocer)
1876
Merthyr Tydfil

Philip Henry
b 1848
Hook Norton
d 1901
Lechlade, Glos
baker, mealman
and farmer
═ Frances Newcomb
1870
Byfield
Northants

Julia Elizabeth
b 1853
Hook Norton
d 1914
Uxbridge, Middx
═ William Thomas Kelly Hore
1879
High Wycombe
schoolmaster

Children of Philip Henry:

Ernest Harry
(1871 - 1939)
farm labourer,
gardener,
unmarried

Mary Elizabeth
b 1873
d 1953
Banbury, Oxon
═ Charles William
Gardiner
1896
Banbury
baker and
confectioner

Frances Kate
b 1877
d 1946 Oxford
pub landlady
═ Charles Robert
Woodbridge
1907
London
pub landlord

William Samuel
b 1878 Lechlade
d 1944
Maidenhead
grocer and pub
landlord
═ Caroline Gills
1912
Chedworth, Glos

Julia
b 1881 Lechlade
d 1935 Lechlade
schoolmistress
(unmarried)

Jack
(1912 - 1976)
pub landlord
═ Ann Moran
1937
Faringdon

Michael
(1938 - 2011)
painter and
decorator
═ Patricia Dale
1962
Maidenhead

↓ *living descendants*

---

as Huntley and Palmer of Reading (established in 1846) who could afford to mechanise. It is likely that Philip kept account books showing items sold and prices obtained, but as far as I am aware, none has survived, so I can only speculate about the more unusual items from his bakery which the inhabitants of Hook Norton and district may have enjoyed. It would be interesting to know, for instance, whether he introduced the delights of pudding pies to the village.

The Hook Norton parish registers record the baptism of Philip and Elizabeth's first child, Thomas James, named after his late grandfathers, in 1843. Unfortunately, they also record his death some three months later. By 1851, two other children had been born to the couple: Lydia Charlotte, named after two of Elizabeth's late sisters, and Philip Henry, named after his father and late uncle (born in Tewin in 1829 or 1830). Philip's youngest brother, David, also born in Tewin in 1829/1830, a fact confirmed by the census form, now formed part of the household; there will be more about him in a later chapter. Philip's birthplace was given as '*Copel*', Beds. It would appear that Philip's business was expanding because Elizabeth's younger sister, Martha Bennett, aged 26 was working as a baker's assistant, and there was also an errand boy, William Wheeler, living on the premises. If young Master Wheeler had kept a daily notebook of the errands he was asked to run they would make fascinating reading now. Philip was clearly doing well: he was mentioned in a voters' list for 1852. He was entitled to vote because he apparently owned freehold houses in Hook Norton. Clearly he was both hard working and enterprising. He may well have been encouraged to buy additional property by his wife, Elizabeth; her father had owned a number of properties in Deddington.

The 1861 census reveals that there was another child in the household. (Julia Elizabeth, aged seven), and although David had moved out, Martha Bennett was still living with the family. However, she was now a school mistress in the National School at Hook Norton. William Cotton Risley's suggestion about her working in the classroom had finally borne fruit.

By the 1860s, Philip had become well-established as a baker in Hook Norton and it seems likely that he was prospering as a result of his labours. The *Oxford Journal* makes it clear that he was one of the bakers selected to provide bread for the local Guardians of the Poor; in 1854 his successful tender had been for 6d per loaf; three years later the price had dropped to 5½d per loaf and by 1860 to 4½d . Thirteen years later the price had increased to 7½d, only to drop to 5½d the following year. These prices, obtained from reports in the local newspapers, probably reflect the fluctuating price of wheat, and thus of flour, presumably one of Philip's main costs. Philip must have been a capable and astute businessman to continue to obtain custom in this way. He had to be able to tender at a price that would keep him operating at a profit, but one which would be more acceptable than the prices quoted by his competitors. Hopefully the quality of the bread he supplied was another important consideration. These guaranteed bulk orders must have helped him enormously, and kept him busy. I would imagine that the loaves were probably delivered by his brother, David. They were catering for paupers in Hook Norton, Sibford Ferris and Sibford Gower, (two small villages situated in very rural surroundings a few miles north of Hook Norton), but must have also had a round of regular domestic customers in the local area. Philip's bread may also have been eaten in Banbury workhouse.

It would appear, however, that not every one of Philip's customers paid up promptly. The *Oxford Times* of Saturday, 21st December, 1867 reported that Philip Whitfield of Hook Norton, baker, had taken a surgeon, Thomas Walker, also of Hook Norton, to the County Court on December 14th for the non- payment of £6 9s 10d for bread. Presumably the debt had been allowed to accumulate for some time. Although the amount owed appears to be a trifling sum today, it must be remembered that agricultural labourers at this time would have been earning no more than about eleven or twelve shillings a week. As no defence was offered by the surgeon, Philip won the case and Walker was ordered to pay the bill, plus costs, in two instalments.

Philip's wife, Elizabeth, died in 1870 aged 58, and in the census details of the following year I found that Philip had engaged the services of a housekeeper: it would have been difficult for him to attend to household tasks while he had a bakery business to run. Mary Collett, nee Busby, was a widow who had been born in nearby Swerford. Her brother, Joseph Busby, a retired farmer, lived next door to Philip and may well have recommended Mary's services; alternatively Philip may have met her when she was visiting Joseph. Mary had been a widow for a long time. In 1851 she was earning her living by working as a nurse in St.John's Wood, Middlesex, in the household of Jackson John Smyth, a Professor of Languages and his family, while her young son, John Collett, was being looked after by his grandmother back in Swerford. Clearly, then, although she had been born locally, Mary had experienced a very different way of life in her younger days, and this may well have broadened her outlook. She was to become Philip's second wife: the couple married in 1873.

Poor John Collett (Mary's son) became a carpenter, but suffered from three attacks of rheumatic fever. He lived for a while in Birmingham, but eventually returned to Hook Norton for a change of air, staying with his mother and stepfather. The *Oxford Journal* of 8th February, 1879 reported his sudden death from heart disease at the age of 32, which occurred while he was out for a walk in Sibford Ferris. Although they would have realised that John was not in the best of health, this still must have been a shock for Mary and Philip. John must have been well aware of his illness: the report stated that one of the items found in his pockets was a *life assurance policy* - a rather strange item to take when out walking on a cold morning, I would have thought. The inquest ruled out the possibility of suicide.

The 1871 census details showed that Philip's son, Philip Henry, had moved out of the bakery. He had married during the previous year. His bride was Frances Newcomb of Byfield, Northamptonshire, a village north of Banbury. She was the daughter of Samuel Newcomb, who, in addition to being a shoemaker, also found the time and the energy to run the *Bell* public house at Byfield. Perhaps it was at this pub that the couple met, but this is conjecture on my part. Philip Henry was working as a baker, like his father and grandfather before him, but various directories in the 1870s describe him as a baker and mealman, i.e. a dealer in milled grain or flour, and sometimes as a baker and farmer. Perhaps he was selling meal at Byfield? He must have travelled further afield than his home village to do much trade.

An advertisement found in the *Oxford Journal* of Saturday 23rd April, 1870 enabled me to find out a few more details about Philip Henry at this time. It showed that he was living in the centre of Hook Norton in a stone-built house which also had a bake house, meal rooms and outbuildings; the property was to be sold by auction at the *Bell Inn*, Hook Norton, on the 3rd May. It wasn't made clear whether Philip Henry's tenancy was to be allowed to continue after the sale had been completed. I'm not sure whether Philip Henry attended the auction, but consider it highly likely that he did.

Lydia Charlotte Whitfield and her sister Julia Elizabeth occupied another property in Hook Norton in 1871. Lydia, now aged 25, was working as a grocer; the business may well have been financed by her father, who presumably had also bought or hired the premises. It would have been fairly unusual, I would have thought, for a young woman in mid-Victorian times to set up in business on her own, and the venture may well have been a talking point in Hook Norton at the time. Lydia must have been an independent and emancipated young woman. Julia Elizabeth, aged 17, had become a pupil teacher - a role somewhat like that of a modern teaching assistant - and was thus following in the footsteps of her aunt Martha and her late aunt Lucy Bennett. They had a fourteen year old domestic servant, Eliza Butters, living with them. One of them was also a singer: the *Oxford Journal* of 13th April, 1872 reported on a concert which took place at the National School in Hook Norton, and mentioned that Miss Whitfield's solo had received a deserved encore. As this Miss Whitfield was also mentioned as being involved in helping to organise the concert, I am inclined to think that it was Julia. I wonder how her voice compared to that of her late aunt, Lucy Bennett, whose singing had been commented on so favourably by William Cotton Risley in his diary? I discovered that Julia (or was it Lydia?) had a soprano voice, because at an earlier Hook Norton concert (in 1866) she had planned to sing 'But thou didst not leave' from Handel's *Messiah*, an aria normally rendered by a soprano, but was in fact prevented from doing so by a severe cold. The audience, comprising (according to the newspaper article) 'members of all the most respectable families of the place' must have been disappointed at her absence, but the concert was still a success and they 'manifested their approbation in the usual way'.

In 1871 there were 21 farmers in Hook Norton, and over ten per cent of the village's population consisted of craftsmen and tradesmen. Kate Tiller believes that this variety and mix of enterprises helped to buffer the village from the worst effects of the agricultural depression which set in after 1873. A complex mixture of poor weather, disastrous harvests, unhelpful Government economic policies (some things never change) and agricultural developments in the U.S.A., was to leave its mark on England, and, as ripples in a pond spread outwards from its centre, even rural backwaters like Hook Norton did not entirely escape. Various members of the family were affected by these developments - not just in Oxfordshire - and they responded in different ways, as we shall see.

At the Oxfordshire Record Office I managed to find an interesting agreement drawn up in 1872 between Susanna Hollier of Hook Norton and Philip Henry Whitfield. It may well represent Philip Henry's first venture into farming. Under the terms of the agreement, he was to have the tenancy of some land in Hook Norton parish, just outside the village itself, comprising nearly 29 acres. There were four fields: Shepherd's Bush (nearly 14 acres), the Triangle (about 2¾ acres), the Barn Ground (nearly 4¾ acres) and the Hill Ground (about 6½ acres). Philip Henry was to have the tenancy for seven years from October, 1871, paying a rent of £70 by equal quarterly instalments. He was to cultivate the land according to the five field course system of husbandry (presumably some kind of crop rotation). Various stipulations were made regarding the crops to be grown, and what he was to do with them, the use of manures and the need to keep gates, ditches and barns in good repair. Both parties to the agreement signed their names and affixed their seals at the bottom of a very impressive looking document. Philip Henry's signature is in a bold, practised and confident hand and appears to have been executed with a flourish. His confidence and optimism may have been misplaced; he could not have foreseen events which were to follow.

The historian G.M.Trevelyan, writing in 1944 stated

'The greatest single event of the seventies [i.e.1870s], fraught with immeasurable consequences for the future, was the sudden collapse of English agriculture. From 1875 onwards, the catastrophe set in. A series of bad harvests aggravated its initial stages, but the cause was the development of the American prairies as grain lands within reach of the English market. The new agricultural machinery enabled farmers of the middle West to skim the cream of the virgin soils of unlimited expanse; the new railway system carried the produce to the ports; the new steamers bore it across the Atlantic. English agriculture was more scientific and more highly capitalised than America's, but under these conditions the odds were too great. Mass production of crops by a simpler and cheaper process undercut the elaborate and expensive methods of farming which had been built up on well-managed English estates during the previous two hundred years. In 1846, Disraeli had prophesied the ruin of agriculture as an inevitable result of Free Trade in corn. For thirty years he had been wrong, but in the 1870s as Prime Minister he did nothing [about it] and the English cornfields were decimated. Statesmen regarded the fate of agriculture with indifference because it did not involve an acute problem with unemployment. As farm labourers lost their jobs they slipped away to find work in the towns or emigrated to the colonies or to the United States'.

This statement is very pertinent to the fate of several members of the Whitfield family.

It was very easy for a scholar like Trevelyan to write this, of course, because he had the benefit of hindsight. The situation could not have happened overnight, and ambitious, practical young men like Philip Henry had day to day decisions to make. Clearly, they could not predict what would happen in the future any more than we can today. We cannot foresee or accurately predict rises in interest rates or crashes in property prices, for example. Even so-called experts disagree about such things and about the measures needed to correct them. As far as Philip Henry was concerned he probably harboured an ambition to become a farmer. Here was an opportunity - and he seized it.

As it happened, it was Susanna Hollier who broke the agreement. At the time the document was drawn up she was living just four doors away from Philip Henry in Hook Norton. She had inherited the land from her father, Robert Salmon, who had been a baker in the village. A widow, Susanna was living with her daughter and son in law, Annie and William Burgess. They were not to remain in the village for long. I found a conveyance (on the National Archives website) dated 1st February, 1875, where Susanna sold the land to James Luckett, farmer and land agent of Hook Norton for £450. Somewhat mysteriously, Susanna's address on the conveyance was given as 'formerly of Hook Norton, now of Crete, Saline, Nebraska, USA.' A little research showed me that Susanna had emigrated to the U.S.A. with Annie and William Burgess and their young family. On the ancestry website, I found them living at Big Blue Precinct, Saline County, Nebraska in the 1880 census. William was farming, and presumably the £450 realised from the Hook Norton land sale had come in useful somewhere along the line. He was benefitting from the advantages America had to offer, whereas Philip Henry had to survive back in Oxfordshire after his venture into farming had come to what may have been a premature and unsatisfactory end. Hopefully his bakery and meal business tided him over. He must, surely, have thought long and hard about raising enough money to buy Mrs Hollier's land himself and indeed may have taken steps in preparation for doing so. The land was advertised in various editions of the *Oxford Journal*, and was sold at an auction held on 24th September, 1874 at the *White Horse Hotel*, Banbury, which Philip Henry may well have attended. James Luckett, the successful purchaser, was a single man of 52 who farmed ninety acres, employing three men and two boys. He lived in Hook Norton with his elderly, widowed mother, who was also a landowner. They must have had more financial clout than Philip Henry who, aged about thirty in 1874, had a wife and young family to support and consider. If he *was* present at the auction, Philip Henry's heart probably sank when he saw that James Luckett was bidding for the land.

It seems unlikely that Luckett allowed Philip Henry to continue with his tenancy after the land was sold because by 1875 the ambitious young man had taken on another tenancy, this time on a yearly basis. This land had a frontage to the main road between Hook Norton and Chipping Norton, and consisted of 'two Enclosures of valuable Arable land, and a Piece or Parcel of rich Pasture land, containing by admeasurement 15A, 0R, 30P, more or less'. The yearly rent was £40. The arable land was considered to be 'well adapted for the growth of all kinds of grain and roots'. I am able to supply these details because the land was later sold by auction and was therefore advertised in the *Oxford Journal* of Saturday 14th October, 1876. Again, Philip Henry's farming ambitions had been nipped in the bud; I assume he attended the auction but was unsuccessful.

I must now jump forward in time by some eleven years or so, to shed some light on Philip Henry's next move. Philip Whitfield, his father, died on 29th December, 1887, the year of Queen Victoria's Golden Jubilee, and I managed, thanks to the National Probate Index, which is now online, to find his will. I had been convinced for a long time that he must have made one. The will is a business-like document in which he left his household effects to his wife Mary (who died a couple of years afterwards), and money to his daughters Lydia and Julia. I was disappointed that the contents and stock-in-trade of his baker's premises were not itemised, or even mentioned. He had perhaps already retired (he was 70 or 71 when he died), but somehow I doubt it: there were no nationally organised pensions at that time, and the directories of the period still list him as a baker. The really interesting snippet of information for me was that the will mentions that Philip had re-mortgaged his property in Hook Norton (presumably the bakery) to provide five hundred pounds for Philip Henry in 1877. This money had not all been repaid some ten years later. It now became clear to me how Philip Henry, clearly an ambitious man, had been able to finance his next venture - a move to Lechlade in Gloucestershire, where he took on the tenancy of Manor Farm, a farm of nearly three hundred acres.

By 1877 Philip Henry had a wife and three children; he had never farmed on this scale before - his expertise was really in baking. However, his father believed in him and was prepared to offer his only surviving son some financial assistance so that he could realise his ambition of becoming a farmer. The first child of Philip Henry and Frances Whitfield was Ernest Harry, born in 1871. Their next child was a daughter, Mary Elizabeth, named after Philip Henry's stepmother and mother, born in 1873. Frances Kate, their next child, was baptised in Hook Norton church in 1877. I wonder if the family returned to Hook Norton for the baptism or whether they were still living in the village. The precise date of the move to Lechlade is not known, but it must have been after October 1876 (the date when the 15 acres of land Philip Henry had been farming in Hook Norton were sold by auction at the *George Inn*, Brailes), and probably after 1877 when Philip remortgaged his property. Philip Henry was certainly living at Lechlade by 1878, because the *Swindon Advertiser and North Wiltshire Chronicle* of 15th June in that year recorded that he had been found guilty at Fairford Petty Sessions of keeping a dog without a licence. I would imagine that he was far from delighted at having to pay a fine of £1 5s for what appears to have been a very trivial offence.

The 1881 census shows Philip Henry and Frances living at Manor Farm, Lechlade, with their family. They employed four men and two boys on the farm and also had two domestic servants - almost unheard of in the Whitfield family. The farmhouse was a large one, having six bedrooms and a bathroom and water closet on the upper floor, according to a later sale catalogue. The bathroom and W.C. may have been later additions; if they *were* there in 1881 they would have been the height of luxury. I wonder if Philip and Mary were ever invited to take time off from baking at Hook Norton and visit? After all, it was some of Philip's money that had helped to make this new life possible. If they were able to make the journey they would probably have been impressed with the downstairs accommodation, which included dining, drawing and sitting rooms in addition to a kitchen, pantry, dairy and washhouse, where presumably the domestic servants would have been kept busy. There was even a cellar, though hopefully Philip Henry had not developed too much of a taste for wine as he had not yet repaid his father.

In the yard, Philip Henry would have been able to show his elderly father and stepmother a two stalled stable, stalling for eleven cows (why *eleven* I wonder?), a hay shed with granary over, another open cattle shed for ten beasts, stalling for twelve beasts, paved standing for ten carthorses and other cattle sheds and piggeries. I feel sure that Philip would have been impressed, and he might have wished that *he* had had a chance to start farming when he was a young man. I can't help feeling that *his* father, James Whitfield, (the gamekeeper) would have loved the place, and would probably have been amused that one of his grandsons was actually employing servants. The owner of the farm was George Milward, the Lord of the Manor of Lechlade, who also owned a baker's shop in the little Thames-side town. I wonder whether Philip Henry continued with his baking once he arrived in Gloucestershire? My guess is that with the farm to manage and a wife and young family to provide for, there probably wasn't time. The two younger children of Philip Henry and Frances Whitfield: William Samuel and Julia, were baptised in Lechlade, in 1879 and 1882 respectively.

The Whitfields apparently lived at Manor Farm for 'about ten years'. (My source of information was an obituary in the *Lechlade Parish Magazine*). The *Western Times* of Friday, 26th March, 1886 stated that Manor Farm, Lechlade was to be let from Michaelmas, 1886; the farm comprised just over 297 acres, of which just over 118 acres were under meadow and pasture and the remainder arable. A farm of this size must have taken an enormous amount of time and effort to work, particularly in the days before large scale mechanisation. By 1891, the census for Lechlade shows that Frances, aged 46, was now living at Thornhill Farm (on the road to Fairford) with Ernest Harry, now aged 19, Frances Kate, (15), William Samuel, (12) and Julia (10). The strange thing was that Philip Henry was found at a separate address. Described as a farmer, and married, he was lodging at the *Crown Inn* in Lechlade High Street. Why he should be staying there is a mystery, and all kinds of explanations could be advanced, including an estrangement between himself and Frances. In addition to the innkeeper's wife, Constance Spiers, and her family there were also two other lodgers besides Philip Henry: John Smith, a married wheelwright of 60 and Harry Lewis, a widower of 46 who was a musical instrument maker. Perhaps Philip Henry had booked himself into a room after a late night drinking session; maybe he was keen on Mrs Spiers - her husband Alfred was away from home on census day, visiting his elderly widowed mother in Worcestershire. In addition to his role as licensee of the Crown, Alfred Spiers was also a Lechlade farmer. I discovered that despite these two occupations he had been in financial difficulties since 1889. We shall probably never know the reason for Philip Henry lodging at the *Crown,* but it is interesting to speculate. Similarly, the reason for the rest of the family being at Thornhill Farm, rather than Manor Farm is not known. Had the original tenancy been for a fixed term of ten years, had the family decided to move to a larger, smaller or different type of farm, or had it been decided for them? As usual, there are more questions than answers, especially for an inquisitive family historian.

Philip Henry died in 1901. He was in his early fifties. He does not appear to have left a will, which is surprising bearing in mind that he had been in business and had a family to provide for. It would be interesting to know whether he had returned to Thornhill Farm and lived there between 1891 and 1901, or whether there was a permanent rift between him and the rest of the family. My hunch was that he had died suddenly, perhaps as the result of a stroke, heart attack or accident. Bearing in mind the difficulties farmers had been facing, I also speculated about his financial position and wondered whether this had preyed on his mind. Had he committed suicide? My curiosity eventually got the better of me, and I sent to the General Register Office for his death certificate. Once I had received it, I noted that the doctor had given the cause of death as *morbus cordis.* Not being a Latin scholar I felt I wasn't much further forward. However, I found out that this referred to heart disease. It still isn't clear to me whether he died from a heart attack or whether he had been suffering from the debilitating effects of heart failure. If it was the latter, he would probably have been unable to follow his occupation of farmer for some while before his death, but probably would have thought it worthwhile (and advisable) to make a will. If, on the other hand, his death was sudden, why was he described on the certificate as '*formerly* a farmer' (my italics)? And why was he living in Oak Street, not on a farm? Just to add a little more mystery, Frances was with him when he died, so it looks as though I may have been a little wide of the mark when I suggested an estrangement between the couple. Perhaps they patched things up before Philip Henry died.

Ernest Harry Whitfield (b.1871) does not appear to have inherited his father's drive and ambition. Ernest seems to have lived quietly in Lechlade for most of his life. Unmarried, he was a farm labourer, probably working on his parents' farm. After his father died he struck out on his own, but to a limited degree: he became a jobbing gardener. He was one of a committee responsible for organising the Lechlade Horse Show in 1910 and 1913, and presumably also in the intervening years, according to the *Cheltenham Chronicle* and it may well be that he had ploughed and hoed with horses at the Manor and Thornhill farms. He continued to live with his mother and sisters, and after Frances' death with his youngest sister, Julia. Towards the end of his life he moved to Oxford to stay with his sister Frances Kate. The move may well have occurred after Julia's death in 1935, and by that time he, too, may have been in failing health. The *Lechlade Parish Magazine* reported after Ernest's death in 1939:

' The name of Whitfield is known and respected in Lechlade, and to many of us it was a personal occasion when the body of Ernest Harry Whitfield was brought back to us for burial and to tell us that another had rested from his labours and gone home'.

Mary Elizabeth, the second child of Philip Henry and Frances Whitfield, married a baker and confectioner Charles William Gardiner in Banbury in 1896. They had three children, Charles Kenneth, Elsie and Gladys. All of them helped in the bakery business. Their shop and bakery were in Bridge Street, Banbury; they lived behind the shop and also used the bedrooms, but they also bought a house in Oxford Road, Banbury and moved there later. The Bridge Street property was then used exclusively as a bakery by their son (Charles) Kenneth. He was certainly following a family tradition: his father, grandfather and great grandfather had all been bakers before him at some time in their working lives. Mary Elizabeth Gardiner died in

1953, aged eighty, and her husband in 1959. The National Probate Register shows that they had been very successful in their business: Charles William Gardiner left over £21,000. Their son Ken continued as a baker and confectioner in Banbury. His specialities were lardy cakes and dough cakes according to his daughter Jill Murchison, who still lives in the Banbury area. Jill kindly contacted me after I had written to the *Banbury Guardian*, asking for any descendants of Charles and Mary Gardiner to get in touch. She said her father also bought a small retail unit in Church Lane, Banbury - a central location. He leased it to a greengrocer for many years. Ken Gardiner died in 1973.

The next child of Philip Henry and Frances was Frances Kate, baptised 1877 in Hook Norton. Few details are known about her early adult life; she was still at school in Lechlade, aged 15, in 1891, but by 1901 was living at Culworth, Northamptonshire, a village a few miles north east of Banbury. She was working as a cook in the household of Oscar and Susanna Bland, both aged 27, and their young daughter Iseult Bland, aged five. Oscar, despite his youth, was 'living on his own means', according to the census details, and evidently doing so in some style, having a governess, a maid, a cook, a housemaid, a laundry maid, a butler and a groom in residence to prevent him or his wife from attempting to do anything too strenuous or worthwhile like preparing a meal, opening a wine bottle, changing their sheets or helping with their daughter's education. I wasn't able to find out how long Frances Kate had been with her apparently affluent and indolent employers, or when she left them. I presume she had secured the post after reading an advertisement in a local newspaper, possibly the *Banbury Guardian*.

In 1907, Frances Kate married Charles Robert Woodbridge at St. George's Church, Hanover Square, London. This was a fashionable church, where a lot of 'society' and 'celebrity' weddings took place. It isn't clear why the couple chose this venue – or how they first met. Possibly it was their wish to have the wedding at this prestigious church, or it may have been that Frances Kate was now in domestic service with some more wealthy employers in the vicinity of Hanover Square.

So far, I have not managed to find out anything about Charles Woodbridge's family background, but I do know from studying the will of Frances Kate's elder brother Ernest Harry Whitfield, that they had a son William Charles Woodbridge, who was born in 1911 in Woolwich, London. He had not been born at the time of the census which shows that his father Charles Woodbridge was the proprietor of a 'dining room' - presumably a restaurant - and Frances was helping him with the business. I assume they had outside help after the birth of their son. The census indicates that an earlier child had died.

The Woodbridge family later returned to Oxfordshire to run the *King's Arms*, a popular and busy hotel and public house near the river at Sandford-on-Thames, just south of Oxford. Charles Robert Woodbridge was described as a licensed victualler of the *King's Arms* when he died in 1921, leaving £1579 2s 11d - a fair sum in those days, when a semi-detached house could be purchased for around £300. Frances Kate continued as licensee after his death. By 1939, when William Woodbridge was required to act as one of the executors of the will of his uncle Ernest Harry Whitfield of Lechlade, both Ernest and William had been living at Fernhill Road, Cowley, (a suburb of Oxford) just north of Sandford-on-Thames, probably with Frances Kate Woodbridge (Ernest's sister).

Frances Kate died at Oxford in 1946. The National Probate Register shows that she was far from destitute when she died: her estate was valued at nearly £6,500. It included the house in Fernhill Road, and was all left to her son William Charles Woodbridge who was by now living at a separate address in Cowley. William Morris had established his car works in Cowley in 1912 and by the late 1930s the enterprise was thriving. It may well be that William Woodbridge was helping to assemble cars or working in the pressed steel works nearby (which supplied car panels) because he was described as an engineer.

William Charles Woodbridge died in Oxfordshire in 1995 and therefore doesn't seem to have left the area. I found that a William C. Woodbridge had married Phyllis Walter in 1934 and that the birth of their daughter, Judith, was registered at Abingdon in 1940. I would need to purchase the certificates before I could be certain that Judith was Frances Kate's granddaughter.

The youngest sister of Frances Kate was Julia, b 1881 in Lechlade. Julia, like her older brother, Ernest Harry, did not marry, but lived with her mother Frances until Frances died in 1928; she then lived with Ernest (or vice versa). She was a school teacher in Lechlade, and, as such, was clearly a well-known and hopefully respected member of the community. She attended Lechlade School as a pupil, became a pupil teacher, and then stayed teaching in the same school for nearly forty years. She retired in 1935, but unfortunately died about two months later. In March, 1935, the *Lechlade Parish Magazine* described her life in the following terms:

'To mention some names is to hear again music - the music of a consistent harmonious life - such name is Julia Whitfield's. The press has recorded her nigh 40 years of public service in the educational world on the staff of our school - guiding, uplifting, moulding - what a splendid term of work it was! Linking up Mr. and Mrs S.N. Davies' and Mr. Harrison's terms of leadership, making doubly sure the loyalty of their changing staffs. Her individual attention secured a specially high standard of needlework in all her pupils, and the same was carried on in her close association with the children out of school hours in the work of the C.E.T.S. [Church of England Temperance Society] and in other causes. It was voluntary work of this nature that Miss Whitfield hoped to resume on her retirement, but it was a higher call that reached her on January 27th.'

The funeral report in the *Wiltshire and Gloucestershire Standard* also noted that Julia had been a Sunday School teacher and a member of the Parochial Church Council.

It must have been difficult for Julia to promote the cause of temperance as some of her near relatives were, or had been, licensed victuallers. (Apparently it was a policy of the C.E.T.S. to recruit children before they had acquired the taste for alcoholic drink.)

Her will, written in September, 1934, provided for her brothers and sisters: Ernest Harry was to have two thirds of her money and William Samuel was to receive the remaining third. Her house in Oak Street, Lechlade and all the furniture (which may well have originally belonged to her parents) were left to Ernest, but on his death they were to go to her nephew, Jack Whitfield (the son of William Samuel). If Ernest Harry were to die before her, then Julia's will stipulated that his two thirds share of her money was to be equally divided between her two sisters (Mary Elizabeth Gardiner and Frances Kate Woodbridge.) Julia's estate was valued at just over £1700; I would imagine her lifestyle meant that she had always lived well within her means and she had been comfortably off as she contemplated the retirement which, sadly, did not last long. Julia is buried with her parents in the cemetery at Lechlade. She was still remembered by some elderly Lechlade residents when I made enquiries in the late 1990s. Unfortunately, I have yet to find a photograph of her; there must have been some taken of her I would have thought.

The only son of Philip Henry and Frances Whitfield to marry was William Samuel, b 1879, at Lechlade. His bride was Caroline Gills, also originally from Lechlade, but presumably living and working in Chedworth, Gloucestershire, as this is where the wedding took place in 1912. In the previous year she had been working as a cook in the household of a barrister in the parish of St. Giles, Oxford. Caroline's father, Joseph Gills, was described as a 'dealer' on the marriage certificate. I wondered what this really meant; census details and old directories containing lists of Lechlade tradesmen showed me that he had originally been a butcher, but was now a dealer in cattle. I presume that William Samuel had probably started his working life by helping out on his father's farm, but the 1911 census describes him as a *master grocer* implying that he had his own grocery business. (He is simply described as a grocer on the marriage certificate).

Thanks to the British Newspaper archive (available on the internet) and Lechlade's *Bridge* magazine I was able to discover some interesting details about life in Lechlade about one hundred years ago. Street markets were held on the last Tuesday of each month; sheep hurdles would be erected overnight in the Market Place, and the end of Sherborne Street was used as a cattle ring. Farmers from the surrounding district would attend, and up to 1000 sheep and 400 cattle were sometimes sold. Clearly, on market days the population of livestock would outnumber the number of permanent human residents of Lechlade. I would imagine that both William Samuel Whitfield, as a grocer, and his father-in-law Joseph Gills, as a cattle trader, were kept busy on such occasions. Pub landlords must also have done well from the farmers as deals were clinched. Philip Henry Whitfield may well have been a well-known figure at the market (and possibly in the pubs) in earlier days.

Although the railway came to Lechlade in 1873, linking it to Oxford, (the line ran close to Manor Farm), motorised road traffic would have been rare in Lechlade in the early twentieth century. In addition to the ubiquitous horse-drawn carts the small town was also accessible to barges travelling along the Thames, transporting bulky cargoes such as coal and gravel. Increasingly, though, the river was being used for recreational pursuits. The water carnival was held annually during the August Bank Holiday, and the *Cheltenham Chronicle* of Saturday, 6th August, 1910 shows that William Samuel Whitfield was on its organising committee. The events took place near Lechlade Bridge which gave spectators access to both banks of the Thames, where they were able to enjoy watching swimming races, diving, water polo and obstacle races; the carnival atmosphere was engendered by a greasy pole contest, a parade of decorated boats and an evening fireworks display. I would imagine food would have been available, and it may well be that William Samuel supplied some provisions for this purpose from his grocer's shop; liquid refreshments probably came from the nearby *New Inn*.

William Samuel was a Lechlade quoits club committee member (and presumably also a player of this ancient game). The *Cheltenham Chronicle* shows that he attended its annual general meeting which was held at the *New Inn* on Saturday, 19th March, 1910. Games may well also have taken place in the *New Inn* garden: quoits often was a pub-based activity. The club may have used horseshoes as quoits - there would have been a plentiful supply of these at this time. I wonder whether a photograph was ever taken of Lechlade quoits club?

In October, 1910, William Samuel appeared in the *Cheltenham Chronicle* for a much more serious reason: he was called as a witness at a coroner's enquiry into the death of Thomas Slatter, aged 63, a former Lechlade butcher. Apparently, William Samuel had been one of the last people to see Slatter alive; the pair of them had enjoyed a glass of whisky each at the *Lion* inn. Slatter's demeanour had shown no sign of what was to follow: he had gone to his lodgings and drank some carbolic acid which had resulted in his death. He had procured the carbolic acid from a Lechlade chemist by claiming he needed it to relieve his toothache. It seems to have been a remedy for toothache at this time: the 1911 edition of *Encyclopaedia Britannica* states that 'a piece of cotton wool soaked in strong carbolic acid will relieve the pain of dental caries'. The chemist had supplied the acid in a small bottle, suitably labelled as poison. It would not have been a pleasant death for Slatter: the same publication informed me that symptoms of carbolic acid poisoning included vomiting of frothy mucus, severe abdominal pain, a weak pulse, vertigo, deafness and stupefaction. As he suffered the agony of these symptoms Slatter's mind was probably no longer on his toothache - if indeed he *had* been suffering from it in the first place. His mind had clearly been in a disturbed state; it appeared that he had planned his suicide because various letters were left behind in his lodgings, including one where he left a friend his watch and chain and an *apple* which he had picked recently in a nearby village. In another, he asked that the inscription on his coffin should be 'Judge not, that ye be not judged'. (The quotation comes from St Matthew's Gospel, chapter 7 verse 1.)

It appears that William Samuel as a farmer's son, grocer, committee member, quoits player and frequenter of various Lechlade public houses was well known in the small town, and he was presumably a popular and sociable man. He later became the licensee of the *Salutation Hotel* in Faringdon, probably much to the annoyance of his youngest sister, Julia, busy promoting the cause of temperance. She now had a brother *and* sister in the licensed trade, though thankfully for her not in Lechlade. Faringdon directories for 1928 and 1931 mention William Samuel Whitfield at the *Salutation*. His presence there may have been the reason for the unequal distribution of Julia's money between her brothers according to her will: I get the impression that she really didn't approve.

William Samuel and Caroline had just one child: Jack, born in 1912, the nephew mentioned in Julia's will. William died in 1944; the death was registered at Maidenhead. At the time his will was made (May, 1937) he was still the manager of the *Salutation Hotel*. The National Probate Register states that he died at an address in Powney Road, Maidenhead (possibly his son Jack's home) and left about £640.

Jack married a farmer's daughter, Ann Moran, in 1937 at Faringdon. Their only son, Michael John, was born the following year. Jack was originally a boot and shoe salesman; he later managed a shoe shop for the Dolcis chain. Eventually, following the occupation of his father (and one of his great grandfathers), he became a pub landlord, running, with Ann, the *Greyhound* at Maidenhead. I wonder what his aunt Julia would have said? He retired to

Somerset, and died there in 1976. The death was registered at Bath.

In my attempt to trace descendants of Philip Whitfield, the baker, who had been born in Bedfordshire in 1816, I had therefore got as far as Jack who had died in 1976, but I knew he had a son, Michael John Whitfield. My aim, of course, was to trace Philip's descendants down to the present day. I managed to find in Bedford library some telephone directories for the Maidenhead area and the Bath area. I listed Whitfield entries for M.J.Whitfield and contacted the people concerned. The one I thought most likely lived in Wiltshire, but I was wrong: this M.J.Whitfield was a scrap merchant who had no connection with Jack Whitfield. I struck lucky with another entry, though; Michael John Whitfield, the son of Jack, was living in Frome, Somerset, and working as a painter and decorator. Michael had married Patricia Dale in Maidenhead in 1962 (they had since divorced). Their children Debra (Debbie) and Adam were born in Maidenhead in 1963 and 1965 respectively. Michael gave me their contact details. I was sorry to see that he had died in 2011 - I found a short obituary on the internet.

Debbie has a son James and a daughter, Georgia and is now living in Spain. I contacted her before she emigrated and she kindly sent me copies of some family photographs. Unfortunately they only go back as far as her grandfather, Jack. Surely some were taken of her great grandfather William Samuel Whitfield, who lived until 1944? Some were probably also taken of Philip Henry and Frances and their family at one of their farms in Lechlade. If they have survived they have eluded me so far.

Adam is living in Maidenhead and working as a carpenter. His partner was Claire Mosdell (they have since parted company).They have two sons: Jack (b.1989), a mechanic, and Samuel (b.1992), who also live in the Maidenhead area. They are both 4x great grandsons of Philip Whitfield, the baker, who was born in Cople, Bedfordshire, nearly two hundred years ago; they share a common ancestor with me: James Whitfield the gamekeeper. I wonder if they will continue the line?

Having traced descendants of Philip bearing the Whitfield surname to the present day, I now need to return to his other children - the sisters of Philip Henry. What happened to them?

The older sister of Philip Henry was Lydia Charlotte, baptised in 1845 at Hook Norton. You will remember that she was working as a grocer there in 1871, in a business possibly started by her father, Philip. She married another grocer, Samuel Frederick Hawley in 1876, but not locally - in Merthyr Tydfil, South Wales. I'm not sure why this location was chosen; presumably Lydia was living and working there.

Samuel Hawley had served a grocery apprenticeship in Leicester, but was born in Adstock Field, near Winslow in Buckinghamshire, where his father, William Hawley, had been a farmer and grocer. The farm is still there today, isolated in beautiful countryside. William hadn't moved far from the farm: in Adstock churchyard an impressive chest-like tomb, surrounded by rusting iron railings commemorates his death in 1868. The inscription was still readable after I had removed an encrustation of lichen when I visited Adstock in 2010. The National Probate Register revealed that William Hawley had been a prosperous man, leaving about £12,000. I would imagine that some of the money must have come Samuel's way.

The 1881 census shows that Samuel and Lydia had returned to Buckinghamshire. They were living in Church Street, High Wycombe, where Samuel, aged 27, was working as a grocer. He was presumably running his own business. He and Lydia now had a daughter, Maud E. Hawley, aged 1, and he was employing two men to work in the shop, in addition to a servant and a nurse for Maud.

The family were found in Tunbridge Wells in 1891. They had moved there sometime between 1882 and 1884. There were now four children: Maud aged 11 and Frederic R. (9) had been born in High Wycombe, but Winifred E. (7) and Adeline (6) had been born in Tunbridge Wells. Lydia's niece, Mary Elizabeth Whitfield, a daughter of Philip Henry, was living with the Hawleys and acting as a 'mother's help'. (That explained *her* absence - though not her father's - from the Whitfield household in Lechlade). There was also a domestic servant, Kate Coppenger.

By 1901, the family had moved again. This time I found them in Maldon, Essex. I had, of course, been fortunate in now having the ancestry website to help me with the searching. Otherwise, following this family as they moved around the country would have been well-nigh impossible. Samuel was again described as a grocer and employer. The children were all still living at home; Maud, aged 21, was now a student. Unfortunately, details of the university or college she was attending were not given. Frederic R. was mysteriously listed as Reginald F. Whatever the order of his Christian names, he was following in his father's footsteps and working as a grocer's assistant. There can be little doubt that Samuel passed on his specialised knowledge of the grocery trade to his son. Samuel and Lydia's house in Lodge Road, Maldon appears to have been in a comfortable middle-class area of the town; their neighbours included a retired farmer, a retired bank manager, a manager of an agricultural implement works and a school principal, Mary Saunders, who lived next door. Miss Saunders was acting as a tutor to Samuel and Lydia's youngest daughter, Adeline. The *Essex Newsman* of 2nd February, 1901 recorded that Adeline had been successful in the Christmas examination of the Royal College of Preceptors, with distinctions in English Language and French. Like her sister Maud, she was training to be a teacher.

Lydia Charlotte's death was recorded at Romford in 1905. Her address was given as 120 Woodlands Road, Ilford, Essex. It looks as though the family had moved again. Samuel and his three unmarried daughters were still living in Ilford in 1911, but were now living in Grosvenor Road – *another* move. Maud had clearly put her education to good use: I was amazed to see that she was already a headmistress at the age of 31. The 1910 *Kelly's Directory* for Ilford shows that she was working at Goodmayes School, an establishment in Airthrie Road catering for '370 boys, 370 girls and 470 juniors, mixed'. She appears to have been in charge of the junior school. Her sister Winifred was working as a housekeeper to the rest of the family. Adeline had become a music teacher.

Frederic Reginald Hawley, b. 1882, died in Flanders on 30th July, 1915, in the carnage of World War One. His military papers, found on the ancestry website, indicated that his civilian occupation had been, rather unsurprisingly, a 'traveller'. I assumed this meant he was a commercial traveller or salesman, probably for a grocery firm. When the 1911 census had been indexed I attempted to discover more and managed to find him visiting Frederick Henry Parks, a grocery and provision merchant in Milkwood Road, Herne Hill, Lambeth. I was surprised to see that his occupation was rather more specialised than his military papers had suggested: he was a 'tea expert'. Alongside this interesting description the enumerator had elaborated further by adding the word 'taster'. Frederic thus had an unusual skilled job; he would have had to know about tea cultivation and processing and different varieties and blends. He would have used a long handled spatula to sample the brewed tea and would have slurped the tea quickly from it to ensure that a fine mist of the liquid reached the back of his palate as well as making contact with his tongue. (Hopefully he was also a good judge of a liquid's temperature). He would have had to refrain from smoking, drinking alcohol and eating spicy foods, all of which would have meant that his palate would have lacked the discernment necessary for his job. I assume that Frederic had to taste different varieties and blends of tea before buying some of them for his company. He could well have attended the tea auctions in Mincing Lane, London and he may have had to travel abroad. He had married just seven months before his death; his bride was Edith Marian Eve, whose father was a watchmaker and jeweller in Maldon, Essex. Frederic took the sensible precaution of making his will after he married, but his untimely death meant that he was only able to leave about £90 to his widow, Edith, who lived until 1960.

We have seen that the youngest daughter of Lydia and Samuel Hawley, Adeline Selina, b.1885, was a music teacher. However, she had also inherited or developed a desire for travel. On the ancestry website I found that she sailed from London to Bombay in 1916 on the *Malwa* and returned to England in 1922, having worked in India as a missionary. In 1928 she was returning from Bombay again; this time she was described as a music teacher. Her English address at that time was given as 82 St Albans Road, Seven Kings, Essex.

Samuel Hawley lived for another thirty years after the death of his wife Lydia, and twenty years after his son was killed in the First World War. His will of 1935 shows that he left over £6,250, indicating that he had been comfortably off. Maud, his oldest daughter, was one of the executors. Samuel's address at the time of his death was 45 Cranbrook Rise in Ilford - surely not another move?

It would appear that Maud and her sisters Winifred and Adeline didn't marry. I found that Winifred died in Eastbourne, Sussex, in 1959, aged 75. Maud also died in Eastbourne during the following year, at the age of eighty. The National Probate Register showed that they had been living together in Freeman Avenue, Hampden Park, just north of Eastbourne, in a road of fairly large, privately owned semi-detached houses. From research undertaken at Eastbourne Library I discovered that Freeman Avenue was being built in 1939 and Kelly's Street Directory for the following year shows that Maud was living there. She would have been about sixty at the time and had possibly just retired. The sisters may well have moved out of the London area after the Second World War had started to avoid the risk of being bombed. They would not have been the first - or the last - people to move to Eastbourne in their later years. A letter of mine was published in a local Eastbourne newspaper in an attempt to gain more information, but there were no replies.

Both sisters were far from being destitute. Maud's will indicates that she had been left some shares by her sister. Her signature on the document suggested to me that she was in failing health. I then looked at the date of the will and discovered that Maud had signed it only *four days* before her death. It would appear that although she was now physically weak, the former headmistress had retained a clear mind and was determined to ensure that her personal affairs were left in order and her money put to good use.

Maud made a number of personal bequests from her estate (which was in excess of £10,000), including four hundred pounds to her cousin Winifred Whitfield Hore, who was living at St Margaret's Home, Lindfield, near Haywards Heath, Sussex at the time and two hundred pounds to Sister Pauline of All Saints' Convent at London Colney, near St Albans, Hertfordshire. The bulk of the estate went to various charities: the Church Army, the Church of England Children's Society, The Divine Healing Fellowship, the Home of Divine Healing (based at the Old Rectory, Crowhurst, Sussex), the University Mission to Central Africa, the Society for the Propagation of the Gospel, the Church of England Missionary Society, St. Mary's Church, Hampden Park (where I presume Maud had worshipped), various other children's charities, the Royal National Lifeboat Institution and the British Empire Cancer Campaign. No mention was made in the will of her younger sister, Adeline. I wonder why. Bearing in mind the charities benefitting from Maud's legacies I also wonder whether she had been involved in missionary work - maybe in Africa - in her younger days. She appears to have been very well acquainted with the work of the Church and I wasn't surprised to learn, thanks to the efforts of one of the current churchwardens, that she had been a member of the parochial church council of St Mary's Church, Hampden Park. I haven't found an obituary for her and realise that I know very little about her between 1911 and the time of her death.

Adeline appears not to have joined her sisters in Sussex. She had travelled to Bombay again in 1950 at the age of 65 and was described as a 'sister of mercy', suggesting that her visit was again connected with religious or charitable work. It is not known when she returned to England but I discovered that she had moved back to the Oxford area, where her death was recorded in 1972. She would have been about 87 and had not married. Whoever cleared out her house probably found some interesting family photographs. I wonder who that person was, and what happened to Adeline's personal effects?

Philip Henry's younger sister was Julia Elizabeth (baptised 1853 at Hook Norton). Like her brother and sister, she appears to have been rather restless, adventurous and ambitious. You will probably remember that in the 1871 census entry for Hook Norton she was described as a pupil teacher, and it may well be that this occupation brought her into contact with a young schoolmaster, Willam Thomas Kelly Hore (to give him his full name). William Hore was also described as a pupil teacher in 1871; at that time he was living with his parents in New Brompton, Kent. The couple married in High Wycombe, Buckinghamshire, in October, 1879. It may be that they had both been teaching at a High Wycombe school at some time between 1871 and 1879, although as yet I have no evidence to support this theory.

William Thomas Kelly Hore had been born in Deptford, Kent, where his father, William Thomas Hore was a shipwright, but the family originated from North Devon, where his grandfather, Thomas Hore, had been a small farmer and shoemaker.

Julia Elizabeth's choice of career may well have been influenced by her aunt, Martha Bennett. Martha, you will remember, had started her working life as a baker's assistant, for her parents in Deddington. William Cotton Risley had offered her a post at Deddington School after the untimely death of her sister, Lucy, but at the time Martha had declined, working instead for her brother-in-law and sister respectively, Philip and Elizabeth Whitfield, at their bakery in Hook Norton. She may have later realised that she enjoyed teaching children and had become a National School mistress in the village. She had subsequently married a gamekeeper, William Davis, some seventeen years her senior. It is perhaps significant that one of the witnesses at the marriage of Julia Whitfield to William Hore was Martha Davis. Julia was living at High Wycombe at the time of her marriage, but William's residence was given as Roath, Cardiff. The couple moved to Cardiff after their marriage and were found there in the 1881 census.

By 1891 they had moved to Harrow in Middlesex; they appear to be running their own school because William is described as both a schoolmaster and an employer. Their daughter, Katherine, aged seven, had been born in Cardiff. Martha Davis, now a widow of 67, was living with them. I assumed that she probably stayed there until her death in December, 1891, as the death was registered at Brentford, Middlesex, but I was wrong. The National Probate Register states that she died in Stockport, Cheshire. I assume she had been visiting friends or relatives - possibly stepchildren.

William Thomas Kelly Hore was named as sole executor of her will, indicating that I had found the correct Martha Davis. She left £117. By Martha's death, the direct link with the Bennett family of Deddington, started in the early 1840s, was finally broken.

The family had moved to Wembley by 1901. Katherine, now aged 17, was working as a pupil teacher, and thereby continuing what had become a family tradition. She now had a much younger sister, Winifred Whitfield Hore, aged six. Winifred had been born while the family had been living in Wembley.

The 1911 census shows that the family had moved again, this time to Sudbury, Middlesex. By now William had become a headmaster. Unfortunately, Katherine had died in 1905, aged only 21. I have not found out the reason, but it must have devastated her parents and young sister. Her mother, Julia Elizabeth Hore died in 1914, aged 60. The death was registered at Uxbridge. William survived her by not much more than six months. His will mentions his daughter Winifred Whitfield Hore, and also his Hawley nephew and nieces: Maud Elizabeth, Frederick Reginald, Winifred Eliza and Adeline Selina, as well as some more Hore relatives. Julia Whitfield of Lechlade is mentioned - a fellow teacher as well as a niece - but not her brothers and sisters. Julia must have been William Hore's favourite Whitfield relative. William left just over £800, so was far from destitute, but financially was not quite in the same league as his brother in law, the grocer Samuel Hawley. Schoolmasters have seldom been renowned for their great wealth and various Secretaries of State for Education over the years (including a certain grocer's daughter) have seemed determined to ensure that this tradition should continue.

Winifred Whitfield Hore, the only surviving daughter of William and Julia, died unmarried in February, 1968 in Sussex. The death was mentioned in the *London Gazette* of 22nd March, 1968 in an attempt to trace relatives. Winifred had been living at St. Margaret's Home, Lindfield, and later at St George's Retreat, Ditchling, a care home run by nuns of the Augustinian order.

Although the family line from Philip Whitfield through his younger daughter, Julia

Elizabeth had come to an end, I was amazed to discover that Winifred Whitfield Hore had some cousins - in *Hawaii* - and I hope you will permit a relatively short digression. Winifred had an uncle, Edward Hore, a younger brother of her father, William Hore. Edward had migrated to Hawaii in June 1872, as a young man of fifteen or sixteen with his parish priest, Rev. Alfred Willis, M.A. (Oxon), who had been appointed Bishop of Hawaii. I found them both in the 1871 census, living in New Brompton, Kent; Edward is described as a page boy, i.e. a male servant, presumably to Alfred Willis, although he was still living at home with his parents. It seems amazing that a young lad should leave his home and family like this to live and work in a remote land; his parents must have entertained misgivings about his plans. Would they ever see him again? The trip to Hawaii must have been an adventure in itself and the way of life (and the weather) he encountered there would have been so different from that experienced in Kent. Hawaii at this time was an independent kingdom, accessible only by sea.

Young Edward must have had ability, because, like his older brother William he became a teacher. His first post was in the Iolani School established by Bishop Willis on the Hawaiian island of Oahu. He left there three years later to teach at the English Mission School at Waialua, before returning to Iolani School as vice principal in 1881. He gained experience as vice principal at other schools in Oahu before returning to the school in Waialua as principal in 1889. He married in 1891; his bride was a Hawaiian girl, Kualii Mokumaia, who appears to have been fifteen or sixteen at the time and some eighteen years Edward's junior – an interesting choice of partner for a school principal. I wonder if she was a former pupil and whether there was any controversy involved. Possibly not, because although Edward left education, becoming at first a tax collector for Waialua, then a magistrate, he seems to have been held in high regard in Hawaii. Hawaii became an American State in 1898, and Bishop Willis, possibly disenchanted with the new regime, left Oahu to take up a post in Tonga. Edward remained in Waialua and became an American citizen in 1903. He died in 1930. Edward and Kualii had five or six children who appear to have stayed in Hawaii, although one son, Thomas Kenoilani Hore, spent some time in Brazil in 1952. It would be very interesting to know whether Edward Hore and his wife and children kept in touch with his brother William, his sister-in-law Julia and their daughters Katherine and Winifred back in England. If any letters survive they would be fascinating to read. After the advertisement of Winifred Whitfield Hore's death appeared in the *London Gazette* perhaps her money was inherited by her Hawaiian cousins, although this seems rather unlikely.

Returning to England, the Hook Norton branch of the Whitfield family was an interesting one for me to trace because it became established outside Bedfordshire. Ambition had encouraged Philip Whitfield to move away from his home area to try his luck in Oxfordshire - and in a different occupation. His children appear to have inherited their drive partly from him but also perhaps from their mother's side, the Bennetts, who, as we have seen, had business interests in Deddington. This branch of the family was more prepared to move around the country in search of work, unlike my branch, which tended to stay in Potton throughout the Victorian period and beyond. Family sizes were smaller than in my branch where large families and poverty were common. Despite achieving a more comfortable standard of living than that secured by Whitfields in Bedfordshire in the Victorian era, not one of Philip Whitfield's children lived to be older than sixty years of age. This may well have been due to the genetic influence of the Bennetts who, as we have seen, were not a long-lived family. Sixty, however, was probably about the average life expectancy for the early twentieth century.

And on that cheerful note, we must leave this Hook Norton branch of the family. It is time to move back to Bedfordshire to see how some of the other children of James Whitfield the gamekeeper, and his wife Sarah, were doing.

Note: Since this chapter was written I managed to find a short article in the *Liverpool Echo* of Monday, 6th July, 1914, thanks to the British Newspaper archive website. It informed me that earlier that day 'Mr W. Hore, a schoolmaster, who had been staying at Gillingham, [Kent] was found mutilated on the railway line at Chatham'. No further details were given and I have been unable to discover more, although I would imagine that articles would have appeared in the Kent local newspapers shortly afterwards, following an inquest. Bearing in mind the (then) recent death of William's wife, Julia, suicide appears the most likely explanation for some unfortunate person's gruesome discovery.

Chapter 8.
Home territory: the line from James Whitfield 1819-1895.

'Lo! Some we loved, the loveliest and best
That Time and Fate of all their Vintage prest
Have drunk their Cup a Round or two before
And one by one crept silently to Rest'

Edward Fitzgerald (1809 – 1883) *Omar Khayyam*

James was possibly born in Potton, Bedfordshire, in 1819, although he was baptised in Tewin in 1821. At the age of fourteen, he had to cope with the death of his father and the move to Potton. As we have already seen, he had to initially earn his keep by stone picking and digging, and was remunerated, after a fashion, by the parish overseers of the poor. It is likely that from these modest beginnings he later graduated to regular farm work in and around Potton.

As his mother had also died by early 1841, and his brother William had left for Manea, James probably felt an extra responsibility as the new head of the family, for, as we have seen, his sister Naomi had married and stayed in Hertfordshire, and his older brother Philip was in Oxfordshire.

What puzzled me was that I couldn't find James living in Potton in the 1841 census, which was taken on Sunday, 6th June. What I *did* eventually find was a James Whitfield, aged 20, living in Whetstone, near Friern Barnet in Middlesex, in the same household as William Lovings aged 50, Gabriel Lovings aged 25 and Jeremiah Riddle, also aged 25. None of them had been born in Middlesex, and the ages given were approximate. Could this James Whitfield be my great -great grandfather, and, if so, what was he doing in Whetstone?

I decided that it would be sensible to research the other members of the household. What were three young men and one older man doing living together in one household, away from their home area? It seemed a rather unusual arrangement.

I figured that not too many people would have had the distinction of being christened Jeremiah Riddle, even in Victorian times, so he seemed to be a suitable person to start with. I was correct in my assumption. What I found intrigued me: in the *1851* census there was a Jeremiah Riddle, born at St. Neots, Huntingdonshire, (about seven miles away from Potton), and living in Gamlingay, Cambridgeshire (about two miles from Potton). His wife, Charlotte, had been born in Sutton (about 1½ miles from Potton) and his oldest son, John, had been born in Gamlingay in 1839. It looked as though one of James' companions had local connections. What about the others?

Using the ancestry website, I looked up William and Gabriel Lovings - and drew a blank. There appeared to be no people of that name alive in 1851. I had no success, either, with deaths in the Lovings family between 1841 and 1851. Then I remembered that the census form would have been completed by the Whetstone census enumerator, not by the individuals concerned - *they* probably couldn't read or write in any case. Had the enumerator recorded their names correctly? Perhaps he was slightly hard of hearing, or perhaps they had mumbled their responses in a strong Bedfordshire or South Cambridgeshire accent. Maybe spelling wasn't the enumerator's strong point? My curiosity hadn't been satisfied, so I looked for William and Gabriel *Livings* and William and Gabriel *Lavins.* No luck. I had been hoping to discover that these men, too, had connections to the Potton/Gamlingay area, but as they seemed to have disappeared completely I was unable to prove or disprove my theory that James was living in Whetstone with three people he had known from his home area.

Then I had another idea. As Gabriel is a relatively uncommon Christian name, why not try a search on the ancestry website for men with that Christian name, born in Bedfordshire or Cambridgeshire and see which surnames came up? This was surprisingly successful, and showed me where I had been going wrong in looking for Gabriel Lovings: a Gabriel *Lowings* had been born in Gamlingay around 1812. He appeared to have been missed from the 1851 census, but I was doubly lucky with the census of ten years later: I found Gabriel *and* his father William.

Gabriel and his family were living at Block Bridge, Gamlingay, perhaps a couple of hundred yards from the road to Hatley St. George, in 1861. Gabriel was described as an agricultural labourer, and had a wife, three sons and a daughter. His father, William Lowings, now a widower of 72, was also an agricultural labourer and living in Green End, Gamlingay, with an unmarried son and daughter. I would imagine that by 1861 William confined his labours - and walking - to the local area.

I had therefore found that the James Whitfield was living in Whetstone in 1841 with three other people who had connections with the Potton and Gamlingay district, and I concluded that I had found my great-great grandfather. What were these four men doing in Whetstone?

I think they were a travelling gang of labourers. They had probably left their home area in search of work during the hay harvest (remember Census Day 1841 was 6th June), and had decided to walk towards London, possibly working as they went; alternatively, they could just have worked on their homeward journey. There was no railway connecting Bedfordshire with the capital at that time. The distance from Potton to Whetstone would have been about forty miles, so the journey would probably have taken about two or three days on foot. People were used to walking longer distances then as a matter of course (and necessity), but some bands of travelling labourers apparently partly overcame this problem by taking a donkey with them, and taking it in turns to ride on its back, thereby easing their weary feet. Hardly an original idea, as Mary and Joseph probably travelled that way into Bethlehem before the birth of Christ - but an effective one. Unfortunately for me, but fortunately for the census enumerator, it was not necessary to list livestock on the census form, so we shall never know whether James and his work colleagues travelled in this way. The men may well have taken their own scythes with them; the grass they were to cut would have been mown by scythes which required regular sharpening. The appropriately named Whetstone, now engulfed in the urban sprawl of the capital, was then just a village. Even London parks were mown by scythe in those days; there would have been a huge demand for hay within London itself, where most public and commercial transport depended on horses.

It was reckoned by many farmers of the time that the uncertainty of obtaining employment disciplined travelling labourers to hard work once they *were* offered some; however, settled families in the area sometimes resented strangers taking work in the locality, particularly if unemployment was a problem, and viewed them with a degree of suspicion. A similar situation exists today in the Fens where many East European labourers work on farms for low wages in an area where jobs are fairly scarce. The Rev J.C. Clutterbuck, in his '*Report on the Agriculture of Middlesex*' (1869), reported that

'...The mowing is for the most part performed ... by strangers who come in companies from the counties of Buckinghamshire, Berkshire and Oxfordshire, and other places. Mowing is undertaken by the acre, the price varying very much with the state of the weather, the supply of labour, the condition of the crop and such like variable incidents. The haymakers, like the hop pickers of Kent and Surrey, are often strangers from various quarters, seeking casual, and for a time, well paid employment'.

This report, although it was written a generation after 1841, suggests that my theory about James and his fellow workers was probably correct. I had first heard about travelling bands of labourers from my grandfather Harry Mingay (1894-1981) who told me that his father Walter Mingay (1858-1943) had been involved in this type of working in his youth.

It is likely that James and his companions stayed on in the area until the wheat and barley harvest started. As they had travelled south it is probable that both the hay harvest and the corn harvest had started earlier in the London area than in north eastern Bedfordshire. They could then start their homeward journey, undertaking harvest work on the way, and possibly then move north to the Fens where the harvests would probably have been a little later.

Harvesting in the 1840s was a very labour-intensive activity involving most of the community in one way or another. A team of men using scythes advanced across each field cutting the corn; each had been selected for this task by virtue of his skill and powers of endurance. The 'lord' of the harvest, usually the head horseman or the farm foreman, set the pace. Earlier he had been responsible for negotiating wage rates for the harvest with the farmer: the agreement reached would have dealt with money payments and amounts of food and beer allowed to the workers.

Scything the corn was a back-breaking job, usually undertaken in hot, sunny weather when there was no prospect of any rain. The scythes were often fitted with cradles made of iron rods to ensure that the cut corn fell evenly, making it easier to gather. Periodically, short breaks were taken so that the scythes could be sharpened; each man would have had his own sharpening stone. Sometimes a barrel of beer was placed at one end of the field so that workers could refresh themselves and replace some of the sweat that had been lost. Women and older children followed the men to rake the cut corn into rows, and then gather it into sheaves. Each sheaf was tied with a band of straws, usually fashioned by children who often were also responsible

DIAGRAM 9

The line descended from James Whitfield (1819 - 1895)

[also see diagram 2]

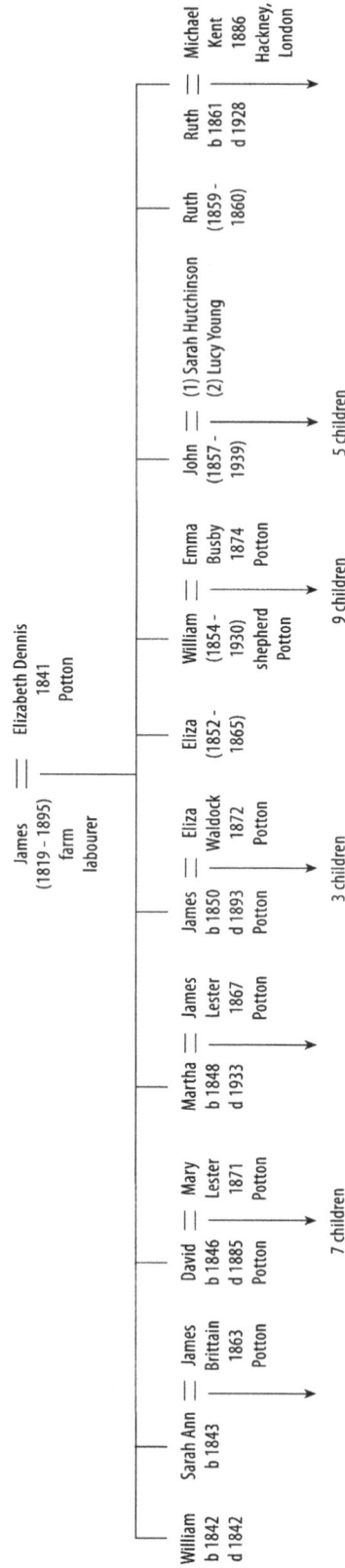

James (1819 - 1895) farm labourer == Elizabeth Dennis 1841 Potton

- William b 1842 d 1842
- Sarah Ann b 1843 == James Brittain 1863 Potton → (children)
- David b 1846 d 1885 Potton == Mary Lester 1871 Potton → 7 children
- Martha b 1848 d 1933 == James Lester 1867 Potton →
- James b 1850 d 1893 Potton == Eliza Waldock 1872 Potton → 3 children
- Eliza (1852 - 1865)
- William (1854 - 1930) shepherd Potton == Emma Busby 1874 Potton → 9 children
- John (1857 - 1939) == (1) Sarah Hutchinson (2) Lucy Young → 5 children
- Ruth (1859 - 1860)
- Ruth b 1861 d 1928 == Michael Kent 1886 Hackney, London →

Large numbers of children in this branch make it difficult to draw a tree which would fit onto a single or even a double page. the descendants of James (1819- 1895) and his wife Elizabeth are covered in this chapter. William and Emma were my great grandparents and had nine children, all of whom survived to marry.

for the tying. The sheaves were then collected into shocks or stooks, with ten being placed in each shock.

Carting the corn was another laborious and long winded process; each sheaf had to be pitched onto a wagon, a strenuous job which was normally undertaken by the strongest men, one on each side of the wagon. Two men, positioned somewhat precariously on top of the wagon received the sheaves and made sure they were stacked evenly. The loaded wagons were usually pulled by the most docile horses which were led by boys back to the farmyard where the corn would be stacked in ricks ready for threshing later to obtain the grain; threshing was normally a winter job. The building of the ricks, which also had to be thatched, was often undertaken by older men. Once the sheaves had been carted, gleaners were summoned to gather any missed ears of corn or spilled grain. Nothing was wasted. All these operations would have been carried out as a matter of urgency, particularly if there was a threat of rain. The harvest field became a scene of frenetic human activity and co-operation was essential. Sometimes whole families were involved; occupational distinctions and barriers disappeared temporarily as village craftsmen laid down the tools of their respective trades to lend a hand with the harvest. It was really a sensible reciprocal gesture on their part because the bulk of their trade depended on the patronage of the farmers.

In case you are still imagining scenes of bucolic jollity remember that harvest time was often a time of tension and anxiety for farmers and labourers alike, as workers were pushed to their limits in the hot sunshine to gather crops before rain set in. Disputes were common as people grew tired and irritable. Many of them would have suffered from backache, blisters, cuts, dehydration, sunburn or sunstroke; and serious accidents - even death - sometimes occurred. Only once the harvest had been completed would there be an opportunity to relax at the harvest supper where food and drink were provided by the farmer. Nowadays, of course, harvesting of cereal crops involves just the combine harvester driver and the driver of the tractor and cart and it is done in a fraction of the time it would have taken in the early years of Queen Victoria's reign.

Hopefully James was able to earn and save some money during this extended period of piecework, undertaken at enhanced rates. We have already seen that Jabez Whitfield, working near Sandy in 1834, was able to earn more money in the harvest period than he normally received. The harvest time of 1841 probably put James in a more secure financial position so that when he returned home he was able to ask Elizabeth Dennis, a carpenter's daughter, to marry him. The fact that she was already pregnant may well have been another good reason, of course. The wedding took place in Potton Church on 12th October, 1841, and their son William was baptised on 28th March, 1842; unfortunately he died later in the same year. He had been named after James' older brother, last heard of in Manea in June, 1841. Was *he* still alive?

The Potton baptism registers give details of James' and Elizabeth's growing family: Sarah Anne, baptised 1843, David (1846), Martha (1848), James (1850), Eliza (1852- she died in 1865), William, my great grandfather, (1854), John (1857), Ruth (1859- she died in 1860) and Ruth (1861): Elizabeth had given birth to ten children in nineteen years.

In June, 1849, when James and Elizabeth had three children to provide for, James appeared in Biggleswade before a surrogate magistrate or solicitor to swear that he was entitled to the

Biggleswade June 5th 1849 —

On which day appeared personally James Whitfield of Potton in the Archdeaconry and County of Bedford — Husbandman — and alleged that he is the natural and lawful son of James Whitfield in the Parish of Tewin in the County of Hertford — Yeoman — deceased — who in his life time made his last will and Testament in writing bearing date on the fourteenth day of August, in the year of our Lord 1832 — and there did appoint his wife Sarah Whitfield sole Executrix thereof — who died on the first day of January 1841 without administering thereto, by reason whereof the said James Whitfield prayed that Letters of administration of all and singular goods, chattels and credits, of the said James Whitfield deceased, together with his last will and testament annexed might be committed and granted to him the said James Whitfield, the son who further makes oath that the personal estate of the testator did not amount to the Sum of One hun

130

-died pounds --

The said James Whitfield
was admitted and sworn
SD. de Bonis non
administrator, with the
will annexed according
to Law, and according to
the above Petition and
Allegation and to the due
Execution thereof before
me --

Joseph Douton
Surrogate --

The mark X of James Whitfield

Extract from document of 1849 showing link between James Whitfield of Tewin, Herts., and James Whitfield of Potton, Beds, my 3xgreat- grandfather and 2xgreat- grandfather, respectively. James the younger 'signed' this document with a cross, as he was illiterate. Image reproduced by kind permission of the Bedfordshire and Luton Archives Service. Reference CD505 proceeds of his late father's estate. It was sixteen years since his father had died. The letter I saw at the Bedford Record Office stated that James (senior) made his will in August, 1832 [in Tewin], naming his wife, Sarah as sole executrix. However, Sarah had died in 1841, without proving the will. There probably hadn't been much point in doing so; there couldn't have been much to inherit. I presume she brought a few sticks of furniture and some household utensils with her to Potton from Tewin - she would have needed a few basics like pots and pans, clothes and blankets to survive. I re-read James' will and then realised that he had also spoken of £50 that had been promised to him by his late brother, Philip. This money, according to Philip's will, was to come to James (senior) within six months after the death of Philip's widow, Ann. However, James and his wife Sarah were already in their graves. I consulted the index of deaths on the ancestry website, and found that Ann had died in Biggleswade in August, 1848. Presumably James (junior) had been made aware of his uncle Philip's bequest, and had learnt of his aunt Ann's death. One would have thought that Philip, as eldest son of James and Sarah would have been the person to deal with this; he could write and probably read, and he was more used to business affairs than his younger brother. However, he was in Oxfordshire, running a bakery. It may be that he wasn't aware of the death of his mother or aunt. It isn't clear whether all the brothers and Naomi kept in touch. I have to confess I'm not sure whether James inherited or successfully claimed all the assets of his father's estate - such as it was - or whether they were shared around the family.

James worked as a farm labourer, but I found out that he also rented land from Potton Charities, whose records indicate that he rented plot 12 at The Roundabout (land just outside Potton, on the way to Gamlingay Heath) in 1854 at a cost of £1 2s 6d, reduced subsequently to 15 shillings per year. He was one of seventy tenants. However, at a meeting of the Charity Trustees in 1860 it was stated that the piece of land had not been cultivated for several years, and rent was in arrears for the years 1856 to 1859. The reason for the rent being unpaid was probably that James didn't have any surplus money, but why he had allowed the weeds to flourish unchecked is more of a mystery. Did it have anything to do with the birth and subsequent death of young Ruth in 1859-1860 I wonder? I assume that the land was being used to grow vegetables for the family and to provide a little surplus cash - or at least that had been the intention.

It is difficult to appreciate what life must have been like for the ordinary rural family at this time. One of the assistant commissioners of the 1867-1869 *Royal Commission on the Employment of Children, Young Persons and Women in Agriculture*, James Fisher, described what he had seen in visiting some three hundred villages:

'The majority of cottages that exist in rural parishes are deficient in almost every requisite that should constitute a home for a Christian family in a civilised community. They are deficient in drainage and sanitary arrangements; they are imperfectly supplied with water; such conveniences as they have are often so situated as to become nuisances; they are full enough of draughts to generate any amount of rheumatism; and in many instances are lamentably dilapidated and out of repair.'

Little wonder, then, that two of James' and Elizabeth's ten children died in infancy, and one in her early teens. The hard lives people from labouring families led meant that only the strongest children survived.

Occupiers of Town Land, No.	Rents due July 6th 1854		
1 Thomas Norman	Mar 13	" 12	"
2 Blows Thomas	Jany 5	" 15	"
3 Sear Richard		" 15	.
4 Stonebridge Widow	Jany 5	" 15	"
5 Smith William	11	" 15	"
6 Judge Mark	"	" 15	"
7 Banes William	5	" 15	"
8 Kefford Thomas	20	" 15	"
9 Apthorpe Widow		— 15	—
10 Lincoln Widow	Sep 10	— 15	—
11 Pigott William		— 15	
12 Whitfield James	Jany 25	1 2	6
13 Peters Thomas			
14 Yerrill William		1 10	"
15 Carter Daniel			
16 Carter William		13	10½
17 Norman Thomas	Mar 13	— 18	9
18 Cox John	"	— 15	—
19 Theobalds James		— 15	—
20 Armon James	Jany 5	" 15	"
	Carried forward £	14 12	1½

Owners of town land, 1854. James Whitfield, my great-great grandfather is listed (no 12) as an occupier of land in Potton one hundred years before I was born. Image reproduced by kind permission of the Bedfordshire and Luton Archives Service

Not all children in the period 1840 to 1869 were able to go to school - the Education Acts of 1876 and the 1880s sought to ensure that this should happen. The 1876 Act established the principle that all children should receive an elementary education and imposed some restrictions on the employment of children. The 1880 Act made school attendance compulsory up to the age of ten, but it wasn't until 1891 that elementary education was made free to all. Prior to 1876 children were found in the roads collecting manure (for their parents' gardens), wandering the countryside, or otherwise loitering or playing. At other times they might be drafted in to help with setting potatoes, weeding or the corn harvest; in Bedfordshire and the Fens they were also used to help with the harvesting of potatoes; and George Culley, reporting for the *Commission on the Employment of Women, Young Persons and Children in Agriculture* mentioned earlier noted that women, boys and girls were being used in Sandy and Biggleswade for peeling onions. If Culley had noticed any children crying at work it *may* not have been because they were lamenting their lack of opportunity for educational advancement. Young girls as well as women were also used in rural industries requiring manual dexterity, such as lace making or straw plaiting. Sometimes children as young as five could be employed in agriculture: they were a cheap source of labour for farmers, and they sometimes worked in gangs, urged on by a gang master. Frequently, their education would be sadly neglected, and, quite apart from anything else, this would restrict their job prospects later on. However intelligent they may have been, lack of educational opportunity usually meant that in most cases they were born destined for manual labour.

At the time of the 1861 census, out of a million permanent agricultural workers in England and Wales, nearly ten per cent were 14 years of age, or younger. One of these young agricultural labourers in 1861 was James Whitfield's son James, aged eleven. His older brother, David (15) was also working on the land. The family was now living in King Street, Potton.

Although James (senior) was also working on the land, his poor pay and large family meant that he and Elizabeth received support from Potton Charities, in the form of occasional money payments, and donations of bread and coal at certain times. James received 4s 6d at Easter, 1859, but nothing in 1862 as his rent was unpaid, 3s 6d in 1863, 1864, 1866-1871 and three shillings in 1872. Put in the context of the ten to twelve shillings a week, or thereabouts, earned by agricultural workers, let alone the £120,000 left by the Right Honourable and Right Reverend Robert, Baron Auckland, D.D., Bishop of Bath and Wells in 1870, these money payments seem far from generous, but they must have been very welcome. James and Elizabeth received 4lb. loaves from Potton Charities in 1857, 1858, 1862, 1864-1866, 1868, 1869, 1875 and from 1889 to 1895 - an ironic state of affairs when James' older brother Philip was having some success in baking and selling bread to the Guardians of the Poor in rural Oxfordshire during much of the same period. The family were also able to keep warm in winter thanks to the half a ton of coal they received each year from 1863 to 1875. It is quite likely that James probably also used wood cut from the hedgerows around Potton on his fire - if only to eke out the supply of coal. Other money payments and payments in kind may have been made, but if so, the records have not survived, or I have missed them.

An article in the *Potton Journal* in July, 1871 claimed that the 'usual [weekly] wage in this neighbourhood [for agricultural labourers] is eleven shillings and during the four weeks of harvest fourteen shillings and four pints of beer a day.' It also stated that 'most labourers take work by the great [i.e. at piecework rates] and keep at it over hours...' The same article gave details of some of the work undertaken by Potton women: 'straw plaiting is done by the labourers' wives and daughters, the former...earning from three to five shillings a week and the latter from eighteen pence to three shillings'. Straw plaiting was very common in Bedfordshire at this time: David Hey in *'Family History and Local History in England'* states that in 1871 about one third of all Bedfordshire girls aged between ten and fifteen were engaged in this work.

Wages such as these would not have gone very far towards providing more than a very basic standard of living for the typically large families of the period. Once items such as bread, bacon, cheese, butter, sugar, tea, coal and wood, and soap and candles had been purchased and the rent had been paid there would have been very little money left for other essential items such as clothes and footwear - or for extras like beer and tobacco. Most labourers' wives had to be highly skilled in managing their household budgets and with so many mouths to feed it was not surprising that many of their husbands had allotments to grow potatoes and other vegetables; some of them kept pigs and poultry, while others resorted to poaching. It was a matter of survival and escaping from this hand-to-mouth existence to a more prosperous one was a rare occurrence. A far more likely outcome was that periods of unemployment or illness would cause genuine hardship and might lead to a stay in the workhouse.

Work on the land did not provide a steady and guaranteed livelihood for market gardeners or their labourers. Weather conditions, the prices obtained for vegetables at market and the freight rates charged by the railway company all varied and could influence the profitability of crops. Late frosts, or wet or very dry summers could ruin some of the smaller market gardeners and would almost guarantee periods of enforced idleness for their employees. The poor weather conditions experienced in the late 1870s, already documented in connection with Philip Henry Whitfield in Oxfordshire and Gloucestershire, also left their mark on the market gardening towns of Potton, Sandy and Biggleswade. In 1878, the onion crop in and around Potton was described in the *Bedfordshire Herald* of 4th October as 'disastrous': it was costing £20 per acre to manure the land and sow and weed the crop, but the onions had been small and had only realised a price of £10 per acre when sold. Similarly, the carrot crop had not been heavy and potato yields had been disappointing. Runner beans had not been plentiful. This report suggests to me that the summer had been unusually dry. The most successful crop had been cucumbers, which had been produced in 'abundant quantities' and despatched, in hampers, to Birmingham. Significantly, as the season progressed even the price obtained for these had dropped (probably due to a glut in the market) and they were no longer packed in hampers but put loose into the railway trucks. The quality of these cucumbers when they reached their destination probably did little to encourage an improved price, or further orders.

In the following year, many seeds sown in spring failed to germinate due to the cold, wet conditions. The summer was also cool and wet, with very little sunshine, and cereal and vegetable crops were adversely affected. Arable farmers and market gardeners fared badly - and so did their labourers.

The *Bedfordshire Times* of 23rd August, 1879 commented, with particular reference to Potton: 'The outlook for those employed in gardening is dark in the extreme and the worst is yet to come. Lowering rents will not meet the difficulty as many will probably find themselves still unable to pay any rent at all. Owing to the four successive bad seasons there will be but very little money left with which to pay for the winter and spring labour'.

In 1881, James and Elizabeth were living in Kidney Bean Row in Horslow Street, and were both described as paupers. James' poor pay, insecure employment and large family would not have allowed him to put aside any money for their old age. Kidney Bean Row was a row of about eight or nine small cottages behind the *Cross Keys* public house. They were in a poor state of repair in the late 1930s when my father Hubert Whitfield used to deliver bread there, and have since been demolished. I can remember having a drink and playing darts and bar billiards at the *Cross Keys* in my younger days. It has now become a private dwelling.

James and Elizabeth presumably continued to be helped by Potton Charities in their old age, and must have done well not to end their days in Biggleswade Workhouse. Elizabeth died in 1890, and I discovered in the 1891 census that James was living with his youngest son John Whitfield, and his grandson, John (junior); I presume they looked after him until he died: his son John's cross appears on his death certificate.

My great-great grandfather, James Whitfield took his last painful breath on 8th February, 1895, having succumbed to 'senile decay' and hydrostatic pneumonia. Poverty and the years of hard labour on the land in all weathers had taken their toll. He was 75 - a good age for a working man in those days. His funeral service took place at the Congregational Chapel in Sun Street, Potton. I had been unable to find details of his burial in the records of the Parish Church; once I had been lent the Congregational Chapel registers I discovered why.

There was no will. James had worked hard all his life to maintain himself, his wife and his family but had very little in the way of money or possessions to leave to his children.

My grandfather, Ernest Whitfield was born in 1886, and must have remembered *his* grandfather who died when Ernest was nine years old. Unfortunately, I was only nine years old when Ernest died, and I never asked him about *his* memories. I wonder if James Whitfield ever had his photograph taken? Somehow, I doubt it: I don't think he would have had the money for this small indulgence, but perhaps one day I will have a pleasant surprise.

Sarah Anne Whitfield, James and Elizabeth's eldest daughter, had already left home by 1861, although she hadn't gone far. She was working as a domestic servant at the *Cock* public house in Gamlingay, Cambridgeshire. She married James Brittain, a hawker, in Potton Church on Christmas Eve in 1863. The union produced three children: Martha, b. 1866, Elizabeth, b. 1868, and Emma, b. 1869. Unfortunately, James Brittain died in 1868, aged only 30. The 1871 census shows that Sarah, aged 27, was living with the three girls in Deepdale, a small hamlet on Sandy Heath, between Potton and Sandy. Next door was Simeon Ginn, the foreman of a fossil works: we shall return to the Deepdale fossil works later in the chapter. Sarah Anne was working as a straw plaiter, but she was also receiving some assistance from Potton Charities.

Beyond 1871, the rest of Sarah Anne's life is a mystery. She may have remarried; the problem in finding out is that there were several women of the same name in the local area at that time.

The 1881 census shows that Martha Brittain, now aged sixteen, was in domestic service at Shortmead Farm, Biggleswade. Her employer was 64 year old William Albone, a market gardener with fifteen acres of land.

Thanks to the London parish records, now available on the ancestry website, I was able to discover that Elizabeth Brittain had married Arthur Robert Jacob, a marble polisher (presumably for a monumental mason, not a toyshop) in Bethnal Green in September, 1889. One of the witnesses was Michael Kent, a member of the family we shall meet later. His name enabled me to establish without any doubt that I had found the correct Elizabeth Brittain.

I have not managed to find any other firm details of this branch of the family, other than a speculative discovery in the 1920 census for Edmonds Precinct, Washington, U.S.A., where a Martha Brittain, aged 55, born in England of English parents, was working as a housekeeper in the household of Jesse A. Wasser, his wife Helen and their three children: Earl (3), Fayette (2) and Jesse, junior, (5 months). Was this Martha Brittain the daughter of James and Sarah Anne Brittain, nee Whitfield, born in Potton in 1866?

James and Elizabeth Whitfield's eldest son, David, baptised 1846, and their next child, Martha, baptised in 1848 stayed in Potton. Both married into the Lester family: Martha married James Lester in 1867, and David married Mary Lester in 1871. The Lesters attended the Congregational Chapel in Sun Street, Potton, and it was in that establishment's records that I found details of the baptisms of the children of both marriages. David and Mary Whitfield's children were; Walter, baptised 1871, George, (1873, who died 1877), Thomas (1874), Fred (1875), John (1876, who died 1877), Mary Ann (1878) and George (1883). It would appear that not all of the children survived infancy, but I have not found deaths recorded for Walter and Fred.

David, like his father, was a farm labourer, and in 1881 was living in Sheffield Close, Potton with Mary and two children, Thomas and Mary Ann. A second son, George, was born in 1883, but in April, 1885, David died suddenly from heart disease. He was only 38. By December, 1885, Mary had remarried. Her new husband was a widower, Charles Reynolds, a coal carter, who acted as stepfather to the Whitfield children, who now had some half-brothers, from Charles Reynolds' first marriage. In addition to his coal carting duties, Charles Reynolds was another staunch Congregationalist, holding the office of deacon at the Potton chapel. He died in 1928, aged 84. In his obituary it was noted that he had been blind for nearly two years. His second wife, Mary, nee Lester, the mother of Thomas, Mary Ann and George Whitfield died in 1937, aged 86. It was noted in her obituary that she had been a loyal member of the Congregational Chapel for fifty years.

As far as I can tell, only three of David and Mary's children survived to marry. These were Thomas, Mary Ann and George.

Thomas Whitfield married Emma Emery in Potton Church in 1901. They remained in Potton, living initially in Horslow Street. They were living there in 1911 and Thomas was described as a farm labourer. He was also clearly growing vegetables for domestic use or maybe as a spare time business because he made the effort to exhibit some of his produce at the 1911 Potton Show, and won second prize for early market carrots and white cabbages.

Thomas and his family moved to Oak Crescent, a council estate built in the late 1920s or early 1930s, just off the Sandy road. Thomas became a coal carter, like his stepfather, operating from a yard behind a house in Sun Street, Potton. Two of his sons told me that he also had four or five acres of land - some in Boston Lane, some at the Roundabout, some on Potton Common, and some at the Pesthouse (part of present day Myers Road, where it is said there was a hospital for people with infectious diseases during some earlier period of Potton's history). It is likely that all this was rented land, some of it at least from Potton Charities. Thomas grew mainly potatoes and beans, as well as mangolds for his horse which was apparently so used to its coal round that it wasn't necessary to hold its reins. The horse was turned out to graze on Biggleswade Common at weekends unless it was being used for ploughing.

Thomas died, aged sixty, in 1934. He had been suffering from bladder cancer. I found his funeral report in the archives of the *Biggleswade Chronicle*, a local newspaper, published in

Thomas Whitfield (1874-1934), a studio photograph from the early 1890s.

the area since 1891, and available in Biggleswade Library. The report stated that Thomas had been ill for nearly two years and had

'….borne his sufferings with much fortitude and patience. He had received treatment at both Northwood Hospital, Middlesex, and Bedford County Hospital and had been cared for at home by his wife and brother in law, Mr W. Inskip. He left behind three sons and four daughters.'

Thomas and Emma's eldest daughter, Dorothy Elizabeth, born in 1902, had died in Bedford Hospital in 1922, aged just nineteen. Dorothy had been in domestic service in Bedford. On the August Bank Holiday she complained of feeling unwell and was brought home. She went to bed but soon became unconscious. She was admitted to the County Hospital in Bedford where she died. I haven't seen the death certificate.

The other children of Thomas and Emma were:

Evelyn, b.1905. Evelyn worked as a housemaid and cook at the Red House, a large Georgian house next door to the Co-operative shop in King Street, Potton. In 1938, she married Billy Abbott, who worked for a grocer in Gamlingay.

Nellie, b.1907, who married Harry Whitbread in 1931.

Elsie, b. 1911, who married Walter Hughes in 1936. They lived in Gamlingay.

Frederick ('Freddie'),b 1914.

William ('Bill') b.1914/15.

Albert, b. 1920, and

Violet Mary, b.1922, who married a Biggleswade florist, Douglas R. Huckle, in 1941.

I have made contact with all three sons, visiting Freddie and Bill in their own homes, and speaking to Albert on the telephone.

Freddie Whitfield was in Potton Church choir as a boy. He did a baker's round for Richardson's in his youth and also worked for Bond Smith the grocers in the Market Square. He left school aged twelve or thirteen. When he was sixteen he hitched a lift to London on a vegetable lorry, taking just £2 and a suitcase of clothes. He got a job as a barman and stayed there for six years. He managed to save some money from his job as he didn't drink alcohol. It must have taken a lot of courage and determination to strike out on his own in this way. Fred must have returned home on occasions during his time working in London. He was certainly in the Potton district in March, 1932, because the *Bedfordshire Times* of Friday 18th March of that year recorded that he had been fined five shillings at Arrington Police Court on the previous Monday for riding a bicycle without a front light in Guilden Morden (just over the Cambridgeshire border) at 12.15 am on 25th February. It would be interesting to know why he was in Guilden Morden at that late hour in winter- perhaps he had been visiting a girlfriend. His address was given as Oak Crescent, Potton.

Freddie worked as an H.G.V. driver during the Second World War, carrying armaments from a London factory to Teesside. He married a girl from County Durham, Elsie Penny, in 1940, and returned to Biggleswade, where Dawn, Ashley and Gillian were born. He subsequently divorced his wife; she took the two girls when they first separated, but Fred eventually got custody of all three children, and brought them up on his own. He became chauffeur and gardener to a Biggleswade doctor who lived at the junction of London Road and The Baulk in Biggleswade. The doctor's large garden stretched down into present day Chestnut Avenue. Fred later became a well-known and popular bus driver in the Biggleswade district, and groundsman for the Stratton House bowls club. When he retired in March, 1979, a *Biggleswade Chronicle* report stated that he had been employed by the United Counties bus company for 34 years and was the longest serving member at the Biggleswade depot, which was in Shortmead Street. Fred had driven nearly one million miles for them, without an accident. A bus company inspector stated that Fred was

'…one of the most even tempered men you could ever wish to meet, and one of the most helpful to passengers. His passengers comment on how he has a smile on his face when they get on his bus.'

What a lovely tribute.

I visited Fred several times when he was in his seventies and eighties. I was always made most welcome and we both enjoyed our meetings. Fred was a short, fairly stocky man. He was a keen gardener; he had trained and trimmed the hedges in his front garden into fantastic shapes, which made his house very easy to identify, and he enjoyed looking after his greenhouse. He used to look after other people's gardens as well as his own, and also used to visit various old people in the area to cut their hair. He drove a three wheeled car until he was well into his eighties, and remained fit and active, interested in and knowledgeable about all sorts of things. I gained the impression that Fred, like various older members of the family I have met over the years, could have done very well in some field if he had been given the opportunity to stay on for further education. He had a keen sense of humour and a good memory, was quietly independent and self-assured and always seemed cheerful and contented. I was sorry when he died in 2003 aged 89.

Fred's daughter, Dawn, is married to Michael Glen. She used to work for the St. John's ambulance organisation, but has now retired.

Fred's son, Ashley, born in 1945, was an apprentice engineer, before joining the marine commandos in 1964. He did his initial training at Lympstone, Devon, then further courses at Portsmouth and Catterick before spending two years in Singapore from 1967 to 1969. He completed both junior and senior command courses, and was promoted to corporal. On his return to the U.K., he had technical training with the Electrical and Mechanical Engineers at Arborfield, near Reading, and, promoted to sergeant, in 1971 was detached for eighteen months to the Signals Research and Development Establishment.

Ashley returned to the Marines to command a telecommunications section based in Arbroath, Scotland, and completed mountain and Arctic warfare training. He was promoted to Colour Sergeant in 1974, and served in Malta. He also qualified as a nuclear, biological and chemical warfare instructor, taking part in N.A.T.O. exercises in Norway, and then served in the Falklands War in 1982.

Promoted to Warrant Officer in 1984, Ashley became head of the Telecommunications Technician branch at the Commando training centre at Lympstone. His service in the Marines concluded in 1986, when he was selected to serve in the Naval Careers service, where he eventually became head of the Careers Information Office at Blackheath, South London. He remained in that role until 1996, and spent his last year at the Armed forces careers office in the Strand, London.

Ashley is married, with three daughters and four grandchildren. He was working as a chauffeur when I last heard from him, but is now probably enjoying more time with the grandchildren in his retirement.

Thomas and Emma's second son, William (Bill), b.1915, like his brother Fred also worked for Richardson's the bakers, on the corner of King Street and the Market Square in Potton before he left school. His first job after leaving school was with Vic. Reynolds, a Potton butcher. He got paid 7s 6d a week, plus a joint of meat, but he didn't like the work. He moved to a job as a baker at premises which stood on the corner of Blackbird Street and Sun Street, Potton, next door to the coal yard where his father worked. At this time he would also help his father, Thomas, on his four acres of market garden land, harvesting runner beans and potatoes. He would sometimes use his father's horse at the weekends to undertake ploughing jobs for other people. Bill later went to work for a bakery in Buckinghamshire, and was then called up into the army in the Second World War. He served in the Middle East, where he baked for the troops. On his return, he spent four years as a tanker driver for the council in Ampthill, Bedfordshire, before turning to lorry driving, carrying market garden produce from the Fens and Bedfordshire to London. He spent his last ten or eleven working years driving the dustcarts around the familiar streets of Ampthill. Bill married Megan Hayward in 1955 in the Ampthill area of Bedfordshire. They had seven children:

Jacqueline, b. 1957.
David, b. 1959.
Jane L., b. 1960.
Andrew M., b 1962.
Joanne. b.1965.
Sandra, b.1966.
Frazer Ian, b.1968.

Bill and Megan subsequently divorced. Bill died in 2004 aged 87. He was survived by his second wife, Jane; they had married in 1989. Jane died in 2008 aged 89.

Not much is known of Bill's children. David works in a scrapyard. Andrew is a machine mover and driver's mate. He married Julie Beard in 1984, and they had two children: Samantha Dawn, b.1985, and Michael Andrew, b. 1987. Samantha married Peter Long in Shillington, Bedfordshire in 2005, and is the mother of Shelby, b 2006. Michael is a trainee mechanic and apparently also a trainee chef. Presumably he will decide which career will suit him best.

Frazer married Alison Jordan in 1996, and they had a daughter, Jordan Laura, born in 1997. Jordan currently attends school in Ampthill.

The youngest son of Thomas and Emma Whitfield was Albert, b.1920. Like his older brother, Fred, Albert Whitfield was a choirboy at Potton Church, but he was also a server and pumped the organ. This latter job was rewarded by a small payment which enabled Albert to treat himself to a piece of fish and a penny-worth of chips the next day: the peace of God was followed by a piece of cod. When he was fourteen, Albert, like his brother Bill, worked for Vic. Reynolds, a butcher in Potton. His tasks included slaughtering the animals, butchery (i.e. cutting them up into joints) and serving in the shop. Albert used to like to accompany drivers for Peacocks, market gardeners in Potton, when they were taking vegetables to the London markets and wanted to learn to drive as soon as he could. He learnt to drive a car when he was sixteen: his teacher was his older brother, Fred, who later taught him to drive lorries.

Albert was called up into the army in 1940, and trained initially at Oswestry, Shropshire. He didn't enjoy the square bashing, and he told me he could vividly remember after about three weeks' training sitting on a five bar gate and debating whether to abscond. He decided against it; with his lorry driving skills he volunteered to help with transport. He eventually joined the commandos (Red Caps Provo Corps), and served in India and Burma.

At one time in the war, Albert was reported missing. He was in charge of mechanical vehicles attached to the 42nd regiment. They were going to make a landing on Achiab, near Rangoon, but things went wrong and they had to go to Calcutta.

After the war, Albert returned to Biggleswade where his brother Fred was living, and got a job at Mantle's garage. He later joined the Railway Police, and moved to Peterborough, living in rented accommodation. He wasn't happy with this and was later transferred to Cheshire, where he lived at Weaversham and worked at Northwich Station. He was later transferred to Cardiff. Albert wasn't happy with this development; his children were doing well at school and he was unwilling to disrupt their education. He therefore asked to go to Chester instead, where there was a vacancy. It was to no avail: he was sent to Cardiff. He complied with the request, but lived in rented accommodation there for thirteen months, coming home at the weekends to see his wife and family who remained in Cheshire.

Albert later moved to Hampshire and worked for the National Health Service, delivering blood to hospitals. He did this for sixteen years. Two of his daughters and his wife also worked at the Southampton blood transfusion centre.

After his retirement, Albert supplemented his pension by making bird boxes from old pallets, then selling them. He also enjoyed gardening and driving and used to make the trip to Biggleswade to see his brother Fred occasionally. He was still alive in 2009, but in poor health (heart trouble).

Albert married Lilian May Stockall in 1942. They had five children: Diana, b.1942, Robert, b.1947, Patricia, b.1949, Pauline, b.1954, and Jean, b. 1960. I know little about the daughters, but Robert has his own hairdressing business in Southampton. He is married, and has a daughter Holly, b.1984, and a son, Gregory, b.1987.

Mary Ann, the next child of David and Mary Whitfield, was born in 1878/9. She was living in Sandy by 1891 with her uncle and aunt, John and Ann Endersby; it would be interesting to know whether she was brought up by them after the death of her father in 1886 and her mother's subsequent remarriage. Mary Ann was still living with her aunt and uncle ten years later and working as a self-employed dressmaker. The census enumerator listed a visitor to the Endersby's household in 1901: a young parchment maker, George William Inskip. Mary Ann married him in the following year. The 1911 census shows that the couple were living in Royston Street, Potton. Their daughter Gladys Irene had been born in 1905. They later had two more daughters: Freda in 1912 and Doris in 1920. George William Inskip worked for the tanners F W Braybrooks in Potton for over thirty years. After a serious illness he began business on his own account as a cycle agent and repairer, operating from a small shop in Sun

Street. He served in France, Belgium and Italy in the First World War. He was a bell ringer at Potton Church for over 55 years, including some time as tower captain. He and Mary Ann celebrated their golden wedding anniversary in 1952. Mary Ann died in the autumn of 1957, and her husband in January of the following year. Both are now at rest in Potton cemetery.

The youngest child of David and Mary was George, b.1883. Like his father, George was an agricultural labourer. He married Ada Duffin in Potton Church in 1903, and twins, Martha and Mary, were born to the couple in January, 1904; unfortunately, both girls died after two days. George and Ada also lost their next child, William George in 1906. He had only been alive for eight months. The only child of the couple to survive was Vera, b.1908.

A *Biggleswade Chronicle* report of 3rd November, 1916, noted that George's employer, George Gurney, had appealed against his employee's call up to fight in the First World War, stating that he was involved in agriculture. George [Whitfield] had been given a temporary exemption in July, 1916 until 15th September, but the appeal was dismissed. Mr. Gurney had explained that George was employed on a market garden of thirteen acres, but after investigation it was found that George, rather than tilling the land, had been employed to wash vegetables. George had to join the army. I have a photograph of him looking rather stern in a military uniform. He survived the war and returned to agricultural work in Potton. He and Ada lived in a cottage at the top end of Horslow Street, near the *Rising Sun* public house. (Anyone walking past this Potton pub in the early morning can understand why its name was chosen: its sign faces east and is illuminated by the rays of the rising sun). Ada died in 1953, aged 69. George remained a familiar figure in Potton, riding around on his bicycle. He must have been a robust character - he used to be in his shirtsleeves, whatever the weather when he filled his kettle in the morning from the outside tap in his yard. He died in 1964, aged 81.

Vera married William Wright, a Gamlingay carpenter in 1951, and they lived in a cottage in Church End, Gamlingay. They married relatively late in life - both were in their forties - and there were no children.

The next child of James Whitfield (1819-1895) and his wife Elizabeth was Martha, b.1848. She married James Lester, a porter for a Potton wine merchant, in November, 1867, and the baptisms of their growing family (they had eleven children) were recorded in the registers of the Congregational Chapel in Potton, where they were both regular worshippers. James was also a member of the choir.

Their 11 children did not all survive to become adults:

Albert James , b.1869 died in the same year.

Walter Lester, b.1871, married Bertha Hall in West Ham in 1899. I presume that they must have met locally, and that Bertha had moved to West Ham to go into domestic service. The couple returned to live in Wagstaff Terrace, Potton, a row of small cottages in Sandy Road. Walter was a wheelwright and coach builder. Their only child, Eva Gladys Lester, was born in 1900, and died in 1998. Unfortunately, I never met her. She married George Bradley in Bedford in 1920, and they had two children, Marie b. 1921, and Peter, b.1924. Walter, their grandfather died in 1946 aged 75, and is buried in Potton cemetery.

Louisa Lester was born in 1874, and was found in the 1901 census working as a parlour maid for a surgeon in Bedford. She married Harry Marshall in 1904. The marriage was registered in

Biggleswade.

James Lester, b.1876, died in the same year.

Clara Lester, b. 1877 was also in domestic service in Bedford according to the 1901 census. She was a house maid for a retired army colonel, William Stoddart. Clara married Walter Joyce in Bedford in 1909.

Annie Lester, b. 1879 was working as a general servant for Charles Bond Smith, a Potton chemist and druggist in 1901. This may well have been the Charles Bond Smith who was a regular worshipper at the Congregational Church. She married Robert Bunce later that year, and their son Eric was born in 1902. He was followed by a daughter, Madeline, in 1904. Robert Bunce was working as a journeyman baker in 1911, and the family were living in St. John's Street, Biggleswade.

Rosa Lester, b.1881, was a dressmaker in 1901, living with her parents in Horslow Street. She married John W. Brown, a wheelwright and coach builder, and another member of the Potton Congregational Chapel. They had two sons, Russell and (John) Milner Brown. Rosa died just before Christmas in 1925, aged 44. Her husband remarried. He became very active in the Congregational Church, holding various offices. He was also a beekeeper, and a keen photographer. He became a local preacher, and wrote some hymns and poetry. I can remember him as an interesting old man from my childhood. His son, Milner, emigrated to Australia.

Emily Martha Lester was born in 1882, but died in 1886.

Ruth Lester b. 1885 died aged 16.

Emily Martha Lester, b. 1887 was a nursemaid in 1901. She married Edward Doughty in Bedford in 1914.

James and Martha's youngest child, Grace, died in infancy.

Like so many of their generation, most of the Lester girls went into domestic service. As the only son to survive, Walter, did not produce a son, the Lester name died out in this branch of the family. I think there may be some living descendants of Martha Whitfield and James Lester, but have not yet yielded to the temptation to trace them. James Lester died in 1927, aged 80; Martha died in 1933, aged 84, at the home of one of her daughters, Emily Doughty in Bedford. She was brought back to Potton and her remains rest with those of her husband in the cemetery.

James Whitfield, b. 1850, the next son of James and Elizabeth, married Eliza Waldock in Potton Church in 1872. He was an agricultural labourer, like so many Whitfield men, and the 1881 census shows that he was living in Horslow Street with his wife and son Frederick, aged eight. Unusually for the time, the couple's other children Louisa and Blanche were born after gaps of eleven and seven years respectively. James was remembered by my father Hubert, my uncle Leslie and my aunt Doris because he used to supply their father, Ernest, with his seed potatoes. It was probably James who was a successful exhibitor at the Potton Show of 1908, where he was awarded second prize for his kidney beans. His name was given as J. Whitfield, so I have to concede that the proud bean grower may have been his younger brother, John. Ernest later became an agent for a seed firm, and Leslie remembers delivering seeds to his great uncle, James. James lived to be 93, dying in 1943.

James' son Freddie Whitfield, b. 1873, was a butcher's labourer in 1901, but he, too, later worked on the land. He did not marry, and became a rather eccentric figure in Potton, collecting rabbit skins and wheeling them round on a cart. The rabbit skins would probably have been sold to a dealer who would have sold them on to a maker of felt hats which were popular at the time. Rabbit skin dealers, some of whom also dealt in moleskins, were advertising in the *Biggleswade Chronicle*; one such dealer, W.M. Cohen, was offering seven shillings for a dozen rabbit skins in the paper dated 11th January, 1924. No doubt the money Freddie earned from his rather picturesque spare time job came in useful as a supplement to his wages earned hoeing carrots or picking beans.

I wasn't surprised to find Fred mentioned in the 7th March, 1941 edition of the *Biggleswade Chronicle* in connection with a case of indecent exposure in Potton, because my father had previously mentioned the incident: I had been expecting to find a report. What did surprise me, though, was that Fred had been 68 years old when he had apparently exposed himself to a group of girls aged between nine and fourteen and that he had chosen early February as a suitable time of year to commit the offence. The report unfortunately (or perhaps fortunately for Fred) gave few details. The girls were selling carrots at the time, but it is not made clear whether they were selling them door-to-door, from a temporary stall or from permanent premises. If the incident took place outdoors surely Fred could have chosen more suitable weather for his display?

The cold may well have meant that the girls didn't see much. Perhaps they had caught him urinating outside – something which the average agricultural worker (male or female) would have done in a secluded place as a matter of necessity when presented with the problem of relieving a full bladder out in the fields. No details are given of what was said, either by Freddie or the girls. Had the vaguely suggestive shape of the carrots led to some banter? Evidence was given in court by two married women and four girls. Fred had denied the allegations made when interviewed by a police constable. He pleaded not guilty in court but said nothing else in his defence. He was charged with 'indecent exposure with intent to insult an eleven years old girl and a similar offence in respect of a fourteen years old girl', and sentenced to one month in prison with hard labour for each case, the sentences to run concurrently. He may have been a little unfortunate. It is possible that the girls may have concocted the story, but clearly the magistrates thought otherwise. My father told me that Fred may have been a little mentally backward, and that as a rather eccentric figure he was sometimes teased and chased by children and teenagers. At the time of the offence Fred was living with his father James in a cottage in Meeting Lane, and as far as I know he had no previous convictions. If the offence had taken place today psychiatric reports would probably have been sought and the case might have been treated with more sensitivity. After he had served his prison sentence Fred returned to Potton and was still living with his father when James died aged 93 in 1943. Fred attended the funeral but died only six days later aged seventy. I haven't seen the death certificate but wonder about the circumstances. It may be that an inquest was held, or perhaps Fred had been ill for some time and his death so soon after his father's was just an unfortunate coincidence.

Louisa Whitfield, one of Freddie's sisters, married Thomas Clark in 1903, and a splendid photograph has survived of the family taken just before, or just after the ceremony. It was taken outside Louisa's parents' house in Horslow Street. It would be impossible to take a similar family photograph at the same location today because of the preponderance of parked cars.

The wedding of Louisa Whitfield and Thomas Clark, 1903. The photo was taken outside the Whitfield's house in Horslow Street, Potton. Front row: l to r : Blanche Whitfield, Eliza Whitfield (bride's mother), Thomas Clark, Louisa Whitfield, James Whitfield (bride's father), ----, and far right Freddie Whitfield.

Thomas Clark was a van boy, then a steam plough driver for T.B. Kitchener, a well-known Potton firm which pioneered and operated this type of agricultural machinery. The 1911 census shows that he and Louisa were living in Horslow Street, but they later moved to Sun Street, Biggleswade. Thomas Clark then worked for Frost's at Hinxworth, Hertfordshire, presumably still working with steam ploughs, before becoming a delivery driver for Wells and Winch brewery. The couple were not blessed with children, but appear to have lived quietly in Sun Street. Thomas Clark died in 1967 aged 87. Louisa survived him by seven years, dying in Bedford Hospital in 1974 aged 90. Although both of the Clarks died within my lifetime I never met them: at the time I wasn't aware they were in Biggleswade. The details I have been able to piece together came from an obituary found in the archives of the *Biggleswade Chronicle*.

Blanche Whitfield, b. 1891, was living in Biggleswade in 1911 and working as a cook for Mary Burnett, a 68 year old widow who lived in Shortmead Street. Blanche married Frederick Basterfield, a porter at Biggleswade workhouse, in July, 1915. They weren't together for long because Frederick joined the army. He died of influenza in Hals, near Brussels, in 1919, just after the end of World War One, leaving his wife with a young daughter, Stella Blanche (aged three) back in Biggleswade. Blanche appears to have brought up Stella on her own, perhaps with some help from her older sister Louisa Clark and her husband Thomas.

Stella married Reginald Albone in Biggleswade in 1941. Their only child, Celia Albone, b.1944, married Stephan Thurlow in Biggleswade in 1966. Their son, Philip Thurlow, b. 1967 is possibly the only living descendant of James Whitfield and Eliza Waldock, because Blanche died in 1978, her daughter Stella in 2000, and her granddaughter, Celia (in Spain) in 2008.

My great grandfather, William Whitfield, baptised 1854, was the next son of James and Elizabeth Whitfield. When he was 21, he married 18 year old Emma Busby in Potton Church on 8th February, 1874. Emma was the illegitimate daughter of Susan Busby of Gamlingay. Susan had married James Wagstaff, a widowed agricultural labourer in 1863, and by 1871 Emma was living in Honey Hill, Gamlingay, with James and Susan and her stepsister, Elizabeth. It is not clear whether James was Emma's biological father, but he may well have been. The stigma attached to illegitimacy at the time meant that Emma's birth does not appear to have been registered anywhere. She was baptised in Gamlingay church on 23rd July, 1865, aged nine, and was described in the register as Emma, daughter of James and Susan Wagstaff. (Emma's baptism was just one of twenty such ceremonies carried out by the Gamlingay rector, Rev. John Boote James, on that day, presumably at the same service. Perhaps her correct surname was overlooked, or the rector assumed, or was led to assume, that her surname was Wagstaff). William and Emma already had a son when they walked down the aisle after their wedding ceremony: David Whitfield had been born on 21st December, 1873. They returned to the church to have him baptised on 5th July, 1874.

William and Emma had nine children between 1873 and 1898, and all of them survived to become adults. There were six boys and three girls. They were brought up in a small, two bedroomed cottage in Pound End, Potton, near to where the opening to Sheffield Close is today. All eleven members of the family would not have been there at the same time, of course. By the time the younger members of the family had arrived, the older ones would have departed, either because they had married, or because the girls had gone into domestic service. Even so, the cottage would have been crowded by today's standards. I have been told that the very young children would have slept in their parents' bedroom, and the other bedroom was divided (by a curtain) into boys' and girls' sections. The cottage at Pound End was owned by William's wealthy employer, William (Billy) Smith, who lived at Home Farm. Smith owned about 650 acres of land in Potton and a number of cottages around the town. Nine of these, including William and Emma Whitfield's at Pound End were put up for auction in 1919. It may be that William attended the auction held at the *Rose and Crown* at 6 pm on September 30th to watch men with far more money than he had bid for the property, and thus to discover who would become his new landlord. By this time, my great grandfather would have been about 65 years old, and about five years away from drawing his State Pension. The cottage was still standing in the 1960s, but, with the one adjoining, has been demolished since. They had large gardens which stretched down to properties along King Street and this is where William grew his vegetables and kept his pigs. (These gardens, like most other decent-sized gardens in Potton have now been covered with houses as developers and planners have contrived to destroy much of the town's essentially rural character).

William was a shepherd. One of his daughters, Rosa, b. 1889, told me that she remembered as a young girl taking her father a hot meal, covered by a cloth, from the house in Pound End to where he was working with sheep on Hatley Hill - a distance of about three quarters of a mile. As Rosa walked, probably with great care, to carry out her errand, I wonder how hot the meal was when it arrived. No doubt it was still appreciated by William, who worked long hours in all sorts of weather. In summer, because he couldn't afford sweets, he would keep a small, smooth pebble in his mouth to prevent it becoming dry. He was bald-headed in later life and his billycock hat would have concealed a fresh cabbage leaf: a device to keep his head cool. In winter, he was subject to quinsy - an inflammation of the tonsils - and he grew a beard under his chin and wore a neckerchief in an attempt to keep his throat warm, believing that this helped to prevent the condition. It probably wasn't helped by the clay pipe he used to smoke.

William was one of a number of Potton fathers (and one mother) who appeared at the Biggleswade Petty Sessions in early November, 1884, accused of 'not causing their children to attend school'. In William's case, the children not attending school may have been his sons David (b 1873) and Philip (b 1876). The case was reported in the *Cambridge Independent Press* of Saturday 22nd November, 1884. Reading between the lines, I reckon it's a fair bet that David and Philip had been helping with the potato harvest that autumn, and contributing to the family finances. William may have been somewhat aggrieved at being fined five shillings plus costs for his lack of concern for his sons' education, but he repeated the offence in May, 1899, and was fined a further five shillings. This time the truanting children could have included Rosa (b 1889) or her younger brother Albert (b 1892), and again I suspect they were working on the land, maybe helping their father set his potatoes or his runner beans.

By 1906 William appears to have learned his lesson - and his youngest daughter, Annie, had been learning hers - because the *Biggleswade Chronicle* of 26th April reported that she had received a prize for not having missed a day's schooling in two years.

Rosa told me that her father used to take a day off work if one of his children had a birthday - this ensured that he had nine days' holiday a year. He could play the accordion, and maybe this helped to make the birthdays all the more memorable. He was probably glad of the rest on these days, because in addition to his work for Billy Smith, his employer, he also rented pieces of land in and around Potton from Potton Charities. He had land on Potton common and at the Roundabout from the 1870s to the 1920s, and also in Handpost Field in Sutton Road. He would have walked to and from his land, and any work done on these plots would have been done in the early morning or after a full day's work for his employer. One of his grandsons, Sid Whitfield, (1915-1994), told me that he was sometimes asked to help out on this land in the 1920s. His payment consisted of a piece of his grandmother's seed cake.

When Emma wasn't doing housework or looking after her children she helped to supplement the family's income by working as a straw plaiter, although this industry began to decline during the last quarter of the nineteenth century, partly due to the introduction of cheaper plait from China and Japan. By 1901 the number of female straw plaiters in Bedfordshire had fallen to just under five hundred; there had been over twenty thousand of them thirty years earlier. My aunt Doris told me she could remember her grandmother having an implement used for splitting straws ready for plaiting. (I wonder what happened to it?). Splitting the straws was done to produce a finer plait; it also made it possible to select and include the duller inside of the stalk as well as the shiny outside, giving a more interesting, variegated finish to the completed plait. Splitting each straw and plaiting such fine lengths to

William Whitfield, (1854-1930), photographed in his garden at Pound End, Potton, about 1914.

an intricate pattern must have tried Emma's patience at times and couldn't have been good for her eyesight.

William was on the committee of the Potton pig club (founded in 1883), a club which sought to encourage working men in the town to keep pigs. The meetings were held at the *Two Brewers* public house in Back Street, (now Chapel Street), where William may well have enjoyed a convivial drink.

I was interested to see that my great grandfather, William was called as a witness at an inquest held at the *Rose and Crown* hotel, Potton (*Biggleswade Chronicle,* Friday 2nd March, 1900). He and a friend, George Gilbert, had been unable to prevent George Francis Carrington from taking his own life on 25th February of the same year.

George Francis Carrington, who was about 73 in 1900, appears to have lived in Potton Market Square. The 1891 census shows that he was a harness maker, possibly occupying premises at the rear of the *Rose and Crown*. The licensee of that establishment (now called the *Old Coach House*) at that time was William Henry Fowler.

Early on the morning of Sunday, February 25th, Carrington had opened a letter which was from his son William, who was in police custody at Biggleswade for threatening behaviour, and was expecting to be put into prison. William had previously assaulted his father and his brothers. George Carrington was obviously distressed by the contents of the letter.

Alice Carrington, (who was Carrington's third wife) had known her husband to threaten suicide before, when he had taken a cut throat razor with him as he walked around Bury Hill, Potton, in an obviously disturbed state of mind. However, the walk must have calmed him because he had not attempted suicide on this occasion. Now she could see from his agitated behaviour that his mind was once again unbalanced.

Those attending the inquest learned that on the day of her husband's death, Mrs Carrington had already thwarted him in one suicide attempt. After reading the letter, Carrington had tried to hang himself from a four-poster bed in his bedroom, using a rope and a chair; Alice had kicked the chair away. He had then picked up a ladder and a chap rein and had gone into the yard, towards his workshop. Alice Carrington had seen my great grandfather, William Whitfield, outside a shop near the harness maker's, chatting to a fellow agricultural labourer George Gilbert. The conversation may well have been about their pigs as they were fellow committee members of the Potton pig club. She had called out to them to stop her husband hanging himself, and they had followed him into his yard, and then into his workshop. Meanwhile, Mrs Carrington had gone in search of the police sergeant.

My great grandfather said to him 'Hallo, what are you about here?' Carrington smiled and said 'Go on with you', put down the ladder and chap rein, and returned to his house. He may well have closed the door behind him. William and George Gilbert would not have known at this stage that he had already attempted suicide inside the house, and that he had rope, a four-poster bed and probably a still conveniently placed chair in his bedroom. Carrington's reassuring smile and apparently meek demeanour may have lulled them into a sense of false security. They were probably reluctant to enter the house, for whatever reason, and did not do so, although they did peer through the ground floor windows. When Mrs Carrington returned, they told her that her husband was 'all right'.

Their optimism was ill-founded. On entering the bedroom, Alice Carrington found her husband hanging from the four-poster bed. He was still warm, but there was no pulse.

The jury returned a verdict of suicide while Carrington's state of mind was disturbed. His psychological turmoil seems to have been as a result of his son's misdemeanours; it certainly wasn't due to financial worries. An auction was held later in the year, somewhat ironically at the *Rose and Crown,* to dispose of Carrington's property, which included land at Deepdale and Wrestlingworth, two cottages in Potton and one in Wrestlingworth, all of which were let to tenants.

Emma Whitfield died in 1929. The report in the *Biggleswade Chronicle* stated that she was '…an old and much respected inhabitant [of Potton]'. William was prevented by illness from attending the funeral. He died in Camden, London, the following year, of cardiac failure and chronic bronchitis. His youngest daughter, Annie, was with him when he died. Both of them had apparently been living there for some time because I found both their names listed on the electoral roll for 1930. They were probably not far from one of William's other daughters, Rosa. William's body was returned to his native town, and he and Emma are now at rest in an unmarked grave in Potton cemetery.

I have not found a funeral report for my great-grandfather William. However, several of his grandchildren remembered him with affection, saying that he was a lovely, happy man. (They were a little more in awe of Emma who apparently kept the little cottage in Pound End in a spotless condition, and used to warn her grandchildren not to mark the wallpaper with their sticky fingers). I am fortunate in having a few photographs of both of them, taken in the 1920s, particularly as they were not 'posed' photographs, taken in a studio, but taken informally outside their home. I would love to know who the photographer was.

William and Emma would have benefitted for a few years from the State pension which had been introduced in 1909 by Lloyd George's Liberal Government. The amount offered in 1909 was 5 shillings a week for an individual, 7s 6d for a married couple. It was paid from the age of seventy, so William would have received his for six years, Emma for just three. I would imagine that both were pleased with this largesse; both had known very hard times with little in the way of security for themselves and their family.

The oldest child of William and Emma was David Whitfield, born in December, 1873. David joined the railway company at Potton station at the age of seventeen, and became a porter and signalman. He also was responsible for the station's gardens where the floral displays apparently became well known for their magnificence. However, he had two side-line businesses: market gardening and buying standing timber in and around Potton, felling it, and selling the timber. The brushwood was cut into faggots by his father, William, who apparently was very quick at this sort of work, and he would then sell them around Potton. David had rented land on Potton common in the 1920s and 1930s, and also near Potton station, which must have been handy for him, bearing in mind where he worked. Although David lived in a railway house in Sandy Road, he had the foresight to buy a house in King Street in 1909 which he leased to tenants until he moved there in his retirement. David's youngest son, Sid Whitfield gave me an old receipt, dated 1909, which states, on a billhead from W.M. Whittet (butcher): 'Received of Mr. D. Whitfield for one house, the sum of two hundred and forty five pounds'. It looks as if David had bought the house outright, for cash!

William and Emma Whitfield in their garden in the 1920s. Potton Church is visible in the background.

Several different people, (not all of them from within the family) have told me that David was an independent character with a blunt manner who enjoyed a good argument. I never met him; he died before I was born, but a few examples given to me will illustrate his general demeanour. My mother reported that he had been in the Co-operative shop in King Street (where she worked), and had left a handcart with an axe or saw in it outside, temporarily. Another customer, noticing David's cart with its contents asked him 'Going for some wood, David?'. His reply was a brusque 'Does it *look* like it?' Undeterred, the person asked him where he was going, and the reply was a rather deliberate and condescending 'I'm going where there is some'.

My maternal grandfather, Harry Mingay, reported that when he had been in charge of the stores at the Land Settlement Association in Potton, selling seeds and other horticultural items, David had appeared and greeted him with 'You've got some cabbage seed and I want some'.

Ken Lawson, in his '*Memories of an ordinary Pottonian*' recalls David, who was a neighbour in Sandy Road. David had some land next to Ken's father's land, and *he was always arguing about the width of the path between the plots*!

Although he worked for the railway for over fifty years, it is clear that David maintained a lifelong interest in gardening and market gardening. At the Potton Horticultural Show in August, 1912, he won prizes for his gooseberries, cooking apples and garden flowers. In the following year he exhibited at Potton again, and won prizes for garden flowers, cut flowers, dessert plums, and gooseberries. (His younger brother Ernest, my grandfather, took first prize for spring sown onions). In 1921, David won first prize for his red cabbage exhibits which were apparently so much admired at the Potton Show that they were also mentioned in the main body of the article, not just in the list of prize winners.

David sometimes travelled further afield to exhibit his produce. In the Langford Show of 1922 he won first prize (five shillings) for six cooking apples, and third prize (two shillings and six pence) for a collection of cut flowers. No doubt encouraged by these efforts, he exhibited at Langford again the following year and won first prize (four shillings) for cooking plums and second prize (three shillings) for cooking apples in the cottagers' classes 'open to all persons in Langford and the parishes in the Biggleswade Union not owning or occupying more than three acres of land'. The exhibits were presumably taken there by bicycle. Clearly, David was a skilful and versatile gardener; and although his primary motive appears to have been to augment his income, he clearly was keen to demonstrate his expertise in growing produce of a very high quality.

I discovered that David was involved in an incident (reported in the *Bedfordshire Times* and the *Biggleswade Chronicle*), outside the *Red Lion* public house in Potton in 1933. He had called into this establishment (which ceased trading recently), for a quiet drink after work on the evening of 5th August. It is quite likely that he had been working on his land near the railway line in Station Road. As David came out of the pub at about 10 pm, he had been assaulted by John Chamberlain. Chamberlain had approached him silently from behind and knocked him to the ground by a blow to the jaw, saying 'That will learn [i.e teach] you to call after my mother going to London'. From this, I inferred that David had called out something uncomplimentary to Mrs Chamberlain as she boarded a train at Potton Station, and this prompted me to investigate further. The *Biggleswade Chronicle* report (it made the front page) fortunately gave additional details, and it appeared that there had been a long-standing feud between David and members of the Chamberlain family. According to the Chronicle report, David had shouted to Mrs Chamberlain 'There's only one Chamberlain in your family', implying that her children were all conceived illegitimately and that her husband was therefore a cuckold. It was claimed in court that the animosity between David Whitfield and the Chamberlains had originated from the time of the General Strike in 1926, when John Chamberlain's father had driven a train from Potton Station to Bedford, and David had called him a blackleg for breaking the strike. An expletive had also been used, which the Chronicle editor had refrained from printing, replacing it by a dash. Like the Chronicle readers of 1933, we can only speculate about the colourful language David had employed.

David was aged about sixty when the assault took place; his assailant was about half his age. The injuries he sustained were cuts and bruises to his knees and he had since suffered from giddiness and headaches. He appears to have returned to the pub - possibly to get cleaned up, maybe to regain his composure and to have another drink or possibly because he wasn't keen to have another meeting with Chamberlain. Chamberlain in the meantime had visited David's house in Station Road, asking for David and threatening to 'knock his bloody head off'. He had assaulted David's wife, Jane, by grabbing her by the throat and pushing his fist into her face. She had ordered him out of the yard, saying 'I don't wish to talk to such trash'. Making further threats, Chamberlain was dragged away by his brother-in-law.

A few days later, Chamberlain had called at the signal box at Potton Station to apologise to David for his behaviour. David told him that the matter had 'gone too far', and had taken him to court.

David was perhaps a little fortunate when the magistrates decided John Chamberlain had been drunk at the time of the assault and that there was no truth in his allegation. Chamberlain was ordered to pay ten shillings costs for each of the two cases of assault, and had since moved to London.

In February, 1935, plans were being made for building new council houses in Sandy Road, Potton, on land owned by the Bedfordshire Smallholdings and Allotments committee. David Whitfield's one acre plot in Sandy Road was mentioned; unfortunately he was to lose half of it. Another tenant had agreed to forfeit one of his two one acre plots, but David Whitfield's agreement wasn't mentioned. From what I have heard of David I would imagine that he would have been reluctant to lose half of his plot, and his acquiescence in the matter seems a little unlikely.

David was aged over seventy and still working at Potton station in 1944, when he again appeared in court, this time as a witness in the sad case of Mr Samuel James Poulter, an elderly London evacuee who had died after being hit by a train. David from his vantage point in the signal box had seen Mr Poulter sitting on a seat beside the railway track; after the train had passed through the station he noticed something huddled up by the crossing. Unfortunately, it was Samuel Poulter. Mr Poulter had not been a well man: he had received injuries in 1941 when London was bombed, and he had been suffering from mental disturbances, gastric trouble and rheumatoid arthritis. Despite receiving medical attention, Poulter died from shock about fifteen minutes after sustaining severe injuries to his abdomen and one of his legs. The coroner returned a verdict of suicide.

I was told by Sid Whitfield that his father had died suddenly, whilst feeding his hens. The funeral report from the *Biggleswade Chronicle* of 13th April, 1951, gave further details:

'During Saturday evening, Mr David Whitfield of King Street [Potton] was found lying in the yard of his home. The discovery was made by his wife after he had failed to go in for tea. Medical aid was summoned, but life was found to be extinct. Mr Whitfield, who was 77 years of age, was very well known in the district. On Saturday he had been working on his land near the Railway station, and appeared to be in his usual health. For over 56 years he was employed by the Railway Company, joining them at the age of 17 and became signalman at Potton station where he remained until he retired about three years ago. Although he was due to retire in 1939, owing to the war he did not do so until 1947. He then carried on a market gardener's business and supplied vegetables for his son's greengrocery business. Mr Whitfield was a keen horticulturist and provided some fine displays of flowers and plants. He also took great interest in beekeeping and owned a number of hives with his sons'.

The National Probate Register reveals that David left an estate of about £900. His hand-written will indicates that David anticipated some disagreement amongst his sons after their parents' deaths: 'We, David Whitfield and Jane Whitfield, hereby united, wish that our sons Clarence David, Leslie James and Sidney Albert at our deaths must agree to equal rights of all we possess'. The words 'must agree', 'equal rights' and 'all' were underlined. It would appear that David's argumentative nature had been passed on to his sons, and he was well aware of it.

David's wife, Jane, nee Taylor, whom he married in 1897, shared his interest in flowers. She loved growing indoor plants and apparently produced some fine specimens. She also made her own wine. Jane Whitfield died in February, 1952.

The four children of David and Jane Whitfield were Jack, b.1902, who died after twelve hours; and we have already briefly met Clarence David, b. 1907, Leslie James, b. 1912, and Sidney Albert, b. 1915.

Clarence was an intelligent boy who showed an early interest in the crystal radio sets that were just beginning to appear at the time: he managed to build his own. Clarence appears to have started to keep bees while he was a young man. The *Bedfordshire Times* of 19th September, 1930, shows that he won first prize for honey in the comb, and second prize for new honey at the Wrestlingworth Show. He was also showing promise as a gardener: he won first prize for his parsley. He would have been aged about 23 at this time. It is fairly safe to assume that he had been taught by his father- and maybe also by his grandfather, William Whitfield. William would have only been about 53 years old and still an active working man when Clarence was born. Clarence's younger brother, Sid, told me that their grandfather kept in touch with his eldest son, David, and his family.

Despite his interest in gardening and matters horticultural, Clarence was working as a painter and decorator for Frederick Dennis of Potton in May, 1929, when an article appeared in the *Bedfordshire Times* reporting that Clarence's employer had not been paying National Health and unemployment contributions on behalf of his young employee. The arrears amounted to

£15 10 shillings and 6 pence. Dennis pleaded the excuse of not having the money for stamping his employee's cards. He claimed that large debts were owing to him and several of his creditors had gone bankrupt. He was ordered to pay the arrears and was also fined a total of £3 with two shillings costs. Some compassion was shown to him by the magistrates by allowing him to pay back what he owed at a rate of £1 per week.

Clarence married Florence Swales in the Ampthill district in 1931, and they moved to Lemsford, a village near Hatfield in Hertfordshire. He started a greengrocery business, using vegetables grown in the market gardening areas of Potton and Sandy (some of them grown by his father), and supplying outlets in north London. Lemsford was an ideal base from which to operate, and Clarence did well. He sold his business and retired to Cornwall, where he continued with his gardening until he died in 1983. The only child of Clarence and Florence, Phyllis, was born in 1931. She married William A. Gossage in 1955. They had a son who was unfortunately killed when he fell from some scaffolding.

The next son was Leslie James Whitfield, b.1912. He became a shepherd in Potton, and then a butcher. He was unusual as a shepherd because he used to drive his sheep i.e. walk behind them, rather than in front of them. My father, Hubert Whitfield, b. 1921, remembered seeing him drive his sheep from a field (which is now a housing estate called Spencer Close) along King Street to Potton Market Square - a feat which if repeated today would cause traffic chaos, quite apart from danger to sheep and their shepherd. Leslie was also a keen gardener and a beekeeper. He married Clara Brunt in August, 1938, and they lived in Upper Caldecote, near Biggleswade, in a semi-detached house which Les bought for £450 at an auction held in May, 1938.

Les clearly continued with his horticultural pursuits after his marriage: an article in the *Biggleswade Chronicle* of 10th July, 1953 shows that he won prizes at the Shefford Fete for his roses, strawberries, gooseberries, and redcurrants. My aunt Doris kept in touch her cousin Les and his wife Clara and would often return from her visits with a jar of honey. Clara was a church organist (like Doris), and played at Upper Caldecote for over sixty years - a remarkable record. The two ladies notched up over a century's worth of organ playing at local churches and chapels between them and must have had plenty to talk about. Les and Clara didn't have any children. Les died from lung cancer in 1973; Clara survived him by 25 years.

Sidney Albert, b. 1915, David and Jane's youngest son lived in Horslow Street, Potton after he married Kathleen Standen in 1938. He first started keeping bees at ten years of age (a somewhat risky activity when he was still wearing short trousers), and he became very interested in gardening, especially the propagation of fruit trees and roses, whilst he was still at school. He would dig wild briars out of the hedgerows around Potton, plant them along the railway line near the railway station where his father worked, and then bud choice varieties of roses onto these stocks. The idea was that the engine drivers would see the blooms as they pulled into the station; the roses would sell themselves, and his father, David, would take the money. Sid had an eye to business from an early age. As a boy he would help his father, and sometimes his grandfather on their pieces of land which they worked in their spare time. On leaving school, he worked on the land for Tom Cheetham, but also worked some land of his own on Everton Heath.

Sid Whitfield in Rex Whitfield's garden in Everton Road Potton, early 1990s.. Photo by Michael Breeds.

He enlisted in the Royal Artillery Medical Corps in the Second World War, spending time in India and Burma, where he was wounded badly in one leg, and also caught malaria. He was advised to have the leg amputated, but he refused, and was eventually able to dispense with the calliper he had to wear. His wartime experiences left their mark: he seemed to like to live for the moment; he was very much his own man; and he didn't cope very well with any type of authority. Anyone trying to deal with him in an official capacity was likely to receive some very offhand, unhelpful answers and would find him generally stubborn and unco-operative. By all accounts his father had been much the same, so maybe Sid's wartime experiences merely accentuated personality traits that were already there.

Most of his working life before the war and after his return from Burma was spent in the orchards at Cockayne Hatley, a hamlet some two miles from Potton, on an estate owned initially by a colourful and controversial character: John Alexander Whitehead. Mr Whitehead's business methods were somewhat dubious, as they involved a type of pyramid selling where people were invited to subscribe to the enterprise; their subscriptions bought more fruit trees and they were entitled to some of the fruit and a share of the profits - in theory at least. Mr Whitehead was a 'showman' with big ideas; he held apple days at Cockayne Hatley and various celebrities and members of the aristocracy attended, viewed the trees and the work in progress and pledged their support. Mr Whitehead paid good wages and provided employment in the local area at a time when jobs were hard to come by. He was always looking for new ways to make money; one involved bringing a number of redundant double decker buses from London to his estate, and using them to house chickens. Another was more questionable as it was said to involve an insurance scam. Two or three bad years in succession meant that Mr Whitehead had to sell up. Adverse weather conditions during the Second World War played an important part in the undermining of his enterprise. Whereas before the war the danger of late frosts, so dangerous to apple blossom, could be lessened by placing flares overnight in the fields, during the war this could not be done because of the blackout regulations, and as luck would have it, late frosts decimated the apple crop in successive years.

The estate was taken over by the Co-operative Wholesale Society, whose head office was in Manchester, and, ironically, the crop of apples was so heavy in their first year at Cockayne Hatley that, according to Sid, 'they didn't know what to do with them all.' He was taken on by the Society, and was involved in the budding of selected varieties on to apple stocks, and the pruning and grafting of the older trees. He was also in charge of the estate's beehives which at one time numbered nearly one thousand. The bees were used to pollinate the estate's apple and pear trees, but were useful in their own right, producing honey and wax. The hives of bees were also taken to another Co-op estate at nearby Buntingford, Hertfordshire, and, in late summer, to Darley Dale, near Matlock in Derbyshire, so that they could produce honey from the heather which would be flowering there at that time. A lot of work and planning was involved in this large scale enterprise, and no doubt Sid's experience and expertise helped to make it successful.

Sid was a hard-working character, but he also liked to scheme, bargain and indulge in banter. He once told his employer (who had asked him how it was that he [Sid] owned his own house when most of the other employees rented theirs) that he liked to earn one week's pay with his hands and another week's pay with his head, i.e. by scheming and dealing. He bought and sold produce, livestock, stocks and shares and property. He was not averse to occasional poaching exploits either, and possessed a gun and a couple of ferrets for this purpose.

After his redundancy from the Cockayne Hatley estate was announced (the fruit trees were pulled up and burnt in the 1970s after Britain joined the European Economic Community and cheap, tasteless European apples, picked before they were ready, flooded the market), Sid became a regular visitor to the estate's woods and plantations after dark when the pheasants were roosting. He enjoyed a flutter on the horses and dogs, whose form he studied regularly, and made weekly visits to the Henlow greyhound stadium, where he convinced various dog trainers that their greyhounds would perform more effectively if their diet included honey. And why not? Sir Edmund Hillary, the conqueror of Mount Everest, was the son of a beekeeper and advocated the regular consumption of honey. Sid used to consume a pound of honey a week himself, stirring it into his tea. In all the time I knew him he never had a cold.

I got to know Sid after he had retired. I wanted to learn how to keep bees and as he had worked with them all his life, he seemed the ideal person to ask. He had carried on with his beekeeping in his retirement, having about a dozen hives of his own. After I coped successfully with a sort of initiation experience where I had to retrieve the hive tool from the bottom of the brood chamber where I had inadvertently dropped it (I collected no stings at all on my bare arm and hand), Sid gave me a hive of bees of my own. I eventually built up to about twelve, and we worked our hives between us, using Sid's specialist knowledge. We also managed some hives belonging to two of Sid's friends, George Montila and Richard Hill. In return, Sid would help himself to any of Mr. Montila's crops (for his own use only) whenever he felt like it. It was an informal arrangement which seemed to suit everyone. The hives were kept in very secluded locations: on the old airfield between Tempsford and Everton, behind White Wood on Gamlingay Heath and on the Co-op's estate at Cockayne Hatley. A lot of the work was done at weekends and during my school holidays. The honey was extracted in the evenings in my kitchen. I was kept entertained by Sid's jokes and stories and I marvelled at his knowledge of the countryside.

As well as selling the honey, Sid used to brew mead, usually a couple of barrels at a time. He would sometimes add blackberries to the other ingredients for a slightly different flavour and colour. After the brewing was over, the liquid would be poured into the barrels which would have muslin placed over the hole where the bung would eventually be inserted, and the hot, late summer sunshine would encourage fermentation to take place. The smell of fermenting honey and yeast pervaded the yard and attracted bees and wasps. No wonder some of Potton's wasps seemed rather drowsy and unsure of themselves on September afternoons.

The mead was delicious and deceptively strong. Sometimes a tot of whisky would be added to the drinker's glass. During an evening with Sid and Kath I would be offered a glass or two of mead and I found I had to be very careful when leaving their house, as it stood at the top of a steep slope which I had to negotiate before walking home along Horslow Street. The mead was also sometimes distilled into a spirit. It was colourless, but it still tasted of honey. It was *very* strong - you could set fire to it, like brandy on a Christmas pudding.

Travelling with Sid in his car was an unforgettable experience. A powerful aroma of honey, wax, old hessian sacks, and smoke (from his bee smoker) greeted you on entering the vehicle,

159

and the hum of the engine was merely incidental to the urgent buzzing coming from dozens of bees which congregated around the windows, trying to escape. Not all of them managed to do so: there was a sort of bee graveyard on his rear window sill. There was always a selection of sharp nail scissors in the glove compartment (they were used to clip the wings of queen bees) and a comprehensive first aid kit. Having served in the Royal Artillery Medical Corps, Sid took an interest in medical matters and took them very seriously. An old overcoat on the back seat concealed a bottle of mead, placed there in case we felt in need of refreshment. Funnily enough, after working with the bees we often did…

Sid would drive fairly slowly. Even in his seventies he had very keen eyesight, and while travelling he liked to survey the general state of the crops; he also liked to look for briars, crab apple stocks, budding wood, pheasants and pretty girls and women, and not necessarily in that order. He used to stop and offer women a lift and was amused at their reaction when they encountered the bees; they enjoyed the mead, though, even if it was sampled straight from the bottle.

Sid was well-known and respected on local farms and market gardens. He had worked for or with some of the owners, or they had contacted him in an attempt to improve pollination of their orchard crops or clover and invited him to bring his hives onto their land. He would often call unannounced and strut around their holdings, admiring or criticising their crops and livestock. These were either 'not amiss' or 'no damn good'. He gave his views without being asked. The infuriating thing was that if a crop or animal was placed in this latter category it usually did turn out to be a failure later on. He knew what he was talking about and he gave his views without fear or favour, irrespective of his audience.

As Sid was an acknowledged authority on bees and matters horticultural, he was sought after by local people, either for advice or because they wanted to deal with troublesome swarms of honey bees or nests of bumble bees in their gardens. Initial consultations often took place outside Lloyd's Bank in the Market Square (now a carpet shop) where he would hold court in the sunshine after fetching his newspaper and before he returned home to water his greenhouse.

His garden was his pride and joy, and rightly so. With vegetables, he liked to obtain very early or very late crops; he liked to push the art of growing to its limits. A favourite saying of his was 'You can't go against nature, but you can help it along'. He grew many different types of apples on dwarfing rootstocks (he had budded them himself); also plums, pears and gooseberries. Just outside his back door he had an apple 'family tree', where he had grafted some of his favourite varieties, all on the one tree. The purpose of this was to provide budding wood for trees he intended to propagate in the future. In his greenhouse he grew grapes, peaches, nectarines, lemons and kiwi fruit as well as tomatoes and cucumbers. With flowers, he enjoyed growing and propagating roses and orchids. He was a familiar figure at the Potton Show, where he won the fruit prize for several successive years when he was in his seventies, but various local newspaper reports indicate that Sid had been a successful exhibitor several decades earlier. The earliest instance I have found of him showing his produce was at the Sandy Show of 1939, where he won third prize for four one pound bottles of honey. His exhibiting would have been interrupted by his war service, but at the Wrestlingworth Show of 1952, he appears to have made a triumphant return to the show circuit, winning first and second prizes for honey both in jars and in the comb, and prizes for his mead, for a collection of fruit, for spring and winter onions, ridge cucumbers, cooking apples and mixed gladioli, giving some indication of the range of his horticultural expertise and interests. Having exhibited produce myself I can appreciate the amount of effort he must have put into growing and preparing such a range of items, particularly as it would also have been a busy time of year for beekeeping.

During his retirement, he travelled to the U.S.A., New Zealand and South Africa where he kept in touch with modern methods of fruit growing and beekeeping; he was interested in the research being undertaken into the uses and properties of propolis and Royal jelly, and he experimented with breeding his own strain of Queen bees, using artificial methods. He was also an effective speaker on fruit growing and beekeeping, where his expertise, combined with a humorous approach, could hold an audience spellbound.

Sid died in 1994, after suffering from bladder cancer. Until he developed this disease he had been remarkably fit and active, and when he first heard he had cancer he went out and harvested all his potatoes. He is still remembered in Potton for his forthright manner, resolute character, good humour and horticultural expertise. A trophy is presented in his honour at the Potton Show each year for the best apple exhibit.

The children of Sid and Kath Whitfield were (Sidney) John b. 1939, Marion, b.1941, and Reginald Ernest, b. 1942. John was certainly following a family tradition when he won prizes for his blackcurrants, gooseberries and honey when he exhibited at the Potton gala day in 1951. He was just twelve years old and must have been thrilled to win his prizes.

John was a bright boy who did well at school and was interested in engineering and technical drawing. He designed an aeroplane and sent the drawings to De Havilland's, who offered him a job. John wanted to work there and become a test pilot. This caused some friction at home, because his mother wasn't keen on the idea. However, he took the job, and moved down to the Hatfield area of Hertfordshire, staying with his uncle and aunt, Clarence and Florence at Lemsford.

John married Marlene Clegg in Hatfield in 1960, and their two children Paul John and Jane were born in 1964 and 1968 respectively. The family emigrated to New Zealand where John died from a heart attack on 18th January, 1975 whilst playing football with his son. He was only 35. Paul and Jane still live in New Zealand.

Marion married Michael Croot from Potton. Marion had her own dog grooming business in Potton, and later became a post lady. She later became a home care and eventually a carer's supervisor, running her own team of ladies who cared for elderly people in their homes. Her marriage to Michael Croot ended in divorce; there were two adopted children: Simon and Leanne. After she retired, Marion sold her house in Potton and moved to the St. Neots area, where she enjoys keeping an eye on her grandchildren.

The younger son of Sid and Kath Whitfield, Reginald Ernest, was born in 1942. Reg married Christine West in 1963, and they had two daughters Juanita Susan b. 1968 and Audrey Mary b.1971. Like his brother, Reg emigrated to New Zealand, where he has his own business as a refrigeration engineer. His first marriage ended in divorce, and Reg married again. His second wife, Talia, was originally from Tonga, and the wedding was in traditional Tongan style. They have two sons, Kilioti David, and Antonio. My cousin, Michael Whitfield, who lives in Bristol, visited Reg and his family in New Zealand a few years ago; some sixty years previously their respective grandfathers, brothers Ernest and David Whitfield had lived a few doors away from each other in King Street, Potton. Marion visited her brother and his family in 2011, and very kindly gave me some up to date photographs.

The next son of William and Emma was Philip, b.1876. He may have been named after his father's uncle, Philip Whitfield, the baker of Hook Norton. In 1891 he was living at home in Potton and working as an agricultural labourer. Articles in the *Bedfordshire Times* and the *Biggleswade Chronicle* for November, 1897 reveal that Philip had been involved in an incident outside the *Cross Keys* public house in Horslow Street, Potton, which had resulted in the death of a young labourer, Frederick Houghton.

Frederick Houghton, aged 26, originated from Arlesey, Bedfordshire, where he had been a brickyard labourer. He had moved to Gamlingay Heath, possibly to work at Gamlingay brickyard. The detailed report in the *Biggleswade Chronicle* of Friday November 12, 1897, showed that he had been on a drinking spree in Potton with friends on the previous Sunday evening. It had been Houghton's birthday, and to celebrate this occasion, his two companions, William Brim and William Boness had encouraged him to break his vow of temperance. They must have regretted this for the rest of their lives.

They had visited a number of public houses in Potton, starting at about 6.15 pm at the *George and Dragon* at the Market Square end of King Street, moving after about three quarters of an hour to the *Shannon* in Biggleswade Road, and half an hour later to the *Rose and Crown* in the Market Square where they seem to have spent most of the evening. Boness then went to the *Cross Keys* in Horslow Street and was joined by his friends later. Brim and Boness appear to have been drinking beer throughout the evening; Houghton started by drinking ginger beer, which I presume would have been an alcoholic drink at that time, but later he drank whisky.

Outside the *Cross Keys*, presumably when the fresh air hit him, Houghton stumbled to the ground, and after his friends got him to his feet appeared to be incapable of walking. He lay down in the road outside the pub, where he was seen by Ebenezer Wright, a market gardener from Gamlingay. His friends thought it important to remove him from public view to avoid a policeman charging him with being drunk, so they carried him to the rear of the property, propping him up against the wall of a barn.

It isn't clear whether Philip Whitfield had been drinking in the *Cross Keys*, but I think this is highly likely. It would explain why he was on hand to render some assistance: he had helped to move Houghton to the comparative warmth and security of a nearby pig-sty to sleep off his alcoholic excess. Philip fetched water and a candle, and they cleaned Houghton's face which was bleeding after his fall. Although it no longer held pigs, the sty still contained straw, and they laid Houghton face down in it. He 'appeared to be asleep-like and did not know what was going on'. They stayed with him until the candle burnt out.

When Brim, Boness and Mark Young went into the sty the next morning, Houghton was dead. The verdict of the doctor was that Houghton smelt strongly of spirits; he had tried to be sick, but had suffocated by inhaling his own vomit. A verdict of accidental death was recorded.

By 1901, Philip Whitfield was lodging in Gascony Avenue, Hampstead, London, just off the Kilburn Road. He was working as an excavator/navvy. It is likely that he was involved with the construction of the London underground railway network which was being developed at this time. The world's first underground electric railway (the Northern line) had opened in London in 1890. The Bakerloo line was opened in 1906, and the Hampstead tube, a later part of the Northern line, in June, 1907. Philip would have been working hard in a dirty and dangerous environment, reminiscent of conditions in a coal mine. He would, however, have been earning more than the average agricultural worker back in Potton, and this may have been the inducement to leave his home town.

Philip married a widow, Clara Court Clark on 1st January, 1921 in a Kensington Register Office. Clara's father on the marriage certificate was given as Jesse Stacey, deceased. He had been a baker in Wiltshire, but had died in 1883, at the early age of 45 (leaving an estate of over £800), and his widow Elizabeth Stacey had remarried. Her new husband was a boot and shoe dealer, George Bavis, twelve years her junior. The 1891 census shows Clara Stacey living with her mother and stepfather in Chertsey, Surrey. Aged fourteen, Clara was working as a milliner's assistant. I decided to check on Clara's whereabouts in 1881. I found her living with Jesse and Elizabeth Stacey in Langley Burrell, Wiltshire, where Jesse was indeed working as a master baker, employing one boy. I was surprised to find, however, that Clara was described as the *adopted* daughter of the couple. And there the mystery begins. I haven't been able to find the birth of a Clara Court, or a Clara Stacey, so I wonder who her parents were, and why she was adopted. It may be that Clara may not have known this herself if her adoption took place when she was very young, so I don't rate *my* chances of finding out very highly.

Philip and Clara do not appear to have had any children (they were both 46 at the time of their marriage), but I was told by Sid Whitfield that Clara had children from her first marriage. It took me some time to find details of this marriage, as Clark is a common surname and I didn't have the groom's Christian name. A further complication was that Clara, for some reason, was listed as Clara Court Stacey-Clark, but persistence eventually brought its reward.

The marriage took place in Greenwich in 1898. Clara's first husband was William Henry Clark. The 1901 census shows that he was about sixteen years older than Clara. He was working as an overseer and senior telegraphic worker for the London postal service. William and Clara were living in Lewisham with their young family: William (junior), Clara (junior) and Dorothy. Clara was a widow with six children (one son and five daughters) by 1911, and living in Birchington, near Margate in Kent; in the previous year she had buried her husband and also given birth to his youngest daughter. I'm not sure when she first met Philip Whitfield or how their paths first crossed. It may be that all her children had left home by the time she married him.

My father, Hubert Whitfield, remembered Philip returning to Potton to see his brother Ernest when the Potton horse fair was in progress. On horse fair days the Market Square would have been very busy as horses were tried out, bought and sold. The pubs would have been open all day and doing a brisk trade. Apparently Philip was one of their customers that day and he had too much to drink, sleeping it off in the front room of Ernest's house in King Street.

Philip acquired the reputation of being the black sheep of the family, but I have been unable to find justification for this, except perhaps for this one incident. It may be that he *was* over-fond of alcohol; his work as a navvy must have made him very thirsty and navvies often enjoyed a few pints of beer after their labours were over for the day. His early life in London is somewhat of a mystery; some members of the family have suggested that he ran away to London in his teens, but again I have found no evidence for this. If he *did* run away, I wonder why. Had he, perhaps, done something wrong? I have been unable to find him in the 1911 census, but assume he was still in London at this time. It would be interesting to know how and why he managed to avoid completing the census form. He died in 1937 from a cerebral haemorrhage, aged 63. He and Clara had been living in Princes Road, Kensington since their marriage. I have found no photographs of him, and no letters from him; I do, however, have his prayer book which I discovered at my grandfather's house in King Street in Potton, so at least I have a sample of his handwriting. He remains an enigmatic figure. Clara does not appear to have remarried after his death. She died in 1945, aged seventy. The death was registered in Rowley Regis in Staffordshire, suggesting that she may have gone to live with relatives - possibly with a married son or daughter.

Philip's younger sister, Emily Elizabeth was born in 1879. At the time of the 1901 census she was working as a housemaid for a retired naval captain, Alexander Campbell, in Kimbolton Avenue, Bedford. Her husband-to-be, John Alfred Ling, was described as a railway porter, and in 1901 was living in the house of John Sanders, a railway platelayer and his wife Eliza, and their two daughters in Pilcroft Street, Bedford. John Ling's father, James Ling, was a railway signalman, but his grandfather had been a farm bailiff in Essex. It may be that Emily and John had met on the railway station platform when she was arriving from Potton, or perhaps John Ling was a friend or workmate of David Whitfield, who, as we have seen, also worked on the railway.

The couple married later in 1901, and appear to have moved to Berkhamsted in Hertfordshire shortly afterwards, where their children were born: Phyllis Mabel (1902), Sidney Walter (1904), Winifred Mary (1906), Alfred William (1908), and Leslie James (1910).

The 1911 census shows that the family were living at 69 Ellesmere Road, Berkhamsted, and John Alfred Ling was still working as a railway porter, presumably at Berkhamsted station. Estate agents' details would have described the house as being within easy walking distance of the railway station; however, the house may have belonged to the railway company.

The family later moved to Watford, a few miles further down the railway line, towards London. This may have been due to a promotion for John Ling; Watford would almost certainly have been a bigger and busier station. The date of the move is not known, but a number of Ling marriages registered at Watford suggest that they were there by the late 1920s: Alfred William Ling married Cissie Nicholson in 1928; his younger brother Leslie James married Kathleen Clara Childs in 1932, and Winifred Mary Ling married Thomas Kavanagh (born in Limerick, Eire), during the following year. There are a number of descendants.

A grandson of Emily Elizabeth Whitfield and John Alfred Ling: Roger John Ling (son of Leslie James and Kathleen Clara Ling) is Professor of Classical Art and Archaeology at Manchester University. He was educated at Watford Grammar School, then at St. John's College, Cambridge, where he gained his B.A. degree in 1964, his M.A. in 1969 and Ph.D. in 1970. He is the author of several books on Roman art and archaeology, and has supervised archaeological digs in the U.K. and in Pompeii.

Emily Elizabeth Ling died in 1953. The National Probate Register indicates that she and her husband had been living in Hatfield Road, Watford. John Alfred Ling is described as a retired ticket collector: presumably he had been moved to lighter duties before his retirement. He died in 1962.

William and Emma's next son was Alfred Whitfield, b. 1884. In 1900, the Potton charities approved his apprenticeship to a local wheelwright, Ebenezer Garrott, who lived in Royston Street, Potton. Alfred was presumably trained to make wheels for wagons and farm carts. Wheel making by hand was a very skilled job: precise measurement, careful selection of woods and painstaking craftsmanship were all essential. Alfred married Ethel Purser sometime between October and December, 1906. The marriage was registered in Biggleswade. I assume that by this time Alfred's apprenticeship was over and he was therefore capable of earning more money. He would have realised that horse drawn coaches and carriages were being superseded by cars, and it would appear that he looked for jobs within the motor industry, still in its infancy at that time. Early models of cars bore some resemblance to the farm waggons and carts that he had been learning to make; the skills he had acquired as a wheelwright were presumably readily transferable as he learnt to build cars.

It appears that Alfred and Ethel may have lived and worked in the Newport Pagnell area of Buckinghamshire at some time after their marriage, because their first child, Gladys May was born there in 1910. I wondered why the family had moved there; more often than not families moved in search of work, and I found that Newport Pagnell had a coach works, owned by the Salmons family, which from 1898 was making car bodies. Early cars had bodies made separately from the chassis and assembly into the finished vehicle took place at a later stage. It seems likely that Alfred was working for the Salmons family, but I'm not sure how many years he may have spent with them, or why he moved.

The 1911 census shows that the family were living in Great Stukeley, near Huntingdon, and Alfred was working as a car body maker. At this time, bodies for Rolls Royce cars were being made in Huntingdon, by a firm called Windovers, who had previously been making horse-drawn coaches and it is likely that Alfred gained some experience here with these prestigious cars before moving to Mansfield in Nottinghamshire and then to the Birmingham area; the birth of Doris Ethel was registered in King's Norton, Staffordshire, in 1913. Alfred moved to become an early employee of Herbert Austin, (1866-1941), a pioneer in car manufacture; he apparently worked in the department where they experimented with new models of cars.

Herbert Austin had toured the Birmingham area by bicycle in November, 1905, looking for a suitable site for a car factory. He discovered a small derelict printing works at Longbridge, seven miles outside Birmingham which seemed promising. Friends helped with finance, and, amazingly, the first Austin car was produced in March, 1906, some four months later (and just seven months or so before the wedding of Alfred and Ethel Whitfield in the Biggleswade area). It was priced at £650, a lot of money in those days, making it affordable only to the wealthier members of society. Austin pressed on however, and just two years later was employing nearly one thousand workers at the Longbridge plant. They were now producing seventeen different models of car.

During the First World War the Longbridge factory was increased in size, but it was producing armaments, not cars. Aeroplanes were also manufactured there for a while, but car production was resumed afterwards. The famous Austin Seven model, a smaller car, priced competitively and therefore suitable for the mass market, first appeared in 1922. It was to become a real success story for Herbert Austin, and the security of employment that its production offered must have been welcomed by Alfred and his fellow workers. He and Ethel now had two more children to support and provide for: Ronald William, b.1917, and Edna Florence, b. 1919.

During World War Two, production at Longbridge again switched to armaments and aeroplanes, but car production continued after the war and the millionth Austin car rolled off the production line in June, 1946. Alfred would have been 62 at this time, and close to retirement. He kept in touch with his brother Ernest back in Potton and would sometimes visit. As far as I know, he was the only child of William and Emma Whitfield to own and drive a car. He died in 1967, aged 83. His wife, Ethel, had died during the previous year. Their daughters Gladys and Doris did not marry. They kept in touch with their cousin Doris (my aunt) in Potton by letter and telephone, until they died in 1989 and 1999 respectively. Their brother Ron married Iris Buggins in 1941. There were no children, and Ron died in 1980.

The youngest child of Alfred and Ethel Whitfield, Edna Florence, married Albert Edward Grazier in Birmingham in 1947. Their daughter Valerie Grazier, b.1949, married David Hitchman in Bromsgrove in 1971.

Valerie and David have a business selling compact discs of brass band and military band music, using the internet. Their daughters Nicola Jane Hitchman and Michelle Sarah Hitchman were born in 1978 and 1981 respectively. Nicola is married to Matthew Edwards and they have two daughters, Jessica Jane Edwards, b.2002, and Georgia Rose Edwards, b.2005.

I had lost touch with this branch of the family until I found a letter from Doris and Gladys Whitfield in the papers of my aunt Doris Sibley, nee Whitfield, after her death. The letter mentioned their niece Valerie, and some research on the internet enabled me to track her down.

I now have in my possession a small bookcase made by Alfred Whitfield from holly wood. It may have been made while he was still at school in Potton, but it was always in the living room at my grandfather's house in King Street, Potton, and was used to house his selection of reference books. It seems rather strange that this inanimate object has survived both brothers but still bears witness to its maker's craftsmanship back in his home town, thankfully far from the bustle of Birmingham.

Ernest Whitfield, b.1886, my grandfather, was the next child of William and Emma. Ernest was baptised in Potton church in 1889, with his brother Alfred, and must have been close to him as a child. There was a significant age difference between him and his older brothers David and Philip who must have seemed quite grown up to him as he and Alfred played at home. I discovered an early photograph of Ernest as a youth in a group of young men – it looks as though they were members of a club or class of some kind. The photograph was taken around 1900.

As a young man, Ernest, with his friend Albert Fox, cycled northwards and they eventually were surprised to find a factory belonging to *Whitfield and Fox* in a Yorkshire town - possibly Bradford: an exciting discovery after a long journey. This remarkable coincidence obviously made an impression because the story was related to his sons several years afterwards. The expedition must have tested the stamina of both lads, but at least would not have been a dangerous undertaking: there would have been few cars on the roads in the first decade of the twentieth century. In any case, their speeds would have been little faster than Ernest and Albert were travelling on their bicycles, and their noise would have been very noticeable in those more tranquil days which were soon to change for ever for everyone, thanks to the First World War.

Ernest married Ethel Wells from Biggleswade on Christmas Day, 1909. The marriage took place at Trinity Methodist Church in Biggleswade. Ethel, the daughter of a market gardener, Henry Wells, was working as a domestic servant at The Laurels, a large detached house in Bedford Road, Sandy. My aunt Doris told me that her father, during his courting days would walk to Sandy to meet Ethel, escort her to Biggleswade to meet her parents (where she presumably spent the night), and then walk back to Potton, a round trip of some ten miles. I assume this must have been at weekends. Some letters written to each other during this time over a century ago have survived - they were found in a case at the King Street house after their daughter Doris died in 2000.

Ernest started his working life as a parchment maker's boy, working at the Potton tannery. I have not managed to discover what his duties would have been in this role, but he later progressed to working as a carter, also for Braybrooks, the tanners. He had to collect skins from newly-slaughtered cattle from farms and butchers and take them by horse and cart to the tannery which was in Royston Street, Potton, about a hundred yards away from where I am writing. I can remember my piano teacher, Mrs Doris Greaves, nee Bartle, telling me in the 1960s that in her younger days she once travelled back from Biggleswade with Ernest after being offered a lift. With a load of cattle skins on the cart, the journey would have been none too fragrant, but it must have been preferable to Shanks' pony.

After their marriage, Ernest and Ethel lived in a cottage in West End Lane in Potton, where their first three children were born: Leslie Ernest in 1910, Herbert in 1911 (he died in infancy), and Doris in 1913. Ernest started working as a market gardener around this time. His employer was Fred Tear, a local man from an ordinary background who became a very wealthy farmer and market gardener, thanks to hard work and enterprise.

In 1915, Ernest and Ethel took on the tenancy of a public house called the *Railway Inn* in Sandy Road, Potton, a few doors away from the railway cottage occupied by his brother David and his wife and family. They often had soldiers from New Zealand and Australia billeted with them. Ernest and Ethel had another child while they were at the pub - a daughter, Millicent, b.1915. Unfortunately, she was born without a roof to her mouth, and she died in the same year.

The trading position of pubs at this time must have been somewhat precarious, with so many men fighting in the First World War; in any case, Potton's population in 1911 had been 2,156 people, and a ratio of about 102 people per public house was given in a *Biggleswade Chronicle* article, suggesting over 20 licensed premises in the small town. Not all these people would have been regular drinkers, of course: some would have been too young; others would have been teetotal or occasional drinkers; and in those days, pubs tended to be the preserve of males. Fortunately, Ernest had market gardening to supplement the income he derived from the Railway Inn. Its owners, Fordham's, brewers based in Ashwell, Hertfordshire, applied to have the licence renewed in March, 1917, but the reprieve was short-lived, and the property was offered for sale, as a private house, at an auction held at the *Rose and Crown* a year later. I would imagine that my granddad attended the auction, but the successful purchaser was

Ernest Theobalds, who acquired the property for £600. He, too, was a market gardener. The substantially-built house which boasted eight rooms and a cellar, also had a large yard with a well and outbuildings, together with a large garden, and would have been ideal premises from which to operate. Even better, the property was only about one hundred yards from Potton railway station which despatched large quantities of market garden produce to London each day. Legal formalities were apparently completed by June, 1918, but in retrospect, the solicitors acting for Mr Theobalds appear to have overlooked some rather important details…

In the meantime, at a tribunal held at Biggleswade in March, 1918, my granddad (described as aged 29, married and a 'smallholder,etc') had been required to 'volunteer' for military service. As far as I am aware he did not leave for Flanders, but may have trained in preparation for doing so; fortunately for him (and for everyone else), the war ended some eight months later.

I was intrigued to see that my grandfather, grandmother and their family were still occupying the *Railway Inn* in October of the same year, and that their continued presence there had prompted the new owner to apply for an ejectment order. They had been given notice to quit as early as February, to expire in May and had been asked to vacate the premises several times by the new owner; to make matters worse, they had paid Mr Theobalds no rent, and to add *further* insult to injury, my granddad, who obviously had an eye to business, had sub-let all the outbuildings. Having met my granddad, I would imagine that he had received *his* rent.

It was mentioned in court that Theobalds had suggested alternative accommodation (a house that his brother had been occupying), but to no avail. Although it was claimed that my granddad owed Theobalds rent, it was decided that in fact he and his family were, in effect, squatters; and as no formal contract existed between them and Theobalds they were therefore not his legal tenants and thus owed no rent at all. The magistrates dismissed the case.

The Theobalds family obviously later took possession of the property and continued living there, because I can remember Ernest Theobalds' son, Frank, as an elderly man living there on his own in the 1960s after his wife had died. When I knew him, Frank was a friendly, but somewhat eccentric odd-job man who had the reputation of being rather careful with his money. He certainly lived frugally and hoarded various items in his sparsely furnished house. His way of life may have resulted from the fact that his wife had died in her forties. My father used to take a vanload of empty cardboard boxes to him each week from the grocery shop he managed; Frank used to flatten the boxes and then dig them into his vegetable garden in an attempt to retain moisture in its light, sandy soil.

My grandfather's market gardening was going well, and in addition to his work for Mr Tear he now farmed a number of plots in and around Potton and on Everton and Gamlingay Heath. After the war he bought two adjoining houses in King Street, Potton, and moved himself and his family to one of them. Apparently, he often said he wished he had had the nerve to buy more. I still have the deeds to the house they lived in; it was purchased from Mr Willie Whittet, a Potton butcher, for £242 10s. You may remember that Mr Whittet had earlier sold a house in King Street (a few doors along the road) to Ernest's older brother, David. In those days most houses were rented: in 1918 only 23 per cent of households owned the houses they lived in. Both brothers worked hard to become owner-occupiers.

Ernest and Ethel's son Kenneth Arthur was born in 1918, and in the same year Ethel became ill with influenza, in the flu epidemic which affected Britain and other European countries after the First World War. Her mother, Emma Wells, came from Biggleswade to help look after her and the children, but caught the flu herself and died at the house in King Street. She was about 53 years old.

In order to encourage Leslie, his oldest son to become self-reliant and enterprising, Ernest told him that if he could sell his father's field of one quarter of an acre of beetroot in Sutton Road, he could buy a bicycle with the proceeds. Leslie duly sold the crop to a Mr Pibworth of Potton, and was soon proudly riding his bicycle.

Ernest used to take Leslie and Doris when they were very young to see William and Emma their grandparents. William would take the children to see his pigs, and Emma would give them seed cake, but warn them as they were eating it at the table, not to scrape the backs of their chairs on the wallpaper. There was a picture of Queen Victoria on the wall. She, too, probably would not have been amused if the wallpaper had been scraped in the small cottage, but of course she had died in 1901. To many older people she remained a much venerated figure.

Ernest still worked for Fred Tear, but he was also working land on his own account both before and after his hours of work for his employer. It was not unusual for him to start work at 4.30 or 5 in the morning in summer, having travelled to one of his plots in the Roundabout, Sutton Road, Gamlingay Road or on the Gamlingay Heath by bicycle. This latter plot was known as Donkey Island: land in the vicinity was said to be so 'hungry' that labourers were advised not to leave their waistcoats on it in case the garments were eaten up by the soil, which was desperate for nutrients. The soil on the Heath was very sandy, but it warmed up quickly in spring, making it suitable for crops of early potatoes, which fetched a high price. The potatoes were forked out by hand, and packed into wicker baskets.

A major part of market gardening involved keeping the crop clean, i.e. free from weeds, so that the vegetables could grow and mature quickly. My grandfather Ernest often grew root crops such as beetroot, parsnips and carrots. He would hoe between the rows with a push hoe or 'Massey', a sort of hoe on wheels. This brilliant invention, a good early example of intermediate technology, was actually a double hoe as there were two hoe blades mounted on a framework which was attached to either one or two wheels. The framework had two handles. The implement was pushed along the rows of the growing crop, making use of the wheels, and the two hoe blades were positioned either side of a row, so that the two sides were hoed at the same time as the contraption was moved slowly along. The push hoe was relatively light and could be carried by a man on his shoulders while he cycled to his plot. Crops such as carrots, parsnips and beetroot also needed to be thinned out or singled, so that individual carrots (or whatever) were eventually the optimum distance apart. In Bedfordshire, this operation tended to be done by men on their knees, and was therefore known as 'crawling'. Protective pads made from hessian sacking were often used, but the job took its toll on the knee joints and my grandfather Ernest had operations to correct cartilage trouble almost certainly caused by this practice. He didn't have the opportunity or luxury of having the problem caused by playing football. Otherwise, his job, which involved constant physical activity, kept him pretty fit.

As his main job involved working for Mr Tear, Ernest would sometimes sell his crop to a dealer once it was ready for harvesting. This was a common practice at the time. Brussels sprouts, for example (an important Bedfordshire crop) were often sold in this way. A few acres of sprouts, grown by someone like my grandfather, would be advertised in the *Biggleswade Chronicle*, and would be purchased by someone who might be looking for a winter's work. He would then pick the sprouts and market them, taking on the risks of fluctuating prices, uncertain demand and severe weather. Ernest would have sold his few acres of sprouts, and banked his money, but would have been picking sprouts for Fred Tear throughout the winter. Nowadays F1 hybrid varieties of Brussels sprouts are grown to ensure that nearly all the 'buttons' mature at the same time. The whole stalk is then harvested by machine and the sprouts are removed from the stalk by the housewife in the comparative warmth of her kitchen. The old Bedfordshire varieties of Brussels sprouts had opposite characteristics: the buttons or sprouts matured gradually over the season, so that picking might be possible over a period lasting from November, say, through to the following March. They were harvested in the field, by hand.

Picking the sprouts was a cold, back-breaking job at the best of times, but must have been a particularly unpleasant task on a foggy, freezing morning in January or February. Like stone picking, the job would have involved frequently repeated contact with freezing cold surfaces, and fingers, hands and toes would soon have turned numb. Gloves were not worn; frostbite was possible. Large measures of determination and stoicism were required. My grandfather had both of these. Manual dexterity and long fingers were also advantageous, and fortunately granddad had these too. Working hard, he was able to earn good money at piecework rates. My father told me that the cold badly affected *his* father's hands; occasionally a whole layer would peel off like a glove, rather like a snake shedding its skin.

Ernest carried on working his plots in his spare time until the late 1940s. His sons while they lived at home (my father was the last to leave) sometimes helped him harvest his produce, particularly crops which needed regular picking, such as runner beans. After my aunt Doris died in 2000 I found some old bills at my granddad's home which showed that some of the heavier tasks such as ploughing and cultivating were being done by contractors such as William Peacock and his son Dick of Mill Lane, Potton

By the time he was 65, my granddad had certainly given up the tenancy of at least some of his plots. In February, 1950, an advertisement seeking new, younger, tenants appeared in the local press. One plot was described as Meeks' land in Potton; it was just over one acre in size; another acre plot was in Sutton. Both plots were part of the Bedfordshire County Council Smallholdings scheme.

From the time the family first moved to the house in King Street , the back garden was also intensively cultivated for vegetables; and hens, goats, and, later, bees were kept. My granddad won a prize for newly extracted honey at the Wrestlingworth Show of 1929. The hens were often turned out into the field at the bottom of the garden where they could scratch around to their hearts' content. This field, like so many others in Potton, is now a housing estate. A Victoria plum tree planted in the 1920s to grow against the south-facing wall of the coal shed was still bearing abundantly over seventy years later. It can be seen in the photograph which appears on page 172. Two more children were born at King Street: Hubert (my father) in 1921, and Raymond in 1922. With a family of five children to feed it was important to keep the

Ernest Whitfield in his retirement, photographed in his garden in King Street, Potton.

Ernest and Ethel Whitfield with some of their family, after the funeral of Ernest's mother, Emma Whitfield in 1929. As Ernest and Ethel's oldest son, Leslie is not on the photograph, I assume he was the photographer. Back row l to r : Doris, Ernest, Ethel. Front row l to r Ray, Ken, Hubert.

garden soil fertile, and it was one of my father's jobs after school to collect horse manure from the roads and bring it home in a little cart made for the purpose.

The house in King Street had two reception rooms. The front room was retained as a special and infrequently used parlour and contained a piano. There were also some Victorian and Edwardian pictures of a sentimental nature and two glass cases. One of these contained a stuffed fox, and the other a pair of stuffed red squirrels - they used to fascinate me when I was a child visiting my grandfather and aunt Doris.

The living room was connected to the kitchen, in which there was a large copper boiler for heating water and washing clothes. The living room was also used as a frost-free store for Ernest's seed potatoes in early spring - much to Ethel's annoyance. There was no bathroom, and baths were taken in a large zinc bath in the kitchen; filling it with hot water was a laborious and long-winded process. Heating was by coal fires.

My grandfather was a hard-working man, but he was also intelligent and enterprising. In addition to working for Fred Tear and himself on his market garden land, he also was an agent for a seed firm, sending for seeds for other people and distributing them to his customers afterwards. His life would probably have followed a different course if he had been born some fifty years later, but the opportunities for intelligent boys from ordinary families were very limited in late Victorian England. He was very good at mental arithmetic and was particularly adept at calculating the number of plants required per acre at various spacings, as well as problems involving money. He was also interested in Geography. He liked to discuss, argue, tease and have a joke. His heavy smoking (Woodbines), may have explained his deep voice; it almost certainly explained the bronchitis which afflicted him in his later years. The health problems caused by smoking were not appreciated in those days. He was also a regular drinker, enjoying his 1½ pints of beer a night. These were fetched in later years in a jug by his daughter Doris from the *Horse and Jockey* pub across the road in King Street.

He was no more than average height, perhaps a little less, and of a spare, almost gaunt physique. He had a very wrinkled face, with large bags under his eyes, a full head of white hair and a white drooping moustache: a face full of character. I remember 'helping' him pluck a hen he had killed when I was about five years old in the barn at his house in King Street, and recall his long fingers, stained brown with nicotine. He died in September, 1963, aged 76. He had been cared for in his later years by his daughter, Doris. His wife, Ethel, had died in 1951 after a long battle with cancer. She had had various stays in hospital over the years and Doris had helped with the housework and with looking after the younger boys.

The children of Ernest and Ethel Whitfield were:

Leslie Ernest b. 1910.

Herbert, b.1911, d1911.

Doris Winifred b. 1913.

Millicent Ivy, b.1915, d.1915.

Kenneth Arthur, b.1918.

Hubert William Henry, b. 1921.

Raymond Stanley, b.1922.

Leslie Ernest used to help his father harvest his produce, and we have already seen how a market gardening deal helped him to buy his first bicycle. Leslie was an intelligent boy who did well at school, but in December, 1924, he was apprenticed, through Potton Charities, to the Potton Co-operative Society, in the grocery department. His initial wage was ten shillings a week. Leslie completed his apprenticeship, but decided that he would like to be a policeman, like some of his mother's brothers. In 1931 he joined the Cambridge Police Force as a constable and was later promoted to sergeant, then inspector. He was the first sergeant in Cambridge to attend Police College. He was in charge of the Cambridge Police first aid team, and was also prosecuting officer, appearing in court. On one of the police parades in Cambridge he

Leslie Whitfield (1910- 2013), taken about 1930.

Leslie Whitfield (1910-2013), aged 100, visiting the Potton Co-operative store in 2010. He completed his apprenticeship there in 1928. L to r: Dennis Whitfield, Leslie Whitfield, Rex Whitfield.

met Queen Elizabeth, the Queen Mother. After thirty years' service he retired from the Police Force. It was said at that time that he had carried out his duties in an admirable manner, and, as prosecuting officer, he had been scrupulously fair to the defendants while properly representing the views of the prosecutor. After he retired from the police force, he joined the Law Society, preparing cases for court.

After working on the beat or at the Police station, Leslie would relax by swimming in the River Cam, often alone, and sometimes after dark. He also had an allotment and a large garden, where he grew vegetables very intensively (I remember being impressed with his intercropping techniques), and kept bees. He lived in a house in Warren Road, Cambridge which he and his wife Grace, nee Cox, purchased in the mid-1930s.

Leslie had noticed Grace as she cycled past the Co-op shop in Potton on her way to work at a solicitor's office in Biggleswade. Grace lived on Gamlingay Heath, where she was brought up by her aunt and uncle, William and Esther Jiggle. Leslie, in his own words 'made it his business' to be outside the shop when Grace next cycled past; they arranged to meet, and romance blossomed. They married in 1934 at Gamlingay Baptist Chapel.

Leslie and Grace and their children, Michael John, b.1937, Dennis Keith, b.1940, and Paul Malcolm, b.1945, attended Arbury Road Baptist Church in Cambridge, where Leslie was in the choir for many years, and was choirmaster for a while. He also did some local preaching.

Leslie continued with gardening and cycling in his retirement and is an inspiring example of keeping fit, interested and active in his later years. He cycled and drove his car until he was

98, and was still doing exercises with dumbbells at the age of 100. He took up computing at the age of 90, and still plays a competitive game of chess. He enjoyed a flight over Cambridge in a police helicopter on his 100th birthday, and made a short speech at his birthday party. After returning to his first workplace, the Potton Co-operative store, a few days later for a short presentation ceremony and photograph session, he was interviewed by Radio Cambridgeshire about his familiarity with computing and the internet. He had set up the interview himself, after contacting the radio station, during a phone-in programme about computing. He is a man of great self-discipline and determination and a truly remarkable member of the family. At the age of 103 he still takes an interest in the activities of the younger Whitfields, keeping in touch by e-mail.[4]

Michael, the oldest son of Leslie and Grace, was at one time bullied at school. His father's response was to buy him some boxing gloves and give him some boxing lessons! The bullying soon stopped. Michael studied Medicine at Emmanuel College, Cambridge and St Thomas' Hospital, London and trained to be a G.P. He married Mavis Thompson in 1961 and they moved to Bristol, where he became senior partner in a six doctor practice. Michael also became Senior Lecturer in General Practice at the University of Bristol and did medical work in South Africa, the U.S.A. and the Sultanate of Oman. Keenly interested in family history, he has published books on the history of a number of Bristol doctors, and is the author of numerous articles and papers in medical journals. He is still working professionally in his early seventies, in India and the U.S.S.R. He is secretary of the Tyndale Baptist church in Bristol.

The children of Michael and Mavis Whitfield are David Andrew and Peter John, born in 1963 and 1964 respectively.

David works in the head office of Lloyds TSB in Bristol and lives in Thornbury, Gloucestershire. He is married to Alison who teaches the clarinet and saxophone. They have two children: Sophie Elizabeth, b.2000 and Robert Michael, b.2002.

Peter trained as a nurse in Edinburgh and is now a hospital manager in Chichester. He is married to Linda who works as a practice nurse and they have two sons: Joseph Peter, b.2003 and Benjamin Luke, b.2007.

The second son of Leslie and Grace is Dennis, b.1940. Before he was old enough to attend school Dennis showed an early interest in making money: the youthful entrepreneur pulled up some of his father's wallflower plants and went next door to try to sell them!

After leaving school, Dennis worked in the electronics industry for Pye in Cambridge, but in 1963 he purchased an old house in the city which he converted into flats for students. He became an agent for an insurance company, but continued with further house conversions in his spare time, before making them his main commercial interest. Most of his early projects were conversions into flats which were then rented to students; obviously Cambridge was a very suitable location for this type of enterprise. Nearly fifty years later, Dennis now has a multi-million pound property empire, with properties all over East Anglia and beyond. Much of his work is still concerned with conversion of large older buildings into accommodation for

---

4   Leslie Ernest Whitfield died peacefully on 11th October, 2013, aged 103.

students, in Cambridge, Chelmsford and Ipswich, but he has other residential and commercial property besides, including, at the time of writing, a shopping mall in Sandy, Bedfordshire, shops in Cambridge, Ely and Sandy, and an engineering business in Sawtry, Cambridgeshire. His more recent projects have included the conversion into flats of the former Congregational Church in Potton, which he purchased with me in 2006, and the conversion of the Old Post Office at Whittlesey. He also owns a large former public house in St.Neots (the Old Falcon) which is awaiting planning permission for development.

Dennis now heads a group of companies, the Whitfield Group, which has its headquarters in Swavesey, Cambridgeshire. He has also done voluntary work in India, helped to establish an orphanage in South Africa, and undertaken much voluntary work for Arbury Road Baptist Church in Cambridge. He is a man with remarkable energy, drive, enthusiasm and business acumen and is still actively managing his companies in his early seventies. This does not mean he is desk-bound; he is just as likely to be up a ladder, laying bricks, or squeezing his 6ft. 3in frame into a roof space.

Dennis married Susan Carey in August, 1962 in Cambridge. They had three children: Jane Alison, born in 1964, Helen Susan, born in 1966 and Jonathan Paul, born in 1970.

Jane trained as a teacher. She married Stephen Bridgeman who works in publishing in 1987 at Over Baptist Chapel. They have four children: Joseph, b.1992, Naomi, b.1993, Elena, b1994 and Archie, b2001.

Helen married Martin Barber in 1997. The marriage was registered at Rushcliffe, Nottinghamshire. Their children are Kate, b 1998, and Ella b 2002.

Jonathan worked with his father as a builder, helping him to renovate old buildings and convert them into flats. More recently he has branched out on his own, renovating older properties in Devon.

Jonathan married Joanne Sharp in 1991. They had two daughters, Hannah, b 1994 and Abigail, b.1998. They subsequently divorced and Jonathan married Joanna McKenzie in 2003 in Devon. Their son Tobias was born in 2003, and they later had daughters Madeline, b.2004 and Annabel, b.2008.

The youngest son of Leslie and Grace is Paul Whitfield, b.1945. Paul became a Geography teacher and later Head of Humanities. He married Sarah Barr, and lives at Bracknell, Berkshire. They had three children of their own: Brendan who died in infancy, Simon, b. 1977 and Philip, b.1980. They also adopted two children, Jonathan, b.1982 and Samantha, b. 1983. Unfortunately Sarah later suffered from Alzheimer's disease; Paul looked after her until she had to go into a home where she died in 2012. Paul has retired from teaching and now owns a number of properties in the Bracknell area, which he lets out to tenants, managing them himself, and also doing much of the maintenance work.

Simon, his eldest son, is married to Jaime Nicholds and they have a young son, Noah, b.2007 and a daughter, Grace, b.2009. Simon has carried on the family tradition of working as a police officer, and is currently in the traffic division.

Philip has not yet married and is a recruitment consultant.

The next child of Ernest and Ethel Whitfield was Doris, b.1913. Doris looked after the rest of the family when her mother was ill; she initially trained as a milliner, working at

Valentine's drapery shop in Potton Market Square - a property which has now been turned into flats. She later worked for Moore's grocery shop in Biggleswade, before becoming the manageress of the Potton co-operative shop's drapery department, where she was involved with, and responsible for the furnishing of the 'pre-fabs' built in Mill Lane, Potton, in the 1940s. She later worked in the Pye radio factory at Cambridge, travelling each day from Potton by train.

Doris married Herbert Stubbings in Potton in 1941. They were subsequently divorced, and Doris married (Leslie) Jack Sibley from Yelling, Huntingdonshire at Biggleswade Register Office in May, 1956. Jack, originally a farm labourer, then worked as a labourer on building sites; after his marriage to Doris he worked at the Potton tannery. He was a strong man, of an affable disposition and one of the kindest men you could meet. One of his interests was cricket and I can remember accompanying him to a test match in the 1960s to watch England play the West Indies whose side at the time included the legendary fast bowlers Wes Hall and Charlie Griffiths.

Both Jack and Doris were Methodists, and they met through the Methodist Church. Doris was an organist at Potton Methodist and Congregational chapels for many years, and she taught my sister, my brother and me to play the piano, travelling from her house in King Street by bicycle to do so. She looked after her parents until they died and her father's will gave her a life interest in the King Street house which was to be sold on her death and the proceeds divided between the rest of the family. She also cared for her husband Jack when he developed Alzheimer's disease. She was a very kind person who loved to have the family visit her; she had no children and so nieces and nephews were made especially welcome. While she was alive, her brothers and their families used to visit regularly. She was often cooking, shopping and running errands for neighbours, and her Christian faith and her great determination enabled her to cope valiantly with the onset of osteoporosis. As the cruel disease progressed, the way Doris coped with it was a triumph of mind over matter for several years; only after a number of falls would she reluctantly consent to being cared for at Abbotsbury Elderly People's Home in Biggleswade.

Doris died in Bedford Hospital just after Christmas, 2000. She was 87. When my cousin Dennis and I cleared out her home we found many interesting family photographs, newspaper cuttings and letters, some of them dating back nearly a century: our aunt's sentimental nature meant that none of these would be destroyed.

Doris' younger brother Kenneth Arthur, b.1918, like his father before him, worked initially at Braybrooks', the Potton tannery, but joined the Cambridge Police Force when he was 18, where his older brother, Leslie was already working.

Apart from war service in India he remained in the Police Force in Cambridge as a constable until he retired from it, aged 48, after thirty years' service, his time in the army being also taken into account.

Ken met his future wife (Edith) Bessie Housden on a Bedfordshire Sunday Schools' outing to a park in Bedford, and while he was at the tannery used to cycle to Bedford to see her after work - a round trip of some 24 miles. They married in Bedford in 1940.

Ken had always been interested in market gardening, having helped his father Ernest on his pieces of land around Potton, and in 1955 he and Bessie purchased a property in Histon, north of Cambridge, with thirteen acres of land. Here he kept about two thousand hens in his spare time after pounding the beat in Cambridge. I can remember visiting him here with my parents and being fascinated by the different breeds of hens; they were kept in separate fenced runs. I was also impressed by my uncle's huge Wellington boots The land was compulsorily purchased for housing, and the family moved to Landbeach, Cambridgeshire, in 1966, to a bungalow, built to their specifications, on a plot of five or six acres of black fen land, where Ken and his son Robert had a commercial sized greenhouse. Ken later had back problems, and the family moved to a bungalow in Willingham, set on half an acre of land. Later they moved to Norfolk.

Ken reminded me most of his father Ernest. He had a very deep voice, was a keen gardener and seemed to like to argue, but had a good sense of humour and a twinkle in his eye. At his funeral in 1996 it was said that he liked to sort out any family problems around the kitchen table. It was very easy for me to imagine him as a policeman, and apparently some of the more trivial problems on his beat were sorted out in the pub, over a drink!

Ken and Bessie had three children: Gillian, b. 1941, Robert, b. 1948 and Susan, b.1958. Gillian married Michael Wakefield in 1963 and they moved to Somerset. They had four children: Lisa, b 1967, Amanda, b 1970, Joanna, b 1973 and James, b 1975. Unfortunately Gillian died from breast cancer in 1986. Michael Wakefield now has a number of grandchildren. One of them, Gemma Pouncy, studied law at Magdalen College, Oxford, and is now a postgraduate student at Bristol.

Robert Whitfield was certainly following a family tradition when he showed an interest in gardening from an early age; and after he left school he studied Horticulture at Writtle Agricultural College in Essex. He worked for a while in the Sudbury area and then moved to Southampton where he was in charge of the city's parks. He has now retired and is working as a landscape gardener for private clients. He designs their gardens, and then works to make his plans a reality. He married Wendy Johnson in 1971 and they have two sons, Richard James b 1976 and Ross William, b. 1978.

Susan (Sue) Whitfield married Rod Buchanan, and they have a daughter Maisie. They live in Norfolk and enjoy the country life, particularly gardening and bee keeping.

The next son of Ernest and Ethel Whitfield was my father, Hubert William Henry Whitfield, born on 16th March, 1921. His younger brother Raymond Stanley was born about 15 months later in 1922, and for a time they shared the same pram. An incident reported in the *Biggleswade Chronicle* of Friday 24th August, 1923 makes it clear that both boys had a lucky escape from what could have been a very serious accident:

'On Tuesday evening, a horse belonging to Mr W. H. Fowler, having just returned from a drive, was being unharnessed in the *Rose and Crown* yard when it took fright and bolted. Before it got clear of the premises it collided with the wall and smashed the trap. Continuing its mad career, it rushed across the market place and headlong into the Post Office window, smashing the plate glass and scattering the contents of the window. Turning sharply into Chequers Square,[now called Brook End], the firemen who were at drill outside the Fire Station attempted to stop the animal, but it swerved and dashed into Mrs Whitfield who was wheeling her two children in a perambulator. They were conveyed into the nearest house, and, after medical examination, were all found to be suffering from bruises and shock. The horse which was badly cut about was eventually captured and taken home'.

My aunt Doris recalled this incident in the 1990s and told me that her mother had flung herself over the pram in an attempt to protect her children, and was kicked by the horse. Doris would have been about ten years old at the time of the incident and it must have been almost as frightening for her to hear about as it was for those directly involved in it.

From an early age my father seems to have been somewhat accident-prone and subject to various illnesses. Having escaped being seriously injured by a runaway horse, he survived double pneumonia as a young child. After he had recovered he was taken for a walk, with his younger brother Ray, by his brother Leslie, who was his senior by about eleven years. They had to cross a narrow stream. Leslie's plan was to throw the two boys over and then jump over the stream himself. He threw my father over, but unfortunately, Dad rolled back into the stream. Leslie rescued him and ran back with both boys. Dad was given a mustard bath and put to bed for the rest of the day; Leslie spent the rest of the day by his bedside.

School was not Dad's favourite place. When he was very young he used to run all over the garden in King Street trying to avoid attending school, and on at least one occasion climbed up onto the coal shed roof to evade capture. Sometimes, Miss Cross, a teacher at Potton School who lived in Gamlingay would be cycling past the house in King Street and would stop to help to catch him.

At playtime on one particular day, Miss Bevan, the headmistress, asked Dad to pick up some litter from the playground. He refused, saying that he hadn't dropped the litter, and his sister, Doris, picked it up for him. Dad could be extremely stubborn, and this characteristic seems to have been with him from a very early age. He received the cane at school only once, however; this was because he was late for afternoon school. He had returned home for his lunch and had been fascinated by the Horse Fair going on in the Market Square when he was on his way back - obviously a spectacle of more interest than lessons. Horses were tried out before deals were struck by being trotted up and down along Sun Street, and Dad stopped to watch the proceedings. Canings were apparently fairly regular occurrences in the school and seem to have taken place at times in front of the rest of the class, who regarded them as good entertainment. Sometimes, however, the punishments were more unusual, and Dad recalled one small boy in his class, Harold Trundley, being put in the waste paper basket by their teacher, Mr Blake. He was a tall man, and he placed the basket, with Harold inside it, on top of a high cupboard for the rest of the lesson.

Mr Williams, the school headmaster, was interested in gardening. At this time the school had land in Back Lane, Potton (it will probably come as no great surprise when I tell you that this land is now occupied by a housing estate), and boys in the top form were given their own plots to cultivate. Dad could remember growing onions, lettuces, cabbages and strawberries on his patch. The produce from the plots was used in the school kitchens, but I would imagine that not all of Dad's strawberries found their way there.

Like most boys, Dad used to run errands for his parents. When he was young he would trundle his iron hoop with him; his parents would have raised no objection as he would have had to run to keep up with the hoop. In any case, he would have been quite safe as there was very little motorised traffic in those days. The quiet roads were used by children for their games and Dad could remember playing football and cricket in Myers Road and Carters Lane. They also used to play with wooden tops which were whipped to keep them spinning - another activity which took place in the roads. Gardens at this time were used like allotments by most working people; they were not playgrounds for children or outdoor rooms for lounging around in the sun. Dad told me that his father, Ernest, in addition to growing market garden produce in his various fields would also use his garden for market gardening purposes: he grew lettuce, sweet peas and rhubarb for sale and this produce was taken to Cambridge market by Dick Giddings who owned a lorry. Ernest would also grow thousands of Brussels sprouts plants in his garden, ready for planting out later in one of his fields. Dad used to help his father pick beans and cucumbers and he reminded me that he also had to collect horse manure and fallen leaves from the streets and bring them back for use as manure. A favourite spot was around the manor corner in Gamlingay Road where there were many large horse chestnut trees. The manor grounds are now occupied by housing estates, but thankfully some of the horse chestnut trees remain.

Before he left school, Dad did a paper round for Mr Elphick each week day. On Saturday he had to burn all unsold papers and clean the shop windows; he received 3s 6d per week for his efforts.

Dad wanted to work in a shop when he left school, but there were no vacancies in Potton at the time, so he started to work at Potton Tanyard, where his father and older brother Ken had also worked for a while. Raw pelts would arrive at the works; the wool would be separated from the skin, and the sheep skins would be 'cured' before being manufactured into parchment, wash-leathers and other articles. The wool was packed into huge sacks which were taken to the railway station to be despatched, presumably to northern cloth, clothes and carpet manufacturing centres. Woollen and cloth waste (shoddy) was returned to Potton. It was used as a fertiliser and soil conditioner and helped the light sandy soil to retain its moisture. Dad worked in the tannery's skin splitting department with several others. They were paid at piecework rates. He didn't enjoy the work; one of the reasons was that the lime which was applied to the skins caused painful 'birds eyes' on his fingers, despite the fact that he was wearing leather cots on them for protection. He applied to Potton Co-op for a job in the grocery department, but there were no vacancies at the time. However, the manager, Mr Hardy, who had previously employed Dad's older brother, Leslie, found him a job as a cycle mechanic with Mr Len Impey. I believe that this cycle shop was also owned by the Potton Co-operative Society. Dad enjoyed this work. In addition to the eight shillings per week he was earning he was also entertained by Mr Impey's antics: he used to hide behind the counter if he didn't want to meet a particular customer and ask Dad to tell the customer that he had gone out.

Dad was transferred to the grocery department at the Co-op's premises in King Street when there was a vacancy. He had to learn the various aspects of the grocer's trade; in those days few of the provisions were pre-packaged: they had to be cut, measured, weighed and dispensed at, or from, the shop. Tea arrived in large foil-lined chests, muslin-wrapped cheeses were delivered whole to the store, whole sides of bacon arrived with all the bones still in place, and flour was in sacks which had to be winched up into the flour loft. Provisions were unloaded into

Hubert Whitfield (1921-2006), with Potton Co-op delivery van, c 1939.

storage sheds and barns at the rear of the shop: these buildings had originally formed part of the Potton Brewery. Bread was baked on the premises. There was also apparently time for fun: Dad recalled having his lunch in the flour loft where he and the other shop lads would stage mock fights using bags of flour. He often had to wash his hair after these escapades. Ted Bailey, the shop baker would sometimes provide them with bread rolls from odd pieces of dough left over from bread-making, which Dad enjoyed with a piece of cheese and a tomato. He needed some refreshment and a little fun at times because he worked from 8 am until 6pm every weekday except Thursdays which was when the shop closed in the afternoon; he also had to work on Saturdays until 2pm.

As his brothers had joined the police force and were doing well there, Dad also applied to join. At that time there was a height restriction: only men who were 5 feet 8 inches tall and above were allowed to join. Dad was very close to this minimum height requirement and on the day before his interview spent all day in bed in an attempt to stretch his spine to its maximum. Unfortunately when measured at the interview he was found to be a quarter of an inch too short and thus his police career was nipped in the bud. It seems a little dramatic to record that this height deficiency was to influence the way my father's life was to develop, but a career in the police force would have offered him opportunities for promotion, a steady income and thus a better chance of owning his own home, and a chance of early retirement with a decent pension. After this disappointment, Dad returned to his job at Potton Co-op.

Within about a year all was to change, as war was brewing. Dad and his fellow Co-op workers who had enjoyed their flour fights in 1938 had to attend medicals in Bedford prior to being called up for military service. Earlier in the year, Dad had spent some time in Bedford Hospital for observation and tests. At first it was thought he might have contracted meningitis. He had a lumbar puncture and various x-rays, but eventually the symptoms he had described were attributed to 'nerves', and he was given electric shock treatment, which sounds rather drastic and must have been very unpleasant. Possibly in view of this and his previous medical history which included double pneumonia as a child, Dad was considered unfit for military service, and he stayed on at the Co-op throughout the war. He was now the only young man there.

He joined the A.R.P. (Air Raid Precautions) organisation voluntarily, as an air raid warden and attended first aid courses. Members of the A.R.P. had to be on duty at night in case the local area was bombed or there was a gas attack. They also had to enforce the blackout: persistent offenders were reported to the police. The wardens slept, three at a time, on a rota system, while their fellow wardens kept watch from the air raid shelter, awaiting *their* turn for sleep. They were equipped with uniforms, whistles and gas masks. They received no pay for their services and most undertook their duties in addition to full time employment during daylight hours. Children and young teenagers from London and larger towns were being evacuated to the countryside and Potton received its fair share of evacuees. The Whitfield family in King Street were joined by Dad's cousins, Pat and Ken Wells from Luton.

Dad got to know one evacuee from Plaistow, London, very well. Her Christian name was Hilda, but I have been unable to discover her surname. It may have been Doy because she was a niece of Mr Doy, the cemetery caretaker, who lived in Oak Crescent, Potton. She met Dad when she came to shop at the Co-op. She worked at Papworth Everard, Huntingdonshire, travelling there and back each day by bus. They started going out together and the relationship appears to have lasted for about two years. Hilda was then called up for military service. She joined the army and was posted to Tenby in South Wales. She and Dad corresponded for a while and then the relationship appears to have fizzled out. I haven't found any letters from Hilda - perhaps Dad thought it best to destroy them when he started to go out with my mother. I did find a photograph of her, though. It may be that some of his letters survive in South Wales.

Around this time Dad seems to have joined the horticultural section of the Potton and District Young Farmers Club, which was formed in 1936. By July of the same year, a plot of land had been hired from the Land Settlement Association on Bury Hill, Potton. This land was treated to several tons of manure; it was then ploughed and divided into plots on which Potton lads were to grow bulbs and strawberries. Planting commenced in October,1936. I was interested to see in the *Biggleswade Chronicle* of 28th April, 1939, that the plots had been inspected and prizes had been awarded to three members. Dad won the first prize, and the second prize went to his older brother, Ken. Unfortunately, the Land Settlement Association now required the land, but another piece of land had been allotted for future use at the bottom of Bury Hill.

Dad was lonely after Hilda had joined the army and his male friends were also involved in military service. There was a young, attractive, dark-haired girl, Jean Mingay, five years his junior, working in the Co-op office, and she invited him to her parents' home in Bury Hill, Potton. Jean had moved to Potton with her parents and younger brother Mervyn from the rural area around Bury St. Edmunds in Suffolk because her father, Harry, had been appointed pigman to the Land Settlement estate just outside Potton. (Further information on the Land Settlement Estate is available in the Appendix). Jean had always done very well at school and had attended a grammar school in Bury St Edmunds (the only pupil to do so from her small village school for years), but had disliked a similar school in Bedford and had left to take an office job at the Potton Co-op. Once a week, Harry and Mildred Mingay, Jean and Mervyn played darts and cards in the evening at home, and they invited friends and neighbours to join them. Knowing my grandmother, I would imagine that there would also have been generous supplies of home-made refreshments, and the Mingays welcomed Dad into their home and social circle. Mum and Dad started to go out together, and as Mum stayed on at the Co-op and eventually became office manager they must have seen a good deal of each other, both at work and afterwards.

Dad had a number of hobbies at this time. He was keeping rabbits on a small commercial scale at home and he also had three or four stocks of bees in the garden at King Street. His first two hives were a present from his older brother Leslie who was now married and living in Cambridge. They were fetched from Cambridge by Dick Giddings on his lorry. Mum bought him a new hive as a Christmas present on their first Christmas together. I can remember Dad telling me that he once fetched a swarm of bees that his brother Les had taken in Cambridge, bringing it back to Potton in a box which he carried on the handlebars of his bicycle: a somewhat hazardous journey of about eighteen miles. Dad would look through his beehives on Thursday afternoons when the Co-op was closed, checking for the presence of Queen cells which he removed to prevent swarming. On one cloudy afternoon he was stung repeatedly on his head and face. The stings affected him badly and he was unable to go to work the next day. Nevertheless, he carried on keeping bees for many years. I was impressed to see that in 1950 he won first prize at the Wrestlingworth Show for his honey. I can remember the hives at King Street and on Dad's allotment in Myers Road. My parents would extract and bottle the honey in the evenings after work.

While Dad was working at the Co-op, his sister Doris was appointed manager of the drapery department. She needed someone to measure men for made-to-measure suits. Dad went to the Bedford branch to learn how to do this and was soon able to put his newly-acquired skills into practice. Writing about this towards the end of his life, he recalled measuring an old man aged over eighty in Eyeworth who told him he wanted a suit made to last, an old man in Sutton who had no legs, and a man who lived on the Land Settlement estate who was very overweight. Each of these customers presented a new challenge, but apparently they were all pleased with their suits. He also remembered several interesting customers who used to call in the shop, including Mr Povey, who was apparently unaware that the assistants used to stick uncomplimentary messages on his back, his uncle David Whitfield, whose gruff, forthright manner put them on their guard, and Mr Croot from Standalone Farm who kept them all entertained with his jokes.

Dad's weekly routine about this time meant that he was collecting money on most mornings from customers together with their new grocery orders, both in Potton itself and surrounding villages. He would also be looking for new customers. On Mondays he would be in Wrestlingworth, on Tuesdays he would be in Potton; he ventured to Cockayne Hatley on Wednesdays and on Thursdays he was in Everton. In each of these places he would have a round of regular customers, and he would stay for a chat with them and sometimes for a cup of tea. He would decline offers of refreshments in some of the village cottages where some of the older people had hens running in and out of their houses, even roosting on beams and tables in the kitchens. At such houses he had to explain that he had just had a drink at the previous house. After his round was finished he would cycle back to Potton and the money he had collected would be checked in the office. After lunch, he would don white coat and apron and serve in the shop; if there was a lull in proceedings he would start to assemble the groceries his customers had ordered earlier: they would be delivered later in the week. On Thursdays he had the afternoon off and would attend to his bees and rabbits and do some gardening. Fridays were spent in the shop, serving customers, who were attracted by the special offers on scarce items which were available on that day. Saturday mornings were also spent in the shop. In addition to his usual wages, Dad used to receive one shilling for procuring new customers and a wear and tear allowance of 6d per week for the use of his own bicycle. He was also in charge of catching mice in the shop and warehouses and was paid by results: 1d per tail. Later, his routine included delivering groceries to the surrounding villages using the Co-op van which he had learnt to drive, after my mother had cycled to the villages to collect the orders earlier in the week.

My Whitfield grandparents went on a rare holiday with my aunt Doris in the late 1940s and left my father, who was still single and living at home, in charge of the house in King Street. A letter from Dad to his parents has survived from this time; unfortunately he didn't date it. It reveals, in a very humorous way, the trouble he had when his bees swarmed, and shows that he had managed to sell eighty celery plants. It also mentions that he was going to my mother's parents, Harry and Mildred Mingay, for his meals in the evenings. I would imagine this meant he didn't need to worry about much food at other times of each day because my grandmother's hospitality was legendary.

My parents married in 1951, and moved to an old cottage in King Street, Potton, as tenants of Mr Mason who lived further along the road next door to my grandfather. My parents' landlord, John Henry Mason (a market gardener and retired baker) died in June, 1952, and in early October the cottage was sold by auction at the *Rose and Crown*, Potton. My parents attended the auction, but they weren't lucky (or rich) enough to buy the cottage; instead it was bought by Mr Saville and he became their new landlord. At about this time Dad bought his first car, an old Austin Seven, for £25. This meant my parents could now visit Mum's relatives in Essex.

I was born in 1954, and when I was about six months old we moved from King Street to a house at Moon's Corner, Potton. The reason for the move was that Dad had managed to find another job. His new employer, William Caton, lived in Clavering, Essex, and owned a number of grocery shops in Essex, Cambridgeshire and Hertfordshire in addition to the one at Potton. The accommodation went with the job and was rent-free; the house was in Station Road and was attached to the shop, which was in Chapel Street. I later was amused to have a bedroom which was technically in two streets, a curious fact which gave me a certain street credibility when I mentioned it at school. The primary school I attended was next door to our house in Station Road. (It was demolished in the 1970s and a development of flats, Caves Court, named after a former teacher, now occupies the site).

Between the back yard and the school playground was an enormous lime tree, smothered in blossom in summer, and I apparently spent most of my first few months in my pram underneath this tree, probably lulled to sleep by the sound of bees and the perfume of the lime flowers overhead. I was slow in learning to walk, but very early to acquire some proficiency in talking, so that by the age of two I was able to hold a conversation with my parents and any interested onlookers while I was flat on my back in my pram. My sister, Andrea, born on Christmas Day, 1957, my brother, Grant, born in 1960, and I all later attended Potton Primary School. We were all taught for a time by Miss Edith Cave, a very experienced teacher who had taught Dad and his older sister, our aunt Doris. Miss Cave was a strict, but *fairly* kindly disciplinarian who drilled the rudiments of the 'three R's' into her pupils, giving them a sound foundation for later, more advanced work. She had their best interests at heart and was usually quite accurate in her predictions of her pupils' future successes. I can remember a lot of rote learning going on as well as some interesting children's stories. Talking was not encouraged and bad behaviour was not tolerated, although Miss Cave used some techniques which would not be allowed in today's lower schools. If a child was talking or not concentrating she would creep up behind them and dig her knuckles into his or her back, near the spine; another method she used to keep children docile was to grab their earlobes from behind and squeeze and twist them. She said she wanted to be able to hear a pin drop in her lessons and sometimes produced the pin; we *were* able to hear it drop. Mr Pierce, the headmaster was allowed to use the cane but it wasn't necessary to use it on us. We knew Mr Pierce anyway because he attended the Methodist Chapel. He was firm, but fair and took us for music and physical education.

I have one memory of my very first day at Potton Primary School: as I was being shown to my classroom I saw Kevin Croot, two or three years my senior, vomiting into a brown paper bag outside *his* classroom. As far as I can remember this set the tone for the day. I don't suppose Kevin enjoyed his day much either. Later in my time there I can also recall another teacher publicly asking a boy in our class who had learning difficulties (it would be wrong of me to give names) whether one apple plus one apple made two apples or a *pair*. This was a question which caused great confusion, whether intentionally or unintentionally, to someone who knew his fruits better than his sums - and great amusement to the rest of the class. I'm not sure what an Ofsted inspector would have made of that one.

Our parents read to us every night when we were young children and encouraged us to take an interest in the world about us. We were frequently tested on our multiplication tables and general knowledge and we could all read before we started to attend Potton Primary School, where we did well. We became members of Potton library and were encouraged to read as much as possible and were usually given books for birthday and Christmas presents. Our mental arithmetic skills were good: Mum and Dad had honed these by buying us darts and a dartboard and playing with us regularly. Word games like Scrabble were encouraged too. Education should be fun, and the didactic intent need not always be made obvious.

As I was seven years older than my brother I was able to teach him various things and it soon became evident that he was very quick to learn. He was therefore able to play chess at the age of four and became a proficient table-tennis player before he was as tall as the table surface; he was also good at cricket from a very early age and used to attract attention from other people when we played on the beach on holiday because he was able to bowl overarm from about the age of five, when he was still very small.

All three of us passed our eleven plus examination and were thus allowed to attend Stratton Grammar School in Biggleswade. We were in a privileged minority: in my year group at Potton Primary School, for instance, only nine children were selected to go to Stratton.

While my brother was in his last year at primary school in 1971, schoolchildren were invited to write an essay on how they had spent Census Day. Grant's effort was one of the five essays selected from Bedfordshire to be locked away at Somerset House for 100 years before being released to the public domain. A ceremony was held at the school to celebrate this honour and photographs were taken. Some Whitfield descendants in 2071 will probably be interested to discover what young Grant got up to on that April day back in the late 20th century. I can also remember him showing an early interest in statistics: there were many large snails in our back yard at Station Road; Grant collected several of these and painted numbers on their shells. He then staged a number of snail races (the contestants were encouraged to move forwards by the presence of a lettuce leaf placed enticingly on the finishing line) and painstakingly recorded and analysed the results in an attempt to find the champion snail. The project was his idea. I think he was about eight years old at the time.

Mr Caton had a shop in Bassingbourn, Cambridgeshire, and once a week Dad would fetch provisions from Bassingbourn in the shop's van, and then use the van to deliver grocery orders around Potton. The orders, packed in cardboard boxes, were initially stacked in our hall which had formed a passageway but now was more like an obstacle course, between the shop and the house. Looking back, I can appreciate that both my parents worked very hard at the shop. Sides of bacon, drinks and tinned goods were kept in a cellar beneath the house, where Dad would bone and joint the sides of bacon after the shop had closed. I can remember he managed to fall down the cellar steps once and cracked a few of his ribs and my mother was made temporary manager of the shop. I used to enjoy accompanying Dad on his delivery rounds and on his trips to Bassingbourn. The manager there, Mr Eric Peachey, kept pigs, and I can vividly remember us taking him some young pigs from the Land Settlement estate in Potton. I sat on one wheel arch in the back of the van with them; my granddad Harry, who had been a pigman, sat on the other wheel arch to supervise proceedings while Dad concentrated on the driving. Mum used to serve in the shop at times in between her housework tasks, and there were also a number of shop assistants over the years, including Marge Steward, Margaret Stonebridge and Janice Drew. In the evenings Dad would 'cash up' and then there would be some clerical work to do in the evening, such as ordering of stock and balancing of accounts before the shop was opened the next day. This sometimes involved both of them; my mother's patient, calm manner often proved invaluable. As I grew older, I used to enjoy helping Dad count the money: I had become interested in old coins which could still be found in change in those pre-decimal days. I would then do my homework on the shop counter. Although it didn't have a Market Square location, the shop appeared to do a good trade; it was conveniently located for the school and most of Potton's younger children must have used it as their sweetshop, while their mothers bought their groceries.

In the early 1960s Potton still had shops in locations other than the Market Square and there were several in the vicinity of Moon's Corner. Further along Chapel Street there was a general store owned by Mrs Blackshaw. The shop was in the front room of her house, and Mrs Blackshaw could usually be seen in the room beyond, sitting by the fire while she waited for customers. Sometimes she went shopping herself, but left her shop open and unattended while she made the short journey to the Market Square: there would be a note on the counter saying 'Back in ten minutes, please help yourself.' Predictably, this shop was popular with certain unscrupulous schoolchildren. At the corner of Chapel Street and Bull Street, opposite the Methodist Chapel, was another shop premises (now a private house). I can remember Dad trading from there temporarily while Mr Caton's shop at Moon's Corner was being refurbished. There was a small baker's shop in Horslow Street, at the corner of Meeting Lane. I would sometimes be sent there by my grandparents on a Saturday morning. Joints of meat were obtained from Mr Smith's shop in Blackbird Street, a few yards across the road from Dad's grocer's shop. It was an errand I disliked because time appeared to stand still while Mr Smith, a genial, white-haired man of infinite patience who was probably well past official retirement age, fetched sides of meat, cut off and trimmed joints to requirements and, after much deliberation, weighed and wrapped them while talking to his customers. It was all done in a very leisurely fashion - he even provided chairs for his customers who were thus able to sit and natter with him and with each other while their meat was being prepared. I can remember that illnesses seemed to be a common topic. It wasn't the butcher's shop to visit if you were young or an impatient, hungry hypochondriac. Further along Blackbird Street was a small shoe shop owned and run by Mr Cecil Spriggs, a prominent Potton Methodist. Again, this shop was in the front room of his house. On hearing the shop bell, Mr Spriggs would often emerge from his cellar where he had been mending shoes.

Moon's Corner was close to the road junction at the intersection of Station Road and Biggleswade Road, a location in Potton which nowadays is busy with traffic. In the early 1960s it was much quieter. Much of the traffic then seemed to consist of ancient bicycles being ridden by market gardeners' labourers as they went to, or returned from work. Each of these men appeared to be as old as, or even older than his bicycle. Each man wore a distinctive set of clothes, rather like an unofficial uniform: a black, brown or dark grey suit which had seen better days, often with a waistcoat, a flat cap and a pair of Wellington boots. Most of them hadn't shaved for a few days (designer stubble isn't a new phenomenon) and many were smoking short, hand-rolled cigarettes. They were often carrying push hoes or hessian sacks and I could hear them greeting each other or making uncomplimentary remarks about the weather as they went past at about 6.45 in the morning. ('Bloody sharp ol' frorst las' night, mate, wornit?'). I could hear them on hot summer nights, too, from my open bedroom window as they sang to a piano accompaniment in the *Royal Oak*, about fifty yards away across the wide road junction. Their bicycles stood in a line, propped up against the front wall of the ancient hostelry, ready for what I suspect may have been a somewhat erratic journey home. Dad would be away from the house, working on his allotment in Myers Road and I would stay awake until he returned, laden with vegetables, at dusk when it became too dark to distinguish the weeds from his crops.

From late September, Dad would save all empty cardboard boxes from the shop and store them in the barn of an adjacent property belonging to our neighbour, an elderly widowed lady called Mrs Louisa Griggs. On the 3rd or 4th November he would take all the boxes to my grandparents' house in Everton Road, which had a large garden, and my granddad would build a huge bonfire for Guy Fawkes' night. Dad would have a good selection of fireworks in the shop, and although I wasn't allowed to buy any, my brother, sister and I would make our selection, write down their names and hope that our parents would buy them. We were usually rewarded for good behaviour - and misbehaviour led to punishment: we learned the difference between right and wrong at an early age.

The back yard belonging to the house and shop premises was small, narrow, concreted and in permanent shade, even in high summer, so we spent a lot of time at weekends at our maternal grandparents' home in Everton Road. My sister learned cooking and gardening, knitting and crochet from our grandmother, Mildred Mingay, a remarkably versatile, energetic and intelligent lady who also loved reading and classical music; and I spent a lot of time gardening and talking with my granddad Harry Mingay, a quiet, amazingly patient and mild-mannered man, still strong and active in his early seventies, although he later became crippled by rheumatoid arthritis. He never seemed to hurry or tire when working in his garden, which was his pride and joy. As we became older we were each allowed to cultivate a garden plot there, and were given gardening lessons by Dad and our grandparents. I was fascinated by some of the old photographs on display at my grandparents' house and, as indicated earlier, looked forward to when my great grandfather, Philip Hiskey came to stay. When he and my granddad got talking in their calm, measured Suffolk accents about East Anglian farming in the nineteenth and early twentieth centuries they brought a bygone era vividly to life for me and it was little short of magical to be there with them. Even as a boy I realised that this was something special. On Sundays we would usually go to see my aunt and uncle, Doris and Jack Sibley in King Street and later visit our grandparents for tea and spend the rest of the evening with them. My grandmother loved cooking for the family (and was still trying out new recipes well into her nineties). Granddad would usually give us a guided tour of his vegetable garden, and as we grew older we would also proudly show our plots to our parents. At the end of the evening we might be allowed to try a glass of home-brewed beer or a small glass of home-made wine before we returned to the house and shop at Moon's Corner.

Dad continued with *his* gardening. Over the years he had a number of different garden plots or allotments. I can remember him renting a large garden belonging to a house on the corner of King Street and The Causeway; he later shared a quarter acre plot at the Roundabout with his brother in law, Jack Sibley. Later still, he had allotments in Myers Road, one of the Pesthouse pieces and a greenhouse at his father's house in King Street where his sister Doris still lived. He grew most vegetables and some fruits such as strawberries, raspberries, gooseberries and blackcurrants. He also used to grow a crop of shallots to sell each year, the intention being to make enough money from them to pay for his allotment rent and his seeds. My granddad Harry and I would help him with cutting hedges, and later, as my father's health deteriorated I would do the heavy digging, leaving him to set the crops and keep them clean. I would then help again with the potato harvest. One of his rented plots (and one of mine) in Myers Road are now part of a housing estate, ironically called 'Garden Fields'. Dad rented a Pesthouse plot in Myers Road for about twenty years. I spread manure on it and dug it for him on many occasions and got to know the tenants of adjoining plots. His neighbour on one side was Bernard Jarvis (recently deceased) who kept his allotment in an immaculate condition. The plot on the other side was cultivated by Billy Hutchison, an old man who was rather unsteady on his feet. This may have been due to arthritic legs but it was probably not helped by Mr Hutchison's fondness for beer. He seldom rode his ancient bicycle but used it as a sort of walking frame on wheels, leaning on it heavily as he made slow and erratic progress to his chosen destinations. The Pesthouse pieces were below the level of Myers Road, and were accessed by scrambling down a low bank. I can remember I was digging on Dad's plot on one sunny spring morning and when I paused for breath at the end of a row I noticed Mr Hutchison laying on his allotment at the bottom of the bank. I rushed over to him because I thought he was dead. When I checked I noticed he was breathing steadily, and I became aware of the smell of alcohol. It turned out that he had consumed a pint or two of beer at the *Cross Keys* in Horslow Street that lunchtime before deciding to have a snooze on his allotment. When Mr Hutchison died a few years later his plot was taken over by Bill Albone. The plots have now been sold by Potton Charities, and are covered by bricks, mortar and concrete. Dad's allotment is now partly taken up by an area of hard standing for cars. Progress? I'm not convinced. I would not recommend sleeping alongside Myers Road now because it carries a lot of traffic seeking to by-pass most of Potton; the resulting noise and pollution would hardly be conducive to a restful snooze.

The allotments in Potton brought happiness and contentment to a number of Potton people, quite apart from the more obvious benefits of exercise and fresh fruit and vegetables. Dad did well with his various plots and our house in the summer months became at times like a small food- processing factory, where pea shelling, gooseberry top and tailing, jam making and similar tasks would take place well into the night.

In addition to his work at the shop, Dad was also Sunday School superintendent and a trustee at the Methodist Chapel in Potton, and this involved some evening meetings and clerical work as well as Sunday duties, ranging from getting up early to light the coke stoves in the chapel and schoolroom to planning and delivering the Sunday School talks or lessons. He didn't get much time to relax, and wasn't very good at relaxation anyway. Both he and my aunt Doris, who was an organist there, used to love singing hymns - and have passed this on to me. My brother, sister and I attended Sunday School. Once a year there was a tea and prize-giving when books were presented to all scholars whose attendance was considered to be good. In late May each year, the Methodist Church held a special anniversary service, and the Sunday School children played a prominent part in it: for several preceding weeks we would learn the new hymns and choruses which would be 'performed' at this service; and members and scholars of the Potton Congregational Chapel, with their Sunday School superintendent, Mr Jack Gillman, would be invited to attend on the day. Rehearsals were taken by Mrs Joyce Simms, a violinist, and the hymns were accompanied on the harmonium by her son Nicholas. When I was thirteen I joined the rota for playing hymns at Sunday services; my fellow organists included Nicholas Simms, my aunt Doris Sibley, Mr Pierce (the school headmaster) and Mrs Nellie Richardson. I can remember accompanying my sister Andrea during one anniversary service; she was singing a hymn as a solo. I can't remember the hymn, but I do remember that Andrea informed me beforehand that she would only be singing three verses of it, not four as printed in the hymnbook. I told her that she should sing all four verses and that I would certainly play for all of them. We are both determined people, and the result was that Andrea sang three verses and I played four. We were not popular when we returned home. The ladies of the chapel made special efforts to decorate the building with flowers for anniversary services, and I can remember the powerful fragrance of the lilac blossom (both mauve and white) which was provided each year by Mrs Nellie Richardson of Newtown and Mrs Wilson who lived in Everton Road.

After Sunday School was over, the scholars were encouraged to attend the morning service each week in the main part of the chapel. These services were taken by local preachers of the St Neots Circuit, and, later from the Biggleswade Circuit. Local preachers I can remember included Mr Fred Simms of Potton, who edited the *Biggleswade Chronicle* for many years (I was friendly with his sons Nicholas and Stuart), Mr Albert Street, an elderly farmer from Langford, a Mr Mould, whose grey walrus moustache gave him a rather lugubrious appearance, a Mrs E.M. Smith, an elderly lady who wore funny hats and always used to talk about her 'lovely flowers' (and give us long lists of them in a monotonous voice) and Mr Horace Dilley from Biggleswade.

Repairs to the fabric of the Chapel and Sunday School room were badly needed, but money was scarce. Funds were raised and a renovation programme was started, but as with the Congregational chapel off Sun Street, congregations were dwindling in size. Members of the congregation tended to be elderly; and as these people became too infirm to attend chapel, or when they died, their places were not taken by younger newcomers. Sunday habits were changing and trips in the car were probably a more attractive proposition than attending chapel for many families. Unable to pay its way, Potton Methodist Chapel closed in 1974 (I attended its final service) and two years later it was sold to the Salvation Army who moved there from their citadel in Bull Street. Dad then attended the Methodist Chapel on Everton Heath, and after I returned from University I attended Potton Church where my grandmother Mildred Mingay worshipped and where so many of my Whitfield ancestors had had their baptism, marriage and funeral services.

When I was about ten or eleven I became interested in listening to Test Match cricket and I asked my parents if they would buy me a transistor radio: these radios were becoming popular at this time. My father told me that if I wanted one I would have to earn and save my own money and advised me that he would help me achieve my goal. He bought a sack of wooden off-cuts from Potton Timber Company's premises in Back Lane (now Willow Road) and showed me how to chop sticks for firewood which he planned to sell in the shop. Most people in those days had coal fires which needed sticks to get them started, and Dad figured that many people would buy ready-chopped sticks which were packed into carrier bags. He was right. The stick chopping became a regular autumn and winter activity; it took place in the shop's cellar in the evenings and my brother and sister were allowed to pack the sticks. I earned 9d per bag and Grant and Andrea shared 3d per bag. I saved my stick money in a money box my father made me from an old cocoa tin (which I still have) until I was able to afford my radio; the enterprise had also, of course, taught me the work ethic and the benefit of saving my money. When I was about twelve I was allowed to deliver groceries around

Potton for Dad on Saturday mornings, using a trades bike (one with a large metal carrier fixed to the frame on the front). Riding this bike was a rather strange experience: all the weight seemed to be at the front and the carrier didn't turn when the handlebars were turned. In addition to delivering groceries, I also had to sweep the pavement outside the shop when I returned and load the chewing gum dispensing machines which were fixed to the walls outside the shop. Stick chopping continued.

When I was thirteen I started to work on Saturday mornings for Mr Wesley West, who had a workshop in King Street, Potton, a few doors away from where my uncle and aunt, Jack and Doris Sibley lived. Mr West was an upholsterer who had trained with Rolls Royce; he now had his own business, specialising in the re-upholstering of armchairs and sofas. He also dealt in antiques, and his premises comprised three semi-chaotic rooms full of meticulously restored furniture, old chairs awaiting attention, tools, opulent fabrics, antiques, curios and Victorian and Edwardian pictures, often featuring nude or scantily-clad curvaceous women. Somewhat incongruously, there was also a large picture or photograph of an elderly Queen Victoria. Thankfully, she was fully clothed.

Wesley West was an interesting character. He loved music, particularly music hall songs and jazz. He played the double bass, but could get a tune out of several other instruments and had his own dance band. He was also a gifted mimic and raconteur who loved a few drinks at the *George and Dragon* at the other end of King Street. A skilled craftsman, he made all the new covers for the furniture on a small electric sewing machine from rolls of fabric stored at the workshop. He would then restore the wooden frame to its former glory by tacking on new padding and then the new covers, followed by decoration such as fringe, piping or ruche, usually mimicking someone on the radio - or a customer who had just left - while he did so (despite having a mouthful of upholstery tacks). My job was to prepare the furniture for him by removing the old upholstery, stripping the chair or sofa down to its wooden frame, using a mallet and old screwdriver to remove the tacks, taking care to salvage the old covers without any damage to them or the wood underneath and clearing up afterwards ready for the skilled work to begin. Mr West then took over and the results were superb. Not only would the furniture look good, but it would continue to do so for many years. We started work at 8.45 a.m., and at 10 a.m. would walk along King Street to Mr West's house for tea and chocolate biscuits prepared by his wife, Ella. We then would work until lunchtime. Sometimes customers would come to the workshop to buy antiques, discuss business or just to tell jokes and occasionally I would help Mr West deliver furniture to customers' houses. I worked for him all week during school holidays. It was great fun.

In 1971, Dad's employer, William Caton, had a heart attack and was advised to scale down his business interests. He sold the shop at Potton and bought a house in Sandy for us to live in as his tenants while Dad found himself another job. Sandy at that time was still a small market town and the house was in Cambridge Road, close to open countryside. We spent the 1971/2 winter there, and for the first time I could remember we had an extra room downstairs. I did my homework there; I was preparing to take my A levels. It was a worrying time for my parents, though.

Although my father was now about fifty he managed to find another job in Potton as the manager of the small Fine Fare supermarket in the Market Square. We moved back to Potton, to a council house in Oak Crescent. Smaller than the house in Sandy, damp, dingy, depressing and cold (I could scrape ice from the *inside* of my metal-framed bedroom windows in winter), and with only a living room downstairs it was far from ideal, but it did have an overgrown garden which I soon cleared, digging out privet hedges and breaking up and removing a particularly unattractive concrete path. Fortunately we had excellent neighbours, John and Nancy Harben, whose friendly assistance was to prove invaluable over the years as, sadly, the health of both my parents began to deteriorate.

My sister, brother and I all managed to go to University; Andrea and I studied Geography at Sussex and Reading respectively, and Grant read History at Nottingham. I then did a postgraduate year at King Alfred's College Winchester, in preparation for teaching, my brother did a postgraduate diploma in statistics at the University of Kent and my sister worked as a cook at the London Institute of Education before studying accountancy. She later obtained an MBA degree from Warwick University. All three of us had piano lessons from our aunt Doris, initially, then from Mrs Doris Greaves of Potton until we left for our respective university courses.

I made a point of attending all my lectures, but on free days and in my holidays worked at various part-time jobs. I had a Betterware round in Reading for a while, taking orders for household cleaning products and delivering them afterwards around the housing estates, and a couple of regular gardening jobs; my landlord was a butcher and I served in his shop on Saturday mornings; and I worked at Courage's Reading brewery and Greene King's brewery in Biggleswade, (now demolished) when I was back at home. My work at the breweries included rolling and stacking full beer barrels, unloading and carrying sacks of barley, putting pellets of hops in barrels as they went past on a conveyor belt and clearing out the brewing vessels. This latter job was hard but enjoyable work: I had to shovel the still-warm and moist barley, after it had been used in the brewing process and the beer had been drained off, into waggons which would take the spent grains to farms where they would be used for cattle feed. The fermented barley would smell delicious and you can perhaps now appreciate why cattle have such a contented demeanour as they graze. I thought the beer tasted good, too. We had a free daily allowance at Greene King – I think it was a couple of pints a day. It helped to replace the sweat I lost.

By way of contrast, I hated the day I spent working at a sawmill while I was at university: I was working next to a circular saw with no ear protection and when I came out of the mill I found I was unable to hear anything. Fortunately the damage wasn't permanent. Some of the workers there thought it was funny to use nail guns to fire six-inch nails around the factory. The place was a health and safety nightmare and I didn't return. During the Christmas holidays I worked as a temporary postman in Potton and enjoyed the early morning banter with Bob Darlow, Dennis Lakin and other regulars in the 'sorting office' (an old garage behind the Post Office) before disappearing, on a Post Office trades bike laden with Christmas cards and letters, to distant parts of the town. Another period of work in my holidays was undertaken at the Wavy Line groceries warehouse at Biggleswade, and I spent a fortnight on a Sandy building site, priming skirting boards for a decorating company. The work was done outside and paid at a piecework rate; overalls were not provided. By working hard I managed to earn good money -

but in the process had changed the colour of my coat from green to white.

My main source of income, though, in my teens and early twenties, came from working on the land, like so many of my ancestors. Much of my time was spent under glass, in temperatures which were sometimes as high as 100 degrees Fahrenheit. I was de-leafing, side-shooting (removing the side-shoots from the tomato plants, which were grown up strings as vertical cordons) and picking tomatoes for Bernard and Ivy Dayman on their Land Settlement holding in The Baulk. I later did the same jobs with tomatoes but also worked with cucumbers and peppers grown under glass and in polytunnels, as well as undertaking outside jobs with strawberries, runner beans, lettuce and marrows for Bert Boxall and his wife who had a smallholding in Sandy Road. (This holding is now a housing estate). When work was short here I went hoeing Brussels sprouts plants and picking runner beans for another hard-working market gardener, Frank Gurney, who had land in Narrow Lane, near Deepdale.

The area of land between Old Bedford Road, Mill Lane and Narrow Lane was devoted to market gardening at that time. I can remember that runner beans, onions, parsnips, carrots and Brussels sprouts were grown here and there was also a field of rhubarb near to the old mill. In the distance I was able to see market gardeners' labourers travelling to and from work on their bicycles as I worked on Bert Boxall's land adjoining Sandy Road. Their progress was slow; they appeared to be on the high seas as they negotiated the very uneven unmade farm tracks, almost disappearing from view at times as they encountered particularly low sections. Market gardeners such as George Baker, Frank Gurney, Derek Whitfield and George Norman had land in this area.

Bert Boxall, who employed me at weekends and in school and, later, university holidays was an inspiration to me. He had left school in his early teens and had started work as a gardener on a large estate in Sussex, undertaking jobs such as weeding gravel paths to support his widowed mother. He had taken a Land Settlement[5] holding in Potton and had later purchased his holding in Sandy Road. He was a small, thin, wiry man who worked hard, but managed to find time for various other interests, including amateur dramatics and French conversation classes. He was also a churchwarden at St Mary's Church, Potton. Although he was in his early sixties when I knew him he bought a horse and learned to ride it. He was interested in current affairs and politics and I enjoyed the conversations we had as I worked alongside him. He employed a number of other workers in summer including George and Joan Clark, Dorothy Sale, Christine Gilbert, Margaret Stewardson, Connie Kitchener, Doreen Beck, Olive Baker and Christine Coolbear. Christine's husband was a keen winemaker, and I was pleased to accept an invitation from the Coolbears to sample some of his efforts on one hot summer evening. Fruit wines were his speciality and I can report that bending down to pick strawberries the next day wasn't pleasant for me as I was nursing a hangover. Mr Boxall later sold his holding and bought a small farm in Cornwall. In autumn I worked for George Norman on Saturdays on his land at Sutton where I harvested beetroot and also took down and stacked the canes which had been supporting runner beans until the bean vines had been killed by the autumn frosts.

I enjoyed this market garden work very much. I worked between ten and twelve hours a

---

5   See appendix

day on the land through several summer holidays and saved as much money as I could; and while I was in my last year at university bought an acre of ground in Everton Road, Potton, where I grew courgettes and asparagus as commercial crops. I had this land ploughed by contractors, but all the other work including muck spreading and harrowing was done by hand. The neighbouring landowners were market gardeners George Croot and his son Ted, and Jack Worboys of Eagle Farm. The Croots were skilful market gardeners who used to grow carrots, parsnips and parsley on their land. My neighbours were kind to a keen youngster just starting in market gardening. I enjoyed listening to their jokes, stories and sayings garnered from years of experience on the land.

My land was on a south-facing slope and after pulling a harrow over the acre on one warm late spring morning until the sand had been reduced to a fine tilth I can remember how much I enjoyed a pint of bitter at the *Rising Sun* at lunch time. I considered that I had earned it. My mother and brother helped me set courgette seeds (pips) on one occasion and I left Grant to cut the courgettes at the back end of the season when I returned to Reading in early October. For some reason muck spreading wasn't popular with other members of the family - I loved it. There was something particularly satisfying in seeing the heaps of steaming pig manure gradually disappear as I spread them over my land with a long-handled fork. There was no-one to bother me or tell me what to do, and it was easy to see the progress I had made.

I carried on with my market gardening for several years in my spare time when I returned to Potton. Each spring after the land had been ploughed, cultivated and harrowed I had the tedious job of forking out the twitch which was invading my plot along the boundary it had with Jack Worboys' pastureland – a distance of about two hundred and twenty yards. I don't think my back muscles have ever recovered. The courgette seeds were planted by hand in mid to late May; the emerging plants were easily damaged by frost, but it was important to establish the plants as early as possible, notwithstanding this hazard, to obtain an early crop which would fetch a high price. In spring most of the jobs on my acre of land were done to a musical accompaniment: the beautiful song of skylarks - a wonderful antidote to stress. Like most market gardening, the enterprise was a gamble. The plants then had to be protected from predatory crows and kept clean until it was time to start harvesting the courgettes. Although I was unable to irrigate them, the plants did remarkably well on the light, sandy soil in the notorious drought year of 1976.

Although marrows had been grown for many years in Bedfordshire, courgettes were a relatively new crop in the 1970s: my idea had been to find a niche market. I can remember farmer Jack Worboys warning me that I was cutting my marrows too small; evidently *he* had not heard of courgettes. My produce was taken by Frank Gurney to the Bedfordshire Growers' depot in Potton Road, Biggleswade, and eventually found its way to the London markets. When the price was low in London I arranged for the courgettes to be marketed by George Baker of Horslow Street who took his produce elsewhere - I think to Cambridge. They fetched good money at the start and end of the season, but otherwise were a lot of work for a minimal reward. The asparagus was also very labour intensive, but *was* a profitable crop. As far as I know I was the only person growing asparagus on a (small) commercial scale in Potton at that time. I would get up at 5 a.m. to cut and bunch it and take it to Mrs Nellie Richardson of

Newtown, a retired Potton shopkeeper I knew through the Methodist Chapel. Her brother, John Warren, was a greengrocer, and he bought all I could supply from my five hundred asparagus crowns. After a wash and change of clothing I was ready to travel to my teaching job.

I later bought two acres of heavier (almost fen-like) land at the rear of the Sheepwalk in Potton where I grew a beautiful crop of potatoes. The variety was *Wilja* and many of the tubers were *huge*. Stan Whinney spun them out for me a few rows at a time and two of my younger cousins, Russell and Darren Mingay and I worked throughout an October half-term holiday to pick them up into paper sacks. It was a lot of heavy, back-breaking work for all of us, and unfortunately the potatoes didn't fetch a good price.

My sister and brother also worked in their spare time. Andrea worked for a time for the Boxalls on their nursery in Sandy Road, Potton and also for George Norman on his land in Sutton, where one of her jobs was runner bean twiddling, i.e. making sure that the young bean plants were making their way up the canes provided for them in early summer. She also worked for a time at a Biggleswade toy factory and for another Biggleswade firm: Kayser Bondor, which made ladies' lingerie. Grant worked for the Potton Town Council before he went to school in the mornings: he had the responsibility of keeping Potton Market Square clean and tidy. I deputised for him on occasions. He told me he once had to dispose of a dead cat he found in the gutter; I found I was dealing mainly with greasy fish and chip wrappers and discarded cigarette ends. Sweeping the Market Square was a fairly pleasant job on early summer mornings, but it took a lot more determination to turn out in January. In his student days he also worked for a while at a factory in Sandy which made Christmas decorations. It might have been the start of a glittering career.

When I was very young, like most children (I suspect) I thought that my parents were invincible. Of course this was not the case, and it was distressing to witness their gradual decline. My father suffered from high blood pressure and while I was away at university had a slight stroke. He was aware of a slightly altered sensation in one of his hands and when he went to put his car into reverse gear noticed that he had lost power in his grip. Fortunately his speech wasn't affected, but he had to have time off work and was never able to undertake heavy gardening from that time. He was fifty three. He was advised to adopt a more relaxed way of life and to take things more calmly, and put on medication to control his blood pressure. Despite this, he had a heart attack a few years later and was advised to take early retirement. He retired from his job as manager of the Fine Fare supermarket when he was sixty three, but after a while decided to take a job at the local bacon factory, where he removed bones from sides of bacon all day but had no work responsibilities to worry about when he returned home. The cold in the bacon factory affected his left hand badly; the stroke had damaged the circulation in this hand and it would turn a dusky blue colour in cold conditions. He finally retired when he was sixty five.

My parents were able to enjoy holidays in their early retirement years in Yorkshire, Devon and Scotland with their life-long friends and relatives Nina and Chris Gossett, but sadly, health problems began to affect both of them. After Dad retired from his job at Fine Fare, my mother carried on working there as a shop assistant for a while until she had to retire; she then worked part-time in a wool shop next to Lloyd's bank in Potton. She had always enjoyed knitting and she was now able to give help and advice to other knitters. Unfortunately she was diagnosed with breast cancer; radiotherapy and a course of Tamoxifen appeared to have worked and Mum was able to live a relatively normal life, and she lived to see three of her grandchildren. She had always enjoyed reading and she loved to sit and read to them. However, the cancer eventually spread and the doctors were unable to do any more for her. She died suddenly in 1998 aged 71; her mother was still alive in her late nineties. We were devastated at our loss.

Well before Mum died, my father was diagnosed with bowel cancer. This was his third life-threatening illness. He had to have a colostomy, and this, combined with his heart trouble, turned him into a semi-invalid. Dad coped valiantly with both illnesses; his stubborn, determined nature and Christian faith meant that he wouldn't give in to either of them without a real fight. He soldiered on for another eight years after my mother's death, with some help from the family and from his next door neighbours, Nancy and John Harben. He died from heart failure aged 85 in 2006.

I taught Geography and some English for nearly 14 years in Upper Schools in Bedfordshire: at Wootton, Sandy, Sharnbrook and Kempston. Although I usually enjoyed being in the classroom I became rather disillusioned with the relatively poor pay, and the constant political interference and Government 'initiatives', where common sense and creativity from the teacher seemed to be in great danger of being smothered by paperwork. The amount of work I had to bring home meant that I had virtually no social life in my twenties and early thirties, and in 1990 I decided on a career change. My parents had a visit once every four weeks from Malcolm Chamberlain, a representative from Co-operative Insurance, and after chatting with him I asked him to let me know if a similar position ever became vacant. After a few weeks he kindly informed me that there was a vacancy in Kempston. I was successful at my interview. I resigned from my teaching post and after some initial training in salesmanship and the products the company offered, began working in the Kempston area. At that time, representatives had to pay for their bank of insurance clients. I was advised to pay a deposit and then take out a loan to pay for the rest of the business. As I obtained new business the value of the 'round' would increase, and on retirement or if I moved to take on a different area, I could sell the round at a profit. As I was paying for my client bank, my job was secure, unless I was found to be dishonest. This way of life was very different from life in the classroom, where my day was ordered by bells, timetables, syllabuses and Heads of Departments. I was now in many respects my own boss. I could plan my own day, and keep my own hours, within reason. I enjoyed the work which was similar to teaching in two important respects: I was still dealing with people; and I was still trying to persuade them to do something, in this case not to do their homework but to take out new business: life assurance contracts, pensions, lump sum investments including unit trusts, and buildings, contents and motor insurance. The aspect I *didn't* enjoy was the traffic in Kempston, which was in effect a busy suburb of Bedford. I also realised that I didn't have too much in common with a lot of my customers: they were from an urban background whereas I am definitely a rural character.

After a couple of years or so, Malcolm Chamberlain announced that he had decided to retire and his round, which consisted of Potton, parts of Biggleswade and most of the surrounding villages, would be for sale. I was definitely interested, but there was a snag: on Malcolm's

197

retirement his large round was to be split in two, the theory being that it was better for the future of the company to have two agents operating on Malcolm's patch who would be hungry for new business rather than one agent who would be earning good money *without* having to look for new customers or encourage existing ones to take out further contracts.

I took a gamble. I had done well in Kempston and sold my round for a good profit. I would save time (and money) by working in my local area where I and my family were well known, and I figured I could make even half a round work. Over the years I *did* manage, with the help of salesmen from firstly the Bedford office and later from Stevenage, to build up the round, and I was lucky to acquire business from agents working nearby as they retired. I enjoyed the work, but things were changing: more women were out at work and their husbands were working out of the local area, so a lot of my visiting had to be done in the evenings: no social life again. There was still a nucleus of older customers who were at home in the daytime, however, and there were also sales and training meetings to attend in the District Office. In addition to procuring new business I had to collect insurance premiums from customers; I was also still advising on, and trying to sell car and home insurance, pensions, unit trusts, mortgages and other investments as well as life cover. I had to balance my books each night (and make up any shortfall); once a fortnight my accounts were checked at the District Office and I had an interview with my manager who would review my progress. This way of life was idyllic for a few years. Most of my older customers seemed to be early risers and I was sometimes out collecting by seven on a summer's morning around Potton and the villages; I was able to enjoy the countryside through the changing seasons and I enjoyed calling on most people who made me very welcome. As I called on some of them every four weeks I shared their triumphs and sorrows and watched their families grow up. Business was increasing and I had some free time, mostly in the early afternoons, to enjoy gardening, bee keeping, music - and researching my family tree. On one day a week I had the company of my sister and her twins when they were babies and toddlers and Mum and I enjoyed helping the children learn to read.

In the late 1990s the company decided that all agents were to be trained to become financial advisers, and in addition to carrying out my collections and weekly sales I had to study in my spare time for a number of examinations and obtained my Financial Planning Certificate and a separate qualification in mortgage advice.

After another few years, the job changed fairly dramatically. Sales meetings became more numerous, sales targets became more difficult to achieve and tremendous pressure was exerted from our Chief Office in Manchester in an attempt to secure more new business. Interviews with the District Manager became more like interrogations and his demands became increasingly unreasonable. Working days became much more regimented and compulsory evening telesales sessions (from the Stevenage office) were introduced on a regular basis. I hated making the telephone calls because I felt it was unfair on customers to pressurise them and invade their privacy in this way. We were put under tremendous pressure ourselves, as agents, to improve our sales figures, and as soon as targets were achieved they were increased for the next time. Sales interviews with clients became more intrusive thanks to new rules on compliance and the time taken to complete them on a laptop computer was resented by clients and advisers alike. Collecting commissions were reduced and it was announced that all agents' rounds were to be sold back to the company. Our semi-independent way of life was to disappear. Disillusioned by the aggressive emphasis on sales, the continual interference from the management at Manchester and the poor new basic wage being offered by the company, I carried on for a couple of years. However, in 2006 I decided to take early retirement and return to teaching, this time on a supply basis. I had worked for the Co-op for nearly sixteen years.

Since then I have worked in many different types of schools in Bedfordshire, Hertfordshire and Cambridgeshire for varying lengths of time; sometimes for just a day, at other times for whole terms. I have taught all ages of children and teenagers from 5 to 18, and have *usually* enjoyed the experience. I could relate several amusing stories about my time in the classroom, but as I am still working in this capacity it would not be appropriate to do so. I seem to be able to relate well to most young people and they appear to enjoy my lessons. They have much better facilities than I had when I was at school and I marvel at how quickly they acquire skills, particularly in computing. I like to encourage curiosity and independent thought in my students whenever and wherever possible. They will need to remain adaptable and receptive to new ideas in today's fast-moving, competitive world and throughout their lifetimes.

Following in the footsteps of my aunt Doris who was my first music teacher, I started playing for church or chapel services when I was thirteen years old at Potton Methodist chapel. I then consented to play once a month at the Congregational chapel, and when I returned from university started to play the organ at the parish church in Sutton, initially for Ian Stewardson, taking over from my sister, Andrea, who was about to go to university. I have played there ever since, and in 1995 also started to play at the parish church in Gamlingay where I have very much enjoyed working with other musicians and singers as we play our part in services.

My sister Andrea now works as an accountant, but also has a smallholding near St Neots, Cambridgeshire which she runs with her partner Jason Woolf. They have a son, Felix Henry and a daughter, Sadie Rose: they are twins and are now both at university.

My brother Grant works as Head of Statistics for a department of the Civil Service in London, but has remained in Bedfordshire. He married Sue Clarke-Williams in 1995 and they have two children Isaac Edward b 1997 and Briony Frances b 1998. All four of my nephews and nieces have learned to play musical instruments and are doing well academically. I am sure my parents and my aunt would be pleased. It is good to see such interests and aptitudes continue through successive generations.

The youngest child of Ernest and Ethel Whitfield was Raymond Stanley, b.1922. We have already seen that he survived an early accident involving a runaway horse. After he left school, Ray worked for Hooper and Fletcher solicitors in Biggleswade, and then joined the Cambridge City police force when he was nineteen when age limits were reduced because of the war. Soon after joining the police he was called up into the Royal Marines where he spent most of his time in administration, although he was involved on landing craft during the D-Day landings. He returned to his police work after the war and was promoted several times, eventually becoming a Chief Superintendent, in charge of administration. He retired from this position in the police when he was 54, but immediately took on the position of finance and budgetary control officer in a civilian role. When he retired aged 65 in 1987 he was responsible for an annual budget of £31 million. He lived in a large detached house in Girton and his garden backed on to Girton College grounds. He was interested in gardening and music: he played the organ. Unfortunately, like my father, he suffered from heart trouble. He died unexpectedly in 1990, so wasn't able to enjoy much time in retirement.

Ray married Hazel Bye and they had two children: Clive, b1946, and Gayna, b1948. Clive studied biochemistry at Churchill College, Cambridge, and later worked in the laboratories for Anglian Water. He is also very interested in and knowledgeable about classical music. A keen gardener and artist, specialising in portraits, Clive also runs yoga classes He married Brenda Saunders in Northern Ireland in 1979. There are no children. Gayna married Peter Gollop, an accountant for a local authority, and they had three children, Christopher, b1978, Nigel, b1979 and Lauren, b 1991.

The next child of William and Emma Whitfield was Rosa, b.1889. Rosa was still living at home in Sheffield Close, Potton at the time of the 1901 census, but while she was young, probably in her teens, left home for London, possibly to go into domestic service. The 1911 census reveals that she was living at the House of Mercy, on North Hill, Highgate, which was a hostel for 'fallen women' being run by the Clewer sisters, a female Anglican religious community which had been founded in Clewer, Berkshire. Rosa's presence here was possibly due to the fact that she was by this time the mother of two illegitimate children; the census describes her as an unmarried domestic servant. She later became a waitress at a Lyons' Corner House in London - it is not known which one.

The first Lyons' Corner House was opened in Coventry Street, London in 1909, although the firm had already established tea shops in the capital. It was soon followed by others in the Strand and Tottenham Court Road. The Corner Houses, as their name suggests, were on corner sites, and thus had two entrances. They were huge restaurants on four or five floors, and each one employed about four hundred people. Each floor had its own restaurant style, and all had orchestras playing to the diners. The ground floor was usually a food hall where many speciality products from the Corner House kitchens could be purchased. There were also hairdressing salons, telephone booths and theatre booking agencies. Dining and socialising had been brought into a new era.

Each waitress was initially known, somewhat unglamorously, as a 'Gladys', but from 1926 the name 'nippy' was used, presumably because the waitresses provided a speedy service. They wore a distinctive maid-like uniform with a matching hat. Prior to World War Two, all 'nippies' were single women. The Joe Lyons Corner Houses and teashops became part of early twentieth century life. They were renowned for the highest standards of hygiene, and good quality food, drink and service.

It would have been a busy daily routine for Rosa who must have found the lively London scene very different from her life in Potton. She would have come into contact with many different people, and may have got to know some of them very well if they were regular customers.

It is thought that Rosa's children, Emma Louise Whitfield and Francis Alec (Frank) Whitfield both had the same father, but I have not been able to discover his name.

The birth of Emma Louise was registered at Biggleswade in 1907. Emma Louise was brought up by her grandparents, William and Emma in Potton. She was only nine years younger than their youngest child, Annie.

Francis Alec Whitfield was born in 1910 at Isleworth, Middlesex in the workhouse infirmary. The 1911 census shows that he was being looked after by Walter Woodman and his wife Ellen at 319A Acton Lane in Brentford. The Woodmans were presumably acting as temporary foster-parents. Their household included two daughters, a step-son Frederick George Lilley (presumably Mrs Woodman's son from a previous marriage) and another illegitimate baby, Winifred Faucier, aged only nine months, in addition to Frank. He was sent from London to the workhouse in Biggleswade and later was looked after in a Dr. Barnardo's Home, although he did meet his sister and kept in touch with her. Apparently they looked very much alike as children.

Emma Louise ('Louie'), married Albert Hutchinson in Potton in 1930, and they had two children, Peter and Malvene. They subsequently divorced and Louie married Walter Sutton and moved to the Maidstone area of Kent. Louie kept in touch with her cousin Doris Sibley (nee Whitfield) - my aunt - and it was thanks to a book of addresses and telephone numbers that I found after my aunt's death in 2000 that I was able to re-establish contact with this branch of the family and trace descendants of Louie's brother Frank (Francis Alec). At that time I had no idea where they were.

Peter Hutchinson married Freda Lindsay and they had a son, Brian. Peter worked as a railway stationmaster. He and Freda still live in Biggleswade.

Malvene married Peter Waller. They had two children, Julie, b.1966 and John, b.1971. Both have married and have families of their own Julie is a lecturer in hairdressing. John is an under woodsman at an organic farm and study centre where he runs courses on tree surgery, woodland management, basketry, wood turning and furniture making.

Francis Alec (Frank) Whitfield was still being looked after by the Biggleswade Board of Guardians at Biggleswade workhouse in 1921, when a request was made that he should be allowed to join the scouts. Permission was given, and fifteen shillings was also paid by the Guardians to enable him to attend a scout camp in Stratton Park. Later in the year, Francis, as the smallest boy in the local scouts, was chosen to place the poppy wreath on the war memorial at Biggleswade in a ceremony held in November commemorating the ending of the First World War.

By July, 1922, arrangements were being made for him to emigrate to Canada to start a new life under the auspices of the Dr Barnardo's Homes; in the interim, he was removed to Hillcote, a children's home, possibly run by Barnardo's. The *Biggleswade Chronicle* of 19th January, 1923 reported that the Biggleswade Board of Guardians had sanctioned the payment of £3 and 13 shillings to the Ministry of Health to cover the charges of the Canadian Government in obtaining reports on Francis and another Biggleswade youth whom the Board were sending to Canada. The payment of £32 and 5 shillings for each of the youths for emigration expenses was also approved.

Frank accordingly left England in April, 1923. Together with another 131 boys and 12 girls from Barnardo's, he made the journey to Quebec, sailing from Southampton, on the *Melita*. An arrangement had existed from the 1880s onwards to take pauper children away from London to rural Canada , where it was thought they had a better chance of a healthy and moral life. Once in Canada, foster families looked after them and used them as a source of cheap farm labour and domestic help. This was fine in theory; in practice, some children were treated little better than slaves, and physical, mental and sexual abuse were apparently fairly common.

From Quebec, Frank's party proceeded to Toronto, and then to Peterborough, just North of Lake Ontario, where there was another Barnardo's home. After a short time Frank was placed with a farming family. He was lucky: they were good to him. Apart from his work on the land, they introduced Frank to the Church of Christ, a non- conformist cross between Methodist and Baptist, and Frank became a lay preacher.

Frank returned to England in 1930 for his sister's wedding; the two of them had kept in touch. He lodged with a member of the family - possibly with my grandparents Ernest and Ethel. My father, Hubert, remembered him, so he certainly visited the household in King Street.

By this time, Frank's mother, Rosa, had married a barman, Walter C. Lane. Walter Lane originated from Dorset. He was one of at least thirteen children born to Charles Lane, a well sinker and his wife Emma. Rosa's wedding took place in the winter of 1923, some six months after her son had set sail for Canada, and was registered in the Pancras area of London. By the late 1930s, she had moved out of London and was working at the *Cross Keys* public house in St.Neots, Cambridgeshire, where her younger sister, Annie, also worked. Frank used to visit the pub to look at his mother, who didn't recognise him. He apparently never introduced himself to her, but was attracted to a young waitress, Daisy Walton, who worked there. It must have been love at first sight because they started going out together and married in 1938. My uncle, Kenneth Whitfield, acted as best man at the wedding ceremony, suggesting that Frank had kept in touch with *his* uncle Ernest and aunt Ethel and their family in Potton.

After his marriage, Frank became a lorry driver with a building firm. They were building a church and some houses in Derby and they let Frank rent one of their houses. He stayed there for the rest of his life. The house had a large garden where he grew vegetables and kept pigs. He also continued with his local preaching. Unfortunately he died of an aneurysm aged 59, so was not able to enjoy any years in retirement. He had never disclosed details of his time in the workhouse to his children.

Frank and Daisy had four children: Rosalie, b. 1939, John Francis, b. 1941, Pauline, b. 1943, and Roland, b. 1947.

Rosalie married a middle school headmaster, Michael Bloor. They lived for a while in Germany, but are now living in the Milton Keynes area of Buckinghamshire. Rosalie worked as a personal assistant at the Open University, but both she and her husband have now retired. They have two daughters and a number of grandchildren.

John has now retired, but was a central heating engineer, running his own business. He is married with two sons, Simon John, b.1971, and David James, b.1974.

Pauline married Richard Lankester, and they ran a grocery business. They also have two sons: Mark Lankester, b.1965 who works in a hospital histology laboratory and Stephen Lankester who works for a meteorological office.

Roland is a very successful businessman, owning garages and a car bodyshop in the Derby area. He has a son Matthew and a daughter. Matthew is married to Clair Loomes and has three young children: Hannah, Jessica and Bradley.

Rosa Lane's husband, Walter, died in 1938 in the St Pancras area of London. He was only 46. Rosa moved back to Potton, living for a while with her brother, Arthur, in Mill Cottages. She found a job as a housekeeper for a person in Bedford, and her employer found her an old person's bungalow in Turvey, Bedfordshire when she retired. I can remember visiting her there. She would sometimes visit her niece Doris Sibley, nee Whitfield in Potton. I remember Rosa as a very thin, frail-looking old lady who appeared to thrive on her daily glass or two of Guinness. She even managed to smuggle brandy into Potton Road Hospital, Biggleswade, where she spent the final period of her life, before dying at the age of 86 in 1976. She had had a colourful and eventful life in her younger days and many of her secrets went with her to the grave. Rumour has it that she may have had a third child, Roy, but I have not managed to find where his birth was registered, so perhaps there *were* only two.

The next child of William and Emma Whitfield was Albert, born in 1892. Albert served in the First World War and returned to the Potton area where he became a market gardener. He married Constance Larkins in Gamlingay, Cambridgeshire in 1923. Their first son, Howard, was born in 1926 and their second son, Maurice, in 1930.

Albert and Connie became the licensees of the *Thornton Arms* public house in Everton, Bedfordshire, (named, of course, after the Thornton family we met in an earlier chapter,) towards the end of the Second World War. There was a fairly large garden behind the pub, and here Albert grew market garden crops. According to Denis Green who called at the *Thornton Arms* at this time to deliver coal, my great uncle did particularly well with carrots. He also trained and looked after foxhounds for the local hunt. He died on 24th March, 1976 aged 83. His funeral report in the *Biggleswade Chronicle* stated that he had been the licensee of the *Thornton Arms* for 24 years. Connie died in 1989, aged 89. It seems that they kept in touch with Albert's older sister Emily Elizabeth Ling because I was given a photograph of them by a granddaughter of Emily and her husband John Alfred Ling.

Howard married Violet Mills in 1947. They had one child, Lynne, born in 1948. Howard worked for a caravan firm in Biggleswade, but unfortunately was diagnosed with multiple sclerosis in middle age which he fought for many years before his death in 1990. Lynne married Geoffrey Sharp in Cambridge in 1970. Their son Karl was born in 1971. Lynne now lives in Poole, Dorset.

Maurice married Margaret Smith in March, 1955. Both were living in Everton at the time before they married; Maurice's parents were still running the *Thornton Arms*, and the reception was held at the pub. Initially, Maurice worked for the railway company at Potton station, but he later became a familiar figure in the area by working as a postman. Maurice and Margaret had one son, Geoffrey William, born in 1960.

Maurice and Margaret divorced in the 1980s and Maurice married Jacqueline Endersby in 1989, moving to Grantham, Lincolnshire. Their son Ashley Maurice was born in October, 1989, and another son, Richard Bradley in October, 1991.

Maurice's son Geoffrey married Gianetta Migliaccio in Huntingdon in 1986. Geoffrey works as an engineering draughtsman and he and Gianetta live in St. Neots, Cambridgeshire. They have two sons, James Andrew, born in 1988 and Anthony John, born in 1993. James studied Design at Huddersfield University and graduated in 2011 with first class honours. He also was a finalist in a national design competition earlier in the same year. Anthony has recently also started studying at university.

The youngest son of William and Emma Whitfield was Arthur, born in 1895. You will remember that it was Arthur who had initially supplied me with the information that the family had lived in Tewin before they came to Potton, an event which had occurred in 1833, over sixty years before Arthur had been born. Arthur served in the army in the First World War. He was in France in 1917, but sustained a serious injury to his right hand in the November of that year, and spent a couple of months in hospital in Sheffield. His army papers record that his grip in the injured hand was not strong even after his discharge from hospital. This must have been a handicap to him because his medical on joining the army had pronounced him to be in the A1 category, which presumably meant that he had been very fit. After the war, he returned to Potton where he continued working as a market gardener. He married Elsie Trundle in Ware, Hertfordshire in 1922. It isn't clear how they met. Their first daughter, Iris, was born in 1922, Joyce their second daughter in 1930 and Marjorie in 1932. Their son Derek was born in 1935.

Arthur lived near the mill in Mill Lane, Potton. I can remember accompanying my father as he delivered groceries to his uncle Arthur; I was about ten years old at the time. Arthur kept rabbits, hens and goats at the Mill, which was not a working mill by this time; he had put a few adult rabbits into the building and they had established a colony. Arthur used to feed them, but otherwise left them to their own devices, apart from killing them when he wanted to eat or sell any of them. His market garden land, rented from Potton Charities, was nearby in Mill Lane, and possibly in Narrow Lane. I can remember that my father who had kept rabbits as a small commercial concern and who was also interested in gardening used to stay talking to his uncle for what seemed to me then a very long time.

The Minute Books of Potton Charities record that Arthur had ten common leys (land temporarily sown to grass) which were given up by F. R. Tear in 1949; and in 1950:

'….Mr Drew reported that a common ley was being neglected by J.W. Bartle, and it was resolved that he be written to as to the intentions of his cropping [it]; he to advise in writing if he wanted to vacate the same.'

Mr Bartle must have indicated that he wished to relinquish the tenancy, because it was transferred to Arthur Whitfield later in the year.

In November, 1953, Mr Drew reported that G. Gurney, tenant of land in Mill Road had not paid his rent as requested and his tenancy was duly transferred to A. Whitfield (presumably Arthur). However, twelve common leys were transferred from Arthur to S. R. Dennis in the same year. Possibly Arthur had his eye on a particular plot of land.

Arthur's first wife, Elsie, nee Trundle, died in 1958, aged 59, and he married Ada Sadler in 1960.

Arthur and Ada were living in a bungalow in Newtown, Potton, when I visited them with my aunt Doris in the early 1970s. I can remember being offered a glass of whisky; when Ada asked me whether I would like some water with it, Arthur interjected with 'No he wouldn't - there's enough water in it already!' His direct, forthright manner reminded me of my grandfather and I could see the resemblance between him and his older brother.

Arthur died in May, 1975, as I was taking my final examinations at university. He was eighty. His snippet of information about the family coming from Tewin had provided me with a vital clue in my search for my ancestors and I shall always be grateful for his help.

Arthur's children all married and had families of their own. His son, Derek, married Janet Bailey from Biggleswade in 1956. They had a daughter, Beverley, in 1965. Derek worked as a market gardener in Potton; he had land in Narrow Lane, where I can remember him growing a beautiful crop of onions. He later became a lorry driver. He ended his working life as a steward, at first at the working men's club in Potton, and then at the Conservative club in Biggleswade.

Beverley married Bryan White in 1991. Their daughters Rebecca and Amy were born in 1993 and 1998 respectively. They still live in Potton. Rebecca spent her gap year teaching young children in rural India.

The youngest child of William and Emma Whitfield was Annie, born in 1898. Annie's oldest brother, David, was born in 1873, so there was the equivalent of a generation between them. David was married before his youngest sister was born; Annie would have shared the cottage at Pound End, Potton with her parents, brothers Albert and Arthur, and her young niece, Emma Louise. Annie moved away to London, maybe in her late teens, probably to go into domestic service. She was definitely there in 1930 because she was present at the death of her father, who had been living with her in Camden. I assume she kept in touch with her older sister, Rosa, who was also working in London at this time because later in the 1930s they were both working at the *Cross Keys* public house in St. Neots, Cambridgeshire. Annie married Fred Haddon in 1943. They moved back to Potton and lived in an old cottage in King Street, next to the *George and Dragon*. I remember being taken to see Annie by my aunt Doris. I have only vague recollections of my great aunt: she was a thin old lady who used to disappear upstairs to fetch me a bar of chocolate. She died in 1963, aged 65. It is strange how, as a nine year old, I considered her to be old. She and Fred had no children and I have to confess I know little more about her. The 1921 census should enlighten me further.

The youngest son of James and Elizabeth Whitfield was John, b.1857. He was described as a labourer in 1871, and I assume that this meant that he was working on the land, like his father. He married Sarah Hutchinson in 1880, and they had four children; unfortunately, the first two died in infancy: Eliza aged three, and William aged four. In 1881, the family were living in Meeting Lane, Potton, literally a stone's throw from John's parents, James and Elizabeth in Kidney Bean Row, and his older brothers James, with his wife Eliza and young Frederick in Horslow Street, and David, with his wife Mary and two children in Sheffield Close. You won't be surprised when I tell you that this time John was described as an *agricultural* labourer.

John, Sarah and their family may well have known hard times in the 1880s. The *Bedfordshire Times* of 6th February, 1886 stated 'The dearth of work is felt very heavily in this place [Potton] and neighbourhood; the closing of some of the coprolite works having been a source of grief to many diggers and pickers; whilst the suspension of field work presses very hardly on the poor. Soup has been provided by public subscription...'

A fortnight later the same paper recorded, for Potton, that it was '...painful to see anxious willing ones, pinched in features, hunting around for employment'. It may well be that John's older brothers, James and William and their respective families were also suffering privations at this time.

Market gardening has always been a risky way of making a living. It has seldom provided a steady income, as too many factors, both physical and economic, conspire against the grower. Probably the most important of these remains the fickle character of the weather in England. One tried and tested way of reducing the risk of financial disaster is for the market gardener to grow a variety of crops, and to spread the sowing or planting dates of these crops over several months during the growing season. Such an approach is rather like 'drip-feeding' a set amount of money into the stock market on a monthly basis over a period of time rather than making a lump sum investment on a particular day. As luck would have it, the fortunes of market gardeners and their labourers improved from the precarious position of 1886. Two years later, the *Bedfordshire Times*, in its Potton column of 13th October, reviewed the spring and summer seasons in much more encouraging tones. Early potatoes and peas had done well in the Potton district: maincrop potatoes had also produced abundant crops after heavy rain; and whereas potatoes grown on heavy land had consequently suffered from blight, the potatoes grown on the sandy soil of Potton had largely escaped the ravages of this deadly crop disease and had sold at a good price. The varieties being grown were Magnum Bonum, White Elephant, Early Rose and Beauty of Hebron.[6] The rain had benefitted the cabbage and cauliflower crops, but unseasonably mild temperatures in early autumn had meant that the 'buttons' on the Brussels sprouts were rather too loose. Carrots had done well, and runner beans had been plentiful until cut down by the first frosts of autumn.

I was interested to read that the old railway station in Biggleswade Road was being used for peeling onions. Concern was expressed in the article at the congestion at the newer railway station, which was said to be handling 'the largest vegetable traffic in England' with an inadequate number of staff, who were sometimes kept working until midnight to handle all the produce. The season was said to have been 'the best for seven years' and it must have saved some of the market gardeners from ruin. Their labourers would have been busy throughout the summer, and their earnings would probably have been augmented by overtime.

John's wife, Sarah, died in July, 1889, aged only 28, and he remarried in June, 1891. His second wife was Lucy Young, who was a coprolite worker. She was also pregnant with John's child. Lois was born in September, 1891, and Lucy now had her to care for as well as two stepchildren from her husband's first marriage: Eliza b. 1884 and John (junior), b. 1886. Unfortunately Lois did not survive for long: she died in December, 1892, aged 15 months.

It may be that John Whitfield also worked in the coprolite industry for a while, combining this with his work on the land. This was a common practice in Potton at that time. When market gardening was slack, for instance in winter or during a summer drought, younger labourers turned their hands to digging for coprolites. Coprolites are phosphatic nodules, the fossilised remains of prehistoric marine life which are to be found in the greensand in the Potton area. They are also found in the same rock type in the Guilden Morden and Bassingbourn areas of South

---

6   See Appendix

Cambridgeshire. It was thought that the coprolites were fossilised dinosaur dung, as many of the nodules have flat bases, as if they had dropped onto the sand after being excreted from the rear ends of dinosaurs. Fossil collecting was a popular hobby in Victorian times, but the coprolites were not mere geological curiosities sought after by gentlemanly enthusiasts, but were of great benefit in agriculture. They were ground up into fertiliser (calcium phosphate). Agriculture was becoming more scientific and the value of fertilisers other than manure from farm animals was being discussed and realised. Many coprolites were exported to France where calcium phosphate was being used in the vineyards. Potton railway records indicate that local coprolites were being sent to Newcastle, Market Harborough, King's Lynn, Stowmarket, Ipswich, Harwich and other places. About forty cartloads apparently left the station every day.

Coprolites occurred in layers or beds, rather like coal seams. The beds were between eighteen inches and two feet in thickness, and could be found at depths varying between five feet and fourteen feet from the surface. Digging for coprolites, using pickaxes and shovels, was tiring and dangerous work. There was always the danger of subsidence in the light, sandy soil, and gunpowder was sometimes needed when the fossils occurred in a conglomerate type of rock, where they were embedded in the sandstones like plums in a pudding. A *Bedfordshire Times* article in 1878 stated that coprolite digging had been known in Potton for about ten years, and revealed that it was taking place at Deepdale and on Sandy Heath. There were also coprolite workings at Bury Hill in Potton, about two hundred yards from where I am writing. There is a depression left behind after the fossil digging which can still be seen in some of the front gardens of some of the Bury Hill houses. Hundreds of acres of land in the Potton district were eventually worked for coprolites and the land was afterwards returned to market gardening. Local market gardeners were, of course, highly delighted if coprolites were found beneath their land; such a discovery would guarantee good rental returns for them for a short period, (up to £150 per acre) and it would have been far easier to collect the revenue from this unusual land use than it would have been to dig potatoes or pull and bunch carrots.

Coprolite diggers would earn better money than agricultural workers - £50 per year rather than about £30 per year on the land, but the physically demanding and dangerous work was usually only undertaken by younger, fitter men. The *Royston Crow* of 5th March, 1886 reported that

'On Thursday last, a man named Whitfield in the employ of Mr H. Coningsby, coprolite merchant, was pecking [i.e. using a pickaxe] in the excavation at Berry Hill (sic) [in Potton], when the rock gave way, and, falling on him, broke his leg'.

Obviously labourers at this time were not considered of sufficient importance, even with broken legs, to be given their full names; my theory is that the unfortunate member of the family was John Whitfield, but I suppose it could have been one of his brothers. John would have been about 29 years old at that time. Whichever member of the family was involved, the accident was somewhat ironic because I would imagine that he had only been using a pickaxe in the Bury Hill coprolite pit because he had been laid off from his market gardening work. I doubt whether he received any compensation for what would now be regarded as an industrial injury. I consulted the archives of the *Royston Crow* in Royston museum in an attempt to find further details. Unfortunately the article didn't enlighten me further, but the 19th March (1886) edition confirmed my suspicions about employment prospects in Potton:

'In consequence of the long and severe winter, a large number of men, able and willing to work are compelled to be idle. The distress is very great and the sufferings of many families intense, all their resources are exhausted and an appeal for help has been made to the public...'

John's second wife, Lucy, was a fossil picker, or sorter, before she married. Once the coprolites had been dug out, they had to be sorted or graded before they were taken to the railway station to be despatched to the fertiliser factory. The sorting sheds had benches along each side, and each bench was partitioned off with a space for each worker. The fossils were pressed through a hole at the back of the bench; the sandstones were thrown onto the floor. Even these had their uses: depending on their size they were either used in road making or for gravelling paths. The *Bedfordshire Times* article I referred to earlier stated that

'...The operation of sorting the fossils is somewhat interesting, and the rapidity with which it is done is marvellous. The stones are always kept wet while being sorted, and to keep the hands of the workers warm a fire basket is burning at every table. As there are twelve of these baskets in the sorting house, the temperature is always warm. The girls amuse themselves at work by singing...'

It would be interesting to know what the girls sang in those days before radio and pop songs. I doubt if it was something 'highbrow', like a song by Schubert. It may have been a music hall song, or perhaps a traditional Bedfordshire folk song. Its rendition may, of course, have been for the benefit of the reporter. I would imagine that gossip may have been the more usual accompaniment to fossil sorting.

The article makes the work sound almost idyllic, but I wonder if the reporter had tried it, and, if so, for how long? I wonder, too, what Lucy Young, soon to become Lucy Whitfield, thought of her job, and how 'interesting' *she* found it. The 'rapidity' which the writer had marvelled at was due to the fact that the sorting was being paid at piecework rates, and workers with nimble (if sore) fingers and good hand/eye co-ordination could earn decent money, particularly if they were not interrupted by newspaper reporters. In Lucy's case, of course, there was an added incentive in 1891: her pregnancy would mean that her job would soon have to be suspended for a while, and there would have been no maternity benefit in those days.

Lucy remained John's wife and stepmother to his two children after her own daughter Lois died. She, however, died at the age of 48 in October, 1906. John continued living in Potton, and seems to have changed his occupation from working on the land to working as a maltster's labourer at Potton Brewery in King Street (some of the brewery buildings can still be seen at the rear of the Co-op's premises). In the 1911 census he was living in Horslow Street with a housekeeper, Annie Osborne and her daughter, Lily. Annie's husband, James William Osborne had died in 1907. A little research uncovered some interesting details: Annie Osborne's maiden name was Wagstaff, and although she had been born in Little Amwell, Hertfordshire, her father, James Wagstaff, had been born in Gamlingay and her mother, originally Sarah Young, in Potton. Sarah Young was an older sister of John Whitfield's late wife, Lucy, so Annie Osborne was John's niece by marriage. I haven't been able to discover what happened to Annie and Lily after 1911.

I was intrigued (and impressed) to see in an article in the *Bedfordshire Times* of Friday, March 22nd, 1912, that John Whitfield was among the number present at the *Swan Hotel,*

Bedford, earlier in the month to hear an address from Rowland Edmund Prothero, agent to the Duke of Bedford. Mr Prothero, who later became Lord Ernle, and President of the Board of Agriculture from 1916 to 1919, was speaking on the desirability of forming a Bedfordshire federation of village friendly societies, and John Whitfield was there representing the *Queen's Head* sick club in Potton. Sick clubs and savings clubs were often organised at and administered from public houses at this time, drawing their members from working men who enjoyed a drink, but were sufficiently prudent to plan for the future. The *Queen's Head* was in Sun Street, Potton, and has since been turned into two private houses, having ceased trading in 1919. John Whitfield's interest in its sick club and the security it provided may well have been as a result of his having lost both of his wives and three of his children; he had learnt from personal experience that family life could be cruelly interrupted by unpredictable, unforeseen events over which he had no control.

Not only did John Whitfield make the effort to attend, he also briefly addressed the meeting - a courageous feat for a working man not used to public speaking. Mr Prothero was warning against village friendly societies joining the Post Office or some national friendly society. By forming a Bedfordshire County federation of friendly societies, he felt that local members would have more control over their funds which, he argued, would not then be diverted into advertising or the building of 'marble palaces in London or Manchester'; in any case, people in rural areas were usually healthier than urban inhabitants; and there was greater opportunity to distinguish between cases of genuine illness and malingerers if the administration of each club or friendly society remained local. John Whitfield informed the assembled company that a committee had been formed in Potton to decide the best course of action to adopt, and he would be recommending that they followed the proposals outlined by Mr Prothero.

Of John's five children from his two wives, only two survived to become adults.

Eliza, b.1884 must have had a rather unsettled upbringing. As we have seen, her mother died when Eliza was only five years old, and she was presumably looked after by her father with some help from his elderly parents or perhaps a nearby brother or sister-in-law until John re-married in 1891. At the time of the 1901 census Eliza was living in the house of Samuel Fuller, a butcher in Potton Market Square, and working as a domestic servant. She married Walter Charles Lincoln in Kempston on Christmas Day in 1905. I found Walter Lincoln's military records for the First World War on the ancestry website and discovered that he and Eliza were living in Bunyan Road in Kempston and that his civilian occupation had been a horse keeper.

Eliza and her husband had eight children: Walter, b.1906, James, b.1908, Leonard, b.1910, Reginald, b. 1913, Lilian, b. 1917, Gordon, b.1920, Ronald, b.1923 and Cecil, b.1927, who died in 1929.

Eliza died in 1938, after seven months of illness. She was 53. Her funeral report in the *Bedfordshire Times* stated that she had been born in Potton, and had lived in Kempston for 35 years, i.e. since 1903. She had probably moved there as a single woman to take up a domestic servant's position. Looking through a list of Kempston burials at the Bedford Record Office, I was surprised to find one for a John Whitfield in 1939. I looked at the *Bedfordshire Times* entries for Kempston over that year and was eventually rewarded by a brief funeral report. The report told me that John's death had followed a long illness. He had been living in Kempston with his daughter and son-in-law (Mr and Mrs Lincoln) for about eleven years. He had actually died in the workhouse infirmary at Ampthill; he had been admitted there five days previously. The workhouse records, also at the Bedford Record Office, gave the cause of his death as a cerebral thrombosis, but it would appear that he had been suffering from some other illness beforehand - maybe heart disease, or cancer.

John Whitfield, junior, b. 1886, like his sister Eliza, must have had an unsettled and possibly unhappy childhood; there were so many comings and goings, with his sisters and brother dying young, losing his mother and gaining a stepmother. He started working at the Braybrooks tannery in Royston Street, and one day an incident occurred there which was to have a lasting influence on the rest of his life: he injured his finger, and the manager of the tannery at that time, Mr George James Spriggs, sent John to his own house, which was nearby in Royston Street, to seek medical attention. John's finger was bound up by Mr. Spriggs' daughter, Laura. Apparently it was a case of love at first sight, and the couple started going out together. Reading between the lines, it may be that the Spriggs family provided the stability that had so far been somewhat lacking - due to unfortunate circumstances - in John's life up to this point, and I suspect he may have been taken under their wing, to a degree. Mr. Spriggs and his daughter attended the Potton Congregational Chapel in Sun Street, where Laura was the organist. As we have seen, the chapel was also used by other members of the Whitfield family: David Whitfield and his wife Mary had attended before his untimely death and James Lester and his wife Martha, John's aunt and uncle, also worshipped regularly there, together with their children - John's cousins.

Congregation members presented Laura with a silver teapot when she relinquished her post as organist just before her marriage to John Whitfield. The marriage took place at the chapel in 1909. I had borrowed the Chapel records to note details of baptisms, marriages and funerals and also to look at the minutes of Trustees' meetings. I was intrigued to find a rather terse entry for John and Laura for 1911: 'Left the town'. Their date of leaving Potton would have been later than Census Day, 1911, because on that day the couple were living in Biggleswade Road, near the *Shannon* public house. Unfortunately, the Congregational minute book gave no further details.

At the time of my searching the internet did not exist, or was in its infancy. I therefore looked at the registration of births volumes at St. Catherine's House in London to find any births of Whitfields where the mother's maiden name was Spriggs, and found that an Audrey Whitfield's birth had been registered at Wallingford in 1913. In more recent years this information could have been forthcoming after a few clicks of a mouse thanks to the ancestry website, but using St. Catherine's House was certainly an experience: there were four large, heavy volumes for each year, and any researcher had to be physically fit to lift them; lightning reflexes were also handy in order to secure the desired volume before it was snatched and consulted by someone else: it was like being at a jumble sale in an age of austerity. I came home wondering whether my visit had been worthwhile as far as the John Whitfield line was concerned. Naturally I made good use of my time there in following up other enquiries.

The next step was to contact a newspaper local to the Wallingford area. I sent a letter for publication in the *Wallingford Herald*, requesting anyone who knew of John and Laura Whitfield

Wedding of John Whitfield, (junior) and Laura Spriggs, Potton, 1909. John Whitfield, senior, is far left, back row. Walter Lester is between him and John Whitfield, junior.

to get in touch. I was fortunate to receive three helpful replies, including one from an elderly member of the Spriggs family who gave me the name and address of John and Laura's only granddaughter, Julie Harman. I contacted Julie and we arranged to meet. She brought with her a photograph taken immediately after John and Laura's wedding in 1909. The setting looked familiar: members of the wedding party were framed by two large ornamental pillars which I couldn't quite place, but I knew I had seen before. When I returned to Potton, I realised that they were the pillars outside the front door of Granville House, on the corner of Royston Street and Brook End in Potton, just opposite where the tannery had been, and close to Mr. Spriggs' house where John and Laura had first met. I had seen these pillars each time I went for a piano lesson in part of the house back in the 1960s. I found out later that many wedding photographs were taken here after the ceremony had been performed at the Congregational Chapel. Mr F.W. Braybrooks, the owner of the tannery, who lived in the house in the early twentieth century, was also one of the Chapel's trustees.

Julie could remember her grandparents, and said they had moved to the Wallingford area when Laura's father had also moved there, to take charge of another tannery at nearby Brightwell. I had been correct in supposing that Audrey was John and Laura's daughter: she was, of course, also Julie's mother. After Audrey's birth, John was called up into the army in the First World War. He enlisted in the Devon Regiment. His army papers reveal that he had been a small man - just five

211

feet two and a half inches tall.

After the War was over he returned to Wallingford and worked as a van driver for a grocery store. Julie described him as a quiet man who loved gardening and music; apparently he could play several musical instruments. Laura became an organist at Wallingford Methodist Church where she also became a trustee; she also gave piano lessons. John died in the Wallingford area in 1948, aged 62. The National Probate Register shows that he and Laura had been living in Wantage Road, Wallingford, and reveals that he left over £900. Laura outlived him, dying in 1966 aged 85.

Their daughter Audrey became a concert pianist, playing mainly classical, but also some 'lighter' pieces. She was especially fond of the Grieg piano concerto, and it was played at her funeral. At some time in her career she played with the famous Charlie Kunz, and may even have had a brief fling with him. Unfortunately her hectic and somewhat unconventional lifestyle meant she was drinking rather too heavily, and she became dependent on alcohol. She died in Cornwall in 2000.

Her daughter Julie married James (Jimmy) Harman in 1967. He has a share in a farming business, and Julie runs an animal sanctuary, mainly for horses. They have two daughters, one of whom lives in the U.S.A., and grandchildren.

The youngest child of James and Elizabeth Whitfield was Ruth Whitfield, b.1861. Like so many working class girls of her generation, Ruth went into domestic service, and in 1881 was found working as a housemaid for William W. Wallis, a married man aged 34, of no occupation, and living in Ashburnham Road, Bedford.

Ruth must have found another position as a domestic servant between 1881 and 1886, probably in London. I found her marriage took place in 1886 in South Hackney, Middlesex, when the London parish records became available on the ancestry website. She married Michael Kent, a boot maker, and son of a cigar maker. Ruth signed her marriage certificate, indicating that she had been to school, or at least learned to write somewhere. This was of interest to me because her brothers William (my great grandfather), and John did not master the art of writing. The young couple were living in Ash Grove, but later moved to Treadway Street in Bethnal Green - an appropriate address for a boot maker and his wife.

Bethnal Green was the poorest district of London in Victorian times. In the eighteenth century it had been an area where weaving and dyeing took place in small workshops, and there was much overcrowding. The weaving industry declined from the 1840s onwards, resulting in much poverty. Other industries began to replace it, including furniture, clothes and boot and shoe manufacture. Cigar making (by hand) was also found here, as well as at Spitalfields and Whitechapel. In 1889, three years after Ruth's marriage to Michael, the social investigator Charles Booth found that almost 45 per cent of the population of Bethnal Green lived below subsistence level. He and another social reformer, Sir Walter Besant, give us an idea of what it must have been like to live in the area at that time. They describe the street scenes that would have been familiar to Ruth and Michael: the constant movement of women through the area with bundles of match boxes, for instance, and men with rolls of cloth or baskets of boots. One of these men might have been Michael Kent (if his name seems vaguely familiar, remember he was a witness at the marriage of his wife's niece, Elizabeth Brittain in Bethnal Green in 1889).

The footwear industry was very important in the area. In 1861, women and children had also been employed: women made the shoe or boot uppers at home and then took them in baskets to the local warehouse. Later the 'sweating' system was introduced where each stage of production was contracted out from the warehouse. This system remained at least until the turn of the century, and those employed in the footwear industry had to put up with irregular employment, long hours and the continued use of women and children, presumably in an effort to reduce costs. Mechanisation became more common towards the end of the century, and resulted, as it usually does, in the loss of jobs, affecting mainly men. It would appear that Michael Kent was not one of them, because the 1911 census shows that he was working as a sole sewer: instead of making a complete pair of boots from start to finish he was now just involved with one of the processes in their manufacture. He was working from home. I would imagine it was a rather tedious, repetitive job, which must have been hard on the hands and fingers.

I have managed to find details of three children born to the couple: Michael James Kent (named after his father and Ruth's father), b.1889, Emily, b.1892, and William John (named after two of Ruth's brothers) in 1906. Michael James Kent was also in the boot trade; like his father, he was working as a sole sewer in 1911, so was not the *sole* sole sewer in the household. He married Alice Wicks in Christ Church, South Hackney in 1913.

Ruth died in 1928 aged 66, her husband in 1934. Ruth's death was registered in Bethnal Green; evidently she had remained there, despite the grinding poverty. In some ways it must have seemed a very different life from that being experienced by her brothers and sister in Potton; the common factor, however, was lack of money. I wonder if they kept in touch with each other? There are probably some of Michael and Ruth's descendants around in London, but so far I have not found the time to trace them. It would not be the easiest of tasks.

Chapter 9.
The First World War takes its toll: the line from George Whitfield 1821-1900.

'If I should die, think only this of me:
That there's some corner of a foreign field
That is forever England...'

Rupert Brooke (1887-1915). *The Soldier*

George was baptised in Tewin and spent most of his boyhood there. He arrived in Potton in 1833 with his mother and brothers, but I couldn't find him there in 1841. I did find a George Whitfield, described as a hawker, i.e. a travelling seller of goods, in the details for Leamington Priors, which was then a small town in Warwickshire. The approximate age was correct for the George Whitfield I was looking for, and this George hadn't been born in Warwickshire. Was this the George Whitfield born in Tewin? Obviously, I can't be sure. However, we have already seen that the family had split up, to a degree, after the death of their mother earlier in the year, with Philip in Deddington, James travelling to Whetstone, and William to Manea, so the idea of George being in Warwickshire is not totally ridiculous; the brothers had to be resourceful, and clearly were not averse to travelling from their home area if the need arose. Unfortunately, the census doesn't record what George was trying to sell to the good people of Leamington Priors, which later developed into the large town of Leamington Spa thanks to the popularity of its mineral-containing springs which were publicised by Victorian doctors. It is unlikely to have been soap, towels or bottles because these items would probably have made him a rich man as the popularity of the spa town developed rapidly around this time and he would probably have stayed in the area. If I have found the correct George, then perhaps he had visited his brother Philip at Deddington, or was intending to turn up at the wedding later on in June. Leamington was a fair distance from Potton, so perhaps George had a horse and cart, but I must not over-indulge in fruitless speculation.

George was certainly back in Bedfordshire by 1849, because he married his cousin, Ann Cox, in Northill Church in that year. Ann was a cousin on his mother's side (his aunt Eliza Berry had married Benjamin Cox, and was the mother of Ann), so George at least had kept in touch with his mother's side of the family. It may be that some of his brothers did so too, but I have no evidence for this.

DIAGRAM 10

The line descended from George Whitfield (1821 - 1900)

[also see diagram 2]

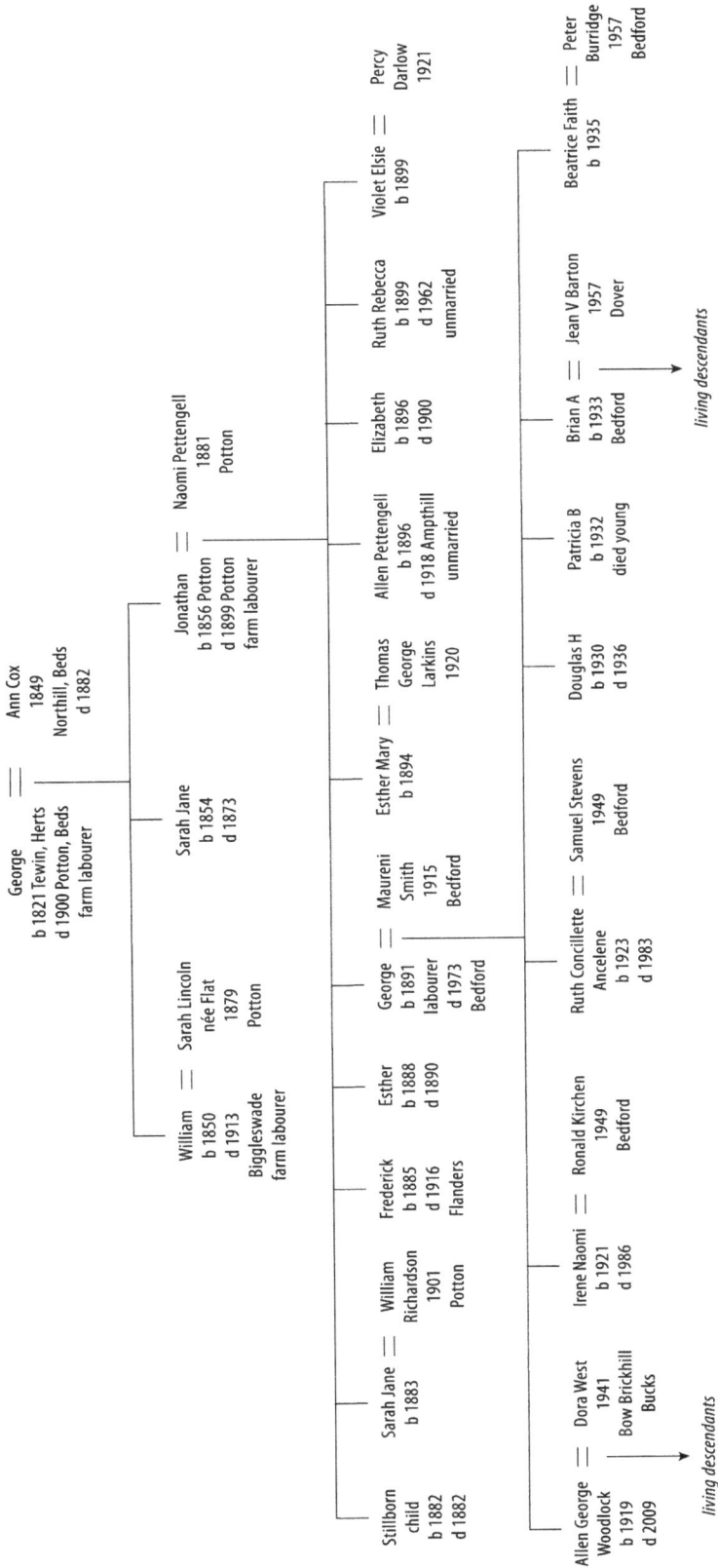

George
b 1821 Tewin, Herts
d 1900 Potton, Beds
farm labourer

==

Ann Cox
1849
Northill, Beds
d 1882

William
b 1850
d 1913
Biggleswade
farm labourer

==

Sarah Lincoln
née Flat
1879
Potton

Sarah Jane
b 1854
d 1873

Jonathan
b 1856 Potton
d 1899 Potton
farm labourer

==

Naomi Pettengell
1881
Potton

Violet Elsie
b 1899

==

Percy
Darlow
1921

Ruth Rebecca
b 1899
d 1962
unmarried

Elizabeth
b 1896
d 1900

Allen Pettengell
b 1896
d 1918 Ampthill
unmarried

Esther Mary
b 1894

==

Thomas
George
Larkins
1920

Maureni
Smith
1915
Bedford

==

George
b 1891
labourer
d 1973
Bedford

Esther
b 1888
d 1890

Frederick
b 1885
d 1916
Flanders

William
Richardson
1901
Potton

==

Sarah Jane
b 1883

Stillborn
child
b 1882
d 1882

Beatrice Faith
b 1935

==

Peter
Burridge
1957
Bedford

Brian A
b 1933
Bedford

==

Jean V Barton
1957
Dover

→ *living descendants*

Patricia B
b 1932
died young

Douglas H
b 1930
d 1936

Ruth Concillette
Ancelene
b 1923
d 1983

==

Samuel Stevens
1949
Bedford

Irene Naomi
b 1921
d 1986

==

Ronald Kirchen
1949
Bedford

Allen George
Woodlock
b 1919
d 2009

==

Dora West
1941
Bow Brickhill
Bucks

→ *living descendants*

215

In 1851, George and Ann and their young son William (1) were living in Meeting Lane in Potton. Meeting Lane is a lane which connects Horslow Street with King Street. The cottage where they lived has now been demolished. I can remember a row of very small, low, thatched cottages in Meeting Lane in the 1960s. They were in a very dilapidated state, with small outside washhouses and were served by an outside tap. They had large gardens which stretched down to the gardens of properties in Bull Street and the Market Square. The cottages had become uninhabitable by the 1970s, and have now been replaced by some decidedly up-market four bedroomed detached houses, giving Meeting Lane a *completely* different character.

An interesting incident from George's early days of married life has come to light from the Criminal Registers, now available on the ancestry website. They informed me that on 1st November, 1852, Ann Dennis, aged 18, stole one apron, one handkerchief and one pair of clogs from George Whitfield. In case you are wondering whether George had Dutch ancestry, the clogs, or pattens, would have been worn outside in muddy or dirty conditions by many people in those days; nowadays, people would wear Wellington boots. Ann Dennis was a straw plaiter and lived in Back Street, (now Chapel Street) with her parents Richard and Ann Dennis. She was sentenced to three months' hard labour for her crime. The case was also mentioned briefly in the *Bedfordshire Times* of 15th January, 1853. The Quarter Sessions records told me a little more. Apparently George's wife, Ann, had hired Ann Dennis in late September, 1852, to look after herself and her sister because they were suffering from fever. Ann Whitfield's sister had died (presumably from the fever) in October; the items stolen had belonged to her, and had also included a flannel petticoat and a new pair of white cotton stockings. Ann Dennis had claimed, to no avail, that Mr Snitch, the relieving officer (i.e. of the poor) for Potton had given her permission to take the articles - a rather unlikely story I would have thought. Mr Lindsell, the Justice of the Peace dealing with the case seems to have thought so too: he wrote that Ann Dennis declined to sign her statement, hinting, perhaps, that this was because she had lied. Her reluctance to sign is unlikely to have been due to embarrassment over illiteracy because Ann Whitfield attested to the truth of *her* statement by adding her cross at the bottom of the document.

By 1861, the family were living in Gamlingay Road, Potton, and there were now three children. In addition to William who we have already met, there was Sarah Jane, b.1854, and Jonathan, b.1856.

They were living in Holland in 1871. I must repeat that (despite the clogs) George did *not* have Dutch blood in his veins: Holland was an aptly named low-lying, rather marshy area of Potton along the Gamlingay Road. The marshy character of the land in the vicinity is still hinted at by the present day name of an adjoining road: Myers Road. Earlier maps of Potton name the general area as 'The Mires'. (I can remember parts of Myers Road, near the lower houses of the more recent Downside Gardens development, flooding in my younger days). It is likely that George and family were living in rented accommodation, possibly belonging to the farmer who was George's employer at the time.

They were still living there in the early summer of 1873, because a brief article mentioning Ann Whitfield appeared in the *Bedfordshire Times* of 21st June of that year. Ann had observed a Potton labourer, George Kitchener, damage a young chestnut tree by breaking off one of its lower branches on 9th June, between eight and nine o'clock in the evening. The tree belonged to James Wagstaff, a retired builder, who lived at Potton Manor along the Gamlingay Road. Ann and George Whitfield and their family lived just two doors away from Wagstaff, so Ann would have had a good view of the horse chestnut trees in the Manor grounds, some of which are still standing. The tree may well have been close to her cottage. Kitchener was fined five shillings for the offence, plus damages of two shillings and sixpence and eleven shillings court costs, and was informed that if the fines were not paid he would face fourteen days' imprisonment. By 1881, George and Ann and their family had moved to King Street; the move might also indicate that George was now working for another farmer or market gardener.

George could not have been earning much money as an agricultural labourer; even with his relatively small family to support he was in receipt of bread from Potton Charities for many years, certainly from 1856 until his death over forty years later. Like his older brother James, he also worked some land in his spare time to provide vegetables for the family and maybe a few extra shillings to supplement his main income. He had a plot on Poor's Common in the 1860s while his family were growing up. Records are incomplete, so he may have kept this plot going later. Like other occupants of land on Potton common he would have had a long walk to his plot before he actually did any work on it: the Enclosure Commissioners had thoughtfully provided land for the poor of Potton well outside the built up area of the town, towards the border the parish shared with Gamlingay. It was a similar situation with the land at the Roundabout, close to the border with the parish of Everton.

Ann Whitfield died in 1882, aged 58. She had lived long enough to see her two sons marry, but also to suffer the loss of her daughter Sarah Jane, a young straw plaiter who had died in 1873 aged just nineteen. Her eldest son, William, a farm labourer, married a 43 year old widow, Sarah Lincoln, nee Flat, the daughter of a maltster. Sarah had previously been married to George Lincoln of Sandy, a tin plate worker, and was fourteen years older than William. The couple lived in Mill Street (now Royston Street), in Potton. There were no children. Sarah died in 1908, and William became another member of the family to end his days in the Biggleswade workhouse. The 1911 census records him as an inmate, and he died there two years later.

Jonathan, the younger son, married Naomi Pettengell in 1881. Naomi was born in Guilden Morden in South Cambridgeshire where her father, Allen Pettengell was an agricultural labourer, possibly a shepherd. She became a domestic servant for a doctor in Ashwell, Hertfordshire, some seven or eight miles away from Potton before she married. Jonathan was a farm labourer who must have done a lot of walking after work to meet Naomi during their courtship. Early photographs of Naomi show that she was a very attractive young woman with dark hair and eyes, and I can understand his enthusiasm.

Jonathan and Naomi lived in King Street after their marriage. They had a large family; their first child was still-born and did not receive a name in 1882. The others were:

Sarah Jane, b.1883, named after her late aunt.
Frederick, b.1885.
Esther Mary, b.1886, died 1890, named after Naomi's mother.
George, b.1891, named after Jonathan's father.
Esther Mary, b.1894.

Allen Pettengell, b.1896, named after Naomi's father.

Elizabeth, b.1896, d 1900.

Ruth Rebecca, b.1899.

Violet Elsie, b.1899.

Notice that the children included two sets of twins. The last set, Ruth and Violet were born in the same year as their father, Jonathan, died. He was only 42, and had been suffering from pancreatic cancer. *His* father, George was still alive, and must have felt the loss keenly; Naomi must have been devastated. She was with George when he died the following year.

The last years around the end of Jonathan's life must have been very trying for Naomi with a large number of children to care for as well as a sick husband who would probably have been unable to work. The Biggleswade Union (Workhouse) Relief Order Book makes it clear that the family had been given some help in the quarter ending Michaelmas, 1898: they received 2s 3d and then 2s 6d and six loaves of bread per week for two weeks. In the next quarter the payments were more generous: five shillings and seven loaves per week for four weeks and then five shillings and six loaves for eight weeks. It is also recorded that the Guardians of the Poor paid for Jonathan to visit Moorfields Ophthalmic Hospital: he must have been having problems with his eyesight. In the quarter ending Lady Day, (March 25th), 1899 the family received four shillings and six loaves for ten weeks and after that the relief was discontinued, presumably because Jonathan had died. Naomi also probably had to look after Jonathan's elderly father, George. Her mark appears on his death certificate. I would think that Sarah Jane, aged about sixteen when her father died, and Frederick, a couple of years younger, were able to help their mother look after the little ones.

Naomi eventually moved to an almshouse in Horslow Street, administered by Potton Charities. She had another child in 1905, who was known as Dorothy E. Whitfield. The father was William Giddings, a Potton labourer, who was bound by a bastardy order to provide 1s 6d per week towards Dorothy's upkeep until she reached the age of fourteen, when she presumably would have left school and be capable of providing for herself. The amount per week does not strike me as very generous; by this time unmarried mothers were often awarded more. The 1s 6d per week couldn't have gone far.

Sarah Jane, the oldest child, married a market gardener, William Richardson of East Hatley, near Gamlingay, in 1901. They were living in Everton Road, Potton in 1911 with their nine year old son William Christopher. They later moved to a farm in East Hatley. Sarah Jane used to rise very early each morning to get the farm horses ready for their work, so that when the men arrived they could start any task on the farm requiring horse power without any preparation.

Frederick Whitfield, Jonathan and Naomi's oldest boy was working as a draper's porter in 1901, but ten years later was described as a horse keeper and worker on a farm. He emigrated to Canada in 1912. He was involved in the First World War, and was killed in action on Good Friday, 1916. A report of his death appeared in the *Biggleswade Chronicle*. It was said that he was one of the best men in his battalion. I doubt if this was much consolation to his mother and the rest of the family as they received the news back in Potton. Apparently fighting had been so ferocious that his comrades were unable to retrieve his body; he was buried on the battlefield.

George Whitfield, b.1891 started his working life on the land but later also emigrated to

Jonathan and Naomi Whitfield, with their young son George, c 1893.

Frederick (l) and George (r) Whitfield. Both emigrated to Canada and fought in the First World War - the maple leaf can be seen on their uniforms. Frederick was killed in action; George survived and returned to Bedfordshire.

Canada with his brother. He worked originally as a lumberjack, then in a rubber factory; his brother Frederick may have also been employed there. George returned to England for a while, long enough to court and marry Irene or Maureni Smith, the daughter of a travelling grinder, Woodlock Smith, said to be of Romany extraction. Woodlock Smith was born in Bedford. The 1901 census shows him living in a van (presumably a caravan), parked near the appropriately named *Traveller's Rest* public house on Clapham Road, Bedford, with his wife Connsy (Concillette) Smith, nee Loveridge, aged 29, son Christopher (11), and daughter Moraney or Maureni (5).

George Whitfield was 24 when he married Maureni Smith in St. Paul's Church, Bedford in 1915. His bride was 19. George was described as a private in the 36th Canadian battalion. The couple returned to Canada, where their first two children were born in Hamilton, Ontario: Allan George Woodlock Whitfield in 1919, and Irene Naomi Whitfield in 1921. The family then returned to England: the ancestry website shows that they departed from Montreal on the *Ausonia*, arriving in London on 27th May, 1923. Their next child, Concillette Ruth Ancelene Whitfield was born in December, 1923 and baptised in Potton in January, 1924. The births of their other children were registered in Bedford: Douglas in 1931 (he died of meningitis aged 5), Patricia B., in 1932 who also died young, Brian Albert in 1933, and Beatrice Faith, their youngest child, in 1935.

George worked as a labourer on farms, then later at Felmersham gravel pits, north-west of Bedford. His wife Maureni died in 1937, aged only 41 and George brought up the family with some help from the Smith family who looked after young Brian and, presumably, (Beatrice) Faith. He joined the London Brick Company in 1947, working initially at Elstow, and was later transferred to Stewartby brickworks. He retired from there in 1963 at the age of 71. His retirement notice said he was employed on wickets, the hydraulic winch and finally on 'spotting', possibly some sort of job in quality control. His retirement photograph shows that even in his early seventies George was a powerfully built man. He carried on working as a labourer after his retirement from the brickworks, taking on all sorts of casual jobs, but was knocked off his bicycle while travelling to a job in 1971, when he was eighty. It was said that he was never the same again, and he died the following year.

George and Maureni's eldest son, Allan was born in Hamilton, Ontario, Canada, in 1919, but returned to England in the 1920s with his parents and sister Irene. He joined the 2nd Hertfordshire Regiment in 1941, and in the same year married Dora West at Bow Brickhill, Buckinghamshire. After the war ended, Allan worked, like his father, at Stewartby brickworks, and then for a time for a meat company. I visited him and Dora at their bungalow in the Milton Keynes area where they made me very welcome, and I later received an invitation to their Golden Wedding celebration, where I was able to meet other members of the family. He died in 2009, aged 89, having had to retire early, at 59, with angina.

Allan and Dora had four children: Carole, b.1947, Robert, b.1948, Genine, b. 1953, and Irene, b. 1954. All have married.

Robert worked as a butcher and later in the brickyard at Stewartby like his father and grandfather before him. He bought a plot of land and built a house on it, and then continued with other building projects, buying old houses, renovating them and selling them on. He

George and Maureni Whitfield with young Allan and Irene, c 1923. The two children had been born in Canada.

married Barbara Lewis in 1973 and they have two sons: Stephen Mark, b.1974 and David Alan, b.1976. Stephen was married for two years (no children), but is now divorced, and in 2009 was living with his parents. David married Anna Mace in 2008 in the Edinburgh region, but they have now moved back to Buckinghamshire. Their daughter, Lily Olivia was born in 2009.

George and Maureni's younger son, Brian Albert, b.1933 married Jean Barton in 1957 in the Dover area, but moved back to Bedford, where their son Michael B. Whitfield was born in 1960. Michael married Tracy Barry in Bedford in 1999, and they have an adopted son David.

I have been able to find out a little about Jonathan and Naomi's other children. George's younger sister, Esther Mary, b.1894 was a domestic servant at various addresses in London, and she kept up a lively correspondence via post cards, which appear to have been a bit of a craze at the time, with friends and family. Many of these have survived, including one written to Esther which had me puzzled for a while. It seemed to be written in a foreign language which I was unable to identify (not that I am much of a linguist). Then I realised that it had been written with the aid of a mirror, not in capitals, but in conventional, 'joined up' handwriting. I have since tried to write in this way, and can report that even using capital letters it isn't easy. Whoever had written that postcard had clearly practised the art many times. Once I was equipped with a mirror the postcard could be read easily. I had hoped to find a message that was of great interest, but was disappointed to find it was fairly mundane; I could only marvel at the skill and ingenuity of the writer in disguising it.

Esther Whitfield married Thomas George Larkins in 1920. They lived on the Gamlingay Heath in a house with some market garden land which Esther's sister, Sarah Jane and her husband William helped them to buy. They had a daughter, Eva, b.1922, who married James Manning, a member of another local market gardening family. Eva kept a lot of her mother's postcards and photographs as well as some newspaper cuttings, and it was thanks to her I was able to track down descendants of her uncle, George Whitfield, and reconstruct the history of this branch of the family. Eva died in 2007, but her son Jim still lives on the Heath, and has also been very helpful.

George's younger brother, Allen Pettengell Whitfield was working as a farm labourer in 1911. He did not emigrate to Canada, but was involved in the First World War like his brothers. He served in France for some time and had been involved in much fighting, but received an injury to his hand on 23rd August, 1918, and he was sent back to England for treatment at Southwell, Nottinghamshire. He returned to Ampthill in his home county for a period of convalescence, but developed pneumonia and died on 26th October, 1918, about three weeks before the war ended. His funeral took place at Potton cemetery on Boxing Day, 1918, and he was buried with full military honours in what must have been a very solemn and moving ceremony. The coffin was placed on a gun carriage, drawn by six black horses, the bearers were some of Allen's comrades, and a trumpeter from his Regiment sounded the Last Post. I obtained these details from the report which appeared in the *Biggleswade Chronicle*.

Allen's mother Naomi and his sisters attended the funeral. Poor Naomi, already widowed prematurely, had now lost two sons within about two years. George was in France at the time; after the war he, too, had developed pneumonia. Fortunately, as we have seen, he recovered. If he had not done so the line from George Whitfield (1821-1900) would have died out.

Jonathan and Naomi's next children were the twins, Ruth Rebecca and Violet Elsie, born in 1899, the year of their father's death. Ruth was apparently working in London during the First World War and suffered from shell-shock when the capital was attacked, and this affliction appears to have stayed with her. She remained an invalid and had to be pushed around in a wheelchair. She was cared for by her mother until Naomi died in 1946, aged 84. Naomi is said to have been pronounced dead once before, and was being 'laid out' ready for burial when she opened her eyes and said 'I'm not going until my boy comes home' [i.e. from the war]. She made a slight recovery and lived on for a few more weeks. She had certainly seen some life: married at twenty, she had produced eleven children, lost her husband at an early age, lost three children in infancy, and two grown-up sons in the war, and had to contend with a daughter who suffered from shell shock, as well as enduring grinding poverty. She must have been a remarkable character.

After Naomi's death, Ruth may have been cared for by another member of the family, but she ended her days at 'The Limes', in Biggleswade, as the workhouse was now euphemistically called. She died in 1962, aged 62.

Various articles in the *Biggleswade Chronicle* make it clear that Ruth and her mother had been keen fundraisers for the Potton Salvation Army; although an invalid, Ruth managed to sell hundreds of raffle tickets for them. I was very surprised to read in an article in the 15th October, 1926 edition that 'Sister Whitfield' had played a harp solo at a Salvation Army concert. Was this Ruth? If so, how did she learn to play such an expensive instrument in her younger days, in what must have been a poverty-stricken household?

Ruth's twin, Violet, married Percy Darlow in 1921. Their daughter, Mary K. Darlow, married Alwyn Edward (Ted) Croot, and they lived in Chapel Street, Potton. I went to school with their son, Kevin, not knowing that we were distantly related, and both descended directly from James Whitfield (1770-1833), the gamekeeper: we were both great-great-great grandsons of his. At that time we lived just a few doors away from each other.

Dorothy Elizabeth, b.1905, the twins' half-sister, married Herbert James Darlow of Gamlingay in 1924. He died in 1957, and Dorothy married Bertie David Munns two years later. Dorothy died quite recently, having lived into her nineties. It's still a small world in the Potton/Gamlingay area, because I played the organ at her funeral service.

Chapter 10.
Railways and military and domestic service: the line from Robert Whitfield 1824-1890.

'The introduction of so powerful an agent as steam to a carriage on wheels will make a great change in the situation of man'.

Thomas Jefferson (1743 – 1826).

Robert Whitfield arrived in Potton aged nine, with his mother and some of his brothers. 1833 must have been a bewildering year for him, what with his father dying and then being uprooted from the only family home that he had known. At some point, however, he appears to have found time for some schooling, because unlike some of his brothers he was able to sign his name. It is difficult to see where he could have acquired this skill since for much of his time in the early years at Potton he seems to have been occupied in stone picking and digging for derisory pay. Possibly he attended school on a part time basis; he could have rested his weary muscles while learning the basics of literacy and numeracy.

Robert was working as an agricultural labourer in 1841, and living in Horslow Street. He married Catherine Jarvis in 1848; his confidently executed signature appears on the certificate. Catherine was unable to sign her name, although she would have been able to read the details on the certificate where she placed her cross. I am able to state this with confidence thanks to a discovery I made about Catherine which will appear later.

Catherine Jarvis had been born in Potton in 1826, but her parents (like Robert's) had been the subjects of a removal order in 1820. They had been removed from Roxton, Bedfordshire, not having gained a legal settlement there, and had at some point become chargeable to that parish, probably because Catherine's father had been unemployed for a while.

I have not been able to find a photograph of Robert or Catherine so far, not even in their later years, but a detailed description of Catherine survives. This is because in 1844 she had been found guilty of stealing from her employers, and she had been sentenced to one year's hard labour in Bedford County Gaol. The criminal register describes Catherine (then aged eighteen), as being 5 ft. ½ inch tall, with light brown hair and hazel eyes and 'well-looking', presumably meaning pretty (a pity there wasn't a photograph). The register then states that she could read, but not write (hence her cross on the marriage certificate). Intrigued by the crime, I wondered if it had been reported in a local newspaper, and I made enquiries at the Bedford Record Office.

DIAGRAM 11

The line descended from Robert Whitfield (1824 - 1890)

[also see diagram 2]

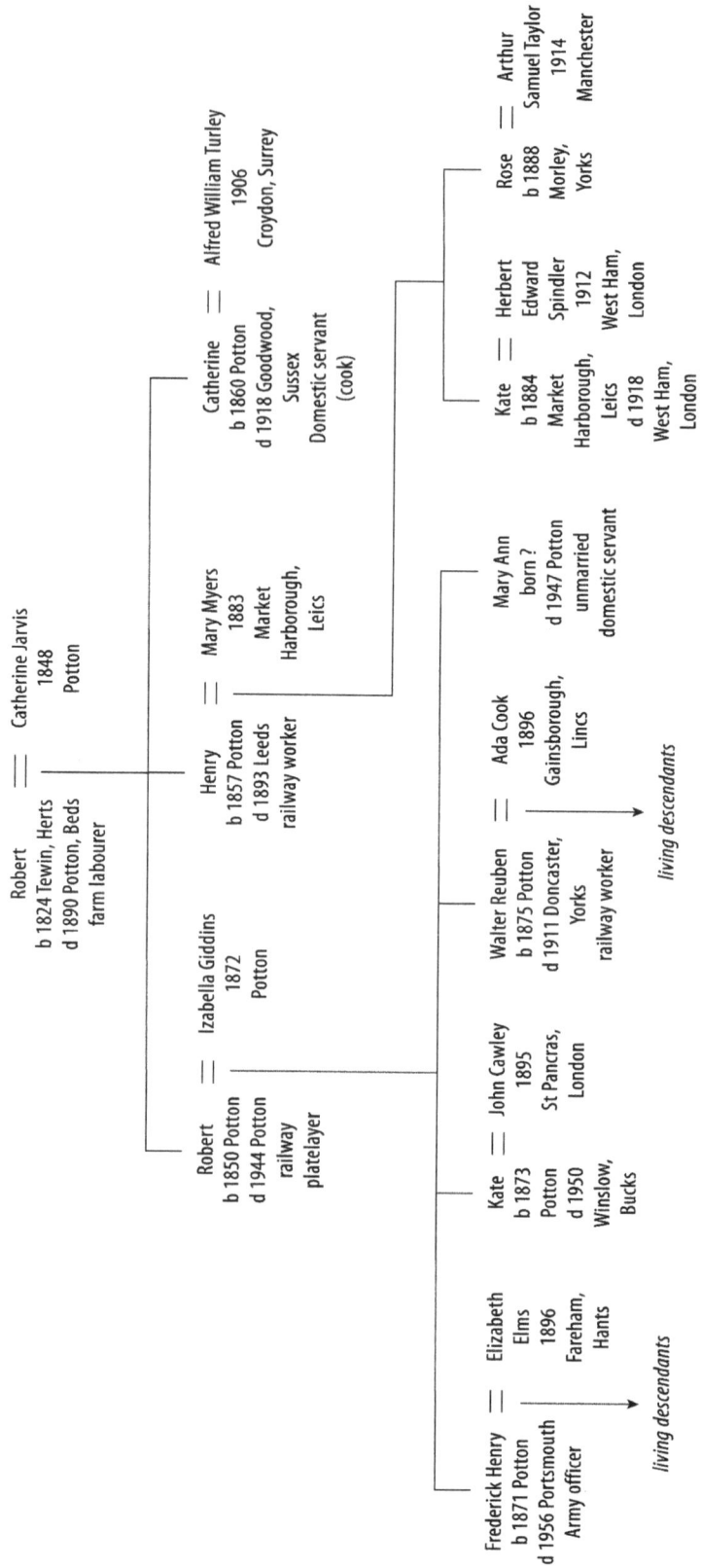

Robert
b 1824 Tewin, Herts
d 1890 Potton, Beds
farm labourer

== Catherine Jarvis
1848
Potton

Robert
b 1850 Potton
d 1944 Potton
railway
platelayer

== Izabella Giddins
1872
Potton

Henry
b 1857 Potton
d 1893 Leeds
railway worker

== Mary Myers
1883
Market
Harborough,
Leics

Catherine
b 1860 Potton
d 1918 Goodwood,
Sussex
Domestic servant
(cook)

== Alfred William Turley
1906
Croydon, Surrey

Frederick Henry
b 1871 Potton
d 1956 Portsmouth
Army officer

== Elizabeth
Elms
1896
Fareham,
Hants

Kate
b 1873
Potton
d 1950
Winslow,
Bucks

== John Cawley
1895
St Pancras,
London

Walter Reuben
b 1875 Potton
d 1911 Doncaster,
Yorks
railway worker

== Ada Cook
1896
Gainsborough,
Lincs

Mary Ann
born ?
d 1947 Potton
unmarried
domestic servant

Kate
b 1884
Market
Harborough,
Leics
d 1918
West Ham,
London

== Herbert
Edward
Spindler
1912
West Ham,
London

Rose
b 1888
Morley,
Yorks

== Arthur
Samuel Taylor
1914
Manchester

living descendants

living descendants

226

An article in the *Bedford Mercury* of 30th March, 1844, informed me that Catherine had been a servant in the household of William Hillyard, a corn factor (or merchant) of Great Barford, Bedfordshire. Apparently she had only been in his service for ten or eleven days and wasn't happy there. (I wonder why this was. Perhaps she was being worked too hard, or was Mr Hillyard, or someone else, paying her unwelcome attentions?). Catherine had indicated to her mistress that she wished to go, but after her departure it was noticed that several things were missing. Putting two and two together, Mr Hillyard sent a servant to apprehend Catherine, who was walking back to Potton, a journey of perhaps eight or nine miles. The servant, who was presumably on horseback, caught up with her somewhere between Tempsford and Girtford. Catherine was told to return to Mr Hillyard's and was asked to return the missing articles to the servant. She replied 'I must throw them away; I shall go and drown myself'. (There was a river nearby, so the servant must have persuaded her not to do so). She had taken a lace cap, a lace veil, a piece of lace, a pair of stockings, a shirt, a silk handkerchief and some money - a rather strange assortment of items. It may be that these articles were intended for her 'bottom drawer'.

The Reverend William Shove Chalk who convicted Catherine in 1844 held the manor and estate and living of the parish of Wilden, Bedfordshire. I would imagine that his wife had an extensive wardrobe of fine clothes and all the lace articles she could possibly desire. He lived in a completely different social milieu from Catherine, but, clearly, stealing was wrong. If the sentence Catherine received seems a little harsh, consider the sentences handed out for youngsters caught helping themselves to electronic gear during the 2011 summer riots, their crimes being condemned by millionaire members of Parliament, while wealthy 'respectable' bankers and company directors pocketed obscene bonuses, and salary increases often with little justification and apparently without any qualms. Stealing and rioting are obviously wrong, but the inequality which helps to encourage such crimes, so obvious in Victorian times, remains as a blight on English society. Some things never change - but I digress.

Catherine appeared in court again two years later. Committed by Robert Lindsell, Esq., she was accused at the Bedford Lent Assizes of stealing 17 yards of lace and 12s 6d from her master, a thread and lace merchant, Joseph Clark, of Tempsford. This time she was pronounced not guilty. The case was reported in two successive editions of the Northampton Mercury, but unfortunately no further details were given.

When Catherine married Robert Whitfield in 1848, she already had a daughter, Mary Ann, who had been baptised in 1846. When had she been born? It has not been possible to discover who the father was; it was unlikely to have been Robert as Mary Ann retained her mother's surname, even after the marriage, and in a later Census return, she was described as Robert's daughter-in-law. We would use the term 'stepdaughter' today. If the father was William Hillyard, her former employer, it might explain Catherine's hasty departure from Great Barford and possibly her theft of the various articles. However, this is speculation on my part.

In 1851, Robert and Catherine were living in Horslow Street, with Mary Ann, aged four and young Robert aged one. They were living next door to Robert's older brother James, his wife Elizabeth, and their four young children, Another of Robert's brothers, George, who we met in the previous chapter, was living just round the corner in Meeting Lane, with his wife Ann and baby son William. All three brothers were working as agricultural labourers, and although they would have been working long hours in all weathers, this appears to have been a more settled and happier time for them all, particularly compared to the 1830s.

Robert and Catherine's house was certainly full at the time of the 1861 census. In addition to their own family, which now comprised Mary Ann, aged 14, Robert, aged 12, (and now working as an agricultural labourer), Henry (4) and young Catherine (1), they also had lodging with them another Mary A. Jarvis, an unmarried lace maker of 24, with her three children: Catherine (5), Sarah (3), and Arthur (8 months). Three adults and seven children were crammed into one, presumably small, cottage.

In 1866, Robert Whitfield and William Apthorpe, both of Potton appeared before the magistrates at Biggleswade Petty Sessions, and were fined ten shillings each for wilfully breaking and destroying two lime trees at Cockayne Hatley, the property of Captain Henry Cockayne Cust. Unfortunately the article I found in the *Bedfordshire Times* of 14th April, 1866, didn't give details of their ages or occupations; I am inclined to think that the offenders were Robert Whitfield, b 1849 and William Apthorpe, b 1848, but as both lads were named after their fathers, it is impossible to be sure. The destruction of the trees was therefore probably a case of teenage vandalism, and hopefully the lads learned their lesson from the hefty fines imposed, roughly equivalent to approximately one week's wages. However, there remains the possibility that their fathers had been responsible for the destruction of the young trees, possibly because they harboured a grudge against Cockayne Cust.

There were fewer people in the Plowman's Yard cottage in 1871. The household now comprised Robert, Catherine (now described as a dressmaker), Robert junior (21), Henry (14) and Catherine, junior (11), but there was also a Ruth Whitfield aged 2, whose birthplace was given as Manea in the Isle of Ely. The information given by the census regarding Ruth's place of birth enabled me to locate another branch of the family, but led to other questions which took me over twenty years to answer: more about this branch later. Robert and Catherine were also being visited by Sarah Jarvis, a thirteen year old straw plaiter and a young 'scholar' Ada Smith. Charles Deeble, a journeyman baker, lived next door with his wife Elizabeth and his family, including young Reuben Deeble, aged six. We shall meet Reuben later: he was to play a part in the family's future.

In addition to his main employment as an agricultural labourer, Robert, like some of his brothers, also rented land from Potton Charities, in an effort to support his growing family. He cultivated plot 46 on Poor's Common from 1860 to 1877, and maybe longer, as records could not be found beyond this date. Despite his efforts, the family remained poor, and received Charity bread from 1873, and coal from 1859 until Catherine died.

In 1881, Robert and Catherine were living in Horslow Street, and Catherine was described as a lace maker. Her early interest in lace had clearly been maintained, although the domestic lace industry was now in decline. Their neighbours included Robert's brother James and his sons James and William, their wives and respective families - a little Whitfield enclave in the heart of Potton.

Robert (senior) appeared at the Biggleswade Petty Sessions in the late summer of 1883 because he had been accused by his employer, Mr William Smith, of 'refusing to work'. Mr

Smith, a prominent Potton farmer and landowner who lived at Home Farm in Horne Lane and employed 45 men (including my great grandfather William Whitfield and Robert, who was William's uncle) to work his 650 acres, had encountered Robert leaving his work early – between one and two o'clock in the afternoon. When asked the reason for his early departure, Robert had advised his employer of his intention to visit Sandy Flower Show, and when threatened with court action he had replied that he would 'put up with that' and continued on his way. Perhaps he was an exhibitor at the Show which at that time was a major event, drawing large numbers of exhibitors and visitors from a wide area, well beyond the towns of Sandy, Potton and Biggleswade. The Show was held in the grounds of Sandy Place, by kind permission of John Nathaniel Foster. (You will remember from Chapter Two that Foster had employed *George* Whitfield as his gardener in the early 1870s).

The incident and Robert's subsequent court appearance were mentioned in an article in the Saturday 15th September 1883 edition of the *Cambridge Independent Press* which gave further details of the work Robert was undertaking and hinted at the sort of character he was. I carried out a little more research on William Smith and his family. The altercation between Smith and Robert Whitfield serves to highlight the stark contrast between master and employee that existed in the late nineteenth century, and a little background information on both families may be of interest.

William Smith's father, George Smith, had been a prosperous Potton farmer and landowner, and a director of the Bedford and Cambridge Railway, leaving just under £60,000 when he died in 1876; despite his wealth (or perhaps because of it) he had taken a Potton labourer, Alfred Yerrill, to court for stealing *one pennyworth* of flour from him in 1860, and a hawker, Joseph Shaw, for 'unlawfully cutting grass' in Potton ten years later. Yerrill was sentenced to one month in Bedford gaol for his misdemeanour, which was possibly prompted by hunger. Shaw was fined sixpence (presumably the value of the grass) but then charged sixteen shillings and sixpence court costs. William Smith appears to have been very much like his father in having a predilection for taking those less fortunate than himself to court. In 1868 he had brought Manjoey Welch and Elias Shaw, two gypsies and John Menneyton, a labourer from Hatch near Sandy, before the magistrates for sleeping in one of his straw stacks at Potton one night in late January. They were able to sleep inside for a while after their appearance because they were each sentenced to seven days' imprisonment.

In 1878 William Smith succeeded in having two young bricklayers, Henry Dean and Elias Lowings, prosecuted for damaging grass at Potton to the value of one shilling. They were each fined fifteen shillings, probably equivalent to about a week's wages for each man.

We have already seen that Robert's father's estate had consisted merely of furniture and household effects and the promise of £50 when his brother's widow died. Robert's father, James Whitfield the gamekeeper, had died in the middle of a court case concerned with the removal of the Whitfield family from Tewin to Potton. Robert had had to fend for himself since the age of ten. He was now a farm labourer who lived in a small, rented cottage, whereas William Smith's home was a fourteen roomed, substantially-built farmhouse. It is likely that Robert was earning somewhere between ten and twelve shillings per week (about £30 per year) outside of harvest time, and saving would have been impossible. The two men would have moved in very different social circles. They were living totally different lives within the same small town, connected only by Robert's need to earn some money to keep himself and his wife and family from starvation. I should perhaps mention that in addition to his wealth and influence, William Smith was a thick-set man of average height, with a rather gruff manner and he was used to being obeyed. It would have taken more than a little courage to defy him.

The 1883 article stated that Robert had been one of a band of twelve labourers who had entered into a harvest contract with their employer, agreeing to cut, tie, and cart a quantity of wheat, barley, oats and clover at thirteen shillings per acre (between them). The report makes it clear that Robert, who would have been nearly sixty years of age at the time, and probably not as physically fit as he had been in his younger days, was responsible for tying the sheaves of barley. As he had left early to enjoy the delights of Sandy Flower Show, a number of barley sheaves remained untied, and were not taken off the field. It had rained heavily that night and during the next two days. The barley had been spoilt and Mr Smith claimed that Robert's negligence had cost him £5.

The magistrates (who happened to include John Nathaniel Foster of Sandy Place) managed to discover that the men had been working from 4 a.m. until about 8 p.m. since starting their piecework, so even allowing for short breaks for refreshment and to answer calls of nature it would appear that Robert had already worked for well over eight hours before leaving for Sandy, and we can hardly blame him for taking a little time off. Robert claimed that his employer's foreman, Mr Bluffield, had already broken the contract that morning by making the men work across the field in a different direction to that which had been previously agreed. Robert also told the magistrates that he had not been paid for a fortnight and claimed that hours of work had not been specified. It was interesting for me to see how he dealt with his employer and the magistrates at a time when showing deference to such people was expected of labourers and their families.

I was impressed to see that after nearly half a century working on the land, including picking up stones in the depths of winter when he first arrived in Potton as a boy of about ten years old, Robert was not prepared to be forced into submission by those with more money, power and influence than he was ever likely to possess. After due consideration, the magistrates dismissed the case – a verdict which must have given Robert some satisfaction. What the article didn't tell me was whether Robert resumed his employment with William Smith; he would probably have been admired by his fellow workers for standing up to his employer, but he may well have been viewed as a trouble maker by the wealthy farmer. Hopefully he was paid for the work he had already done. You will probably be as relieved as I was to know that the loss of the barley appears to have caused no lasting hardship to Smith: he later moved from Home Farm (where he was born) to Potton Manor, set in grounds of over 27 acres, when he retired from farming in 1917 and still managed to leave nearly £119,000 when he died in 1933. Although he clearly disapproved of Robert taking some time off work to enjoy Sandy Flower Show, Smith was happy to indulge his hobbies of hare coursing and fox hunting with the Cambridgeshire Hounds; and stag hunting with the Biggleswade Harriers. I wasn't surprised to discover that he had been a staunch Conservative. Unlike Robert, he had plenty to conserve.

Robert died in 1890. Catherine lived much longer and augmented her income by taking in lodgers. In 1891 her granddaughter Kate was staying with her (a fact which opened up another line of enquiry for me), and in 1901 her lodger was Thomas Merrick, aged 23. This young man had been born in Hereford and was working in Potton as a market gardener.

The *Biggleswade Chronicle* of Friday 30th March, 1923 reported, with regret, '……the death of Potton's oldest inhabitant in the person of Mrs Whitfield [Catherine], of Wagstaff Terrace who passed away last Friday at the advanced age of 96 years'.

This little old lady (remember she was only just over five feet tall in her prime), born in the reign of George IV, had lived right through the Victorian era, through the First World War, and well into the twentieth century - what remarkable social and technological changes there had been in her lifetime! She had been born in an age of candlelight, travel by foot or by horse, illiteracy for the poor, operations without anaesthetics, child labour and cottage industries, and had lived to see trains and cars (and hence greater geographical mobility), photography, radio, education for all and the introduction of pensions, just to give a few examples. Some of these things had already made their presence felt in Catherine's family, as we shall see.

Robert and Catherine's son, Robert, b.1849, married Isabella Giddins in Potton in 1872. Unlike his father, Robert did not sign his marriage certificate, so Robert senior does not appear to have given his son any lessons in handwriting. The younger Robert worked as a platelayer on the railway for many years.

Platelayers were responsible for the maintenance of a stretch of railway track - in Robert's case this would have been the track between Potton and Sandy via Deepdale, which had opened in 1857.

Each rail was joined to the next by a pair of 'fishplates' placed vertically across the joint between the rails, one on each side, and bolted through. The rails were on a bed of wooden sleepers. Platelayers like Robert would be checking the rails and equipment on their stretch of track, replacing worn-out rails or rotten sleepers and packing them to ensure that the track was level. There would also be routine weeding and clearing out of drains along the track. Platelayers tended to work in gangs; each gang could contain between three and eight men. In Robert's working days most of the tasks would have been carried out by hand, so the work would have been heavy and arduous. However, it was carried out in the fresh air, and, unlike work on the land, would have been rewarded by an occupational pension - a rarity in those days. Despite this, Potton railway records examined at the Bedford Record Office show that Robert was not averse to earning a few extra shillings at an advanced age if the opportunity arose: for example he was recalled in May, 1926, when he would have been about 76 years old. This was the time of the General Strike in England and railway platelayers joined the strike when they backed the miners in order to secure them an extra shilling a week in wages.

Although I have been unable to find a photograph of Robert, I do have one of his wife, Isabella, taken in 1909 outside their cottage in Wagstaff Terrace, in Sandy Road, Potton. On the reverse of the photograph Isabella had written that her daughter, Mary Ann (known as Polly), had had to hold her up to pose for the snap. Isabella was clearly ill; she died the following year, aged 58. I was given this photograph by one of Robert's grandsons, Walter Harry Whitfield (1897-1990).

I made contact with (Walter) Harry thanks to an amazing coincidence. He lived in Doncaster,

South Yorkshire, and one of his neighbours had informed him that her daughter had just started teaching at a place called Potton in Bedfordshire. Harry told her that his grandfather, Bob, (i.e. Robert), had lived there, and made some enquiries through his neighbour's daughter. She put him in touch with Mrs Patricia Yates of Potton History Society, who kindly got in touch with me.

Harry told me that his grandfather used to supplement his railway pension by poaching and shooting. He used to walk inside the hedgerows between Potton and Sandy, leaving a trail of corn, and would later return to shoot any pheasants that would be feeding. Harry recalled a visit he made to his grandfather in 1912. He could remember being impressed by the long shelf full of pickled onions and walnuts he saw in the cottage. A dead furry animal was hanging on the pantry door. When one of his grandchildren asked what the animal was, his grandfather told him it was a cat. This made the children very reluctant to have any meat with their meal. Unfortunately they therefore missed the delicious taste of hare.

Robert (Bob) was obviously a very frugal and resourceful man - I expect he had been brought up that way. Apart from his poaching exploits, he used to collect firewood from the woods and store it in his shed, ready for winter. According to the late Mrs Gwen Leigh of Potton, b.1922 (who remembered Bob as 'a bit of a character' and said he had a picturesque turn of phrase), he also used to pick up cigarette ends in the street, collect the tobacco, and then make cigarettes of his own. Not the most hygienic of practices, but Bob lived to a ripe old age. When interviewed for an article which appeared in the *Biggleswade Chronicle* of 20th October, 1939, Robert attributed his longevity to the quiet life he had led since his retirement. At ninety, he still enjoyed fairly good health, and until recently he had gone for a walk each day - a habit which most doctors today would agree would be conducive to good health and possibly a longer life. The article also mentioned that Robert was 'highly respected in his native town'; everyone, even children, enjoyed having a chat with him. He had started working as a railway platelayer at eighteen years of age, and had worked full time for 47 years. He was believed to be Potton's oldest inhabitant when he died in 1944 aged 94, an honour formerly bestowed, you may remember, on his mother, Catherine, in 1923. I was delighted, but not altogether surprised to note in his obituary, which appeared in the *Bedfordshire Times*, that Robert had been a skilful gardener in his younger days. Apparently, his flowers and vegetables had been 'among the finest grown in the district'.

Robert's younger brother, Henry, b.1857 moved out of Potton, presumably in connection with his job: he also worked on the railway. I'm not sure when the move took place; he was not to be found in the 1881 census, but in November, 1883, he married Mary Myers, who was about seven years his junior, at the Register Office in Market Harborough, Leicestershire. Market Harborough was connected to the railway line which ran through Potton; we have already seen that coprolites were being sent there in the 1860s. The reason for the marriage ceremony being held at the Register Office may have been that Mary was probably a Catholic, whereas Henry had been baptised in the Anglican Church. It may be that Mary's father didn't approve of the marriage. Mary was clearly pregnant at the time of the ceremony because the couple's daughter, Kate, was born in March, 1884; Kate's presence in her grandmother Catherine's house in Potton in 1891 prompted me to search for the marriage.

I found out, from later census details, that Mary Myers had been born in Whitwick, Leicestershire, where her father, Michael Myers, originally from Ireland, was a coal miner. The Whitwick area was already a centre of Catholicism, and attracted a number of Irish immigrants in the nineteenth century; some of them, like Michael Myers worked in the coal mines, others worked as navvies, constructing the Charnwood Forest railway between 1881 and 1883. The London and North Western Railway Company, which also operated the line running through Potton by this time, was heavily involved in the planning stage of the Charnwood Forest railway and ran the line from the time of its opening in April, 1883. I wonder if Henry Whitfield was involved in the construction of this railway (it had a station at Whitwick), and if this is how he met Mary Myers? It would appear he wasn't in Potton at this time.

Tracing this branch of the family has presented me with problems. It appears that Henry's job on the railways meant that he could be geographically mobile; unlike his brother Robert he was prepared to move. In 1891, a Henry Whitfield, married, aged thirty and born in Bedfordshire (no parish given), was working as a railway labourer, and lodging at Monk Bretton in the Barnsley area of Yorkshire. In the same lodgings was James Brown, another railway worker, born in Cambridgeshire. Across the words 'railway labourer', the enumerator had scribbled 'plate', implying that at that time Henry was a platelayer like his brother back in Potton. I feel sure that I have found the correct Henry Whitfield here. For the same census year I found a Mary Whitfield, married, aged 26, born in 'Wittick', Leicestershire, living with her daughter Rose, aged two, who had been born in Morley, Yorkshire. I feel sure that these people were Henry's wife and younger daughter. The other daughter, Kate, b.1884, was staying in Potton with her grandmother, as we have already seen.

And there the trail peters out. Henry, Mary and Rose appear to have eluded the census enumerators for 1901, for whatever reason. My search was not helped by the fact that Henry Whitfield was a fairly common name at the time, although clearly I was looking for one who had been born in Potton, Bedfordshire, and who was still probably working on the railway. Having carried out a fairly extensive search on the ancestry website, I concluded that the most likely outcome was that he had died in the Leeds area in 1893, and I sent for the death certificate. It told a sorry story, but wasn't *absolutely* conclusive. The certificate stated that Henry Whitfield, a 36 year old navvy, had died accidentally. The cause of death was given as 'rupture of the heart from a crush'. Often the 'informant' on a death certificate is the next of kin, or another close member of the family, (which of course would have been helpful for me), but in this case, the name appearing in this column was that of the coroner, because there had been an inquest. As yet, I haven't seen the inquest details, but I feel pretty sure that this was the Henry I was looking for. I found a brief article in the *Leeds Times* of 18th February, 1893 which gave a few more gruesome details: Henry had been coupling two railway wagons. One presumably had started to move towards the other because he was caught between the buffers. He had died before reaching the Leeds Infirmary. I have yet to find out what happened to Mary. She may have re-married, but looking for details on marriage certificates involving a Mary Whitfield would be a very time-consuming (and costly) business.

Kate Whitfield, the elder daughter of Henry and Mary, was working as a domestic servant for George Kitchener on the corner of Blackbird Street and Chapel Street in Potton in 1901.

George Kitchener was a member of a Potton family which had developed agricultural machinery, including traction engines, steam ploughs and threshing tackle in the latter half of the nineteenth century - some members of the Kitchener family still live in the town today. I presume that Kate had stayed with her grandmother in Potton after the tragic death of her father some eight years earlier.

Kate appears to have been friendly with her second cousin Eliza Whitfield (daughter of John Whitfield (1856-1939), who we met in a previous chapter). They were born in the same year, and may have been in the same class at school. Kate was a witness at Eliza's marriage to Walter Lincoln in Kempston in 1905, so it is probably safe to assume she was still living and working in Bedfordshire at that time. However, by 1911 she was living in Wandsworth, London, presumably in domestic service.

Kate married Herbert Edward Spindler, a booking clerk (on the railway?), in Woodford, Essex, in December, 1912. Kate's rank or profession is left blank, but her father's name is given as Henry Whitfield, a deceased labourer. Their son, Henry E. Spindler was born in October-December, 1913, but unfortunately Kate died in 1918, aged only 34. It is a possibility that she may have died as a result of another pregnancy - but I have not seen the death certificate. Herbert remarried in 1920. His new bride was Charlotte M. Watts, and they appear to have had two children: Kenneth A. Spindler, b.1922, and Beryl M. Spindler, b.1930. Herbert then died in 1931. He would have been about 42.

Kate and Herbert's son, Henry Spindler, married Ellen Maud Wassell in 1943. There were no children. Ellen died in 2004 aged 89, and Henry on 14th April, 2011, aged 97, in Boreham, near Chelmsford in Essex. I discovered Henry's address and telephone number on the same day as I found his short obituary on the internet - in June, 2011, so unfortunately I never managed to meet him. I found the solicitors dealing with his estate and contacted them. They put me in touch with a niece on his late wife's side, Dianne Styles, and she kindly sent me some photographs of Henry and Maud, and brief details of Henry's life. After leaving school he had worked for the British Oxygen Company in Waltham Abbey until he retired. He and Maud were married for 61 years, living in Leytonstone, and later Cheshunt before moving to Boreham in their retirement years. In the late 1960s Henry was diagnosed with cancer of the oesophagus, but he was a very determined man and managed, presumably with some form of medical intervention, to overcome his illness.

Rose Whitfield, Kate's younger sister, was not found in the 1901 census, but I did manage to locate her in Manchester in the census taken ten years later. Her birthplace was given as Yorkshire and she was lodging in Hadfield Street, with a tripe dresser, William Taylor, and his family. Although tripe dressing, the washing and preparation of cattle offal prior to it being sold for human consumption, was a characteristically Northern occupation, William Taylor originally hailed from Oxfordshire. It is not made clear whether the tripe dressing actually took place on the premises. Let us hope for Rose's sake, that it took place elsewhere, for the smell wafting up to her room would not have been pleasant - in fact, it would have been offal. Mr Taylor appears to have changed his occupation afterwards, because in 1914 he is described as an engineer. I feel sure that his family would not have raised any objections.

On the ancestry website, I found a marriage for a Rose Whitfield in Manchester which took place in 1914. I sent for the certificate, and found that Rose had married William Taylor's son, Arthur Samuel Taylor. Both were living in Hadfield Street at the time of their marriage. Arthur Taylor was an engineer and Rose was working as a kitchen maid. Her father was given as Henry Whitfield, deceased, engine driver, so it would appear that Henry might have started to progress in his railway career prior to his untimely death. The inquest details will hopefully confirm that this was the case.

There were a number of Taylor births in the Manchester/ Liverpool area after 1914 where the mother's maiden name was Whitfield, but as yet I haven't been able to establish whether these were children of Arthur and Rose. The way forward may be to advertise in a Manchester newspaper, but I don't rate my chances of success too highly; it is a pity the couple didn't live in a village.

The youngest child of Robert and Catherine Whitfield was Catherine, b.1860. Described as a scholar in the 1871 census, Catherine had left Potton by 1881 and was working as a cook, in Kensington. Her employers were Joseph Hardcastle, an M.P. and J.P., and his wife, the Honourable Mrs Hardcastle. Mr and Mrs Hardcastle also apparently required the services of a footman, a lady's maid, a housemaid, and a kitchen maid in addition to Catherine. It isn't clear whether this was Catherine's first position as a cook. In all likelihood she had already worked as a kitchen maid, perhaps locally, or in Bedford before moving to London. A cook was higher up the domestic service hierarchy than a kitchen maid or scullery maid, and the position carried extra responsibilities. It was also better paid.

By 1891, Catherine, still unmarried, was working as a cook in the household of Montague Charles Browning and his wife Fanny Allen Browning in St. George's, Hanover Square, London. Montague Browning was away from home on the night of the 1891 census and therefore unable to enjoy one of Catherine's meals, but he was described in the 1881 census as a Lieutenant-Colonel in the West Suffolk Militia. In addition to Catherine, the family apparently felt the need for two housemaids, a scullery maid, a kitchen maid, a lady's maid and a butler. The Browning's neighbours in Hanover Square included a consulting physician and surgeons. Montague and Fanny's son, Berthold Alexander Browning was a student of Theology. Catherine was clearly working for a family of high social standing. As she had a scullery maid and kitchen maid to help her with the more mundane, but necessary tasks such as preparing vegetables and washing up, Catherine's energies were probably devoted to preparing fairly elaborate dishes for the household, who may well have indulged in a fair amount of 'entertaining'. Thanks to the National Probate Register, available on the internet, I found out that when he died in 1905, Montague Charles Browning left nearly £146,000. It would be interesting to know how much he paid Catherine. A housekeeper in those days would normally be earning something like £80 per year, a cook slightly less.

By 1901, Catherine had secured a housekeeper's position. She was working for a barrister, Thomas W. Poley and his wife, Eleanor. The Poleys also employed a lady's maid, two housemaids and a kitchen maid, a scullery maid, a butler and a footman: eight servants toiling away to run the household of a middle aged barrister and his wife who were presumably too busy, too important or too idle to attend to such things themselves. Catherine must still have supervised the cooking, but would have had extra responsibilities such as the ordering and management of provisions and household linen; the kitchen staff would have reported to her; she would have been responsible to her mistress. The Poleys and their entourage were living at 26 Chesham Place in Knightsbridge, a fashionable and up-market area.

Unfortunately, censuses were only taken every ten years. I therefore have no idea how many jobs Catherine had in between these snapshot glimpses we have of her life. It isn't clear either how she coped in these environments which must have been so different from her home life in Potton. Presumably she learned to cook from her mother. As we have seen, the Whitfield household was usually fairly large, but the meals she would have had to produce for her employers must have been far more elaborate and adventurous than anything prepared and eaten in the cottage at Plowman's Yard. It isn't clear how she convinced her London employers of her suitability for the posts she managed to secure. She must have been a very capable, confident and independent woman as well as a good cook, and able to read and write to a good standard. I presume she must have obtained references from her former employers. It is a pity that, as far as I know, none has survived.

The impression I had of Catherine until recently was that she was an early example of a career woman, married to her job. I was wrong. In 1906, she married Alfred William Turley, a coachman, in Croydon, Surrey. She was 46, and was Alfred's second wife. (For a long time I was unable to find any details of the death of his first wife, Louisa. They had married in 1883, in the parish of St George, Hanover Square, London). In 1891, the census reveals that Alfred and Louisa, nee Harnwell, were managing a public house in West Ham, but by 1901 they were living in Goodwood, Sussex, where Alfred was working as coachman to the Duke of Richmond. I had searched in London and Sussex records for Louisa's death before 1906 without success, and the thought of a bigamous second marriage had crossed my mind. The old adage that truth is stranger than fiction was strikingly illustrated when I carried out a desultory search for Mrs Turley on the British Newspaper Archive website. It hardly seemed worthwhile to look at the article which appeared on the computer screen because it came from the 27th August, 1903 edition of the *Aberdeen Journal*. Surely this article was about a different Mrs Turley? However, I did look – and was surprised at what the article revealed.

Apparently Alfred Turley's employer, Charles Henry Gordon-Lennox, the sixth Duke of Richmond, in addition to the estate he owned at Goodwood, Sussex, also owned an estate at Gordon Castle near Fochabers in Morayshire. Alfred Turley, in his capacity as head coachman, had accompanied his elderly employer to his Scottish estate, leaving his wife at Goodwood. Mrs Turley later journeyed to Scotland to join her husband, but had presumably been suffering from toothache, because a few days later she had proceeded a further ten miles to Elgin to consult a dentist. She had several teeth extracted, but never recovered from the operation and died in the evening. Alfred Turley had been sent for, but his wife was already dead by the time he arrived.

Although the remains of Louisa Turley were later laid to rest in Tooting Cemetery, London, her funeral took place at Fochabers, and her death was also registered in Scotland - which explained why I had been unable to find these details in England. The residents and guests at Gordon Castle were most sympathetic when the news and circumstances became known, and the funeral was attended by various female members of the Gordon-Lennox family: Lady

Caroline, Lady Muriel, Lady Helen and Miss Ivy Gordon-Lennox.

A search of the Scottish deaths index confirmed the registration of the death of Louisa Turley in 1903. Alfred Turley's employer, the Duke of Richmond, Charles Henry Gordon-Lennox, died a month later at Gordon Castle in his mid-eighties. [7]

It would be understandable if Alfred Turley was reluctant to visit a dentist after 1903.

Alfred had previously worked in the parish of St George's, Hanover Square, and may have met Catherine during this time; at the time of his marriage (as we have seen) he was working on an estate in Sussex. The couple returned to Sussex after their marriage to The Kennels, part of the Goodwood Estate, which was owned by the Duke of Richmond. Originally, the building had been built to house the master of the local hunt and to accommodate the foxhounds (in some style), but by 1901, suitably adapted, it was being run as a convalescent home for soldiers who were presumably returning home with injuries received in the Boer war. Alfred and Catherine Turley were living there in 1911. Alfred was still working as a coachman. I expected to see that Catherine was working there as a cook or housekeeper, but no occupation was given for her. She must have been content with preparing meals for herself and her husband, and no doubt they enjoyed them. As they had married in middle age, there were no children. Neither of them lived to a great age. Catherine died in 1918, aged 58; her mother was still alive in Potton. Alfred Turley died the following year at the age of 65. Having spent the best years of their lives working to make the lives of their employers more pleasant and gracious, both were denied the opportunity to enjoy a well-earned retirement - an all too frequent occurrence in the 'upstairs downstairs' world they had inhabited. We must now return to Potton briefly to look at the next generation - the lives of the children of Catherine's older brother, Robert.

Robert Whitfield, (1849-1944) and his wife Isabella had four children: Frederick Henry, b.1870, Kate, b.1873, Walter Reuben, b.1875, and Mary Ann, b.1876/7.

Frederick Henry Whitfield was born to Isabella before she married Robert, but Robert seems to have been his father. It was apparently fairly common for couples to produce a child before marriage, either through ignorance of contraception or to prove that the woman was capable of bearing children. Frederick Henry was a scholar aged ten according to the 1881 census, but had left home by 1891, and probably before then. By 1891 he had joined the Dorset Regiment; his papers have survived from 26th January of that year. They reveal that he had previously been a volunteer in the Hampshire Regiment. Unfortunately, they didn't tell me why he had moved towards the South coast - or when. Frederick Henry is described as being twenty years and two months old (i.e. born in November, 1870), and 5 feet 10½ inches tall. His weight was 10st 3lb., and he had a fresh complexion, grey eyes and light brown hair. The 1891 census shows that he was living with the rest of his regiment at a barracks in Plymouth. He was a private, and the return confirms his birthplace was Potton. His military papers indicated that he was also in Portsmouth in 1891, Belfast and Chatham in 1893, and Dorchester in 1895, presumably as part of his training.

---

7   Charles Henry Gordon-Lennox (1818-1903) was a descendant of the first Duke of Richmond, Charles Lennox, (1672-1723) who was an illegitimate son of King Charles the Second and one of his mistresses, Louise de Kerouaille. The title continues today with Charles Gordon-Lennox, (b 1929), the tenth Duke.

Frederick Henry and Elizabeth Whitfield with young Elizabeth and Walter Henry. The photograph was taken in Dalhousie in the Punjab, India, about 1902.

He married Elizabeth Elms in November, 1896. The marriage was registered at Fareham, Hampshire. Elizabeth's father, Henry Elms, was described as a labourer in the 1881 census, but the 1891 census is more specific: he was a platelayer on the railway. I had therefore found another railway connection, but it was possibly coincidence this time. Whether Henry Elms and Robert Whitfield (Frederick Henry's father) knew each other before the young couple started going out together isn't clear, and I have no idea how Frederick Henry and Elizabeth met.

Frederick Henry's military papers show that he and Elizabeth didn't stay in England long after their marriage. By 1897 they were in Malta; they then proceeded to India, where Frederick Henry served for a number of years. Some of their children were born in these years in North West India (some of the locations are now in Pakistan).

Elizabeth was born in 1899 in Nowshera, the chief city of the Nowshera district in the Pakhtunkhwa province of Pakistan; Walter Henry was also born in Nowshera in 1901. Florence Isabel was born in 1902 in Ferozepore (Firozpur) in the Punjab district of India. The gazetteer tells us that this is an ancient city on the banks of the river Sutlej, a centre of numerous holy shrines and historic places. It produces cotton and grain, and has agricultural services and light manufacturing. Frederick Charles was born in 1904 at Kalabagh, a small town in the Punjab province of Pakistan, on the west bank of the river Indus. Nearby are the famous Red Hills of the Salt Range. James Robert was born in Poonamallee, a settlement in South East India, in the state of Tamil Nadu, just west of Madras. The thumbnail descriptions from gazetteers obviously do not succeed in conveying to us what it must have been like for Frederick Henry and his family to live in various parts of India in the early days of the twentieth century.

India at this time was governed by the British as an outpost of its extensive empire. According to Benjamin Disraeli, India was 'a jewel in the crown of England'. It had become an important market for British exports and in turn it provided us with most of our tea. A lot of British money was invested in the country. As Viceroy Mayo wrote around this time 'We are determined as long as the sun shines in heaven to hold India. Our national character, our commerce, demand it, and we have, one way or another, £250 million of English capital fixed in the country.'

I have a photograph from this period of Frederick Henry in military uniform, standing proudly by the side of his wife Elizabeth and his children Elizabeth and Walter Henry, taken at Dalhousie in the Punjab in 1902. It was given to me by Walter Henry in the 1980s.

After 12 years' service had been completed in 1903, Frederick Henry decided to extend his army career. He was now a sergeant and still living in India. His discharge papers have survived from February, 1912. He had completed 21 years' service and was now 41 years old. His conduct and character were said to have been 'exemplary' and he was described as 'a thoroughly sober, reliable and trustworthy man with considerable services experience and of above the average ability'.

Frederick Henry possibly found the return to civilian life in England a little difficult to cope with, and by October, 1914 had re-joined the army, shortly after the outbreak of the First World War. He was 43 years old and living with his wife and family in Tottenham, London. By now there were seven children: in addition to the ones we have already met, Elizabeth had given birth to twins Ernest Arthur and Robert in 1913. At the age of 43, Frederick Henry's weight was exactly 10 stone – three pounds lighter than it had been 23 years previously. He had obviously kept himself fit. He now had a tattoo: an anchor, crown and crossed flags on his right forearm. The enlistment papers described him as a commissionaire.

Frederick Henry served in France and also in the Dardanelles campaign, where he was wounded in both legs and apparently had no medical attention for a week. Settling in Fareham after the war, he became a foreman in a flour mill until he retired. He died in March, 1956 in Portsmouth Hospital. The National Probate Register shows that his estate was valued at around £2,700.

Frederick Henry's younger brother was Walter Reuben Whitfield, b.1875. You will remember that I had made contact with his son (Walter) Harry Whitfield (b. 1897). Harry told me that his father had come to Doncaster from Potton in about 1890. He said that another Potton man, Reuben Deeble, had come to Doncaster before 1890 and had started a milk round, and his (i.e. Harry's) father had worked for him when he arrived in Yorkshire. You will probably remember that the enterprising Mr Deeble used to live next door to Walter Reuben Whitfield's father and grandfather in Plowman's Yard.

Walter Reuben Whitfield was certainly still living in Potton in July, 1887, when the *Bedfordshire Times* recorded that he, together with about two hundred other scholars, had attended the Church Sunday School's 'annual treat' held in the Vicarage Field where he received a prize for 'good conduct and attainment in Scriptural knowledge', and probably enjoyed the 'swinging boats and other amusements', which included 'cuffs, collars, belts, etc., to be run for'. Whether he was successful in racing to complete his attire wasn't mentioned, but it's a fair bet that he enjoyed the tea provided and he may also have appreciated the music of the Fife and Drum Band which accompanied the proceedings.

Once the ancestry website had become available, I looked at the 1891 census for Doncaster. I found that at 22 Wellington Road there lived a widow of 65, Mary Mitchenson, who was described as a cow keeper. With her was a domestic servant Isabella Franklin, born at Eltisley, Cambridgeshire (about seven miles from Potton), and two lodgers: Reuben Deeble, single, aged 27, and Reuben W. (i.e. Walter Reuben) Whitfield, aged 16. Both lodgers had, of course, been born in Potton, and both were described as general labourers. It may well be that they were both working for Mrs Mitchenson, who presumably had a small herd of dairy cattle. By 1901, Reuben Deeble *was* running his own milk round: the census describes him as a cow keeper and milk seller. He may well have purchased Mrs Mitchenson's business at some point in the intervening years. By 1911 he was being helped in the business by his young son, Horace.

In 1896, Walter Reuben Whitfield married Ada Cook at Gainsborough, Lincolnshire. The 1901 census showed me that the couple were living in Arthur Street, Doncaster. Walter was working as a railway engine stoker, and the couple now had a son, three year old Walter Harry (my contact some 85 years later). Ten years later, Walter had become a locomotive engine driver, and his son Walter Harry had started working for the Co-operative Society as an errand boy.

Walter Reuben was involved in a serious accident at work later in 1911 which led to his death from heart failure. He and Ada had three children living at the time (Walter Harry, Frank, b1903, and John Reuben, b.1909). Their other two children, Emily and Fred had died in infancy.

Ada remarried in 1919. She died in 1961 in Rotherham.

There will be more about Walter Harry, Frank and John Reuben and their respective families later.

Frederick Henry's sister, Kate, b.1873 married John Thomas Wright Cawley in 1895. The marriage took place in the St. Pancras area of London. John Cawley was described as a railway servant and Kate as a domestic servant: another railway connection in this branch of the family. They had been living together at 9 Torbay Street before their marriage. (Walter) Harry Whitfield had told me that his uncle John Cawley had been a signalman at Potton station and then at Gamlingay before moving to Winslow in Buckinghamshire.

John and Kate Cawley's first child was named James Whitfield Cawley and was baptised in London in April, 1896. He had been born in Kentish Town. Their next two children, Isobel Mary Elizabeth Cawley, b.1897 and Reginald John Cawley, b.1900 were both born in Harlesden. However, their next three children, Alec Francis, b.1904, Leonard, b.1906 and Gladys Millicent, b.1910 were born in Potton.

The 1911 census shows that they were living at 10 Wagstaff Terrace, Sandy Road, Potton, next door to Kate's father, Robert. Harry Whitfield had been correct - he had a remarkable memory for a man of nearly ninety - his uncle *did* work as a signalman at Potton station. John Cawley must have known David Whitfield, my great uncle, another Potton signalman, a character we met in a previous chapter.

I'm not sure when John and Kate Cawley moved to Winslow, but they certainly *did* move. Kate died in North Buckinghamshire in 1950; her husband outlived her by about four years. The National Probate Register shows that he had been living in Avenue Road, Winslow. I have made contact with Patricia Gem Cawley, b.1934, who is the daughter of Reginald John Cawley. She married Dennis Lyons in 1956, and they have a son Andrew Lyons, b.1964. She told me that her uncle, Leonard Cawley, b. 1906 in Potton had married and emigrated to New Zealand - another line of enquiry for me to follow up when I can find the time.

Mary Ann (Polly) Whitfield, b.1878, the youngest sister of Frederick Henry, did not marry, but didn't always stay in Potton. In 1901, she was in Bromley, Kent, working as a housemaid in the house of a civil engineer. Ten years later she was working as a parlour maid for a retired solicitor and his American wife in the parish of St George, Hanover Square in London. She was back in Potton by the 1940s, looking after her father, Robert (and several cats). She died in 1947, aged 69.

It is time to return to Frederick Henry Whitfield's family. Elizabeth, his oldest child, b.1899 in Nowshera married Ernest Elliott in 1928, and they moved to the Doncaster area. I know little about them other than the fact that they had no children. Elizabeth died in 1988.

The sons of Frederick Henry were clearly influenced by the military life of their father. The oldest son, Walter Henry, b.1901 joined the Royal Artillery and later became a prison officer, working initially at Wormwood Scrubs prison in London, before being promoted to chief warder at Winchester Prison. He married Nellie New in Portsmouth in 1931. The births of their children Freda A. Whitfield and John H. Whitfield were registered in Hammersmith in 1933 and 1936 respectively, presumably while their father was working at Wormwood Scrubs. I visited Walter Henry in Winchester in the 1980s. He was walking with the aid of two sticks:

he told me he had been badly beaten up by prisoners while he had been serving at Winchester Prison, and this had led to arthritic hips. He showed his determination by insisting on showing me round his house (including upstairs), and let me have some interesting family photographs. He died in 1988.

The second son, Frederick Charles, b.1904, at Kalabagh, joined the navy and became a deep sea diver. He suffered from the bends once and was unconscious for four days. However, he recovered and carried on diving until he was over sixty years old, obviously after he had undergone regular medical checks. He was a keen gardener and had an allotment in Fareham, Hampshire, where he also ran an allotment shop in his retirement, selling seeds, tools and fertilisers to other allotment holders. He was said by his son Robert (Bob) to be good company - apparently he enjoyed his beer and going out for a curry. He must have been a good judge of a curry, bearing in mind where he had spent his early years. He married Florence Elliott in Doncaster in 1932, and they had two sons: Frederick Donald, b.1935, and Robert Edward (Bob), in 1937.

(Frederick) Donald Whitfield is an architect in the Bodmin area of Cornwall. He married Janet P. Chapman in Gosport, Hampshire in 1957, and they had two sons: Timothy M., b. 1961, and Michael J., b.1962. Both births were registered at Portsmouth. Donald married a second time, in 1976. His bride was Geneveare Clahane. His son Timothy died in 1983; I think it was as a result of an accident involving a tractor. The death was registered at Truro. A Michael J. Whitfield married Karen S. Hoare in 1988 at Stratton, Cornwall, but they appear to have moved to the Barnstaple area of North Devon, where their children Nicholas Jarvis Whitfield and Stephanie Mary Whitfield were born in 1989 and 1991 respectively. I'm not sure if I have found the correct Michael Whitfield here. I am intrigued by Nicholas' middle name - had his parents been researching their family history? I feel sure Catherine Whitfield, nee Jarvis, (1826-1923) would have approved. I have not yet managed to make contact with them.

The younger son of Frederick Charles Whitfield was Robert Edward (Bob), b.1937. I was given his name and address by his relative Harry Whitfield of Doncaster. Bob was in the merchant navy and had visited most countries in the world which had a coastline. He married Terrie V. Andreassen in 1961. I haven't found any details of children, and I presume Bob and Terrie divorced. Bob was living on his own in Colenso Road, Fareham when I visited him in the late 1980s with Sid Whitfield. He had retired from the merchant navy and had been looking after his father. He enjoyed crosswords as well as his beer and cigarettes, and was a regular visitor to the British Legion club in Fareham. He appeared to be rather lonely - understandable after the death of his father. We exchanged Christmas cards until he died in 1998 - I suspect that cigarettes may have been a contributory factor, but haven't seen the death certificate.

The next child of Frederick Henry was Florence Isabella (Bella), b.1902, Ferozepore. She married John P. Garrad in 1928 and they had two daughters, Jean and Margaret.

So far, I haven't managed to find out much about Frederick Henry's other children. James Robert, b.1909 was in the navy, possibly working in naval engineering. He was married and there were two daughters, Shirley and Caryl. Unfortunately, I haven't been able to trace them. The last children of Frederick Henry and Elizabeth Whitfield were twins, born in 1913. Their births were registered in Edmonton, London. Ernest was very tall and joined the Guards. He married Fanny Milner in 1939. They had a daughter, Susan. He died in Worthing, Sussex in 1999. Robert was a chef in the Royal Air Force.. I'm not sure whether he married. He died in Winchester in 2004, aged ninety.

Much of my early information on the branch of the family descended from Robert Whitfield (1824-1890), came from (Walter) Harry Whitfield, from Doncaster, b.1897. Harry, the eldest of the children of Walter Reuben Whitfield and his wife Ada, started working part time as an errand boy for his local Co-operative store in Doncaster at the age of twelve. He left school at thirteen, and worked full time for the Co-op, becoming deputy manager for four years, and then manager for 36 years. His time at the Co-op was interrupted by his war service, but after he officially 'retired' at 65, he worked for the firm part time until he was 77.

Harry joined the West Yorkshire Infantry when he was 17½, in April, 1915. He lied about his age: the official joining age was eighteen. After some training, he was on his way to Suvla Bay on the Gallipoli peninsula, in the Dardanelles expedition, arriving there just before his eighteenth birthday. The Dardanelles, theoretically an international waterway, had been closed by the Turks with mines in the first week of August, 1915. The waterway was of strategic importance because it was used by countries in Western Europe for the importation of grain from Russia. Control over the waterway was considered essential to check the German plan for developing, via Turkey and Asia minor, a campaign in the Middle East. War was declared on Turkey on 3rd November, 1915, but troops had assembled on the Gallipoli peninsula before then in response to the closure of the waterway. Harry's uncle, Frederick Henry Whitfield was also in the area, but as far as I know, the two men didn't meet each other there - they were in different regiments. According to Harry, Suvla Bay was a horrible place, because it was never out of range from the Turkish shells, so he had very little rest. The ground was so hard and rocky they only managed to dig shallow trenches by hand, and they had to pile up sandbags to shield themselves from the Turks. The Turks, on the other hand, had blasted trenches six feet deep. Lord Kitchener, Secretary of State for War visited the peninsula in November, 1915, and the conditions he witnessed convinced him that it would be advisable to withdraw his troops. However, the men were only to be given two days' notice of when the withdrawal was to take place.

On 26th November, 1915, it was a cold, grey, stormy day, with bitter North easterly winds sweeping down across the Black Sea from Siberia. Sleet, and later torrential rain accompanied by thunder and hurricane force winds lashed the troops who were seeking refuge in their dug-outs and trenches. Harry told me that all the cookers of the Allied Forces (British, New Zealanders, Indians and French) were swept into the sea. However, the Turks fared worse: their deeper trenches held the water, and many of the men were drowned during the torrential downpours. The reason for the presence of the many steep ravines and gullies on the peninsula suddenly became clear. Two days later, the temperature dropped dramatically and the rain turned to snow. Thousands of men, including Ghurkhas, used to the Himalayas, suffered from exposure and hundreds died. Frostbite was common. Harry told me that clearing up afterwards took each side about a week during which time not a shot was fired. It was clear that there was little to be gained from staying on the peninsula now that the winter had set in.

Studio photograph of Walter Harry Whitfield, in his early twenties.

Withdrawal was carried out in stages, but efforts were made to fool the Turks into thinking that the very opposite was taking place - that the Allies were actually *reinforcing* their troops. Boats, apparently nearly empty, were sent from the beach in daylight, and then returned with men clearly visible, and decoy rifles were set up in the trenches with triggers attached to tins. When the tins were full of water, the rifles would fire, and the Turks would think that soldiers had fired them.

After a spell in the furthest part of the line from the shore, Harry and his regiment were recalled to the second line of defence. On the night of 19th December, 1915, the troops from the forward line came back, and the West Yorkshire regiment were asked to hold the line while evacuation was taking place. Harry was therefore one of the last men to leave the peninsula. The men marched, as quietly as possible, their boots covered with old socks, onto lighters, or tugs, which took them to a battleship, H.M.S. *Magnificent.*

The *Magnificent* conveyed them to Imbros, a small island some twenty miles away, where they set up camp. The men were in very poor condition, according to Harry, after the way they had been living and fighting, and after the atrocious weather. Rations were now very limited, and they were living 22 to a tent. At least the men now on Imbros had survived; many had not: the Allied casualties from the Dardanelles campaign numbered nearly 214,000.

Harry had to queue on Imbros on Christmas Eve, 1915, for his tent's share of the Christmas food provided. There were thousands in the queue, and he had to wait all morning. The 22 men in his tent received one tin of sausages and a tinned Christmas pudding between them, plus a tin of McConachie's (whatever that was - possibly beer). For about a month they had been living on extremely meagre rations - mostly hard biscuits and jam - and their stomachs had not been used to cooked food. Their hot meal didn't stay with them long, as many of them were sick afterwards - it sounds as though it was a case of food poisoning. Harry was able to look back at this episode with some amusement when he was in his eighties, but it must have been far from funny at the time. He recalled the incident in an article he wrote for his local newspaper, and kindly sent me a copy.

From Imbros, Harry and his regiment went to Alexandria, the Suez Canal, and on to the Sinai Desert for a while, where he manned heliographs, keeping in touch with troops with their camels further on into the desert. Heliographs were a system of communication involving the use of mirrors to send Morse Code flashes of sunlight. The distance the signals could be sent depended on the clarity of the sky and the size of mirrors used, but apparently under ordinary conditions a flash could be seen by the naked eye up to thirty miles away. The main problem with the system was that anyone with the correct knowledge of what was going on could intercept them without being detected.

The West Yorkshire regiment landed in France on the day the battle of the Somme started - 1st July, 1916. After spells in quiet parts, Harry and his comrades occupied part of the Hindenburg line in front of Thiepval. During the battle, Harry's best friend was killed a few yards away from where Harry was standing. Harry was half-buried in earth and stones, and, not surprisingly, suffered from shock, but he survived. He was present at the storming of the German stronghold known as 'The Wonderworks', and was involved in ferocious fighting to the S.E. of Thiepval where there was an approximate casualty rate of fifty per cent.

The main weapon used by British soldiers in the trenches was the bolt-action rifle. Armed with one, a soldier like Harry could fire fifteen rounds in a minute, and could kill a person up to 1400 yards away. Machine guns needed at least four men to work them, but had a fire power of one hundred ordinary guns. Large field guns had a longer range and could fire shells which exploded on impact. They needed twelve men to operate them.

Tanks were used for the first time on 15th September, 1916. Harry mentioned this in a letter to me about seventy years later, and he was correct to the day. He did not see them in action for long; he was severely wounded on 27th September, three days after his nineteenth birthday. He spent time in hospital in Wimereux in Northern France, and later in Leicester. After that he was never considered fit to return to France, but spent some time in Southern Ireland, in Wexford and Waterford, with jobs for short periods. Only 21 years old when demobilised, he had probably seen enough of war to last a lifetime.

Harry married Fanny Benett in 1922, and returned to Doncaster, resuming his work at the Co-op. Their son, Gerald was born in 1923. He joined the Royal Air Force. when he was sixteen and served for four years in India. He stayed in the forces until he was thirty, with spells in Egypt, Iraq, Iran, Mesopotamia, Germany and South Africa. On his return to England, he set up his own television repair business in Doncaster, presumably using skills he had acquired in the R.A.F. Like his father, he worked on beyond retirement age. *Unlike* his father, he didn't marry. He died peacefully in an armchair after lunch at his sister's house, aged eighty.

Gerald's sister, Margaret Whitfield, b.1926, served in the Women's Air Force, but remained in England. She married Michael Jablonski in Doncaster in 1955, and they had two children, Adrian, b.1959, and Cheryl, b.1961.

I visited Harry, Fanny and Gerald Whitfield in Doncaster in the late 1980s, taking Sid Whitfield with me. We all got on well and enjoyed each other's company, and I took some photographs. It was very satisfying to have arranged this temporary meeting of two lines of the family which hadn't been in touch for upwards of eighty years. Harry then corresponded with me until his death in 1990. Quietly spoken and small and slight in stature, it was amazing to think that he had been involved in some of the famous battles of the First World War, and had lived to tell the tale; he had even retained his sense of humour. He was a thoughtful, intelligent man who took a great interest in his family history, and many other things besides. I will always be grateful to him for the help he gave me.

Walter Reuben and Ada Whitfield's next two children, Emily, b.1899 and Fred, b.?, both died in infancy. Their next child was Frank, b. November, 1903.

Frank Whitfield married Lucy Daisy Faulkner in 1930. The marriage was registered in Rotherham. They had four children: Eileen, b.1931, June, b 1933, who died aged twenty months in July, 1935, (Walter) Rex, b.1935, and Gordon, b.1937.

Frank worked for most of his life in quarries and was a foreman for many years. Moving to a plant making concrete products (it was owned by the quarrying company), he was unfortunate in having an accident in 1953, where he became trapped under a crate of machine parts, which resulted in one of his legs being severely injured. He was off work for nearly a year as a result and was no longer able to undertake heavy tasks afterwards. His injury was aggravated by

Two lines of the family reunited after about 90 years: L ,Walter Harry Whitfield, aged 89, a veteran of World War One, and r, Sidney Albert Whitfield, veteran of World War Two.Taken by Rex Whitfield in the 1980s outside Walter Harry's house in Doncaster.

a later accident which occurred as he was travelling as a passenger in a works van, and he secured a less physically demanding job, as a cleaner, in a civilian capacity, attached to the R.A.F. at Finningley, near Doncaster. However, his leg injury was still troubling him, so he became a boiler attendant and handyman at a school for the deaf, next door to Doncaster racecourse. He enjoyed his time here; he was able to mend the children's toys, as the boiler was semi-automatic, and he stayed there until he was 67. Even after that he worked as a gardener, and carried out small concreting jobs. He and Lucy celebrated their golden wedding in 1980, and he died in 1983.

Frank and Lucy's oldest child, Eileen Whitfield, b.1931, married George Blatherwick in 1957. He was a joiner, working for the local council, repairing properties. They had four children: Ian Andrew, b. 1960, David, b.1962, Gavin Mark, b.1965 and Carol Ann, b.1967. When I contacted her in December, 2010, Eileen was a widow, with six grandchildren, and had just become a great grandmother to Nicholas Arran, b.2010.

Eileen's brother, (Walter) Rex, b.1935, married Rose Thorpe in Doncaster in 1958. Rex was a foreman for a welding firm. He and Rose had two children: Steven Rex, b.1959 and Elaine, b. 1963. Steven married Sue Pilkington in Scotland in 2008, but they are now living in the Doncaster area. There are no children. Elaine married David Cotton in 1983. Rex died in 1999, aged 63.

Gordon Whitfield, the youngest child of Frank and Lucy, is a boilermaker. He emigrated to New Zealand in the late 1970s, and worked for New Zealand railways. He married Joan Wildsmith in Doncaster in 1956, and their three children, Janet, b.1957, Anita, b.1962, and Stuart, b.1959 were all born in the Doncaster area. Gordon and Joan have since divorced, and Gordon has remarried. He and Anne live at Weymouth, near Auckland.

Janet trained as an industrial laboratory technician. She married Royce Boyd McClure in 1978 in New Zealand, and by 1981 they had moved to Los Angeles, U.S.A. Royce was born in Tokoroa, New Zealand in 1956. He has been interested in diving and tropical fish since he was twelve years old, and is now an artist, having painted full time since 1975. He became a commercial illustrator in Australia in 1977.

Royce and Janet run a commercial art company called Artgame. He produces designs for t-shirts, book marks and jigsaws. Most of them have a marine life theme. The couple have now moved back to New Zealand and live at Mount Maunganui, where they bought some land with an old house on it. They have since built a new house on the plot, which they live in, and are using the old house for their business. They have two children: Norton Boyd McClure, b.1984, and Kimberly McClure, b.1986.

Anita Whitfield, b.1962 qualified as a medical laboratory technician, and worked at Auckland hospital. She married a graduate engineer, Stephen Karpik in 1986, and they have two children.

Stuart Whitfield, b.1969, studied architecture at university, and now works as an architect in Auckland. He and his wife Nicole have two girls: Alaina, b.2008 and Caroline Sophia, b.2010.

The youngest child of Walter Reuben Whitfield and his wife Ada was John Reuben, b.1909. After he left school, John worked for a jeweller in Doncaster, in the workshop, but as soon as he was 21 (and entitled to a man's wage), he was made redundant, and had several different jobs for a time. He had learnt to drive, and he eventually drove the first diesel lorry in the district. Although slightly built, he remained a lorry driver for the rest of his working life, even during the Second World War: lorry drivers were exempt from military service. He was driving all over the country. He married Elsie Garner in 1934, and they had two children: (Walter) Clive, b 1937, and Ann, b.1945.

John lived in several villages within easy reach of Doncaster, but retired to Grimthorpe, Lincolnshire, where he died after a long illness in 1978.

Clive Whitfield worked for a firm making agricultural machinery. He married Cynthia Swift in 1959. There are no children. They lived in Bawtry, near Doncaster, but have since moved to Louth, Lincolnshire.

It is over sixty years since anyone in this branch of the family lived in Potton, and as the older generation die it may well be that their children and grandchildren will have never even heard of the place. The descendants of a young lad picking up stones in the fields of Potton in the 1830s have travelled all over the world, but it is remarkable how the railways, domestic service and the armed services have figured in so many of their lives, providing both employment and a means of moving away from the small Bedfordshire town where job opportunities were so limited.

Chapter 11.
Life in the Fens- but not for long: the line from Jonathan Whitfield, b1825.

'The mission of the United States is one of benevolent assimilation'

William McKinley (1843-1901).

In the days before the arrival of the internet, I had difficulty in finding out what happened to Jonathan Whitfield. Born in Tewin in 1825, the year the first railway (Stockton to Darlington) opened, he was with his mother when she and most of the family came to Potton in 1833, but then seems to have vanished from the records. He wasn't involved in the stone picking - at least, not in the Overseers' accounts I have seen - but I would imagine he was soon working on the farms and market gardens of Potton and district.

The 1841 census, not for the first time, wasn't very helpful. I couldn't find a Jonathan Whitfield in Potton, but did find a *John* Whitfield, aged fifteen, and not born in Bedfordshire, working as an agricultural labourer on the farm of George Bone in Ickwell, near Biggleswade. It is a pity that the 1841 census doesn't give precise details of people's birthplaces.

I feel fairly confident that this person *was* Jonathan. The Whitfield family had relatives living in nearby Northill at this time (the Cox family) and George Whitfield, Jonathan's older brother, later married Ann Cox in Northill church, so it may well be that Jonathan spent some time there with his aunt and uncle (Eliza Cox nee Berry and her husband Benjamin). He would then have heard about the work available at Mr. Bone's farm at Ickwell, just down the road.

I must now jump forward in time by thirty years to explain how I managed to find Jonathan subsequently, because I have no actual hard evidence to show that he ever set foot on Potton soil later than 1833 - although I feel sure that he did. You may remember that there was a niece, Ruth Whitfield, aged only two, living with Robert and Catherine Whitfield in their cottage in Plowman's Yard, Potton in 1871. Young Ruth's birthplace was given as Manea in the Isle of Ely. At the time, I had never heard of Manea, but decided that its parish records needed investigating at the Cambridge record office. Before I did this, I made a trip to Manea to get an idea of what the parish was like. I was amazed at how remote and isolated it was, even in the late twentieth century when I first visited. Set down in the flat Fen landscape, about five or six miles from the small town of Chatteris, the village is surrounded by acres of peaty black soil which stretch to the horizon, uninterrupted save for the intersecting deep dykes. It is still a rural backwater, and must have been all the more so about 150 years earlier. Strolling around the village, I tried to mentally strip away the almost inevitable 1960s bungalows, parked cars and other trappings of modern life so that I could try to imagine what it must have been like all those years ago. The church seemed comparatively recent, and a search of its graveyard for Whitfield gravestones proved fruitless.

At the Record office in Cambridge, I examined the 1841 census for Manea, and discovered that a William Whitfield, not born in the county, was working on a farm belonging to Thomas Cope. This could well have been the William Whitfield born to James Whitfield (the gamekeeper) and his wife Sarah in Cople. He had been removed to Potton in 1834, and we have seen that he was involved in stone picking and digging, like some of his brothers. As I have already indicated, he does not appear in subsequent censuses. It seems likely that at least some of the Whitfield brothers had travelled up to the Fens - another market gardening district, about 35 miles or so from Potton - in search of work. We have already seen that James Whitfield, my great-great grandfather, had travelled towards London with a group of labourers; William had probably done the same. So, too, I suspect, did Jonathan, although in 1841 he appears to have been in Ickwell.

I examined the Manea parish registers, and found that Jonathan Whitfield had married Jane Clark(e) there in 1846. Unhelpfully, he was described as a labourer; Jane was a servant and their fathers, Joseph Clark(e) and James Whitfield, were also, apparently, labourers. Reading between the lines it would appear that to the officiating clergyman all of the lower orders were just 'labourers'; it wasn't of sufficient interest or importance to make any finer distinctions. What was the point when bride and groom were illiterate anyway?

Actually, Joseph Clark was a basket maker, and is described as such in the census details for Manea. Originally from Whittlesey, he had served an apprenticeship in Ely. I discovered that he and his wife Frances, and their six older children, Mary, Sarah, Henry, Ann, Susan and Abraham had been removed from Ely to Manea in 1823: another example of a Whitfield family member marrying into a family with a similar experience to his own. Jonathan's future wife, Jane, had been born in Manea in 1828. She was the ninth child in a family of *thirteen* children eventually born to Joseph and Frances Clark: Joseph must have had to weave a very large number of baskets to earn enough money to provide for them all.

Basket making was a fairly common occupation in this part of the Fens. Willow trees, or 'osiers' were planted along sheltered waterways, and carefully tended so that they produced long shoots which were regularly cut, peeled and seasoned before being used to make baskets. Joseph would have made the baskets by hand, probably at home. It would have been a rather laborious process, and he may well have had some assistance from Frances and some of the older children. Osier peeling was certainly a job which was often done by women and children; the peeled willow rods were used for basket weaving and the bark was dried and then used on domestic fires. It would be interesting to know where Joseph obtained his raw materials - whether he owned some willow trees along a stretch of waterway, or just helped himself to willow shoots around Manea, rather like we might go blackberry picking. I also wonder where he sold his baskets. They were probably used for agricultural produce and for holding eels, but

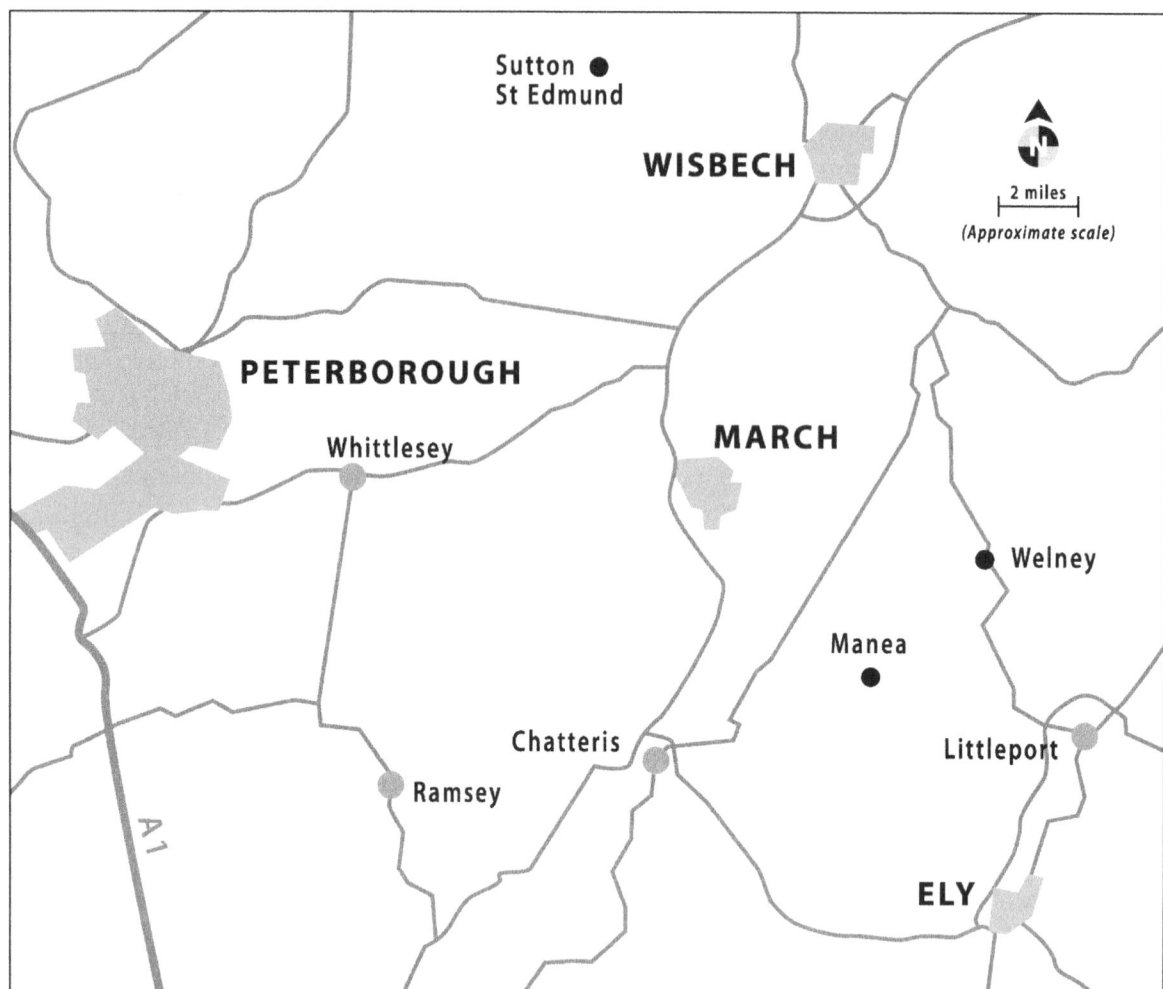

*A map showing Fenland parishes associated with the
Whitfield family in the nineteenth century*

Manea was hardly a bustling and accessible market for anything. Perhaps he sold them to a travelling dealer who took them to Ely, Cambridge or Peterborough.

Jonathan Whitfield appears in the Criminal Registers for January, 1849. He was accused of larceny, but was pronounced not guilty. The register doesn't give any further details, but I discovered from the *Cambridge Independent Press* of Saturday, 18th November, 1848 that he had been accused of stealing one pound of sugar from Thomas Munns, a Manea grocer. The local police constable had pursued the matter and had found a pound of sugar 'with Mr Munns' private mark on the paper' at Jonathan's house. Jonathan admitted he had been to the grocery shop for certain articles but maintained he had taken the sugar by mistake. The incident must have led to a rather worrying Christmas time for Jonathan and Jane as they awaited the trial. By now they had young Henry to care for (baptised in 1847), and William arrived in the year of Jonathan's acquittal. Henry was probably named after Jonathan's younger brother who had died in infancy at Tewin; I wonder if the selection of the name William for Jonathan's second son was made because one of his *older* brothers born in Cople was also no longer alive.

The 1851 census shows that Jonathan, now described as an *agricultural* labourer (no surprise there) was living at Manea Green with Jane and their two sons Henry (4) and William (2). Jonathan's birthplace is given as Tring, Hertfordshire, which the enumerator had probably thought he heard (and could spell), rather than Tewin. By 1861, Jonathan's birthplace was given as 'Tuin, Harts.', which suggests that the enumerator had better hearing than his 1851 counterpart, but inferior spelling skills. Jonathan and Jane couldn't have completed the form for the enumerator even if he had asked them to, as neither of them could write. The family now comprised Jonathan, Jane, Henry (13), William (11), Sarah Jane (9), David (3), and young George (1). They were living in Manea High Street, next door to Jane's parents.

Two other children were born to Jonathan and Jane during the 1850s: Sarah, baptised in 1852, who died aged eleven months from consumption (tuberculosis), and David, who had died from pneumonia after just a year of life. I wonder if the Whitfield household made use of laudanum, or opium derived from poppies to treat their medical ailments and to keep their infants quiet, as so many fenland cottagers did in the mid nineteenth century? Laudanum acts as a painkiller and cough suppressant, and at that time could be obtained without a doctor's prescription. Babies and infants were doped with opium to make them easier to look after, particularly when they were teething, while their mothers worked in the fields. Their older brothers and sisters would also be working on the land, probably in closely supervised gangs. Many rural labourers grew poppies in their gardens and prepared a tea from their seed heads for medicinal purposes, and chemists in the fenland towns dispensed opium to regular customers who had become addicts. Opium taking was rife in Chatteris, March, Doddington and Ely, and there is no reason to suppose that people in Manea did not indulge in the habit. It was so freely available that *children* would sometimes be sent on errands to fetch it. Men sometimes dropped an opium pill in their beer, or took one before starting work. Farm animals were also given opiates, particularly horses which were proving difficult to manage. Opium was said to help to relieve the three common problems encountered in the Fens: poverty, the ague (fever) and rheumatism. The relief, of course, would have been temporary.

A fortunately less common (but still serious) problem affected Manea in 1852. An article in the *Cambridge Independent Press* of Saturday, 22nd May, 1852, described a fire which had destroyed about half of the village on the previous Sunday afternoon. The report suggested that the fire had been started accidentally by a Mr B. Overall, an agricultural labourer, who was attending to his sow and pigs whilst smoking a pipe in their sty. (Mr Overall lived next to the *Queen Adelaide* public house: perhaps he had become a little careless after indulging in a lunchtime drink or two). Some burning embers from his pipe had set the straw in the sty alight, and, fanned by a stiff south-westerly wind the flames had apparently swept through the village from one end to the other within about half an hour.

Many of the buildings would have had timber frames and thatched roofs; and despite the efforts of the Manea and March fire brigades (and I suspect of many of the villagers), thirty one houses and cottages, in addition to numerous barns, piggeries and other outbuildings had eventually succumbed to the flames. No mention is made of any human fatalities, but some livestock perished, and quantities of hay and wheat were lost.

The detailed report takes the reader from one end of the village to the other, from building to building, listing details of each owner and tenant and commenting on the damage done by the fire. Although it was an interesting exercise for me to make the same journey using census information, I was unable to find a Mr B. Overall living in the village in either 1851 or 1861, and I suspect it was an agricultural labourer named *James* Overall, living at one end of the High Street who may have wisely refrained from puffing away on his pipe, at least in public, after the events of 16th May, 1852. There remains the possibility, of course, that Mr B. Overall hadn't arrived in Manea in 1851, and that he decided to move away after the fire - for understandable reasons.

Jonathan Whitfield and family were living in one of seven cottages (presumably a row) belonging to Frederick Griffin. Griffin was clearly a man with an eye to business; as a blacksmith who later became a small farmer I suppose you could say with some justification that he was planning to forge ahead by having other irons in the fire, including an income from property rentals. Unfortunately for him and his tenants, including Jonathan and Jane Whitfield and their young sons Henry and William, all seven cottages were destroyed. Hopefully Mr Griffin believed in the benefits of property insurance.

Jonathan's father-in-law, Joseph Clark, also lost his home and livelihood to the conflagration. He was living in a cottage further along the High Street, and making use of a number of nearby outbuildings for his basket making business. Most of his raw materials and stock in trade would have been readily flammable and he wouldn't have been able to salvage much in the short time available before the fire engulfed his property.

It isn't clear how much each village family lost in terms of furniture and personal possessions; some furniture was rescued and stacked temporarily in the fields; neighbours rallied round and accommodated homeless families, and a relief fund was started to help those whose property had been uninsured. The catastrophic episode must have been a frightening experience for young Henry and William Whitfield (aged about five and three respectively) as they watched their home being devoured by the flames.

Homes and some possessions can often be replaced; family members are irreplaceable. Further tragedies were to shake this branch of the Whitfield family in the next decade. On 22nd March, 1868, the Manea register records the burial of Jonathan at the early age of 42, and the officiating curate had been moved to add some further details in the register. Jonathan had gone to bed in apparent health, on the night of 17th March, but had died about three hours later, from a diseased heart. The death was not registered until 24th March because an inquest was held on the 19th March; unfortunately the inquest records do not seem to have survived. The inquest was briefly mentioned in the *Stamford Mercury* of 27th March, 1868. The verdict of the coroner, William Pratt, Esq. was that Jonathan had 'died by the visitation of God'.

By this time, Jonathan's sons Henry, aged 21 and William, aged 18, were probably self-supporting, but the family now included Sarah Jane, aged 15, David (10), George (8), Naomi (6), and young Jonathan (nearly 3). To make matters worse, Jane was three months' pregnant with her youngest child. Ruth was born in September, 1868, with her father already in his grave. She was baptised a month later. It must have been a poignant ceremony for her mother; hopefully she was supported by some of her older children.

The ensuing years must have been an extremely stressful time for Jane, with a large family to provide for and very little money coming in. It is likely, though not certain, that she may have had some help from the parish, but as so few records have survived for Manea I can only speculate. Unfortunately, Jane didn't survive for much longer either: she died in 1870, also aged only 42. The cause of death looked like 'phremtis', or phrenitis; the handwriting was difficult to read. It would appear that Jane had been suffering from inflammation of the brain. Her symptoms would probably have included headaches, nausea, fever and delirium; and without the possibility of a brain scan, I would imagine that diagnosis and treatment would have posed difficulties for most nineteenth century doctors. It is likely, however, that as the family was already living in poverty, the services of a doctor were beyond Jane's means.

Whatever the cause of death, Jonathan and Jane's family were now orphans, including young Ruth, aged about two. This, of course, explained her presence in Robert and Catherine Whitfield's household in Potton in 1871, the original clue which had prompted my search for this branch of the family. You will remember that Robert had experienced a similar situation in 1841, with the death of *his* mother. The interesting thing for me, writing some 140 years after Jane's death is: how were Robert and Catherine made aware of the tragedy? Possibly a letter was sent, initially; some of Jonathan and Jane's family were probably able to write a simple message, which Catherine would have been able to read; otherwise I can only assume one or two of the older children made the journey from Manea to Potton to inform their aunt and uncle. And how did little Ruth travel from the Fens to Potton? Surely she wouldn't have walked about 35 miles at her age?

The enumerator of the 1871 census for Manea listed the new head of the Whitfield household as Sarah Jane, aged 17. She was living with three younger brothers: David (13), George (10), and Jonathan (5), and her younger sister, Naomi (8). Their grandmother, Frances Clark, aged 78, and described as a pauper was also living with them, and was possibly of great help. Having had thirteen children of her own, she must have been well used to providing for a family's day to day needs, and may well have organised meals while her older grandchildren were working in the fields. However, she died in 1879 aged 86. As we have seen, Ruth, the youngest member of the family was taken in by her aunt and uncle in Potton. I'm not sure how long she stayed with them.

I was unable before the days of the internet to discover where the two older brothers, Henry and William, were living - if they *were* still alive. I could find no details for them in the Manea records - for marriages or burials. Thanks to the ancestry website, they were eventually found in an outlying part of Chatteris, Cambridgeshire: Horseway, which is a small group of houses and a couple of farms on the Manea road. They were working as agricultural labourers, and were lodging with another farm worker, William Gibson (60) and his wife, Hannah.

Sarah Jane Whitfield married Henry Nightall, a son of the village blacksmith, in 1873. Unusually, they were married in a granary, 'lent by Mr. Plowright, fitted up for the purpose and licensed by the bishop' while the new church was being built in Manea. We will meet the Nightalls later.

The next obvious step was to discover where family members were in 1881, but here I

255

experienced some difficulties. Jonathan, now aged fifteen, was living with an aunt and uncle (on his mother's side) in Littleport, Cambridgeshire. Sarah Warner had been a widow, Sarah Lee, when she married James Warner in Littleport in 1865, but the marriage certificate makes it clear that she was the daughter of Joseph Clark, basket maker. In addition to Sarah Warner and her husband James and nephew Jonathan, the household also included John and Joseph Lee, aged 37 and 32 years respectively. They were sons of Sarah from her first marriage, and working as pedlars. It would be interesting to know what they were selling, but the enumerator was concerned with their names, not their wares.

By this time, young Ruth Whitfield had returned from Potton, and was found at a separate address in Littleport. She was visiting Sarah Walker, a widow of 62. The reason for the visit isn't clear. Was Sarah Walker a relative? It may be that Ruth normally lived with her brother Jonathan at her aunt's house. I have no idea how long she had stayed in Potton. Unfortunately, censuses were only taken every ten years and thus only give us tantalising glimpses of the lives of family members; enough to whet the appetite, but not enough to satisfy it.

I had accounted for two members of Jonathan and Jane's family in 1881 - where were the others? They were not in Manea, Chatteris, Littleport, Potton or Hook Norton. At the time of my searching the internet wasn't available, so I had to resort to other lines of enquiry.

Unfortunately, the Christian names of the 'missing' family members were not very helpful: William, Henry, George, David, and Naomi. None of them had a middle name. My first thought was that perhaps the family had been taken into care by the Barnardo's Homes. I wrote to the Barnardo's organisation, but they could find no records of the family. The 1891 census was not available at this time, due to the rather over-cautious one hundred year secrecy rule - it would not be available until 1992.

I figured that at least some of the family members would have married between 1871 and, say, 1900, and decided that it would be a good idea to venture to St. Catherine's House in London to search the marriage indexes. At the time, this was the only way to get an overview of where family members might have married if they had left their home parishes, once a search of neighbouring parishes had been carried out. The system at St. Catherine's House was simple and logical enough, but rather cumbersome to use. Marriages for each quarter year were listed by surname, then Christian names, and were housed in huge, heavy volumes which had to be manhandled from the shelves, and then returned. I was often in a queue for the volume I needed, and some of the volumes were temporarily missing because they were being consulted by someone else. For each marriage listed, there was the bridegroom's name, the registration district where the marriage had taken place, and a reference number, so that, if required, a copy of the full certificate could be obtained. Naturally, a fee was involved at this stage. In a day of frantic searching, I listed all the marriages involving Whitfields with the Christian names I was interested in over a period between 1871 and 1900. Nowadays, this could have been achieved in a fraction of the time using the ancestry website, or similar, and in an infinitely more comfortable environment.

Having listed them, I found that there were very few marriages involving any Jonathan Whitfields during this period. I reckoned that as he had been born in 1866, or thereabouts, he would probably have married between 1884 and the early 1900s. I found the marriage of a

Jonathan Whitfield in Sheffield which took place in 1892. *Sheffield*? If this was the Jonathan Whitfield born in Manea, he would have been about 25 or 26 when he married, which seemed about right, but the ceremony had taken place a long way from home. I consulted the list again. I figured that family members would have probably kept together. Were there any other Whitfield marriages in Sheffield involving the Christian names I was interested in?

I found a Sheffield marriage for a David Whitfield in 1880. If this involved David born in Manea, he would have been 23 or 24 at the time. This seemed plausible. I then discovered a Sheffield marriage for a William Whitfield for 1878. William Whitfield of Manea would have been 29 or 30 in 1878. I began to think I was on the right trail.

Weighing up the evidence, I thought it would be worthwhile to send for the certificates to see if my hunches were correct. I didn't totally waste the money I had to send to the General Register Office. I hadn't found the correct William Whitfield, but the David and Jonathan Whitfield marriages involved the people I was looking for. Was this a triumph for logical thinking, or a stroke of luck? Maybe it was a bit of both.

David's marriage had taken place in Brightside, Sheffield. His bride was Naomi Ellingham, aged nineteen, daughter of Paget Ellingham, a carter. David, aged 23, was also described as a carter, and his father was given as Jonathan Whitfield. The couple were both living in Sorby Street, Sheffield, at the time of their marriage, and both signed their names in the register. Naomi Ellingham wasn't originally a local Sheffield girl - she had been brought up in Littleport, Cambridgeshire, by her grandparents: Thomas Ellingham, a bricklayer, and his wife, Hannah.

Jonathan's bride was Sarah Padget, daughter of John Padget, described on the marriage certificate as a labourer. Like his older brother, Jonathan was working as a carter, and his father was given as Jonathan Whitfield, deceased. At the time of their marriage, Jonathan (junior) was living in Dorking Street, Sheffield, and Sarah was living in Sorby Street. An examination of a Sheffield street map showed me that Dorking Street and Sorby Street intersected at right angles. David Whitfield, Jonathan Whitfield and John Padget and their respective families were all living in the same area of Sheffield, within a few hundred yards of each other, and close to an iron and steel works.

The 1891 and 1901 census details were not yet available, thanks to the slightly absurd one hundred year secrecy rule, and in any case would only have been available in an unindexed, hard copy, form. I therefore wrote a letter to the *Sheffield Star* newspaper, inviting any descendants of David and Jonathan Whitfield to get in touch.

I was delighted to receive a reply from a Mrs Joan Martin, nee Whitfield, a granddaughter of Jonathan and Sarah. She gave me details of Jonathan and Sarah's family- their children and grandchildren, and some addresses of further contacts. I wrote to some of Joan's cousins to obtain more information, and was able to piece together Jonathan and Sarah's family tree. They were able to give me a few details of the family of David and Naomi Whitfield of Sheffield, but I also contacted a Sheffield family researcher who sent me baptism details of their children. I have followed these up with census details when they became available; more about the families of David and Jonathan later.

A letter I had written to one of Jonathan's grandchildren - Mrs Margaret Goddard, daughter of Jonathan's youngest daughter Ada Whitfield - bore fruit some twenty years after it was written. Mrs Goddard's son, Jonathan, came across the letter when he was going through some family papers, after the death of his father. He contacted me and I asked him whether his mother knew anything about Jonathan Whitfield's older brothers, Henry and William. Mrs Goddard said she wasn't sure, but she could remember her mother Ada Kelsey, nee Whitfield, receiving letters from someone she thought was connected to the family in some way who lived in Ohio, U.S.A. She said their surname was an unusual one, beginning with a B; something like Bilko or Barko. This was interesting, although I couldn't see how I could research the matter further. However, I now had access to the internet, and American census details had just been placed on the library edition of the ancestry website. Furthermore, there were also passenger lists: details of people who had sailed to the U.S.A. from England. These were some possible lines of enquiry, although as I started I felt I was looking for the proverbial needle in a haystack. As it happened, my efforts were rewarded sooner than I expected.

I found out from the New York passenger lists that a Henry Whitfield, estimated birth year 1847, had sailed from Liverpool on the steamship *Spain*, arriving in New York on 3rd October, 1871. Was this the Henry Whitfield, b.1847 in Manea? Unfortunately, the passenger list did not enlighten me further. Perhaps I would have more luck if I tried to find this Henry Whitfield in the 1880 American census? But no; I couldn't find a Henry Whitfield, born in England in 1847 listed there. Censuses were taken every ten years in the U.S.A., but unfortunately, little of the 1890 census has survived. Just my luck! However, in the 1900 census I found Henry Whitfield, aged 53, born in England, living with his wife Emma, aged 51 in Rocky River Hamlet, Cuyahoga County, Ohio. Living with them was Henry's mother-in-law, Hannah Robinson, aged 78. Henry was described as a farmer, and his year of immigration was given as 1871. This seemed promising.

I did a little research on Rocky River Hamlet. It was established in 1810, on the southern shoreline of Lake Erie. It is hardly a hamlet nowadays: its 2010 population was 20,213, and it is virtually a western suburb of Cleveland.

I decided to look at some more recent censuses. The secrecy rule is much more realistic in the U.S.A., because censuses as recent as that for 1930 are available online; the indexed 1940 census for some states became available for viewing in 2012. You can probably imagine my delight when I found in the 1930 census details for Rocky River, in one household:

Henry Whitfield, aged 83, b. England, white.
Ruth F. Bailey, aged 54, daughter, b.Ohio.
John D. Barco, aged 37
Lois Barco, aged 32
Arthur Barco, aged 10
Willard Barco, aged 7
Shirley D. Barco, aged 2 months.

I was excited by this because in the same household *in Ohio,* I had not only established a Whitfield/Barco connection, but also found a *Henry* Whitfield, born in England in exactly the same year as Henry Whitfield of Manea. This was surely not coincidence. You will remember

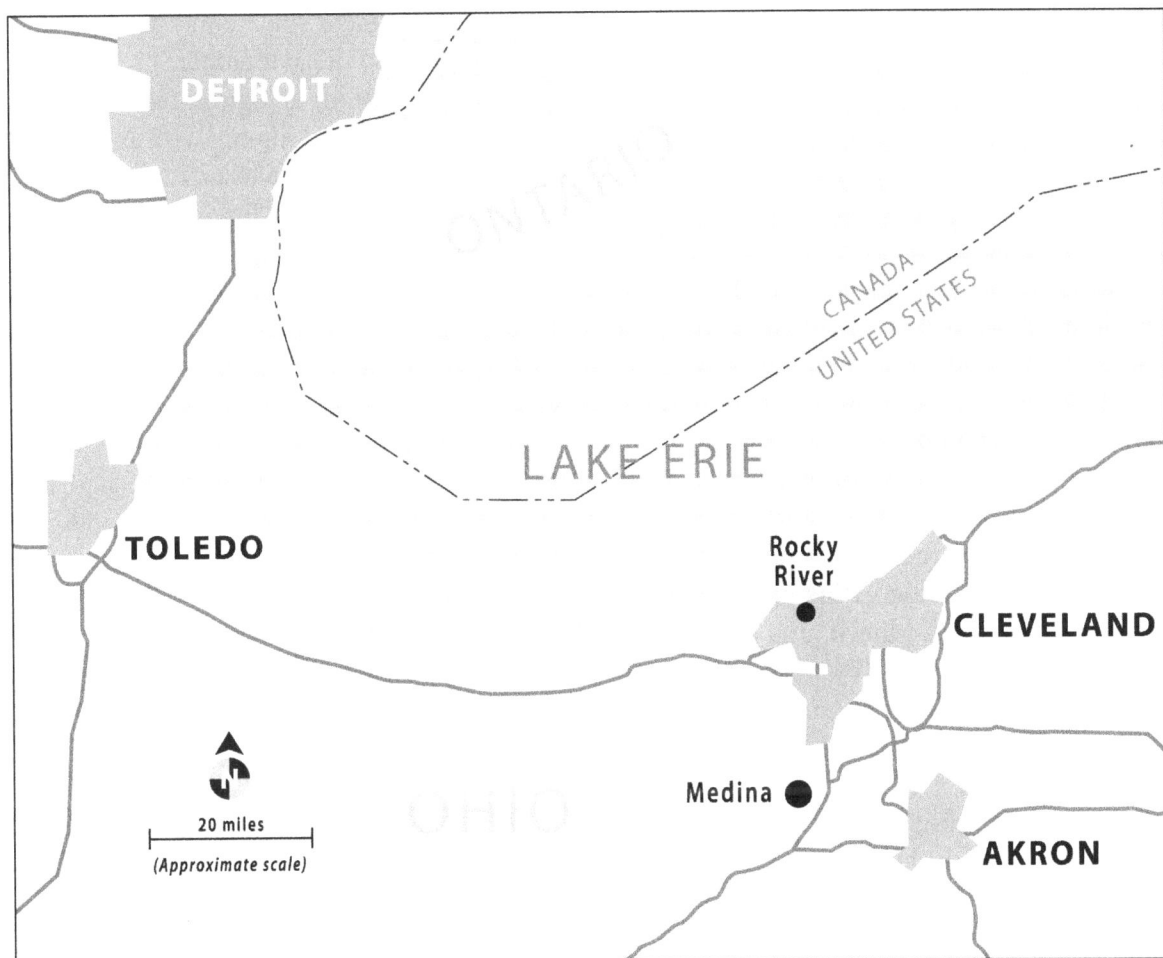

A map showing the Cleveland district of Ohio, USA

(NB: Rocky River was a hamlet when Henry Whitfield arrived there in the 1870s)

that the Barco surname had been recalled by Margaret Goddard, one of Jonathan Whitfield's grandchildren.

I contacted my cousin, Michael Whitfield, to let him know of my discovery, and he searched the internet for any mention of the Barco surname. He found an obituary for a Willard H. Barco, who had died in Medina, Ohio. This Mr Barco had greenhouses and a floristry business in Medina, and the business had its own website, giving an address, email details and a list of family members. My cousin Michael contacted them, and one of them, Mrs Shirley Zornow (nee Barco) replied. She was the Shirley Barco mentioned in the 1930 census, and she was the sister of the late Willard H. Barco. She confirmed that we were related, and could actually remember her great grandfather Henry Whitfield. She even kindly sent us some photographs of him and his family, and a copy of a letter which had travelled with him over the Atlantic. It had been written in Chatteris by Henry's employer in September, 1871, and recommended Henry to prospective employers in the U.S.A.

It had been a remarkable breakthrough, and further details have since come to light of an amazing story which has taken me the best part of thirty years to piece together.

We have seen that Henry and William Whitfield were working as agricultural labourers on the outskirts of Chatteris at the time of the 1871 census, and lodging with the Gibson family (William and Hannah). Henry's letter of recommendation, which must have been in his pocket as the steamship *Spain* crossed the Atlantic, was written by Fryer Richardson his employer, who lived some two or three doors away from the Gibsons. It is possible, perhaps even likely, that both Henry and William worked for Mr Richardson, and it may well be that William Gibson was another employee. I wonder if Jonathan Whitfield, the father of Henry and William, had also worked on the same farm until his untimely death? The 1871 census shows that Fryer Richardson was a farmer, auctioneer and estate agent who employed six men, two boys and two women.

Henry's leaving testimonial is dated 16th September, 1871, and states that he had been working for Mr Richardson for ten years. Henry is described as 'an honest, steady and good labourer'. The letter stayed with Henry for the rest of his life - and beyond; the original is now a treasured possession of his great granddaughter in Ohio. After it was written, Henry must have travelled from Manea, in a remote part of the Fens, to Liverpool, presumably travelling for much of the journey by train. For someone who had lived all his life in such a quiet area, this journey in his home country must have been an adventure in itself. He may have made a short visit to Little Bolton in Lancashire before he embarked on his voyage across the Atlantic, for a reason which will become apparent a little later.

Henry's travelling arrangements: the booking of the voyage, the purchase of his steamship ticket and possibly his rail journey to Liverpool may have been handled by an emigration or passenger agent. The agent may even have shown him promotional literature from the steamship company at some time before 1871, and awakened in the young man a desire to emigrate to the U.S.A. I was amazed to find that there was even an emigration agent who had connections to *Chatteris* - in fact he appears to have lived there in the late 1860s. I hope I am not jumping to unwise conclusions when I suggest that Henry may well have come into contact with him and made use of his services.

Josiah Schorah, born in Yorkshire, was originally a hairdresser and later an ironmonger. This apparently enterprising and versatile man was living in Moorfields, Liverpool, within easy reach of the docks, in 1871, and was described by the census enumerator as an 'eating house proprietor and emigration agent': two new businesses! The really interesting details for me were that his youngest son, Charles D. Schorah (aged 1), had been born in Chatteris, and Josiah's (second) wife had been born in Doddington, Cambridgeshire, close to Manea and Chatteris. A little more research showed me that some of Josiah's other children were still living in Chatteris (for some reason) in 1871. They were staying with their grandparents in Slade End, so Josiah presumably still kept in touch with the small Cambridgeshire town. (Incidentally, Emma Schorah, one of Josiah's children living with her grandparents in 1871, appears to have inherited her father's business acumen: in 1891 she was living with her father in Liverpool, and while he was still operating as an emigration agent, she was working as a *lifebelt maker* - from the same premises. She may well have done a good trade.)

It may be, then, that Henry made use of Josiah Schorah's services when he emigrated, and perhaps he enjoyed his last meal on English soil at Josiah's 'eating house'. I wonder what Henry selected from the menu? It may not have stayed with him long, but it would have been the last decent meal he had for a while.

The S.S.*Spain*'s maiden voyage had been from Liverpool to New York on 16th August, 1871, so it was a nearly new ship when Henry purchased his ticket, which would have cost him the English equivalent of $32, depending on the exchange rate. The vessel would have been regarded as huge in those days, weighing in at over 4500 tons, and being 426 feet long and 43 feet wide. It had an average speed of 13.6 knots and would have taken between seven and ten days to complete the journey of over three thousand miles across the Atlantic. However, the voyage would have been an experience to be endured rather than enjoyed.

It is highly likely that Henry travelled as a steerage passenger. Steerage offered the cheapest travel, and only a privileged few passengers could afford to travel first class. Steerage accommodation was similar to a dormitory, with bunks along the sides and tables in the centre. (I found a plan of the S.S. *Spain* on the internet which confirmed this arrangement). Henry would have found the accommodation extremely cramped and crowded. Sea sickness was common, and the smell of vomit would have been overpowering at times, because sick cans were not provided and ventilation was poor. He would have been allocated a berth which was six feet long by two feet wide and two and a half feet high. Ensconced within, he could have laid down on an iron framed bed, which had a mattress, a blanket, a lifebelt, and a straw or seaweed-filled pillow. He would have had no space for any personal luggage. If he wanted to wash or use the toilet, he would have noticed that the washroom floor was wet and soiled, and would remain so until the last day of the voyage, when it was cleaned ready for inspection. He would have looked in vain for soap and towels, and the water would have been cold and salty. Conditions in the washroom would have been relatively civilised compared to those he would have encountered in the lavatory. Hopefully I need not elaborate on *this* point! If he could cope with the thought of eating after experiencing the steamship's 'facilities', Henry would have had to queue for the basic food provided, before eating it at a communal table. He would then have to queue again to wash his plate - in the washroom. Not surprisingly, diseases soon spread in this type of environment. A report, written in 1909, *nearly forty years after Henry's voyage*, makes it clear that conditions aboard the transatlantic steamships had not improved very much - if at all - in the intervening years. It stated

'…..the universal human needs of space, air, food, sleep and privacy are recognised to the degree now made compulsory by law…. Beyond that, the persons carried [as steerage passengers] are looked upon as so much freight, with mere transportation as their only due'.

The report concluded that

'…..the experience of a single crossing is enough to change bad standards of living to worse. It is abundant opportunity to weaken the body and implant there germs of disease to develop later. It is more than a physical and moral test; it is a strain. And surely it is not the introduction to American institutions that will tend to make them respected.'

As far as I know, Henry Whitfield didn't keep a diary; if he had, I feel sure he would have commented on the voyage, and it would have made fascinating reading today. All I know is that

Henry Whitfield, b Manea, Cambs, England c 1847. A copy of this studio photograph was kindly sent to me by one of his great-granddaughters, Mrs Shirley Zornow. It was probably taken in the USA in the 1870s.

the S.S. *Spain* duly arrived in New York harbour on 3rd October, 1871, and *Henry* had survived the voyage. He must have stepped ashore with relief, but also with excitement and probably a degree of trepidation. Had he done the right thing? A new chapter in his life had certainly begun.

I found out from Shirley Zornow in Ohio that her great grandmother (Henry's wife) had also originated from England, and that her name was Emma Gibson. Naturally, I soon wondered whether there was any connection between Emma and the Gibson family of Horseway, Chatteris.

If there was, Emma was not living in Chatteris in 1871. However, I found an Emma Gibson, aged 22 in 1871, and unmarried, working as a cook in the household of Ralph Haslam, aged 68, a 'town councillor, cotton spinner and manufacturer, employing 1000 persons' of Little Bolton, Lancashire. According to the census details, this Emma had been born in 'Wellany', Norfolk. I eagerly consulted my U.K. road atlas. Wellany was conspicuous by its absence: it appeared that there was no such place. Undeterred, and suspecting that the enumerator might have had some trouble spelling certain place names, I decided to look at the 1861 census details for *Welney,* Norfolk. There I found William Gibson, aged 48, Hannah Gibson, aged 38, and young Emma Gibson, aged 11. Henry's future wife had been born in Welney. The Norfolk parish is about ten miles from Chatteris, and even closer to Manea - well within walking distance for a young man with a good reason for making the journey. In any case, by 1871 the Gibsons could well have been living just outside Chatteris for some time: they could have moved there any time after 1861.

Henry had therefore presumably met Emma before she became a cook in Lancashire, or perhaps they met at her parents' home when she returned home for an occasional holiday. The former seems more likely. I discovered that Henry could read and write, and it would appear that he kept in touch with Emma and the Gibson family, because the romantic attachment continued although the young couple were over three thousand miles apart. (I feel sure that Henry and Emma would have approved of the telephone, e-mails, Facebook and Skype). Emma must have saved the wages she received from Mr Haslam, because just over a year after Henry stepped ashore, she arrived in New York, on 20th October, 1872. Her voyage on the S.S. *Egypt* had taken ten days. The couple married just over a month later, on 23rd November, 1872.

We have seen that Henry was originally an agricultural labourer, but he later became a carter, or in American parlance, a 'teamster'. His great granddaughter, Shirley, told me he could also lay bricks, and we have seen that he was described as a farmer in some census schedules. It would appear that he was a versatile and resourceful labourer, worthy of his recommendation from his former employer in England. Shirley Zornow told me that her mother had told her that Henry and Emma were both hard-working and thrifty. Photographs have survived of Henry working in his garden; and of him with his horse and wagon. They show that he was not very tall, but of sturdy build.

Henry and Emma had three children, but one died in infancy. The survivors were William H. Whitfield, named after (or, as the Americans say, named *for*) Henry's brother, and Emma's father; and Ruth (Shirley Zornow's grandmother), named after Henry's youngest sister. They were born in 1873 and 1876 respectively. William is the earliest graduate I have found in the family - his degree was in chemical engineering from what is now Casewestern University. Originally the Case Institute of Technology, founded in Cleveland, Ohio, in 1880, Casewestern had introduced a new course of study by 1886: chemical technology. The head of department until 1911 was Charles Mabery, an early scholar in petroleum research.

William married Katherine (Kate) Archbold in Elk Rapids, Antrim, Michigan in 1899. Kate's father, a clerk, had been born in England, and her mother (Christiana) had been born in New York, although *her* family originated from Denmark. The census taken in the following year shows that William and Kate were still living in Elk Rapids. William was working as a chemist. The 1910 census is more specific: he was a chemist working for an iron company.

The Elk Rapids iron company (Noble and Dexter) was founded in the 1870s. Mr Dexter already had extensive timber interests and owned large sawmills in Elk Rapids, as well as a general store. Some of the hardwood was made into charcoal, which was used in the furnaces to smelt iron ore which was shipped in (possibly from Labrador or Minnesota) via Escanaba, a port on Michigan's Northern peninsula, which was also handling timber and copper. Limestone, used as a flux in the iron making process, was available from the Rockport and Rogers City areas of the state. The position of Elk Rapids, on the North West part of Michigan's southern peninsula, so close to Lake Michigan's eastern shore must have helped with the transport of both raw materials and finished products. The Elk Rapids works was eventually producing 24 tons of pig iron per day and employing around 360 workers. A cement works and a chemical plant also became established in Elk Rapids, but all three enterprises were relatively short-lived and by 1916 had stopped altogether, leaving the small settlement economically depressed. It may have led to a spell of unemployment for William, and it is likely that he left Elk Rapids. The economic malaise experienced by the settlement was such that its population dropped from around 2000 in 1900 to under 700 some thirty years later. (Its fortunes and population have since both picked up, thanks to tourism).

The marriage of William and Kate Whitfield ended at some time between 1910 and 1920 and there were no children. By 1920, Kate had moved to Detroit. She was working as a stenographer and was living with her widowed mother and some of her brothers; I have been unable to find William in 1920. He could have moved to Canada for a while, but I have no evidence for this at present.

The 1930 census confirms that William was divorced, and lodging at a premises in Railroad Street, Newberry, Michigan. He was described as a chemist at an iron furnace. Shirley Zornow, nee Barco told me that William later came to live with the Barco family in Rocky River - and he was certainly present in the Bailey/Barco household at the time of the 1940 census. She said he lost his job and livelihood during the Great Depression of the 1930s. Apparently he enjoyed playing cards and draughts (checkers) with his great nephews and nieces when they came home from school. He died in October, 1942, aged 68 and is buried in Lakewood cemetery, Ohio.

Kate reverted to her maiden name, and by 1930 had moved to El Monte, Los Angeles, California. She was living with a younger brother and his wife. Ten years later, aged 64, and working as a nurse, she was lodging with, and possibly looking after eighty year old Emma Popperwell in Alhambra, Los Angeles. She died in Los Angeles in 1952.

Henry and Emma's daughter, Ruth Florence Whitfield, married Horace Bailey, who was about 15 years her senior in November, 1896. Horace was a market gardener in Rocky River; the 1930 census shows that his farm at that time was valued at $12,000. Ruth and Horace had two children: Lois Bailey, b.1897, and Wesley Willis Bailey, b.1903. Unfortunately, Wesley died of measles when he was five years old. Lois married John D. Barco, another market gardener, whose family originated from Hungary, and they had five children. We have met some of these before on the 1930 census of Rocky River when I found the elderly Henry Whitfield was living with their parents. They were Arthur Horace Barco, b.1920, Willard H. Barco, Shirley R. Barco, Doris Barco and David Barco. John Barco's sons eventually joined him in his market gardening business. They were growing vegetables, and presumably supplying the rapidly developing market of Cleveland.

Using the Mormon website, I discovered that Emma Whitfield, nee Gibson, had died in 1926 at Rocky River, aged 78. The certificate confirmed that her father was William Gibson and that she had been born in Norfolk, England, in 1848. Henry died in October, 1932, aged 86. His death certificate confirmed that he had been born in England in May, 1846, and that his father was Jonathan Whitfield. Henry was described as a retired *gardener*.

John Barco died in Rocky River in 1959, aged 66. His sons bought some land in Medina, Ohio, in 1965 and built a commercial sized greenhouse on it. They eventually made Medina their home, and have built up a flourishing floristry business, growing poinsettias, begonias, potted chrysanthemums, kalanchoes, Easter lilies and other houseplants. They have 43 acres of land at Branch Road, Medina and another six acres at Elmsted Falls, Ohio, and their families are also involved in the business, whether working in the greenhouses or in the office. Their mother, Lois Barco, survived her husband by over twenty years, dying in Medina in 1982. She had undoubtedly contributed to, and witnessed her family's success, thanks to enterprise and a lot of hard work. It was fascinating for me to see how these descendants of Jonathan Whitfield had maintained their interest in and connection with the land across the Atlantic some 140 years after his death. I feel sure that Jonathan would have been proud of them.

Henry Whitfield's younger brother, William appears to have emigrated to the U.S.A. in July, 1872. Presumably Henry had sent encouraging reports to him. I get the impression that he was able to write very persuasive letters.

Like his brother, William married an English girl. Matilda Cook was born in the village of Sutton St. Edmund in fenland Lincolnshire in about 1853, but in 1861 was living with the rest of her family in Bury, Huntingdonshire. The Cook family appears to have moved around in the Fenland area, because a younger brother, Thomas, was born in Whittlesey. Matilda's father, Stephen Cook, was an agricultural labourer and it may well be that the family's moves were related to his occupation; as we have seen, there was little job security in farm work. It is likely that Matilda was in domestic service in the Chatteris area, sometime between 1861 and 1871, but I have no evidence for this. However, Bury is within comfortable walking distance of Chatteris, and the couple must have known each other before William emigrated. I presume they kept in touch by letter for over three years. It would be fascinating to read these letters now.

Matilda arrived in New York (travelling from Liverpool) on 3rd November, 1875. The couple's marriage appears in the Cuyahoga County Marriage Index, available on the internet: it took place on 9th November, 1875, just *six days* after Matilda's arrival. Further confirmation of this was given by details of children born to the couple in Ohio when they became available on the internet: a boy was born to William and Matilda 'Wheatfield' on 11th August 1876, (just over nine months after Matilda's arrival in the U.S.A.) and another boy on 14th September, 1877; I assume the registrar was responsible for the misspelling of the surname. It would appear that neither of the boys lived very long as they do not appear in later records. Another son was born to the couple on 31st March, 1879. This time he was named David Whitfield, and his parents were given as William and Matilda (Whitfield), nee Cook. He, too, doesn't appear to have lived for very long. The interesting thing about him now is the selection of his Christian name for reasons which will be apparent in the next chapter. Suffice it to say that it suggests to me that William and Matilda may well have been aware of a death in the family which had taken place in Hook Norton, England, some six months or so previously. Presumably family members were keeping in touch across the Atlantic.

William and Matilda had another four children: William S. Whitfield (I assume the 'S' stands for Stephen, after Matilda's father), b. 1883, Harriet Matilda, b. 1885 (Matilda's mother's name was Harriet), and Harry Thomas, b.1889/1890 (Matilda's brother was called Thomas). Another boy was born to the couple when they were both in their forties: born on 6th January, 1895, he doesn't appear to have survived long. Matilda also died on 24 January, 1895; it may well be that she suffered from complications following the birth.

William (senior), like both his parents - and his wife - did not live to a great age. He died on 2nd May, 1899, a month short of his fiftieth birthday. The death certificate doesn't give too many details, but it does say that he was born in England. (William Whitfield was born in Manea on 3rd June, 1849). He is buried in Woodland cemetery, Ohio.

William and Matilda's daughter, Harriet Matilda, had moved to California by 1900. It is possible that the death of her parents had prompted the move. Her presence in the household of Naomi and Samuel Beck led me to make further discoveries and strengthened my conviction that I had traced the correct family. Naomi Beck had been born in England in 1862. Harriet was described as her niece. I feel sure that Naomi was therefore Naomi Whitfield, born in Manea in 1862. The Beck family were living in San Jose Township, Pomona City in California. We will return briefly to Naomi later.

I have looked for Harriet's brothers, William S. and Harry Thomas Whitfield in the 1900 census, but have been unable to locate them. My guess is that they stayed together and were probably working, but I have no idea how they managed to evade the census enumerators. They both appear in later records.

William S. Whitfield had his life cut short at the age of 19, when he was attacked by a man wielding a knife in a dark alley, presumably in Cleveland. The information came from a descendant of his younger brother, Harry Thomas Whitfield. I later discovered that the death occurred on 4th September, 1902.

In 1916 Harriet married Charles Nagel, a carpenter, who had been born in Germany, but had emigrated to the U.S.A. with his parents in 1891. The couple's son, Samuel Nagel was born in Ohio in 1917, and died in Los Angeles in 1970. Harriet also moved back to the Los Angeles area, dying there in 1945. I found her details on the ancestry website in the U.S. Social Security Index; the entry confirms that her mother's maiden surname was Cook and her father's surname was Whitfield.

Harriet's brother, Harry Thomas Whitfield was working as a machinist and lodging with Bernhard and Helen Duneiski and their family in Cleveland in 1910. The Duneiskis were originally from Hungary and had only been in the city for a few years. Harry married Emma Nagel in 1915. Emma was the sister of Charles Nagel the carpenter, (Harriet Whitfield's husband) so there was a double alliance between the two families. Emma had been born in Ohio in 1893 and was about eight years younger than her brother. Harry Thomas became a brass finisher, but unfortunately lost one of his arms in an industrial accident. The 1930 census shows that he had become an inspector at a soda fountain in Cleveland. Presumably this job had been selected to enable him to carry on working despite his disability; alternatively, perhaps it was a job he felt obliged to take during the economic depression that hit the U.S.A. at around that time, following the collapse of the New York stock market in 1929. I wasn't sure what a soda fountain was, or what the inspector's job might have entailed.

I discovered that a soda fountain was an apparatus for dispensing soda water. It came with a counter equipped for preparing and serving soft drinks, ice-cream dishes and sandwiches. Concern was being expressed at the consumption of alcohol in America, and it was claimed in 1915, admittedly by the *Soda Fountain Magazine* (hardly an unbiased source), that 'ice cream soda is a greater medium for the cause of temperance than all the sermons preached on the subject'. Prohibition of alcohol in the U.S.A. began in 1919, and it appears that many people missed the socialising made possible in bars more than they missed the alcohol itself; the opening of soda fountains in most American drugstores helped to fill the void. However, their provision was not merely fulfilling some sort of social obligation - soda fountains were highly profitable. John Somerset, writing in '*Drug Topics*' in June, 1920, stated that 'the soda fountain is the most valuable, most useful, most profitable and altogether most beneficial business-building feature assimilated by the drugstore in a generation'. Apparently not content with this glowing endorsement, he went on to proclaim, in the same article 'the bar is dead, the fountain lives and soda is king!'

I'm still not sure *exactly* what Harry Thomas' job would have entailed. Was he checking whether the soda fountain was working properly, or was he a sort of health and safety inspector? Did he visit other drugstores to check on *their* soda fountains? Soda fountains remained popular in the U.S.A. until the 1950s and became an integral part of American culture. However, the 1940 census shows that Harry Thomas was no longer inspecting them: he was working as a clerk for an automobile parts firm.

Shirley Zornow could remember Harry Thomas Whitfield, who had kept in touch with her branch of the family (descended from Henry Whitfield). This was reassuring confirmation that I had found the correct William Whitfield and his descendants. Unfortunately, the next generation did not maintain the contact after Harry Thomas died in 1951. However his obituary notice enabled me to piece together some details of his family.

Obituary notices placed in the Cleveland *Plain Dealer* newspaper have been a great help where other information has been lacking. They are to be found in the Cleveland Necrology File, available on the internet. Unlike the civil registration system in England, where all births, marriages and deaths from 1837 onwards have been indexed - an invaluable aid to the family historian - there is no direct equivalent in the U.S.A. Each state kept its own records, and so far I have found this system extremely frustrating: if a person left the state of his or her birth it becomes very difficult to trace any subsequent marriage. Such has been the case with several members of the family we shall meet later. The Social Security Death Index, available on the internet, is of some assistance here, because it gives information not only on where a person died, but also where they first obtained their National Insurance number, often many years previously. This, at least, gives some indication of the person's likely state of origin. I was lucky to find the Cleveland Necrology File; not every city or state appears to have such a record, or, if they have, these records are not available online.

Using the obituaries found in the Cleveland Necrology file, I have been able to bring the details of Harry Thomas Whitfield's family up to the present day. The children of Harry Thomas and Emma Whitfield were: Irene Ruth Whitfield, b.1916, William Harry Whitfield b.1918, and Dorothy E. Whitfield, b.1919. Irene Ruth married Norman J. Hess. There were no children and Irene died in 1972. Dorothy married Roman Kopanski and died in 2004. William Harry Whitfield married Grace Ann Miller, and they had four children: Grace Ann, born before 1951, Linda Marie, born before 1951, William Harry, born after 1951, and Robert Thomas, also born after 1951. The birth dates are given in this way because Grace and Linda are mentioned as grandchildren of Harry Thomas Whitfield in *his* obituary of 1951, whereas their brothers were not mentioned until the obituary of their father (William Harry Whitfield, senior), appeared in 1974. He would have been about 57 when he died.

Contact has been made with Linda and Robert, but few details have been forthcoming. Linda married Raymond Cifani in 1976. One of their daughters, Nicole Cifani, b.1980 has a high profile job in media/broadcasting, having graduated from Ohio State University with a B.A. in Information Communication Processes and from Emerson College with an M.A. in Visual and Media Arts. Grace Ann married Ralph L. Hollo and they had two sons Thomas M. Hollo and Jeffrey S. Hollo.

William Harry Whitfield (junior) is still living in Lakewood, Ohio. He married Theresa or Tina Lyncha in 1978, but they divorced in April, 1986. It appears that they didn't have any children. His younger brother, Robert Thomas Whitfield joined Zep Inc., a leading producer of commercial and industrial cleaning products, in Cleveland in 1978, working initially as a warehouseman. He became warehouse manager in 1987 but was transferred to Phoenix, Arizona in 2005, where he became distribution manager at Zep Inc.'s new distribution centre. However, this closed in 2009, and he became a warehouse manager for Brody Chemicals in Phoenix. He lives in a new, fast-growing city called Surprise in Maricopa County, about twenty miles NW of Phoenix.

Three more of Jonathan and Jane's children from Manea made the journey across the Atlantic, and two of them travelled together, possibly making use of Josiah Schorah's services. George Whitfield, b.1860, and Naomi, b.1862, travelled from Liverpool on the same steamship

DIAGRAM 12

The line descended from Jonathan Whitfield born 1825

[also see diagram 2]

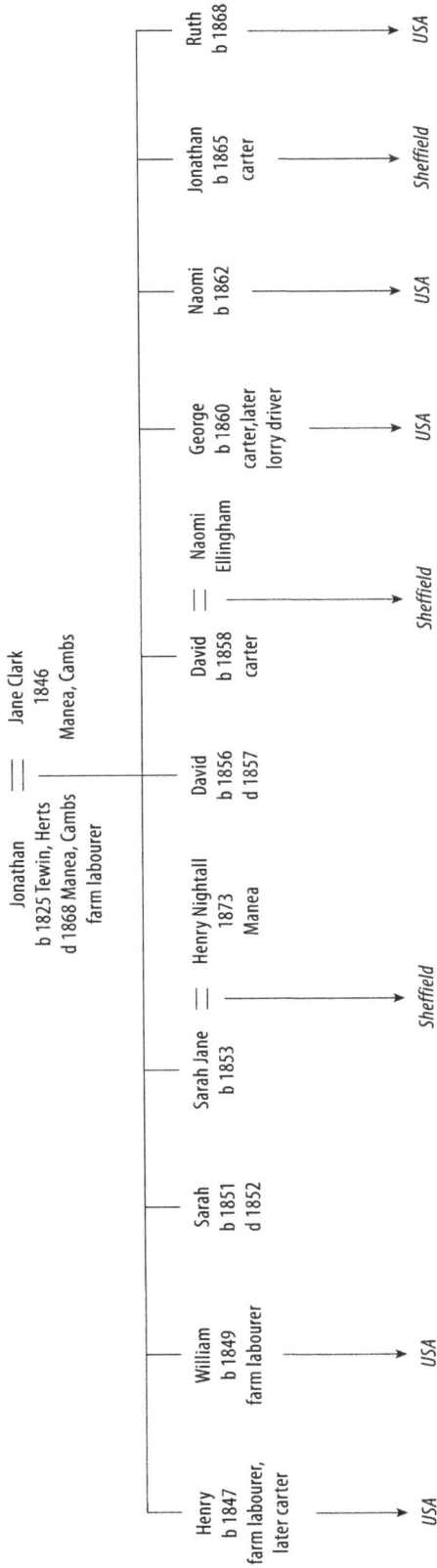

Jonathan
b 1825 Tewin, Herts
d 1868 Manea, Cambs
farm labourer

== Jane Clark
1846
Manea, Cambs

Henry
b 1847
farm labourer,
later carter
→ USA

William
b 1849
farm labourer
→ USA

Sarah
b 1851
d 1852

Sarah Jane
b 1853
== Henry Nightall
1873
Manea
→ Sheffield

David
b 1856
d 1857

David
b 1858
carter
== Naomi
Ellingham
→ Sheffield

George
b 1860
carter, later
lorry driver
→ USA

Naomi
b 1862
→ USA

Jonathan
b 1865
carter
→ Sheffield

Ruth
b 1868
→ USA

All of Jonathan and Jane's children were born in Manea. Fenland life obviously didn't suit the Whitfields; tracking down the descendants of Jonathan and Jane, now spread over three continents, took over twenty years.

269

(the S.S. *Spain*) that their brother Henry had used in 1871. They arrived in New York on 25th October, 1880. Unfortunately for me, their journey date meant that they arrived in the U.S.A too late to appear on the 1880 census, and of course they then missed the 1881 census in England. The emigration list document that has survived appears to have been drawn up very hurriedly (no marks for neatness), and in any case seems to be in a very poor condition. Thankfully, it wasn't destroyed, however; it can be found on the internet. Naomi is described as George's wife - which certainly *wasn't* the case. The birth years are given correctly for both of them. Further confirmation that I had found the correct people was provided by the details of their travelling companion, entered next on the list: Hannah Gibson (Henry Whitfield's mother-in-law). Recently widowed, she was presumably going to visit Henry and Emma and to see her grandchildren - the trip of a lifetime. Perhaps the official completing the form *assumed* that George and Naomi were married, or maybe he was led to believe that this was the case for reasons of convenience. He probably wasn't too bothered - the list looks as though it was drawn up hurriedly on the back of an envelope.

It appears that like the rest of the family, Naomi initially was living in the Cleveland area and I would imagine she kept in touch with her brothers, Henry, William and George. I presume she obtained work in the area, possibly on the land or in domestic service. I was excited to find online a copy of the *Los Angeles Daily Herald* for 6th January, 1887, where there was an article on 'the A.T. and S.F. excursion of 24 cars' which had recently arrived in Los Angeles. Included in the long list of passengers was Naomi Whitfield of Cleveland. My curiosity hadn't been fully satisfied, so I did a little more research. Naomi had been travelling on the Atchison, Topeka and Santa Fe railway, one of the larger railways (or railroads) of the USA, established in 1859. This railway extended into the American interior from Chicago; it was a pioneering enterprise in more ways than one because it set up real estate offices along its route as it was extended across Kansas and Colorado. The railway sold farmland which it had been granted by the American government to aspiring farmers, thus opening up the American interior and securing future trade and revenue for itself, because the farmers, once established, would use the railway for transporting wheat and cattle back to the urban markets in the east. Financing itself in this way, the railway had reached Pueblo, Colorado, in 1876 and Albuquerque, New Mexico, by 1880. It then collaborated with the Atlantic and Pacific railroad in building railway lines west of Albuquerque into Arizona and California. San Diego and Los Angeles had been connected to the network by 1887. Naomi was therefore making use of a new facility enabling her to travel from Ohio to the west coast. The railroad companies reduced their fares later to encourage more travel (with hindsight, perhaps Naomi should have waited for a few more months before making her journey), and many people took the opportunity to move west to start a new life in California, prompting rapid economic growth and triggering a property boom.

Naomi, as we have seen, later married Samuel Sanders Beck. I found details of their marriage on the Church of Latter Day Saints website. It took place in San Bernardino, California, some eight years after Naomi set foot on American soil, and as yet I have no idea what she had been doing in the intervening years and what prompted her move west, away from the rest of her family in Ohio. She clearly kept in touch with them. I found a potted biography of Samuel Beck on a Californian website. Born in San Francisco in 1861, he became a painter, working initially for a firm of painting contractors, but later founded his own business. He eventually employed 25 men and was involved in painting many important public buildings and large homes in Pomona City, a settlement in an area where grapes, citrus fruits and olives were cultivated. After 1905, he turned his attention to sign painting. He and Naomi lived in a house he had constructed in Pomona City, where he also owned five building plots. The couple appear to have been fairly prosperous, but there were no children to benefit from their efforts. We have already seen that they provided a home for their niece, Harriet Matilda after her parents died in Ohio. Naomi died on the 28th December, 1915 aged 53. The death was registered in Los Angeles and Samuel later remarried. Although no photographs of Samuel and Naomi appear to have survived, I had an interesting find on the ancestry website: a voters' list for the Pomona Precinct no 1, Los Angeles, compiled for 1896, not only gave details of Samuel's name, but also had recorded that he was five feet eight inches tall, with a light complexion, blue eyes and sandy coloured hair. Unfortunately Naomi's details weren't given because women were unable to vote in the U.S.A. at this time.

George Whitfield, like his brothers Henry and William, settled in the Cleveland area of Ohio. He married Emma J. Keating (known as Jennie) on 4th September, 1886. I found Jennie, (baptised Emma Jane Keating in England in 1868) in the 1880 U.S.A. census. She was living in Cleveland with her parents, John Keiting, a ship carpenter, born in Bristol, and Mary A. Keiting. They had arrived in the U.S.A. in 1872. The variation in the spelling of the family name was thanks to the census enumerator.

Cleveland had experienced phenomenal growth since its first settler, Lorenzo Carter, had built himself a log cabin on the east bank of the Cuyahoga River in 1797. By 1820 it was still a small village of about 600 people, but the building of the Erie Canal and the Ohio and Erie Canal in the 1820s and 1830s, and the settlement's connection in the 1850s to the railway network linked it with the east coast and the Gulf of Mexico via the River Mississippi, and it became not only a port and route centre on the Great Lakes, but also an important manufacturing centre. Its population in 1850 was over 17,000; and as industries were established (including steel making in 1868 and John D. Rockefeller's Standard Oil Company in 1870) people migrated to Cleveland to work in them. Cleveland had grown to over 90,000 by 1870. Its port function meant that raw materials such as iron ore and coal could be brought in and finished goods despatched. As migrants continued to pour in, not only from other parts of America, but also from Europe (including some of the Whitfield family from a small village in England) its population then nearly *trebled* in the next twenty years. Already huge by the time the Whitfields arrived, it continued to grow, until by 1920 it was the fifth largest city in the U.S.A. Car manufacture, machine tools and oil refining had become established in addition to steel making and various service industries.

The 1900 census (remember that little survives of the one taken in 1890) shows that George and Jennie were living in Cleveland with their children: Robert Henry, b. June, 1887, George Albert, b.1889 and Clara N., b.1892, named after her mother's younger sister, Clara Keating. (I suspect that the 'N' stands for Naomi). They also had another girl in October, 1906, according to Ohio births records available on the internet; she doesn't appear to have lived for very long because she wasn't mentioned in the 1910 census. George was working as a teamster, the American equivalent of a carrier or carter, like his brother Henry. In 1910, George and Jennie were still living in Cleveland, and were now buying their own home, with the aid of a mortgage. George was employed by a 'dry goods store' which I assume was the American term for a general store, selling food, clothing, tools and furniture. He was presumably delivering their goods to customers using a horse and cart. The couple's son, Robert Henry, was still single at 22, and was working as a salesman in a china store. Jennie died in 1918 aged just 49; her death certificate, found on the Mormon website, confirms that she had been born in England to John and Mary Ann Keating.

The 1920 census shows that George, described as a widower, was now living with his daughter, Clara and her husband, Raymond Pagel at their home in Cleveland. The census reveals that George was able to read and write; he was now 59 years old, and these skills would have enabled him to find a less physically demanding job. He had possibly attended school back in Manea at some point, despite his unsettled childhood, or perhaps he had received lessons from an older brother or sister. He was working as a 'shipping clerk' for the dry goods store, presumably organising their deliveries, rather than actually taking the goods himself as previously. He is the first Whitfield of his generation I have found to have been involved in a clerical, sedentary job.

By 1930, George was living with Ruth Caine and her daughter, Alice Behrens, in a rented house in Cleveland. He was described as Ruth's brother. Both Ruth and Alice were working as sales ladies in a confectionery store - possibly their own business. George certainly had a sister, Ruth, who was born in Manea in 1868, after her father Jonathan, had already died. We have seen that she was living with her uncle and aunt, Robert and Catherine, in Potton in 1871; in fact it was her presence there that triggered my research into this branch of the family. I hadn't found her in England since the 1881 census when she was in Littleport, Cambridgeshire. Had she, too, emigrated to America? It certainly appeared to be the case.

Returning to the New York passenger lists (on the internet) I found that a Ruth Whitfield had arrived in New York on 21ˢᵗ May, 1884. She was a spinster, aged just fifteen. I checked on her birth details - she was born on 15ᵗʰ September, 1868 in Manea, so would have been fifteen in May, 1884. I concluded that I had successfully tracked her down. She, too, had probably made use of the services of Josiah Schorah. She travelled, unaccompanied, across the Atlantic from Liverpool on the S.S. *Helvetia*, another National Line vessel. This steamship was only capable of travelling at ten knots per hour, so the journey must have been a memorable experience for the young girl, probably for all the wrong reasons. She must have been relieved to be ashore, and it could well be that she was met at the harbour by one of her brothers, although I have no evidence for this. It isn't clear how she managed to save enough money for the voyage and for her train fare to Liverpool. Maybe she was helped by her brothers who were already employed in the U.S.A., or perhaps she was in domestic service somewhere in England prior to her departure. I also assume that she found employment in America, probably in the Cleveland area, before she married.

Ruth's husband was Douglas Caine; they married in December 1887, when Ruth was nineteen. Douglas had been born in Ohio, but his parents William and Eleanor Cain or Caine originated from the Isle of Man. The 1861 census shows that they were living at Ballaugh, where William was working as an agricultural labourer and Eleanor as a washerwoman, but the Caine family appears to have previously lived in the parish of Michael or Kirk Michael in the North West part of the island. I found out that the Isle of Man had a long-established link to the Cleveland area of America. In about 1826, a Dr. Harrison, brother of a well-known Manx scholar and divine, the Reverend John Edward Harrison, had visited the U.S.A., passing along the southern shore of Lake Erie. He commented very favourably on the environment he saw, and reports obviously got back to the Isle of Man. It wasn't long before Manx families decided to try their luck in the New World. At that time, as we have seen, Cleveland was just a small village. A century later it was reported that Cleveland had the largest number of Manx people and their descendants in the U.S.A.

The 1880 census shows William and Eleanor Caine were living in Cleveland with their son Douglas, then aged 14, and their daughters Ella (12) and Emma (5). William was working as a carpenter.

Ruth and Douglas appear to have had just one child: their daughter Alice, who was born in August, 1888.

The 1900 census shows that the Caines were living in Cleveland; Douglas was working as an assistant plumbing inspector. It was interesting to learn that all of them could read and write, so Ruth had attended school somewhere, possibly in Potton, despite her unsettled childhood.

By 1920 the family had moved to Willoughby, in Lake County, Ohio. Douglas was now working as a plumber. Alice had married Carl Behrens, a teamster. He had been born in Germany, but could speak English. Alice and Carl were living with Douglas and Ruth.

A lot can happen to a family in ten years, as I know only too well. It appears that Alice and Carl did not have any children, and by 1930 they had divorced. Ruth, now widowed, and Alice had moved back to Cleveland. Both of them were working in a sweet shop. As we have already seen, Ruth's brother, George Whitfield was living with them. The confectionery shop which was being run by Ruth and Alice was remembered by Henry Whitfield's great granddaughter, Shirley Zornow in 2008. It was obviously a popular place for a young child to visit. Alice, however, didn't work there for much longer, because she died suddenly in April, 1935, at the early age of 46. Her death must have been a great shock to her mother and uncle, and it probably revived memories for them of the early deaths of their parents back in England.

Ruth died on 10th October, 1938, aged seventy. Her older brother, George outlived her, but not for long, dying about six weeks later aged 78; by their deaths the direct link between Potton, Manea and the U.S.A. was broken. Both their death certificates state that they were born in England and details given of their parents confirm that I had found the correct people. George's occupation is stated as a garage attendant: it appears that he was still working in his late seventies.

The children of George and Jennie Whitfield all married and had children of their own. Robert Henry, b.1887 married Emma Ida Pagel, the daughter of a German carpenter Charles E. Pagel and his wife Augusta, who had emigrated to the U.S.A. in 1874 and 1873 respectively. The marriage took place on 14th August, 1911 in Windsor, Ontario, Canada, but I have been unable to establish why this location was chosen. Perhaps they wanted a more unusual venue, rather like some couples today marry in the Seychelles. Windsor was arguably less exotic, but a journey around - or even across - Lake Erie must have made the occasion more memorable. Alternatively, perhaps the couple just wanted a quiet wedding, away from the rest of the family. They moved back to Ohio, where their son and daughter were born: Robert C. (presumably Charles) in 1917, and Jane F. in 1919. Robert Henry was evidently a somewhat adaptable and resourceful character, capable of earning a living in various different ways. We have seen that as a young man of 22 he was a salesman in a china shop. After his marriage he became a shipping clerk for a rolling works (presumably steel) in 1920, and in 1930 he was a truck driver for a department store in Cleveland, following in his father's footsteps. He died on 28th December, 1949 at Cleveland Heights, aged 62. Details of the next generation are only sketchy as no successful contact has been made with this branch: a letter was sent but no reply was forthcoming. Robert C. Whitfield appears to have married and had a son Robert C. Whitfield, junior. At some point the family moved to Lafayette, Sussex, New Jersey, where Robert (senior) died in 1997. Jane F. Whitfield married twice. Her first husband was George J. Miller, junior, and her second was James Joseph O'Neill. There was one child from each marriage: Marilyn Miller and Karen O'Neill.

The second child of George and Jennie Whitfield was George Albert Whitfield, b.1889 in Ohio. He married Elizabeth Link in 1910. Elizabeth had been born in Ohio in 1890, but her parents Herman and Eva Link came originally from Germany. Herman was described as a labourer in the 1900 census schedule; in 1910, the year of his daughter's marriage, he was a stove maker in a stove factory. I was lucky that George and Elizabeth's marriage took place a month before the census enumerator visited them to record their details, so I can reveal that the couple had settled in Cleveland and George Albert was working as a travelling salesman.

At the time of his registration for World War One, George Albert was living at 580 Pinewood, Cleveland, and was working as a clerk at the firm of Wiedenmeier and Whitfield, presumably an enterprise owned by himself and his brother-in-law, George Wiedenmeier (who was the husband of Elizabeth Whitfield's sister, Alma, nee Link). The nature of the business is not made clear, but it is possible, or even likely that it was something to do with groceries or provisions. This is because in the 1920 census George Albert was described as a retail merchant (groceries), and Elizabeth was a saleslady in the grocery store. It isn't clear whether Mr. Wiedenmeier was actively involved in any way; perhaps he financed or helped to finance the original venture. The business may not have been that successful because in 1930 the ever-resourceful George Albert was described as the proprietor of a barbecue stand. It may be that his original business foundered during the inter-war depression, which affected Cleveland so badly that by 1933 roughly one in every three of its workers was unemployed. Hopefully his barbecue stand had plenty of regular customers because in addition to himself and Elizabeth, George Albert now had two teenage sons, two younger sons and his mother-in-law, Eva Link, living with him. Hopefully *they* all liked barbecued food. It would be interesting to know what George Albert was offering on his stand - I had always assumed that barbecues were a more modern phenomenon.

The children of George Albert and Elizabeth Whitfield were Wesley George, b.1911, George Albert, junior, b.1915, Clayton L., b. 1918 and Neil W., b.1927. Their father, George Albert, senior, died at Lodi, Medina, in 1945. It isn't clear whether he had moved there or whether he spent his last days in hospital there. He was 56 years old. No occupation was listed for him in the 1940 census, when he, Elizabeth and young Neil were living in Montville, Medina, Ohio and this suggests that he could have been suffering from a long term illness during his last few years of life.

I have managed to find out a little about the three older boys. Wesley married Anna Margaret Kirk in 1931. At the time of his marriage Wesley was a clerk, but the certificate doesn't give further details. His bride's occupation wasn't specified on the certificate, but I found from the 1930 census that she had been working as a waitress at a 'Road House', and her father, Marsh Kirk, was a farmer. Wesley and Anna's daughter, Shirley A. Whitfield was born in May, 1931. The family were living with Anna's father, Marsh Kirk, in Montville, Medina, Ohio, at the time of the 1940 census, and Wesley was working as an attendant at a 'gas station'- presumably serving petrol. I haven't yet managed to discover whether any other children were born to the couple. Wesley died in San Diego, California, in 1994; it is possible that he had moved there to enjoy the sun in his retirement, but he could have travelled there with his job in earlier years. If there were any more children, they could have been born in Ohio, California, in another American state or even abroad - a reflection of the increasing social and geographical mobility of people in the U.S.A. in the twentieth century - and it is difficult to know where to start looking. Wesley's widow, Anna Whitfield died in Las Vegas, Nevada, in 1998. Their daughter, Shirley married Dean M. Meyer, but the couple divorced in 1977 in San Diego, California. Shirley died in El Cajon, California in 2003. I discovered details of Shirley after the 1940 U.S.A. census was published on the ancestry website in 2012, so was unable to contact her.

George Albert Whitfield, junior, (Wesley's brother) was described as a widower when he died in Columbus, Ohio on 1st January, 2000. Working backwards, I found the death of a Betty Jane Whitfield in Columbus in 1992. Her maiden name had been Boeshans. Her zip code (the U.S.A. equivalent of our postcode system) was the same as the one given for George some eight years later, and I concluded that she had been George Albert's wife. The 1940 census when it became available showed that I had found the correct couple, although the enumerator managed to frustrate me for a while by spelling their surname *Whitfied*. George Albert and Betty and their young daughter Carol Sue, aged two were living in Montgomery township, Columbus City, with Floyd E. Taylor, his wife Pearl and their son Floyd junior. George and Betty were described as brother-in-law and sister-in-law, respectively, of the Taylors. In fact, Pearl was Betty's older sister. The three men were working for a company called Buckeye Packet: Floyd senior was a plating engineer, the other two were labourers. I'm not sure whether George and Betty subsequently had any more children. Carol Sue Whitfield married Ronald Hamilton, but they were later divorced. Unfortunately, Carol Sue Hamilton died only two years after her father, in Columbus, Franklin, Ohio. I have also found details of a George Albert Whitfield, born in 1948 in Medina, Ohio, who died in El Cajon, California in 2006. He was a lance corporal in the U.S. Marine Corps during the Vietnam War, and more recently had been working as an inspector in the aerospace industry. He had a brother, Daryl Whitfield, a sister, Deanna Link (a surname already connected to the Whitfield family in America) and a daughter, Courtney. Bearing in mind his two Christian names and his date and State of birth,

I initially speculated that he may have been a son of the George Albert Whitfield who died in 2000. I haven't yet managed to make contact with this branch, so have been unable to have my suspicions confirmed - or otherwise.

Until the publication of the 1940 census on the internet in 2012 I had great difficulties in finding out much about Clayton Whitfield, the next son of George Albert and his wife Elizabeth. Without a nationally organised registration system for births, marriages and deaths it is very difficult to track down individuals in the U.S.A. if they stray from their home area - or even if they stay put, in some cases. It may be easier for someone in America, but this side of the Atlantic it is very frustrating to have progressed as far as someone born in 1918 and then to 'lose' him when he or his children could still be alive. Obviously, the U.S.A is a much bigger country, not only geographically, but also in terms of population, and tracing people seems much more difficult.

Using the Mormon website, I managed to discover that Clayton had married Loretta Iona Frost in November, 1936. Both bride and groom were actually in their late teens, although Clayton's age was given as 21. The marriage took place at New Cumberland, a small town in the West Virginia panhandle, just beyond the boundary with Ohio. Loretta's parents, George and Arta Frost, both came from West Virginia, but had moved to Medina, Ohio, and Loretta was living there at the time of the marriage, according to the licence. It is therefore difficult to see why this venue was chosen. Perhaps Clayton's parents didn't approve of the match.

The 1940 census revealed that Clayton and Loretta were living with Loretta's parents in Medina. Both Clayton and Loretta gave their age as 21, further suggesting to me that that they *had* married in their late teens. They now had a daughter, Deanna, aged two. Clayton was working as a truck driver. I have not yet managed to discover whether they had any more children, but the name of their daughter has made me re-consider the theory I had earlier about the George Albert Whitfield who died in El Cajon, California in 2006. It now seems more likely that he and his brother Daryl and sister Deanna were all children of Clayton and Loretta. Such information would be easy to find in England where births are registered nationally, and the maiden names of mothers are also given; not so in the U.S.A.

Clayton died in San Diego in 1981, suggesting that he may have kept in touch with his older brother Wesley who was possibly also living in San Diego at this time. Again, he may have migrated to the California to enjoy an early retirement, or it could have been a job-related move. I have wondered whether both brothers were working in the aerospace industry, but this is mere conjecture. Loretta had died some ten years earlier, also in San Diego.

Much more is known about Wesley and Clayton's youngest brother, Neil, b.1927, who became well-known in Medina, Ohio, and, I suspect, well beyond his native State. I found some early details of Neil in the U.S. enlistment records for World War Two. Neil enlisted after the war had ended - in October, 1945 - probably when he became eighteen. His place of enlistment was at Camp Atterbury, Columbus, Indiana, and he was assigned to the Panama Canal department in the air corps as a private. His civil occupation was given as a farm hand. I have no idea why he was in Indiana when he enlisted.

Neil may have acquired a taste for education in the air corps, and clearly was ambitious to improve upon his lot as a farm hand. He studied law at Western Reserve University and qualified in 1951. He was named Young Man of the Year in 1959 and also won a distinguished service award from the Jaycees (United States Junior Chamber – a leadership training and civic organisation). He was also an active member of St Matthew's Lutheran Church. After working as an attorney in Medina for twenty years he served as a special assistant to the attorney general of Ohio for four years, before he became a judge in Medina County, Ohio in 1974.

Despite these excellent credentials, Neil was a controversial figure. In April, 1978 he jailed 38 striking teachers for defying his order to get back to work. He defended his action, saying he had given them a choice. He added: 'All I'm asking them to do is obey the law. I enforce the law the way I see it, and I'll jail anyone who violates a lawful order of my court'. He considered that 'the decision to go to jail was theirs [i.e. the teachers'], not mine'. The case was reported in the *Chronicle Telegraph*, published in Elyria, Ohio, on 12th April, 1978. Over fifty more teachers were to suffer the same fate, for contempt of court if they, too, refused to sign the order. With just two hours to go before these teachers joined their colleagues behind bars, attorneys for the Board of Education intervened. They met Neil, and the restraining order was lifted. However, Neil reserved the right to press criminal contempt charges against any of the striking teachers, their leaders or their organisations.

Some of his other decisions were questionable: for instance, later in the same year he sentenced Robert W. Attwood, aged twenty, to a minimum of four years and a maximum of 25 years in jail for stealing ten dollars' worth of beer from a neighbour's garage. Attwood's father said that his son had a drinking problem and his mother reported that the beer (two six-packs and a case) had been replaced. Neil defended his decision, saying that he had imposed the sentence on Attwood because it took him six weeks to return to court for sentencing. When asked on a radio programme if he considered the sentence harsh, Neil said 'Why should I think that? I don't pass the laws in this State. I merely enforce them'. The controversial case featured in the *Milwaukee Journal* of 2nd February, 1979, which also reported that Judge Whitfield had given a suspended sentence to a deputy registrar, Mary Murray, accused of stealing licence plate fees to the value of $8,000. Murray had been put on probation for five years. Her initial fine of $2,000 had been reduced to $500 and her prison sentence of two to ten years had been suspended. She was ordered to repay the money she had allegedly stolen and Neil gave her one week to present a plan for restitution.

Neil was described in one newspaper article as 'probably the County's [Medina County in Ohio] most prominent and powerful public official'. The cases over which he presided were obviously reported in the press - and not always favourably. His private life also attracted attention in September, 1981, when his wife, Marjorie A. Whitfield, nee Hickling, died of an insulin overdose - a somewhat suspicious way to die, as she wasn't diabetic. The death was recorded as suicide, but apparently no suicide note was ever found. Neil re-married in July, 1982. His new wife was Beverley J. Ivie, aged 42, some twelve years his junior.

In October, 1985, Neil Whitfield announced that after discussions with his family (more about his family later), he had decided not to seek a third term as Medina County Common Pleas judge. He said he was considering a number of opportunities, and it was likely that he would return to private law practice. Ostensibly, his motive was greater financial reward; he stated '...a judge's pay is incommensurate with the private sector', but for various reasons the storm clouds were gathering.

In October, 1986, a month before he retired, the press reported that

'Judge Whitfield has often been a lightning rod of controversy and his strong persona is currently a centrepiece of serious doubts about the competence, if not the integrity of the administration of justice and law enforcement in Medina County'.

The article was more of a diatribe than a eulogy, and must have made uncomfortable reading for Neil and members of his family.

Neil retired from his $60,500 per year post in November, 1986, but to many people he remained a controversial figure. A friend outside the legal profession, Howard Servens, said that Neil was 'a man of principle - if he believed something, he did it'. Before he retired he received approval for disability retirement payments, but by the following March he asked the Medina County Commissioners to pay $4225 towards legal fees and other bills which he had incurred in defending himself against a disciplinary action and a slander suit whilst still in office. To continue to be embroiled in such controversies was hardly the ideal way to finish a career or start retirement.

The *Akron Beacon Journal* of 13th November, 1986 noted that 'Three for sale boards grace the front lawn of Republican Neil W. Whitfield's secluded Medina home. The retired judge is reportedly preparing for a move to Bradenton, Florida'. I'm not sure exactly when the move took place, but Neil (and presumably his wife) *did* move to Bradenton. As he managed to secure disability retirement benefits, it seems likely that Neil was not in the best of health when he retired; his illness may well have been the result of the stress he had been under for a protracted period. In addition to his own job-related problems and issues he also had to cope with a son who had made headlines for controversial reasons, as we shall soon see.

Neil's retirement didn't last long. The *Plain Dealer* of 13th November, 1992 recorded that 'the controversial Medina City judge, Neil Whitfield, died quietly in a Florida nursing home on October 19th'. There *must* have been an obituary, but so far I have been unable to find one, which is very frustrating. Neil was 65.

Neil and his first wife Marjorie had three children, according to the *Chronicle Telegram* of 1 November, 1974, where a brief summary of Neil's career and personal life appeared when he was a candidate for the Medina County judgeship. I managed to find details of two sons: Mark W. Whitfield, b.1950 and Bruce W. Whitfield, b.1953. A birth index for Ohio appeared online in August, 2012, and this enabled me to find their third child: Andrea L. Whitfield, born in 1959.

Mark graduated from the University of Akron in 1973 with a B.A. degree in political science. He appears to have married while still at university: his bride was Nancy Louise Cunningham, a 22 year old teacher. Mark moved or returned to Medina where he became involved in local politics, standing as Republican candidate for Congress in 1978, albeit unsuccessfully. He became a Medina County Commissioner - one of a trio of officials who formed the executive authority for county government. Like his father, Mark was a controversial figure. As early as 1976, his secretary Pamela Terrill was found naked and hanging by her scarf in her bedroom closet. Her mouth and left eye were covered by adhesive tape. Miss Terrill's death was considered to be suicide by the Medina County coroner Andrew Karson. However, as the pathologist performing Pamela Terrill's autopsy was Dr. Peter Volodkevich, a friend of Neil Whitfield, and Mark was a son of a Medina county judge, you can imagine that the suicide verdict was not always viewed with complete satisfaction. It was later changed to 'undetermined'.

In 1979, a secret from Mark's private life came to light. On the afternoon of 5th April, a blonde in a blue dress driving a grey car was stopped by a Medina sheriff's deputy who was investigating a burglary. The deputy asked the blonde (who was heavily made up with lipstick and rouge and wearing a wig), for identification. The 'blonde' replied that his name was Mark Whitfield.

Mark admitted that he had been trying to get into the home of a woman he knew slightly, and asked that he should be given time to break the news to his family. The local newspaper got hold of the story, but Mark resigned from public office before the *Akron Beacon Journal* went to press. The story wasn't published and no charges were filed.

However, the incident resurfaced in 1988, after Neil Whitfield had retired, because the Pamela Terrill murder case was re-opened. Pamela's body had been exhumed in July, 1987 to enable another autopsy to be performed, this time by Cuyahoga County coroner Elizabeth Balraj and a pathologist, Dr. Robert Challener. The *Akron Journal* of 2nd May, 1988 announced, with an almost palpable sense of anticipatory relish:

' A case involving some classic mystery elements - sex, a young female victim, and a rising politician from an influential family - is expected to unfold as Mark Whitfield goes on trial today in Medina County Common Pleas Court for a nearly 12 year old murder'.

To make matters worse, Mark was already in trouble and in the public eye: the *Akron Journal* noted in February, 1988 that officials of the Old Phoenix National Bank in Medina did not enquire about the financial condition of a T-shirt business owned by Mark W. Whitfield before loaning the former Medina County commissioner $575,000. From this side of the Atlantic it would appear that the press were keen to discover as much adverse publicity as they could.

Mark appears to have handled the situation very well. He announced on television that he looked forward to 'getting the case [involving the death of Pamela Terrill] into a court of law and out of public speculation'.

The trial investigated the death of Marjorie Whitfield in 1981 as well as the death of Pamela Terrill in 1976. Bruce Whitfield, Mark's younger brother, was one of the witnesses. At one point in the trial, a former Medina police officer testified that he had seen a police report in August, 1976, in which Pamela Terrill accused Mark of raping her. However, on 13th May, 1988, the *Akron Journal* reported that

'….former Medina County commissioner Mark W. Whitfield, having been identified by some investigators as a prime suspect, was found innocent on Thursday of the nearly 12 year old murder of Pamela J. Terrill. Appearing relaxed in a beige suit as he emerged from a Medina County courtroom, Whitfield said in a steady, deep voice 'Naturally we're very happy and pleased to have this ordeal over…'

The investigation had clearly been thorough: at that time the cost had been calculated at $38,000, and bills were still arriving…

The family suffered another tragedy in 1990. On 27th June, Mark's brother, Bruce Whitfield, was found dead at his home in Medina. He was just 36, divorced, and working in the construction industry as an operating engineer. There was an autopsy, but I haven't been able to discover the coroner's verdict. Bruce had been divorced from his former wife Anita for about a year. They had been married for four years and there were no children.

Mark Whitfield has married twice. His first marriage, to Nancy Cunningham ended in divorce in January, 1981 and he married Susan G. Nagy later in the same year. Their children, Nathaniel W. Whitfield and Abigail Joy Whitfield were born in 1983/4 and 1986/7 respectively.

Mark and his wife Susan were in the public eye again in 1995, when an article in the *Akron Beacon Journal* proclaimed in February that 'Investigators suspect arson as sheriff opens probe into blaze at site owned by Susan Whitfield, wife of a former Medina commissioner'. The same journal reported in April that

'...Former Medina County commissioner Mark Whitfield is demanding full payment of $120,000 from prospective buyers for the burned out shell of a restaurant destroyed by arson on 2nd January. Whitfield and his wife Susan are also seeking approximately $100,000 from an insurance claim on the same restaurant said Tom and Mike Bogden, father and son operators of the sports bar and restaurant...'

Since this time, Mark seems to have lived a quiet and uncontroversial life. He appears to own a fast food establishment in the settlement of Westfield Center, in Ohio.

Mark and Susan's son, Nathaniel W. Whitfield attended Cloverleaf High School in Lodi, Ohio. He graduated from the College of Wooster, Ohio in 2007, with a degree in political science, and this was followed by a master's degree in Sport and Recreation management from Kent State University in 2009 and an M.B.A. from Ashland University. He is Operations and Facilities manager for the Athletics Department at Wooster College, Wooster, Ohio, where he also helps as assistant coach for the men's soccer team. Nathaniel (Nate) married Sara Dresser in July, 2011. Sara grew up in Sturgis, Michigan, and graduated from the College of Wooster in 2009 with a degree in Economics. At the time of her marriage she was employed by Westfield Insurance as a financial analyst and was also studying for a master's degree in public administration from the University of Akron. The couple met at Wooster College.

Nathaniel's sister, Abigail Joy Whitfield also attended Cloverleaf High School. Like her brother, she is keenly interested in sport, and plays basketball, soccer and golf.

Neil Whitfield's daughter, Andrea, married Thomas Judkins in 1981 in Medina, Ohio; they appear to have moved to Colorado Springs, Colorado.

For the sake of completeness I must now return to the youngest child of George Whitfield, b.1860 in Manea, and his wife Jennie Keating. Clara N. Whitfield was born in May, 1892, and later married Raymond L. Pagel. He had been born in Cleveland in 1890, but his father, Rudolph Pagel, had originated from Germany. I haven't been able to establish whether there was any connection between this Pagel family and the family of Emma Pagel, the wife of Robert Henry Whitfield. Clara and Raymond (who was a salesman of electrical goods), were living in Lakewood, Ohio in 1930. They had two children: Donald Pagel b.1919, and Marjorie C. Pagel, b.1922. The census reveals that they were buying their own home: it was valued at $8,000. Raymond was probably doing very well; at this time there would have been a growing demand for electrical goods. Radios were a relatively new invention at this time. They provided news and entertainment; they enabled farmers in remote rural areas to check market prices and keep in touch with the outside world. They were beginning to appear in many houses and the census questionnaire even contained a question about radio ownership; I wasn't surprised to see that the Pagels owned one.

I have discovered from obituaries that Donald Pagel presumably married later because he had three children: Paula, David and Christian. Marjorie married into the Toth family and had a daughter, Jaci.

Clara died in 1984 aged 92; she had outlived her husband by ten years and each of her brothers by over thirty years. She would have known all about her father's earlier life in England and may well have possessed some interesting family photographs. If so, I wonder where they are now? So far, I have not managed to contact this branch of the family. Both Donald Pagel and his sister Marjorie Toth died in 2006, so I would need to try to trace their respective children.

I have already dealt with the American branches of the family because chronologically, the emigration of Henry Whitfield occurred while the rest of the family were still living in the Fens in England. However, I have previously indicated that other family members migrated to Sheffield. I mentioned this earlier in the chapter because it was thanks to some descendants of these Sheffield Whitfields that I managed to find the American connection. My search, beginning in Manea, had continued in Sheffield, as I indicated earlier, mainly because the information was easier to discover. As more details were published on the internet the American story began to unfold. I now need to return to Sheffield to give further details of the family members there.

You will remember that David Whitfield had married Naomi Ellingham in Brightside, Sheffield in 1880. Both originated from fenland Cambridgeshire. It isn't entirely clear why they had chosen Sheffield as a place to live. Migration, whether international or interregional, is often looked at in terms of 'push' and 'pull' factors, i.e. reasons for leaving one's home area, and reasons for settling in a new place. The main push factors in this case would appear to be the lack of employment opportunities in the Fens which were (and to a certain extent still are) remote from main centres of employment. Job opportunities here in the nineteenth century would have been connected to agriculture, and as we have already seen, farming in the 1870s and 1880s was being adversely affected by American competition and by a series of poor summers. Mechanisation was also leading to a reduced demand for labour on farms, and working conditions and pay remained poor. There was therefore every incentive to leave the Fens, whether for America or somewhere in England offering more employment opportunities. What prompted David Whitfield and other members of his family to choose Sheffield, rather than some other English industrial city (or America) is rather more difficult to explain.

Sheffield, like Cleveland in Ohio, was a rapidly expanding city – and for similar reasons. In 1841, its population was around 68,000, but by 1871 its population had more than trebled: there were 240,000 people living there - an enormous increase. Ten years later, helped by the addition of David Whitfield and the Ellingham family, and thousands like them, the population had risen to 284,000, and by the time Jonathan Whitfield arrived in the early 1890s, the city's population exceeded 325,000. Compared to Manea the city would have seemed *huge*. Although some of the population growth was by natural increase, i.e. more births than deaths during this period, much of it was due to the fact that Sheffield was attracting people to it from other areas of the country, like moths to an illuminated light bulb – or flies to a cowpat. They were coming to take jobs in Sheffield's thriving industries. The city was exerting a gravitational pull, in an economic sense, on people, rather like Cleveland was doing on the other side of the Atlantic. Urbanisation was the result of thousands of individual decisions to migrate from the countryside, but looked at *en masse*, the process seemed inexorable.

Sheffield's industrial growth was as a result of people over the years making use of the natural resources available in the local area. Iron ore was found in nearby rocks which also included coal. Initially, the ore was smelted using wood and then charcoal, from nearby forests. (It was discovered later that coke could be used, manufactured from coal). Fast-flowing streams from the slopes of the Pennines were used to operate water wheels which provided power in the early stages of the industry. Millstones, used for grinding tools and limestone, used in the smelting process to collect impurities, were also available locally. Even clay was found nearby and was used to make the firebricks which lined the furnaces. Nature had spread all these resources with a generous hand in the Sheffield area, and the ingenuity of local inventors and the enterprise of Yorkshire entrepreneurs led to the development of a number of industries, such as cutlery, and, later, iron and then steel.

One of the main problems with iron was that it was brittle in certain circumstances, and experiments carried out in order to investigate and hopefully rectify this fault led to the development of steel with its lower carbon content. Steel was a tougher metal, able to withstand stresses and strains, and it was therefore suitable for bridges and railway tracks. The 'modern' steel industry began in the middle of the eighteenth century when Benjamin Hunter invented the crucible method of production, and Sheffield plate, a steel alloy with copper and a silver coating was invented in 1742. Electroplating was introduced in 1850. Henry Bessemer (1813-1898) set up a steelworks in Sheffield, and by 1858, coincidentally the year of David Whitfield's birth in Manea, had introduced the Bessemer converter process of manufacturing steel. All of these developments would of course, whether directly or indirectly, influence the lives of members of the Whitfield family and countless other families like them. The metals produced in Sheffield and other industrial cities would be used to make steamships like the ones which carried some of the Manea Whitfields across the Atlantic; they would be vital to the railways which were providing employment for other members of the family and encouraging them to move from their home areas, and the armaments manufactured in Sheffield would be used in the two World Wars which were to involve so many unsuspecting men in the future. Furthermore, the metals would be used in the manufacture of farm machinery which would, in turn, lead to a reduced demand for farm labourers in the countryside. Thousands of people eager to secure jobs associated with the manufacture of iron, steel and their alloys were flocking to Sheffield and other Northern industrial cities. The influx of these migrants would lead to social problems in the cities as well as rural depopulation: the seeds of modern life were being sown.

Sheffield's steel industry spread along the Don valley towards Rotherham and Doncaster. Sheffield tended to specialise in light steel goods such as cutlery and tools and high grade special steels. The making of stainless steel was pioneered in Sheffield in 1903, and the city became a major centre for the manufacture of armaments during both World Wars. It therefore became a target for enemy bombing, as we shall see later. Today, most of the raw materials used in iron and steel making are imported as the local ones have been exhausted or they are uneconomic to exploit.

Once a major industry develops in an area, it tends to attract not only workers from other areas to work in it, but also service industries - other enterprises which often depend on the original industry for their livelihood, but assist it in its continued development. With all the raw materials being brought to the iron and steel works and all the finished products being sent to customers, there would have been a great demand for transport of various types, ranging from railways for heavy and bulky goods to horse-drawn waggons and carriers' carts for lighter goods and people. Clearly, carters and carriers would not be short of work in Sheffield. The surroundings would have been much more noisy and polluted than those in small villages like Manea, but there was a living to be made.

David and Naomi Whitfield's eldest child, Annie, was baptised in Sheffield in 1881. Their next child, Thomas, was baptised in 1883. Their other children were William, b.1887, and Frank, who was born much later - in 1900. David is described as a general carter in the 1881 census (like his brothers Henry and George in the U.S.A.), but as a groom in 1891. This suggests to me that his expertise was really in looking after horses, which he probably gained from working on Fenland farms as a young man. It is likely that he was employed by an iron and steel works: at that time most of the short distance haulage in and around the works would have been by horse and cart. However, by 1901, David had become a furniture remover. Presumably he had purchased a horse and cart and was undertaking more congenial work on his own account; alternatively he could have been working for a removals firm.

In 1891 David's younger brother, Jonathan, was living with him as well as his own growing family. There was also a lodger, John Henry Prutton. The family was living in Dorking Street.

By 1901, Jonathan had married and moved out of the Dorking Street cottage. David's son Thomas was working at an armour plate works and William, aged thirteen or fourteen was working as an errand boy. The census enumerator also recorded the arrival of Frank, now aged nine months. The two branches of the family clearly kept in touch: David's oldest child, Annie (aged twenty) was visiting her uncle Jonathan and his family in nearby Sorby Street.

In 1911, David was described as a general carter. His daughter, Annie was still living with her mother and father, and no occupation was given for her; her brother Thomas (28) was still single and working at the armour plate works. He was described as a planer and slotter. His younger brother, William (23), was working for a silversmith. Young Frank was still at school. Once again, the family had taken in a lodger in an attempt to augment their household income.

David Whitfield died in 1918 aged sixty, and unfortunately two of his children, William and Frank died in the same year, aged 31 and 18 respectively. They may have been victims of the influenza epidemic which swept England after the end of the First World War, but I haven't seen the death certificates. I'm not sure whether William was married at the time.

Thomas Whitfield, David and Naomi's surviving son, married Beatrice A. Foster in 1921, and their daughter, Olive, was born in 1923. Thomas died in 1940 aged about 57. It is thought that Olive married, but attempts to locate her have been unsuccessful. It would appear that Annie, David and Naomi's daughter didn't marry. I found the death of an Annie Whitfield in 1940. She was 59, suggesting a birth date of around 1881. I can't be absolutely sure, but it seems as though I have found the correct person. As far as I can tell, therefore, David and Naomi's line has died out in the Whitfield name, although if Olive *did* marry and have children there may be some living descendants.

You will remember that Sarah Jane, the oldest daughter of Jonathan and Jane Whitfield of Manea (b.1852/3) married Henry Nightall, the son of a blacksmith, in a temporary church in Manea in 1873. Sarah Jane was able to write her name in the marriage register. Neither of her parents was there to witness the happy occasion because they were both already in their graves. After a few years, Sarah Jane and Henry had migrated to Sheffield. The date of their move is not known precisely, but it would have occurred between 1875 and 1877. This is because the place of birth of their first child, Alfred, b.1875 was in Cambridgeshire, and their next surviving child, Mary Jane, was born in Sheffield in 1877, according to later census details. The presence of his sister Sarah Jane in Sheffield may, of course, have been the reason why David Whitfield decided to move there. However, as censuses were only taken every ten years and the earliest record of David having been in Sheffield is his marriage in 1880, it may be that he actually arrived in the city before his sister, or he could have made the journey *with* the Nightalls. The 1891 census shows that the Nightall family were living in Saville Street, near an ironworks, where Henry and young Alfred, now about sixteen, were labourers.

Little is known of this branch of the family, but the births and deaths registers tell a sorry story. Henry and Sarah Jane Nightall's children were: Alfred, b.1875, David, b.1876, Mary Jane, b.1877, William Henry, b.1880, Henry, b.1882, George, b.1884, Jonathan, b.1885, Fanny, b.1888, Naomi, b.1891, and Tom, b.1894. Most of the children didn't survive very long, and the death registers record the departures of David in 1878, William Henry in 1880, George in 1884, Fanny and Naomi in 1891 and Jonathan in 1893. Henry, having lost a number of his brothers and sisters survived a little longer, but died as a young man in 1907; his older brother Alfred then died in 1911, aged only 36. I haven't been able to find a marriage for him.

Sarah Jane, therefore, having given birth to ten children, lived to bury eight of them. Obviously this must have been a desperately unhappy series of events for her and her husband Henry. I haven't seen the death certificates, but wonder whether there was some type of illness such as tuberculosis within the family or some type of genetic disorder. It would be interesting to know whether the district of Sheffield where they were living was notorious for infant mortality. Perhaps the family might have been better off returning to Manea, but it is easy to say this with hindsight. A further hint of unhappiness in this unfortunate branch of the family is given by the 1911 census: Sarah Jane was found living at 12 Cooper Place, Sheffield with her unmarried son Alfred, aged 36, who was working at an iron works (but was to die later that year) and his much younger brother, Tom, who was working as a painter at a railway waggon works. Sarah Jane's husband, Henry was not mentioned at this address. I found that he was living in the Sheffield workhouse. He was 64 years old, and presumably unable to work as the result of some illness or disability. Unfortunately the column giving such information had been blanked out. I'm not sure when these details will be available to the general public. Henry lived on until 1923, but I'm not sure whether he died in the workhouse. It would appear that his quality of life was poor in his later years, for some reason.

Sarah Jane did at least live to see her daughter Mary Jane Nightall marry George Burditt in Sheffield in 1898. The 1901 census shows that Mary Jane and George, a coal carter, were living in Fisher Lane, Attercliffe, Sheffield. By 1911 they had moved to Frederick Street in the Attercliffe area; there were now four children: Alice aged seven, George (six), Hilda (three) and young Mary Jane, aged just eleven months. Sarah Jane Nightall died in 1914 aged 61, so would at least have had, for a short time, the pleasure of seeing her young grandchildren. Her daughter Mary Jane Burditt survived to the respectable age of 72. Her youngest son, Tom Nightall, appears not to have married and died in Sheffield in 1959, aged 65. Whoever cleared the house after the death of Henry Nightall in 1923 - it may have been Tom Nightall or Mary Jane Burditt - probably found some letters from Sarah Jane's brothers and sisters in America: as they all seem to have been able to read and write they presumably kept in touch. The letters would be fascinating to read now, but I doubt whether they have survived. It may well be that there are some descendants of Sarah Jane Nightall, nee Whitfield still alive in the Sheffield area, as some of her grandchildren married.

Jonathan Whitfield, the youngest child of Jonathan and Jane Whitfield of Manea, was living in Littleport, Cambridgeshire, in 1881, as we have seen. He was fifteen years old. However, in the 1891 census he was found living in Sheffield with his older brother David in Dorking Street, Sheffield; they clearly had kept in touch. I have no idea when Jonathan made the journey to Yorkshire - it could have been at any time between these two dates. By 1891, Jonathan was working as a carter. Most of his brothers had also worked as carters (or 'teamsters') at some stage in their working lives: Henry, George, David, and now Jonathan. I suspect that their other brother, William may also have done so, but have no evidence for this.

Jonathan married Sarah Padget in 1892 in Sheffield (this marriage, you may remember helped me to locate the whereabouts of this branch of the family). A study of an old street map of Sheffield showed me that Jonathan, his brother David, his sister Sarah Jane and their respective families all lived in the same district of the city, within easy walking distance of each other and close to an iron works. I suspect that most of the men and boys in the family worked there at some time in their working lives. Thanks to the 1881 census, I was able to discover further interesting details relating to Sarah Padget. She was born in 1871 in Littleport, Cambridgeshire, where Jonathan had once lived; and while still a child had come to Sheffield with her parents John and Harriet. Her father was described as a general carter. You will probably recall that David Whitfield, also a carter, had in the previous year married a carter's daughter, Naomi Ellingham. Naomi's father was called Paget Ellingham, suggesting some earlier connection by marriage of the Padget and Ellingham families. But the connections (or coincidences) didn't end there: I was amazed to find that in 1881 the Padget family, (Jonathan's future in-laws), were living *next door* to *David* Whitfield, his wife Naomi and his little daughter Annie in Sorby Street, in the Brightside Bierlow area of Sheffield. I have not managed to discover whether Jonathan first met Sarah in Sheffield or in Littleport. If they had first fallen in love in Littleport then Jonathan had an additional incentive to migrate to Sheffield rather than joining other members of his family in Ohio, though I have to admit it would have been a childhood infatuation at this stage.

Jonathan *may* have changed his job after his marriage. He was described as a labourer at an iron works (presumably the one close to his home) in the 1901 census, and was living in

Dorking Street. Weighing up this evidence, I couldn't rule out the possibility that this really meant that he was working as a carter at the iron works; in the days before fork lift trucks there would have been plenty of raw materials and finished products to move around on the premises.

The children of Jonathan and Sarah Whitfield were: Harry, b.1893, Ruth, b.1894, Frank, b.1895, Fred, b.1898, Ada, b.1902, George, b.1903, and Harriet, b.1904. Unlike David's branch, I have been able to make contact with some of their descendants. One of Jonathan's granddaughters told me that her grandfather used to work for a haulage firm called Cope Brothers of Sheffield. This firm was involved with haulage within steelworks, and it was Jonathan's job to look after the horses. As I speculated with his brother David, this may well have been a job which Jonathan originally learnt to do on a fenland farm in his youth. According to his daughter, Ada, Jonathan also used to help people move house, using his horse and cart. This was possibly a side-line business after his work for Cope Brothers was over. The horses seemed enormous to Ada - she had to 'do the splits' to sit on them. One of Jonathan's granddaughters, Joan Martin, nee Whitfield told me that her grandfather used to bring all the money from Cope Brothers home at night before pay day and sleep on it, so that it was safe overnight and ready for distribution the next morning. Obviously he was a man to be trusted, but why it was necessary to give him this responsibility it is difficult to say.

I have just one photograph where Jonathan appears. Aged probably between sixty and seventy, he is standing at the back of a group of people at a family wedding. The photograph shows that he was slim in build; he had a full head of white hair and a white moustache, and looked very much like my grandfather, Ernest Whitfield. Unfortunately most of his family photographs were destroyed or lost when Jonathan and Sarah's house suffered bomb damage in the Second World War, during the Sheffield Blitz.

Sheffield, being one of England's leading cities and a major centre for the production of armaments, was a target for bombing by the Luftwaffe on the nights of 12th and 15th December, 1940. Both nights were cold and clear, giving good visibility for the German airmen. During the Sheffield blitz, more than 660 lives were lost and many buildings were destroyed. Documents captured after the war ended revealed that the Luftwaffe targets had been the iron and steel works and it is easy to understand why they had been chosen. The Vickers works in Sheffield had the only drop hammer in the country capable of forging crankshafts for the Rolls Royce Merlin engine which powered the Spitfire fighting planes and the Hawker Hurricane bombers. Hadfield's steelworks in Sheffield was the only place in the U.K. at the time where eighteen inch armour-piercing shells were being made. Most of the factories producing armaments were located in East Sheffield, beside the River Don. I'm not sure whether Jonathan and Sarah's house was completely destroyed during the Blitz, but family photographs were lost. It is possible that the Jonathan and Sarah had vacated the house at the time - they would have been in their early seventies, and it must have been a very worrying time for them. Jonathan survived the Sheffield Blitz, but didn't live to see the end of the war. He died in 1944, aged about seventy eight.

Harry Whitfield, the oldest son of Jonathan and Sarah, b1893, married Sarah Ann Kelsey in 1917. They had three children, Harry, b.1919, who died in the same year, Joan, b1924, who responded to my letter in the *Sheffield Star* in the 1980s, and Mavis, b.1934. Harry (senior) started working for a firm as an office boy (he is described as a clerk in the 1911 census) and finished his career with the same firm as chief accountant. He died on Christmas Day, 1969. Joan married Stuart Martin in 1953, and they had one son, John, b.1955, who is now married and has a daughter, Gabrielle. Mavis married Ronald Ellis in Sheffield in 1959.

The next child of Jonathan and Sarah was Ruth, b.1894. Ruth apparently didn't marry and was not of a very robust constitution. She looks painfully thin in the photograph I have of her. The 1911 census records that she was working as a domestic servant. She died in Sheffield in 1936, aged 42.

Frank, the next son, was born and died in 1895.

His younger brother, Fred, was born in 1898. The 1911 census shows that he had left school and was working as an errand boy for a fishmonger. I have no idea how long this job lasted, but of course life for everyone was disrupted three years later by the outbreak of war. I found details of Fred on the ancestry website in the military section. His army enlistment papers have survived, although they were in very poor condition for some reason. I managed to discover that Fred lived in Sorby Street, Sheffield, and his father was Jonathan Whitfield - this confirmed that I had found the correct person. I was amazed to discover how *tiny* Fred was: his height was just under 4 feet 11 inches, and he weighed 110lb (7 stone 12lb). His chest measurement was 31-33 inches. Despite these vital statistics, the papers claimed that his physical development was 'good'. His medical history revealed that he had spent eighteen days in hospital with impetigo - it must have been a severe attack. It isn't clear whether he was involved in any front line fighting. With his physique, life in the army must have seemed like hell, even if he was away from the action. He survived the war, but died in Sheffield in 1922, aged 24.

Ada, the next child of Jonathan and Sarah was born in 1902. Ada married Herbert Kelsey (brother of Harry Whitfield's wife, Sarah Ann Kelsey), another example of a double alliance between families. They were married at Burngreave Methodist Church in Sheffield in 1927; Ada was a Methodist and Herbert was a Quaker. After their marriage they lived in Roe Lane in Sheffield. Their daughter, Margaret Kelsey was born in 1935. Their house had its front windows blown out by a bomb during the Second World War, but thankfully sustained no further damage. Herbert Kelsey was an engineer and worked for the British Oxygen Company in Erinsworth for forty years. He was involved in the development of an oxyacetylene cutter, and also worked on improving tank tracks during the Second World War. Margaret Kelsey married Charles Brian Goddard in 1965, and they had two children: Jonathan Charles Goddard, b.1969, and Sarah Margaret Goddard, b.1971. Jonathan Goddard studied Medicine at London University and is now an urologist, working at Leicester General Hospital. He has published various papers on gender reassignment and is also interested in the history of medicine and genealogy. He married Kerenza Louise Hannaford in 2001 and they have a daughter, Harriet Poppy Hannaford Goddard, b.2007.

It was thanks to Jonathan and his mother Margaret that I was able to trace the American branches of the family: Jonathan discovered a letter I had written to Mrs Goddard in 1986 when he was sorting through some family papers in 2007, following the death of his father. As mentioned earlier, the letter prompted his mother to remember the Barco surname which was to provide me with a vital clue in my search for Henry Whitfield and his brothers and sisters.

George Whitfield, b.1903, was the youngest son of Jonathan and Sarah Whitfield. He married Florence Aizlewood in 1933. They had a son, John, who died young and a daughter, Elaine, b.1942. Elaine married Gordon Baker in 1968 who died in 1995. There were no children. George used to return to the Manea district for holidays with relatives, presumably on his mother's side: he used to enjoy fishing in the Fenland waterways near March with his brother-in-law, Herbert Kelsey.

The youngest child of Jonathan and Sarah Whitfield was Harriet, b.1904, and named after Sarah's mother. She married Charles Kent in Sheffield in 1936. The couple had one son, Peter Charles Kent. Peter Kent served in the Royal Air Force and then worked as an electronics technician. He married Janet Blackwell in Scarborough in 1963, and they emigrated to Australia in 1965, setting up home in Carnarvon. Their three children, Sarah, Susan and Martin were born in 1967, 1970 and 1971 respectively. All three have married and have children of their own. Peter has now retired and is able to spend time with his grandchildren.

I have been writing this chapter about half a mile from where Jonathan Whitfield, born in 1825 in Tewin, would have been living about 175 years ago. I feel sure that as he travelled towards Manea in search of work he would have been amazed if someone had met him and predicted that by the year 2000 his descendants would be scattered over three continents. His branch of the family took me over thirty years to trace, but it was a fascinating experience. To complete this survey of the Whitfield family we now need to return to David, the youngest son of James Whitfield, the gamekeeper of Tewin and his wife, Sarah.

Note: Since this chapter was written, I have managed to find details of a marriage which took place in Cuyahoga County, Ohio, USA, in December, 1891: Hannah Gibson married Silas J. Robinson. (You will remember that Hannah, the mother-in-law of Henry Whitfield, had migrated to the Cleveland area with George and Naomi Whitfield in October, 1880, after her husband, William Gibson, had died). This explained why Henry's mother-in-law was described as Hannah Robinson, widow, in the 1900 census, referred to on page 258. It is likely that Silas was also elderly at the time of the marriage, which appears not to have lasted long. Hannah Robinson, formerly Gibson, died at Rocky River, Ohio, USA, in 1907, aged 85.

Chapter 12:
Big brother helps little brother: the line from David Whitfield, b.1830.

'Life is mostly froth and bubble
Two things stand alone
Kindness in another's trouble
Courage in your own'

Adam Lindsay Gordon (1833-1870) *Ye Wearie Wayfarer.*

'....And forgive us our trespasses.......'

From *The Lord's Prayer*

David Whitfield was baptised in Tewin in 1830 with his brother Henry, who may well have been his twin. Unfortunately, Henry died soon afterwards, although it is *David's* name that appears in the burial register. As David's name is found in several later records and Henry's is not, I have assumed that the vicar of Tewin, or his churchwarden or parish clerk, made a mistake when completing the register. Henry's grieving parents, James and Sarah, would not have spotted this as they were both illiterate, and in any case were probably not shown the register. You will remember that David was brought to Potton with his mother and some of his brothers in 1833, following the death of his father, James, who was about sixty years old when David was born. David presumably lived with his mother, Sarah until *her* death in January, 1841. He would probably have had only hazy memories of his father, but he would obviously have remembered his mother very well. She had probably been in declining health for some time. Orphaned at the age of ten, David would have had to grow up very quickly. I would imagine that his childhood and adolescence were somewhat unsettled - even bewildering - at times.

In the 1841 census he was living in Horslow Street, Potton, not with his older brother Robert, who was lodging at a separate address in the same street, but with another family: John Parker, aged 60 and his wife Esther, aged 50. There was also another lodger, Gardner Ellis, aged 35. It must have seemed strange to David to be a part of a different household, but opefully reassuring to know that his brother Robert was not too far away. They probably saw each other each day. His older brother Philip was away in Oxfordshire and was to be married later in the month; his brother William was working in Manea, and his brother James, who normally lived in Potton had travelled down towards London with some friends in search of work. David may not have known where his brother George was when the census enumerator called on Mr and Mrs Parker. I am not certain either, but as we have seen in a previous chapter, he appears to have been in Warwickshire.

Within a few years David's brothers would marry and have families of their own. I assume that one of them must have kept an eye on his younger brother, possibly allowing him a roof over his head as well as food and some emotional support during his teenage years. It may be that David lived with a number of them in turn over the next ten years or so; unfortunately the next census wasn't taken until 1851, and so I can only speculate about what happened. If they had been taken *every* year I would imagine an interesting story would emerge, in terms of where David was living and what he was doing to earn some sort of living. It appears that he kept in touch with his oldest brother, Philip. Both of them could write and I presume they could also read. It is a pity that no letters from Philip or David have so far come to light, but I think there must have been some. I doubt whether Philip could have spared the time away from his bakery to travel to Potton very often - if at all. Nevertheless, I think that the Potton and Hook Norton branches of the family may well have kept in touch in some way, possibly until the deaths of David and Philip. The selection of the Christian names of the first two sons of my great grandfather, William Whitfield and his wife Emma: (David and Philip) suggests that they were named after the two brothers who had settled in Oxfordshire.

By 1851, David had moved to Hook Norton in Oxfordshire and was living with Philip and Elizabeth and their family. He was now 22 years old and working as a carrier. A carrier normally carried people as well as goods. Setting up as a carrier required a more substantial investment than becoming a carter who would often just have an open, two wheeled cart, because in addition to the purchase of at least one horse (often two were used), a *covered* cart, with two or four wheels, or a waggon also had to be provided: if passengers were to be carried they would expect to remain dry during their journey. Some carriers' waggons had a canvas hood, others had a wooden roof. David may have saved the money necessary for the purchase of his horse and waggon; he may have had periods of good earnings from working as a navvy or an itinerant harvester, for instance, but I have no evidence for this. Alternatively, it may be that Philip gave him some financial help.

David may initially have been working for Philip for at least some of the time, probably collecting flour from the mill, yeast from the brewery, thorn faggots from neighbouring farms and then delivering bread, while his brother concentrated on baking. While I was at the Oxfordshire Record Office I looked at some of the Hook Norton parish records to try to find out the sort of work David would have done. I found no evidence there for any *regular* work which he must have undertaken, but did find one interesting snippet of information from the churchwardens' accounts: on 22nd February, 1853, David fetched some new bell ropes - possibly from Banbury - and was paid the princely sum of 6d for his trouble. As bell ropes last fairly well and were probably purchased in bulk but only replaced singly as they wore out or became dangerous, I think we can assume that this job did not come David's way very often; in any case, at 6d a time it was never going to make him the richest man in Hook Norton.

Having consulted the few Hook Norton records available at the Oxford Record Office without much success, I turned to some old County directories to try to find some more details of David's carrying business. The *Post Office Directory* for 1847 mentioned Philip Whitfield, baker, but the carriers listed for Hook Norton were Henry and Robert Bosbery (or Borsberry) and Matthew Wyton. The Bosberys operated from the village to the *Waggon and Horses* in Banbury every Monday, Thursday and Saturday; Matthew Wyton operated between Hook Norton and the *Buck and Bell,* Banbury on the same days, and Robert Bosbery travelled between the village and Chipping Norton every Wednesday. Robert Bosbery was also a coal dealer; it was not unusual to find carriers having another occupation - often the conveyance of goods and passengers developed from their original enterprise: farming and carrying, for instance. I concluded from this information that David had not yet arrived in Hook Norton, but have to admit there remains the possibility that he *was* living with Philip, but had not yet purchased his horse and waggon.

Unfortunately, I was unable to find any directories dealing with the period 1848-1850, but we have already seen, from census information, that David was living in Hook Norton in 1851 and operating as a carrier. I decided to look in old newspapers now available online: perhaps David advertised his services? I was a little surprised by what I found. The young man was clearly not averse to female company at this time - no surprise there, of course - but the *Oxford Journal* of 30th October, 1852 reported that at the Banbury petty sessions

'David Whitfield of Hook Norton was ordered to pay 5s [shillings] for the first six weeks and 2s per week afterwards for the maintenance of the child of Mary Ann Gaskin of Bloxham'.

Bloxham is a village between Banbury and Hook Norton on the main road between Banbury and Chipping Norton. It was almost certainly on David's carrying route. I couldn't find a Mary Ann Gaskin in Bloxham around this date. I did, however, find a Mary Ann *Gascoigne.* She was about the same age as David and was the daughter of a baker, John Gascoigne, and his wife Elizabeth who lived in Grub Street, Bloxham. A Charlotte Ann Gascoigne was born between July and September, 1852, in the Banbury district. Charlotte's birth certificate states that her mother was Mary Ann Gascoigne and no father's name was mentioned, so almost certainly this was the child for whom David was paying maintenance.

In an attempt to discover further details I consulted the *Banbury Guardian* of Thursday, 28th October, 1852. My search proved to be worthwhile. The article I found stated that David Whitfield had been looked upon as Miss Gaskin's suitor, but as soon as she had discovered her pregnancy he had 'discontinued his attentions'. When he had been asked what he intended to do about the situation he had replied that 'he should do nothing unless he was obliged'. The writer of the article used the French word *enceinte* rather than 'pregnant' in describing Miss Gaskin's condition, perhaps in an attempt to save her further embarrassment. I would think that only a small and select number of people would have been able to understand French in Banbury in the mid nineteenth century; for those who needed to look up the word, French-English dictionaries (like the one I used) wouldn't have been too plentiful either. In making the maintenance order, the magistrates had taken David's financial status into account: it was interesting to note that in his early twenties he already owned three carts and two horses, and it seems likely, therefore, that he was already employing someone else to help him with his carrying business.

Unfortunately young Charlotte died in 1858. Her mother, Mary Ann, remained single. She became a dressmaker, and died in 1900. I have no idea why she and David didn't marry (as so many Victorian couples did) after an illegitimate child was conceived.

David is mentioned as a carrier in *Gardner's History, Gazetteer and Directory of Oxfordshire* for 1852, but I managed to find some interesting additional details for 1854. The *Post Office Directory* for that year lists David Whitfield and Robert Bosbery (or Borsberry) operating from Hook Norton to the *Waggon and Horses*, Banbury and Matthew Wyton to the *Buck and Bell*, Banbury every Monday, Thursday and Saturday, and Robert Bosbery and David Whitfield to Chipping Norton every Wednesday. Robert Bosbery was still a coal dealer: I hope he cleaned his waggon carefully before carrying passengers, otherwise if they were not wearing black when they boarded his vehicle they may have been by the time they alighted. Of course, like David, he could have owned more than one waggon.

By 1864, *Kelly's Directory* mentions David as being a carrier to the *Waggon and Horses,* Banbury every Monday, Thursday and Saturday, and to Chipping Norton every Wednesday (presumably market day). The Bosberys are not mentioned; perhaps people tired of having their clothes spoiled. A new competitor had arrived, however: John Tims was offering a service to the *Fox* at Banbury every Monday, Thursday and Saturday. The same directory mentioned that David Whitfield was now also a farmer, though unfortunately it gave no details of the location and extent of his land holding. His carrying business must have thrived; further evidence for this is provided by the 1869 *Kelly's Directory*, which showed that he was now offering a carrier's service to Banbury on *every* weekday except Wednesday, when he travelled to Chipping Norton instead. This was in addition to his farming activities. It is highly probable that he was still employing at least one other man to help him, but there can be little doubt that David was not afraid of work, and he must also have been thrifty to be able to set up as a farmer - a remarkable achievement considering that he had been orphaned at the age of ten. Once again, I wonder if he had any financial help from his brother, Philip. I feel sure that their father James (the gamekeeper) would have been proud of both of them. However, back in Potton, you will recall, their brothers were struggling financially, and in Manea their brother Jonathan had recently died.

Banbury had a population of around 9,000 in 1851 when David is first recorded as working as a carrier in the area; not huge by today's standards, but the town was an important route centre and market town within a very prosperous agricultural area. Dozens of villages lay within a ten mile radius - ideal territory in which carriers' carts could operate. Carriers went to Banbury from every settlement of any significance within ten miles on more than one day a week, and there were weekly services from settlements up to fifteen miles away, although within this zone other large settlements such as Northampton, Coventry, Oxford and Stratford upon Avon began to exert their gravitational pull upon shoppers and traders.

Dr. Barrie Trinder, in his book *'Victorian Banbury'* notes that 'the most important road vehicles servicing Banbury were neither the lumbering waggons nor the speedy stage coaches but the humble carriers' carts which brought in country people and their produce and distributed merchandise from the towns to the agricultural districts'. An observer of Banbury market wrote in 1854: 'some idea may be formed of its commerce by the fact of nearly 300 carriers attending it [i.e. in a day], many of whom visit on two other days in the week'.

The most popular day for carriers to visit Banbury was Thursday - market day. The carrying trade was concentrated at certain public houses. The most popular of these in 1831 were the *Plough* and the *Waggon and Horses*, and we have seen that David Whitfield was using this latter hostelry (in Butchers' Row and a comfortable walk from Banbury Cross) some thirty years later. In early and mid-Victorian times, out-working weavers would come to this pub to collect their raw materials and bring their cloth for examination and approval before being paid. Their cloth would be sent to local dyers and then despatched to London and other markets. A number of butchers used the inn yard which would have been bustling with buyers, sellers, goods – and horses and carriers' carts. With so much money exchanging hands some of it must naturally have been used to purchase pints of beer. David may well have had a drink and some food here before attending to his business in the market.

Banbury was a very busy town in Victorian times, particularly on market days, and carriers were its lifeblood. In addition to carrying passengers they also brought in agricultural produce, particularly dairy products, eggs, fruit and vegetables to shopkeepers and on their return journeys carried goods bought on behalf of customers from Banbury retailers back for distribution in their home villages and en route. They were an integral part of a bigger picture: grain was despatched by canal to Birmingham; barley was sent to brewers in Dudley, and wool to Leicester and Kidderminster. Waggons and vans took butter, pigs, sheep and poultry to the London markets and drovers took cattle from Banbury to Smithfield market. David Whitfield may well have brought some of his farm produce for sale in the market and perhaps some of his brother's bread. He may have had his regular customers waiting for him.

At certain times of year fairs and horse and cattle sales were held. Some hiring of farmworkers took place at the March Fair, and it is possible that Philip had first secured his job with the Bennetts here rather than at the Pudding Pie Fair in Deddington. The Michaelmas Fair was the largest hiring fair in the South Midlands. It attracted farmers, labourers, dealers, showmen, cheapjacks and even less desirable characters from all over England. Apparently such crowds of grooms, waggoners, dairymen and shepherds waited to be hired in the Market Place that shop windows had to be boarded up in case they were damaged. Wool was sold in Banbury in July and fat cattle in December. With all this bustling activity it was little wonder that Banbury became known as the metropolis of the carriers' carts. In 1860, the *Banbury Advertiser* commented on the large number of carriers plying their trade in the town and wondered whether other towns of a similar size had such a service. The article estimated that 167 carriers made a total of 395 journeys between them to Banbury; it seems to me that they must have done a survey to obtain such a precise figure. The carriers' carts were not even ousted by the railway; they presumably acted as a sort of feeder service like taxis would today. Their numbers *did* decline, however, as lorries and cars became more numerous in the 1920s, particularly as the latter provided a door to door service. A visitor to Banbury today will notice the numerous taxis which operate from the centre of the town, so in a sense the carrying tradition continues.

David Whitfield in his capacity as a carrier would have been well known in Hook Norton, but also in Banbury and Chipping Norton. He may not have needed to advertise his services beyond an appearance from time to time in local directories. He must have *usually* been considered a reliable and trustworthy person as he was dealing with people and their property. However, it was suspected in 1860 that he had been operating as a carrier without a licence. Apparently the excise officers had sent one of their men, Henry Perkins, to investigate this, by posing as a customer. Perkins, a young man in his mid-twenties, probably ambitious and anxious to follow the instructions he had been given - to the letter - had travelled with David to Hook Norton, on Thursday 30th August, 1860, having been picked up somewhere along the Banbury to Hook Norton Road, presumably not far from Hook Norton, as he was only charged 9d. The van or waggon was already carrying some passengers (Eliza Goodwin, a servant aged 28 and Emily Jane Crow, aged 18, the daughter of a retired wine merchant) on its return journey from the market at Banbury, so it had already been hired when Perkins boarded the vehicle. The *Oxford Journal* of 22nd December 1860 stated that he had booked his return journey to Banbury railway station for early the following morning, but didn't give precise details how and when this had been arranged. On the return journey Perkins was charged five shillings plus sixpence for the charge at the toll gate.

The case came up before the magistrates at Banbury on 21st December 1860; apparently the matter had been adjourned from a previous hearing. You will probably be as amused as I was to learn that Perkins had to share the carrier's van with a *pig* on his journey back to Banbury, so he may not have been smelling of roses when he boarded his train. The case had 'excited a very great degree of interest, and caused the council chamber….to be visited by a much greater number of anxious listeners than are usually to be found within its precincts'. I wasn't surprised to learn that there was laughter in the public gallery when details of the excise officer's fellow passenger were revealed and would have loved to have seen Henry Perkins' face at that moment: everyone must have been looking at him as he squirmed with embarrassment.

The *Banbury Guardian* and *Banbury Advertiser* both reported the case and gave further interesting information. It appears that Perkins, when asked if he would mind sharing the cart with a pig had expressed the hope that the animal wouldn't *eat* him. David had reassured him that the pig wouldn't do him any harm because it was *dead*. John Gardner, the landlord of the *Bell* public house in Hook Norton, appearing as a witness, recalled the conversation about the pig which had presumably taken place on his premises; Perkins, possibly in a forlorn attempt to save further discomfiture, couldn't recall making the remark attributed to him. David claimed, unsuccessfully, that he had been doing Perkins a favour, because the van had already been hired by the pig's owner, John Woolgrove, and, technically, not by Perkins himself.

David had been asked to convey six pigs to a Mrs Powell of Banbury, one every Friday for six weeks. He had intended to start his journey with one of the pigs between nine and ten o'clock on the Friday morning, but Henry Perkins, after smoking a cigar at the *Bell* where presumably he had been dropped by the carrier on Thursday night, had later called at David's lodgings specifically to book his return journey for the morning, stressing that he wanted to be at Banbury railway station for eight o'clock. David had replied that in that case they needed to leave Hook Norton at *six* o'clock because he wasn't allowed to travel at more than four miles an hour (Hook Norton is about eight miles from Banbury). It appears that if he exceeded four miles an hour he needed a licence. Postmasters needed such a licence, but there was no postmaster at Hook Norton at this time. The reason for the excise officer being charged over five shillings for the return journey became understandable: he was committing David to an early start and having little chance of being booked by other passengers that morning.

Someone else called at David's house on the Thursday night and overheard the conversation between the carrier and the wily, over-zealous excise man. Decimus Morton Hassam, a tailor, was calling to ask David to play for the Hook Norton cricket team and ironically going to suggest (or so he claimed in court) that David should send his man on the journey with the pig. Having just made the arrangement with Perkins, David had presumably thought it advisable to keep to his word. In retrospect, of course, a substitute would have saved him a lot of trouble.

John Gardner stated that David had accordingly arrived at the *Bell* at five minutes to six on the next morning to pick up Perkins who had presumably stayed there overnight. I reckon that this public house which had a central position within the village, fairly close to the parish church, may well have been David's regular departure point, although he clearly also picked up passengers en route for Banbury or Chipping Norton. The pig destined for Mrs Powell had not yet been loaded onto the cart. Perkins claimed they left the village at a quarter past six. I suspect it may not have taken twenty minutes to load a dead pig onto a carrier's van. (Incidentally, a search of the 1861 census for Banbury showed me that a widow, Elizabeth Powell, was living in the High Street and working as a pastry cook and provision merchant; ten years earlier she had been described as an eating house proprietor.) I reckon that a significant proportion of each of those six pigs ended up in home-made pork pies - a subject bringing me conveniently back to the court case, where the magistrates also began to suspect that Mr Henry Perkins was being a little economical with the truth and appeared to have a rather selective memory.

Perkins finally admitted in court that he was trying to catch David travelling at more than four miles an hour and he had had no other reason for visiting Hook Norton. (He had previously maintained that he was there to 'meet a gentleman'). He claimed that the young carrier had indeed exceeded the speed limit. The magistrates were not at all impressed with the underhand tactics employed by the excise officer and it was argued that in requesting an early start David had been aware of the necessity of proceeding at a leisurely pace. However, after due consideration, David was convicted of the offence of operating without a licence; in an earlier hearing a fine of £100 had been suggested, but he had appealed against this and consequently a mitigated fine of £25 was imposed.

The editor of the *Banbury Advertiser* still clearly thought *any* fine was outrageous. He considered that Perkins had taken advantage of David's obliging nature and had sought to entrap him. The editor appealed to readers of his newspaper to help pay the carrier's fine but I'm not sure what sort of response was elicited. It would be satisfying to know that some of David's friends and regular customers made some sort of contribution. Even if little money was collected it may be that he enjoyed some free pork pies for a while, or a few drinks on the house at the *Bell* and the *Waggon and Horses*.

It's often satisfying to follow up a story, and in this case I couldn't resist the temptation. Forgive my cynicism, but the qualities shown in court by Mr Perkins suggested to me that he might later have been tempted to become a Member of Parliament, but later census returns showed that he continued to work as an excise officer for the Inland Revenue, where his efforts were hopefully appreciated: I suppose both occupations are held in similar esteem by many members of the public at present. If questioned later about the Hook Norton case he would probably have argued that he was simply following instructions from his superiors. I doubt if he ever saw David Whitfield again, and he may well have avoided setting foot in Hook Norton, at least for a while. Henry Perkins' marriage to Jane Lett was registered in Worcester in the spring of 1861; he subsequently worked for periods in Scotland and Ireland, before returning first to Gloucestershire and then to his home county of Worcestershire, where he retired. He died in Hertfordshire in 1917, leaving an estate of about £770. His executor was a spinster daughter, Lizzie Lett Perkins: her middle name confirmed that I had found the correct person.

David Whitfield had more luck in a later court case: on 12th June, 1867 he successfully brought an action against Thomas Beale for an unpaid charge of 8s 6d made for the carriage of Beale's fiancé and her luggage from Hook Norton to Banbury before her marriage. Few additional details were given in the *Oxford Journal* of 15th June, but a little research showed me that Thomas Beale was an agricultural labourer, who had married Hannah Hall on 27th April, 1867. Hannah was a domestic servant and the daughter of another Hook Norton agricultural labourer, James Hall and his wife Elizabeth, nee Borsberry. The charges made show that David was making good money as a carrier, although he clearly had a number of expenses to consider: food for his horses, farriers' bills, maintenance of his carts and wages for any employees come readily to mind. Farm labourers of the period would probably have been earning, at most, about fifteen shillings a week.

Some labourers could have been a little jealous of David's success. I found that two of them, John Borsberry and Henry Nash, assaulted him in January, 1866. The assault took place at the *Bell* public house in Hook Norton. David took them to court, where the case was dismissed after the labourers had been made to pay David's (and presumably the court's) costs. The reason for the assault and the extent of David's injuries were not specified, but I was interested to note that a member of the Borsberry family was involved. John *Borsberry* was indeed a labourer, but he may have been related to the Robert Bosberry or Borsberry, a rival carrier in Hook Norton. The case was mentioned briefly in the *Oxford Journal* of Saturday 3rd March, 1866. I searched for it in the *Banbury Advertiser* and the *Banbury Guardian* without success. However, the *Oxford Chronicle* of 24th February, 1866 gave some additional detail: apparently the nature of the assault was that Nash and Borsberry had 'put their fists into David's face and used threatening and abusive language'. It would be interesting to know what David had done to provoke such behaviour.

These instances of controversy appear to have been few and far between, however; and for most of the time for David it would have been 'business as usual'. He and his brother Philip and his nephew Philip Henry would have come into contact with a large number of people in Banbury and district through their various business interests. David, in particular, would have been a familiar figure in the streets and possibly the pubs of Banbury as he and his horse would have been in need of refreshment, and his customers may have met him at the *Waggon and Horses* for the return journey.

It is possible that David met his future wife, Ann Summerton, while he was travelling. She may have been one of his passengers at some time. Ann was a widow and the daughter of John Golding or Golden, a farmer. In the 1861 census, John Golding was farming 130 acres at Windmill Farm in Oxhill, Warwickshire. Ann had been born in Deddington in Oxfordshire but had been brought up in Oxhill. She had married a blacksmith, Thomas Summerton in 1850, and the 1851 census shows that they had a son, William Summerton, aged ten months. The Warwickshire parish registers became available online in October, 2011 and I discovered further details of their growing family. John Henry Summerton, their second son, was baptised in April, 1853. Their happiness was to be short-lived because young William Summerton's burial appears in the Oxhill register in June, 1855. The register gives his age as five years and makes it clear that the family were living at Pillerton, although it isn't clear whether this was Pillerton Hersey or Pillerton Priors. John Henry Summerton also died in infancy: his burial is recorded in September, 1856. At about this time, Ann gave birth to a daughter, Harriet, who was baptised in November, 1856. Ann must have been on an emotional roller coaster at this ceremony, but the tragedies were to continue: young Harriet died aged three in 1859, and two years later, Ann's husband Thomas also died - in January, 1861: he was only 33. Ann, having married and produced three children was now a childless widow. It must have made her realise how precious life is and how fragile it can be.

I haven't been able to discover when she first met David Whitfield. David and Ann married on 30th October, 1866 in the beautiful small parish church of Pillerton Hersey in South Warwickshire. Both were 37 years old. David's occupation was given as 'carrier', although he had also started farming, as we have seen from the 1864 *Kelly's Directory*. His father's name and occupation (James Whitfield, gamekeeper) confirmed that I had found the correct David Whitfield. Ann was a dressmaker at the time of her marriage. Both bride and groom signed the marriage register, so despite his rather unsettled upbringing, David had learnt to write. He would have found this skill invaluable, for apart from anything else, his carrying and farming businesses would probably have involved him in a certain amount of record keeping. He had certainly learnt to count and save his money. Like certain other members of the family he appears to have been very much his own man and not at all in awe of authority figures. I still keep hoping that some of his records - possibly farm accounts or pocket books listing passengers, goods carried and fares paid - will turn up. It would be fascinating to read them. A diary would be even better: I would love to read what he thought of Henry Perkins, the excise officer, although I can hazard a guess.

David and Ann's son, David, junior, was born in 1868. He was, of course, Ann's fourth, but only surviving child and I would imagine that he was nurtured with great care. (I wonder if Ann was aware of her husband's youthful indiscretion.) Incidentally, it appears that David (senior) was still playing for Hook Norton's cricket team on occasions. The *Oxford Journal* of Saturday 11th July, 1868 records that he scored 2 and 1 not out in their victory against Adderbury, batting at number eleven; I assume from this that he was a bowler, but unfortunately the bowling figures were not given. Perhaps the main reason for his inclusion was to help with transport to away matches. I haven't bothered to look him up in *Wisden*, the cricket enthusiast's 'bible', first published in 1864, which gives the batting and bowling statistics of famous players.

The 1871 census shows that David, Ann and young David were living in a house near the Baptist minister's residence in Hook Norton.

A return of owners of land was made in Oxfordshire in 1873. It mentions that David Whitfield owned 32 acres 3 roods and 14 poles (nearly 33 acres) in Hook Norton, but unfortunately gives no indication of where this landholding was within the parish. It may have been at, or near, Duckpool Farm, south of the built up area of the village itself. David was certainly farming here by 1877, according to an old directory. It is likely that this was a small dairy or mixed stock farm, although as yet I have little evidence for this: it was in a prosperous mixed farming area. The *Oxford Journal* of Saturday, 10th August, 1878 recorded a sale of ewes and shearling rams of the Oxfordshire Down breed which took place on 2nd August of that year at the farm of Mr A. Brassey in Heythrop, near Chipping Norton. Mr Brassey had won many prizes with his sheep, which consequently were much sought after. Around two hundred people attended this sale and David Whitfield was one of them. He purchased some rams (the number wasn't stated) for seven guineas, and hopefully also enjoyed the luncheon, with numerous toasts to Mr Brassey, which took place in a marquee.

I had assumed that Mr Brassey was a farmer with an interest in sheep breeding - a countryman with local roots. I was wrong, and I hope you will forgive a short digression. Albert Brassey's father was an extremely wealthy man, Thomas Brassey, who had been a railway contractor and an acquaintance of George Stephenson (1781-1848), the famous railway engineer. Thomas Brassey had overseen railway building projects all over the world, and had left a fortune of over *£3million* when he died in December,1870. Albert Brassey was born in France in 1844 when his father had been overseeing the building of the Paris and Rouen railway. Educated at Eton and Oxford University where he had excelled at rowing, Albert had later become a Lieutenant in the 14th Hussars and the Queen's Own Hussars. In 1878, when the sale of sheep took place on his estate he was High Sheriff of Oxfordshire, and was clearly a very wealthy and influential man. Although he was his father's fourth son, I would imagine that he had inherited a sizeable sum in 1871 after Thomas Brassey's will had been proved, and was thus able to indulge in an interesting and profitable hobby like breeding Oxfordshire Down sheep. The 1881 census shows that he kept a veritable tribe of servants to minister to his needs at Heythrop Hall: thirteen men worked in his stables and there were eight gardeners; his indoor staff included a butler, under butler, a groom, an 'odd man' (!) a hall boy and thirteen maids. He also had a residence in Berkeley Square, London, a highly sought after location in the West End of the capital. Brassey was Master of the Heythrop Hunt for many years and became MP for Banbury in 1895, a seat he held until 1906. G.T.Hutchinson, the author of a book in 1935 on the Heythrop Hunt considered that Brassey was…'.devoted to sport…capable and energetic, and was blessed with a natural kindness of heart and genial manner which gained universal popularity'. The local foxes might not have shared Hutchinson's view, of course. (The Heythrop Hunt is the current Prime Minister's local hunt, and he has joined it on occasions before fox hunting was made illegal in 2005).The 1911 census showed some evidence of retrenchment in the Brassey household: his retinue of servants had been reduced to just 23. Despite his lack of an MP's income from 1906 he was managing to live on his own means. He died in 1918, leaving an estate of £992, 473 16s 5d. It is perhaps a little superfluous to add that his political persuasion had been Conservative.

David Whitfield probably didn't come into direct contact with Mr Brassey, but he was mixing with many local farmers, stock breeders and landowners; and although he was not in Brassey's league financially or socially he had clearly come a long way from his unhappy, poverty-stricken early life in Tewin and Potton. He was clearly in a position to be able to enjoy a little leisure time and to invest in his farm. The Oxfordshire Down breed of sheep have dark faces and woolly white fleeces; they are a large breed, developed for both meat and wool and the rams can apparently weigh over 300lb. I assume that David had purchased the rams with a view to improving his own stock of sheep in the future at Duckpool Farm.

Unfortunately, David was not able to derive any benefit from his newly-purchased livestock. He died less than three weeks later - on 22nd August, 1878. I wondered if it was due to a farming accident or perhaps he had over-exerted himself in the harvest field. I speculated about the possibility of suicide: perhaps his farming business was getting into financial difficulties and he couldn't cope. My curiosity got the better of me and I sent for the death certificate. I was shocked to see that David had died from 'dilatation of heart, oedema of lungs and bronchitis'. It looks as though he had been ill for some time, but these symptoms of heart failure I had associated with much older people. Indeed, my father had suffered from these distressing symptoms before *he* died - but he was in his mid-eighties. The person informing the registrar of David's death was his older brother, Philip. It was touching to read on the certificate that Philip had been with David when he died: the two brothers had stayed together until the end. Their bodily remains are now at rest in Hook Norton churchyard - within a few feet of each other - which seems to be a fitting and enduring tribute to their life-long friendship.

You will remember that David's brother, Jonathan, had died from a 'diseased heart' at an even younger age (42) at Manea about ten years previously, and their mother, Sarah, had died from 'dropsy' (which implies heart disease to me) at the age of 48 in 1841. Had the brothers inherited a susceptibility to heart disease? I am not a medical expert, but I noted in a newspaper recently that doctors are taking an interest in people's family histories when assessing an individual's likelihood of suffering from certain serious diseases, like heart disease, cancer, multiple sclerosis and Parkinson's disease. Genealogists may be able to supply detailed information to their doctors about how their ancestors have died, over several generations thanks to the information given on death certificates since 1837.

David's symptoms suggest to me that he had been in failing health for some months, if not longer, and it is therefore somewhat surprising that he didn't make a will, particularly as he had property to leave. Instead, letters of administration were granted to his widow, Ann. The value of David's estate was rather unhelpfully given as 'under £1,000'. (It must be remembered, of course, that £1,000 was worth a lot more than it is today; to put this sum into some sort of context remember that James Luckett bought the 29 acres of land that Philip Henry Whitfield had been farming for £450 in 1875).

The form giving Ann the right to administer David's estate mentions that sureties were given by Thomas Golding of Hook Norton, and William Henry Golding of Swerford. Both men were farmers and were presumably Ann's relatives. William Henry Golding farmed 150 acres, employing three men and one boy and Thomas Golding employed two men and one boy to run his farm of 104 acres. I'm not entirely sure why they had to act in this way; I presume it was to ensure that Ann administered her late husband's estate with honesty and diligence, so that the financial future of David Whitfield, junior, was safeguarded. If this was the case, it would appear that these men had been chosen with care. As practical farmers, they would be well qualified to oversee the daily running of Duckpool Farm until David was able to manage it himself. As Ann was from a farming family she may well have been fairly used to agricultural matters herself, but she must have been grateful for the advice and practical help she probably received. She had now lost two husbands as well as three children and it must have taken a lot of courage and determination from her to attend to household tasks and keep the farm going at such a desperately unhappy time.

The 1881 census shows that Ann, aged 49 was still living at Duckpool Farm, with her son David, now aged 13 and Henry Wyton, an agricultural labourer. Her father, John Golding, aged 85 and now retired from farming, was also living at the farm; his presence and his farming experience probably provided Ann with some reassurance during the first few years following David's death, but he died in 1882. As we have seen, the late 1870s and early 1880s were difficult for farmers, experienced or otherwise. All sorts of factors beyond their control were at work. The 1881 census states that Duckpool Farm comprised 125 acres, and Ann was employing one man and one boy. Presumably the man was Henry Wyton and the boy was young David Whitfield.It is fairly safe to assume that Ann was also undertaking practical work on the farm.

It isn't clear how long Ann and David stayed at Duckpool Farm, but it is perhaps significant that Ann (or her landlord) asked for reports and valuations to be undertaken in 1881 and 1885 at *Southrop* Farm, which suggests that they may have taken on the tenancy of a nearby farm after David's death. The valuation reports, now at the Warwickshire Record Office, make it clear that about twelve acres of the farm's land had already been sold to the Banbury and Cheltenham railway company, although the railway station at Hook Norton did not open until 1887 (the year of Philip Whitfield's death). The 1885 report also mentions that a further 38 acres had been sold, but unfortunately does not specify whether Ann Whitfield owned some of this land - or the land sold to the railway earlier; if any of the land did belong to her, the capital sum released may have eased the financial pressure in this difficult period. The farm had thus been reduced in size from over 161 acres to about 111 acres. Ann was paying rent of £250 per year to her landlord and a yearly tithe (payment to the church) of £5. The reports mention that rich deposits of ironstone had been found underneath some of the remaining arable land, and in all likelihood Ann's landlord was probably contemplating selling the farm to the Brymbo Ironworks Company which eventually started quarrying ironstone in Hook Norton in 1899. It is likely that land had become more valuable in the locality. With the coming of the railway and, later, the ironworks, the village was no longer a rural backwater in late Victorian and Edwardian times.

Both enterprises have long since ceased to operate in Hook Norton after it became cheaper to import higher-grade iron ore and process it in large industrial centres or in modern coastal iron and steel works. The former course of the railway through the parish is still shown on Ordnance Survey maps; and although the problems presented by the hilly terrain in its construction remain of interest to the geographer and the industrial archaeologist, Hook Norton's modern economic enterprises are again mainly based on farming and brewing. After an industrial interlude lasting about fifty years the village has successfully regained its essentially rural character.

Ann and David moved between 1885 and 1888 to Barton on the Heath, Warwickshire, a small settlement in beautiful undulating countryside some eight miles west of Hook Norton. *Kelly's Directory* for 1888 lists Ann Whitfield as a Barton farmer. The reasons for leaving Duckpool Farm and for selecting their new farm, Barton Hill House, are not entirely clear, but it may well be that their Hook Norton landlord had struck a deal with the Brymbo Ironstone Company and had given them notice to quit. Barton Hill House, as its name implies, is perched at the summit of a steep hill overlooking the village from the south: a picturesque rather than a convenient location.

Both Ann and David (now aged 23), were described as farmers in the 1891 census for Barton on the Heath. They were employing two young servants: John Hayward, aged seventeen and Florence Bartlett, aged fourteen. The fact that Florence worked in the house suggests that Ann was more concerned with farming than she was with housework: it looks as if both she and David were busy getting their hands dirty. Ann had done well to keep farming during the difficult years following her husband's death, and it looks as though her son had also played his part. It may be that they also received some financial assistance when John Golding died. I have searched in vain for a will.

Another young farmer in Barton on the Heath in 1891 was William Smith Taylor, aged 28. He came from a farming family: his father, Oliver Taylor had been at Glyme Farm, outside Chipping Norton, but had been born in Churchill, Oxfordshire, where *his* father, Thomas Taylor, had also been a farmer. William Smith Taylor's full name and his father's birthplace suggest to me that the Taylor family may have been connected to the family of William Smith (1769-1839), also born in Churchill, who became known as the Father of British Geology. Smith produced the first geological map of England and Wales having acquired a great practical knowledge of rocks and their fossils while he was acting as a consultant to canal and mining companies. Although he was the son of a blacksmith he came from farming stock which strengthens my suspicion that the Smith and Taylor families *may* have been connected, but I have no firm evidence as yet.

William Smith Taylor had a sister, Ethel Laura Taylor, some seven years his junior. I assume that David Whitfield must have known William Taylor as a fellow farmer in what is still a very small parish; I would think that everyone in Barton on the Heath knew everyone else. It is likely that David first met Ethel through William.

The couple married in 1893. They had nine children: William David, b.1894, Laura Ann, b.1895, Albert Philip, b.1897, John Oliver, b.1899, Frederick, b.1901, Mary, b.1902, Eleanor Kate, b.1905, Richard Edwin, b.1909, and Gertrude Dorothy, b.1914.

Ann Whitfield died on the 31st December, 1894, aged about 65. She had worked hard in far from ideal circumstances to maintain and no doubt encourage her son in farming. She had lived long enough to see him established as a farmer in Barton on the Heath with a wife and young son to carry on the family name and the farming tradition.

I had assumed that Ann died at Barton on the Heath, but I was wrong: she had moved back to Hook Norton. Her death there was reported, with frustrating brevity, in the *Oxford Journal* of

Saturday, 12th January, 1895. It may be that she had moved back to the Oxfordshire village after David's marriage, leaving the young couple in Barton to continue with their farming business. It is impossible to tell whether or not the move had been undertaken voluntarily. Possibly Ann had kept a house in Hook Norton after she and David had moved to Barton, or they had continued to run the farm there in addition to the one in Barton. In two subsequent editions of the *Oxford Journal* her household effects were advertised for sale ('on the premises' in Hook Norton) by auction: David had approached auctioneers Keck and Son of Bourton on the Water. The firm was probably already well-known to him because they also held sales of horses, cattle, pigs and sheep in the locality. I was amazed to see that the catalogue comprised 150 lots, including a feather bed, two guns, some cider casks, garden tools and a sewing machine – interesting items giving some indication of the lifestyles of David's deceased parents. Clearly, either David Whitfield (senior) or Ann had made cider on their farm, and Ann had maintained her interest in dressmaking. It would be fascinating to view the entire auction catalogue, but it probably hasn't survived. I wonder whether David (junior) kept any photographs of his parents or any personal effects? It would appear from his prompt clearance of his mother's house that he wasn't troubled too much by an excess of sentimentality.

Initially David, Ethel and family remained at Barton Hill Farm, but they later moved to Rainbow Farm in the centre of the village, retaining the tenancy of both farms. Their sons all became farmers in the village; with five sons to help him I assume that David had no need of outside help.

A photograph showing the family in 1912 outside Barton Hill Farm has survived. Although taken in the reign of George V, it still has an almost Victorian air about it: David and Ethel sit proudly outside the farmyard gate, surrounded by their growing family and two lovely sheepdogs. Apparently the family moved to Rainbow Farm shortly after the photograph was taken. The *Cheltenham Chronicle* of Saturday,14th December, 1912, records that David Whitfield won second prize for a pen of three porkets (young pigs) at the Moreton in Marsh Christmas Fatstock Show; I believe he was also keeping sheep and dairy cattle at this time.

David was clearly an ambitious man, and appears to have done well while holding the tenancy of two farms. In August, 1919, the Long Compton Estate, the property of the Marquess of Northampton, came up for sale by auction: 1,850 acres in 67 lots. It comprised seven excellent dairy and stock farms, with 'superior homesteads' (according to the auction catalogue), as well as a mill, the *Red Lion* hotel, Long Compton woods, 73 cottages and other farmland which appears not to have been assigned to any specific farm. The auction was held at the *Red Lion* Hotel, Banbury. David Whitfield attended and made successful bids for lots 5, 6b and 6c. He must have felt elated as he made the journey back to Barton on the Heath: he now owned a farm.

Lot 5 comprised Coates Barn Farm (a farmhouse and 139 acres); lot 6b comprised eleven acres of adjoining land and lot 6c a further ten acres, or thereabouts. David paid £3,100 for lot 5, plus a further £272 for the timber growing on the farm, £250 for lot 6b and £270 for lot 6c: in total £3,892 for 160 acres of land and a farmhouse. The farm and the extra land were all in the occupation of Mr Albert Holder. I have not been able to discover when he relinquished his tenancy.

David was 51 years old when he purchased his farm - two years older than his father had

David and Ethel Whitfield and family at Barton Hill Farm, Barton on the Heath, Warwickshire, in 1912.

been when he died at Duckpool Farm. However, he now had five sons to help him, and help him they did. None of them married. They all became farmers in Barton on the Heath. Two of their sisters married, however: Mary to James Heath in 1936 (there were no children) and Laura Ann (Nancy) to Leonard Rainbow, another farmer in 1924. Laura and Leonard had two children: Leonard David Rainbow, b.1926 and Mary Rainbow, b.1929. In an attempt to learn more about the family and hopefully make contact with any living descendants of David Whitfield, I wrote a letter to the *Banbury Guardian* in 1999 and was delighted to receive a letter from a former neighbour, Miss M. Shepherd, who could remember the Whitfield family in Barton on the Heath from the 1930s. In her reply she recollected:

'You may like some idea what it was like to grow up in those days before the war, near those lovely neighbours. I awoke every morning to the sound of Albert calling up the cows in the old way- not driving them in the present barbaric fashion, but calling them 'Cooop, Cooop', and sure enough they all came. As good drinking water was hard to come by, my mother used to take a bucket every day up the lane to the Whitfields' farm and fill it from a pump over their kitchen sink, and here we were able to keep in touch with what was going on in the village. The Whitfields kept exotic domestic fowl, and Mrs Whitfield always seemed to be chopping herbs in a wooden bowl for her turkey. The 'gulleneys' or guinea fowl would sometimes fly over the wall and perch in our apple trees. When David and Mary Rainbow came to stay they would come down and play with me, and Mary and I rode around bareback on my Shetland

DIAGRAM 13

The line descended from David Whitfield born 1829/1830

[also see diagram 2]

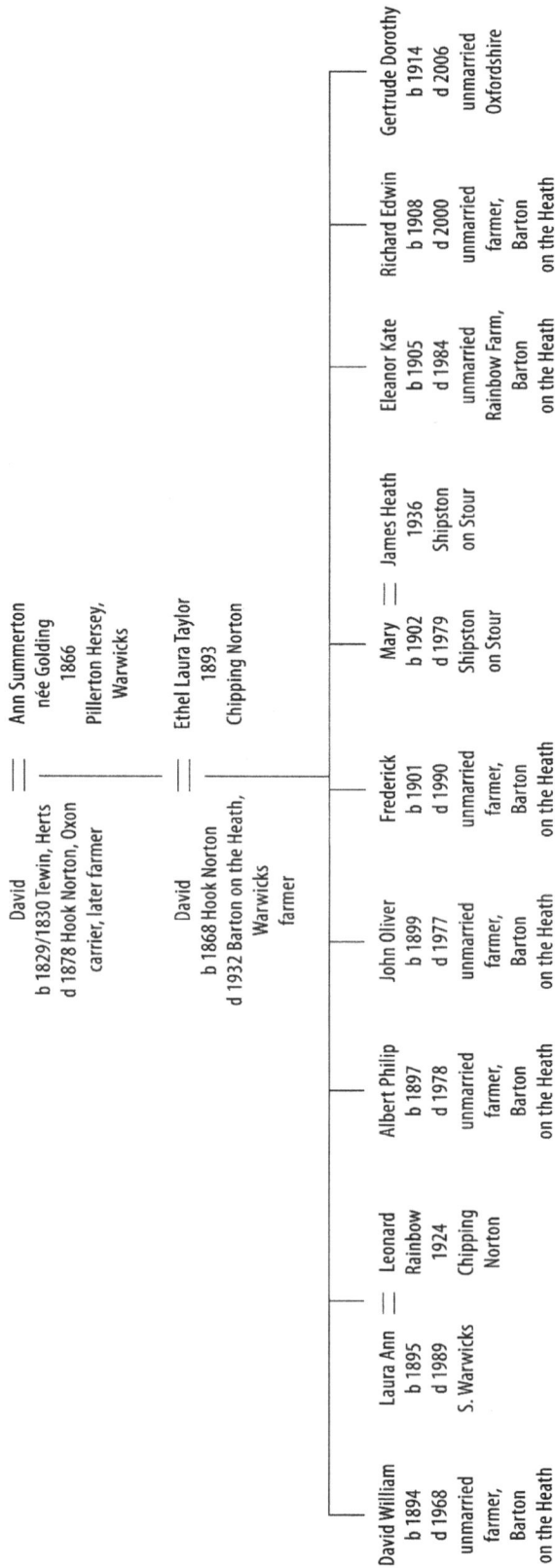

David
b 1829/1830 Tewin, Herts
d 1878 Hook Norton, Oxon
carrier, later farmer

══

Ann Summerton
née Golding
1866
Pillerton Hersey,
Warwicks

David
b 1868 Hook Norton
d 1932 Barton on the Heath,
Warwicks
farmer

══

Ethel Laura Taylor
1893
Chipping Norton

David William	Laura Ann	══	Leonard	Albert Philip	John Oliver	Frederick	Mary	══	James Heath	Eleanor Kate	Richard Edwin	Gertrude Dorothy
b 1894	b 1895		Rainbow	b 1897	b 1899	b 1901	b 1902		1936	b 1905	b 1908	b 1914
d 1968	d 1989		1924	d 1978	d 1977	d 1990	d 1979		Shipston	d 1984	d 2000	d 2006
unmarried	S. Warwicks		Chipping	unmarried	unmarried	unmarried	Shipston		on Stour	unmarried	unmarried	unmarried
farmer,			Norton	farmer,	farmer,	farmer,	on Stour			Rainbow Farm,	farmer,	Oxfordshire
Barton				Barton	Barton	Barton				Barton	Barton	
on the Heath				on the Heath	on the Heath	on the Heath				on the Heath	on the Heath	

All of David and Ethel Whitfield's children were born in Barton on the Heath, Warwickshire.
None of the five sons married, and there are now no living descendants with the Whitfield surname in this branch.

pony and the Whitfields' donkey which ran with the cows. I was very fond of Nelly [Eleanor Kate], indeed of the whole family, who were very good to us, especially when my father died. After my mother and I left Barton, it was lovely to go back and see them all.'

David died in 1932, after suffering from throat cancer for two years. He was 64. His obituary in the *Evesham Journal and Four Shires Advertiser* of 1st October, 1932 stated that 'he continued with his farming business until a few days before his death', which speaks volumes about his determination in the face of adversity. He was described as '…an outstanding figure in the agricultural world, and in the district in which he resided [he] was a recognised authority on all agricultural matters'. The obituary went on to say that David was 'a very popular figure, and much respected by all with whom he came into contact. He was always outspoken, but his opinions were recognised as being honest and sincere. Of a naturally kind and genial disposition, he was a good friend to all who asked his assistance.' The photograph accompanying David's obituary shows a typical Whitfield face: long and thin, with high cheek bones. Unlike many Whitfield men, though, David had not suffered from baldness. His dominant facial feature was his enormous moustache, which he appears to have cultivated with some pride. The photograph shows David had a magnificent and luxuriant un-waxed walrus moustache (rather like the one sported by the composer Edward Elgar) which threatened to obscure his mouth and must have made eating and drinking somewhat challenging.

The National Probate Register shows that David had been a prosperous man: his estate was valued at over £27,000. His will made in February, 1931, is a little disappointing from the family historian's point of view because it gives few details of his farming interests, such as crops being grown and livestock kept. David provided for his wife Ethel by paying her an income from his residuary fund during her widowhood and stated that no part of his personal chattels or freehold and leasehold property were to be sold without her consent. His executors and trustees were his son John Oliver Whitfield and two other local farmers: Thomas Randall and Frank Hawes. However, by April of the same year in a codicil to the will he empowered his trustees to use their own discretion whether to sell his farming business or whether to employ outside help in the business *without* Ethel's consent. Ethel's annuity remained, but she was apparently not to be given much say in how the farms were to be run. This development must have put John Whitfield in an awkward position and presumably led to some friction within the family. I wonder why David decided to add the codicil?

The *Cheltenham Chronicle* shows that after David's death his sons continued to keep sheep and cattle on the farm. It records that 'Whitfield Bros. of Barton on the Heath' won the first prize for ten grass tegs [sheep in their second year] in the Moreton in Marsh Christmas fatstock show of 1938, and in the spring Show of the following year they won second prize for a dairy cow with a calf at foot or about to calve.

Ethel Whitfield died in 1954 at Rainbow Farm, Barton on the Heath. *Her* will makes interesting reading, because most of the bequests were made to *female* members of the family: her daughter Mary Heath and granddaughter Mary Rainbow received sums of money and her daughter Gertrude Dorothy Whitfield was left a car. It appears that Ethel owned land in her own right outside Barton on the Heath, although the acreage isn't specified. It was in Campden

Road, Shipston on Stour and was left to her unmarried daughters Eleanor Kate Whitfield and Gertrude Dorothy Whitfield who also shared the residue of her estate. These bequests to female members of the family may represent Ethel's reaction to having lived for so long in a male-dominated household, and to her treatment in her late husband's will.

The family continued to farm in Barton on the Heath after the deaths of their parents; all five sons were involved. Gravestones in Barton on the Heath churchyard commemorate the brothers as one by one they were returned to the soil of the parish where they had farmed: William David in 1968, John Oliver in 1977, Albert Philip in 1978, Frederick in 1990 and Richard Edwin (Dick) in 2000, aged 91. Dick (Richard Edwin) was still driving a tractor in his late eighties. He was the last male Whitfield in this branch of the family. His sisters have also all died: Eleanor Kate in 1984, Mary in 1979, Laura Ann in 1989, aged 93, and Gertrude Dorothy in 2006, also in her early nineties.

David Whitfield's granddaughter, Mary Rainbow married another local farmer, Berkley Hicks in 1959. She died in 2001. David's only grandson, (Leonard) David Rainbow lives in rural Warwickshire.

Conclusion.

'Time present and time past
Are both perhaps present in time future
And time future contained in time past'

T.S. Eliot (1888-1965) *Burnt Norton*

When I started researching my family in 1971 I obviously had no idea that it would take me about forty years before I would be able to produce a reasonably full account of its history. Even now, I am conscious that the story is not complete, but of course, it never will be, because life moves on. There will always be something to add, something else to discover. Genealogy appears to be a life-long addiction. New documentary material becomes available on a regular basis, and much of it is now on-line, making it easier for the family historian to search and consult than ever before. Despite this, the thrill of discovery remains as intense as ever.

******

As a church organist, I sometimes play for funeral services. At one particular service, there was no tribute to the deceased person and I queried this with a member of her family afterwards. Her reply was 'What could you say about someone who ended up in an old folks' home and died in her nineties?' It was one of the saddest comments I had ever heard. I kept quiet in response because I was unable to reply in a tactful way. I would imagine that many pages - possibly a book - could probably have been written about that person's life.

Every person and *every* family has a story to tell. Individuals usually, though not always, of course, grow up within a family environment, and may well have memories of a previous generation, and perhaps of siblings. In most cases, they will have memories of their school days, their first and subsequent jobs, boyfriends or girlfriends, and then possibly of settling down with a partner, 'for better for worse, for richer for poorer, in sickness and in health...'. The family cycle goes on over the generations. Within each lifetime, people react to and are shaped by various social and economic conditions over which they have little, if any, control. Factors such as wars, economic booms and depressions, diseases, mechanisation and technological change, educational opportunities and increasing geographical and possibly social mobility spring to mind as being significant in affecting the lives of individuals and families in any age. Family members are somewhat like small boats launched on a turbulent ocean of such factors, and the decisions they make in response to them help to shape their lives. Individuals are also influenced, particularly early on in their lives, by the people with whom they frequently come into contact, and in most cases these people are members of their immediate family. I am not qualified to discuss the 'nature versus nurture' debate, but it seems to me that although some facets of an individual's personality may be genetically determined, others must surely be learnt early on from parents and other older members of the family. I was lucky to grow up in a happy and stable family unit and also had frequent and regular contact with some of my grandparents, uncles and aunts. Not everyone could say the same thing, of course. The story every person and every family has to tell is unique. Collectively, the way people live their lives will shape the future of their families, and perhaps, in a small way, contribute to the history of the country in which they live.

******

As we lead our own lives, thereby helping the family story continue a little further, how conscious are we of the evidence *we* will leave behind for subsequent generations to discover and record? Do we label the photographs we may take, for example, and do we keep diaries? Thanks to emails we are able to keep in touch with members of the family all over the world, but although these electronic communications may be kept longer than telephone conversations, I suspect that they may not be as permanent as letters. Letter writing appears to be an activity in decline. Diaries, photographs and letters are obviously extremely valuable resources to the family historian, quite apart from their immediate and sentimental value to the individuals concerned who currently possess them. Do we keep in touch with family members, or are we 'too busy'? Have we asked elderly members of our families about their early memories? And are our children aware of their family's history? After all, their genetic make-up has been inherited, and their personalities, speech and outlook have also been influenced by previous generations. Surely they ought to know as much as possible about their family's history? It is something of real and lasting value which should be researched, recorded, shared and passed on: something which I have tried to do in this book.

The story of my family started in my records with Robert Whitfield the plumber of Clophill, Bedfordshire, who died in 1555, although it clearly started much earlier. If only I could find some definite documentary evidence! Many members of the family were collectively involved in agriculture over several hundred years, either as farm labourers or market gardeners. As mechanisation became more widespread and the rationalisation of land holdings accompanying enclosure also reduced the need for agricultural workers, the family became poverty-stricken, and nearly died out in the male line. The impoverished state of some branches of the family was reinforced by the early deaths of some breadwinners, and some of the large Victorian and Edwardian Whitfield families took a long time to recover from the misfortunes which beset them. Some families, as we have seen, decided to try their luck beyond Bedfordshire; others stayed in their home area. Different escape routes from poverty and continued work on the land were tried by different branches and family members as the nineteenth and twentieth centuries unfolded, with varying degrees of success.

DIAGRAM 14

Fifteen generations of the Whitfields in Bedfordshire

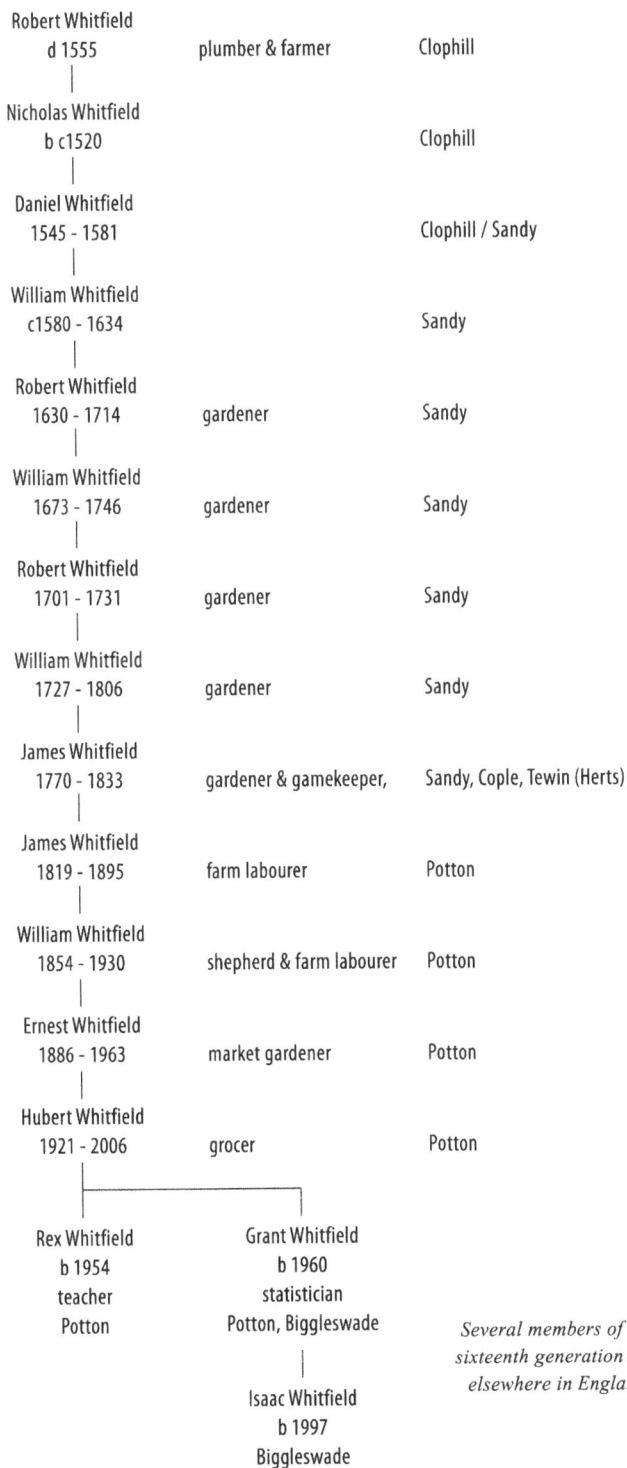

Robert Whitfield d 1555	plumber & farmer	Clophill
Nicholas Whitfield b c1520		Clophill
Daniel Whitfield 1545 - 1581		Clophill / Sandy
William Whitfield c1580 - 1634		Sandy
Robert Whitfield 1630 - 1714	gardener	Sandy
William Whitfield 1673 - 1746	gardener	Sandy
Robert Whitfield 1701 - 1731	gardener	Sandy
William Whitfield 1727 - 1806	gardener	Sandy
James Whitfield 1770 - 1833	gardener & gamekeeper,	Sandy, Cople, Tewin (Herts)
James Whitfield 1819 - 1895	farm labourer	Potton
William Whitfield 1854 - 1930	shepherd & farm labourer	Potton
Ernest Whitfield 1886 - 1963	market gardener	Potton
Hubert Whitfield 1921 - 2006	grocer	Potton

Rex Whitfield
b 1954
teacher
Potton

Grant Whitfield
b 1960
statistician
Potton, Biggleswade

*Several members of the
sixteenth generation live
elsewhere in England*

Isaac Whitfield
b 1997
Biggleswade

The future of the family now continues in three continents. As the number of male members of the family aged under thirty is currently well into double figures it would appear that the family name and gene pool will continue long after I have gone, though not in every branch I have investigated.

Members of the family born in the first decade of the twenty first century will be growing up in a rapidly changing and overcrowded world. As ever, they will need to be adaptable and resourceful in order to survive and live their lives to the full. Access to education and better medical facilities, and the safety net of the Welfare State, all too frequently denied to previous generations of the family, *should* help to improve the lifestyles and life expectancies of present and future family members, but at the time of writing the reappearance of rickets in some children, high youth unemployment, and the presence of food banks in many British towns and cities all sound a cautionary note and warn against complacency.

Potton, the home to so many of the Whitfield family over the last 180 years or so, has changed considerably in my lifetime. Its population has more than doubled and many newcomers have settled on new housing estates, built from the late 1960s onwards with more scheduled for the future. It is still a good place to live in, however, and remains fairly compact, so that it is possible to stand in the Market Square and hear, simultaneously, footballers training at The Hollow along the Biggleswade Road on the southern outskirts of the parish and the church bells being rung on the Gamlingay side of the town. Despite the increase in Potton's size, facilities in the town have declined over the last sixty years. Several shops have closed, including three butcher's shops, a baker's, a grocer's, two selling electrical goods, three selling clothing, a shoe shop, two barber's premises and a couple of general stores. Some of these are now private houses; others have been replaced by different types of businesses. At least seven pubs catering for thirsty market gardeners during my earlier years are now private houses. Potton's railway station was closed in 1968 and the land formerly occupied by the railway line has been used to accommodate light industry and houses to such an extent that if a railway link between Bedford and Cambridge were to be re-opened (as has been suggested) it would probably have to by-pass the town. Market gardening has been in decline in the parish for the last thirty years or so, although vestiges of this distinctive type of agriculture remain along the Greensand ridge. A number of factors are responsible for this, particularly the easy availability throughout the year of fruits and vegetables from other countries in local supermarkets; the labour-intensive nature of the work involved in market gardening; the high cost of labour; and changing dietary and cooking habits. Some tools and equipment still used in the industry when I was a teenager will soon become museum items. Land around the expanding town of Potton has now been returned to arable farming or has been sown with grass for horse and pony paddocks. Some land at Deepdale, on the way to Sandy has been purchased by the RSPB and has been allowed to revert to heath vegetation as a suitable habitat for birds, and quarrying for sand for the building industry continues to the North and West of the parish: the local geology thus still exerts some influence on economic activity in my home town.

In central Bedfordshire, villages and small towns are losing their rural character as people from London and Hertfordshire move north in search of cheaper housing, often returning to their places of origin to work, making daily use of railway and motorway links. Unfortunately many of the newcomers are *in* the countryside, but not really *of* it. Periodically there are complaints about smells of manure, cockerels crowing and church bells ringing; and there are requests for the establishment of facilities usually encountered in larger urban centres. Meanwhile, the noise and pollution from the extra traffic generated seem to go unnoticed. To be fair, some of the newcomers *do* appreciate country life and contribute in a positive way to it; they may help to keep village facilities going. The countryside as we know it has evolved over the centuries, and will undoubtedly continue to do so.

In Britain, the gap between rich and poor is probably as wide now as it was in early Victorian times and the social class system is alive and well, although many politicians would claim otherwise. There is also a marked divide between the relatively affluent south east of England and the north, where unemployment is higher and average life expectancy is lower. Successive governments (of various political persuasions) have not been able to solve these problems. Some have tried harder than others.

On a world scale, although a projected population of nine billion people for 2050 has been suggested, which would place great pressure on our planet, many people, encouraged by persuasive advertising and skilful marketing, maintain or aspire to throw-away, consumerist lifestyles which ultimately will be unsustainable. Already it would appear that global warming is contributing to more extreme and more erratic weather conditions. Life will not be easy in the future, with dwindling resources and scarce food supplies, particularly if people do not make a conscious effort to live more modest, environmentally friendly lifestyles. Of course, for most people in the past life was always a struggle, but hopefully well worth living. Clearly, no-one knows what the future holds, but a study of the past suggests that people will adapt to survive and hopefully continue to live satisfying and happy lives.

Family members can justifiably be proud of their history. Hopefully one of them will consider it worthwhile at some point to bring my record up to date, as life does not stand still. Thomas Hardy expressed this sense of continuity in families far more effectively than I can, in the first verse of a poem called 'Heredity', so he can have the last word:

'I am the family face;

Flesh perishes, I live on,

Projecting trait and trace

Through time to times anon

And leaping from place to place

Over oblivion'

Appendix

(a) The Land Settlement Association and its connection with Potton

The Land Settlement Association (LSA) was a Government initiative started in 1934, whereby unemployed workers from depressed industrial areas of Britain, particularly North East England and Wales, were settled in newly built smallholdings which they worked after receiving some initial training in horticulture. Between 1934 and 1939 around 1100 smallholdings were created on 26 estates or 'settlements'. Most smallholdings had between about four and ten acres of land; and a holding of five or six acres was fairly typical. The new tenants grew commercial crops of fruit, vegetables and salad crops, sometimes under glass; they also often kept poultry and pigs. Produce was marketed by and sold through the Land Settlement Association. The allocation of holdings to the unemployed was suspended at the outbreak of the Second World War in a bid to increase food production, and holdings were taken by men and their families who already had some horticultural experience. After the war, the holdings became incorporated into County Council schemes to provide smallholdings and the LSA holdings became a stepping stone for ambitious tenants who eventually purchased their own smallholdings or farms outside the organisation.

Potton's LSA estate was the first of these estates. It was started in March, 1935, on land donated by Potton's last Lord of the Manor, Sir (Percy) Malcolm Stewart (1872-1951), who had purchased Home Farm, formerly owned by William Smith. Stewart had purchased Sandy Lodge (now the headquarters of the RSPB) in the previous year. He was a wealthy industrialist and businessman who was the Chairman of the London Brick Company from 1924 to his retirement in 1950. He was also managing director of the British Portland Cement Makers' Federation and a generous philanthropist. The land he donated was to the east of the main settled area of Potton – towards Wrestlingworth and Cockayne Hatley, and the soil on the thirty LSA holdings thus tended to be heavier, as in this zone the greensand merges into boulder clay. The first tenants were former miners from County Durham and their tenancies started in 1936.

The LSA was well established by the time I started working there as a lad in the early 1970s; my grandfather, Harry Mingay, had been pigman there some thirty years or so previously. In the 1970s the Potton estate seemed to be run in conjunction with the nearby estate at Chawston and Wyboston in Bedfordshire and lorries would serve both estates to collect produce such as tomatoes, lettuce and celery. Pigs were still being kept on the Potton estate, but not in such great numbers as in earlier years. Most holdings had a number of greenhouses.

As so often happens in such organisations, cracks began to show, as far as I could tell by the 1970s, maybe even earlier. Tenants were frustrated by the rather unimaginative marketing of the produce by the LSA, particularly in the face of foreign competition; the poor prices obtained and by the bureaucratic interference by 'Head Office', this last criticism an all too familiar one, as I know from working in the insurance industry and as a teacher. I can remember the amusement caused by a colour chart which was circulated from the Head Office which rather patronisingly showed the ranges of colours permissible for tomatoes when they were picked: if they were picked when too red they would be past their best when they arrived at market. I can also remember being told by my granddad of a visit by Head Office 'experts' to one particular holding where they offered sincere congratulations to the tenant on the fine crop of blackcurrants he was growing under cloches. The 'blackcurrants' they had observed were actually berries growing on mature plants of deadly nightshade (belladonna) - poisonous weeds. Hopefully they didn't try any.

After much frustration and haggling the LSA organisation was wound up in 1982. The holdings were sold by auction to private buyers and a brief but important chapter in Potton's history had come to an end.

(b) Joseph Nathaniel Hall (1866 – 1921).

Articles in various newspapers found on the British Newspaper Archive website testify to the fame of Joseph Nathaniel Hall, who appears in Chapter 4. News of his death and, later, the publication of a summary of his will, featured in local newspapers as far afield from Sandy as Cornwall and Yorkshire. These articles make fascinating reading.

Joseph Nathaniel Hall was a self-made man; his father, James Hall (who was still alive in his mid-eighties at the time of his son's death), was a labourer who had not allowed his illiteracy to prevent him building up a market gardening business. Joseph's mother, Mary Ann, nee Whitfield, had been a dressmaker before her marriage, and his maternal grandfather, Joseph Whitfield, had been a shepherd.

Joseph Nathaniel Hall started by working for his father, but at the age of twenty five had started in market gardening on his own account. By the age of thirty he was already a wealthy man. In addition to growing market gardening crops, he was trading in potatoes, buying them as standing crops and then selling them at market. The newspaper reports make it clear that he was buying potatoes on a very large scale, sometimes over one thousand acres at a time, and was venturing into the Fens and Lincolnshire to do so. He became well known in vegetable markets from London to Edinburgh, and was thought to be the largest potato merchant in England.

His obituary in the *Biggleswade Chronicle* stated that he was also one of the largest potato growers in the country and commented on the long hours he worked, his fine brain and 'his unassuming, droll and unconventional conversation'. Although his application to his large business empire left him little free time, he had been active in the Baptist Church in Sandy, where he was Sunday School Superintendent. He had been known to attend the Sunday School in this capacity with his breakfast unfinished and his boots unlaced – but he was always there.

The newspapers commented on the £247,000 fortune he left when he died at the age of

55, following an unsuccessful operation, but what to me was even more remarkable was that he had managed to leave this money after becoming virtually penniless - twice. On these occasions he had purchased large acreages of growing potatoes in the Fens which had later been washed away in floods, or had rotted in the ground before harvest. One report, in the *Hull Daily Mail* of Wednesday, 14th September, 1921, commented on his 'indomitable courage and cheerfulness'. It must have taken incredible courage and determination to pick himself up after these disasters and rebuild his business. At the time of his death he owned farms in Bedfordshire, Huntingdonshire, Cambridgeshire and Lincolnshire, and apparently on all of them 'he applied intensive cultivation to large areas'.

(c) Some Victorian varieties of potatoes being grown in Potton.

I was interested to discover how a combination of historical, geographical and biological factors had helped to shape the fortunes of the market gardeners of Potton and district as they planted their potato crops in 1888. The family trees of potatoes appear to be as complex as human family trees, and the long history of these tubers, stretching back thousands of years to their origins in South America, is fascinating.

Magnum Bonum was a potato developed by market gardener and potato breeder James Clark (1825- 1890) of Christchurch, Hampshire. Clark's work involved developing hybrid varieties of potato, pollinating the flowers of one variety with the pollen from another variety, probably by hand in controlled conditions; and sowing the seeds produced to create new varieties of potatoes which would inherit characteristics from both parents. Magnum Bonum was the first of Clark's commercial successes. After the variety was trialled at Stoke Newington he sold it to seed merchants Suttons, who introduced it in 1876. It was a floury potato with an excellent flavour and was popular until around 1900 after which it became increasingly susceptible to blight. It was later used in the breeding of other potatoes: King Edward, Arran Victory and Arran Banner.

The Early Rose potato was bred by amateur grower Albert Bresee of Hubbardton, Vermont, USA, at some time between 1857 and 1861. Its tubers were a flattened oval in shape and they had a pale pink skin and white flesh which sometimes had a rosy vein running through it. As its name further suggests, the variety was an early cropper. Bresee had developed the Early Rose from a potato known as Garnet Chili, which, in turn, had been bred around 1853 by an American Episcopalian minister and potato enthusiast Chauncey E Goodrich from a potato variety called Rough Purple Chili. This latter, picturesquely named variety had been imported from South America in an attempt to introduce some vigour to the North American potato varieties which were succumbing to blight. Bresee's new variety grew well in a variety of soil types, and presumably still had some blight resistance. Apparently he was paid one thousand dollars per pound for the true seeds of the plant – a lot of money in the mid nineteenth century.

The Beauty of Hebron potato originated from Hebron, New York, USA, possibly in 1874-1875, and was mentioned in a seed catalogue of a Massachusetts seed firm in 1879. It strongly resembled Early Rose potatoes in shape and colour, which suggests that it may have been bred from this variety. It also cropped early, but yields were heavier. By 1888 it had mutated into a white skinned variety, which presumably was characteristic of the Beauty of Hebron potatoes being grown in Potton.

White Elephant potatoes were a cross of Garnet Chili x White Peachblow, and thus were related to both Early Rose and Beauty of Hebron. White Elephant was first introduced commercially in 1878. As its name suggests it produced large tubers. It did well without the need for irrigation, which may well be why it was being grown in the Potton district in 1888.

STOP PRESS

'…Seek and ye shall find….'

From St Matthew's Gospel, chapter 7 verse 7.

This book was nearly ready for publication when, after a barren period of several weeks, I was delighted to discover further details about the Whitfield family which I include below. I have indicated in each case their relevance to the material in the main body of the book. Readers wishing to refresh their memories of the characters involved will therefore be able to consult the relevant chapters if they so wish. This final section of the book has not been indexed.

I was impressed to see in the *Bedfordshire Mercury* of 8th January, 1870, which appeared on the British Newspaper Archive website, that George Whitfield, the gardener at Sandy Place (who can be found in Chapter Two), was a member of the committee responsible for founding and organising the Sandy Reading Room. This was further evidence that George, born around 1818, had, as I had suspected, learnt to read and write, unlike so many of his contemporaries. It seems that he was sufficiently public spirited to give up some of his time to ensure that other ordinary Sandy residents were able to access reading material or at least benefit from hearing other people read or give talks to them. I wonder where the reading room was located in Sandy in 1870? Its official opening had taken place on 3rd January.

George Whitfield was in distinguished company. The president of the Sandy Reading Room Society was Arthur Wellesley Peel (1829-1912), a Liberal MP, and at that time Parliamentary Secretary to the Poor Law Board. Arthur Peel was later to become the Speaker of the House of Commons from 1884 to 1895. He was also a great supporter of the Sandy Show and Horticultural Society. His older brother, William Peel (1824-1858), had been the founder of the Sandy to Potton railway line which ran through the Peel's estate. The Reading Room's vice presidents were Colonel Thomas Hooke Pearson, C.B., who had retired to The Hasells, Sandy, after a distinguished military career in India, and George's employer, John Nathaniel Foster. The Committee chairman was the Reverend John Richardson, who was Rector of Sandy from 1858 to 1913. George presumably must have rubbed shoulders with all of these men.

Sandy residents attending the Reading Room's opening ceremony were able to enjoy 'an entertainment with the magic lantern' presented by the Sandy Rector. This treat consisted of 'illustrative views of *The Pilgrim's Progress*'. Clearly an effort was being made to promote a local author. Each scene was explained by the Sandy curate, the Reverend Claude Smith Bird. For people unable to cope with such excitement the Reading Room also housed a good stock of books, games, newspapers and periodicals. I would love to know what sort of books

George was fond of reading. Did he enjoy the novels of Dickens (who died in June, 1870) for instance? Was he inspired by *The Pilgrim's Progress*? He may well have consulted reference books on gardening and kept up with local and national events reported in various local and national newspapers. I hope he was able to read in Biggleswade workhouse where he ended his days. I would be interested to know whether he exchanged letters with his daughters when they moved away from Sandy. The Sandy Reading Room eventually became housed in the Town Hall which wasn't built until 1906.

Joseph Whitfield, (1812- 1867) the shepherd of Girtford near Sandy (who appears in Chapter Four) witnessed John Squires and Amos Geeves helping themselves to some young willow tree shoots on one November morning in 1840. The willow trees were growing on land which Robert Ayres rented from Francis Pym. The trees may well have been growing alongside the River Ivel. The shoots were probably required for making baskets or hurdles. Squires and Geeves paid the penalty of £1 for their barrow load of willow shoots after they appeared in court at Biggleswade. They were possibly a little surprised and upset to see that one of the presiding magistrates was a certain Mr F. Pym. The case was reported in the *Bedfordshire Mercury* of 26th December, 1840.

The death of Jabez Whitfield junior was dealt with in the *Bedfordshire Mercury* of 17th May, 1856. Jabez (who also appears in Chapter Four) had been in apparently perfect health until a few days before his death. Since feeling unwell he had been taking medicine prescribed by Henry Raynes of Potton, but had not had any further medical assistance, presumably because he was unable to pay the surgeon's fee. The verdict of the inquest, held at the *Greyhound* public house in Sandy by the deputy coroner, E. Eagles, was that Jabez had died from heart disease. He was in his early thirties.

 You will remember that Jabez (senior) and his wife Alice had already lost one son (William) to heart disease in 1829. The loss of a second son must have devastated them. The elder Jabez was mentioned in connection with a fire which had taken place in his house in December, 1860. Two young men: James Vines and Charles Blewitt, lodged with Jabez and Alice at this time; they had spent the evening at the *Bell* public house in Sandy, and had returned 'at a very late hour', presumably somewhat the worse for drink.

Vines and Blewitt retired to (the same) bed for the night. This was presumably not an ideal arrangement, but I assume it was because the cottage and bedroom were small and they had no choice in the matter. They were awoken later by the smell of smoke. The room was full of it, and the flames which soon followed consumed their clothes and the bedclothes. As no injuries to Vines and Blewitt were mentioned I assume they had changed into their nightshirts. The fire is thought to have started from a pipe which had not been properly extinguished and had remained smouldering in one of the young men's pockets. It threatened to spread to the rest of the house and the article in the *Bedfordshire Mercury* of 31st December, 1860, makes it clear that it could also have endangered adjoining cottages which were all owned by Mr Skilleter who was probably also Jabez' and Alice's landlord. The elderly couple were clearly supplementing their income by taking in lodgers: the 1861 census shows that they were also in receipt of 'parish relief' in their declining years. It may well be that the pipe had belonged to James Vines because that census showed me that after the fire Charles Blewitt was still lodging with Jabez and Alice, but Vines had moved to Upper Stondon; his place had been taken by an older labourer, William Smith. It would be interesting to know whether Smith was a non-smoking teetotaller. If he shared meals with Jabez and Alice he was probably almost vegetarian too, as I suspect that poverty dictated that members of the household didn't taste meat very often.

The *Bedfordshire Mercury* of 27th June, 1857, mentioned that Catherine Whitfield (who appears in Chapter Ten) was one of the people who had discovered the body of a young woman, Mary Lawson, who had drowned near Watermill Bridge on the Sutton to Biggleswade road. The report makes it clear that Catherine was leaving an adjoining hayfield with three other women, presumably after helping with the hay harvest. The article evokes a simpler way of life in the local area over one hundred and fifty years ago as witnesses were questioned at the *John O'Gaunt* inn, Sutton, in an attempt to ascertain what had happened.

We learn that on Tuesday, 23rd June, Mary Lawson had attended the official opening of the Sandy to Potton railway line- a momentous occasion in the life of the town and obviously an exciting event for a girl of seventeen; she had then spent the night at the *Queen's Head* public house in Potton with George Lenton, an agricultural labourer aged about twenty one. Lenton's statement was rather confused, but he claimed that they left the *Queen's Head* around half past three the next morning, although another witness, Fanny Sanderson from Sutton, stated that she had seen Lenton and Mary Lawson walking together in Sir John Burgoyne's park about half an hour earlier than this. (This well-wooded park, now the John O'Gaunt golf course, may well have been a popular spot for local courting couples; and, after a few drinks, spending some time together in this pleasant, secluded location on a fine early morning towards the end of June must have been a particularly attractive prospect). Was this a lovers' tryst or had they gone there on impulse? We shall probably never know.

Mary had been spotted walking towards Biggleswade at about half past five on the same morning by Samuel Jakins, a Potton sawyer. At about half past six in the evening her lifeless body had first been discovered by John Saville, described as 'a little boy', who was going to Sutton to 'turn his sheep back'. The discovery must have been a great shock to the boy: he had run home to tell his grandmother.

Colonel Lindsell had been passing the bridge and the four women had drawn his attention to Mary Lawson's body in the stream; she was lying on her back in about a foot of water. He had supervised the retrieval of the corpse and its subsequent identification. As there were no obvious signs of violence on Mary's body, and no signs of a struggle near the bridge, the jury after some deliberation returned an open verdict of 'found drowned'. The possibilities of murder, suicide and accident were all presumably considered. I would imagine that the incident must have revived unhappy memories for Catherine who, you will remember, had threatened to drown herself after she had been apprehended for stealing items from her employer in Great Barford some thirteen years earlier.

Various town and city directories for the U.S.A. appeared recently on the ancestry website. Thanks to them I was able to piece together further details of the early life of Henry, William, George, Naomi and Ruth Whitfield on the far side of the Atlantic - information which had been sadly lacking previously because the Whitfields from Manea (covered in Chapter 11) had all somehow managed to evade the census enumerators in 1880. Henry and William were found at separate addresses in Cleveland, Ohio; Henry was first mentioned at 42 Hewlett (Avenue) in 1875 and William at 37 Burton (Avenue?) from 1880. From the early 1880s, George lodged with Henry and his wife Emma in Hewlett Avenue until he and his wife Jennie moved to 102 Lawn (Avenue?), Cleveland. Directories were not available for every single year, but George and Jennie were no longer living with Henry and Emma by 1892. I was interested to see that ten years earlier a John Whitfield, described as a teamster, was also living at 42 Hewlett Avenue with Henry and George. This, surely, was not a remarkable co-incidence. I can only assume that their younger brother Jonathan (born in 1865) had been paying them a visit from England. As we know, Jonathan didn't remain in the USA, but became a carter (the English equivalent of a teamster) in Sheffield. At first, William, Henry and George were described as labourers in the directories, but by 1886 George had become a 'teamster', a term also used for his brother Henry five years later. Naomi was found at a different address in Cleveland, and was described as a matron at a children's home, presumably living on the premises. We know that she later used the railway to travel across America to settle and marry in California. William is described in various later directories as a brickmaker and later still as a bricklayer. It may well be that he passed on his bricklaying skills to his brother Henry. As we have already seen, William's family also kept in touch with Naomi in California because William's daughter, Harriet Matilda, went to live with Naomi and her husband Samuel Beck after William died in his late forties.

Henry appears to have purchased the house in Hewlett Avenue, Cleveland, moving to the smaller settlement of Rocky River later: he was certainly living there by 1900 and described as a farmer. Ten years later the census makes it clear that he was actually a market gardener. He retained the house in Cleveland, however, and presumably leased it to tenants. The census had already shown me that he had moved back there in 1920, but a directory for 1915 revealed that he was back in the city by then. He is described in somewhat unflattering terms as a 'huckster'. It may well be that he was operating from door to door in parts of Cleveland selling vegetables which had been grown by his daughter Ruth and her husband Horace Bailey back in Rocky River. A deed found online on the Cuyahoga County Recorder's website shows that he prudently transferred the ownership of the house in Hewlett Avenue to his son and daughter in February, 1930, and on census day (18thApril) in the same year he was living with his daughter Ruth and her family in Rocky River.

I had been searching newspaper articles for the conventional spelling of the Whitfield surname. It then occurred to me that it might be a good to search for the surname Witfield to see whether any articles appeared where family members could be recognised, from the context of the report even if their surname was spelt incorrectly - a fairly easy task if details of place or other family members were also mentioned. I was rewarded with an article from the *Gloucester Citizen* of 14th July, 1898. It was obvious that the 'Mr Witfield' mentioned in the article was David Whitfield, (1868- 1932), because it dealt with a tragic accident which had occurred on his farm in Barton on the Heath (see Chapter 12). A fifty-six year old labourer, James Hiatt, had been loading hay, presumably onto a wagon or a stack; he had been roping the load and had pulled on one end of the rope, believing the other end (which must have been out of his view), to be already fastened. Unfortunately, it wasn't, and Hiatt had fallen from the wagon or haystack. He had been conveyed to the cottage hospital in Moreton-in-Marsh, but had later died from a broken spine. An inquest was held, but unfortunately I have been unable to find a report of it. It appears that the newspaper article I found on the excellent British Newspaper Archive website may have been slightly inaccurate in one detail: an examination of the Great Wolford burial registers showed that Hiatt's Christian name was Joseph. His burial took place in Great Wolford on 16th July, 1898.

I hadn't visited the BLARS (Bedfordshire and Luton Archives and Records Service) website for a while, and was interested to find details of the will of Sir Philip Monoux of Sandy, who died in 1805. In this document, the testator mentions his kitchen garden and another plot called the Mill Garden. Adjoining the Mill Garden, according to Sir Philip's will, was a cottage 'occupied by William Whitfield'(1727- 1806), a member of the family we met in Chapter Two; and in the same sentence Sir Philip mentions all his 'garden frames, glasses (cloches?), tools and utensils…'. I have concluded from this that William had been Sir Philip's gardener. William may not have been past work when the will was first drafted (1797), and it would appear that he had been employed to produce early crops for his employer. This connection with the Monoux family would explain why some of William's sons, including my great-great-great grandfather, James Whitfield (1770- 1833), the gamekeeper, also became servants to the same family, although, as we have seen, they also worked plots elsewhere in the parish. It would also explain why William's eldest surviving son, Robert, was also occupying what appears to have been the same cottage nearly half a century later. It seems likely, therefore, that my 3x great grandfather James Whitfield, one of the central characters in this book, would have grown up near the Mill at Sandy, within a stone's throw of the River Ivel, and would have been familiar with both gardening and market gardening on the greensand before taking up gamekeeping.

It appears that ordinary people in the past - even if they were illiterate- left much more evidence behind of the sort of lives they led than might at first be supposed. I hope I have succeeded in showing that family stories can be reconstructed with a reasonable degree of success, given a little initiative, persistence and patience. If this account has inspired readers to embark on similar projects it will have been a worthwhile exercise.

.

Acknowledgements.

One of the less pleasant aspects of recording my thanks to the various people who have assisted with the production of this book is the realisation that so many of them who helped in the early stages of my work are no longer alive. I suppose this is inevitable, given the passage of forty years. They, and the help they gave me, have not been forgotten.

Within my own family I was first inspired to take an interest in social history and agricultural history by listening to my great grandfather, Philip Hiskey (1874-1965) and my grandfather Harry Mingay (1894-1981). They talked about these subjects not from an academic point of view, but from practical experience. My earliest sources of information about the Whitfield family history came from Arthur Whitfield (1895-1975) and Rosa Lane, nee Whitfield (1889-1976). My father, Hubert Whitfield, (1921-2006) consented during his final illness to write down his memories, which appear in Chapter 8; my aunt Doris Sibley, nee Whitfield (1913-2000) helped by organising various meetings with her uncle and aunt so that I was able to question them about the family. She also provided me with many details of my grandfather and his family by storing a veritable treasure trove of photographs, letters and newspaper cuttings at the family home in King Street, Potton. My father's cousin, Sidney Whitfield (1915-1994) gave me information about his father and grandfather, informally and in his own inimitable way, usually while we were extracting and bottling honey. My uncle, Leslie Whitfield, tape-recorded some of his memories a few months before his 100th birthday and remains a source of inspiration to me and the rest of the family. I owe these people a lot, in all sorts of ways and would like to record my sincere thanks for the help they gave me with this project, as with so many other things.

As my research continued I was grateful to receive help from more distant members of the family, and it was a pleasure to meet them. In particular, Harry Whitfield of Doncaster and his daughter Margaret Jablonski, Walter Henry Whitfield of Winchester, Bob Whitfield of Fareham, Fred Whitfield of Biggleswade and his son Ashley, Bill Whitfield of Ampthill, Albert Whitfield of Southampton, Allan and Dora Whitfield and Mike and Rosalie Bloor (nee Whitfield), all of Milton Keynes, and Eva and Jim Manning of Gamlingay Heath were all willing to share their memories and photographs.I am sorry they are not all alive to read the final book.

Enquiries placed in local newspapers and on the internet produced another set of contacts within the extended family as I tried to find descendants of other Whitfields who had left Bedfordshire, Cambridgeshire - or England. Joan Martin, Julie Harman, Debbie Whitfield, Jill

Murchison and Shirley Zornow all replied to my enquiries, tolerated my inquisitive nature and extended and enriched my research. Without their help my research and this book would have been much the poorer. Similarly, I am grateful to Professor Roger Ling for taking the time and trouble to write to me giving me details of the Ling family, descendants of Emily Elizabeth Whitfield, and to his cousin, Mrs Patricia Carthew, for the photograph of Emily Elizabeth and her husband, John Alfred Ling. Dianne Styles was equally co-operative by providing details of Henry Spindler, grandson of Henry Whitfield who left Potton in the 1880s. As the book was nearing publication, I managed to make contact with Dan Mateik, a 3x great grandson of Rev Thomas Simpkins and his wife Susan (nee Whitfield), and would like to thank him and his family for their help. Reluctantly I have to record that some enquiries fell upon stony ground; co-operation can never be taken for granted.

Outside the family, I must record my thanks to the late Reverend Ian Stewardson for his general encouragement and for allowing me to consult some of the original Potton parish registers, to the late Frank Gurney for lending me the Potton Congregational Church records, to the late Eric Mayston and Brian Smith for putting the records of Potton Charities at my disposal and to Peter Mount for allowing me to view the Sandy Charity records. I was also very fortunate to receive help from Miss M. Shepherd, who not only shared her memories of the Whitfields of Barton on the Heath, but also let me have a splendid photograph of the family.

Members of staff at various record offices have been unfailingly attentive in directing me to many useful and interesting original documents and dealing with my enquiries after viewing them. I have visited record offices at Cambridge, Aylesbury, Oxford, Warwick, Hertford and Bedford on occasions, but have been a frequent visitor to the latter, where James Collett White and Trevor Cunnick (now enjoying a well-deserved retirement) have been particularly solicitous over the years. The present archivist, Nigel Lutt, very kindly allowed me to include a selection of extracts from various documents relating to the Whitfield family held at the Bedfordshire and Luton Archives in this book, for which I am most grateful. After the edited diaries of the Reverend William Cotton Risley were published I was keen to view the original volumes at the Bodleian Library, Oxford, and would like to thank the staff there for making these fascinating books available to me. I would also like to thank George Howe and Peter Ibbett of Potton History Society and Jane Croot of Biggleswade History Society for their friendly assistance with my local enquiries. I hope this book may be of some use to future historians in the local area.

As information became available on the internet I became a regular and frequent visitor to local libraries, particularly at Sandy, Biggleswade and Gamlingay and would like to thank library staff for their help and patience with downloading and printing various items of interest. The archives of the *Biggleswade Chronicle*, a wonderful resource for the local historian, were also available at Biggleswade and I apologise for my lack of expertise with some of the library equipment needed to view them. One of these days I will come to terms with the twenty first century! I am particularly grateful to Debbie Hare at Gamlingay library for tracking down some fairly obscure background material so quickly and efficiently, to Kate Laugharne, also at Gamlingay library in the Ecohub for her help with some of the finer points of computing, for printing out the final version of the manuscript and for numerous cups of tea; and to Jan Cooper for supplying the marriage certificate for George Whitfield and Charlotte Muncey Rayner and the army papers of Benjamin Whitfield. As the book was nearing completion I almost took up residence at the Gamlingay Ecohub, (a wonderful village facility) to index it, and would like to thank all staff there for their friendly assistance. I have been a less frequent visitor to the Centre for Banburyshire Studies, based in Banbury library, and Royston museum but would like to thank staff there for their help as I trawled the archives of their local newspapers.

As the book began to take shape I was fortunate to be given a much-needed crash course in computing by my nephew, Isaac Whitfield. Isaac also kindly took photographs of various locations in Clophill and Sandy which feature in this book, in the summer of 2013. I am also grateful to his sister, Briony Whitfield, who was equally co-operative in taking the photograph of me which appears on the book's cover. I am grateful to my cousin, Dr Michael Whitfield for organising some of the material into a booklet in 2000, and for his continued interest in the project. I would particularly like to thank Michael Breeds, who at very short notice very kindly consented to take the photograph of me beekeeping which appears on page 329.

My friend and local history mentor, Jim Brown, author of *Gamlingay* and *Villagers*, not only read the first draft of the book but also designed the book's cover, drew family tree diagrams and produced an excellent set of maps. I very much appreciate this and have valued his encouragement, inspiration and advice over the years. His suggestions for future research have often pointed me in the right direction when my enquiries have seemed to grind to a halt, and I have tried to incorporate his suggestions into a new version of the manuscript. He also read the new (and hopefully improved) version. So, too, did my cousin Dr Michael Whitfield and my friends Chris Miller and Glynne and Sarah Rowlands. I hope their duties were not too onerous and thank them for their comments. Since then, the appearance online of the 1911 census for England and the 1940 U.S.A. census has led to a number of new discoveries, and as more old newspapers also found their way onto websites it has been possible to shed more light on the lives (and deaths) of various family members. Almost inevitably, it seems, fresh material will continue to appear from time to time. Although it will not feature in this book it will still be of interest. Although I have spent 40 years researching my family's history I know that the story hasn't yet come to an end.

I would like to record my thanks to Elizabeth Fitt of Book Create Service, who has prepared a challenging manuscript for publication with unfailing courtesy and efficiency.

Some notes on sources

When I first started researching my family history some forty years ago I had no idea that my discoveries would lead to the production of a book. Most of the research and the writing have been done in my spare time, without systematically recording details of every single source used and it hopefully will suffice to give a broad outline of the source material I have consulted.

At the Bedfordshire Archives I have made use of the Pym and Monoux family papers for details of the Whitfield family and their land holdings in Sandy. Documents deposited by the Franklin family enabled me to obtain a picture of the family in sixteenth century Clophill. Wills found at the Bedfordshire Archives and in the National Archives have added further important details of family possessions and relationships. Quarter Sessions records enabled me to find out details of members of the family who were considered to have stepped out of line and of other family members who were the victims of crime. The enclosure map and award for Sandy gave me a fascinating insight into the reorganisation of land holdings in the parish in the early nineteenth century. I consulted the archives of the *Biggleswade Chronicle* (established 1891) held at Biggleswade library for further information on the family in Potton. Parish registers for Sandy, Biggleswade, Potton and elsewhere in Bedfordshire supplied details of baptisms, marriages and deaths, those essential basic ingredients for any family tree. Potton Charity minute books gave me information on several members of the family who had fallen on hard times. Details I found out about the family encouraged me to undertake field work in parts of these parishes hitherto virtually unknown to me, and thus made me look at them from a different perspective, rewarding me with fascinating glimpses of times gone by.

In Oxfordshire I was able to find a tenancy agreement involving a member of the family at the Qxford Record Office; I consulted William Cotton Risley's diary at the Bodleian library, Oxford. The Centre for Banburyshire Studies in Banbury was visited to look at past editions of the *Banbury Guardian*. Pleasant exploratory visits were made to Deddington, Hook Norton, Barton on the Heath and Banbury. I ventured further afield - to the Warwick Record Office - to view farm valuations undertaken for Ann Whitfield of Hook Norton.

Tewin and Sacombe parish registers and Quarter Sessions records were consulted at the Hertford Record Office. I also visited the Buckinghamshire Record office at Aylesbury and made a field trip to Winslow and nearby Adstock in connection with research on the Jennings and Hawley families.

Unfortunately, time and resources did not allow a trip to Ohio and New York State, U.S.A.

to gather information; I had to be content with the internet and some correspondence with distant members of the family. Perhaps in the future…

Online, I have made extensive use of the ancestry and familysearch websites, looking particularly at the U.K. and U.S.A censuses, the U.S. Social Security index, the index of births, marriages and deaths (from 1837) and the National Probate Register for family wills from 1858 to 1966. The Ohio marriage index and the Cleveland Necrology File, both available online, gave me useful information on Whitfield marriages and deaths in Ohio, U.S.A. The website showing details of old British local newspapers has been used to find further details of family members. Sometimes it was also possible to find old American local newspapers on the internet; various editions of the *Ticonderoga Sentinel*, for example, gave me the opportunity to discover much more about the family of Susan Whitfield and her husband the Reverend Thomas Simpkins. Old trade directories have also been used, both online and in Record Offices. These were particularly useful in researching the two Oxfordshire branches of the family. Closer to home, but dealing with a much earlier time period, I was delighted to find online information relating to workers engaged in renovating the old house in Ampthill Park, Bedfordshire, 1533-1567, thanks to the Ampthill and District Archaeological and Local History Society; the original documents had been transcribed by Michael J.B. Turner.

I have received much help and encouragement from various members (past and present) of the Whitfield extended family and associated families; without their assistance this book would have been much the poorer. The information they supplied painted vivid pictures of earlier members of the family who had died before I was born, and whetted my appetite to find out even more about them.

Books Used

'Some books are to be tasted, others to be swallowed, and some few to be chewed and digested; that is, some books are to be read only in parts; others to be read but not curiously; and some few to be read wholly and with diligence and attention…'

Francis Bacon (1561-1626).

I wanted to place my family's growth and activities into a broader historical and geographical context, and in order to do so have made use of many local and general history books and other reference works over the years, particularly for background material. The list below contains some of these, but is by no means exhaustive. Some have already been acknowledged in the text; works of fiction are in italics.

- Agar, Nigel E. 'The Bedfordshire farm worker in the nineteenth century' Bedfordshire Historical Record Society, 1981.

- Batchelor, Thomas 'General view of the agriculture of the county of Bedford' (1808) - found online.

- Beavington, F.H. 'Early market gardening in Bedfordshire' Transactions of the Institute of British geographers, vol 37, 1965.

- Beavington, F.H. 'The development of market gardening in Bedfordshire 1799-1939' British Agricultural Society, 1975.

- Brown, James 'Gamlingay' Cassell, 1989.
  'Villagers: 750 years of life in an English village' Amberley, 2011.

- Brown, Jonathan 'The English market town: a social and economic history 1750-1914' Crowood Press,1986.

- Bryson, Bill 'At Home: a short history of private life' *Black Swan*, 2010.

- Chater, Kathy 'How to trace your family tree in England, Ireland, Scotland and Wales' Hermes House, 2005.

- Collett-White, James 'How Bedfordshire voted 1685-1735' Bedfordshire Historical Records Society, 2008.

- Crossley, Antony 'Apple years at Cockayne Hatley 1929-1946', published by the author, 1996.

- Doubleday, H. Arthur and Page, William 'A History of Bedfordshire', (a volume in the

Victoria History of the Counties of England series), published by Archibald Constable and Co., 1904.

- Davies, Jennifer 'The Victorian kitchen garden' BBC Books, 1987.
- Dickens, Charles *Oliver Twist*, first published 1838.

    Great Expectations, first published 1860-1861.

- Evans, George Ewart 'Ask the fellows who cut the hay' Faber, 1956.

    'The pattern under the plough' Faber, 1966.

    'Where beards wag all' Faber, 1970.

    'The farm and the village' Faber, 1977 edition.

- Godber, Joyce 'History of Bedfordshire 1066-1888' Bedfordshire County Council, 1969.
- Goose, Nigel ' How saucy did it make the poor? The Straw Plait and Hat Trades, Illegitimate fertility and the family in Nineteenth century Hertfordshire' University of Hertfordshire. Found online.
- Hardy, Thomas *Under the greenwood tree*, first published 1872.

    Far from the madding crowd, first published 1874.

    The Mayor of Casterbridge, first published 1886.

    The Woodlanders, first published 1887.

- Hey, David 'Family history and local history in England' Longman, 1987.
- Hoskins, W.G. 'Local history in England' Longman, 1977 edition.

    'The making of the English landscape' Pelican, 1971 edition.

- Kitchener, Dorothy 'The Kitchener Family History' Top Graphics, Potton, 1988.
- Lawson, Kenneth W. 'Memories of an ordinary Pottonian' Potton History Society, 1997.
- Mortimer, Ian 'The Time Traveller's guide to Elizabethan England' The Bodley Head, 2012.
- Niall, Ian 'To speed the plough' Readers Union, 1978.
- O'Connor, Bernard 'Coprolite diggers on Sandy Heath: the story of the coprolite industry around Potton' published by the author, 1998.
- Outhwaite, R.B., 'Scandal in the Church: Dr Edward Drax Free (1764-1843)' Hambledon and London, 2003.
- Page, Ken 'Thirsty old town: the story of Biggleswade pubs' Lion Press, Sandy, 1995.
- Parker, Rowland 'The common stream' Granada Publishing, 1975.
- Porter, Valerie 'Yesterday's farm: life on the farm 1830-1960' David and Charles, 2008.
- Pym, Francis 'Sentimental journey: tracing an outline of family history' published by the author, 1998.
- Quince, Ken 'The Sandy I knew' published by the author, 1984.
- Richardson, John 'The local historian's encyclopedia' Historical Publications, 1977 edition.

- Risley, William Cotton (Rev.), Diaries. (In the Bodleian Library, Oxford).

- Samuel, Raphael (ed.) 'Village life and labour' Routledge and Kegan Paul, 1975.

- Smedley-Stevenson, Geoffrey 'Early Victorian Squarson: the diaries of William Cotton Risley, vicar of Deddington 1835-1848' Robert Boyd Publications, 2007.

- Snell, Keith, 'Annals of the labouring poor: social change in Agrarian England 1660-1900' (1985). Found online.

- Steel, Don 'Discovering your family history' BBC Books, 1987.

- Swint, Jack 'Who killed…? Cleveland, Ohio.' Rooftop Publishing, 2007.

- Tiller, Kate: chapter on *Hook Norton* in Thirsk, Joan (ed.) 'Rural England: an illustrated history of the landscape' Oxford University Press, 2002.

- Trevelyan, G.M. 'Illustrated English Social History' Penguin, 1973 edition.

- Trinder, Barrie 'Victorian Banbury' Phillimore, 1982.

- Webber, Ronald 'Market gardening in Bedfordshire' article in *Bedfordshire Magazine*, Spring, 1974.

- Weinreb, Ben, et al. ' The London Encyclopaedia' Macmillan, 2008 edition.

- Whitbread, Sam, et al. 'Southill and the Whitbreads' S. C.Whitbread, 1995.

- Yates, Patricia and Ralph 'Potton Consolidated Charities' Potton History Society, 1985.

In addition, I used information from various articles in a number of historical local newspapers found in local libraries, record offices and online. These newspapers included the following publications:

Akron Beacon Journal, (USA), Akron Journal, (USA), Banbury Advertiser, Banbury Guardian, Biggleswade Chronicle, Bedfordshire Mercury, *Bedfordshire Times*, Bury and Norwich Post, Cambridge Chronicle and Journal, Cambridge Independent Press, Cheltenham Chronicle, Cleveland Plain Dealer (USA), Chronicle Telegraph (USA), Essex Newsman, Evesham Journal and Four Shires Advertiser, Leeds Times, London Gazette, Los Angeles Daily Herald (USA), Milwaukee Journal (USA), Northampton Mercury, Oxford Journal, Oxford Times, Royston Crow, Stamford Mercury, Ticonderoga Sentinel (USA) the Western Times, the Swindon and North Wiltshire Chronicle and the Wiltshire and Gloucestershire Standard.

If you have enjoyed reading this book, why not write your own family's history?

The author inspecting some of his bees, June, 2014.

Index

Indexing this book proved to be a major exercise. I would like to thank Peter Condon of Gamlingay library for showing me how to undertake this task on the computer, and apologise for any discrepancies; any faults or omissions are attributable to my inexperience – or incompetence.

Archbold, Kate 264
architect 9, 83, 242, 248
Arlesey, Beds 81, 162
armaments 139, 165, 166, 282, 286
armour plate works 283
army 46, 74, 102, 141, 142, 143, 144, 146, 178, 183, 204, 211, 239, 287, 319
A.R.P 183
Arrington, Cambs 139
Ashford, Ezekiel 11
Ashwell, Herts 69, 217
Ashwell, John 86
Ashwell, Samuel 11
asparagus 40, 195
Astell, William 55
Atchison, Topeka and Santa Fe railway 270
Atlantic Ocean 43, 109, 259, 260, 261, 265, 266, 268, 272, 276, 279, 282
Attercliffe, Sheffield, Yorkshire 285
attorney 68, 277
Attwood, Robert W. 277
Auckland, New Zealand 248
auction 12, 29, 31, 40, 103, 108, 110, 111, 302, 313
Austin, Herbert 165, 166
Australia 31, 144, 167, 248, 288
Austreet Field, Sandy 54, 55, 59
Back Lane, Potton 180
bacon 101, 135, 181, 187, 196
Bailey, Horace 265
Bailey, Janet 205
Bailey, Lois 265
Bailey, Ruth Florence 258
Bailey, Ted 182
Bailey, Wesley Willis 265
baker 100, 101, 102, 103, 104, 105, 106, 107, 108, 110, 111, 112, 113, 118, 121, 139, 141, 144, 162, 163, 182, 188, 228, 291
Baker, George 194, 195
Baker, Gordon 288
Baker, Olive 194
Ballantine, Robert 13
Balraj, Elizabeth 279
Banbury Guardian 114, 291, 294, 296, 303, 320, 324
Banbury, Oxon 99, 103, 107, 108, 110, 113, 114, 290, 291, 292, 293, 294, 295, 296, 300, 302, 303, 319, 320, 324
banker 24, 27, 33, 39, 82
banker, bankers 9, 39, 227
bankruptcy 29
baptism xvi, 2, 5, 6, 8, 17, 27, 31, 62, 72, 74, 76, 82, 106, 111, 129, 257
barbecue stand 274
Barber, John 50, 54, 55, 56
Barco, Arthur 258
Barco, David 265
Barco, Doris 265

349

Tilcock, Elizabeth 50, 74, 75
Tilcock, William 55
tile draining 78
Tiller, Dr Kate 103, 109
timber 24, 39, 40, 151, 264, 302
Tims, John 292
tomatoes 160, 194, 312, 313
Tonga 123, 161
Toth, Marjorie 281
Townley, Rev James 25
Townley, Rev. James 97
Townsend, Charles 84
Townsend, Widow 55
travelling labourers 126, 127
Trevelyan, G.M. 109
Trinder, Dr Barrie 292
tripe 234
truck driver 274, 276
Trundle, Elsie 204
Trundley, Harold 180
tuberculosis 101, 253, 284
Tunbridge Wells, Kent 49, 119
Turkey 243
Turley, Alfred and Catherine 237
Turley, Alfred William 236, 237
Turvey, Beds 203
Twelvetrees, Drusilla 83
twins 2, 31, 143, 199, 218, 223, 239, 242
twitch 79, 195
Twitchell, Benjamin 6
Two Brewers, the 150
Tyndale, William 68
Underwood, John 55, 56
United Order of Free Gardeners 83
university vii, 1, 2, 68, 103, 121, 164, 176, 193, 202, 204, 264, 268, 277, 278, 280, 287, 323, 324
upholsterer 192
Upper Caldecote, Beds 76, 156
U.S. Social Security Index 267
Uxbridge, Middx. 67, 68, 74
Varney, Edith Sarah 45
vegetables ix, 12, 17, 18, 19, 26, 32, 36, 40, 41, 42, 49, 78, 104, 105, 132, 135, 142, 143, 147, 155, 156, 160, 169, 170, 175, 188, 189, 202, 217, 235, 265, 293, 312
victualler 22, 34, 114
Vines, Fanny 84
Vines, Frederick 84
Vines, George 84
Vines, John 84
Vintiner, Thomas 10, 13
Volodkevich, Dr Peter 279
voters' list 26, 106, 271

369